21 Servants of Sovereign Joy

Other Books by John Piper

21 Servants of Sovereign Joy

FAITHFUL, FLAWED, AND FRUITFUL

John Piper

CROSSWAY®

WHEATON, ILLINOIS

Contents

Preface

It brings me a great deal of pleasure at the beginning of this volume of collected biographies to pay tribute to a man without whom they would, in all likelihood, not exist. Iain Murray sowed the seeds from which this has all grown. There is a story behind this claim.

The Story behind the Tribute

During my first seven years in the pastoral ministry (1980–1987), I felt very green—inexperienced, and in some ways unprepared. Before coming to Bethlehem Baptist Church at the age of thirty-four, I had never been a pastor. I was in school full-time till I was twenty-eight and then taught college Bible courses until God called me to the pastoral ministry.

In seminary, I had avoided pastoral courses and taken as many exegetical courses as I could, not at all expecting to be a pastor. When I came to Bethlehem, I had never performed a funeral, never stood by the bed of a dying person, never led a council of elders or any other kind of council or committee, never baptized anyone, never done a baby dedication, and had only preached a couple dozen sermons in my life. That's what I mean by green.

During those first seven years, one of the ways I pursued wisdom for the pastoral work in front of me was the reading of pastoral biographies. For example, I devoured Warren Wiersbe's two volumes *Walking with the Giants: A Minister's Guide to Good Reading and Great Preaching* (1976), and *Listening to the Giants: A Guide to Good Reading and Great Preaching* (1980). Together they contained over thirty short biographies of men in pastoral ministry.

But one of the most enjoyable and inspiring things I did to deepen my grasp of the pastoral calling was to listen to a master life-storyteller,

Iain Murray. Murray had been a pastoral assistant with Martyn Lloyd-Jones in London and had served as a pastor in two churches in England and Australia. He is a cofounder of the Banner of Truth Trust and has devoted a great part of his life to biographical writing.

He is well-known for his biographies of Martyn Lloyd-Jones and Jonathan Edwards, to mention only two. But not as many people know that Iain Murray is a master at taking an hour in a ministerial conference and telling the story of a great Christian in a way that instructs and inspires. For example, even today you can go online and find the (forty-plus-year-old) audio stories of Charles Spurgeon, Robert Dabney, William Tyndale, Ashbel Green, George Whitefield, John Knox, John Newton, William Jay, Thomas Hooker, and more.

The Latest Technology: Walkman

The latest technology in the early 1980s was the Walkman—a small cassette player that let me take Murray with me on my morning jogs or into the car. I listened to everything biographical I could get. This stoked the embers of my affections for biography. It has always felt to me that biography is one of the most enjoyable, edifying, and efficient ways to read history. *Enjoyable* because we all love a good story and the ecstasies and agonies of real life. *Edifying* because the faithfulness of God in the lives of contrite, courageous, forgiven sinners is strengthening for our own faith. *Efficient* because, in a good biography, you not only learn about a person's life but also about theology, psychology, philosophy, ethics, politics, economics, and church history. So I have long been a lover of biography.

I could be wrong, but my own opinion is that this volume would not exist without the inspiring ministry of Iain Murray's audio tapes. In 1987, it seemed to me that there was a need for a conference for pastors that would stir up a love for "the doctrines of grace," a zeal for the beauty of the gospel, a passion for God-centered preaching, a commitment to global missions, and a joy in Christ-exalting worship.

A Conference and Book Series Are Born

The first Bethlehem Conference for Pastors took place in 1988. Inspired by Iain Murray, I gave a biographical message every year for the next twenty-seven years. That is where the mini-biographies in this volume come from (which means that all these chapters can be heard in audio form at www.desiringGod.org). Throughout the year before each conference, I would read about the life and ministry of some key figure in church history. Then I would decide on some thematic focus to give unity to the message, and I would try to distill my reading into an hour-long message. The messages—and the edited versions—are unashamedly hortatory. I aim to teach and encourage. I also aim never to distort the truth of a man's life and work. But I do advocate for biblical truths that his life illustrates.

This volume contains seven collections with three historical figures each. The series was published under the title The Swans Are Not Silent. You can read the story behind that title in the preface to *The Legacy of Sovereign Joy*. But the gist of it is this: when Augustine died, his successor felt so inadequate that he said, "The cricket chirps, the swan is silent." The point of the series title is that, through biography, *the swans are not silent*! Augustine was not the only great voice that lives on. Thousands of voices live on. And their stories should be told and read.

Biography Is Biblically Mandated

It would be wonderfully rewarding to me if I heard that your reading of these stories brought you as much joy as I received in researching and writing them. If you need a greater incentive than that prospect, remember Hebrews 11. Surely this chapter is a divine mandate to read Christian biography. I wrote a chapter in *Brothers, We Are Not Professionals* that tried to make this case. It was titled "Brothers, Read Christian Biography." I commented on Hebrews 11,

> The unmistakable implication of the chapter is that if we hear about the faith of our forefathers (and mothers), we will "lay aside every weight and sin" and "run with endurance the race that is set before us" (Heb. 12:1). If we asked the author, "How shall we stir one another up to love and good works?" (10:24), his answer would be: "Through encouragement from the living *and the dead*" (10:25; 11:1–40). Christian biography is the means by which the "body life" of the church cuts across the centuries.[1]

---

[1] John Piper, *Brothers, We Are Not Professionals* (Nashville, TN: B&H, 2013), 106–12.

Countless Benefits

I think that what was said of Abel in Hebrews 11:4 can be said of any saint whose story is told: "Through his faith, though he died, he still speaks" (ESV). It has been a great pleasure as I have listened to these voices. But not only a pleasure. They have strengthened my hand in the work of the ministry again and again. They have helped me feel that I was part of something much bigger than myself or my century. They have showed me that the worst of times are not the last of times, and they made the promise visible that God works all things for our good. They have modeled courage and perseverance in the face of withering opposition. They have helped me set my face to the cause of truth and love and world evangelization. They have revived my love for Christ's church. They have reinforced my resolve to be a faithful husband and father. They have stirred me up to care about seeing and savoring the beauty of God. They inspired the effort to speak that beauty in a way that it doesn't bore. They quickened a love for Christian camaraderie in the greatest Cause in the world. And they did all this—and more—in a way that caused me to rejoice in the Lord and be glad I was in his sway and his service.

I pray that all of this and more will be your pleasure and your profit as you read or listen. For the swans are definitely not silent.

John Piper
July 2016

The Swans Are Not Silent

Book 1

The Legacy of Sovereign Joy

*God's Triumphant Grace in the Lives of
Augustine, Luther, and Calvin*

To Jon Bloom

whose heart and hands
sustain the song
at the Bethlehem Conference for Pastors
and Desiring God Ministries

The Legacy of Sovereign Joy

Book 1

Contents

The sum of all our goods, and our perfect good, is God. We must not fall short of this, nor seek anything beyond it; the first is dangerous, the other impossible.

St. Augustine
Morals of the Catholic Church

Preface

At the age of seventy-one, four years before he died on August 28, AD 430, Aurelius Augustine handed over the administrative duties of the church in Hippo on the northern coast of Africa to his assistant Eraclius. Already, in his own lifetime, Augustine was a giant in the Christian world. At the ceremony, Eraclius stood to preach as the aged Augustine sat on his bishop's throne behind him. Overwhelmed by a sense of inadequacy in Augustine's presence, Eraclius said, "The cricket chirps, the swan is silent."[1]

If only Eraclius could have looked down over sixteen centuries at the enormous influence of Augustine, he would have understood why the series of books beginning with *The Legacy of Sovereign Joy* is titled The Swans Are Not Silent. For 1,600 years, Augustine has not been silent. In the 1500s, his voice rose to a compelling crescendo in the ears of Martin Luther and John Calvin. Luther was an Augustinian monk, and Calvin quoted Augustine more than any other church father. Augustine's influence on the Protestant Reformation was extraordinary. A thousand years could not silence his song of jubilant grace. More than one historian has said, "The Reformation witnessed the ultimate triumph of Augustine's doctrine of grace over the legacy of the Pelagian view of man"[2]—the view that man is able to triumph over his own bondage to sin.

The swan also sang in the voice of Martin Luther in more than one sense. All over Germany you will find swans on church steeples, and for centuries Luther has been portrayed in works of art with a swan at his feet. Why is this? The reason goes back a century before Luther.

---

[1] Peter Brown, *Augustine of Hippo* (Berkeley, CA: University of California Press, 1969), 408.
[2] R. C. Sproul, "Augustine and Pelagius," in *Tabletalk*, June 1996: 11. See the introduction in this book (n. 24) for a similar statement from Benjamin Warfield. See chapter 1 on the meaning of Pelagianism.

John Hus, who died in 1415, a hundred years before Luther nailed his Ninety-Five Theses on the Wittenberg door (1517), was a professor and later president of the University of Prague. He was born of peasant stock and preached in the common language instead of Latin. He translated the New Testament into Czech, and he spoke out against abuses in the Catholic Church.

"In 1412 a papal bull was issued against Hus and his followers. Anyone could kill the Czech reformer on sight, and those who gave him food or shelter would suffer the same fate. When three of Hus's followers spoke publicly against the practice of selling indulgences, they were captured and beheaded."[3] In December 1414, Hus himself was arrested and kept in prison until March 1415. He was kept in chains and brutally tortured for his views, which anticipated the Reformation by a hundred years.

On July 6, 1415, he was burned at the stake along with his books. One tradition says that in his cell just before his death, Hus wrote, "Today, you are burning a goose [the meaning of 'Hus' in Czech]; however, a hundred years from now, you will be able to hear a swan sing, you will not burn it, you will have to listen to him."[4] Martin Luther boldly saw himself as a fulfillment of this prophecy and wrote in 1531, "John Hus prophesied of me when he wrote from his prison in Bohemia: They will now roast a goose (for Hus means a goose), but after a hundred years they will hear a swan sing; him they will have to tolerate. And so it shall continue, if it please God."[5]

And so it has continued. The great voices of grace sing on today. And I count it a great joy to listen and to echo their song in this little book and, God willing, the ones to follow.

Although these chapters on Augustine, Luther, and Calvin were originally given as biographical messages at the annual Bethlehem Conference for Pastors, there is a reason why I put them together here for a wider audience including laypeople. Their combined message is profoundly relevant in this modern world at the beginning of a new millennium. R. C. Sproul is right that "we need an Augustine or a Luther to speak to us anew lest the light of God's grace be not only overshadowed

---

[3] Erwin Weber, "Luther with the Swan," *The Lutheran Journal* 65, no. 2 (1996): 10.
[4] Ibid.
[5] Martin Luther, quoted in Ewald M. Plass, *What Luther Says, An Anthology* (St. Louis: Concordia, 1959), 3:1175.

but be obliterated in our time."[6] Yes, and perhaps the best that a cricket can do is to let the swans sing.

Augustine's song of grace is unlike anything you will read in almost any modern book about grace. The omnipotent power of grace, for Augustine, is the power of "sovereign joy." This alone delivered him from a lifetime of bondage to sexual appetite and philosophical pride. Discovering that beneath the vaunted powers of human will is a cauldron of desire holding us captive to irrational choices opens the way to see grace as the triumph of "sovereign joy." Oh, how we need the ancient biblical insight of Augustine to free us from the pleasant slavery that foils the fulfillment of the Great Commandment and the finishing of the Great Commission.

I am not sure that Martin Luther and John Calvin saw the conquering grace of "sovereign joy" as clearly as Augustine. But what they saw even more clearly was the supremacy of the Word of God over the church and the utter necessity of sacred study at the spring of truth. Luther found his way into paradise through the gate of New Testament Greek, and Calvin bequeathed to us a five-hundred-year legacy of God-entranced preaching because his eyes were opened to see the divine majesty of the Word. My prayer in writing this book is that, once we see Augustine's vision of grace as "sovereign joy," the lessons of Luther's study will strengthen it by the Word of God, and the lessons of Calvin's preaching will spread it to the ends of the earth. This is *The Legacy of Sovereign Joy.*

Augustine "never wrote what could be called a treatise on prayer."[7] Instead, his writing flows in and out of prayer. This is because, for him, "the whole life of a good Christian is a holy desire."[8] And this desire is for God, above all things and in all things. This is the desire I write to awaken and sustain. And therefore I pray with Augustine for myself and for you, the reader,

> Turn not away your face from me, that I may find what I seek. Turn not aside in anger from your servant, lest in seeking you I run toward something else. . . . Be my helper. Leave me not, neither despise me, O God my Savior. Scorn not that a mortal should seek the Eternal.[9]

---

[6] Sproul, "Augustine and Pelagius," 52.
[7] Thomas A. Hand, *Augustine on Prayer* (New York: Catholic Book, 1986), 11.
[8] Ibid., 20.
[9] Ibid., 27.

Acknowledgments

How thankful I am for a wife and children who, several weeks each year (at least), unbegrudgingly let me live in another century. This is where I go to prepare the biographical messages for the Bethlehem Conference for Pastors. All the while, Jon Bloom, the director of Desiring God Ministries, is masterfully managing a thousand details that bring hundreds of hungry shepherds together in the dead of winter in Minneapolis. That conference, those biographies, and this book would not exist without him and the hundreds of Bethlehem volunteers who respond to his call each year.

To steal away into the Blue Ridge Mountains for a season to put this book together in its present form has been a precious gift. I owe this productive seclusion to the hospitality of the team of God's servants at the Billy Graham Training Center at The Cove. May God grant the dream of Dr. Graham to flourish from this place—that those who attend the seminars at The Cove "will leave here transformed and prepared for action—equipped to be an effective witness for Christ."

A special word of thanks to Lane Dennis of Crossway for his interest in these biographical studies and his willingness to make them available to a wider audience. And thanks to Carol Steinbach again for her help with this project.

Finally, I thank Jesus Christ for giving to the church teachers like St. Augustine, Martin Luther, and John Calvin. "He gave some . . . pastors and teachers, for the equipping of the saints for the work of service, to the building up of the body of Christ" (Eph. 4:11–12). I am the beneficiary of this great work of equipping the saints that these three have done for centuries. Thank you, Father, that the swans are not silent. May their song of triumphant grace continue to be sung in *The Legacy of Sovereign Joy*.

This will be written for the generation to come,
That a people yet to be created may praise the LORD.
Psalm 102:18

One generation shall praise Your works to another,
And shall declare Your mighty acts.
Psalm 145:4

Introduction

Savoring the Sovereignty of Grace in the Lives of Flawed Saints

The Point of History

God ordains that we gaze on his glory, dimly mirrored in the ministry of his flawed servants. He intends for us to consider their lives and peer through the imperfections of their faith and behold the beauty of their God. "Remember your leaders, those who spoke to you the word of God; consider the outcome of their life, and imitate their faith" (Heb. 13:7 RSV). The God who fashions the hearts of all men (Ps. 33:15) means for their lives to display his truth and his worth. From Phoebe to St. Francis, the divine plan—even spoken of the pagan Pharaoh—holds firm for all: "I have raised you up for the very purpose of showing my power in you, so that my name may be proclaimed in all the earth" (Rom. 9:17 RSV). From David the king to David Brainerd, the missionary, extraordinary and incomplete specimens of godliness and wisdom have kindled the worship of sovereign grace in the hearts of reminiscing saints. "This will be written for the generation to come, that a people yet to be created may praise the LORD" (Ps. 102:18).

The history of the world is a field strewn with broken stones, which are sacred altars designed to waken worship in the hearts of those who will take the time to read and remember. "I shall remember the deeds of the LORD; surely I will remember Your wonders of old. I will meditate on all Your work and muse on Your deeds. Your way, O God, is holy; what god is great like our God?" (Ps. 77:11–13). The aim of providence in the history of the world is the worship of the people of God. Ten thousand stories of grace and truth are meant to be remembered for the refinement of faith and the sustaining of hope and the guidance of love. "Whatever was written in former days was written for our instruction, that by steadfastness and by the encouragement of the scriptures we might have hope" (Rom. 15:4 RSV). Those who nurture their hope in the history of grace will live their lives to the glory of God. That is the aim of this book.

It is a book about three famous and flawed fathers in the Christian church. Therefore, it is a book about grace, not only because the faithfulness of God triumphs over the flaws of men, but also because this was the very theme of their lives and work. Aurelius Augustine (354–430), Martin Luther (1483–1546), and John Calvin (1509–1564) had this in common: they experienced, and then built their lives and ministries on, the reality of God's omnipotent grace. In this way their common passion for the supremacy of God was preserved from the taint of human competition. Each of them confessed openly that the essence of experiential Christianity is the glorious triumph of grace over the guilty impotence of man.

Augustine's Discovery of "Sovereign Joy"

At first Augustine resisted the triumph of grace as an enemy. But then, in a garden in Milan, Italy, when he was thirty-one, the power of grace through the truth of God's Word broke fifteen years of bondage to sexual lust and living with a concubine. His resistance was finally overcome by "sovereign joy," the beautiful name he gave to God's grace. "How sweet all at once it was for me to be rid of those fruitless joys which I had once feared to lose . . . ! You drove them from me, you who are the true, the *sovereign joy*. You drove them from me and took their place, you who are sweeter than all pleasure. . . . O Lord my God, my Light, my Wealth, and my Salvation."[1]

Then, in his maturity and to the day of his death, Augustine fought the battle for grace as a submissive captive to "sovereign joy" against his contemporary and arch-antagonist, the British monk Pelagius. Nothing shocked Pelagius more than the stark declaration of omnipotent grace in Augustine's prayer: "Command what you wish, but give what you command."[2] Augustine knew that his liberty from lust and his power

---

[1] Augustine, *Confessions*, trans. R. S. Pine-Coffin (New York: Penguin, 1961), 181 (IX, 1), emphasis added.
[2] Peter Brown, *Augustine of Hippo* (Berkeley, CA: University of California Press, 1969), 179. The quote is found in Augustine, *Confessions*, 40 (X, 29).

to live for Christ and his understanding of biblical truth hung on the validity of that prayer. He was painfully aware of the hopelessness of leaning on free will as a help against lust.

> Who is not aghast at the sudden crevasses that might open in the life of a dedicated man? When I was writing this, we were told that a man of 84, who had lived a life of continence under religious observance with a pious wife for 25 years, has gone and bought himself a music-girl for his pleasure. . . . If the angels were left to their own free-will, even they might lapse, and the world be filled with "new devils."[3]

Augustine knew that the same would happen to him if God left him to lean on his own free will for faith and purity. The battle for omnipotent grace was not theoretical or academic; it was practical and pressing. At stake was holiness and heaven. Therefore he fought with all his might for the supremacy of grace against the Pelagian exaltation of man's ultimate self-determination.[4]

Luther's Pathway into Paradise

For Martin Luther, the triumph of grace came not in a garden but in a study, and not primarily over lust but over the fear of God's wrath. "If I could believe that God was not angry with me, I would stand on my head for joy."[5] He might have said "sovereign joy." But he could not believe it. And the great external obstacle was not a concubine in Milan, Italy, but a biblical text in Wittenberg, Germany. "A single word in [Rom. 1:17], 'In [the gospel] the *righteousness of God* is revealed' . . . stood in my way. For I hated that word 'righteousness of God.'"[6] He had been taught that the "righteousness of God" meant the justice "with which God is righteous and punishes the unrighteous sinner."[7] This was no relief and no gospel. Whereas Augustine "tore [his] hair and hammered [his] forehead with his fists" in hopelessness over bondage to sexual passion,[8]

---

[3] *Contra Julian*, III, x, 22, quoted in Brown, *Augustine of Hippo*, 405.
[4] The book Augustine himself saw as his "most fundamental demolition of Pelagianism" (Peter Brown, *Augustine of Hippo*, 372) is *On the Spirit and the Letter*, in *Augustine: Later Works*, ed. John Burnaby (Philadelphia, PA: Westminster Press, 1965), 182–251.
[5] Heiko A. Oberman, *Luther: Man between God and the Devil*, trans. Eileen Walliser-Schwarzbart (orig. 1982; New York: Doubleday, 1992), 315.
[6] John Dillenberger, ed., *Martin Luther: Selections from His Writings* (Garden City, NY: Doubleday, 1961), 11, emphasis added.
[7] Ibid.
[8] "I was beside myself with madness that would bring me sanity. I was dying a death that would bring me life. . . . I was frantic, overcome by violent anger with myself for not accepting your will and entering into

Luther "raged with a fierce and troubled conscience . . . [and] beat importunately upon Paul at that place [Rom. 1:17], most ardently desiring to know what St. Paul wanted."[9]

The breakthrough came in 1518, not, as with Augustine, by the sudden song of a child chanting, "Take it and read,"[10] but by the unrelenting study of the historical-grammatical context of Romans 1:17. This sacred study proved to be a precious means of grace. "At last, by the mercy of God, meditating day and night, I gave heed to the context of the words, namely . . . 'He who through faith is righteous shall live.' There I began to understand [that] the righteousness of God is that by which the righteous lives by a gift of God, namely by faith. . . . Here I felt that I was altogether born again and had entered paradise itself through open gates."[11] This was the joy that turned the world upside-down.

Justification by faith alone, apart from works of the law, was the triumph of grace in the life of Martin Luther. He did, you might say, stand on his head for joy, and with him all the world was turned upside-down. But the longer he lived, the more he was convinced that there was a deeper issue beneath this doctrine and its conflict with the meritorious features of indulgences[12] and purgatory. In the end, it was not Johann Tetzel's sale of indulgences or Johann Eck's promotion of purgatory that produced Luther's most passionate defense of God's omnipotent grace; it was Desiderius Erasmus's defense of free will.

Erasmus was to Luther what Pelagius was to Augustine. Martin Luther conceded that Erasmus, more than any other opponent, had realized that the powerlessness of man before God, not the indulgence controversy or purgatory, was the central question of the Christian faith.[13] Luther's book *The Bondage of the Will*, published in 1525, was an answer to Erasmus's book *The Freedom of the Will*. Luther regarded this one book of his—*The Bondage of the Will*—as his "best theological book, and the only one in that class worthy of publication."[14] This is

your covenant. . . . I tore my hair and hammered my forehead with my fists; I locked my fingers and hugged my knees," Augustine, *Confessions*, 170–71 (VIII, 8).
[9] Dillenberger, *Martin Luther: Selections*, 12.
[10] See chapter 1 of this book for the details of this remarkable story.
[11] Dillenberger, *Martin Luther: Selections*, 12.
[12] Indulgences were the sale of release from temporal punishment for sin through the payment of money to the Roman Catholic Church—for yourself or another in purgatory.
[13] Oberman, *Luther: Man between God and the Devil*, 220.
[14] Dillenberger, *Martin Luther: Selections*, 167.

because at the heart of Luther's theology was a total dependence on the freedom of God's omnipotent grace to rescue powerless man from the bondage of the will. "Man cannot by his own power purify his heart and bring forth godly gifts, such as true repentance for sins, a true, as over against an artificial, fear of God, true faith, sincere love. . . ."[15] Erasmus's exaltation of man's fallen will as free to overcome its own sin and bondage was, in Luther's mind, an assault on the freedom of God's grace and therefore an attack on the very gospel itself, and ultimately on the glory of God. Thus Luther proved himself to be a faithful student of St. Augustine and St. Paul to the very end.

Calvin's Encounter with the Divine Majesty of the Word

For John Calvin, the triumph of God's grace in his own life and theology was the self-authenticating demonstration of the majesty of God in the Word of Scripture. How are we to know that the Bible is the Word of God? Do we lean on the testimony of man—the authority of the church, as in Roman Catholicism? Or are we more immediately dependent on the majesty of God's grace? Sometime in his early twenties, before 1533, at the University of Paris, Calvin's resistance to grace was conquered for the glory of God and for the cause of the Reformation. "God, by a sudden conversion subdued and brought my mind to a teachable frame. . . . Having thus received some taste and knowledge of true godliness, I was immediately inflamed with [an] intense desire to make progress."[16] With this "taste" and this "intense desire," the legacy of sovereign joy took root in another generation.

The power that "subdued" his mind was the manifestation of the majesty of God. "Our Heavenly Father, revealing *his majesty* [in Scripture], lifts reverence for Scripture beyond the realm of controversy."[17] There is the key for Calvin: the witness of God to Scripture is the immediate, unassailable, life-giving revelation to our minds of *the majesty of God* that is manifest in the Scriptures themselves. This was his testimony to the omnipotent grace of God in his life: the blind eyes of his spirit were opened, and what he saw immediately, and without a

---

[15] Conrad Bergendoff, ed., *Church and Ministry II*, Luther's Works, vol. 40 (Philadelphia, PA: Muhlenberg, 1958), 301.
[16] John Dillenberger, ed., *John Calvin, Selections from His Writings* (Atlanta: Scholars Press, 1975), 26.
[17] John Calvin, *Institutes of the Christian Religion*, ed. John T. McNeil, trans. Ford Lewis Battles, 2 vols. (Philadelphia, PA: Westminster Press, 1960), I.viii.13, emphasis added.

lengthy chain of human reasoning, were two things so interwoven that they would determine the rest of his life—the majesty of God and the Word of God. The Word mediated the majesty, and the majesty vindicated the Word. Henceforth he would be a man utterly devoted to displaying the supremacy of God's glory by the exposition of God's Word.

United with a Passion for the Supremacy of Divine Grace

In all of this, Augustine, Luther, and Calvin were one. Their passion was to display above all things the glory of God through the exaltation of his omnipotent grace. Augustine's entire life was one great "confession" of the glory of God's grace: "O Lord, my Helper and my Redeemer, I shall now tell and confess *to the glory of your name* how you released me from the fetters of lust which held me so tightly shackled and from my slavery to the things of this world."[18] From the beginning of Luther's discovery of grace, displaying the glory of God was the driving force of his labor. "I recall that at the beginning of my cause Dr. Staupitz, who was then a man of great importance and vicar of the Augustinian Order, said to me: 'It pleases me that the doctrine which you preach ascribes the glory and everything to God alone and nothing to man.'"[19] Calvin's course was fixed from his first dispute with Cardinal Sadolet in 1539 when he charged the Cardinal to "set before [man], as the prime motive of his existence, *zeal to illustrate the glory of God.*"[20]

Under Christ, Augustine's influence on Luther and Calvin was second only to the influence of the apostle Paul. Augustine towers over the thousand years between himself and the Reformation, heralding the sovereign joy of God's triumphant grace for all generations. Adolf Harnack said that he was the greatest man "between Paul the Apostle and Luther the Reformer, the Christian Church has possessed."[21] The stan-

---

[18] Augustine, *Confessions*, 166 (VIII, 6).
[19] Ewald M. Plass, *What Luther Says: An Anthology*, 3 vols. (St. Louis, MO: Concordia, 1959), 3:1374.
[20] Dillenberger, *John Calvin*, 89, emphasis added.
[21] Adolf Harnack, "Monasticism and the Confessions of St. Augustine," quoted in Benjamin Warfield, *Calvin and Augustine* (Philadelphia, PA: P&R, 1971), 306. Although "[Augustine's] direct work as a reformer of Church life was done in a corner, and its results were immediately swept away by the flood of the Vandal invasion . . . it was through his voluminous writings, by which his wider influence was exerted, that he entered both the Church and the world as a revolutionary force, and not merely created an epoch in the history of the Church, but has determined the course of its history in the West up to the present day" (Warfield, *Calvin and Augustine*, 306). "Anselm, Aquinas, Petrarch (never without a pocket copy of the *Confessions*), Luther, Bellarmine, Pascal, and Kierkegaard all stand in the shade of [Augustine's] broad oak. His writings were among the favourite books of Wittgenstein. He was the *bête noire* of Nietzsche. His psychological analysis anticipated parts of Freud: he first discovered the existence of the 'sub-conscious.' . . . He was 'the first modern man' in the sense that with him the reader feels himself addressed at a level of extraordinary

dard text on theology that Calvin and Luther drank from was *Sentences* by Peter Lombard. Nine-tenths of this book consists of quotations from Augustine, and it was for centuries *the* textbook for theological studies.[22] Luther was an Augustinian monk, and Calvin immersed himself in the writings of Augustine, as we can see from the increased use of Augustine's writings in each new edition of the *Institutes*. "In the 1536 edition of the *Institutes* he quotes Augustine 20 times, three years later 113, in 1543 it was 128 times, 141 in 1550 and finally, no less than 342 in 1559."[23]

Not surprisingly, therefore, yet paradoxically, one of the most esteemed fathers of the Roman Catholic Church "gave us the Reformation." Benjamin Warfield put it like this: "The Reformation, inwardly considered, was just the ultimate triumph of Augustine's doctrine of grace over Augustine's doctrine of the Church."[24] In other words, there were tensions within Augustine's thought that explain why he could be cited by both Roman Catholics and by Reformers as a champion.

God's Grace over the Flaws of Great Saints

This brings us back to an earlier point. This book, which is about Augustine, Luther, and Calvin, is a book about the glory of God's omnipotent grace, not only because it was the unifying theme of their work, but also because this grace triumphed over the flaws in these men's lives. Augustine's most famous work is called the *Confessions* in large measure because his whole ministry was built on the wonder that God could forgive and use a man who had sold himself to so much

---

psychological depth and confronted by a coherent system of thought, large parts of which still make potent claims to attention and respect" (Henry Chadwick, *Augustine* [Oxford: Oxford University Press, 1986], 3).
[22] Agostino Trapè, *Saint Augustine: Man, Pastor, Mystic* (New York: Catholic Book, 1986), 333–34.
[23] T. H. L. Parker, *Portrait of Calvin* (Philadelphia, PA: Westminster Press, 1954), 44.
[24] Warfield, *Calvin and Augustine*, 322–23. "This doctrine of grace came from Augustine's hands in its positive outline completely formulated: sinful man depends, for his recovery to good and to God, entirely on the free grace of God; this grace is therefore indispensable, prevenient, irresistible, indefectible; and, being thus the free grace of God, must have lain, in all the details of its conference and working, in the intention of God from all eternity. But, however clearly announced and forcefully commended by him, it required to make its way against great obstacles in the Church. As over against the Pelagians, the indispensableness of grace was quickly established; as over against the Semi-Pelagians, its prevenience was with almost equal rapidity made good. But there advance paused. If the necessity of prevenient grace was thereafter (after the Council of Orange, 529) the established doctrine of the Church, the irresistibility of this prevenient grace was put under the ban, and there remained no place for a complete 'Augustinianism' within the Church. . . . Therefore, when the great revival of religion which we call the Reformation came, seeing that it was, on its theological side, a revival of 'Augustinianism,' as all great revivals of religion must be (for 'Augustinianism' is but the thetical expression of religion in its purity), there was nothing for it but the rending of the Church. And therefore also the greatest peril to the Reformation was and remains the diffused anti-'Augustinianism' in the world."

sensuality for so long. And now we add to this imperfection the flaws of Augustine's theology suggested by Warfield's comment that his doctrine of grace triumphed over his doctrine of the church. Of course, this will be disputed. But from my perspective he is correct to draw attention to Augustine's weaknesses amid massive strengths.

Augustine's Dubious Record on Sex and Sacraments

For example, it is a perplexing incongruity that Augustine would exalt the free and sovereign grace of God so supremely and yet hold to a view of baptism that makes the act of man so decisive in the miracle of regeneration. Baptismal regeneration and spiritual awakening by the power of the Word of God do not fit together. The way Augustine speaks of baptism seems to go against his entire experience of God's grace, awakening and transforming him through the Word of God in Milan. In the *Confessions* he mentions a friend who was baptized while unconscious and comes to his senses changed.[25] "In a way that Augustine never claimed to understand, the physical rites of baptism and ordination 'brand' a permanent mark on the recipient, quite independent of his conscious qualities."[26] He regretted not having been baptized as a youth and believed that ritual would have spared him much misery. "It would have been much better if I had been healed at once and if all that I and my family could do had been done to make sure that once my soul had received its salvation, its safety should be left in your keeping, since its salvation had come from you. This would surely have been the better course."[27] Peter Brown writes that Augustine "had once hoped to understand the rite of infant baptism: 'Reason will find that out.' Now he will appeal, not to reason, but to the rooted feelings of the Catholic masses."[28]

Of course, Augustine is not alone in mingling a deep knowledge of grace with defective views and flawed living. Every worthy theologian and every true saint does the same. Every one of them confesses, "Now we see in a mirror dimly, but then face to face; now I know in part, but then I shall know fully just as I also have been fully known" (1 Cor. 13:12). "Not that I have already obtained it, or have already become

---

[25] Cited in Brown, *Augustine of Hippo*, 222 (IV.iv.8).
[26] Ibid.
[27] Augustine, *Confessions*, 32 (I, 11).
[28] Brown, *Augustine of Hippo*, 280.

perfect, but I press on so that I may lay hold of that for which also I was laid hold of by Christ Jesus" (Phil. 3:12). But the famous flawed saints have their flaws exposed and are criticized vigorously for it.

Diverse Defects of Different Men

Martin Luther and John Calvin were seriously flawed saints. The flaws grew in the soil of very powerful—and very different—personalities.

> How different the upbringing of the two men—the one, the son of a German miner, singing for his livelihood under the windows of the well-to-do burghers; the other, the son of a French procurator-fiscal, delicately reared and educated with the children of the nobility. How different, too, their temperaments—Luther, hearty, jovial, jocund, sociable, filling his goblet day by day from the Town Council's wine-cellar; Calvin, lean, austere, retiring, given to fasting and wakefulness. . . . Luther was a man of the people, endowed with passion, poetry, imagination, fire, whereas Calvin was cold, refined, courteous, able to speak to nobles and address crowned heads, and seldom, if ever, needing to retract or even to regret his words.[29]

Luther's Dirty Mouth and Lapse of Love

But, oh, how many words did Luther regret! This was the downside of a delightfully blunt and open emotional life, filled with humor as well as anger. Heiko Oberman refers to Luther's "jocular theologizing."[30] "If I ever have to find myself a wife again, I will hew myself an obedient wife out of stone."[31] "In domestic affairs I defer to Katie. Otherwise I am led by the Holy Ghost."[32] "I have legitimate children, which no papal theologian has."[33] His personal experience is always present. "With Luther feelings force their way everywhere. . . . He himself is passionately present, not only teaching life by faith but living faith himself."[34] This makes him far more interesting and attractive as a person than Calvin, but far more volatile and offensive—depending on what side of the joke you happen to be on. We cannot imagine today (as much as we might

---

[29] Henry F. Henderson, *Calvin in His Letters* (London: J. M. Dent, 1909), 109–10.
[30] Oberman, *Luther: Man between God and the Devil,* 5.
[31] Ibid., 276.
[32] William J. Peterson, *Martin Luther Had a Wife* (Wheaton, IL: Tyndale, 1983), 14.
[33] Oberman, *Luther: Man between God and the Devil,* 278.
[34] Ibid., 312–13.

like to) a university professor doing theology the way Luther did it. The leading authority on Luther comments, "[Luther] would look in vain for a chair in theology today at Harvard. . . . It is the Erasmian type of ivory-tower academic that has gained international acceptance."[35]

With all its spice, his language could also move toward crudity and hatefulness. His longtime friend Melanchthon did not hesitate to mention Luther's "sharp tongue" and "heated temper" even as he gave his funeral oration.[36] There were also the four-letter words and the foul "bathroom" talk. He confessed from time to time that it was excessive. "Many accused me of proceeding too severely. Severely, that is true, and often too severely; but it was a question of the salvation of all, even my opponents."[37]

We who are prone to fault him for his severity and mean-spirited language can scarcely imagine what the battle was like in those days, and what it was like to be the target of so many vicious, slanderous, and life-threatening attacks. "He could not say a word that would not be heard and pondered everywhere."[38] It will be fair to let Luther and one of his balanced admirers put his harshness and his crudeness in perspective. First Luther himself:

> I own that I am more vehement than I ought to be; but I have to do with men who blaspheme evangelical truth; with human wolves; with those who condemn me unheard, without admonishing, without instructing me; and who utter the most atrocious slanders against myself not only, but the Word of God. Even the most phlegmatic spirit, so circumstanced, might well be moved to speak thunderbolts; much more I who am choleric by nature, and possessed of a temper easily apt to exceed the bounds of moderation.
>
> I cannot, however, but be surprised to learn whence the novel taste arose which daintily calls everything spoken against an adversary abusive and acrimonious. What think ye of Christ? Was he a reviler when he called the Jews an adulterous and perverse generation, a progeny of vipers, hypocrites, children of the devil?
>
> What think you of Paul? Was he abusive when he termed the enemies of the gospel dogs and seducers? Paul who, in the thirteenth chapter of the Acts, inveighs against a false prophet in this manner: "Oh, full of subtlety and all malice, thou child of the devil, thou enemy of all righteousness." I

---

[35] Ibid., 313.
[36] Ibid., 10.
[37] Ibid., 322.
[38] Ibid., 298.

pray you, good Spalatin, read me this riddle. *A mind conscious of truth cannot always endure the obstinate and willfully blind enemies of truth.* I see that all persons demand of me moderation, and especially those of my adversaries, who least exhibit it. If I am too warm, I am at least open and frank; in which respect I excel those who always smile, but murder.[39]

It may seem futile to ponder the positive significance of filthy language, but let the reader judge whether "the world's foremost authority on Luther"[40] helps us grasp a partially redemptive purpose in Luther's occasionally foul mouth.

> Luther's scatology-permeated language has to be taken seriously as an expression of the painful battle fought body and soul against the Adversary, who threatens both flesh and spirit. . . . The filthy vocabulary of Reformation propaganda [was] aimed at inciting the common man. . . . Luther used a great deal of invective, but there was method in it. . . . Inclination and conviction unite to form a mighty alliance, fashioning a new language of filth which is more than filthy language. Precisely in all its repulsiveness and perversion it verbalizes the unspeakable: the diabolic profanation of God and man. Luther's lifelong barrage of crude words hurled at the opponents of the Gospel is robbed of significance if attributed to bad breeding. When taken seriously, it reveals the task Luther saw before him: to do battle against the greatest slanderer of all times![41]

Nevertheless most will agree that even though the thrust and breakthrough of the Reformation against such massive odds required someone of Luther's forcefulness, a line was often crossed into unwarranted invective and sin. Heiko Oberman is surely right to say, "Where resistance to the Papal State, fanaticism, and Judaism turns into the collective vilification of papists, Anabaptists, and Jews, the fatal point has been reached where the discovery of the Devil's power becomes a liability and a danger."[42] Luther's sometimes malicious anti-Semitism was an inexcusable contradiction of the Gospel he preached. Oberman observes with soberness and depth that Luther aligned himself with the Devil here, and the lesson to be learned is that this is possible for Christians, and to demythologize it is to leave Luther's anti-Semitism in the

---

[39] W. Carlos Martyn, *The Life and Times of Martin Luther* (New York: ATS, 1866), 380–81.
[40] The plaudit comes from professor Steven Ozment of Harvard University, printed on the back of Oberman, *Luther: Man between God and the Devil.*
[41] Oberman, *Luther*, 109.
[42] Ibid., 303.

hands of modern unbelief with no weapon against it.[43] In other words, the Devil is real and can trip a great man into graceless behavior, even as he recovers grace from centuries of obscurity.

Calvin's Accommodation to Brutal Times

John Calvin was very different from Luther but just as much a child of his harsh and rugged age. He and Luther never met, but had profound respect for each other. When Luther read Calvin's defense of the Reformation to Cardinal Sadolet in 1539, he said, "Here is a writing which has hands and feet. I rejoice that God raises up such men."[44] Calvin returned the respect in the one letter to Luther that we know of, which Luther did not receive. "Would that I could fly to you that I might, even for a few hours, enjoy the happiness of your society; for I would prefer, and it would be far better . . . to converse personally with yourself; but seeing that it is not granted to us on earth, I hope that shortly it will come to pass in the kingdom of God."[45] Knowing their circumstances better than we, and perhaps knowing their own sins better than we, they could pass over each other's flaws more easily in their affections.

It has not been so easy for others. The greatness of the accolades for John Calvin have been matched by the seriousness and severity of the criticisms. In his own day, even his brilliant contemporaries stood in awe of Calvin's grasp of the fullness of Scripture. At the 1541 Conference at Worms, Melanchthon expressed that he was overwhelmed at Calvin's learning and called him simply "The Theologian." In modern times, T. H. L. Parker agrees and says, "Augustine and Luther were perhaps his superiors in creative thinking; Aquinas in philosophy; but in systematic theology Calvin stands supreme."[46] And Benjamin Warfield

---

[43] Ibid., 297.
[44] Henderson, *Calvin in His Letters*, 68.
[45] Ibid., 113–14.
[46] Parker, *Portrait of Calvin*, 49. Jakobus Arminius, usually considered the historic antagonist of Calvinism, wrote, "[Calvin] excels beyond comparison in the interpretation of Scripture, and his commentaries ought to be more highly valued than all that is handed down to us by the Library of the Fathers" (Alfred T. Davies, *John Calvin and the Influence of Protestantism on National Life and Character* [London: Henry E. Walter, 1946], 24). "He stands out in the history of biblical study as, what Diestel, for example, proclaims him, 'the creator of genuine exegesis.' The authority which his comments immediately acquired was immense—they 'opened the Scriptures' as the Scriptures never had been opened before. Richard Hooker—'the judicious Hooker'—remarks that in the controversies of his own time, 'the sense of Scripture which Calvin alloweth' was of more weight than if 'ten thousand Augustines, Jeromes, Chrysostoms, Cyprians were brought forward'" (Warfield, *Calvin and Augustine*, 9).

said, "No man ever had a profounder sense of God than he."[47] But the times were barbarous, and not even Calvin could escape the evidences of his own sinfulness and the blind spots of his own age.

Life was harsh, even brutal, in the sixteenth century. There was no sewer system or piped water supply or central heating or refrigeration or antibiotics or penicillin or aspirin or surgery for appendicitis or Novocain for tooth extraction or electric lights for studying at night or water heaters or washers or dryers or stoves or ballpoint pens or typewriters or computers. Calvin, like many others in his day, suffered from "almost continuous ill-health."[48] If life could be miserable physically, it could get even more dangerous socially and more grievous morally. The libertines in Calvin's church, like their counterparts in first-century Corinth, reveled in treating the "communion of saints" as a warrant for wife-swapping.[49] Calvin's opposition made him the victim of mob violence and musket fire more than once.

Not only were the times unhealthy, harsh, and immoral, they were often barbaric as well. This is important to see, because Calvin did not escape the influence of his times. He described in a letter the cruelty common in Geneva. "A conspiracy of men and women has lately been discovered who, for the space of three years, had [intentionally] spread the plague through the city, by what mischievous device I know not." The upshot of this was that fifteen women were burned at the stake. "Some men," Calvin said, "have even been punished more severely; some have committed suicide in prison, and while twenty-five are still kept prisoners, the conspirators do not cease . . . to smear the door-locks of the dwelling-houses with their poisonous ointment."[50]

This kind of capital punishment loomed on the horizon not just for criminals, but for the Reformers themselves. Calvin was driven out of his homeland, France, under threat of death. For the next twenty years, he agonized over the martyrs there and corresponded with many of them as they walked faithfully toward the stake. The same fate easily could have befallen Calvin with the slightest turn in providence. "We have not only exile to fear, but that all the most cruel varieties of death

---

[47] Warfield, *Calvin and Augustine*, 24.
[48] John Calvin, *Sermons on the Epistle to the Ephesians* (orig. French ed., 1562; orig. English trans., 1577; repr., Edinburgh: Banner of Truth, 1973), *viii*. For details on Calvin's miseries, see chapter 3.
[49] Henderson, *Calvin in His Letters*, 75.
[50] Ibid., 63.

are impending over us, for in the cause of religion they will set no bounds to their barbarity."[51]

This atmosphere gave rise to the greatest and the worst achievement of Calvin. The greatest was the writing of the *Institutes of the Christian Religion*, and the worst was his joining in the condemnation of the heretic Michael Servetus to burning at the stake in Geneva. The *Institutes* was first published in March 1536, when Calvin was twenty-six years old. It went through five editions and enlargements until it reached its present form in the 1559 edition. If this were all Calvin had written— and not forty-eight volumes of other works—it would have established him as the foremost theologian of the Reformation. But the work did not arise for merely academic reasons. We will see in chapter 3 that it arose in tribute and defense of Protestant martyrs in France.[52]

But it was this same cruelty from which he could not disentangle himself. Michael Servetus was a Spaniard, a medical doctor, a lawyer, and a theologian. His doctrine of the Trinity was unorthodox—so much so that it shocked both Catholic and Protestant in his day. In 1553, he published his views and was arrested by the Catholics in France. But, alas, he escaped to Geneva. He was arrested there, and Calvin argued the case against him. He was sentenced to death. Calvin called for a swift execution instead of burning, but Servetus was burned at the stake on October 27, 1553.[53]

This has tarnished Calvin's name so severely that many cannot give his teaching a hearing. But it is not clear that most of us, given that milieu, would not have acted similarly under the circumstances.[54] Melanchthon was the gentle, soft-spoken associate of Martin Luther whom Calvin had met and loved. He wrote to Calvin on the Servetus affair, "I am wholly of your opinion and declare also that your magistrates acted quite justly in condemning the blasphemer to death."[55] Calvin never held civil office in Geneva[56] but exerted all his influence as a pastor. Yet in this execution, his hands were as stained with Servetus's blood as David's were with Uriah's.

This makes the confessions of Calvin near the end of his life all the

---

[51] Dillenberger, *John Calvin*, 71.
[52] Ibid., 27.
[53] Parker, *Portrait of Calvin*, 102.
[54] Parker describes some of those circumstances in ibid.
[55] Henderson, *Calvin in His Letters*, 196.
[56] Warfield, *Calvin and Augustine*, 16.

more important. On April 25, 1564, a month before his death, he called the magistrates of the city to his room and spoke these words:

> With my whole soul I embrace the mercy which [God] has exercised towards me through Jesus Christ, atoning for my sins with the merits of his death and passion, that in this way he might satisfy for *all my crimes and faults*, and blot them from his remembrance. . . . I confess I have failed innumerable times to execute my office properly, and had not He, of His boundless goodness, assisted me, all that zeal had been fleeting and vain. . . . For all these reasons, I testify and declare that I trust to no other security for my salvation than this, and this only, viz., that as God is the Father of mercy, he will show himself such a Father to me, who acknowledge myself to be *a miserable sinner.*[57]

T. H. L. Parker said, "He should never have fought the battle of faith with the world's weapons."[58] Most of us today would agree. Whether Calvin came to that conclusion before he died, we don't know. But what we know is that Calvin knew himself a "miserable sinner" whose only hope in view of "all [his] crimes" was the mercy of God and the blood of Jesus.

Why We Need the Flawed Fathers

So the times were harsh, immoral, and barbarous and had a contaminating effect on everyone, just as we are all contaminated by the evils of our own time. Their blind spots and evils may be different from ours. And it may be that the very things they saw clearly are the things we are blind to. It would be naïve to say that we never would have done what they did under their circumstances, and thus draw the conclusion that they have nothing to teach us. In fact, we are, no doubt, blind to many of our evils, just as they were blind to many of theirs. The virtues they manifested in those times are probably the very ones that we need in ours. There was in the life and ministry of John Calvin a grand God-centeredness, Bible-allegiance, and iron constancy. Under the banner of God's mercy to miserable sinners, we would do well to listen and learn. And that goes for Martin Luther and St. Augustine as well.

The conviction behind this book is that the glory of God, however

---

[57] Dillenberger, *John Calvin*, 35, emphasis added.
[58] Parker, *Portrait of Calvin*, 103.

dimly, is mirrored in the flawed lives of his faithful servants. God means for us to consider their lives and peer through the imperfections of their faith and behold the beauty of their God. This is what I hope will happen through the reading of this book. There are life-giving lessons written by the hand of Divine Providence on every page of history. The great German and the great Frenchman drank from the great African, and God gave the life of the Reformation.

But let us be admonished, finally, from the mouth of Luther that the only original, true, and life-giving spring is the Word of God. Beware of replacing the pure mountain spring of Scripture with the sullied streams of great saints. They are precious, but they are not pure. So we say with Luther,

> The writings of all the holy fathers should be read only for a time, in order that through them we may be led to the Holy Scriptures. As it is, however, we read them only to be absorbed in them and never come to the Scriptures. We are like men who study the sign-posts and never travel the road. The dear fathers wished by their writing, to lead us to the Scriptures, but we so use them as to be led away from the Scriptures, though the Scriptures alone are our vineyard in which we ought all to work and toil.[59]

I hope it will be plain, by the focus and development of the following three chapters, that this is the design of the book: From the "Sovereign Joy" of grace discovered by Augustine to the "Sacred Study" of Scripture in the life of Luther to the "Divine Majesty of the Word" in the life and preaching of Calvin, the aim is that the glorious gospel of God's all-satisfying, omnipotent grace will be savored, studied, and spread for the joy of all peoples—in a never-ending legacy of sovereign joy. And so may the Lord come quickly.

---

[59]Hugh T. Kerr, *A Compend of Luther's Theology* (Philadelphia, PA: Westminster Press, 1943), 13.

How sweet all at once it was for me to be rid of those fruitless joys which I had once feared to lose. . . . You drove them from me, you who are the true, the sovereign joy. You drove them from me and took their place, you who are sweeter than all pleasure, though not to flesh and blood, you who outshine all light, yet are hidden deeper than any secret in our hearts, you who surpass all honor, though not in the eyes of men who see all honor in themselves. . . . O Lord my God, my Light, my Wealth, and my Salvation.

St. Augustine
Confessions

1

Sovereign Joy

*The Liberating Power of Holy Pleasure in the Life
and Thought of St. Augustine*

The End of an Empire

On August 26, 410, the unthinkable happened. After nine hundred years of impenetrable security, Rome was sacked by the Gothic army led by Alaric. St. Jerome, the translator of the Latin Vulgate, was in Palestine at the time and wrote, "If Rome can perish, what can be safe?"[1] Rome did not perish immediately. It would be another sixty-six years before the Germans deposed the last emperor. But the shock waves of the invasion reached the city of Hippo, about 450 miles southwest of Rome on the coast of North Africa, where Augustine was the bishop. He was fifty-five years old and in the prime of his ministry. He would live another twenty years and die on August 28, 430, just as eighty thousand invading Vandals were about to storm the city. In other words, Augustine lived in one of those tumultuous times between the shifting of whole civilizations.

He had heard of two other Catholic bishops tortured to death in the Vandal invasion, but when his friends quoted to him the words of Jesus, "Flee to another city," he said, "Let no one dream of holding our ship so cheaply, that the sailors, let alone the Captain, should desert her in time of peril."[2] He had been the bishop of Hippo since 396 and, before that,

---

[1] Peter Brown, *Augustine of Hippo* (Berkeley, CA: University of California Press, 1969), 289.
[2] Ibid., 425.

had been a preaching elder for five years. So he had served the church for almost forty years and was known throughout the Christian world as a God-besotted, biblical, articulate, persuasive shepherd of his flock and a defender of the faith against the great doctrinal threats of his day, mainly Manichaeism,[3] Donatism,[4] and Pelagianism.[5]

Unparalleled and Paradoxical Influence

From this platform in North Africa, and through his remarkable faithfulness in formulating and defending the Christian faith for his generation, Augustine shaped the history of the Christian church. His influence in the Western world is simply staggering. Adolf Harnack said that he was the greatest man the church has possessed between Paul the Apostle and Luther the Reformer.[6] Benjamin Warfield argued

---

[3] From age nineteen to twenty-eight, Augustine was enamored with Manichaeism, but then became disillusioned with it and a great opponent in philosophical debate (Augustine, *Confessions*, trans. R. S. Pine-Coffin [New York: Penguin, 1961], 71 [IV, 1]). Manichaeism was a heretical sect of Christianity founded by Mani, who claimed to have received an inspired message in Mesopotamia and had been executed in AD 276 by the Persian government. The "new" Christianity he founded had sloughed off the Old Testament as unspiritual and disgusting. In Mani's Christianity, "Christ did not need the witness of the Hebrew prophets: He spoke for Himself, directly to the soul, by His elevated message, by His Wisdom and His miracles. God needed no other altar than the mind" (Brown, *Augustine of Hippo*, 43–44). The problem of evil was at the heart of Augustine's involvement with the Manichees. "They were dualists: so convinced were they that evil could not come from a good God, that they believed that it came from an invasion of the good—the 'Kingdom of Light'—by a hostile force of evil, equal in power, eternal, totally separate—the 'Kingdom of Darkness'" (p. 47). "The need to save an untarnished oasis of perfection within himself formed, perhaps, the deepest strain of [Augustine's] adherence to the Manichees. . . . 'For I still held the view that it was not I who was sinning, but some other nature within me'" (p. 51). Augustine gives his own explanation of why he was taken by the heresy of Manichaeism: "I thought that you, Lord God who are the Truth, were a bright, unbounded body and I a small piece broken from it" (Augustine, *Confessions*, 89 [V, 16]). "I thought that whatever had no dimension in space must be absolutely nothing at all. . . . I did not realize that the power of thought, by which I formed these images, was itself something quite different from them. And yet it could not form them unless it were itself something, and something great enough to do so" (p. 134 [VII, 1]). "Because such little piety as I had compelled me to believe that God, who is good, could not have created an evil nature, I imagined that there were two antagonistic masses, both of which were infinite, yet the evil in a lesser and the good in a greater degree" (p. 104 [V, 10]). From this entanglement Augustine went on to be a great apologist for the true biblical vision of one transcendent, sovereign God.

[4] Donatism "was a Christian movement of the 4th and 5th centuries, which claimed that the validity of the sacraments depends on the moral character of the minister. It arose as a result of the consecration of a bishop of Carthage in AD 311. One of the three consecrating bishops was believed to be a *traditor*, that is, one of the ecclesiastics who had been guilty of handing over their copies of the Bible to the oppressive forces of the Roman emperor Diocletian. An opposition group of 70 bishops, led by the primate of Numidia, formed itself into a synod at Carthage and declared the consecration of the bishop invalid. They held that the church must exclude from its membership persons guilty of serious sin, and that therefore no sacrament could rightly be performed by a *traditor*. The synod excommunicated the Carthaginian bishop when he refused to appear before it. Four years later, upon the death of the new bishop, the theologian Donatus the Great became bishop of Carthage; the movement later took its name from him" ("Donatism," *Microsoft® Encarta® Encyclopedia 99* [Microsoft Corporation, 1993–1998]). In this controversy we see Augustine's allegiance to the sacramental character of the Catholic Church that we raised questions about in the introduction. See pages 30–31.

[5] The teachings of Pelagius will be explained later in this chapter.

[6] Adolf Harnack, "Monasticism and the *Confessions* of St. Augustine," in Benjamin B. Warfield, *Calvin and Augustine* (Philadelphia, PA: P&R, 1956), 306.

that through his writings Augustine "entered both the Church and the world as a revolutionary force, and not merely created an epoch in the history of the Church, but . . . determined the course of its history in the West up to the present day."[7] He had "a literary talent . . . second to none in the annals of the Church."[8] "The whole development of Western life, in all its phases, was powerfully affected by his teaching."[9] The publishers of *Christian History* magazine simply say, "After Jesus and Paul, Augustine of Hippo is the most influential figure in the history of Christianity."[10]

The most remarkable thing about Augustine's influence is the fact that it flows into radically opposing religious movements. He is cherished as one of the greatest fathers of the Roman Catholic Church,[11] and yet it was Augustine who "gave us the Reformation"—not only because "Luther was an Augustinian monk, or that Calvin quoted Augustine more than any other theologian . . . [but because] the Reformation witnessed the ultimate triumph of Augustine's doctrine of grace over the legacy of the Pelagian view of man."[12] "Both sides in the controversy [between the Reformers and the (Catholic) counter-Reformation] appealed on a huge scale to texts of Augustine."[13]

Henry Chadwick tries to get at the scope of Augustine's influence by pointing out that "Anselm, Aquinas, Petrarch (never without a pocket copy of the *Confessions*), Luther, Bellarmine, Pascal, and Kierkegaard all stand in the shade of his broad oak. His writings were among the favourite books of Wittgenstein. He was the *bête noire* ["object of aversion"] of Nietzsche. His psychological analysis anticipated parts of Freud: he first discovered the existence of the 'sub-conscious.'"[14]

There are reasons for this extraordinary influence. Agostino Trapè gives an excellent summary of Augustine's powers that make him incomparable in the history of the church:

---

[7] Ibid.
[8] Ibid., 312.
[9] Ibid., 310.
[10] *Christian History* 6, no. 3 (1987): 2.
[11] "The Council of Orange adopted his teaching on grace, the Council of Trent his teaching on original sin and justification, and Vatican I his teaching on the relations between reason and faith. In our own day, Vatican II has made its own his teaching on the mystery of the Church and the mystery of the human person." Agostino Trapè, *Saint Augustine: Man, Pastor, Mystic* (New York: Catholic Book, 1986), 333.
[12] R. C. Sproul, "Augustine and Pelagius," *Tabletalk*, June 1996: 11. "Pelagian view of man" means the view that man has the final and ultimate self-determining ability to overcome his own slavery to sin. See later in this chapter on the views of Pelagius.
[13] Henry Chadwick, *Augustine* (Oxford: Oxford University Press, 1986), 2.
[14] Ibid., 3.

Augustine was . . . a philosopher, theologian, mystic, and poet in one. . . .
His lofty powers complemented each other and made the man fascinating
in a way difficult to resist. He is a philosopher, but not a cold thinker; he is
a theologian, but also a master of the spiritual life; he is a mystic, but also
a pastor; he is a poet, but also a controversialist. Every reader thus finds
something attractive and even overwhelming: depth of metaphysical intuition, rich abundance of theological proofs, synthetic power and energy,
psychological depth shown in spiritual ascents, and a wealth of imagination,
sensibility, and mystical fervor.[15]

Visiting the Alps without Seeing Them All

Virtually everyone who speaks or writes on Augustine has to disclaim
thoroughness. Benedict Groeschel, who has written a recent introduction to Augustine, visited the Augustinian Heritage Institute adjacent to
Villanova University where the books on Augustine comprise a library
of their own. Then he was introduced to Augustine's five million words
on computer. He speaks for many of us when he says,

> I felt like a man beginning to write a guidebook of the Swiss Alps. . . . After
> forty years I can still meditate on one book of the *Confessions* . . . during
> a week-long retreat and come back feeling frustrated that there is still so
> much more gold to mine in those few pages. I, for one, know that I shall
> never in this life escape from the Augustinian Alps.[16]

But the fact that no one can exhaust the Alps doesn't keep people
from going there, even simple people. If you wonder where to start in
your own reading, almost everyone would say to start with the *Confessions*, the story of Augustine's life up through his conversion and the
death of his mother. The other four "great books" are *On Christian
Doctrine*; the *Enchiridion: On Faith, Hope and Love*, which, Warfield
says, is Augustine's "most serious attempt to systematize his thought";[17]
On the Trinity, which gave the Trinity its definitive formulation; and
The City of God, which was Augustine's response to the collapsing of
the empire and his attempt to show the meaning of history.

The brevity of the tour of these Alps is drastically out of proportion
to the greatness of the subject and its importance for our day. It is rele-

---

[15] Trapè, *Saint Augustine*, 335.
[16] Benedict J. Groeschel, *Augustine: Major Writings* (New York: Crossroad, 1996), 1–2.
[17] Warfield, *Calvin and Augustine*, 307.

vant for our ministries—whether vocational minister or layperson—and especially for the advance of the Biblical Reformed faith in our day. The title of this chapter is "Sovereign Joy: The Liberating Power of Holy Pleasure in the Life and Thought of St. Augustine." Another subtitle might have been "The Place of Pleasure in the Exposition and Defense of Evangelicalism." Or another might have been, "The Augustinian Roots of Christian Hedonism."[18]

Augustine's Life in Overview

Augustine was born in Thagaste, near Hippo, in what is now Algeria, on November 13, 354. His father, Patricius, a middle-income farmer, was not a believer. He worked hard to get Augustine the best education in rhetoric that he could, first at Madaura, twenty miles away, from age eleven to fifteen; then, after a year at home, in Carthage from age seventeen to twenty. His father was converted in 370, the year before he died, when Augustine was sixteen. He mentions his father's death only in passing one time in all his vast writings. This is all the more striking when you consider the many pages spent on the grief of losing friends.

"As I grew to manhood," he wrote, "I was inflamed with desire for a surfeit of hell's pleasures. . . . My family made no effort to save me from my fall by marriage. Their only concern was that I should learn how to make a good speech and how to persuade others by my words."[19] In particular, he said that his father "took no trouble at all to see how I was growing in your sight [O God] or whether I was chaste or not. He cared only that I should have a fertile tongue."[20] The profound disappointment in his father's care for him silenced Augustine's tongue concerning his father for the rest of his life.

Before he left for Carthage to study for three years, his mother warned him earnestly "not to commit fornication and above all not to seduce any man's wife."[21] "I went to Carthage, where I found myself in the midst of a hissing cauldron of lust. . . . My real need was for you, my God, who are the food of the soul. I was not aware of this hunger."[22] "I was willing to steal, and steal I did, although I was not

---

[18] Christian Hedonism is the name I give to the vision of God and Christian life and ministry unfolded especially in *Desiring God* (Colorado Springs: Multnomah, 2011).
[19] Augustine, *Confessions*, 44 (II, 2).
[20] Ibid., 45 (II, 3).
[21] Ibid., 46 (II, 3).
[22] Ibid., 55 (III, 1).

compelled by any lack."[23] "I was at the top of the school of rhetoric. I was pleased with my superior status and swollen with conceit. . . . It was my ambition to be a good speaker, for the unhallowed and inane purpose of gratifying human vanity."[24] He took a concubine in Carthage and lived with this same woman for fifteen years and had one son by her, Adeodatus.

He became a traditional schoolmaster teaching rhetoric for the next eleven years of his life—age nineteen to thirty—and then spent the last forty-four years of his life as an unmarried monk and a bishop. Another way to say it would be that he was profligate until he was thirty-one and celibate until he was seventy-five. But his conversion was not as sudden as is often thought.

When he was nineteen, in the "cauldron of Carthage," swollen with conceit and utterly given over to sexual pleasures, he read Cicero's *Hortensius*, which for the first time arrested him by its content and not its rhetorical form. Hortensius exalted the quest for wisdom and truth above mere physical pleasure.

> It altered my outlook on life. It changed my prayers to you, O Lord, and provided me with new hopes and aspirations. All my empty dreams suddenly lost their charm and my heart began to throb with a bewildering passion for the wisdom of eternal truth. I began to climb out of the depths to which I had sunk, in order to return to you. . . . My God, how I burned with longing to have wings to carry me back to you, away from all earthly things, although I had no idea what you would do with me! For yours is the wisdom. In Greek the word "philosophy" means "love of wisdom," and it was with this love that the *Hortensius* inflamed me.[25]

This was nine years before his conversion to Christ, but it was utterly significant in redirecting his reading and thinking more toward truth rather than style, which is not a bad move in any age.

For the next nine years he was enamored by the dualistic teaching called Manichaeism, until he became disillusioned with one of its leaders when he was twenty-eight years old.[26] In his twenty-ninth year he moved from Carthage to Rome to teach, but was so fed up

---

[23] Ibid., 47 (II, 4).
[24] Ibid., 58 (III, 3).
[25] Ibid., 58–59 (III, 4).
[26] Ibid., 71 (IV, 1).

with the behavior of the students that he moved to a teaching post in Milan, Italy, in 384. This was providential in several ways. There he would discover the Platonists, and there he would meet the great bishop Ambrose. He was now thirty years old and still had his son and his concubine—a tragic, forgotten woman whom he never once names in all his writings.

In the early summer of 386, he discovered the writings of Plotinus, a neo-Platonist[27] who had died in 270. This was Augustine's second conversion after the reading of Cicero eleven years earlier. He absorbed the Platonic vision of reality with a thrill. This encounter, Peter Brown says, "did nothing less than shift the center of gravity of Augustine's spiritual life. He was no longer identified with his God [as in Manichaeism]: This God was utterly transcendent."[28]

But he was still in the dark. You can hear the influence of his Platonism in his assessment of those days: "I had my back to the light and my face was turned towards the things which it illumined, so that my eyes, by which I saw the things which stood in the light, were themselves in darkness."[29]

Now came the time for the final move, the move from Platonism to the apostle Paul, through the tremendous impact of Ambrose, who was fourteen years older than Augustine. "In Milan I found your devoted servant the bishop Ambrose. . . . At that time his gifted tongue never tired of dispensing the richness of your corn, the joy of your oil, and the sober intoxication of your wine. Unknown to me, it was you who led me to him, so that I might knowingly be led by him to you."[30]

Augustine's Platonism was scandalized by the biblical teaching that "the Word was made flesh." But week in and week out he would listen to Ambrose preach. "I was all ears to seize upon his eloquence, I also began to sense the truth of what he said, though only gradually."[31] "I thrilled with love and dread alike. I realized that I was far away from

---

[27] Neoplatonism was founded by Plotinus (AD 205–270), whose system was based chiefly on Plato's theory of ideas. Plotinus taught that the Absolute Being is related to matter by a series of emanations through several agencies, the first of which is *nous*, or pure intelligence. From this flows the soul of the world; from this, in turn, flow the souls of humans and animals, and finally, matter. Augustine would find numerous elements in this philosophy that do not cohere with biblical Christianity—for example, its categorical opposition between the spirit and matter. There was an aversion to the world of sense, and thus the necessity of liberation from a life of sense through rigorous ascetic discipline.

[28] Brown, *Augustine of Hippo*, 100.

[29] Augustine, *Confessions*, 88 (V, 16).

[30] Ibid., 107 (V, 13).

[31] Ibid., 108 (V, 14).

you . . . and, far off, I heard your voice saying I am the God who IS. I heard your voice, as we hear voices that speak to our hearts, and at once I had no cause to doubt."[32]

But this experience was not true conversion. "I was astonished that although I now loved you . . . I did not persist in enjoyment of my God. Your beauty drew me to you, but soon I was dragged away from you by my own weight and in dismay I plunged again into the things of this world . . . as though I had sensed the fragrance of the fare but was not yet able to eat it."[33]

Notice here the emergence of the phrase "enjoyment of my God." Augustine now conceived of the quest of his life as a quest for a firm and unshakable enjoyment of the true God. This would be utterly determinative in his thinking about everything, especially in his great battles with Pelagianism near the end of his life forty years from this time.

He knew that he was held back now not by anything intellectual, but by sexual lust: "I was still held firm in the bonds of woman's love."[34] Therefore the battle would be determined by the kind of pleasure that triumphed in his life. "I began to search for a means of gaining the strength I needed to enjoy you [notice the battlefront: How shall I find strength to enjoy God more than sex?], but I could not find this means until I embraced the mediator between God and men, Jesus Christ."[35]

His mother, Monica, who had prayed for him all his life, had come to Milan in the spring of 385 and had begun to arrange a proper marriage for him with a well-to-do Christian family there. This put Augustine into a heart-wrenching crisis and set him up for even deeper sin, even as his conversion was on the horizon. He sent his concubine of fifteen years back to Africa, never to live with her again. "The woman with whom I had been living was torn from my side as an obstacle to my marriage and this was a blow which crushed my heart to bleeding, because I loved her dearly. She went back to Africa, vowing never to give herself to any other man. . . . But I was too unhappy and too weak to imitate this example set me by a woman. . . . I took another mistress, without the sanction of wedlock."[36]

---

32 Ibid., 146 (VII, 10).
33 Ibid., 152 (VII, 17).
34 Ibid., 158 (VIII, 1).
35 Ibid., 152 (VII, 18).
36 Ibid., 131 (VI, 15).

The History-Making Conversion

Then came one of the most important days in church history. "O Lord, my Helper and my Redeemer, I shall now tell and confess to the glory of your name how you released me from the fetters of lust which held me so tightly shackled and from my slavery to the things of this world."[37] This is the heart of his book, the *Confessions*, and one of the great works of grace in history, and what a battle it was. But listen carefully how it was won. (It's recorded more fully in Book VIII of the *Confessions*.)

Even this day was more complex than the story often goes, but to go to the heart of the battle, let's focus on the final crisis. It was late August 386. Augustine was almost thirty-two years old. With his best friend, Alypius, he was talking about the remarkable sacrifice and holiness of Antony, an Egyptian monk. Augustine was stung by his own bestial bondage to lust, when others were free and holy in Christ.

> There was a small garden attached to the house where we lodged. . . . I now found myself driven by the tumult in my breast to take refuge in this garden, where no one could interrupt that fierce struggle in which I was my own contestant. . . . I was beside myself with madness that would bring me sanity. I was dying a death that would bring me life. . . . I was frantic, overcome by violent anger with myself for not accepting your will and entering into your covenant. . . . I tore my hair and hammered my forehead with my fists; I locked my fingers and hugged my knees.[38]

But he began to see more clearly that the gain was far greater than the loss, and by a miracle of grace he began to see the beauty of chastity in the presence of Christ.

> I was held back by mere trifles. . . . They plucked at my garment of flesh and whispered, "Are you going to dismiss us? From this moment we shall never be with you again, for ever and ever." . . . And while I stood trembling at the barrier, on the other side I could see the chaste beauty of Continence in all her serene, unsullied joy, as she modestly beckoned me to cross over and to hesitate no more. She stretched out loving hands to welcome and embrace me.[39]

---

[37] Ibid., 166 (VIII, 6).
[38] Ibid., 170–71 (VIII, 8).
[39] Ibid., 175–76 (VIII, 11).

So now the battle came down to the beauty of Continence and her tenders of love versus the trifles that plucked at his flesh.

> I flung myself down beneath a fig tree and gave way to the tears which now streamed from my eyes. . . . In my misery I kept crying, "How long shall I go on saying 'tomorrow, tomorrow'? Why not now? Why not make an end of my ugly sins at this moment?" . . . All at once I heard the singsong voice of a child in a nearby house. Whether it was the voice of a boy or a girl I cannot say, but again and again it repeated the refrain "Take it and read, take it and read." At this I looked up, thinking hard whether there was any kind of game in which children used to chant words like these, but I could not remember ever hearing them before. I stemmed my flood of tears and stood up, telling myself that this could only be a divine command to open my book of Scripture and read the first passage on which my eyes should fall.[40]

> So I hurried back to the place where Alypius was sitting . . . seized [the book of Paul's epistles] and opened it, and in silence I read the first passage on which my eyes fell: "Not in reveling and drunkenness, not in lust and wantonness, not in quarrels and rivalries. Rather, arm yourselves with the Lord Jesus Christ; spend no more thought on nature and nature's appetites" (Romans 13:13–14). I had no wish to read more and no need to do so. For in an instant, as I came to the end of the sentence, it was as though the light of confidence flooded into my heart and all the darkness of doubt was dispelled.[41]

The Unchosen Place and the Providence of God

The experience of God's grace in Augustine's own conversion set the trajectory for his theology of grace that brought him into conflict with Pelagius and made him the source of the Reformation a thousand years later. And this theology of sovereign grace was a very self-conscious theology of the triumph of joy in God.

He was baptized the next Easter 387, in Milan by Ambrose. That autumn his mother died, a very happy woman because the son of her tears was safe in Christ. In 388 (at almost thirty-four), he returned to Africa with a view to establishing a kind of monastery for him and his friends, whom he called "servants of God." He had given up the plan

---

[40] Ibid., 177–78 (VIII, 12).
[41] Ibid., 178 (VIII, 12).

for marriage and committed himself to celibacy and poverty—that is, to the common life with others in the community.[42] He hoped for a life of philosophical leisure in the monastic way.

But God had other plans. Augustine's son, Adeodatus, died in 389. The dreams of returning to a quiet life in his hometown of Thagaste evaporated in the light of eternity. Augustine saw that it might be more strategic to move his monastic community to the larger city of Hippo. He chose Hippo because they already had a bishop, so there was less chance of his being pressed to take on that role. But he miscalculated— like Calvin more than a thousand years later. The church came to Augustine and essentially forced him to be the priest and then the bishop of Hippo, where he stayed for the rest of his life.

In a sermon much later, Augustine said to his people, "A slave may not contradict his Lord. I came to this city to see a friend, whom I thought I might gain for God, that he might live with us in the monastery. I felt secure, for the place already had a bishop. I was grabbed. I was made a priest . . . and from there, I became your bishop."[43]

And so, like so many in the history of the church who have left an enduring mark, he was thrust (at the age of thirty-six) out of a life of contemplation into a life of action. The role of bishop included settling legal disputes of church members and handling many civil affairs. "He would visit jails to protect prisoners from ill-treatment; he would intervene . . . to save criminals from judicial torture and execution; above all, he was expected to keep peace within his 'family' by arbitrating in their lawsuits."[44]

Augustine established a monastery on the grounds of the church and for almost forty years raised up a band of biblically saturated priests and bishops who were installed all over Africa, bringing renewal to the churches. He saw himself as part of the monastery, following the strict vegetarian diet and poverty and chastity. There was an absolute prohibition on female visitors. There was too much at stake, and he knew his weakness. He never married. When he died, there was no will because all his possessions belonged to the common order. His legacy was his writings, the clergy he trained, and his monastery.

---

[42] Brown, *Augustine of Hippo*, 116.
[43] Ibid., 138.
[44] Ibid., 195.

The Triumph of Grace as "Sovereign Joy"

Now, back to the triumph of grace in Augustine's life and theology. Augustine experienced this grace and developed it self-consciously as a theology of "sovereign joy." R. C. Sproul says that the church today is very largely in a Pelagian captivity.[45] Perhaps the prescription for the cure is for the church, and especially the lovers of God's sovereignty, to recover a healthy dose of Augustine's doctrine of "sovereign joy." Far too much Christian thinking and preaching in our day (including Reformed thinking and preaching) has not penetrated to the root of how grace actually triumphs—namely, through joy—and therefore is only half-Augustinian and half-biblical and half-beautiful.

The life and thought of Augustine bring us back to this root of joy. Pelagius was a British monk who lived in Rome in Augustine's day and taught that "though grace may facilitate the achieving of righteousness, it is not necessary to that end."[46] He denied the doctrine of original sin and asserted that human nature at its core is good and able to do all it is commanded to do. Therefore Pelagius was shocked when he read in Augustine's *Confessions*, "Give me the grace [O Lord] to do as you command, and command me to do what you will! . . . O holy God . . . when your commands are obeyed, it is from you that we receive the power to obey them."[47] Pelagius saw this as an assault on human goodness and freedom and responsibility; if God has to give what he commands, then we are not able to do what he commands and are not responsible to do what he commands, and the moral law unravels.

Augustine had not come to his position quickly. In his book *On the Freedom of the Will*, written between 388 and 391, he defended the freedom of the will in a way that caused Pelagius to quote Augustine's own book against him in later life.[48] But by the time Augustine wrote the *Confessions* ten years later, the issue was settled. Here is what he wrote (this may be one of the most important paragraphs for understanding the heart of Augustine's thought, and the essence of Augustinianism):

---

[45] "What would Luther think of the modern heirs of the Reformation? My guess is that he would write on the modern church's captivity to Pelagianism," R. C. Sproul, *Willing to Believe: The Controversy Over Free Will* (Grand Rapids, MI: Baker, 1997), 21.

[46] Sproul, "Augustine and Pelagius," 13.

[47] Augustine, *Confessions*, 236 (X, 31).

[48] "So, paradoxically the great opponent of Augustine's old age had been inspired by those treatises of the young philosopher, in which Augustine had defended the freedom of the will against a Manichaean determinism" (Brown, *Augustine of Hippo*, 149).

During all those years [of rebellion], where was my free will? What was the hidden, secret place from which it was summoned in a moment, so that I might bend my neck to your easy yoke? . . . How sweet all at once it was for me to be rid of *those fruitless joys* which I had once feared to lose! . . . *You drove them from me*, you who are the true, the *sovereign joy*. [There's the key phrase and the key reality for understanding the heart of Augustinianism.] You drove them from me and took their place, you who are *sweeter than all pleasure*, though not to flesh and blood, you who outshine all light, yet are hidden deeper than any secret in our hearts, you who surpass all honor, though not in the eyes of men who see all honor in themselves. . . . O Lord my God, my Light, my Wealth, and my Salvation.[49]

This is Augustine's understanding of grace. *Grace is God's giving us sovereign joy in God that triumphs over joy in sin.* In other words, God works deep in the human heart to transform the springs of joy so that we love God more than sex or anything else. Loving God, in Augustine's mind, is never reduced to deeds of obedience or acts of willpower. He never makes the mistake of quoting John 14:15 ("If you love Me, you will keep My commandments") and claiming that love *is* the same as keeping Christ's commandments, when the text says that keeping Christ's commandments *results from* loving Christ. "*If* you love, *then* me you will obey." Nor does he make the mistake of quoting 1 John 5:3 ("For this is the love of God, that we keep His commandments; and His commandments are not burdensome") and overlook the point that loving God means keeping his commandments *in such a way* that his commandments are not burdensome. Loving God is being so satisfied in God and so delighted in all that he is for us that his commandments cease to be burdensome. Augustine saw this. And we need him badly today to help us recover the root of all Christian living in the triumphant joy in God that dethrones the sovereignty of laziness and lust and greed.

For Augustine, loving God is always a delighting in God, and in other things only for God's sake. He defines it clearly in *On Christian Doctrine* (III.x.16). "I call 'charity' [i.e., love for God] the motion of the soul toward the enjoyment of God for His own sake, and the enjoyment of one's self and of one's neighbor for the sake of God."[50] Loving God

---

[49] Augustine, *Confessions*, 181 (IX, 1), emphasis added.
[50] Augustine, *On Christian Doctrine*, trans. D. W. Robertson Jr. (Upper Saddle River, NJ: Prentice Hall, 1958), 88. He adds, "'Cupidity' is a motion of the soul toward the enjoyment of one's self, one's neighbor, or any corporal thing for the sake of something other than God."

is always conceived of essentially as delighting in God and in anything else for his sake.

Augustine analyzed his own motives down to this root. Everything springs from delight. He saw this as a universal: "Every man, whatsoever his condition, desires to be happy. There is no man who does not desire this, and each one desires it with such earnestness that he prefers it to all other things; whoever, in fact, desires other things, desires them for this end alone."[51] This is what guides and governs the will, namely, what we consider to be our delight.

But here's the catch that made Pelagius so angry. Augustine believed that it is not in our power to determine what this delight will be.

> Who has it in his power to have such a motive present to his mind that his will shall be influenced to believe? Who can welcome in his mind something which does not give him delight? But who has it in his power to ensure that something that will delight him will turn up? Or that he will take delight in what turns up? If those things delight us which serve our advancement towards God, that is due not to our own whim or industry or meritorious works, but to the inspiration of God and to the grace which he bestows.[52]

So saving grace, converting grace, in Augustine's view, is *God's giving us a sovereign joy in God* that triumphs over all other joys and therefore sways the will. The will is free to move toward whatever it delights in most fully, but it is not within the power of our will to determine what that *sovereign joy* will be. Therefore Augustine concludes,

> A man's free-will, indeed, avails for nothing except to sin, if he knows not the way of truth; and even after his duty and his proper aim shall begin to become known to him, unless he also take delight in and feel a love for it, he neither does his duty, nor sets about it, nor lives rightly. Now, in order that such a course may engage our affections, God's "love is shed abroad in our

---

[51] Thomas A. Hand, *Augustine on Prayer* (New York: Catholic Book, 1986), 13 (sermon 306). See Augustine, *Confessions*, 228 (X, 21): "Without exception we all long for happiness . . . all agree that they want to be happy. . . . They may all search for it in different ways, but all try their hardest to reach the same goal, that is, joy."

[52] T. Kermit Scott, *Augustine: His Thought in Context* (New York: Paulist, 1995), 203 (*To Simplician*, II, 21). In another place he said, "Clearly it is in vain for us to will unless God have mercy. But I don't know how it could be said that it is vain for God to have mercy unless we willingly consent. If God has mercy, we also will, for the power to will is given with the mercy itself. It is God that worketh in us both to will and to do of his good pleasure. If we ask whether a good will is a gift of God, I should be surprised if anyone would venture to deny that. But because the good will does not precede calling, but calling precedes the good will, the fact that we have a good will is rightly attributed to God who calls us, and the fact that we are called cannot be attributed to our selves" (p. 201 [*To Simplician* II, 12]).

hearts" not through the free-will which arises from ourselves, but "through the Holy Ghost, which is given to us" (Romans 5:5).[53]

In 427, he looked back over a lifetime of thought on this issue and wrote to Simplician, "In answering this question I have tried hard to maintain the free choice of the human will, but the grace of God prevailed."[54] Controversy was Augustine's daily vocation. Near the end of his life, he listed over eighty heresies that he had fought against.[55] Why this defensive labor, in view of his deepest longing for joy in God? He gives one answer in the *Confessions*: "It is indeed true that the refutation of heretics gives greater prominence to the tenets of your Church [O Lord] and the principles of sound doctrine. For parties there must needs be, so that those who are true metal may be distinguished from the rest."[56]

But there was a deeper reason for his long engagement in the Pelagian controversy. When he was asked by his friend Paulinus why he kept on investing so much energy in this dispute with Pelagius, even as a man in his seventies, he answered, "First and foremost because no subject [but grace] gives me greater pleasure. For what ought to be more attractive to us sick men, than grace, grace by which we are healed; for us lazy men, than grace, grace by which we are stirred up; for us men longing to act, than grace, by which we are helped?"[57] This answer has all the more power when you keep in mind that all the healing, stirring, helping, enabling grace that Augustine revels in is *the giving of a compelling, triumphant joy*. Grace governs life by giving a supreme joy in the supremacy of God.

Augustine is utterly committed to the moral accountability of the human will, even though the will is ultimately governed by the delights of the soul that are ordered finally by God. When pressed for an explanation, he is willing, in the end, to rest with Scripture in a "profound mystery." This can be seen in the following two quotes:

Now, should any man be for constraining us to examine into this profound mystery, why this person is so persuaded as to yield, and that person is not,

---

[53] Ibid., 208 (*Spirit and Letter*, V).
[54] Ibid., 211 (*To Simplician*, II, 1).
[55] Augustine wrote *On Heresies* during 428–429, and it remains unfinished because of his death. In it he lists over eighty heresies from Simon Magus to the Pelagians (Brown, *Augustine of Hippo*, 35–56).
[56] Augustine, *Confessions*, 153–54 (VII, 19).
[57] Brown, *Augustine of Hippo*, 355 (Epistle 186, XII, 139).

there are only two things occurring to me, which I should like to advance as my answer: "O the depth of the riches!" (Romans 11:33) and "Is there unrighteousness with God?" (Romans 9:14). If the man is displeased with such an answer, he must seek more learned disputants: but let him beware lest he find presumptuousness.[58]

Let this truth, then, be fixed and unmovable in a mind soberly pious and stable in faith, that there is no unrighteousness with God. Let us also believe most firmly and tenaciously that God has mercy on whom he will and that whom he will he hardeneth, that is, he has or has not mercy on whom he will. Let us believe that this belongs to a certain hidden equity that cannot be searched out by any human standard of measurement, though its effects are to be observed in human affairs and earthly arrangements.[59]

The fact that grace governs life by giving a supreme joy in the supremacy of God explains why the concept of Christian freedom is so radically different in Augustine than in Pelagius. For Augustine, freedom is to be so much in love with God and his ways that the very experience of choice is transcended. The ideal of freedom is not the autonomous will poised with sovereign equilibrium between good and evil. The ideal of freedom is to be so spiritually discerning of God's beauty, and to be so in love with God, that one never stands with equilibrium between God and an alternate choice. Rather, one transcends the experience of choice and walks under the continual sway of sovereign joy in God. In Augustine's view, the self-conscious experience of having to contemplate choices was a sign not of the freedom of the will, but of the disintegration of the will. The struggle of choice is a necessary evil in this fallen world until the day comes when discernment and delight unite in a perfect apprehension of what is infinitely delightful, namely, God.

What follows from Augustine's view of grace as the giving of a sovereign joy that triumphs over "lawless pleasures"[60] is that the entire Christian life is seen as a relentless quest for the fullest joy in God. He said, "The whole life of a good Christian is a holy desire."[61] In other words, the key to Christian living is a thirst and a hunger for God. And

---

[58] Scott, *Augustine: His Thought in Context*, 209–10 (*Spirit and Letter*, LX).
[59] Ibid., 212 (*To Simplician*, II, 16).
[60] Augustine, *Confessions*, 44 (II, 2). "You were always present, angry and merciful at once, strewing the pangs of bitterness over all my lawless pleasures to lead me on to look for others unallied with pain. You meant me to find them nowhere but in yourself, O Lord, for you teach us by inflicting pain, you smite so that you may heal, and you kill us so that we may not die away from you."
[61] Hand, *Augustine on Prayer*, 20 (*Treatise on 1 John 4:6*).

one of the main reasons people do not understand or experience the sovereignty of grace and the way it works through the awakening of sovereign joy is that their hunger and thirst for God is so small. The desperation to be ravished for the sake of worship and holiness is unintelligible. Here's the goal and the problem as Augustine saw it:

> The soul of men shall hope under the shadow of Thy wings; they shall be made drunk with the fullness of Thy house; and of the torrents of Thy pleasures Thou wilt give them to drink; for in Thee is the Fountain of Life, and in Thy Light shall we see the light? Give me a man in love: he knows what I mean. Give me one who yearns; give me one who is hungry; give me one far away in this desert, who is thirsty and sighs for the spring of the Eternal country. Give me that sort of man: he knows what I mean. But if I speak to a cold man, he just does not know what I am talking about.[62]

These words from Augustine should make our hearts burn with renewed longing for God. And they should help us see why it is so difficult to display the glory of the gospel to so many people. The reason is that so many do not long for anything very much. They are just coasting. They are not passionate about anything. They are "cold," not just toward the glory of Christ in the gospel, but toward everything. Even their sins are picked at rather than swallowed with passion.

The Place of Prayer in the Pursuit of Joy

The remedy from God's side for this condition of "coldness," of course, is the gracious awakening of a sovereign joy. But on the human side, it is prayer and the display of God himself as infinitely more desirable than all creation. It is not a mere stylistic device that all 350 pages of the *Confessions* are written as a prayer. Every sentence is addressed to God. This is astonishing. It must have required enormous literary discipline not to fall into some other form. The point of this discipline is that Augustine is utterly dependent on God for the awakening of love to God. And it is no coincidence that the prayers of Augustine's mother, Monica, pervade the *Confessions*. She pled for him when he would not plead for himself.[63]

Augustine counsels us, "Say with the psalmist: 'One thing I have

---

[62] Brown, *Augustine of Hippo*, 374–75 (*Tractatus in Joannis evangelium*, 26, 4).
[63] See notes 67, 69, 70.

asked from the LORD, that I shall seek: That I may dwell in the house of the LORD all the days of my life, To behold the beauty of the LORD and to meditate in His temple' (Psalm 27:4)." Then he says, "In order that we may attain this happy life, he who is himself the true Blessed Life has taught us to pray."[64] Augustine shows us the way he prayed for the triumph of joy in God: "O Lord, that I may love you [freely], for I can find nothing more precious. Turn not away your face from me, that I may find what I seek. Turn not aside in anger from your servant, lest in seeking you I run toward something else. . . . Be my helper. Leave me not, neither despise me, O God my Saviour."[65]

His mother's praying became the school where he learned deep things about Jesus's words in John 16:24, "Until now you have asked for nothing in My name; ask, and you will receive, so that your joy may be made full." Prayer is the path to fullness of sovereign joy. But, oh, what a strange and circuitous path! Monica had learned patience in the pain of long-unanswered prayers. For example, her husband, Patricius, was unfaithful to her. But Augustine recalls in the *Confessions* that "her patience was so great that his infidelity never became a cause of quarreling between them. For she looked to you to show him mercy, hoping that chastity would come with faith. . . . In the end she won her husband for you [O Lord] as a convert in the very last days of his life on earth."[66]

So it would prove to be with her son. She "shed more tears [over] my spiritual death," Augustine said, "than other mothers shed for the bodily death of a son."[67] When her son was a Manichaean heretic, Monica sought help from an old bishop. His counsel was not what she wanted to hear: He too had been a Manichee once, but had seen his folly. "Leave him alone," he said. "Just pray to God for him. From his own reading he will discover his mistakes and the depth of his profanity. . . . Leave me and go in peace. It cannot be that the son of these tears should be lost."[68]

At the age of sixteen in 371, soon after his father's death, Augustine sneaked away from his mother in Carthage and sailed to Rome. "Dur-

---

[64] Hand, *Augustine on Prayer*, 25 (*Letter 130*, 15).
[65] Ibid., 27.
[66] Augustine, *Confessions*, 194–95.
[67] Ibid., 68 (III, 11).
[68] Ibid., 69–70 (III, 12).

ing the night, secretly, I sailed away, leaving her alone to her tears and her prayers."[69] How were these prayers answered? Not the way Monica hoped at that time. Only later could she see the truth of Jesus's words worked out in her life—that praying is the path to deepest joy. "And what did she beg of you, my God, with all those tears, if not that you would prevent me from sailing? But you did not do as she asked you. Instead, in the depth of your wisdom, you granted the wish that was closest to her heart. You did with me what she had always asked you to do."[70]

Later, just after his conversion, he went to tell his mother what God had done in answer to her prayers:

> Then we went and told my mother [of my conversion], who was overjoyed. And when we went on to describe how it had all happened, she was jubilant with triumph and glorified you, who are powerful enough, and more than powerful enough, to carry out your purpose beyond all our hopes and dreams. For she saw that you had granted her far more than she used to ask in her tearful prayers and plaintive lamentations. You converted me to yourself, so that I no longer desired a wife or placed any hope in this world but stood firmly upon the rule of faith, where you had shown me to her in a dream years before. And you turned her sadness into rejoicing, into joy far fuller than her dearest wish, far sweeter and more chaste than any she had hoped to find in children begotten of my flesh.[71]

Such was the lesson Augustine learned from the unremitting travail of his mother's prayers. Not what she thought she wanted in the short run, but what she most deeply wanted in the long run—God gave her "joy far fuller than her dearest wish." "Ask, and you will receive, so that your joy may be made full" (John 16:24).

Displaying the Superior Delight of Knowing God

But alongside prayer, the remedy for people without passion and without hunger and thirst for God is to display God himself as infinitely more desirable—more satisfying—than all creation. Augustine's zeal for the souls of men and women was that they might come to see the beauty of God and love him. "If your delight is in souls, love them in

---

[69] Ibid., 101 (V, 8).
[70] Ibid.
[71] Ibid., 178–79 (VIII, 12).

God . . . and draw as many with you to him as you can."[72] "You yourself [O God] are their joy. Happiness is to rejoice in you and for you and because of you. This is true happiness and there is no other."[73]

So Augustine labored with all his spiritual and poetic and intellectual might to help people see and feel the all-satisfying supremacy of God over all things.

> But what do I love when I love my God? . . . Not the sweet melody of harmony and song; not the fragrance of flowers, perfumes, and spices; not manna or honey; not limbs such as the body delights to embrace. It is not these that I love when I love my God. And yet, when I love him, it is true that I love a light of a certain kind, a voice, a perfume, a food, an embrace; but they are of the kind that I love in my inner self, when my soul is bathed in light that is not bound by space; when it listens to sound that never dies away; when it breathes fragrance that is not borne away on the wind; when it tastes food that is never consumed by the eating; when it clings to an embrace from which it is not severed by fulfillment of desire. This is what I love when I love my God.[74]

Few people in the history of the church have surpassed Augustine in portraying the greatness and beauty and desirability of God. He is utterly persuaded by Scripture and experience "that he is happy who possesses God."[75] "You made us for yourself, and our hearts find no peace till they rest in you."[76] He will labor with all his might to make this God of sovereign grace and sovereign joy known and loved in the world.

> You are ever active, yet always at rest. You gather all things to yourself, though you suffer no need. . . . You grieve for wrong, but suffer no pain. You can be angry and yet serene. Your works are varied, but your purpose is one and the same. . . . You welcome those who come to you, though you never lost them. You are never in need yet are glad to gain, never covetous yet you exact a return for your gifts. . . . You release us from our debts, but you lose nothing thereby. You are my God, my Life, my holy Delight, but is this enough to say of you? Can any man say enough when he speaks of you? Yet woe betide those who are silent about you![77]

---

[72] Ibid., 82 (IV, 12).
[73] Ibid., 228 (X, 22).
[74] Ibid., 211–12 (X, 6).
[75] Hand, *Augustine on Prayer*, 17 (*On the Happy Life*, 11).
[76] Augustine, *Confessions*, 21 (I, 1).
[77] Ibid., 23 (I, 4).

What a preacher Augustine became in his passion not to be "silent" about the all-satisfying pleasures at God's right hand! "Can any man say enough when he speaks of you?" He explained to his own congregation how his preaching came to be: "I go to feed [myself] so that I can give you to eat. I am the servant, the bringer of food, not the master of the house. I lay out before you that from which I also draw my life."[78] This was his way of study: he sought for soul-food that he might feed himself on God's "holy Delight" and then feed his people.

Even his ability—and his hearers' ability—to see the truth of Scripture was governed partially by the delight he took in what he found there. He would always tell his readers that they must "look into the Scriptures [with] the eyes of their heart on its heart." This means that one must look with love on what one only partially sees: "It is impossible to love what is entirely unknown, but when what is known, if even so little, is loved, this very capacity for love makes it better and more fully known."[79] In other words, loving, or delighting in, what we know of God in Scripture will be the key that opens Scripture further. So study and preaching were, for Augustine, anything but detached and impartial, as scholarship is so often conceived today.

He explained to the great Bible scholar Jerome that he could therefore never be a "disinterested" scholar, because "if I do gain any stock of knowledge [in the Scriptures], I pay it out immediately to the people of God."[80] And what was it that he showed them and fed them? It was the very joy that he himself found in God: "The thread of our speech comes alive through the very joy we take in what we are speaking about."[81] That was the key to his preaching, and the key to his life—he could not cease seeking and speaking about the sovereign joy in God that had set him free by the power of a superior satisfaction.

The Unchanged Relevance of Grace as "Sovereign Joy"

The implications of Augustine's experience and his theology of sovereign joy are tremendously relevant not only for preaching but also for evangelism. What had happened to him can happen to others because every human heart is the same in this way. "I am not alone in this desire

---

[78] Brown, *Augustine of Hippo*, 252 (Epistle 73, II, 5).
[79] Ibid., 279 (*Tractatus in Joannis evangelium*, 96, 4).
[80] Ibid., 252 (Epistle 73, II, 5).
[81] Ibid., 256.

[for the blessed state of happiness], nor are there only a few who share it with me: without exception we all long for happiness. . . . All agree that they want to be happy. . . . They may all search for it in different ways, but all try their hardest to reach the same goal, that is, joy."[82] This is a great common ground for doing evangelism in every age. Deeper than all "felt needs" is the real need: God. Not just God experienced without emotional impact, but rather God experienced as "holy Delight." "You made us for yourself, and our hearts find no peace till they rest in you."[83] This peace is the presence of a profound happiness. "He is happy who possesses God."[84] Not because God gives health, wealth, and prosperity, but because God *is* our soul's joyful resting place. To make this known and experienced through Jesus Christ is the goal of evangelism and world missions.

Augustine's doctrine of delight in God is the root of all Christian living. He brings it to bear on the most practical affairs of life and shows that every moment in every circumstance we stand on the brink between the lure of idolatry and the delight of seeing and knowing God. Perhaps he erred on the side of asceticism at times in an overreaction to the lust of his youth. But in principle he seemed to get it right. For example, his chief rule on using the things of the world so that they are gratefully received as God's gifts but do not become idols is expressed in this prayer: "He loves thee too little who loves anything together with thee, which he loves not for thy sake."[85] He illustrates:

> Suppose, brethren, a man should make a ring for his betrothed, and she should love the ring more wholeheartedly than the betrothed who made it for her. . . . Certainly, let her love his gift: but, if she should say, "The ring is enough. I do not want to see his face again" what would we say of her? . . . The pledge is given her by the betrothed just that, in his pledge, he himself may be loved. God, then, has given you all these things. Love Him who made them.[86]

Instead of minimizing the greatness and the beauty of this world, Augustine admired it and made it a means of longing for the City of

---

[82] Augustine, *Confessions*, 228 (X, 21).
[83] Ibid., 21 (I, 1).
[84] Hand, *Augustine on Prayer*, 17 (*On the Happy Life*, 11).
[85] Augustine, quoted in *Documents of the Christian Church*, ed. Henry Bettenson (London: Oxford University Press, 1967), 54.
[86] Brown, *Augustine of Hippo*, 326 (*Tractate on the Epistle of John*, 2:11).

which this is all a shadow. "From His gifts, which are scattered to good and bad alike in this, our most grim life, let us, with His help, try to express sufficiently what we have yet to experience."[87] He ponders the wonders of the human body and the "gratuitous ornament of a male beard," and even turns admiringly to pagan scholarship: "Who can possibly do full justice to the intellectual brilliance displayed by philosophers and heretics in defending their errors and incorrect opinions?"[88]

His delight in nature comes out in this regard as he, perhaps, looks out over the Bay of Hippo: "There is the grandeur of the spectacle of the sea itself, as it slips on and off its many colors like robes, and now is all shades of green, now purple, now sky-blue. . . . And all these are mere consolations for us, for us unhappy, punished men: they are not the rewards of the blessed. What can these be like then, if such things here are so many, so great, and of such a quality?"[89] Augustine's relentless focus on the City of God did not prevent him from seeing the beauties of this world and enjoying them for what they are—good gifts of God pointing us ever to the Giver and the superior joys of his presence. We need to heed the unremitting call of Augustine to be free from the ensnaring delights of this world, not because they are evil in themselves, but because so few of us use them as we ought: "If the things of this world delight you, praise God for them but turn your love away from them and give it to their Maker, so that in the things that please you may not displease him."[90]

Augustine's vision of salvation through Jesus Christ and of living the Christian life is rooted in his understanding and experience of grace—the divine gift of triumphant joy in God. The power that saves and sanctifies is the work of God deep beneath the human will to transform the springs of joy so that we love God more than sex or seas or scholarship or food or friends or fame or family or money. Grace is the key because it is free and creates a new heart with new delights that govern the will and the work of our lives. "It does not depend on the man who wills or the man who runs, but on God who has mercy" (Rom. 9:16).

If it is true, as R. C. Sproul says, that today "we have not broken free

---

[87] Ibid., 328 (*City of God*, XXII, 21, 26).
[88] Ibid., 329 (*City of God*, XXII, 24, 160).
[89] Ibid., 329 (*City of God*, XXII 24, 175).
[90] Augustine, *Confessions*, 82 (IV, 12).

from the Pelagian captivity of the church"[91]—a captivity that Augustine warred against for so many years for the sake of sovereign joy—then we should pray and preach and write and teach and labor with all our might to break the chain that holds us captive. Sproul says, "We need an Augustine or a Luther to speak to us anew lest the light of God's grace be not only overshadowed but be obliterated in our time."[92] Yes, we do. But we also need tens of thousands of ordinary pastors and laypeople who are ravished with the extraordinary power of joy in God.

And we need to rediscover Augustine's peculiar slant—a very biblical slant—on grace as the free gift of sovereign joy in God that frees us from the bondage of sin. We need to rethink our Reformed doctrine of salvation so that every limb and every branch in the tree is coursing with the sap of Augustinian delight. We need to make plain that *total depravity* is not just badness, but blindness to beauty and deadness to joy; and *unconditional election* means that the completeness of our joy in Jesus was planned for us before we ever existed; and that *limited atonement* is the assurance that indestructible joy in God is infallibly secured for us by the blood of the covenant; and *irresistible grace* is the commitment and power of God's love to make sure we don't hold on to suicidal pleasures, and to set us free by the sovereign power of superior delights; and that the *perseverance of the saints* is the almighty work of God to keep us, through all affliction and suffering, for an inheritance of pleasures at God's right hand forever.

This note of sovereign, triumphant joy is a missing element in too much Christian (especially Reformed) theology and worship. Maybe the question we should pose ourselves is whether this is so because we have not experienced the triumph of sovereign joy in our own lives. Can we say the following with Augustine?

> How sweet all at once it was for me to be rid of *those fruitless joys* which I had once feared to lose! . . . *You drove them from me*, you who are the true, the *sovereign joy*. You drove them from me and took their place. . . . O Lord my God, my Light, my Wealth, and my Salvation.[93]

Or are we in bondage to the pleasures of this world so that, for all our talk about the glory of God, we love television and food and

---

[91] R. C. Sproul, "Augustine and Pelagius," 52.
[92] Ibid.
[93] Augustine, *Confessions*, 181 (IX, 1), emphasis added.

sleep and sex and money and human praise just like everybody else? If so, let us repent and fix our faces like flint toward the Word of God. And let us pray: O Lord, open my eyes to see the sovereign sight that in your presence is fullness of joy and at your right hand are pleasures forevermore (Ps. 16:11). Grant, O God, that we would live the legacy of sovereign joy.

In this psalm [119] David always says that he will speak, think, talk, hear, read, day and night and constantly—but about nothing else than God's Word and Commandments. For God wants to give you His Spirit only through the external Word.
Martin Luther
Preface to his *1539 Works*

It is a sin and shame not to know our own book or to understand the speech and words of our God; it is a still greater sin and loss that we do not study languages, especially in these days when God is offering and giving us men and books and every facility and inducement to this study, and desires his Bible to be an open book. O how happy the dear fathers would have been if they had our opportunity to study the languages and come thus prepared to the Holy Scriptures! What great toil and effort it cost them to gather up a few crumbs, while we with half the labor—yes, almost without any labor at all—can acquire the whole loaf! O how their effort puts our indolence to shame!
Martin Luther
"To the Councilmen of All Cities in Germany That They Establish and Maintain Christian Schools"

2

Sacred Study

Martin Luther and the External Word

The Word of God Is a Book

One of the great rediscoveries of the Reformation—especially of Martin Luther—was that the Word of God comes to us in the form of a book. In other words, Luther grasped this powerful fact: God preserves the experience of salvation and holiness from generation to generation by means of a book of revelation, not a bishop in Rome, and not the ecstasies of Thomas Muenzer and the Zwickau prophets.[1] The Word of God comes to us in a book. This rediscovery shaped Luther and the Reformation.

One of Luther's arch-opponents in the Roman Church, Sylvester Prierias, wrote in response to Luther's Ninety-Five Theses (posted in 1517): "He who does not accept the doctrine of the Church of Rome and pontiff of Rome as an infallible rule of faith, from which the Holy Scriptures, too, draw their strength and authority, is a heretic."[2] In other words, the Church and the pope are the authoritative deposit of salvation and the Word of God; and the book—the Bible—is derivative

---

[1] Thomas Muenzer, seven years Luther's junior, became the preacher at the Church of St. Mary in Zwickau. "He . . . joined a union of fanatics, mostly weavers, who, with Nikolaus Storch at their head, had organized themselves under the leadership of twelve apostles and seventy-two disciples, and held secret conventicles, in which they pretended to receive divine revelations" (Philip Schaff, ed., *Religious Encyclopedia* [New York: Christian Literature, 1888], 2:1596). For Luther's response, see A. G. Dickens and Alun Davies, eds., *Documents of Modern History: Martin Luther* (New York: St. Martin's, 1970), 75–79.

[2] Heiko A. Oberman, *Luther: Man between God and the Devil*, trans. Eileen Walliser-Schwarzbart (orig., 1982; New York: Doubleday, 1992), 193. Professor Steven Ozment of Harvard calls Heiko Oberman "the world's foremost authority on Luther."

and secondary. "What is new in Luther," Heiko Oberman says, "is the notion of absolute obedience to the Scriptures against any authorities; be they popes or councils."[3] In other words, the saving, sanctifying, authoritative Word of God comes to us in a book. The implications of this simple observation are tremendous.

In 1539, commenting on Psalm 119, Luther wrote, "In this psalm David always says that he will speak, think, talk, hear, read, day and night and constantly—but about nothing else than God's Word and Commandments. *For God wants to give you His Spirit only through the external Word.*"[4] This phrase is extremely important. The "external Word" is the book. And the saving, sanctifying, illuminating Spirit of God, he says, comes to us *through* this "external Word." Luther calls it the "external Word" to emphasize that it is objective, fixed, outside ourselves, and therefore unchanging. It is a book. Neither ecclesiastical hierarchy nor fanatical ecstasy can replace it or shape it. It is "external," like God. You can take or leave it. But you can't make it other than what it is. It is a book with fixed letters and words and sentences.

Luther said with resounding forcefulness in 1545, the year before he died, "Let the man who would hear God speak, read Holy Scripture."[5] Earlier he had said in his lectures on Genesis, "The Holy Spirit himself and God, the Creator of all things, is the Author of this book."[6] One of the implications of the fact that the Word of God comes to us in a book is that the theme of this chapter is "The Pastor and His Study," not "The Pastor and His Seance" or "The Pastor and His Intuition" or "The Pastor and His Religious Multi-Perspectivalism." The Word of God that saves and sanctifies, from generation to generation, is preserved in a book. And therefore at the heart of every pastor's work is book-work. Call it reading, meditation, reflection, cogitation, study, exegesis, or whatever you will—a large and central part of our work is to wrestle God's meaning from a book, and then to proclaim it in the power of the Holy Spirit.

Luther knew that some would stumble over the sheer conservatism of this simple, unchangeable fact: God's Word is fixed in a book. He

---

[3] Ibid., 204.
[4] Ewald M. Plass, comp., *What Luther Says: An Anthology*, 3 vols. (St. Louis, MO: Concordia, 1959), 3:1359, emphasis added.
[5] Ibid., 2:62.
[6] Ibid.

knew then, as we know today, that many say this assertion nullifies or minimizes the crucial role of the Holy Spirit in giving life and light. Luther would probably say, "Yes, that might happen. One might argue that emphasizing the brightness of the sun nullifies the surgeon who takes away blindness." But most people would not agree with that. Certainly not Luther.

He said in 1520, "Be assured that no one will make a doctor of the Holy Scripture save only the Holy Ghost from heaven."[7] Luther was a great lover of the Holy Spirit. And his exaltation of the book as the "external Word" did not belittle the Spirit. On the contrary, it elevated the Spirit's great gift to Christendom. In 1533 Luther said, "The Word of God is the greatest, most necessary, and most important thing in Christendom."[8] Without the "external Word," we would not know one spirit from the other, and the objective personality of the Holy Spirit himself would be lost in a blur of subjective expressions. Cherishing the book implied to Luther that the Holy Spirit is a beautiful person to be known and loved, not a buzz to be felt.

Another objection to Luther's emphasis on the book is that it minimizes the incarnate Word, Jesus Christ himself. Luther says the opposite is true. To the degree that the Word of God is disconnected from the objective, "external Word," to that degree the incarnate Word—the historical Jesus—becomes a wax nose shaped by the preferences of every generation. Luther had one weapon with which to rescue the incarnate Word from being sold in the markets of Wittenberg. He drove out the money changers—the indulgence sellers—with the whip of the "external Word," the book.

When he posted the Ninety-Five Theses on October 31, 1517, thesis forty-five read, "Christians should be taught that he who sees someone needy but looks past him, and buys an indulgence instead, receives not the pope's remission but God's wrath."[9] That blow fell from the book—from the story of the Good Samaritan and from the second great commandment in the book, the "external Word." Without the book there would have been no blow, and the incarnate Word would be everybody's clay toy. So precisely for the sake of the incarnate Word, Luther exalts the written Word, the "external Word."

---

[7] Ibid., 3:1355.
[8] Ibid., 2:913.
[9] Oberman, *Luther: Man between God and the Devil*, 77.

It is true that the church needs to *see* the Lord in his earthly talking and walking on the earth. Our faith is rooted in that decisive revelation in history. But Luther reasserted that this *seeing* happens through a written record. The incarnate Word is revealed to us in a book.[10] Is it not remarkable that the Spirit in Luther's day, and in our day, was and is virtually silent about the history of the incarnate Lord on the earth—except in amplifying the glory of the Lord through the written record of the incarnate Word?

That is, neither the Roman Catholic Church nor charismatic prophets claimed that the Spirit of the Lord narrated to them untold events of the historical Jesus. This is astonishing. Of all the claims to authority *over* the "external Word" (by the pope) and *alongside* the "external Word" (by contemporary prophets), none of them brings forth new information about the incarnate life and ministry of Jesus. Rome will dare to add facts to the life of Mary (for example, the immaculate conception[11]), but not to the life of Jesus. Charismatic prophets will announce new movements of the Lord in the sixteenth century, and in our day, but none seems to report a new parable or a new miracle of the incarnate Word omitted from the Gospels—in spite of the fact that the apostle John wrote, "There are also many other things which Jesus did, which if they were written in detail, I suppose that even the world itself would not contain the books that would be written" (John 21:25). Neither Roman authority nor prophetic ecstasy adds to or deletes from the external record of the incarnate Word.[12]

Why is the Spirit so silent about the incarnate Word after the age of the New Testament—even among those who encroach on the authority of the book? The answer seems to be that it pleased God to reveal the incarnate Word, Jesus Christ, to all succeeding generations *through a book*, especially the Gospels. Luther put it like this:

---

[10] It is true that "flesh and blood" cannot see the glory of the Lord (Matt. 16:17). Only the Spirit of God can open the eyes of the heart to see the glory of God in the face of Christ (2 Cor. 4:6). I am not denying that. I only mean, with Luther, that the Spirit does not reveal the Son apart from the "external Word."

[11] Pope Pius IX announced the doctrine on December 8, 1854, with these words: "That the most blessed Virgin Mary, in the first moment of her conception, by a special grace and privilege of Almighty God, in virtue of the merits of Christ, was preserved immaculate from all stain of original sin" (Schaff, *Religious Encyclopedia*, 2:1064).

[12] Critical historians do this. They use various historical criteria to deny that such and such a saying of Jesus was really said by him, or that such and such a miracle was really done by him. But none of these historians claims that they are retelling the story of the incarnate Word *because of the inspiration of the Spirit*. In other words, my point here is not that there are no attacks on the historical Jesus, but that the role of the Spirit is not to replace the role of the book, and that the true incarnate Word is not revealed by the Spirit apart from the external Word.

> The apostles themselves considered it necessary to put the New Testament into Greek and to bind it fast to that language, doubtless in order to preserve it for us safe and sound as in a sacred ark. For they foresaw all that was to come and now has come to pass, and knew that if it were contained only in one's head, wild and fearful disorder and confusion, and many various interpretations, fancies and doctrines would arise in the Church, which could be prevented and from which the plain man could be protected only by committing the New Testament to writing and language.[13]

The ministry of the internal Spirit does not nullify the ministry of the "external Word." The Spirit does not duplicate what the book was designed to do. The Spirit glorifies the incarnate Word of the Gospels, but he does not re-narrate his words and deeds for illiterate people or negligent pastors.

The immense implication of this for the pastoral ministry and lay ministry is that *ministers are essentially brokers of the Word of God transmitted in a book*. We are fundamentally readers and teachers and proclaimers of the message of the book. And all of this is for the glory of the incarnate Word and by the power of the indwelling Spirit. But neither the indwelling Spirit nor the incarnate Word leads us away from the book that Luther called "the external Word." Christ stands forth for our *worship* and our *fellowship* and our *obedience* from the "external Word." This is where we see "the glory of God in the face of Christ" (2 Cor. 4:6). So it is for the sake of Christ that the Spirit broods over the book where Christ is clear, not over trances where he is obscure.

What difference did this discovery of the book make in the way Luther carried out his ministry of the Word? What can we learn from Luther at study? His entire professional life was lived as a professor in the University of Wittenberg. So it will be helpful to trace his life up to that point and then ask why a professor can be a helpful model for pastors and laypeople who care about the "external Word" of God.

The Pathway to the Professorship

Luther was born November 10, 1483, in Eisleben, Germany, to a copper miner. His father had wanted him to enter the legal profession. So

---

[13] Hugh T. Kerr, *A Compend of Luther's Theology* (Philadelphia, PA: Westminster, 1943), 17.

he studied at the university on the way to that vocation. According to Heiko Oberman, "There is hardly any authenticated information about those first eighteen years which led Luther to the threshold of the University of Erfurt."[14]

In 1502, at the age of nineteen, he received his bachelor's degree, ranking, unimpressively, thirtieth of fifty-seven in his class. In January 1505, he received his Master of Arts at Erfurt and ranked second among seventeen candidates. That summer, the providential Damascus-like experience happened. On July 2, on the way home from law school, he was caught in a thunderstorm and was hurled to the ground by lightning. He cried out, "Help me, St. Anne; I will become a monk."[15] He feared for his soul and did not know how to find safety in the gospel. So he took the next best thing, the monastery.

Fifteen days later, to his father's dismay, he kept his vow. On July 17, 1505, he knocked at the gate of the Augustinian Hermits in Erfurt and asked the prior to accept him into the order. Later he said this choice was a flagrant sin—"not worth a farthing" because it was made against his father and out of fear. Then he added, "But how much good the merciful Lord has allowed to come of it!"[16] We see this kind of merciful providence over and over again in the history of the church. We saw it powerfully in the life of Augustine, and we will see it in Calvin's life too. It should protect us from the paralyzing effects of bad decisions in our past. God is not hindered in his sovereign designs from leading us, as he did Luther, out of blunders into fruitful lives of joy.

Luther was twenty-one years old when he became an Augustinian monk. It would be twenty years before he married Katharina von Bora on June 13, 1525. So there were twenty more years of wrestling with the temptations of a single man who had very powerful drives. But "in the monastery," he said, "I did not think about women, money, or possessions; instead my heart trembled and fidgeted about whether God would bestow His grace on me. . . . For I had strayed from faith and could not but imagine that I had angered God, whom I in turn had to appease by doing good works."[17] There was no theological gamesman-

---

[14] Oberman, *Luther: Man between God and the Devil*, 102.
[15] Ibid., 92.
[16] Ibid., 125.
[17] Ibid., 128.

ship in Luther's early studies. He said, "If I could believe that God was not angry with me, I would stand on my head for joy."[18]

On Easter, April 3, 1507, he was ordained to the priesthood, and on May 2 he celebrated his first mass. He was so overwhelmed at the thought of God's majesty, he says, that he almost ran away. The prior persuaded him to continue. Oberman says that this incident of fear and trembling was not isolated in Luther's life.

> A sense of the *mysterium tremendum*, of the holiness of God, was to be char-acteristic of Luther throughout his life. It prevented pious routine from creeping into his relations with God and kept his Bible studies, prayers, or reading of the mass from declining into a mechanical matter of course: his ultimate concern in all these is the encounter with the living God.[19]

For two years, Luther taught aspects of philosophy to the younger monks. He said later that teaching philosophy was like waiting for the real thing.[20] In 1509, the real thing came when his beloved superior and counselor and friend, Johannes von Staupitz, "admitted Luther to the Bible." That is, he allowed Luther to teach Bible instead of moral philosophy—Paul instead of Aristotle. Three years later, on October 19, 1512, at the age of twenty-eight, Luther received his doctor's de-gree in theology, and Staupitz turned over to him the chair in Biblical Theology at the University of Wittenberg, which Luther held the rest of his life.

So Luther was a university theology professor all his professional life. This causes us to raise the question whether he can really serve as any kind of model for the rest of us who are not professors. Can he really understand, for example, what those of us who are pastors face in our kind of ministry? But it would be a mistake to think Luther has nothing to show us. At least three things unite him to us who are pas-tors—and thus all the closer to the people in the pew.

Why Pastors (and Others) Should Listen to Luther

First, he was a preacher—more a preacher than most pastors. He knew the burden and the pressure of weekly preaching. There were two

---

[18] Ibid., 315. Which is why, when he found the gospel, he was able to turn the world upside-down.
[19] Ibid., 137.
[20] Ibid., 145.

churches in Wittenberg, the town church and the castle church. Luther was a regular preacher at the town church. He said, "If I could today become king or emperor, I would not give up my office as preacher."[21] He was driven by a passion for the exaltation of God in the Word. In one of his prayers he says, "Dear Lord God, I want to preach so that you are glorified. I want to speak of you, praise you, praise your name. Although I probably cannot make it turn out well, won't you make it turn out well?"[22]

To feel the force of this commitment, you have to realize that in the church in Wittenberg there were no church programs but only worship and preaching. On Sundays there were the 5:00 a.m. worship with a sermon on an epistle, the 10:00 a.m. service with a sermon on a Gospel, and an afternoon message on the Old Testament or catechism. Monday and Tuesday sermons were on the catechism; Wednesdays on Matthew; Thursdays and Fridays on the apostolic letters; and Saturday on John.[23]

Luther was not the pastor of the town church. His friend, Johannes Bugenhagen, was pastor there from 1521 to 1558. But Luther shared the preaching virtually every week he was in town. He preached because the people of the town wanted to hear him and because he and his contemporaries understood his doctorate in theology to be a call to teach the Word of God to the whole church. So Luther would often preach twice on Sunday and once during the week. Walther von Loewenich said in his biography, "Luther was one of the greatest preachers in the history of Christendom. . . . Between 1510 and 1546 Luther preached approximately 3000 sermons. Frequently he preached several times a week, often two or more times a day."[24]

For example, he preached 117 sermons in Wittenberg in 1522 and 137 sermons the next year. In 1528 he preached almost 200 times, and from 1529 we have 121 sermons. So the average in those four years was one sermon every two and a half days. As Fred Meuser says in his book on Luther's preaching, "Never a weekend off—he knows all about that. Never even a weekday off. Never any respite at all from preaching, teaching, private study, production, writing, counseling."[25] That's

---

[21] Fred W. Meuser, *Luther the Preacher* (Minneapolis: Augsburg, 1983), 39.

[22] Ibid., 51.

[23] Ibid., 37–38.

[24] Walther von Loewenich, *Luther: The Man and His Work*, trans. Lawrence W. Denef (orig. 1982; Minneapolis: Augsburg, 1986), 353.

[25] Meuser, *Luther the Preacher*, 27.

his first link with those of us who are pastors. He knows the burden of preaching.

Second, like most pastors, Luther was a family man, at least from age forty-one to his death at sixty-two. He knew the pressure and the heartache of having and rearing and losing children. Katie bore him six children in quick succession: Johannes (1526), Elisabeth (1527), Magdalena (1529), Martin (1531), Paul (1533), and Margaret (1534). Do a little computing here. The year between Elisabeth and Magdalena was the year he preached 200 times (more than once every other day). Add to this that Elisabeth died that year at eight months old, but he kept on going under that pain.

And lest we think Luther neglected the children, consider that on Sunday afternoons, often after preaching twice, Luther led the household devotions, which were virtually another worship service for an hour, including the guests as well as the children.[26] So Luther knew the pressures of being a public and family man.

Third, Luther was a churchman, not an ivory-tower theological scholar. He was not only part of almost all the controversies and conferences of his day, he was usually the leader. There was the Heidelberg Disputation (1518), the encounter with Cardinal Cajetan at Augsburg (1518), the Leipzig Disputation with Johann Eck and Andrew Karlstadt (1519), the Diet of Worms before the emperor (1521), the Marburg Colloquy with Zwingli (1529), and the Diet of Augsburg (though he was not there in person, 1530).

Besides active personal involvement in church conferences, there was the unbelievable stream of publications that are all related to the guidance of the church. For example, in 1520 he wrote 133 works; in 1522, 130; in 1523, 183 (one every other day!), and just as many in 1524.[27] He was the lightning rod for every criticism against the Reformation. "All flocked to him, besieging his door hourly, trooped citizens, doctors, princes. Diplomatic enigmas were to be solved, knotty theological points were to be settled, the ethics of social life were to be laid down."[28]

With the breakdown of the medieval system of church life, a whole new way of thinking about church and the Christian life had to be

---

[26] Ibid., 38.
[27] W. Carlos Martyn, *The Life and Times of Martin Luther* (New York: ATS, 1866), 473.
[28] Ibid., 272.

developed. And in Germany that task fell in large measure to Martin Luther. It is astonishing how he threw himself into the mundane matters of parish life. For example, when it was decided that "Visitors" from the state and university would be sent to each parish to assess the condition of the church and make suggestions for church life, Luther took it upon himself to write the guidelines: "Instructions for the Visitors of Parish Pastors in Electoral Saxony." He addressed a broad array of practical issues. When he came to the education of children, he went so far as to dictate how the lower grades should be divided into three groups: pre-readers, readers, and advanced readers. Then he made suggestions for teaching them.

> They shall first learn to read the primer in which are found the alphabet, the Lord's prayer, the Creed, and other prayers. When they have learned this they shall be given Donatus and Cato, to read Donatus and to expound Cato. The schoolmaster is to expound one or two verses at a time, and the children are to repeat these at a later time, so that they thereby build up a vocabulary.[29]

We see then that this university professor was intensely involved in trying to solve the most practical ministry problems from the cradle to the grave. He did not do his studying in the uninterrupted leisure of sabbaticals and long summers. He was constantly besieged and constantly at work.

So, though he was a university professor, there is good reason for pastors and lay ministers of the Word to look at his work and listen to his words, in order to learn and be inspired for the ministry of the Word—the "external Word," the book.

Luther at Study: The Difference the Book Made

For Luther, the importance of study was so interwoven with his discovery of the true gospel that he could never treat study as anything other than utterly crucial and life-giving and history-shaping. Study had been his gateway to the gospel and to the Reformation and to God. We take so much for granted today about the truth and about the Word that we can hardly imagine what it cost Luther to break through to the truth

---

[29] Conrad Bergendoff, ed., *Church and Ministry II*, Luther's Works, vol. 40 (Philadelphia, PA: Muhlenberg, 1958), 315–16.

and to sustain access to the Word. Study mattered. His life and the life of the church hung on it. We need to ask whether all the ground gained by Luther and the other Reformers may be lost over time if we lose this passion for study, while assuming that truth will remain obvious and available.

To see this intertwining of study and the rediscovery of the gospel, let's go back to the early years in Wittenberg. Luther dates his discovery of the gospel in 1518 during a series of lectures on Psalms.[30] He tells the story in his *Preface to the Complete Edition of Luther's Latin Writings*. This account of the discovery is taken from that preface, written on March 5, 1545, the year before his death. Watch for the references to his study of Scripture.

> *I had indeed been captivated with an extraordinary ardor for understanding Paul in the Epistle to the Romans.* But up till then it was . . . a single word in Chapter 1 [v. 17], "In it the righteousness of God is revealed," that had stood in my way. For I hated that word "righteousness of God," which *according to the use and custom of all the teachers, I had been taught to understand philosophically* regarding the formal or active righteousness, as they called it, with which God is righteous and punishes the unrighteous sinner.
>
> Though I lived as a monk without reproach, I felt that I was a sinner before God with an extremely disturbed conscience. I could not believe that he was placated by my satisfaction. I did not love, yes, I hated the righteous God who punishes sinners, and secretly, if not blasphemously, certainly murmuring greatly, I was angry with God, and said, "As if, indeed, it is not enough, that miserable sinners, eternally lost through original sin, are crushed by every kind of calamity by the law of the decalogue, without having God add pain to pain by the gospel and also by the gospel threatening us with his righteous wrath!" Thus I raged with a fierce and troubled conscience. Nevertheless, *I beat importunately upon Paul at that place, most ardently desiring to know what St. Paul wanted.*
>
> At last, by the mercy of God, *meditating day and night,* I gave heed to the context of the words, namely, "In it the righteousness of God is revealed, as it is written, 'He who through faith is righteous shall live.'" There *I began to understand* [that] the righteousness of God is that by which the righteous lives by a gift of God, namely by faith. And this is the meaning: the righteousness of God is revealed by the gospel, namely, the passive

[30] John Dillenberger, ed., *Martin Luther: Selections from His Writings* (Garden City, NY: Doubleday, 1961), xvii.

righteousness with which [the] merciful God justifies us by faith, as it is written, "He who through faith is righteous shall live." Here I felt that I was altogether born again and had entered paradise itself through open gates. Here a totally other face of the entire Scripture showed itself to me. *Thereupon I ran through the Scriptures from memory. . . .*

And I extolled my sweetest word with a love as great as the hatred with which I had before hated the word "righteousness of God." Thus *that place in Paul* was for me truly the gate to paradise.[31]

Notice how God was bringing Luther to the light of the gospel of justification. Six sentences—all of them revealing the intensity of study and wrestling with the biblical text:

I had indeed been captivated with an *extraordinary ardor* for understanding Paul in the Epistle to the Romans.

According to the use and custom of all the teachers, I had been taught to understand *philosophically* [an approach to study from which he was breaking free].

I beat importunately upon Paul at that place, most ardently desiring to know what St. Paul wanted.

At last, by the mercy of God, *meditating day and night*, I gave heed to the context of the words.

Thereupon I ran through *the Scriptures from memory*.

That place in Paul was for me truly the gate to paradise.

The seeds of all Luther's study habits are there or are clearly implied. What was it, then, that marked the man Luther at study and yielded such history-shaping discoveries?

1. Luther came to elevate the biblical text itself far above the teachings of commentators or church fathers. This was not the conclusion of laziness. Melanchthon, Luther's friend and colleague at Wittenberg, said Luther knew his dogmatics so well in the early days that he could quote whole pages of Gabriel Biel (the standard dogmatics text, published 1488) by heart.[32] It wasn't lack of energy for the fathers and the

---

[31] Ibid., 11–12, emphasis added.
[32] Oberman, *Luther: Man between God and the Devil*, 138.

philosophers that limited his focus; it was an overriding passion for the superiority of the biblical text itself.

He wrote in 1533, "For a number of years I have now annually read through the Bible twice. If the Bible were a large, mighty tree and all its words were little branches, I have tapped at all the branches, eager to know what was there and what it had to offer."[33] Oberman says Luther kept to that practice for at least ten years.[34] The Bible had come to mean more to Luther than all the fathers and commentators.

"He who is well acquainted with the text of Scripture," Luther said in 1538, "is a distinguished theologian. For a Bible passage or text is of more value than the comments of four authors."[35] In his *Open Letter to the Christian Nobility,* Luther explained his concern:

> The writings of all the holy fathers should be read only for a time, in order that through them we may be led to the Holy Scriptures. As it is, however, we read them only to be absorbed in them and never come to the Scriptures. We are like men who study the signposts and never travel the road. The dear fathers wished by their writing, to lead us to the Scriptures, but we so use them as to be led away from the Scriptures, though the Scriptures alone are our vineyard in which we ought all to work and toil.[36]

The Bible is the pastor's vineyard, where he ought to work and toil. But, Luther complained in 1539, "The Bible is being buried by the wealth of commentaries, and the text is being neglected, although in every branch of learning they are the best who are well acquainted with the text."[37] This is no mere purist or classicist allegiance to the sources. This is the testimony of a man who found life at the original *spring* in the mountain, not the secondary *stream* in the valley. It was a matter of life and death whether one studied the text of Scripture itself or spent most of his time reading commentaries and secondary literature. Looking back on the early days of his study of the Scriptures, Luther said,

> When I was young, I read the Bible over and over and over again, and was so perfectly acquainted with it, that I could, in an instant, have pointed to any verse that might have been mentioned. I then read the commentators,

---

[33] Plass, *What Luther Says,* 1:83.
[34] Oberman, *Luther: Man between God and the Devil,* 173.
[35] Plass, *What Luther Says,* 3:1355.
[36] Kerr, *Compend of Luther's Theology,* 13.
[37] Plass, *What Luther Says,* 1:97.

but I soon threw them aside, for I found therein many things my conscience could not approve, as being contrary to the sacred text. 'Tis always better to see with one's own eyes than with those of other people.[38]

Luther doesn't mean in all this that there is no place at all for reading other books. After all, he wrote books. But he counsels us to make them secondary and make them few. He says,

A student who does not want his labor wasted must so read and reread some good writer that the author is changed, as it were, into his flesh and blood. For a great variety of reading confuses and does not teach. It makes the student like a man who dwells everywhere and, therefore, nowhere in particular. Just as we do not daily enjoy the society of every one of our friends but only that of a chosen few, so it should also be in our studying.[39]

The number of theological books should . . . be reduced, and a selection should be made of the best of them; for many books do not make men learned, nor does much reading. But reading something good, and reading it frequently, however little it may be, is the practice that makes men learned in the Scripture and makes them pious besides.[40]

2. This radical focus on the text of Scripture itself with secondary literature in secondary place led Luther to an intense and serious grappling with the very words of Paul and the other biblical writers. That's the second characteristic of Luther at study. Instead of running to the commentaries and fathers, he says, "*I beat importunately upon Paul* at that place, most ardently desiring to know what St. Paul wanted." This was not an isolated incident, but a habit.

He told his students that the exegete should treat a difficult passage no differently than Moses did the rock in the desert, which he smote with his rod until water gushed out for his thirsty people.[41] In other words, strike the text. "I beat importunately upon Paul." There is a great incentive in this beating on the text: "The Bible is a remarkable fountain: the more one draws and drinks of it, the more it stimulates thirst."[42]

In the summer and fall of 1526, Luther took up the challenge

---

[38] Kerr, *Compend of Luther's Theology*, 16.
[39] Plass, *What Luther Says*, 1:112.
[40] Ibid., 113.
[41] Oberman, *Luther: Man between God and the Devil*, 224.
[42] Plass, *What Luther Says*, 1:67.

to lecture on Ecclesiastes to the small band of students who stayed behind in Wittenberg during a plague that was threatening the city. "Solomon the preacher," he wrote to a friend, "is giving me a hard time, as though he begrudged anyone lecturing on him. But he must yield."[43]

That is what study was to Luther—taking a text the way Jacob took the angel of the Lord, and saying: "It must yield. I *will* hear and know the Word of God in this text for my soul and for the church!" That's how he broke through to the meaning of "the righteousness of God" in justification. And that is how he broke through tradition and philosophy again and again.

3. *The power and preciousness of what Luther saw when he beat importunately upon Paul's language convinced him forever that reading Greek and Hebrew was one of the greatest privileges and responsibilities of the Reformation preacher.* Again the motive and conviction here are not academic commitments to high-level scholarship but spiritual commitments to proclaiming and preserving a pure gospel.

Luther spoke against the backdrop of a thousand years of church darkness without the Word when he said boldly, "It is certain that unless the languages [of Greek and Hebrew] remain, the Gospel must finally perish."[44] He asks, "Do you inquire what use there is in learning the languages? . . . Do you say, 'We can read the Bible very well in German?'" (As many American pastors today say, "Isn't a good English translation sufficient?") Luther answers,

> Without languages we could not have received the gospel. Languages are the scabbard that contains the sword of the Spirit; they are the [case] which contains the priceless jewels of antique thought; they are the vessel that holds the wine; and as the gospel says, they are the baskets in which the loaves and fishes are kept to feed the multitude.
>
> If we neglect the literature we shall eventually lose the gospel. . . . No sooner did men cease to cultivate the languages than Christendom declined, even until it fell under the undisputed dominion of the pope. But no sooner was this torch relighted, than this papal owl fled with a shriek into congenial gloom. . . . In former times the fathers were frequently mistaken, because they were ignorant of the languages and in our days there are some who,

---

[43] Heinrich Bornkamm, *Luther in Mid-Career, 1521–1530*, trans. E. Theodore Bachmann (orig. 1979; Philadelphia: Fortress, 1983), 564.
[44] Kerr, *Compend of Luther's Theology*, 17.

like the Waldenses, do not think the languages of any use; but although their doctrine is good, they have often erred in the real meaning of the sacred text; they are without arms against error, and I fear much that their faith will not remain pure.[45]

The main issue was the preservation and the purity of the faith. Where the languages are not prized and pursued, care in biblical observation and biblical thinking and concern for truth decreases. It has to, because the tools to think otherwise are not present. This was an intensely real possibility for Luther because he had known it. He said, "If the languages had not made me positive as to the true meaning of the word, I might have still remained a chained monk, engaged in quietly preaching Romish errors in the obscurity of a cloister; the pope, the sophists, and their antichristian empire would have remained unshaken."[46] In other words, he attributes the breakthrough of the Reformation to the penetrating power of the original languages.

The great linguistic event of Luther's time was the appearance of the Greek New Testament edited by Desiderius Erasmus. As soon as it appeared in the middle of the summer session of 1516, Luther obtained a copy and began to study it and use it in his lectures on Romans 9. He did this even though Erasmus was a theological adversary. Having the languages was such a treasure to Luther, he would have gone to school with the Devil in order to learn them—as he might have said it.

He was convinced that many impediments in study would be found without the help of the languages. "St. Augustine," he said, "is compelled to confess, when he writes in *De Doctrina Christiana*, that a Christian teacher who is to expound Scripture has need also of the Greek and the Hebrew languages in addition to the Latin; otherwise it is impossible for him not to run into obstacles everywhere."[47]

---

[45] Martyn, *Life and Times of Martin Luther*, 474–75. Luther did not praise Augustine in this regard, but would have occasion to call him to account for his weakness in Greek and his virtual ignorance of Hebrew (Peter Brown, *Augustine of Hippo* [Berkeley, CA: University of California Press, 1969], 257). Augustine's bent toward allegorizing would have to be corrected by those who attended more closely to the text and its meaning in the original languages. Augustine learned Greek superficially as a child, but disliked it intensely ("Even now I cannot fully understand why the Greek language, which I learned as a child, was so distasteful to me. I loved Latin," Augustine, *Confessions*, trans. R. S. Pine-Coffin [New York: Penguin, 1961], 33, [I, 13]) and never was able to use it with great facility. "Only a few times when confronted with Julian of Eclanum, the Pelagian, would Augustine try to refute his critics by comparing the original Greek with translations" (Brown, *Augustine of Hippo*, 171). Let the remarkable achievement of Augustine encourage those who do not have the privilege of studying the original languages. But let us beware of making the compensating power of his extraordinary abilities an excuse for not improving ours with the gift of Greek and Hebrew.
[46] Martyn, *Life and Times of Martin Luther*, 474.
[47] Plass, *What Luther Says*, 1:95. But see note 45.

And he was persuaded that knowing the languages would bring freshness and force to preaching. He said,

> Though the faith and the Gospel may be proclaimed by simple preachers without the languages, such preaching is flat and tame, men grow at last wearied and disgusted and it falls to the ground. But when the preacher is versed in the languages, his discourse has freshness and force, the whole of Scripture is treated, and faith finds itself constantly renewed by a continual variety of words and works.[48]

Now that is a discouraging overstatement for many pastors who never studied or have lost their Greek and Hebrew. What I would say is that knowing the languages can make any devoted preacher a better preacher—more fresh, more faithful, more confident, more penetrating. But it is possible to preach faithfully without them—at least for a season, while pastors stand on the previous generations of expositors who knew and used the languages. The test of our faithfulness to the Word, if we cannot read the languages, is this: Do we have a large enough concern for the church of Jesus Christ to promote their preservation and their widespread teaching and use in the churches? Or do we, out of self-protection, minimize their importance because to do otherwise stings too badly?

It may be that for many of us today, Luther's strong words about our neglect and indifference are accurate when he says,

> It is a sin and shame not to know our own book or to understand the speech and words of our God; it is a still greater sin and loss that we do not study languages, especially in these days when God is offering and giving us men and books and every facility and inducement to this study, and desires his Bible to be an open book. O how happy the dear fathers would have been if they had our opportunity to study the languages and come thus prepared to the Holy Scriptures! What great toil and effort it cost them to gather up a few crumbs, while we with half the labor—yes, almost without any labor at all—can acquire the whole loaf! O how their effort puts our indolence to shame![49]

4. This reference to "indolence" leads us to the fourth characteristic of Luther at study, namely, extraordinary diligence in spite of

---

[48] Kerr, *Compend of Luther's Theology*, 148.
[49] Meuser, *Luther the Preacher*, 43. With computer programs for instruction and use of the languages, how much more true is this today than when it was written!

tremendous obstacles. What he accomplished borders on the superhuman, and of course makes pygmies of us all.

> His job as professor of Bible at the University of Wittenberg was full-time work of its own. He wrote theological treatises by the score: biblical, homiletical, liturgical, educational, devotional, and political, some of which have shaped Protestant church life for centuries. All the while he was translating the whole of the Scriptures into German, a language that he helped to shape by that very translation. He carried on a voluminous correspondence, for he was constantly asked for advice and counsel. Travel, meetings, conferences, and colloquies were the order of the day. All the while he was preaching regularly to a congregation that he must have regarded as a showcase of the Reformation.[50]

We are not Luther and could never be, no matter how hard we tried. But the point here is: Do we work at our studies with rigor and diligence, or are we slothful and casual about it, as if nothing really great is at stake?

When he was just short of sixty years old, he pleaded with pastors to be diligent and not lazy.

> Some pastors and preachers are lazy and no good. They do not pray; they do not read; they do not search the Scripture. . . . The call is: watch, study, attend to reading. In truth you cannot read too much in Scripture; and what you read you cannot read too carefully, and what you read carefully you cannot understand too well, and what you understand well you cannot teach too well, and what you teach well you cannot live too well. . . . The devil . . . the world . . . and our flesh are raging and raving against us. Therefore, dear sirs and brothers, pastors and preachers, pray, read, study, be diligent. . . . This evil, shameful time is not the season for being lazy, for sleeping and snoring.[51]

Commenting on Genesis 3:19 ("By the sweat of your face you will eat bread"), Luther says, "The household sweat is great; the political sweat is greater; the church sweat is the greatest."[52] He responded once to those who do hard physical labor and consider the work of study a soft life:

---

[50] Ibid., 27.
[51] Ibid., 40–41.
[52] Plass, *What Luther Says*, 2:951.

Sure, it would be hard for me to sit "in the saddle." But then again I would like to see the horseman who could sit still for a whole day and gaze at a book without worrying or dreaming or think about anything else. Ask . . . a preacher . . . how much work it is to speak and preach. . . . The pen is very light, that is true. . . . But in this work the best part of the human body (the head), the noblest member (the tongue), and the highest work (speech) bear the brunt of the load and work the hardest, while in other kinds of work either the hand, the foot, the back or other members do the work alone so the person can sing happily or make jokes freely which a sermon writer cannot do. Three fingers do it all . . . but the whole body and soul have to work at it.[53]

There is great danger, Luther says, in thinking we have ever gotten to a point when we fancy we don't need to study anymore. "Let ministers daily pursue their studies with diligence and constantly busy themselves with them. . . . Let them steadily keep on reading, teaching, studying, pondering, and meditating. Nor let them cease until they have discovered and are sure that they have taught the devil to death and have become more learned than God himself and all His saints"[54]—which of course means never.

Luther knew that there was such a thing as overwork and damaging, counterproductive strain. But he clearly preferred to err on the side of overwork than underwork. We see this in 1532 when he wrote, "A person should work in such a way that he remains well and does no injury to his body. We should not break our heads at work and injure our bodies. . . . I myself used to do such things, and I have racked my brains because I still have not overcome the bad habit of overworking. Nor shall I overcome it as long as I live."[55]

I don't know if the apostle Paul would have made the same confession at the end of his life. But he did say, "I labored even more than all of them [the other apostles]" (1 Cor. 15:10). And in comparison to the false apostles he said, "Are they servants of Christ?—I speak as if insane—I more so; *in far more labors,* in far more imprisonments, beaten times without number, often in danger of death" (2 Cor. 11:23). He said to the Colossians, "I labor, striving [*agōnizomenos*] according to His power, which mightily works within me" (Col. 1:29). So it's not

---

[53] Meuser, *Luther the Preacher,* 44–45.
[54] Plass, *What Luther Says,* 2:927.
[55] Ibid., 3:1496–497.

surprising that Luther would strive to follow his dear Paul in "far more labors."

5. Which leads us to the fifth characteristic of Luther at study, namely, suffering. For Luther, trials make a theologian. Temptation and affliction are the hermeneutical touchstones.

Luther noticed in Psalm 119 that the psalmist not only prayed and meditated over the Word of God in order to understand it; he also suffered in order to understand it. Psalm 119:67, 71 says, "Before I was afflicted I went astray, but now I keep Your word. . . . It is good for me that I was afflicted, that I may learn Your statutes." An indispensable key to understanding the Scriptures is suffering in the path of righteousness.

Thus Luther said : "I want you to know how to study theology in the right way. I have practiced this method myself. . . . Here you will find three rules. They are frequently proposed throughout Psalm [119] and run thus: *Oratio, meditatio, tentatio* (prayer, meditation, tribulation)."[56] And tribulation (*Anfechtungen*) he called the "touchstone." "[These rules] teach you not only to know and understand, but also to experience how right, how true, how sweet, how lovely, how mighty, how comforting God's Word is: it is wisdom supreme."[57]

He proved the value of trials over and over again in his own experience. "For as soon as God's Word becomes known through you," he says, "the devil will afflict you, will make a real [theological] doctor of you, and will teach you by his temptations to seek and to love God's Word. For I myself . . . owe my papists many thanks for so beating, pressing, and frightening me through the devil's raging that they have turned me into a fairly good theologian, driving me to a goal I should never have reached."[58]

Suffering was woven into life for Luther. Keep in mind that from 1521 on, Luther lived under the ban of the empire. Emperor Charles V said, "I have decided to mobilize everything against Luther: my kingdoms and dominions, my friends, my body, my blood and my soul."[59] He could be legally killed, except where he was protected by his prince, Frederick of Saxony.

He endured relentless slander of the most cruel kind. He once ob-

---

[56] Ibid., 3:1359.
[57] Ibid., 3:1360.
[58] Ibid.
[59] Oberman, *Luther: Man between God and the Devil*, 29.

served, "If the Devil can do nothing against the teachings, he attacks the person, lying, slandering, cursing, and ranting at him. Just as the papists' Beelzebub did to me when he could not subdue my Gospel, he wrote that I was possessed by the Devil, was a changeling, my beloved mother a whore and bath attendant."[60]

Physically he suffered from excruciating kidney stones and headaches, with buzzing in his ears and ear infections and incapacitating constipation and hemorrhoids. "I nearly gave up the ghost—and now, bathed in blood, can find no peace. What took four days to heal immediately tears open again."[61]

It's not surprising then that emotionally and spiritually he would undergo the most horrible struggles. For example, in a letter to Melanchthon on August 2, 1527, he writes, "For more than a week I have been thrown back and forth in death and Hell; my whole body feels beaten, my limbs are still trembling. I almost lost Christ completely, driven about on the waves and storms of despair and blasphemy against God. But because of the intercession of the faithful, God began to take mercy on me and tore my soul from the depths of Hell."[62]

On the outside, to many, he looked invulnerable. But those close to him knew the *tentatio*. Again he wrote to Melanchthon from the Wartburg castle on July 13, 1521, while he was supposedly working feverishly on the translation of the New Testament:

> I sit here at ease, hardened and unfeeling—alas! praying little, grieving little for the Church of God, burning rather in the fierce fires of my untamed flesh. It comes to this: I *should* be afire in the spirit; in reality I am afire in the flesh, with lust, laziness, idleness, sleepiness. It is perhaps because you have all ceased praying for me that God has turned away from me. . . . For the last eight days I have written nothing, nor prayed nor studied, partly from self-indulgence, partly from another vexatious handicap [constipation and piles]. . . . I really cannot stand it any longer. . . . Pray for me, I beg you, for in my seclusion here I am submerged in sins.[63]

These were the trials that he said made him a theologian. These experiences were as much a part of his exegetical labors as was his Greek

---

[60] Ibid., 88.
[61] Ibid., 328.
[62] Ibid., 323.
[63] E. G. Rupp and Benjamin Drewery, eds., *Martin Luther: Documents of Modern History* (New York: St. Martin's, 1970), 72–73.

lexicon. This should cause us to think twice before we begrudge the trials of our ministry. How often I am tempted to think that the pressures and conflicts and frustrations are simply distractions from the business of study and understanding. Luther (and Ps. 119:71) teach us to see it all another way. That stressful visit that interrupted your study may well be the very lens through which the text will open to you as never before. *Tentatio*—trial, the thorn in the flesh—is Satan's unwitting contribution to our becoming good theologians.

The triumph in these trials is not our own doing. We are utterly dependent on God's free grace to supply our strength and restore our faith. Luther confessed that in his sense of abandonment and torment, faith "exceeds my powers."[64] Here we must cry out to God alone.

6. Which leads to the final characteristic of Luther at study: prayer and reverent dependence on the all-sufficiency of God. And here the theology and methodology of Luther become almost identical.

In typical paradoxical form, Luther seems to take back almost everything he has said about study when he writes in 1518,

> That the Holy Scriptures cannot be penetrated by study and talent is most certain. Therefore your first duty is to begin to pray, and to pray to this effect that if it please God to accomplish something for His glory—not for yours or any other person's—He may very graciously grant you a true understanding of His words. For no master of the divine words exists except the Author of these words, as He says: "They shall be all taught of God" (John 6:45). You must, therefore, completely despair of your own industry and ability and rely solely on the inspiration of the Spirit.[65]

Luther does not mean that we should leave the "external Word" in mystical reverie, but that we should bathe all our work in prayer, and cast ourselves so wholly on God that he enters and sustains and prospers all our study.

> Since the Holy Writ wants to be dealt with in fear and humility and penetrated more by studying [!] with pious prayer than with keenness of intellect, therefore it is impossible for those who rely only on their intellect and rush into Scripture with dirty feet, like pigs, as though Scripture were merely a sort of human knowledge, not to harm themselves and others whom they instruct.[66]

---

[64] Oberman, *Luther: Man between God and the Devil*, 323.
[65] Plass, *What Luther Says*, 1:77.
[66] Ibid., 1:78.

Again he sees the psalmist in Psalm 119 not only suffering and meditating, but praying again and again:

> Psalm 119:18, "Open my eyes, that I may behold wonderful things from Your law." Psalm 119:27, "Make me understand the way of Your precepts." Psalm 119:34, "Give me understanding, that I may observe Your law." Psalm 119:35–37, "Make me walk in the path of Your commandments, for I delight in it. Incline my heart to Your testimonies, and not to dishonest gain. And revive me in Your ways."

So he concludes that the true biblical way to study the Bible will be saturated with prayer and self-doubt and God-reliance moment by moment:

> You should completely despair of your own sense and reason, for by these you will not attain the goal. . . . Rather kneel down in your private little room and with sincere humility and earnestness pray God, through His dear Son, graciously to grant you His Holy Spirit to enlighten and guide you and give you understanding.[67]

Luther's emphasis on prayer in study is rooted in his theology, and here is where his methodology and his theology become one. He was persuaded from Romans 8:7 and elsewhere that "the natural mind cannot do anything godly. It does not perceive the wrath of God, therefore cannot rightly fear him. It does not see the goodness of God, therefore cannot trust or believe in him either. Therefore we should constantly pray that God will bring forth his gifts in us."[68] All our study is futile without the work of God overcoming our blindness and hardheartedness.

Luther and Augustine were one on this central issue of the Reformation. At the heart of Luther's theology was a total dependence on the freedom of God's omnipotent grace rescuing powerless man from the bondage of the will. Concerning free will, Luther said, "Man has in his own power a freedom of the will to do or not to do external works, regulated by law and punishment. . . . On the other hand, man cannot by his own power purify his heart and bring forth godly gifts, such as true repentance for sins, a true, as over against an artificial, fear of God,

---

[67] Ibid., 3:1359.
[68] Bergendoff, *Church and Ministry II*, 302.

true faith, sincere love, chastity. . . ."[69] In other words, the will is "free" to move our action, but beneath the will there is a bondage that can only be overcome by the free grace of God. Luther saw this bondage of the will as the root issue in the fight with Rome and its most discerning spokesman, Erasmus.

Luther's book by that name, *The Bondage of the Will*, published in 1525, was an answer to Erasmus's book, *The Freedom of the Will*. Luther regarded this one book of his—*The Bondage of the Will*—as his "best theological book, and the only one in that class worthy of publication."[70]

To understand Luther's theology and his methodology of study, it is extremely important to recognize that he conceded that Erasmus, more than any other opponent, had realized that the powerlessness of man before God, not the indulgence controversy or purgatory, was the central question of the Christian faith. Man is powerless to justify himself, powerless to sanctify himself, powerless to study as he ought, and powerless to trust God to do anything about this. He had seen this in Paul, and it was confirmed in the great battles between Augustine and Pelagius.

Erasmus's exaltation of man's will as free to overcome its own sin and bondage was, in Luther's mind, an assault on the freedom of God's grace and therefore an attack on the very gospel itself. In Luther's summary of faith in 1528 he wrote,

> I condemn and reject as nothing but error all doctrines which exalt our "free will" as being directly opposed to this mediation and grace of our Lord Jesus Christ. For since, apart from Christ, sin and death are our masters and the devil is our god and prince, there can be no strength or power, no wit or wisdom, by which we can fit or fashion ourselves for righteousness and life. On the contrary, blinded and captivated, we are bound to be the subjects of Satan and sin, doing and thinking what pleases him and is opposed to God and His commandments.[71]

Luther realized that the issue of man's bondage to sin and his moral inability to believe or make himself right—including the inability to study rightly—was the root issue of the Reformation. The freedom of

---

[69] Ibid., 301.
[70] Dillenberger, *Martin Luther: Selections*, 167.
[71] Plass, *What Luther Says*, 3:1376–377.

God, and therefore the freedom of the gospel, and therefore the glory of God and the salvation of men, were at stake in this controversy. Therefore Luther loved the message of *The Bondage of the Will*, ascribing all freedom and power and grace to God, and all powerlessness and dependency to man.

In his explanation of Galatians 1:11–12, he recounted:

> I recall that at the beginning of my cause Dr. Staupitz . . . said to me: It pleases me that the doctrine which you preach ascribes the glory and everything to God alone and nothing to man; for to God (that is clearer than the sun) one cannot ascribe too much glory, goodness, etc. This word comforted and strengthened me greatly at the time. And it is true that the doctrine of the Gospel takes all glory, wisdom, righteousness, etc., from men and ascribes them to the Creator alone, who makes everything out of nothing.[72]

This is why prayer is the root of Luther's approach to studying God's Word. Prayer is the echo of the freedom and sufficiency of God in the heart of powerless man. It is the way Luther conceived of his theology and the way he pursued his studies. And it is the way he died.

At 3:00 a.m. on February 18, 1546, Luther died. His last recorded words were, "*Wir sein Bettler. Hoc est verum.*" "We are beggars. This is true."[73] God is free—utterly free—in his grace. And we are beggars— pray-ers. That is how we live, that is how we die, and that is how we study, so that God gets the glory and we get the grace.

---

[72] Ibid., 3:1374.
[73] Oberman, *Luther: Man between God and the Devil*, 324.

Let the pastors boldly dare all things by the word of God. . . . Let them constrain all the power, glory, and excellence of the world to give place to and to obey the divine majesty of this word. Let them enjoin everyone by it, from the highest to the lowest. Let them edify the body of Christ. Let them devastate Satan's reign. Let them pasture the sheep, kill the wolves, instruct and exhort the rebellious. Let them bind and loose thunder and lightning, if necessary, but let them do all according to the word of God.

John Calvin
Sermons on the Epistle to the Ephesians

3

The Divine Majesty of the Word

John Calvin: The Man and His Preaching

The Absoluteness of God

John Calvin would approve beginning this chapter with God and not with himself. Nothing mattered more to Calvin than the supremacy of God over all things. Focus your attention, then, on God's self-identification in Exodus 3:14–15. Here we will see the sun in the solar system of John Calvin's thought and life.

God calls Moses and commissions him to go to Egypt and bring his people out of bondage. Moses is frightened at this prospect and raises the objection that he is not the person to do this. God responds by saying, "I will be with you" (Ex. 3:12). Then Moses says, "[When I] say to them, 'The God of your fathers has sent me to you' . . . they may say to me, 'What is His name?' What shall I say to them?" God's response is one of the most important revelations that has ever been given to man:

> God said to Moses, "I AM WHO I AM"; and He said, "Thus you shall say to the sons of Israel, 'I AM has sent me to you.'" God, furthermore, said to Moses, "Thus you shall say to the sons of Israel, 'The LORD [יְהוָה], the God of your fathers, the God of Abraham, the God of Isaac, and the God of Jacob, has sent me to you.' This is My name forever, and this is My memorial-name to all generations." (Ex. 3:14–15)

In other words, the great, central, biblical name of *Yahweh* (יְהוָה) is explicitly rooted by God himself in the phrase "I AM WHO I AM"

(אֶהְיֶה אֲשֶׁר אֶהְיֶה). "Tell them, *the one who simply and absolutely is* has sent you. Tell them that the essential thing about me is that I AM."

I begin with this biblical self-identification of God because the unhidden and unashamed aim in this chapter and in this book is to fan the flame of your passion for the centrality and supremacy of God. Does not our heart burn when we hear God say, "My name is, 'I AM WHO I AM'"? The absoluteness of God's existence—God's never beginning, never ending, never becoming, never improving, simply and absolutely there to be dealt with on his terms or not at all—enthralls the mind.

Let this sink in: God—the God who holds you in being this moment—never had a beginning. Ponder it. Do you remember the first time you thought about this as a child or a young teenager? Let that speechless wonder rise. God never had a beginning! "I AM" has sent me to you. And one who never had a beginning, but always was and is and will be, defines all things. Whether we want him to be there or not, he is there. We do not negotiate what we want for reality. *God* defines reality. When we come into existence, we stand before a God who made us and owns us. We have absolutely no choice in this matter. We do not choose to be. And when we are, we do not choose that God be. No ranting and raving, no sophisticated doubt or skepticism, has any effect on the existence of God. He simply and absolutely is. "Tell them 'I AM' has sent you."

If we don't like it, we can change for our joy, or we can resist to our destruction. But one thing remains absolutely unassailed. God *is*. He was there before we came. He will be there when we are gone. And therefore what matters in ministry above all things is this God. We cannot escape the simple and obvious truth that God must be the main thing in ministry. Ministry has to do with God because life has to do with God, and life has to do with God because all the universe has to do with God, and the universe has to do with God because every atom and every emotion and every soul of every angelic, demonic, and human being belongs to God, who absolutely *is*. He created all that is, he sustains everything in being, he directs the course of all events, because "from Him and through Him and to Him are all things. To Him be the glory forever" (Rom. 11:36).

You who are pastors, may God inflame in you a passion for his centrality and supremacy in your ministry, so that the people you love and serve will say, when you are dead and gone, "This man knew God. This man loved God. This man lived for the glory of God. This man showed us God week after week. This man, as the apostle said, was 'filled up [with] all the fullness of God'" (Eph. 3:19).

This is the aim and the burden of this chapter and this book. Not only because it is *implicit* in the sheer, awesome existence of God, and not only because it is *explicit* in the Word of God, but also because David Wells is staggeringly right when he says, "It is this God, majestic and holy in his being . . . who has disappeared from the modern evangelical world."[1] Lesslie Newbigin says much the same thing. "I suddenly saw that someone could use all the language of evangelical Christianity, and yet the center was fundamentally the self, my need of salvation. And God is auxiliary to that. . . . I also saw that quite a lot of evangelical Christianity can easily slip, can become centered in me and my need of salvation, and not in the glory of God."[2] And, oh, have we slipped. Where are the churches today where the dominant experience is the precious weight of the glory of God?

Calvin's Unremitting Zeal to Illustrate the Glory of God

John Calvin saw the same thing in his own day. In 1538, the Italian Cardinal Sadolet wrote to the leaders of Geneva trying to win them back to the Roman Catholic Church after they had turned to the Reformed teachings. He began his letter with a long, conciliatory section on the preciousness of eternal life, before coming to his accusations of the Reformation. Calvin wrote the response to Sadolet in six days in the fall of 1539. It was one of his earliest writings and spread his name as a Reformer across Europe. Luther read it and said, "Here is a writing which has hands and feet. I rejoice that God raises up such men."[3]

Calvin's response to Sadolet is important because it uncovers the root of Calvin's quarrel with Rome that would determine his whole life. The issue is not, first, the well-known sticking points of the Reformation: justification, priestly abuses, transubstantiation, prayers to saints, and papal authority. All those will come in for discussion. But beneath all of them, the fundamental issue for John Calvin, from the beginning

---

[1] David Wells, *No Place for Truth* (Grand Rapids, MI: Eerdmans, 1993), 300.
[2] Lesslie Newbigin, quoted in Tim Stafford, "God's Missionary to Us," *Christianity Today* 40, no. 4 (December 9, 1996): 29.
[3] Henry F. Henderson, *Calvin in His Letters* (London: J. M. Dent, 1909), 68.

to the end of his life, was the issue of the centrality and supremacy and majesty of the glory of God. He sees in Sadolet's letter the same thing Newbigin sees in self-saturated evangelicalism.

Here's what Calvin said to the Cardinal: "[Your] zeal for heavenly life [is] a zeal which keeps a man entirely devoted to himself, and does not, even by one expression, arouse him to *sanctify the name of God.*" In other words, even precious truth about eternal life can be so skewed as to displace God as the center and goal. This was Calvin's chief contention with Rome. This comes out in his writings over and over again. He goes on and says to Sadolet that what he should do—and what Calvin aims to do with all his life—is "set before [man], as the prime motive of his existence, *zeal to illustrate the glory of God.*"[4]

I think this would be a fitting banner over all of John Calvin's life and work—*zeal to illustrate the glory of God.* The essential meaning of John Calvin's life and preaching is that he recovered and embodied a passion for the absolute reality and majesty of God. That is what I want us to see most clearly. Benjamin Warfield said of Calvin, "No man ever had a profounder sense of God than he."[5] There's the key to Calvin's life and theology.

Geerhardus Vos, the Princeton New Testament scholar, asked the question in 1891, Why has Reformed theology been able to grasp the fullness of Scripture unlike any other branch of Christendom? He answers, "Because Reformed theology took hold of the Scriptures in their deepest root idea. . . . This root idea which served as the key to unlock the rich treasuries of the Scriptures was *the preeminence of God's glory in the consideration of all that has been created.*"[6] It's this relentless orientation on the glory of God that gives coherence to John Calvin's life and to the Reformed tradition that followed. Vos said that the "all-embracing slogan of the Reformed faith is this: the work of grace in the sinner is a *mirror for the glory of God.*"[7] Mirroring the glory of God is the meaning of John Calvin's life and ministry.

When Calvin did eventually get to the issue of justification in his

---

[4] John Dillenberger, *John Calvin, Selections from His Writings* (Atlanta: Scholars, 1975), 89, emphasis added.

[5] Benjamin Warfield, *Calvin and Augustine* (Philadelphia, PA: P&R, 1971), 24.

[6] Geerhardus Vos, "The Doctrine of the Covenant in Reformed Theology," in *Redemptive History and Biblical Interpretation: The Shorter Writings of Geerhardus Vos*, ed. Richard B. Gaffin (Phillipsburg, NJ: P&R, 1980), 241–42, emphasis added.

[7] Vos, "Doctrine of the Covenant in Reformed Theology," 248, emphasis added.

response to Sadolet, he said, "You . . . touch upon justification by faith, the first and keenest subject of controversy between us. . . . Wherever the knowledge of it is taken away, *the glory of Christ is extinguished.*"[8] So here again we can see what is fundamental. Justification by faith is crucial. But there is a deeper reason why it is crucial. The glory of Christ is at stake. Wherever the knowledge of justification is taken away, the glory of Christ is extinguished. This is always the deepest issue for Calvin. What truth and what behavior will "illustrate the glory of God"?

For Calvin, the need for the Reformation was fundamentally this: Rome had "destroyed the glory of Christ in many ways—by calling upon the saints to intercede, when Jesus Christ is the one mediator between God and man; by adoring the Blessed Virgin, when Christ alone shall be adored; by offering a continual sacrifice in the Mass, when the sacrifice of Christ upon the Cross is complete and sufficient,"[9] by elevating tradition to the level of Scripture and even making the word of Christ dependent for its authority on the word of man.[10] Calvin asks, in his *Commentary on Colossians*, "How comes it that we are 'carried about with so many strange doctrines' (Hebrews 13:9)?" And he answers, "Because the excellence of Christ is not perceived by us."[11] In other words, the great guardian of biblical orthodoxy throughout the centuries is a passion for the glory and the excellency of God in Christ. Where the center shifts from God, everything begins to shift everywhere, which does not bode well for doctrinal faithfulness in our own non-God-centered day.

Therefore the unifying root of all of Calvin's labors is his passion to display the glory of God in Christ. When he was thirty years old, he described an imaginary scene of himself at the end of his life, giving an account to God, and said, "The thing [O God] at which I chiefly aimed, and for which I most diligently labored, was, that the glory of thy goodness and justice . . . might shine forth conspicuous, that the virtue and blessings of thy Christ . . . might be fully displayed."[12]

Twenty-four years later, unchanged in his passions and goals, and

---

[8] Dillenberger, *John Calvin, Selections*, 95, emphasis added.
[9] T. H. L. Parker, *Portrait of Calvin* (Philadelphia, PA: Westminster, 1954), 109.
[10] John Calvin, *Institutes of the Christian Religion*, John T. McNeil, trans. Ford Lewis Battles, 2 vols. (Philadelphia, PA: Westminster Press, 1960), I.vii.1. "A most pernicious error widely prevails that Scripture has only so much weight as is conceded to it by the consent of the church. As if the eternal and inviolable truth of God depended upon the decision of men!"
[11] Parker, *Portrait of Calvin*, 55.
[12] Dillenberger, *John Calvin, Selections*, 110.

one month before he actually did give an account to Christ in heaven (he died at age fifty-four), he said in his last will and testament, "I have written nothing out of hatred to any one, but I have always faithfully propounded what I esteemed to be *for the glory of God.*"[13]

The Origin of Calvin's Passion for the Supremacy of God

What happened to John Calvin to make him a man so mastered by the majesty of God? And what kind of ministry did this produce in his life?

He was born July 10, 1509, in Noyon, France, when Martin Luther was twenty-five years old and had just begun to teach the Bible in Wittenberg. We know almost nothing of his early home life. When he was fourteen, his father sent him to study theology at the University of Paris, which at that time was untouched by the Reformation and steeped in Medieval theology. But five years later (when Calvin was nineteen), his father ran afoul of the church and told his son to leave theology and study law, which he did for the next three years at Orleans and Bourges.

During these years Calvin mastered Greek and was immersed in the thought of Duns Scotus and William Occam and Gabriel Biel, and he completed his law course. His father died in May of 1531, when Calvin was twenty-one. Calvin felt free then to turn from law to his first love, which had become the classics. He published his first book, a *Commentary on Seneca*, in 1532, at the age of twenty-three. But sometime during these years he was coming into contact with the message and the spirit of the Reformation, and by 1533, something dramatic had happened in his life.

In November 1533, Nicholas Cop, a friend of Calvin, preached at the opening of the winter term at the University of Paris and was called to account by the Parliament for his Lutheran-like doctrines. He fled the city, and a general persecution broke out against what King Francis I called "the cursed Lutheran sect." Calvin was among those who escaped. The connection with Cop was so close that some suspect Calvin actually wrote the message that Cop delivered. So by 1533, Calvin had crossed the line. He was now wholly devoted to Christ and to the cause of the Reformation.

What had happened? Calvin recounts, seven years later, how his

---

13 Ibid., 42, emphasis added.

conversion came about. He describes how he had been struggling to live out the Catholic faith with zeal

> when, lo, a very different form of doctrine started up, not one which led us away from the Christian profession, but one which brought it back to its fountain . . . to its original purity. Offended by the novelty, I lent an unwilling ear, and at first, I confess, strenuously and passionately resisted . . . to confess that I had all my life long been in ignorance and error. . . .
>
> I at length perceived, as if light had broken in upon me [a very key phrase, in view of what we will see], in what a sty of error I had wallowed, and how much pollution and impurity I had thereby contracted. Being exceedingly alarmed at the misery into which I had fallen . . . as in duty bound, [I] made it my first business to betake myself to thy way [O God], condemning my past life, not without groans and tears.[14]

> God, by a sudden conversion subdued and brought my mind to a teachable frame. . . . Having thus received some taste and knowledge of true godliness, I was immediately inflamed with [an] intense desire to make progress.[15]

What was the foundation of Calvin's faith that yielded a life devoted utterly to displaying the glory and majesty of God? The answer seems to be that Calvin suddenly, as he says, saw and tasted in Scripture the majesty of God. And in that moment, both God and the Word of God were so powerfully and unquestionably authenticated to his soul that he became the loving servant of God and his Word the rest of his life. This experience and conviction dethroned the Church as the authority that accredits the Scriptures for the saints. The majesty of God himself in the Word was sufficient for this work.[16]

How this happened is extremely important, and we need to see how Calvin himself describes it in the *Institutes*, especially Book I, chapters VII and VIII. Here he wrestles with how we can come to a saving knowledge of God through the Scriptures. His answer is the famous phrase, "the internal testimony of the Holy Spirit." For example, he

---

[14] Ibid., 114–15.

[15] Ibid., 26.

[16] Calvin, as he so often did, laid hold on Augustine to strengthen his claim that this was the historic position of the Church, in spite of the Roman Catholic teaching that the Church authorizes the Scriptures for the believer. Commenting on Augustine's view of the role of the authority of the church in leading to a well-founded faith in Scripture, Calvin wrote in the *Institutes*, "He only meant to indicate what we also confess as true: those who have not yet been illumined by the Spirit of God are rendered teachable by reverence for the church, so that they may persevere in learning faith in Christ from the gospel. Thus, he avers, the authority of the church is an introduction through which we are prepared for faith in the gospel. For, as we see, he wants the certainty of the godly to rest upon a far different foundation" (I.vii.3).

says, "Scripture will ultimately suffice for a saving knowledge of God only when its certainty is founded upon the inward persuasion of the Holy Spirit" (I.viii.13). So two things came together for Calvin to give him a "saving knowledge of God"—Scripture and the "inward persuasion of the Holy Spirit." Neither alone suffices to save.

But how does this actually work? What does the Spirit do? The answer is not that the Spirit gives us added revelation to what is in Scripture[17] but that he awakens us, as from the dead, to see and taste the divine reality of God in Scripture, which authenticates it as God's own Word. He says, "Our Heavenly Father, revealing his majesty [in Scripture], lifts reverence for Scripture beyond the realm of controversy" (I.viii.13). There is the key for Calvin: The witness of God to Scripture is the immediate, unassailable, life-giving revelation to our minds of *the majesty of God* that is manifest in the Scriptures themselves. The "majesty of God" is the ground of our confidence in his Word.

Over and over again in Calvin's description of what happens in coming to faith, you see his references to the majesty of God revealed in Scripture and vindicating Scripture. So already in the dynamics of his conversion, the central passion of his life is being ignited.

We are almost at the bottom of this experience now. If we go just a bit deeper, we will see more clearly why this conversion resulted in such an "invincible constancy" in Calvin's lifelong allegiance to the majesty of God and the truth of God's Word. Here are the words that will take us deeper.

> Therefore illumined by [the Spirit's] power, we believe neither by our own [note this!] nor by anyone else's judgment that Scripture is from God; but above human judgment we affirm with utter certainty (just as if we were gazing upon the majesty of God himself) that it has flowed to us from the very mouth of God by the ministry of men.[18]

This is almost baffling. He says that his conviction concerning the majesty of God in Scripture rests not on any human judgment, not even

---

[17] J. I. Packer, "Calvin the Theologian," in *John Calvin: A Collection of Essays*, ed. James Atkinson et al. (Grand Rapids, MI: Eerdmans, 1966), 166. "Rejecting both the Roman contention that the Scripture is to be received as authoritative on the church's authority, and with it the idea that Scripture could be proved divinely authoritative by rational argument alone, Calvin affirms Scripture to be self-authenticating through the inner witness of the Holy Spirit. What is this 'inner witness'? Not a special quality of experience, nor a new, private revelation, nor an existential 'decision,' but a work of enlightenment."
[18] *Institutes*, I.vii.5.

his own. What does he mean? Perhaps the words of the apostle John shed the most helpful light on what Calvin is trying to explain. Here are the key words from 1 John 5:7–11:

> And it is the Spirit who bears witness, because the Spirit is the truth. . . . If we receive the witness of men, the witness of God [= the Spirit] is greater; for the witness of God is this, that He has borne witness concerning His Son. . . . And the witness is this, that God has given us eternal life, and this life is in His Son.

In other words, the "witness of God," that is, the inward witness of the Spirit, is greater than any human witness—including, John would probably say in this context, the witness of our own judgment. And what is that witness of God? It is not merely a word delivered to our judgment for reflection, for then our conviction would rely on that reflection. What is it then? Verse 11 is the key: "The witness is this: that God has given us eternal life." I take that to mean that God witnesses to us of his reality and the reality of his Son and his Word by giving us life from the dead so that we come alive. His witness is the gift of spiritual life. His witness is that we come alive to his majesty and see him for who he is in his Word. In that instant, we do not reason from premises to conclusions—we see that we are awake, and there is not even a prior human judgment about it to lean on. When Lazarus was awakened in the tomb by the call or the "witness" of Christ, he knew without reasoning that he was alive and that this call had wakened him.

Here's the way J. I. Packer puts it:

> The internal witness of the Spirit in John Calvin is a work of enlightenment whereby, through the medium of verbal testimony, the blind eyes of the spirit are opened, and divine realities come to be recognized and embraced for what they are. This recognition, Calvin says, is as immediate and unanalyzable as the perceiving of a color, or a taste, by physical sense—an event about which no more can be said than that when appropriate stimuli were present it happened, and when it happened we knew it had happened.[19]

So in his early twenties, John Calvin experienced the miracle of having the blind eyes of his spirit opened by the Spirit of God. And what he saw immediately, and without any intervening chain of human

---

[19] Packer, "Calvin the Theologian," 166.

reasoning, were two things, so interwoven that they would determine the rest of his life: the majesty of God and the Word of God. The Word mediated the majesty, and the majesty vindicated the Word. Henceforth he would be a man utterly devoted to displaying the majesty of God by the exposition of the Word of God.

The Ministry Made by the Divine Majesty of the Word

What form would that ministry take? Calvin knew what he wanted. He wanted the enjoyment of literary ease so he could promote the Reformed faith as a literary scholar.[20] That is what he thought he was cut out for by nature. But God had radically different plans—as he had for Augustine and Luther—and for many of us who did not plan our lives the way they have turned out.

After escaping from Paris and finally leaving France entirely, Calvin spent his exile in Basel, Switzerland, between 1534 and 1536. To redeem the time, "he devoted himself to the study of Hebrew."[21] (Imagine such a thing! Would any pastor today, exiled from his church and country, and living in mortal danger, study Hebrew? What has become of the vision of ministry that such a thing seems unthinkable today?) In March of 1536, he published in Basel the first edition of his most famous work, *The Institutes of the Christian Religion*, which would go through five enlargements before reaching its present form in 1559. And we should not think that this was a merely academic exercise for Calvin. Years later, he tells us what was driving him:

> But lo! while I lay hidden at Basel, and known only to few people, many faithful and holy persons were burnt alive in France. . . . It appeared to me, that unless I opposed [the perpetrators] to the utmost of my ability, my silence could not be vindicated from the charge of cowardice and treachery. This was the consideration which induced me to publish my *Institutes of the Christian Religion*. . . . It was published with no other design than that men might know what was the faith held by those whom I saw basely and wickedly defamed.[22]

So when you hold the *Institutes* of John Calvin in your hand, remember that theology, for John Calvin, was forged in the furnace of

---

[20] Dillenberger, *John Calvin, Selections*, 86.
[21] Theodore Beza, *The Life of John Calvin* (Edinburgh: Calvin Translation Society, 1844; repr., Milwaukie, OR: Back Home, 1996), 21.
[22] Dillenberger, *John Calvin, Selections*, 27.

burning flesh, and that Calvin could not sit idly by without some effort to vindicate the faithful and the God for whom they suffered. I think we would, perhaps, do our theology better today if more were at stake in what we said.

In 1536, France gave a temporary amnesty to those who had fled. Calvin returned, put his things in order, and left, never to return, taking his brother Antoine and sister Marie with him. He intended to go to Strasbourg and continue his life of peaceful literary production. But he wrote later to a friend, "I have learned from experience that we cannot see very far before us. When I promised myself an easy, tranquil life, what I least expected was at hand."[23] A war between Charles V and Francis I resulted in troop movements that blocked the road to Strasbourg, and Calvin had to detour through Geneva. In retrospect, one has to marvel at the providence of God that he should so arrange armies to position his pastors where he wanted them.

The night that Calvin stayed in Geneva, William Farel, the fiery leader of the Reformation in that city, found out he was there and sought him out. It was a meeting that changed the course of history, not just for Geneva, but for the world. Calvin tells us what happened in his preface to his commentary on Psalms:

> Farel, who burned with an extraordinary zeal to advance the gospel, immediately learned that my heart was set upon devoting myself to private studies, for which I wished to keep myself free from other pursuits, and finding that he gained nothing by entreaties, he proceeded to utter an imprecation that God would curse my retirement, and the tranquillity of the studies which I sought, if I should withdraw and refuse to give assistance, when the necessity was so urgent. By this imprecation I was so stricken with terror, that I desisted from the journey which I had undertaken.[24]

The course of his life was irrevocably changed. Not just geographically, but vocationally. Never again would Calvin work in what he called the "tranquillity of . . . studies." From now on, every page of the forty-eight volumes of books and tracts and sermons and commentaries and letters that he wrote would be hammered out on the anvil of pastoral responsibility.

---

[23] Parker, *Portrait of Calvin*, 24.
[24] Dillenberger, *John Calvin, Selections*, 28.

He took up his responsibilities in Geneva first as Professor of Sacred Scripture, and within four months was appointed pastor of St. Peter's church—one of the three parishes in the ten-thousand-person town of Geneva. But the city council was not altogether happy with Farel or Calvin because they did not bow to all their wishes. So the two of them were banished in April 1538.

Calvin breathed a sigh of relief and thought God was relieving him from the crush of pastoral duties so he could be about his studies. But when Martin Bucer found out about Calvin's availability, he did the same thing to get him to Strasbourg that Farel had done to get him to Geneva. Calvin wrote, "That most excellent servant of Christ, Martin Bucer, employing a similar kind of remonstrance and protestation as that to which Farel had recourse, before, drew me back to a new station. Alarmed by the example of Jonah which he set before me, I still continued in the work of teaching."[25] That is, he agreed to go to Strasbourg and teach. In fact, for three years Calvin served as the pastor to about five hundred French refugees in Strasbourg, as well as teaching New Testament. He also wrote his first commentary, on Romans, and put out the second enlarged edition of the *Institutes*.

Perhaps the most important providence during this three-year stay in Strasbourg was finding a wife. Several had tried to get Calvin a wife. He was thirty-one years old, and numerous women had shown interest. Calvin had told his friend and matchmaker William Farel what he wanted in a wife: "The only beauty which allures me is this—that she be chaste, not too nice or fastidious, economical, patient, likely to take care of my health."[26] Parker comments, "Romantic love . . . seems to have had no place in his character. Yet prosaic wooing led to a happy marriage."[27] I think Parker was wrong about romantic love (see below on Idelette's death). An Anabaptist widow named Idelette Stordeur was the subject of John Calvin's "prosaic wooing." She and her husband Jean had joined Calvin's congregation. In the spring of 1540, Jean died of plague, and on August 6, 1540, Calvin and Idelette were married. She brought a son and daughter with her into Calvin's home.

Meanwhile back in Geneva, chaos was making the city fathers think that maybe Calvin and Farel were not so bad after all. On May 1, 1541,

---

[25] Ibid., 29.
[26] Parker, *Portrait of Calvin*, 70.
[27] Ibid., 69.

the City Council rescinded the ban on Calvin and even held him up as a man of God. This was an agonizing decision for Calvin, because he knew that life in Geneva would be full of controversy and danger. Earlier in October he had said to Farel that though he preferred not to go, "yet because I know that I am not my own master, I offer my heart as a true sacrifice to the Lord."[28] This became Calvin's motto, and the picture on his emblem included a hand holding out a heart to God with the inscription, *prompte et sincere* ("promptly and sincerely").

On Tuesday, September 13, 1541, he entered Geneva for the second time to serve the church there until his death on May 27, 1564. His first son, Jacques, was born July 28, 1542, and two weeks later died. He wrote to his friend Viret, "The Lord has certainly inflicted a severe and bitter wound in the death of our baby son. But He is Himself a Father and knows best what is good for His children."[29] This is the kind of submission to the sovereign hand of God that Calvin rendered in all his countless trials.

Idelette was never well again. They had two more children who also died at or soon after birth. Then on March 29, 1549, Idelette died of what was probably tuberculosis. Calvin wrote to Viret:

> You know well how tender, or rather soft, my mind is. Had not a powerful self-control been given to me, I could not have borne up so long. And truly, mine is no common source of grief. I have been bereaved of the best companion of my life, of one who, had it been so ordained, would have willingly shared not only my poverty but even my death. During her life she was the faithful helper of my ministry. From her I never experienced the slightest hindrance. She was never troublesome to me throughout the whole course of her illness, but was more anxious about her children than about herself. As I feared these private worries might upset her to no purpose, I took occasion three days before she died, to mention that I would not fail in discharging my duty towards her children.[30]

Calvin never remarried. And it is just as well. The pace he kept would not have left much time for wife or children. His acquaintance Colladon, who lived in Geneva during these years, describes his life:

[28] W. de Greef, *The Writings of John Calvin: An Introductory Guide*, trans. Lyle D. Bierma (Grand Rapids, MI: Baker, 1993), 38.
[29] Parker, *Portrait of Calvin*, 71.
[30] Ibid., 71.

Calvin for his part did not spare himself at all, working far beyond what his power and regard for his health could stand. He preached commonly every day for one week in two [and twice on every Sunday, or a total of about ten times every fortnight]. Every week he lectured three times in theology.... He was at the *Consistoire* on the appointed day and made all the remonstrances.... Every Friday at the Bible Study ... what he added after the leader had made his *declaration* was almost a lecture. He never failed in visiting the sick, in private warning and counsel, and the rest of the numberless matters arising out of the ordinary exercise of his ministry. But besides these ordinary tasks, he had great care for believers in France, both in teaching them and exhorting and counseling them and consoling them by letters when they were being persecuted, and also in interceding for them.... Yet all that did not prevent him from going on working at his special study and composing many splendid and very useful books.[31]

He was, as Wolfgang Musculus called him, "a bow always strung." In one way he tried to take heed to his health but probably did more harm than good. Colladon says that "he took little regard to his health, mostly being content for many years with a single meal a day and never taking anything between two meals." His reasons were that the weakness of his stomach and his migraines could only be controlled, he had found by experiment, by continual abstinence.[32] But on the other hand, he was apparently careless of his health and worked night and day with scarcely a break. You can hear the drivenness in this letter to Falais in 1546: "Apart from the sermons and the lectures, there is a month gone by in which I have scarce done anything, in such wise I am almost ashamed to live thus useless."[33] A mere twenty sermons and twelve lectures in that month!

To get a clearer picture of his iron constancy, add to this work schedule the continuous ill health he endured. He wrote to his physicians in 1564, when he was fifty-three years old, and described his colic and spitting of blood and ague and gout and the "excruciating sufferings" of his hemorrhoids.[34] But worst of all seemed to be the kidney stones that had to pass, unrelieved by any sedative.

[They] gave me exquisite pain.... At length not without the most painful strainings I ejected a calculus which in some degree mitigated my suffer-

---

[31] T. H. L. Parker, *Calvin's Preaching* (Louisville: Westminster John Knox, 1992), 62–63.
[32] Colladon, quoted in T. H. L. Parker, *John Calvin: A Biography* (Philadelphia: Westminster, 1975), 104.
[33] Ibid., 103–4.
[34] Dillenberger, *John Calvin, Selections*, 78.

ings, but such was its size that it lacerated the urinary canal and a copious discharge of blood followed. This hemorrhage could only be arrested by an injection of milk through a syringe.[35]

On top of all this pressure and physical suffering were the threats to his own life. "He was not unfamiliar with the sound of mobs outside his house [in Geneva] threatening to throw him in the river and firing their muskets."[36] On his deathbed, Calvin said to the pastors gathered, "I have lived here amid continual bickerings. I have been from derision saluted of an evening before my door with forty or fifty shots of an arquebus [a large gun]."[37] In a letter to Melanchthon in 1558, he wrote that war was imminent in the region and that enemy troops could reach Geneva within half an hour. "Whence you may conclude," he said, "that we have not only exile to fear, but that all the most cruel varieties of death are impending over us, for in the cause of religion they will set no bounds to their barbarity."[38] In other words, he went to sleep, when he slept, pondering from time to time what sorts of tortures would be inflicted on him if the armies entered Geneva.

One of the most persistent thorns in Calvin's side were the libertines in Geneva. But here too his perseverance was triumphant in a remarkable way. In every city in Europe, men kept mistresses. When Calvin began his ministry in Geneva in 1536 at the age of twenty-seven, there was a law that said a man could keep only one mistress.[39] After Calvin had been preaching as pastor in St. Peter's church for over fifteen years, immorality was still a plague, even in the church. The libertines boasted in their license. For them the "communion of saints" meant the common possession of goods, houses, *bodies, and wives.* So they practiced adultery and indulged in sexual promiscuity in the name of Christian freedom. And at the same time they claimed the right to sit at the Lord's Table.[40]

The crisis of the Communion came to a head in 1553. A well-to-do libertine named Berthelier was forbidden by the consistory of the church to eat the Lord's Supper but appealed the decision to the council

[35] Ibid., 78.
[36] Parker, *Portrait of Calvin*, 29.
[37] Dillenberger, *John Calvin, Selections*, 42.
[38] Ibid., 71.
[39] Parker, *Portrait of Calvin*, 29.
[40] Henderson, *Calvin in His Letters*, 75.

of the city, which overturned the ruling. This created a crisis for Calvin, who would not think of yielding to the state the rights of excommunication, nor of admitting a libertine to the Lord's Table.

The issue, as always, was the glory of Christ. He wrote to Viret, "I . . . took an oath that I had resolved rather to meet death than profane so shamefully the Holy Supper of the Lord. . . . My ministry is abandoned if I suffer the authority of the Consistory to be trampled upon, and extend the Supper of Christ to open scoffers. . . . I should rather die a hundred times than subject Christ to such foul mockery."[41]

The Lord's day of testing arrived. The libertines were present to eat the Lord's Supper. It was a critical moment for the Reformed faith in Geneva.

> The sermon had been preached, the prayers had been offered, and Calvin descended from the pulpit to take his place beside the elements at the communion table. The bread and wine were duly consecrated by him, and he was now ready to distribute them to the communicants. Then on a sudden a rush was begun by the troublers in Israel in the direction of the communion table. . . . Calvin flung his arms around the sacramental vessels as if to protect them from sacrilege, while his voice rang through the building: "These hands you may crush, these arms you may lop off, my life you may take, my blood is yours, you may shed it; but you shall never force me to give holy things to the profaned, and dishonor the table of my God."
>
> "After this," says Beza, Calvin's first biographer, "the sacred ordinance was celebrated with a profound silence, and under solemn awe in all present, as if the Deity Himself had been visible among them."[42]

The point of mentioning all these woes in Geneva is to set in bold relief the invincible constancy of John Calvin in the ministry that God had called him to. We asked earlier, What happened to John Calvin to make him a man so mastered by the majesty of God? And what kind of ministry did this produce in his life? We answered the first question by saying that Calvin experienced the supernatural inward witness of the Spirit to the majesty of God in Scripture. Henceforth, everything in his thinking and writing and ministry was aimed at illustrating the majesty and glory of God.

---

[41] Ibid., 77.
[42] Ibid., 78–79.

Now what is the answer to the second question—what kind of ministry did his commitment to the majesty of God produce? Part of the answer has been given: It produced a ministry of incredible steadfastness—a ministry, to use Calvin's own description of faithful ministers of the Word, of "invincible constancy."[43] But that is only half the answer. It was a ministry of unrelenting exposition of the Word of God. The constancy had a focus, the exposition of the Word of God.

Calvin had seen the majesty of God in the Scriptures. This persuaded him that the Scriptures were the very Word of God. He said, "We owe to the Scripture the same reverence which we owe to God, because it has proceeded from Him alone, and has nothing of man mixed with it."[44] His own experience had taught him that "the highest proof of Scripture derives in general from the fact that God in person speaks in it."[45] These truths led to an inevitable conclusion for Calvin. Since the Scriptures are the very voice of God, and since they are therefore self-authenticating in revealing the majesty of God, and since the majesty and glory of God are the reason for all existence, it follows that Calvin's life would be marked by "invincible constancy" in the exposition of Scripture.

He wrote tracts, he wrote the great *Institutes*, he wrote commentaries (on all the New Testament books except Revelation, plus the Pentateuch, Psalms, Isaiah, Jeremiah, and Joshua), he gave biblical lectures (many of which were published as virtual commentaries), and he preached ten sermons every two weeks. But *all* of it was exposition of Scripture. Dillenberger said, "[Calvin] assumed that his whole theological labor was the exposition of Scripture."[46] In his last will and testament he said, "I have endeavored, both in my sermons and also in my writings and commentaries, to preach the Word purely and chastely, and faithfully to interpret His sacred Scriptures."[47]

Everything was exposition of Scripture. This was the ministry unleashed by seeing the majesty of God in Scripture. The Scriptures were absolutely central because they were absolutely the Word of God and

---

[43] In a sermon on Job 33:1–7, Calvin calls preachers to constancy: "When men so forget themselves that they cannot subject themselves to Him Who has created and fashioned them, it behooves us to have an *invincible constancy*, and to reckon that we shall have enmity and displeasure when we do our duty; yet nevertheless let us go through it without bending." John Calvin, *Sermons from Job by John Calvin* (Grand Rapids, MI: Eerdmans, 1952), 245.

[44] John Calvin, quoted in Packer, "Calvin the Theologian," 162.

[45] Calvin, *Institutes*, I.vii.4.

[46] Dillenberger, *John Calvin, Selections*, 14.

[47] Ibid., 35ff.

had as their self-authenticating theme the majesty and glory of God. But out of all these labors of exposition, preaching was supreme. Emile Doumergue, the foremost biographer of John Calvin with his six-volume life of Calvin, said, as he stood in the pulpit of John Calvin on the four hundredth anniversary of Calvin's birth, "That is the Calvin who seems to me to be the real and authentic Calvin, the one who explains all the others: Calvin the preacher of Geneva, molding by his words the spirit of the Reformed of the sixteenth century."[48]

Calvin's preaching was of one kind from beginning to end: He preached steadily through book after book of the Bible. He never wavered from this approach to preaching for almost twenty-five years of ministry in St. Peter's church of Geneva—with the exception of a few high festivals and special occasions. "On Sunday he took always the New Testament, except for a few Psalms on Sunday afternoons. During the week . . . it was always the Old Testament."[49] The records show fewer than half a dozen exceptions for the sake of the Christian year. He almost entirely ignored Christmas and Easter in the selection of his text.[50]

To give you some idea of the scope of Calvin's pulpit, he began his series on the book of Acts on August 25, 1549, and ended it in March 1554. After Acts, he went on to the epistles to the Thessalonians (46 sermons), Corinthians (186 sermons), the pastoral epistles (86 sermons), Galatians (43 sermons), Ephesians (48 sermons)—until May 1558. Then there is a gap when he was ill. In the spring of 1559, he began the Harmony of the Gospels and was not finished when he died in May 1564. On the weekdays during that season he preached 159 sermons on Job, 200 on Deuteronomy, 353 on Isaiah, 123 on Genesis, and so on.[51]

One of the clearest illustrations that this was a self-conscious choice on Calvin's part was the fact that on Easter Day 1538, after preaching, he left the pulpit of St. Peter's, banished by the City Council. He returned in September 1541—over three years later—and picked up the exposition in the next verse.[52]

Why this remarkable commitment to the centrality of sequential

[48] Emile Doumergue, quoted in Harold Dekker, introduction to Calvin, *Sermons from Job*, xii.
[49] Parker, *Portrait of Calvin*, 82.
[50] John Calvin, *The Deity of Christ and Other Sermons*, trans. Leroy Nixon (Grand Rapids, MI: Eerdmans, 1950), 8.
[51] For these statistics, see Parker, *Portrait of Calvin*, 83; and de Greef, *Writings of John Calvin*, 111–12.
[52] Parker, *Calvin's Preaching*, 60.

expository preaching? Three reasons are just as valid today as they were in the sixteenth century.

First, Calvin believed that the Word of God was a lamp that had been taken away from the churches. He said in his own personal testimony, "Thy word, which ought to have shone on all thy people like a lamp, was taken away, or at least suppressed as to us. . . . And now, O Lord, what remains to a wretch like me, but . . . earnestly to supplicate thee not to judge according to [my] deserts that fearful abandonment of thy word from which, in thy wondrous goodness thou hast at last delivered me."[53] Calvin reckoned that the continuous exposition of books of the Bible was the best way to overcome the "fearful abandonment of [God's] Word."

Second, Parker says that Calvin had a horror of those who preached their own ideas in the pulpit. He said, "When we enter the pulpit, it is not so that we may bring our own dreams and fancies with us."[54] He believed that by expounding the Scriptures as a whole, he would be forced to deal with all that *God* wanted to say, not just what *he* might want to say.

Third—and this brings us full circle to the beginning, where Calvin saw the majesty of God in his Word—he believed with all his heart that the Word of God was indeed the Word of *God,* and that all of it was inspired and profitable and radiant with the light of the glory of God. In Sermon number 61 on Deuteronomy, he challenged pastors of his day and ours:

> Let the pastors boldly dare all things *by the word of God.* . . . Let them constrain all the power, glory, and excellence of the world to give place to and to obey *the divine majesty of this word.* Let them enjoin everyone by it, from the highest to the lowest. Let them edify the body of Christ. Let them devastate Satan's reign. Let them pasture the sheep, kill the wolves, instruct and exhort the rebellious. Let them bind and loose thunder and lightning, if necessary, *but let them do all according to the word of God.*[55]

The key phrase here is "the divine majesty of this word." This was always the root issue for Calvin. How might he best show forth for all

---

[53] Dillenberger, *John Calvin, Selections,* 115.
[54] Parker, *Portrait of Calvin,* 83.
[55] John Calvin, *Sermons on the Epistle to the Ephesians* (Edinburgh: Banner of Truth, 1973), xii, emphasis added.

of Geneva and all of Europe and all of history the majesty of God? He answered with a life of continuous expository preaching. There would be no better way to manifest the full range of the glories of God and the majesty of his being than to spread out the full range of God's Word in the context of the pastoral ministry of shepherding care.

This is why preaching remains a central event in the life of the church even five hundred years after the printing press and the arrival of radio and TV and cassettes and CDs and computers. God's Word is mainly about the majesty of God and the glory of God. That is the main issue in ministry. And even though the glory and majesty of God in his Word can be known in the still, small voice of whispered counsel by the bedside of a dying saint, there is something in it that cries out for expository exultation. This is why preaching will never die. And radical, pervasive God-centeredness will always create a hunger for preaching in God's people. If God is "I AM WHO I AM"—the great, absolute, sovereign, mysterious, all-glorious God of majesty whom Calvin saw in Scripture—there will always be preaching, because the more this God is known and the more this God is central, the more we will feel that he must not just be analyzed and explained, he must be acclaimed and heralded and magnified with expository exultation. The flaming legacy of sovereign joy, lit so bright in the life of Augustine, and spread through centuries of fervent saints, is ignited anew in every generation by glowing, God-besotted preaching—the preaching of the "divine majesty of this word." May God grant every preacher of the Word such a "taste" of sovereign joy in God and such an "intense desire" for him that expository exultation would flame up in every church.

Conclusion

Four Lessons from the Lives of Flawed Saints

The swans are not silent. And this is a great mercy. We may feel like crickets chirping in the presence of St. Augustine, or tiny echoes of Luther and Calvin. But our sense of inadequacy only magnifies the grace of hearing their voices and seeing their lives so long after they have lived. They were not perfect, which makes them the more helpful in our battle to be useful in spite of frailty. I thank God for the privilege of knowing these famous, flawed saints.

The lessons from their stories for our lives are rich with hope, no matter how humbling. Of many more that could be distilled and savored, I close with four.

1. Do not be paralyzed by your weaknesses and flaws. Oh, how many times we are tempted to lick our wounded pride and shrink from some good work because of the wounds of criticism—especially when the criticism is true! A sense of being weak and flawed can paralyze the will and take away all passion for a worthy cause. Comparison with others can be a crippling occupation. When it comes to heroes, there is an easy downward slip from the desire for imitation to the discouragement of intimidation to the deadness of resignation. But the mark of humility and faith and maturity is to stand against the paralyzing effect of famous saints. The triumphs they achieved over their own flagrant sins and flaws should teach us not to be daunted by our own. God never yet used a flawless man, save one. Nor will he ever, until Jesus comes again.

In the case of our weaknesses, we must learn with the apostle, and the swans who sang his song after him, that the grace of Christ is sufficient, and that his strength is made perfect in weakness. We must learn from the Scripture and from the history of weak victors to say, "Most gladly, therefore, I will rather boast about my weaknesses, so that the power of Christ may dwell in me" (2 Cor. 12:9). The suffering of weak saints can make them sink with defeat or make them strong. From Paul, Augustine, Luther, and Calvin, we can learn to say, "I take pleasure in infirmities, in reproaches, in necessities, in persecutions, in distresses for Christ's sake: for when I am weak, then am I strong" (2 Cor. 12:10 KJV).

In the case of our flaws and our sins, we must learn gutsy guilt. This is what we see, especially in Luther. The doctrine of justification by faith alone did not make him indifferent to practical godliness, but it did make him bold in grace when he stumbled. And well it should, as Micah 7:8–9 declares: "Do not rejoice over me, O my enemy. Though I fall I will rise; though I dwell in darkness, the LORD is a light for me. I will bear the indignation of the LORD because I have sinned against Him, until He pleads my case and executes justice for me. He will bring me out to the light, and I will see His righteousness."

Even when we have "sinned against Him"—even when we "bear the indignation of the LORD"—we say to the accusing and gloating adversary, "Do not rejoice over me. . . . Though I fall I will rise." The Lord himself, who frowns in chastisement, will be my irresistible Advocate and he will triumph in court for me. He will plead my case. He will be my light. The cloud will pass. And I will stand in righteousness not my own and do the work he has given me to do.

Oh, let us learn the secret of gutsy guilt from the steadfastness of sinful saints who were not paralyzed by their imperfections. God has a great work for everyone to do. Do it with all your might—yes, and even with all your flaws and all your sins. And in the obedience of this faith, magnify the glory of his grace, and do not grow weary in doing good.

2. In the battle against sin and surrender, learn the secret of sovereign joy. Few have seen this or modeled it for us like Augustine. The quest for holiness is the quest for satisfaction in God. And satisfaction in God is a divine gift of sovereign joy. It is sovereign because, in its fullness, it triumphs over all contestants for the heart. The duration of Augustine's bondage only serves to make the power of his deliverance more compelling. It was the bondage of "fruitless joys" that could only be driven out by a superior—a sovereign—pleasure.

> How sweet all at once it was for me to be rid of *those fruitless joys* which I had once feared to lose! . . . *You drove them from me*, you who are the true, the *sovereign joy*. You drove them from me and took their place, you who are *sweeter than all pleasure*. . . . O Lord my God, my Light, my Wealth, and my Salvation.[1]

No one taught more powerfully than Augustine that the heart is made for God, and that nothing else will drive out the suitors of sin but the happiness of knowing our true Husband. "You made us for yourself, and our hearts find no peace till they rest in you."[2]

Many have said with Augustine that "he is happy who possesses God."[3] But not as many have seen and said that this happiness is a sovereign delight that sanctifies the soul with idol-evicting jealousy. This is what we must learn. The battle to be holy—the battle for sanctification—is a battle fought at the level of what we love, what we cherish and treasure and delight in.

To be sure there is real self-denial and real discipline and gouging out of the eye and cutting off of the hand—a spiritual severity of warfare that many have not attained. But it must be said—and let the apostle say it with all authority—that the secret beneath this severe discipline, the secret to severing all else as rubbish, is to savor Christ as gain (Phil. 3:8).

The battle for holiness is a battle to be fought mainly by fueling the fires of our passion for Christ. Sanctification is the triumph of "sovereign joy." Its legacy is a legacy of love.

3. Supernatural change comes from seeing Christ in his sacred Word. The sanctifying power of sovereign joy does not arise in a blind soul. "*Beholding* the glory of the Lord, [we] are being changed into his likeness from one degree of glory to another" (2 Cor. 3:18 RSV). But where do we "behold" this glory of the Lord? The New Testament answers: in "the light of the *gospel* of the glory of Christ, who is the image of God . . . [that is, in] the Light of the *knowledge* of the glory of God in the face of Christ" (2 Cor. 4:4, 6).

Notice the words "knowledge" and "gospel." We see the glory of Christ in the "gospel." We see the glory of God through "knowledge."

---

[1] Augustine, *Confessions*, trans. R. S. Pine-Coffin (New York: Penguin, 1961), 181 (IX, 1), emphasis added.
[2] Ibid., 21 (I, 1).
[3] Thomas A. Hand, *Augustine on Prayer* (New York: Catholic Book, 1986), 17 (*On the Happy Life*, 11).

The glory of the Lord, whom to see truly is "sovereign joy," is seen in a gospel, a knowledge, a message, a Word. Oh, how Luther drove this truth with relentless force against fanatics with their added revelations and against Catholics with their added traditions.

We must learn from Luther that the Word became flesh, and the Word became Greek sentences. We behold the glory of the incarnate Word through the grammar of the written Word. Sacred study is a way of seeing, especially when combined with prayer. *Oratio* and *meditatio*—prayer and meditation—were the pathway to supernatural sight of the glory of God in the face of Christ.

Oratio: "Incline my heart to thy testimonies, and not to gain!" (Ps. 119:36 RSV). "Open my eyes, that I may behold wondrous things out of your law" (Ps. 119:18 ESV). "[I pray] that the God of our Lord Jesus Christ, the Father of glory, may give to you a spirit of wisdom and of revelation in the knowledge of Him . . . that the eyes of your heart may be enlightened" (Eph. 1:17–18). This was not just any prayer, but prayer over the Word and prayer to love the Word and prayer for light from the Word.

Meditatio: "His delight is in the law of the LORD, and in His law he meditates day and night. And he will be like a tree firmly planted by streams of water, which yields its fruit in its season, and its leaf does not wither; and in whatever he does, he prospers" (Ps. 1:2–3). "Faith comes by hearing, and hearing by the word of Christ" (Rom. 10:17). "Sanctify them in the truth; Your word is truth" (John 17:17). After years of pounding on the Greek text of the apostle Paul, it finally yielded, and Luther saw the glory of Christ in the gospel and entered into paradise. His life and labor bear witness to this crucial truth: the sight of Christ that wakens sovereign joy is mediated through the written word. Even though flesh and blood does not reveal the glory of the Son, neither is it revealed apart from the ordinary work of hearing and meditating on the Word of God (Matt. 16:17; Rom. 10:17).

We are sanctified in the truth because the truth (revealed and written) displays the glory of Christ, which begets the sovereign joy, which severs the root of sin and sets us free.

4. Therefore, let us exult over the exposition of the truth of the gospel and herald the glory of Christ for the joy of all peoples. When John Calvin saw the majesty of God in his Word, he was taken captive to preaching. Preaching, for John Calvin, was the faithful, regular exposition of the Word of God with a passion for the glory of Christ. It was exposition, but it was also exultation. Exultation over the majesty of God and the glory of Christ revealed in the written Word produced expository exultation. That is what I call preaching. Calvin's devotion to preaching through all his life, as one of the greatest theologians who ever lived, is a trumpet call for all of us—laypeople and preachers—to exult over the exposition of the Word.

Let churches ring with expository exultation! Let laypeople love the hearing of this great, God-saturated sound! Let seminaries breed the passions of Calvin, Luther, and Augustine for the majesty of God that takes the soul captive and binds it to the Word, which reveals Christ and wakens sovereign joy. If a worshiping heart and a holy life are the fruit of sovereign joy, and if the written Word of God is the deposit of historical truth where the glory of Christ wakens this joy, then let us pray that God would raise up generations of preachers who give themselves, with Calvin-like devotion, to expository exultation over the glory of Jesus Christ for the joy of all peoples.

The Swans Are Not Silent

Book 2

The Hidden Smile of God

*The Fruit of Affliction in the Lives of
John Bunyan, William Cowper,
and David Brainerd*

To
George T. Henry[†] and Pamela C. Henry

Parents of my wife,
partners in the warfare,
precious in life and death

The Hidden Smile of God

Book 2

Contents

Judge not the Lord by feeble sense,
But trust him for his grace;
Behind a frowning providence
He hides a smiling face.
William Cowper
"God Moves in a Mysterious Way"

Preface

The swans sing sweetly when they suffer. The swans I have in mind are John Bunyan (1628–1688), William Cowper (1731–1800), and David Brainerd (1718–1747). I call them swans because they are great voices for Christian truth that death has not silenced.

When the unrivaled Augustine, the bishop of Hippo in North Africa, retired in AD 430, he handed over his duties to his humble successor, Eraclius. At the ceremony, Eraclius stood to preach as the aged Augustine sat on his bishop's throne behind him. Overwhelmed by a sense of inadequacy in Augustine's presence, Eraclius said, "The cricket chirps, the swan is silent."[1] This story is the origin of the title for this series of books called The Swans Are Not Silent. You are now reading Book 2. The first was called *The Legacy of Sovereign Joy: God's Triumphant Grace in the Lives of Augustine, Luther, and Calvin.*

The reference to swans appeared again a thousand years later. On July 6, 1415, John Hus (whose name in Czech means "goose") was burned at the stake for criticizing the Roman Catholic sale of indulgences. Just before his death, he is said to have written, "Today, you are burning a goose; however, a hundred years from now, you will be able to hear a swan sing; you will not burn it, you will have to listen to him."[2] And so the line of "swans" has continued down to our own day—faithful witnesses to the gospel of the glory of Christ whose death does not silence their song.

My aim in this series of books is to magnify the voice of the swans with the megaphone of their lives. The apostle Paul calls the church to "adorn the doctrine of God" with the fidelity of our lives (Titus 2:10). That is what the swans have done, especially in their suffering. Their steadfastness

---

[1] Peter Brown, *Augustine of Hippo* (Berkeley, CA: University California Press, 1969), 408.
[2] Erwin Weber, "Luther with the Swan," *The Lutheran Journal* 65, no. 2 (1996): 10.

through trial sweetens and intensifies the song of their faith. It is part of our pleasant Christian duty to preserve and proclaim the faith-sustaining stories of Christ's suffering swans. The Bible exhorts us that we "not be sluggish, but imitators of those who through faith and patience inherit the promises" (Heb. 6:12). "Remember those who led you, who spoke the word of God to you; and considering the result of their conduct, imitate their faith" (Heb. 13:7). But we can't imitate or be inspired by what we don't know. Hence the series, The Swans Are Not Silent.

The three stories that I tell in this book were originally biographical messages delivered orally at the Bethlehem Conference for Pastors. I am influenced in my selection of these three for this book by the conviction expressed by Benjamin Brook in the preface to his three-volume work, *The Lives of the Puritans*:

> Of all the books which can be put into your hands, those which relate the labors and suffering of good men are the most interesting and instructive. In them you see orthodox principles, Christian tempers, and holy duties in lovely union and in vigorous operation. In them you see religion shining forth in real life, subduing the corruptions of human nature, and inspiring a zeal for every good work. In them you see the reproaches and persecutions which the servants of God have endured; those gracious principles which have supported their minds; and the course they have pursued in their progress to the kingdom of heaven. Such books are well calculated to engage your attention, to affect your feelings, to deepen your best impressions, and to invigorate your noblest resolutions. They are well calculated to fortify you against the allurements of a vain world; to assimilate your characters to those of the excellent of the earth; to conform your lives to the standard of holiness; and to educate your souls for the mansions of glory.[3]

These are my aims. And I agree that "the labors and suffering of good men are the most interesting and instructive" for these great ends. It is apparent, therefore, that I do not write as a disinterested scholar, but rather as a passionately interested—and I hope, honest and careful—pastor whose mission in life is to spread a passion for the supremacy of God in all things for the joy of all peoples.

John Bunyan, William Cowper, and David Brainerd labored and suffered. And it was by this very affliction that they bore fruit for the

---

[3] Benjamin Brook, *The Lives of the Puritans*, 3 vols. (orig. 1813; Pittsburgh, PA: Soli Deo Gloria, 1994), 1:vi–vii.

nourishing of radical Christian living, God-centered worship, and Christ-exalting world missions. How they suffered, how they endured, and how it bore fruit is the story that, I pray, will inspire in you that same radical Christian life, God-centered worship, and Christ-exalting mission.

John Bunyan is best known as the simple, British, Baptist pastor who in prison wrote the book that to this day "remains the widest circulating single piece of literature in the history of the human race outside of the Bible,"[4] *The Pilgrim's Progress*. It is a great book about how to live the Christian life. Lesser known is the fact that his twelve years in prison were "voluntary," in the sense that a commitment not to preach the gospel of Jesus Christ would have obtained his freedom at any time. This fact intensifies the effect of knowing that when Bunyan's oldest child, Mary—blind from birth—visited him in prison, it was like "the pulling of the Flesh from my bones."[5] Fewer still are those who know that this imprisoned pastor, with no formal education beyond grammar school, also wrote some sixty other books, most of which are still in print 350 years later.[6]

William Cowper, for those who, along the way, happened to take a course in eighteenth-century literature, is known as "the poet of a new religious revival" led by John Wesley and George Whitefield. His poetry and letters merited over fifty pages in the anthology I studied in college.[7] Among those who know him as a Christian poet, many do not know that William Cowper lived with bleak depression as a steady companion all his life, sometimes immobilized in despair, and repeatedly attempting suicide. In spite of this darkness, Cowper today is still touching the hearts of thousands who know nothing of him at all, simply because, in worship, they sing his hymns "There Is a Fountain Filled with Blood," "O for a Closer Walk with God," and "God Moves in a Mysterious Way."

David Brainerd would probably not be known by anyone today if it were not for Jonathan Edwards, the New England pastor in whose house this young missionary to the American Indians died of tuberculosis when he was twenty-nine. Edwards took Brainerd's diary and turned it into

---

[4] Barry Horner, *The Pilgrim's Progress by John Bunyan, Themes and Issues: An Evangelical Apologetic* (Lindenhurst, NY: Reformation Press, 1998), 2.
[5] John Bunyan, *Grace Abounding to the Chief of Sinners* (Hertfordshire: Evangelical Press, 1978), 123.
[6] The "Catalogue-Table of Mr. Bunyan's Books," in *The Works of John Bunyan*, ed. George Offor (Edinburgh: Banner of Truth, 1991), 3:763, lists sixty works of Bunyan. See also the complete list of his writings in Christopher Hill, *A Tinker and a Poor Man: John Bunyan and His Church, 1628–1688* (New York: Alfred A. Knopf, 1989), xv–xvii.
[7] Louis Bredvold, Alan McKillop, Lois Whitney, eds., *Eighteenth Century Poetry and Prose*, 2nd ed. (New York: Ronald, 1956), 882–935.

what is called *The Life of David Brainerd*,[8] a biography that has inspired more missionary service, perhaps, than any other book outside the Bible.[9] There were no specialists to tell the twenty-two-year-old Brainerd, when he began to spit blood in his sophomore year at Yale, that he was an unfit candidate for missionary stress in the wilderness. So for the next seven years, after being expelled from Yale, he laid down his life for the salvation of "the Stockbridge, Delaware and Susquehanna Tribes of Indians."[10] His story has become a spiritual classic, and "it is as hard to number the great company seen by John on Patmos as to count that company—red, brown, yellow, and white—brought into the Kingdom of God directly or indirectly by the young consumptive who burned himself out in the wilderness of New York, Pennsylvania, and New Jersey over two centuries ago."[11]

With great spiritual privileges comes great pain. It is plain from Scripture that this is God's design: "Because of the surpassing greatness of the revelations," Paul wrote in 2 Corinthians 12:7, "for this reason, to keep me from exalting myself, there was given me a thorn in the flesh, a messenger of Satan to torment me—to keep me from exalting myself!" Great privilege, great pain, God's design. So it was with Bunyan, Cowper, and Brainerd. But they did not all have the same pain. For Bunyan it was prison and danger, for Cowper it was lifelong depression and suicidal darkness, for Brainerd it was tuberculosis and the "howling wilderness."

What was the fruit of this affliction? And what was the rock in which it grew? Consider their stories and be encouraged that no labor and no suffering in the path of Christian obedience is ever in vain. "Behind a frowning providence He hides a smiling face."

---

[8] The full title of the 1749 edition was *An Account of the Life of the late Reverend Mr. David Brainerd, Minister of the Gospel, Missionary to the Indians, from the honourable Society in Scotland, for the Propagation of Christian Knowledge, and Pastor of a Church of Christian Indians in New Jersey. Who died at Northampton in New England, October 9th, 1747, in the 30th year of his Age: Chiefly taken from his own Diary, and other private Writings, written for his own Use; and now published by Jonathan Edwards, A.M., Minister of the Gospel at Northampton.* See Jonathan Edwards, *An Account of the Life of the Reverend Mr. David Brainerd,* in *The Life of David Brainerd,* ed. Norman Pettit, vol. 7 of *The Works of Jonathan Edwards* (New Haven, CT: Yale University Press, 1985), vii. The reference to Brainerd being thirty years old is inaccurate. He was born April 20, 1718 and died October 9, 1747.

[9] This claim is, of course, hard to substantiate, but others have made even greater claims: "But in truth David Brainerd's life sacrifice reached out and touched the whole world, challenging more people into Christian service than perhaps any other man that ever lived" (Ed Reese, "The Life and Ministry of David Brainerd," *Christian Biography Resources,* June 1, 2000, http://www.wholesomewords.org/biography /biobrainerd.html). A more modest claim would be, "Almost immediately upon [the *Diary's*] publication, it captured the hearts of the Protestant world. For over a century it was one of the most popular documents in evangelical circles. Its influence has been enormous" (Francis M. DuBose, ed., *Classics of Christian Missions* [Nashville: Broadman, 1979], 173–74).

[10] This summary of his Indian mission is taken from his gravestone in Northampton, MA.

[11] Clyde Kilby, "David Brainerd: Knight of the Grail," in *Heroic Colonial Christians,* ed. Russell T. Hitt (Philadelphia: J. B. Lippincott, 1966), 202.

Acknowledgments

After thirty-two years of marriage, she still reads everything I write. She not only reads it, she makes it better. Thank you, Noël, for being my live-in editor.

Justin Taylor took an extra year at Bethlehem Baptist Church on his way through seminary and worked full-time in Desiring God Ministries, helping people think their way through knotty issues in the Bible and theology. Thanks, Justin, for applying your eagle eye to this manuscript as it emerged and for making such helpful suggestions and for catching my bloopers.

Aaron Young does all that a loyal and gifted and intelligent assistant can do to make my life manageable. I would not be able to keep my head above water without his help. Thank you, Aaron, for being there so faithfully behind the scenes, enabling so much.

I love books with indexes that help me find a barely-remembered quote or a forgotten fact. That is why I return again and again to Carol Steinbach to help me make every book more useful with her indexing skills. Thanks, Carol. Now you can read my face when it is time to ask you again.

As with Book One of The Swans Are Not Silent, these chapters were originally messages to the Bethlehem Conference for Pastors. It is one of the great joys of my life to encourage brothers in the pastoral ministry by portraying the lives of great saints, and urging them to "consider the outcome of their life, and imitate their faith" (Heb. 13:7 RSV). These chapters would not exist without the hunger of those pastors to draw out the effort. And the conference would not exist without Jon Bloom, the director of Desiring God Ministries, and his prayer-filled oversight of this conference. Thanks, brother, for being there.

Lane Dennis, Ted Griffin, Brian Ondracek, Marvin Padgett, and the whole team at Crossway are the indispensable link between writer and reader. Thanks to all of you for caring about the song of the swans and making this project a delight for me.

Finally, God our Father, and Jesus Christ our Lord, and the Holy Spirit are to be honored and thanked above all and in all. God is always sufficient for every good work; he is not "served by human hands, as though He needed anything, since He Himself gives to all people life and breath and all things" (Acts 17:25). Sometimes his smile is hidden, but his arm is never shortened, nor his light extinguished. In due season the clouds move, and the light returns, and we are sustained. As we get older, we learn to trust the inscrutable working of his winds. May these chapters strengthen you to wait patiently for the Lord in the seasons of darkness, because behind a frowning providence he hides a smiling face.

We also, before the temptation comes, think we can walk upon the sea, but when the winds blow, we feel ourselves begin to sink. . . . And yet doth it yield no good unto us? We could not live without such turnings of the hand of God upon us. We should be overgrown with flesh, if we had not our seasonable winters. It is said that in some countries trees will grow, but will bear no fruit, because there is no winter there.

John Bunyan
Seasonable Counsel, or Advice to Sufferers

I saw with the eyes of my soul Jesus Christ at God's right hand; there, I say, was my righteousness; so that wherever I was, or whatever I was doing, God could not say of me, he [lacks] my righteousness, for that was just before him. . . . Now did my chains fall off my legs indeed. I was loosed from my afflictions and irons.

John Bunyan
Grace Abounding to the Chief of Sinners

Introduction

Where the Fruit of Affliction Grows

Three Kinds of Fruit

The afflictions of John Bunyan gave us *The Pilgrim's Progress*. The afflictions of William Cowper gave us "There Is a Fountain Filled with Blood" and "God Moves in a Mysterious Way." And the afflictions of David Brainerd gave us a published *Diary* that has mobilized more missionaries than any other similar work. The furnace of suffering brought forth the gold of guidance and inspiration for living the Christian life, worshiping the Christian God, and spreading the Christian gospel.

There is a certain irony to the fruit of these afflictions. Bunyan's confinement taught him the pilgrim path of Christian freedom. Cowper's mental illness yielded sweet music of the mind for troubled souls. Brainerd's smoldering misery of isolation and disease exploded in global missions beyond all imagination. Irony and disproportion are all God's way. He keeps us off balance with his unpredictable connections. We think we know how to do something big, and God makes it small. We think that all we have is weak and small, and God makes it big. Barren Sarah gives birth to the child of promise. Gideon's three hundred men defeat one hundred thousand Midianites. A slingshot in the hand of a shepherd boy brings the giant down. A virgin bears the Son of God. A boy's five loaves feed thousands. A breach of justice, groveling political expediency, and criminal torture on a gruesome cross become the foundation of the salvation of the world.

This is God's way—to take all boasting off of man and put it on God.

Not many of you were wise according to worldly standards, not many were powerful, not many were of noble birth. But God chose what is foolish in the world to shame the wise; God chose what is weak in the world to shame the strong; God chose what is low and despised in the world, even things that are not, to bring to nothing things that are, so that no human being might boast in the presence of God. . . . "Let the one who boasts, boast in the Lord." (1 Cor. 1:26–29, 31 ESV)

Not surprisingly (1 Pet. 4:12), therefore, suffering fits into God's design in ways that sometimes baffle us and test us to the limit. This very baffling and testing is part of the design: "Consider it all joy, my brethren, when you encounter various trials, knowing that the testing of your faith produces endurance. And let endurance have its perfect result, so that you may be perfect and complete, lacking in nothing" (James 1:2–4).

Does God Design Suffering for His Children?

But many stumble at the word *design*. Would suffering be God's design? Can we speak that way? Or should we speak of God working with what he is given? In other words, does God oversee and manage the affairs of the world so that we can speak of suffering as his will and his design, or does he, rather, manage the world like a chess player who does not will the moves of his opponent, but can always check them and turn them for good? Does God plan the place of suffering in the lives of his children for good ends, or is he always in the position of a responder to the pain that other forces give him to work with?

All the swans in this book sing in unison on this question. God governs the world and all that happens in it with purpose and design for the good of those who love him. This was the final lesson Job learned from all his suffering: "Then Job answered the LORD and said, 'I know that You can do all things, and that no purpose of Yours can be thwarted'" (Job 42:1–2). Satan may play his wicked role in the drama and take Job's children and strike him with boils from head to toe, but Job will not give Satan the eminence of ultimate causality. That belongs to God alone, even if we cannot understand it all. When Job's ten children were crushed to death, he "fell on the ground and worshiped. And he said, 'Naked I came from my mother's womb, and naked shall I return. The LORD gave, and the LORD has taken away; blessed be the name of the LORD'" (Job 1:20–21 ESV). To this amazing confession that God had taken his children, the author of the book responds with confirmation:

"In all this Job did not sin or charge God with wrong" (Job 1:22 ESV). Similarly, even when the text says explicitly that "*Satan* . . . afflicted Job with loathsome sores," Job's response was, "Shall we receive good at the hand of God, and shall we not receive evil?" And again the author endorses Job's theology with the words, "In all this Job did not sin with his lips" (Job 2:7, 10 RSV).

This is the uniform message of the Bible, whether we are talking about suffering that comes from disease[1] or from calamity[2] or from persecution[3]: "[God] works all things after the counsel of His will" (Eph. 1:11). God has a good and wise purpose in all that happens.[4] From morning until night, over all the goings and comings of our lives, we should say, "If the Lord wills, we will live and also do this or that" (James 4:15). Why? Because God says, "My purpose will be established, and I will accomplish all My good pleasure" (Isa. 46:10). "Many plans are in a man's heart, but the counsel of the LORD will

---

[1] Ex. 4:11, "The LORD said to him, 'Who has made man's mouth? Or who makes him mute or deaf, or seeing or blind? Is it not I, the LORD?'" John 9:1–3, "[Jesus's] disciples asked Him, 'Rabbi, who sinned, this man or his parents, that he would be born blind?' Jesus answered, 'It was neither that this man sinned, nor his parents; but it was so that the works of God might be displayed in him.'" 2 Sam. 12:15, "Then the LORD struck the child that Uriah's widow bore to David, so that he was very sick." Rom. 8:20, "For the creation was subjected to futility, not willingly, but because of Him who subjected it, in hope." See also Job 2:7, 10.

[2] Lam. 3:32–33, 37–38, "For if He causes grief, then He will have compassion according to His abundant lovingkindness. For He does not afflict willingly or grieve the sons of men. . . . Who is there who speaks and it comes to pass, unless the Lord has commanded it? Is it not from the mouth of the Most High that both good and ill go forth?" Amos 3:6, "If a trumpet is blown in a city will not the people tremble? If a calamity occurs in a city has not the LORD done it?" Isa. 31:2, "Yet He also is wise and will bring disaster." 1 Sam. 2:6–7, "The LORD kills and makes alive; He brings down to Sheol and raises up. The LORD makes poor and rich; He brings low, He also exalts."

[3] Acts 4:27, "For truly in this city there were gathered together against Your holy servant Jesus, whom You anointed, both Herod and Pontius Pilate, along with the Gentiles and the peoples of Israel, to do whatever Your hand and Your purpose predestined to occur." 2 Cor. 1:8–9, "For we do not want you to be unaware, brethren, of our affliction which came to us in Asia, that we were burdened excessively, beyond our strength, so that we despaired even of life; indeed, we had the sentence of death within ourselves so that we would not trust in ourselves, but in God who raises the dead." 2 Tim. 3:12, "Indeed, all who desire to live godly in Christ Jesus will be persecuted." 1 Pet. 2:21, "For you have been called for this purpose, since Christ also suffered for you, leaving you an example for you to follow in His steps." 1 Pet. 3:17, "For it is better, if God should will it so, that you suffer for doing what is right rather than for doing what is wrong." 1 Pet. 4:19, "Therefore, those also who suffer according to the will of God shall entrust their souls to a faithful Creator in doing what is right." Heb. 12:4–8, 11, "You have not yet resisted to the point of shedding blood in your striving against sin; and you have forgotten the exhortation which is addressed to you as sons, 'My son, do not regard lightly the discipline of the LORD, nor faint when you are reproved by Him; for those whom the LORD loves He disciplines, and He scourges every son whom He receives.' It is for discipline that you endure; God deals with you as with sons; for what son is there whom his father does not discipline? But if you are without discipline, of which all have become partakers, then you are illegitimate children and not sons. . . . All discipline for the moment seems not to be joyful, but sorrowful; yet to those who have been trained by it, afterwards it yields the peaceful fruit of righteousness."

[4] For fuller statements of the sovereignty of God in relation to our suffering and how disease and calamity and persecution are dealt with in Scripture, see John Piper, "Suffering: The Sacrifice of Christian Hedonism," in *Desiring God* (Colorado springs: Multnomah, 2011), 253–88. Piper, "The Supremacy of God in Missions through Suffering," in *Let the Nations Be Glad* (Grand Rapids, MI: Baker Academic, 2010), 93–130; and Piper, "The Future Grace of Suffering," in *Future Grace* (Colorado Springs: Multnomah, 2012), 341–50.

stand" (Prov. 19:21). "The mind of man plans his way, but the LORD directs his steps" (Prov. 16:9). "Are not two sparrows sold for a penny? And not one of them will fall to the ground without your Father's will" (Matt. 10:29 RSV). "The king's heart is like channels of water in the hand of the LORD; He turns it wherever He wishes" (Prov. 21:1). "The lot is cast into the lap, but its every decision is from the LORD" (Prov. 16:33).

Opposing Voices

Yet there are those who will not have it so. There are old-fashioned liberals who say, "I believe that pain and suffering are never the will of God for his children. . . . I cannot conceive that it is the will of God that anyone should be run over by a driver under the influence of drink, or that a young mother should die of leukemia, or that some one in the first flush of youth should face the increasing helplessness of arteriosclerosis."[5]

And there are modern-day "open theists"[6] who say, "God does not

---

[5] William Barclay, *A Spiritual Autobiography* (Grand Rapids, MI: Eerdmans, 1975), 44. I call Barclay an "old-fashioned liberal" because his views are similar to those who summed up Christianity as the fatherhood of God, the brotherhood of man, and the ethic of love. He was a universalist (pp. 58–60), and the cross of Christ was essentially a demonstration of God's love, not a substitutionary penal atonement demanded by the righteousness of God (pp. 51–53). With regard to the specifics of doctrine, like Christology, his motto was: "Hold fast to Christ, and for the rest be totally uncommitted" (p. 97).

[6] *Open theism* is the term chosen by a group of theologians to describe their view that God does not plan or know all of the future but leaves much of it "open." That is, he does not plan it or know it ahead of time. Thus, for example, one open theist says, "God is omniscient in the sense that he knows everything which can be known, just as God is omnipotent in the sense that he can do everything that can be done. But free actions are not entities which can be known ahead of time. They literally do not yet exist to be known" (Clark Pinnock, "God Limits His Knowledge," in *Predestination and Free Will: Four Views of Divine Sovereignty and Freedom* [Downers Grove, IL: InterVarsity Press, 1986], 157). Or again he says, "Decisions not yet made do not exist anywhere to be known even by God" (Pinnock, "From Augustine to Arminius: A Pilgrimage in Theology," in *The Grace of God, The Will of Man: A Case for Arminianism*, ed. Clark Pinnock [Grand Rapids, MI: Zondervan, 1989], 25). Another open theist puts it like this: "Indeed, to say that God is ignorant of future creaturely decisions is like saying that God is deaf to silence. It makes no sense, because before they exist such decisions are nothing for God to be ignorant *of*" (Richard Rice, "Divine Foreknowledge and Free-Will Theism," *The Grace of God, The Will of Man*, 129). Another says,

> In the Christian view God knows all of reality—everything there is to know. But to assume He knows ahead of time how every person is going to freely act assumes that each person's free activity is already there to know—even before he freely does it! But it's not. If we have been given freedom, we create the reality of our decisions by making them. And until we make them, they don't exist. Thus, in my view at least, there simply isn't anything to know until we make it there to know. So God can't foreknow the good or bad decisions of the people He creates until He creates these people and they, in turn, create their decisions. (Gregory A. Boyd and Edward K. Boyd, *Letters from a Skeptic* [Colorado Springs, CO: Chariot Victor Publishing, 1994], 30)

Other books representing this viewpoint include Clark Pinnock, ed., *The Openness of God: A Biblical Challenge to the Traditional Understanding of God* (Downers Grove, IL: InterVarsity Press, 1994) and John Sanders, *The God Who Risks: A Theology of Providence* (Downers Grove, IL: InterVarsity Press, 1998). This view has never been embraced as part of orthodoxy by any major Christian body in the history of the church. Thomas Oden, a Wesleyan scholar, along with others, has called it heresy:

have a specific divine purpose for each and every occurrence of evil. . . .
When a two-month-old child contracts a painful, incurable bone cancer
that means suffering and death, it is pointless evil. The Holocaust is
pointless evil. The rape and dismemberment of a young girl is pointless
evil. The accident that caused the death of my brother was a tragedy.
God does not have a specific purpose in mind for these occurrences."[7]
"When an individual inflicts pain on another individual, I do not think
we can go looking for 'the purpose of God' in the event. . . . I know
Christians frequently speak about 'the purpose of God' in the midst of
a tragedy caused by someone else. . . . But this I regard to simply be a
piously confused way of thinking."[8] "Neither Jesus nor his disciples
assumed that there had to be a divine purpose behind all events in
history. . . . The Bible does not assume that every particular evil has a
particular godly purpose behind it."[9]

"But God Meant It for Good"

And then there is the Bible itself with its resounding claim over every
evil perpetrated against God's people: "You meant evil against me, but
God meant it for good in order to bring about this present result, to
preserve many people alive" (Gen. 50:20). This is what Joseph said to
his brothers who had sinned against him in selling him into slavery and
lying to his father, Jacob. What he says is not merely that God turned
this evil for good after it happened, but that God "meant it" (the same
verb as the one used for the brothers' intention) for good. This is confirmed in Genesis 45:7 where Joseph says, "God sent me before you
to preserve for you a remnant." In fact, in later centuries the people
of Israel celebrated precisely this sovereign design of God in Joseph's
trouble, along with the conviction that God planned to bring the famine

---

If "reformists" insist on keeping the boundaries of heresy open, however, then they must be resisted with charity. The fantasy that God is ignorant of the future is a heresy that must be rejected
on scriptural grounds ("I make known the end from the beginning, from ancient times, what is
still to come"; Isa. 46:10a; cf. Job 28; Ps. 90; Rom. 8:29; Eph. 1), as it has been in the history of
exegesis of relevant passages. This issue was thoroughly discussed by patristic exegetes as early
as Origen's *Against Celsus*. ("The Real Reformers and the Traditionalists," *Christianity Today* 42
[Feb. 9, 1998]: 46)

For a thorough and compelling critique of open theism, I highly recommend Bruce A. Ware, *God's Lesser
Glory: The Diminished God of Open Theism* (Wheaton, IL: Crossway, 2000).
[7] Sanders, *The God Who Risks*, 262.
[8] Boyd and Boyd, *Letters from a Skeptic*, 46–47. In another place Gregory Boyd says, "Sickness, disease,
war, death, sorrow and tears are not God's will." (Gregory Boyd, *God at War: The Bible and Spiritual
Conflict* [Downers Grove, IL: InterVarsity Press, 1997], 293).
[9] Boyd, *God at War*, 53, 166.

that made Joseph's presence in Egypt so necessary, and the conviction that God tested Joseph with severe trials:

> And [God] called for a famine upon the land;
> He broke the whole staff of bread.
> He sent a man before them,
> Joseph, who was sold as a slave.
> They afflicted his feet with fetters,
> He himself was laid in irons;
> Until the time that his word came to pass,
> The word of the LORD tested him. (Ps. 105:16–19)

What the Suffering Swans Say

And then there are the swans who suffered. For John Bunyan, William Cowper, and David Brainerd, the loving purpose of God in pain was one of the most precious truths in the Bible and one of the most powerful experiences of their lives. Cowper expressed it in one of his most famous hymns. Notice especially the lines, "He treasures up his bright designs," and "Behind a frowning providence," and "His purposes will ripen fast," and "And scan his work in vain." Each of these lines points to the deep and hope-filled conviction that God has "designs" and "purposes" in his painful "providence" and puzzling "work."

> Deep in unfathomable mines
> Of never-failing skill,
> He treasures up his bright designs
> And works his sovereign will.
>
> Judge not the Lord by feeble sense,
> But trust him for his grace;
> Behind a frowning providence
> He hides a smiling face.
>
> His purposes will ripen fast,
> Unfolding every hour;
> The bud may have a bitter taste,
> But sweet will be the flower.
>
> Blind unbelief is sure to err,
> And scan his work in vain:

God is his own interpreter,
And He will make it plain.[10]

David Brainerd shared Cowper's confidence that God governed all that happened to him. This awakened in him what he called a "sweet resignation" in all his extraordinary suffering with tuberculosis and loneliness and dangers and all kinds of privations in the wilderness. He wrote in his diary on Sunday, March 10, 1744, "My soul was sweetly resigned to God's disposal of me, in every regard; and I saw there had nothing happened to me but what was best for me."[11] Even the disappointments of ministering in a "dry and barren" spiritual condition he saw within the designs of his Father's care:

> It pleased God to leave me to be very dry and barren; so that I don't remember to have been so straightened for a whole twelve month past. God is just, and he has made my soul acquiesce in his will in this regard. 'Tis contrary to "flesh and blood" to be cut off from all freedom in a large auditory [audience], where their expectations are much raised; but so it was with me: and God helped me to say "Amen" to it; good is the will of the Lord.[12]

If anyone should begin to wonder if such submission to the sovereign will of God over all things would produce a passive fatalism, all one has to do is look honestly at Brainerd's life. It produced the opposite. He was empowered to press on against immense obstacles with the confidence that God was working for him in every trial. "This, through grace, I can say at present, with regard to the life or death: 'The Lord do with me as seems good in his sight.'"[13]

The Old Testament context for that last quote confirms the empowering and freeing effect of believing in God's triumphant sovereignty over the battles of life. Joab and his brother Abishai, with the army of Israel, were arrayed against the Syrians and the Ammonites. The outcome looked precarious. So Joab said to his brother, "If the Syrians are too strong for me, then you shall help me; but if the Ammonites are too strong for you, then I will help you. Be of good courage, and

---

[10] Excerpted from *The Poetical Works of William Cowper*, ed. William Michael Rossetti (London: William Collins), 292.

[11] Jonathan Edwards, *The Life of the Reverend Mr. David Brainerd*, in *The Life of David Brainerd*, ed. Norman Pettit, vol. 7 of *The Works of Jonathan Edwards* (New Haven, CT: Yale University Press, 1985), 242.

[12] Ibid., 316, a diary entry dated Lord's Day, August 18, 1745.

[13] Ibid., 431, a diary entry dated Tuesday, September 30, 1746.

let us play the man for our people, and for the cities of our God; and may the LORD do what seems good to him" (1 Chron. 19:12–13 RSV). The Lord was in control of the outcome. But this did not paralyze Joab with fatalism; it empowered him with hope. Come what may—defeat or victory—the Lord is in control and has his "bright designs." Even if the bloody "bud" of battle turns out to have a bitter taste, "sweet" will be the "flower" of God's design.

Bunyan's Counsel for Those Who Suffer

John Bunyan wrote more on suffering and the fruitfulness of afflic-tion than Cowper or Brainerd. He was even more explicit that there is divine purpose and design in suffering for the good of God's children and for the glory of his name. The great *Pilgrim's Progress*, as George Whitefield said, "smells of the prison." It was born in suffering, and it portrays the Christian life as a life of affliction. But Bunyan saw his imprisonment as no more than what God had designed for him: "So being delivered up to the jailer's hand, I was had home to prison, and there have lain now complete for twelve years, waiting to see what God would suffer those men to do with me."[14]

The richest source of teaching on suffering in the writings of Bun-yan is a book that he wrote for his own congregation titled *Seasonable Counsel, or Advice to Sufferers*.[15] It appeared in 1684 just before the "Bloody Assizes."[16] The need for this "seasonable counsel" was not theoretical. Some of his parishioners had already been imprisoned with him. The threat was so real again that Bunyan deeded over all his pos-sessions to his wife Elizabeth in the expectation that he might be im-prisoned and made to pay fines that would take all his possessions.[17] It was no exaggeration when Bunyan wrote, "Our days indeed have been days of trouble, especially since the discovery of the Popish plot, for then we began to fear cutting of throats, of being burned in our beds, and of seeing our children dashed in pieces before our faces."[18]

What, then, would he say to his people to prepare them for the probability of their suffering for Christ? Would he say, with the old-

---

[14] John Bunyan, *Grace Abounding to the Chief of Sinners* (Hertfordshire: Evangelical Press, 1978), 20.
[15] John Bunyan, *Seasonable Counsel, or Advice to Sufferers*, in *The Works of John Bunyan*, ed. George Offor, 3 vols. (Edinburgh: Banner of Truth, 1991), 2:691–741.
[16] See chapter 1, note 12.
[17] John Brown, *John Bunyan: His Life, Times and Work* (London: Hulbert, 1928), 338.
[18] John Bunyan, *Israel's Hope Encouraged*, in *The Works of John Bunyan*, ed. Offor, 1:585.

fashioned liberal, "I believe that pain and suffering are never the will of God for his children"? Would he say with the modern-day open theist, "Christians frequently speak about 'the purpose of God' in the midst of a tragedy caused by someone else. . . . But this I regard to simply be a piously confused way of thinking"? No, this would have been biblically and pastorally unthinkable for John Bunyan, whose blood was "bibline."[19]

He takes his text from 1 Peter 4:19, "Wherefore let them that suffer according to the will of God commit the keeping of their soul to him in well doing, as unto a faithful Creator" (KJV). Then he explains the text with these observations:

> It is not what enemies will, nor what they are resolved upon, but what God will, and what God appoints, that shall be done. . . . And as no enemy can bring suffering upon a man when the will of God is otherwise, so no man can save himself out of their hands when God will deliver him up for his glory. . . . We shall or shall not suffer, even as it pleaseth him. . . . God has appointed who shall suffer. Suffering comes not by chance or by the will of man, but by the will and appointment of God.[20]

He goes on to say that God has appointed not only who shall suffer but also when, where, in what way, for how long, and for what truth they shall suffer.[21]

"God's Hook Is in Their Nose"

Whether there have been serious and loving pastors in the history of the church who during times of great persecution have pointed their people to a God who has no control over and no purpose in their suffering, I do not know. But such counsel would have been viewed as untrue and unloving by Bunyan, Cowper, and Brainerd. They knew another God, and they lived with a different confidence. Bunyan summed up the involvement of God in the persecutions of his people like this:

> All the ways of the persecutors are God's (Dan. 5:23). Wherefore, as we should, so again we should not, be afraid of men: we should be afraid of them, because they will hurt us; but we should not be afraid of them, as

---

[19] Charles Spurgeon, *Autobiography*, 2 vols. (Edinburgh: Banner of Truth, 1973), 2:159.
[20] Bunyan, *Seasonable Counsel*, 722–23.
[21] See chapter 1 for the details of his argument and the texts he gives to support them.

if they were let loose to do to us, and with us, what they will. God's bridle is upon them, God's hook is in their nose: yea, and God has determined the bounds of their rage, and if he lets them drive his church into the sea of troubles, it shall be but up to the neck, and so far it may go, and not be drowned (2 Kings 19:28; Isa. 37:29; 8:7–8). I say the Lord has hold of them, and orders them; nor do they at any time come out against his people but by his license and compassion how far to go, and where to stop.[22]

This robust view of God's rule over his enemies is the foundation of Bunyan's consolation as he ministers to his people:

I have, in a few words, handled this . . . to show you that our sufferings are ordered and disposed by him, that you might always, when you come into trouble for this name, not stagger nor be at loss, but be stayed, composed, and settled in your minds, and say, "The will of the Lord be done" (Acts 21:14). . . . How kindly, therefore, doth God deal with us, when he chooses to afflict us but for a little, that with everlasting kindness he may have mercy upon us (Isa. 54:7–8).[23]

"My Father's Wise Bestowment"

This is the vision of God's sovereign and mysterious kindness that has sustained Christians in every century and from all parts of the world. It is the vision that underlies scores of hymns that the people of God have sung through many storms. Indeed, the great hymns usually come from the experience of suffering and prove by their existence the truth of their message—that afflictions bear fruit for the people of God. Examples come not only from William Cowper, but from others as well.

Karolina Wilhelmina Sandell-Berg (Lina Sandell) "was the daughter of Jonas Sandell, pastor of the Lutheran church in Fröderyd, Sweden. At age twenty-six, she accompanied her father on a boat trip to Gothenberg, during which he fell overboard and drowned before her eyes. The tragedy profoundly affected Lina and inspired her to write hymns,"[24] one of the best known of which is "Day by Day."

Day by day, and with each passing moment,
Strength I find, to meet my trials here;

---

[22] Bunyan, *Seasonable Counsel*, 725–26.
[23] Ibid., 724, 737.
[24] "Karolina Wilhelmina Sandell-Berg," Cyber Hymnal, accessed February 29, 2016, http://www.hymntime .com/tch/bio/s/a/n/sandell-berg_kw.htm.

Trusting in my Father's wise bestowment,
I've no cause for worry or for fear.
He Whose heart is kind beyond all measure
Gives unto each day what He deems best—
Lovingly, its part of pain and pleasure,
Mingling toil with peace and rest.

This is the same vision of God's sovereign kindness that we saw in Bunyan's *Seasonable Counsel*. Our God is "kind beyond all measure." What he gives is a "Father's wise bestowment," which means he gives to each day "what He deems best—lovingly, its part of *pain* and pleasure."[25] This wisely and lovingly apportioned pain gives us "strength to meet [our] trials here." The truth and beauty of this hymn was the fruit of affliction and goes on helping us "consider it all joy" (James 1:2) so that the affliction of our own lives may yield "the peaceful fruit of righteousness" (Heb. 12:11).

Baptist, Anglican, Congregationalist: All Justified through Faith

The suffering of persecution was not bestowed equally to John Bunyan, William Cowper, and David Brainerd. But there was another form of affliction that brings these three together, and the remedy for it was cherished by them all, even though it bore fruit very differently in their lives. The affliction was the terrifying mental turmoil and darkness of guilt before God, and the remedy for it was the great biblical truth of justification by grace through faith alone. Bunyan was a Baptist, Cowper an Anglican, and Brainerd a Congregationalist. One of the great mercies of God is that, in their times, the doctrine of justification was clear and common to all of them.

"Now Did My Chains Fall off My Legs Indeed"

The *Second London Confession* was forged by Baptists in Bunyan's lifetime and published in its final form in 1689, the year after he died. Built on the *Westminster Confession of Faith*, it was crystal clear on justification.

Those whom God effectually calleth He also freely justifieth; not by infusing righteousness into them, but by pardoning their sins, and by accounting and accepting their persons as righteous; not for anything wrought in them,

---

[25] Emphasis added.

or done by them, but for Christ's sake alone, not by imputing faith itself, the act of believing, or any other evangelical obedience, to them as their righteousness; but by imputing Christ's active obedience unto the whole law, and passive obedience in his death for their whole and sole righteousness, receiving and resting on Him, and His righteousness, by faith; which faith they have not of themselves, it is the gift of God.

Faith, thus receiving and resting on Christ and His righteousness, is the alone instrument of justification; yet is it not alone in the person justified, but is ever accompanied with all other saving graces, and is no dead faith, but worketh by love.[26]

This was the truth that rescued Bunyan from the terrors of feeling hopelessly damned. "Oh, no one knows the terrors of those days but myself."[27] Then comes what seemed to be the decisive moment.

One day as I was passing into the field . . . this sentence fell upon my soul. Thy righteousness is in heaven. And methought, withal, I saw with the eyes of my soul Jesus Christ at God's right hand; there, I say, was my righteousness; so that wherever I was, or whatever I was doing, God could not say of me, he wants [lacks] my righteousness, for that was just before him. I also saw, moreover, that it was not my good frame of heart that made my righteousness better, nor yet my bad frame that made my righteousness worse, for my righteousness was Jesus Christ himself, "The same yesterday and today and forever" (Heb. 13:8). Now did my chains fall off my legs indeed. I was loosed from my afflictions and irons. . . . Now went I also home rejoicing for the grace and love of God.[28]

"I Think I Should Have Died with Gratitude and Joy"

The solid foundation of *The Thirty-Nine Articles of Religion of the Church of England* (framed in 1571) had been around for almost 150 years when William Cowper, the Anglican, experienced the power of its truth on justification. Article 11, "Of the Justification of Man," says,

We are accounted righteous before God, only for the merit of our Lord and Savior Jesus Christ by Faith, and not of our own works or deservings.

[26] The Second London Confession, 1677 and 1689, chapter 11:1–2, quoted in *John A. Broadus: Baptist Confessions, Covenants, and Catechisms*, ed. Timothy and Denise George (Nashville: Broadman & Holman, 1996), 69–70.

[27] Bunyan, *Grace Abounding to the Chief of Sinners*, 59.

[28] Ibid., 90–91.

> Wherefore, that we are justified by Faith only, is a most wholesome Doctrine, and very full of comfort.[29]

Comfort indeed to the young Cowper who had been committed to an insane asylum for his suicidal depression. There a man of God applied to him the truths of the gospel again and again. Slowly Cowper began to feel some hope. One day he opened the Bible at random, and the first verse he saw was Romans 3:25, "Whom God hath set forth to be a propitiation through faith in his blood, to declare his righteousness for the remission of sins that are past, through the forbearance of God" (KJV). He marks his conversion from this moment, because, as he says,

> Immediately I received the strength to believe it, and the full beams of the Sun of Righteousness shone upon me. I saw the sufficiency of the atonement He had made, my pardon sealed in His blood, and all the fullness and completeness of His justification. In a moment I believed, and received the gospel. . . . Unless the Almighty arm had been under me, I think I should have died with gratitude and joy. My eyes filled with tears, and my voice choked with transport; I could only look up to heaven in silent fear, overwhelmed with love and wonder.[30]

Again it is "the completeness of [Christ's] justification" that the Holy Spirit used to awaken and rescue Cowper from the darkness of damnation that had settled over him. The war for Cowper's soul was not ended, but the decisive battle had been fought and won by the gospel of justification by grace through faith.

"This Way of Salvation, Entirely by the Righteousness of Christ"

The *Westminster Shorter Catechism* formed the doctrinal foundation of life and ministry for David Brainerd, the Congregationalist (with Presbyterian leanings[31]). He used it among his Indian converts,[32] as he had grown up on it himself. Question 33 asks, "What is Justification?" and answers, "Justification is an act of God's free grace, wherein he pardoneth all our sins, and accepteth us as righteous in his sight, only

---

[29] Quoted from Philip Schaff, ed., *Creeds of Christendom*, 3 vols. (Grand Rapids, MI: Baker, 1977), 3:494, citing the American Revision of 1801.

[30] Gilbert Thomas, *William Cowper and the Eighteenth Century* (London: Ivor Nicholson and Watson, 1935), 132.

[31] Edwards, *Life of David Brainerd*, 58.

[32] Ibid., 345.

for the righteousness of Christ imputed to us, and received by faith alone."[33]

On the Lord's Day, July 12, 1739, at the age of twenty-one, Brainerd experienced a conversion that marked the rest of his life.

> At this time, the way of salvation opened to me with such infinite wisdom, suitableness, and excellency, that I wondered I should ever think of any other way of salvation; was amazed I had not dropped my own contrivances, and complied with this lovely, blessed, and excellent way before. If I could have been saved by my own duties, or any other way that I had formerly contrived, my whole soul would [now] have refused it. I wondered [that] all the world did not see and comply with this way of salvation, entirely by the righteousness of Christ.[34]

As with Bunyan and Cowper, it is the "way of salvation, entirely by the righteousness of Christ," that breaks through the darkness of doubt and unbelief and wakens new life.

And not just at the beginning of his walk with God but also at the end of his life, this is the truth that sustained Brainerd. On Saturday, September 19, 1747, less than three weeks before he died, he wrote about how God sustained him in a moment of self-recrimination:

> Near night, while I attempted to walk a little, my thoughts turned thus, "How infinitely sweet it is to love God and be all for Him!" Upon which it was suggested to me, "You are not an angel, not lively and active." To which my whole soul immediately replied, "I as sincerely desire to love and glorify God, as any angel in heaven." Upon which it was suggested again, "But you are filthy, not fit for heaven." Hereupon instantly appeared the blessed robes of Christ's righteousness which I could not but exult and triumph in.[35]

Where the Fruit of Affliction Grows

Is it not remarkable that the song of these three suffering swans should be so similar at the crucial moments of their conversions? The righteousness of Christ, outside themselves, imputed to them through faith alone, did not make wastrels of them but worshipers. It did not lead them into profligate living but impelled them into the pursuit of holiness. It did not leave them self-satisfied but set them to preaching and

---

[33] Quoted from Schaff, *Creeds of Christendom*, 3:683.
[34] Edwards, *Life of David Brainerd*, 140.
[35] Ibid., 465.

writing and evangelizing. It sustained them through all suffering (for Cowper, barely—1 Pet. 4:18) and formed the solid ground where the fruit of affliction could grow and the tree not be broken.

Under God's sovereign grace, then, what we have to thank for the great allegory of Bunyan and the hymns of Cowper and the life of Brainerd is, first, the glorious biblical truth of Christ's righteousness imputed by grace through faith alone, and second, the merciful gift of affliction. We are the beneficiaries today of the fruit of their affliction. And God's design in it is that we not lose heart, but trust him that someone also will be strengthened by the fruit of ours. Behind a frowning providence he hides a smiling face. We may see it in our lifetime, or we may not. But the whole Bible is written, and all the swans are singing, to convince us it is there, and that we can and should "exult in our tribulations" (Rom. 5:3).

I was made to see that if ever I would suffer rightly, I must *first* pass a sentence of death upon everything that can be properly called a thing of this life, even to reckon myself, my wife, my children, my health, my enjoyment, and all, as dead to me, and myself as dead to them. The *second* was, to live upon God that is invisible.
John Bunyan
Grace Abounding to the Chief of Sinners

"To Live upon God That Is Invisible"

Suffering and Service in the Life of John Bunyan

"Bless You, Prison, for Having Been in My Life!"

In 1672, about fifty miles northwest of London in Bedford, John Bunyan was released from twelve years of imprisonment. As with suffering saints before and since, Bunyan found prison to be a painful and fruitful gift. He would have understood the words of Aleksandr Solzhenitsyn three hundred years later, who, like Bunyan, turned his imprisonment into a world-changing work of explosive art. After his imprisonment in the Russian gulag of Joseph Stalin's "corrective labor camps," Solzhenitsyn wrote:

> It was granted to me to carry away from my prison years on my bent back, which nearly broke beneath its load, this essential experience: how a human being becomes evil and how good. In the intoxication of youthful successes I had felt myself to be infallible, and I was therefore cruel. In the surfeit of power I was a murderer and an oppressor. In my most evil moments I was convinced that I was doing good, and I was well supplied with systematic arguments. It was only when I lay there on rotting prison straw that I sensed within myself the first stirrings of good. Gradually it was disclosed to me that the line separating good and evil passes not through states, nor between classes, nor between political parties either—but right through every human heart—and through all human hearts. . . . That is why I turn back to the years of my imprisonment and say, sometimes to the astonishment of

those about me: "*Bless you, prison!*" I . . . have served enough time there. I nourished my soul there, and I say without hesitation: "*Bless you, prison*, for having been in my life!"[1]

How can a man pronounce a blessing on imprisonment? Bunyan's life and labor give one answer. Just before his release (it seems[2]), at age forty-four, Bunyan updated his spiritual autobiography called *Grace Abounding to the Chief of Sinners*. He looked back over the hardships of the previous twelve years and wrote about how he was enabled by God to survive and even flourish in the Bedford jail. One of his comments gives me the title for this chapter.

He quotes from the New Testament where the apostle Paul says, "We had the sentence of death within ourselves so that we would not trust in ourselves, but in God who raises the dead" (2 Cor. 1:9). Then he says,

> By this scripture I was made to see that if ever I would suffer rightly, I must *first* pass a sentence of death upon everything that can be properly called a thing of this life, even to reckon myself, my wife, my children, my health, my enjoyment, and all, as dead to me, and myself as dead to them. The *second* was, *to live upon God that is invisible*, as Paul said in another place; the way not to faint, is to "look not at the things which are seen, but at the things which are not seen; for the things which are seen are temporal, but the things which are not seen are eternal."[3]

I have not found any phrase in Bunyan's writings that captures better the key to his life than this one: "To live upon God that is invisible." He learned that if we are to suffer well, we must die not only to sin but also to the imperious claims of precious and innocent things, including family and freedom. While in prison he confessed concerning his wife and children, "I am somewhat too fond of these great Mercies."[4] Thus we must learn to "live upon God that is invisible," not only because God is superior to sinful pleasures, but also because he is superior to

---

[1] Aleksandr I. Solzhenitsyn, *The Gulag Archipelago: 1918–1956. An Experiment in Literary Investigation*, trans. Thomas P. Whitney (Boulder, CO: Westview, 1997), 2:615–17.
[2] According to John Bunyan, *Grace Abounding to the Chief of Sinners* (Hertfordshire: Evangelical Press, 1978), 109, the first part of this "autobiography" was written after Bunyan had been in prison for about five years. But on page 120 he says, "I . . . have lain now complete for twelve years, waiting to see what God would suffer those men to do with me."
[3] Ibid., 122, emphasis added.
[4] Ibid., 123.

sacred ones as well. Everything else in the world we must count as dead to us and we to it.

He learned this from prison and he learned from Paul: "Far be it from me to glory except in the cross of our Lord Jesus Christ, by which the world has been crucified to me, and I to the world" (Gal. 6:14 RSV). Death to the world was the costly corollary of life to God. The visible world died to Bunyan. He lived on "God that is invisible." Increasingly this was Bunyan's passion from the time of his conversion as a young married man to the day of his death when he was sixty years old.

Suffering: Normal and Essential

In all my reading of Bunyan, what has gripped me most is his suffering and how he responded to it, what it made of him, and what it might make of us. All of us come to our tasks with a history and many predispositions. I come to John Bunyan with a growing sense that suffering is a normal and useful and essential element in Christian life and ministry. It not only weans us off the world and teaches us to live on God, as 2 Corinthians 1:9 says, but also makes ministers more able to strengthen the church[5] and makes missionaries more able to reach the nations[6] with the gospel of the grace of God.

I am influenced in the way I read Bunyan both by what I see in the world today and what I see in the Bible. As you read this page, the flashpoints of suffering will have changed since I wrote it. But the reality will not—not as long as the world stays and the Word of Jesus stands. "In the world you have tribulation" (John 16:33). "Behold, I send you out as sheep in the midst of wolves" (Matt. 10:16). Today churches are being burned in some countries, and Christian young people are being killed by anti-Christian mobs. Christians endure systematic starvation and enslavement. China perpetuates its official repression of religious freedom and lengthy imprisonments. India, with its one billion people and unparalleled diversity, heaves with tensions between major religions

---

[5] "Therefore I endure everything for the sake of the elect, that they also may obtain salvation that is in Christ Jesus with its eternal glory" (2 Tim. 2:10 ESV). "I rejoice in my sufferings for your sake, and in my flesh I complete what is lacking in Christ's afflictions for the sake of his body, that is, the church" (Col. 1:24 RSV).

[6] "Behold, I send you out as sheep in the midst of wolves; so be shrewd as serpents and innocent as doves. But beware of men, for they will hand you over to the courts and scourge you in their synagogues; and *you will even be brought before governors and kings for My sake, as a testimony to them and to the Gentiles* [nations]" (Matt. 10:16–18). "Those who were scattered *because of the persecution* that occurred in connection with Stephen made their way to Phoenicia and Cyprus and Antioch, speaking the word. . . . Some of them . . . began speaking to the Greeks also, preaching the Lord Jesus" (Acts 11:19–20).

and with occasional violence. The estimate of how many Christians are martyred each year surpasses all ability to weep as we ought.[7]

As I write, I see thousands dead in the paths of hurricanes or killed by earthquakes. I see hundreds slaughtered in war. I see thirty-three million people worldwide infected with HIV, the virus that causes AIDS. Almost six million new people are infected with the virus each year (eleven people every minute). "By the end of [2000], there will be ten million AIDS orphans."[8] More than six thousand people are dying every day from AIDS. And, of course, I see the people suffering in my own church with tuberculosis and lupus and heart disease and blindness, not to mention the hundreds of emotional and relational pangs that people would trade any day for a good, clean amputation.

And as I come to Bunyan's life and suffering, I see in the Bible that "through many tribulations we must enter the kingdom" (Acts 14:22); and the promise of Jesus, "If they persecuted Me, they will also persecute you" (John 15:20); and the warning from Peter "not [to] be surprised at the fiery ordeal among you, which comes upon you for your testing, as though some strange thing were happening to you" (1 Pet. 4:12); and the utter realism of Paul that we who have "the first fruits of the Spirit, even we ourselves groan within ourselves, waiting eagerly for our adoption as sons, the redemption of our body" (Rom. 8:23); and the reminder that "our outer nature is wasting away" (2 Cor. 4:16 RSV), and that the whole creation "was subjected to futility" (Rom. 8:20).

As I look around me in the world and in the Word of God, my own sense is that what we need from Bunyan is a glimpse into how he suffered and how he learned "to live upon God that is invisible." I want that for myself and my family and the church I serve and for all who read this book. For nothing glorifies God more than maintaining our stability and joy when we lose everything but God. That day is coming for each of us, and we do well to get ready, and to help the people we love get ready.

The Times of the Redwoods

John Bunyan was born in Elstow, about a mile south of Bedford, England, in 1628, the same year that William Laud became the bishop of

---

[7] David Barrett and Todd M. Johnson, "Annual Statistical Table on Global Mission: 1999," *International Bulletin of Missionary Research* 23, no. 1 (1999): 25, estimated 164,000 Christian martyrs in 1999.
[8] *StarTribune* (Minneapolis), May 13, 2000, A19.

London during the reign of King Charles I. The connection with Bishop Laud is important because we can't understand the sufferings of Bunyan apart from the religious and political times in which he lived.

In those days there were tremendous conflicts between Parliament and monarchy. Bishop Laud, together with Charles I, opposed the reforms of the Church of England desired by the Puritans—those pastors and teachers between 1550 and 1700 who longed to see the Church of England "purified" with biblical truth and fire, and whom J. I. Packer calls the California redwoods in the forest of Christianity.[9] Both Laud and King Charles pressed to bring all the Church of England into High Church conformity along the lines of the *Book of Common Prayer*—against the consciences of many Puritans.

Oliver Cromwell—a Puritan champion in the political realm—was elected to Parliament in 1640, and civil war broke out in 1642 between the forces loyal to the king and those loyal to Parliament—and to the reforms longed for by the Puritans. In 1645, Parliament took control of the monarchy. Bishop Laud was executed that year on January 10, and the mandatory use of the *Book of Common Prayer* was overthrown. The Westminster Assembly completed the *Westminster Confession* for the dominant Presbyterian church in 1646. The king, Charles I, was beheaded in 1649, and his son, Charles II, escaped to the continent. Cromwell led the new Commonwealth until his death in 1658. His main concern was a stable government with freedom of religion for Puritans like John Bunyan and others. "Jews, who had been excluded from England since 1290, were allowed to return in 1655."[10]

After Cromwell's death, his son Richard was unable to hold the government together. The longing for stability with a new king swelled. How quickly the favor of man can turn! Parliament turned against the nonconformists like John Bunyan and passed a series of acts that resulted in increased restrictions on the Puritan preachers. Charles II was brought home in what is known as the Restoration of the Monarchy

---

[9] "California's redwoods make me think of England's Puritans, another breed of giants who in our time have begun to be newly appreciated. Between 1550 and 1700 they too lived unfrilled lives in which, speaking spiritually, strong growth and resistance to fire and storm were what counted. As redwoods attract the eye, because they overtop other trees, so the mature holiness and seasoned fortitude of the great Puritans shine before us as a kind of beacon light, overtopping the stature of the majority of Christians in most eras, and certainly so in this age of crushing urban collectivism, when Western Christians sometimes feel and often look like ants in an anthill and puppets on a string" (J. I. Packer, *A Quest for Godliness: The Puritan Vision of the Christian Life* [Wheaton, IL: Crossway, 1990], 11–12). This book is an excellent, readable introduction to the life and thought of that generation of Christian giants.

[10] "Cromwell, Oliver," *Microsoft® Encarta® 98 Encyclopedia* (Microsoft Corporation, 1993–1997).

and was proclaimed king in 1660, the same year that Bunyan was imprisoned for preaching without state approval.

Two Thousand Pastors Ejected

In 1662, the Act of Uniformity was passed that required acceptance, again, of the *Book of Common Prayer* and Episcopal ordination. That August, two thousand Puritan pastors were forced out of their churches. Twelve years later there was a happy turn of affairs with the Declaration of Religious Indulgence that resulted in Bunyan's freedom, his license to preach, and his call as the official pastor of the nonconformist church in Bedford. But there was political instability until he died in 1688 at the age of sixty. He was imprisoned one other time in the mid-1670s, during which he wrote *The Pilgrim's Progress*.[11]

These were the days of John Bunyan's sufferings, and we must be careful not to overstate or understate the terror of the days. We would overstate it if we thought he was tortured in the Bedford jail. In fact, some jailers let him out to see his family or make brief trips. But we would understate it if we thought he was not in frequent danger of execution. For example, in the Bloody Assizes[12] of 1685, more than three hundred people were put to death in the western counties of England for doing no more than Bunyan did as a nonconformist pastor.

Young Heartache and Fear

Bunyan learned the trade of metalworking or "tinker" or "brasyer"[13] from his father. He received the ordinary education of the poor to read and write, but nothing more. He had no formal higher education of any kind, which makes his writing and influence all the more astonishing. The more notable suffering of his life began in his teens. In 1644,

---

[11] Scholars differ about the time *The Pilgrim's Progress* was actually written. Some conclude that it was during the first imprisonment of 1660–1672 (John Bunyan, *The Pilgrim's Progress*, ed. Barry Horner [North Brunswick, NJ: n.p., 1997], xvii), and some that it was written during the second imprisonment of 1675 (John Brown, *John Bunyan: His Life, Times, and Work* [London: Hulbert, 1928], 174). We do know that it was finally published for the first time in 1678.

[12] "Bloody Assizes" refers "in English history [to] the trials conducted in the west of England by the chief justice, George Jeffreys, 1st Baron Jeffreys of Wem, and four other judges after the abortive rebellion (June 1685) of the Duke of Monmouth, illegitimate son of King Charles II, against his Roman Catholic uncle King James II. About 320 persons were hanged and more than 800 transported to Barbados; hundreds more were fined, flogged, or imprisoned." "Bloody Assizes," *Encyclopedia Britannica*, accessed February 22, 2016, http://www.britannica.com/event/Bloody-Assizes.

[13] This is the term he uses to describe his occupation in his own will. John Brown, *John Bunyan*, 29. It refers to repairing tools with hammer and forge.

when he was fifteen, his mother and sister died within one month of each other. His sister was thirteen. To add to the heartache, his father remarried within a month. All this while not many miles away, in that same month of loss, the king attacked a church in Leighton and "began to cut and wound right and left."[14] And later that fall, when Bunyan had turned sixteen, he was drafted into the Parliamentary Army and for about two years was taken from his home for military service. There were harrowing moments, he recounts, as for example once when a man took his place as a sentinel and was shot in the head with a musket ball and died.[15]

Bunyan was not a Christian at heart during this time. He tells us, "I had few equals, especially considering my years . . . for cursing, swearing, lying, and blaspheming the holy name of God. . . . Until I came to the state of marriage, I was the very ringleader of all the youth that kept me company, in all manner of vice and ungodliness."[16]

Precious Books Came with His Wife

He "came to the state of matrimony" when he was twenty or twenty-one, but we never learn his wife's name. What we do learn is that she was poor, but had a godly father who had died and left her two books that she brought to the marriage, *The Plain Man's Pathway to Heaven* and *The Practice of Piety*.[17] Bunyan said, "In these two books I would sometimes read with her, wherein I also found some things that were somewhat pleasing to me; but all this while I met with no conviction."[18] But God's work had begun. He was irreversibly drawing the young, married Bunyan to himself.

John and his wife had four children: Mary, Elizabeth, John, and Thomas. Mary, the oldest, was born blind. This not only added to the tremendous burden of his heart in caring for Mary and the others, but it would also make his imprisonment, when Mary was ten years old, an agonizing separation.[19]

---

[14] Ibid., 42.
[15] Ibid., 45.
[16] John Bunyan, *Grace Abounding to the Chief of Sinners*, 10–11.
[17] Both of these books have been made available in recent years: Arthur Dent, *The Plain Man's Pathway to Heaven* (Morgan, PA: Soli Deo Gloria, 1997), and Lewis Bayly, *The Practice of Piety* (Morgan, PA: Soli Deo Gloria, 1994).
[18] Bunyan, *Grace Abounding to the Chief of Sinners*, 13.
[19] See page 159–60.

"Thy Righteousness Is in Heaven"

During the first five years of marriage, Bunyan was profoundly converted to Christ and to the baptistic, nonconformist church life in Bedford. He came under the influence of John Gifford, the pastor in Bedford, and moved from Elstow to Bedford with his family and joined the church there in 1653, though he was not as sure as they were that he was a Christian. Pastor Gifford, he wrote, was willing to think him a Christian, "though, I think, from little grounds."[20] It's hard to put a date on his conversion because in retelling the process in *Grace Abounding to the Chief of Sinners*, he includes almost no dates or times. But it was a lengthy and agonizing process.

He was poring over the Scriptures but finding no peace or assurance. There were seasons of great doubt about the Scriptures and about his own soul. "A whole flood of blasphemies, both against God, Christ, and the Scriptures were poured upon my spirit, to my great confusion and astonishment. . . . How can you tell but that the Turks had as good scriptures to prove their Mahomet the Savior as we have to prove our Jesus?"[21] "My heart was at times exceeding hard. If I would have given a thousand pounds for a tear, I could not shed one."[22]

When he thought that he was established in the gospel, there came a season of overwhelming darkness following a terrible temptation when he heard the words, "Sell and part with this most blessed Christ. . . . Let him go if he will." He tells us that "I felt my heart freely consent thereto. Oh, the diligence of Satan; oh, the desperateness of man's heart."[23] For two years, he tells us, he was in the doom of damnation. "I feared that this wicked sin of mine might be that sin unpardonable."[24] "Oh, no one knows the terrors of those days but myself."[25] "I found it a hard work now to pray to God because despair was swallowing me up."[26]

Then comes what seemed to be the decisive moment.

> One day as I was passing into the field . . . this sentence fell upon my soul.
> Thy righteousness is in heaven. And methought, withal, I saw with the eyes
> of my soul Jesus Christ at God's right hand; there, I say, was my righteous-

---

[20] Bunyan, *Grace Abounding to the Chief of Sinners*, 33.
[21] Ibid., 40.
[22] Ibid., 43.
[23] Ibid., 54–55.
[24] Ibid., 57.
[25] Ibid., 59.
[26] Ibid., 63.

ness; so that wherever I was, or whatever I was doing, God could not say of me, he wants [lacks] my righteousness, for that was just before him. I also saw, moreover, that it was not my good frame of heart that made my righteousness better, nor yet my bad frame that made my righteousness worse, for my righteousness was Jesus Christ himself, "The same yesterday and today and forever" (Heb. 13:8). Now did my chains fall off my legs indeed. I was loosed from my afflictions and irons; my temptations also fled away; so that from that time those dreadful scriptures of God [about the unforgivable sin] left off to trouble me; now went I also home rejoicing for the grace and love of God.[27]

It is no accident that this echoes the story of Martin Luther's conversion.[28] Under God, one key influence here, besides Pastor Gifford in Bedford, was Martin Luther.

The God in whose hands are all our days and ways, did cast into my hand one day a book of Martin Luther's; it was his *Comment on Galatians*. . . . I found my condition in his experience so largely and profoundly handled, as if his book had been written out of my heart. . . . I do prefer this book of Martin Luther upon the Galatians, excepting the Holy Bible, before all the books that ever I have seen, as most fit for a wounded conscience.[29]

A Preacher Is Born

So in 1655, when the matter of his soul was settled, he was asked to exhort the church, and suddenly a great preacher was discovered. He would not be licensed as pastor of the Bedford church until seventeen

---

27 Ibid., 90–91.

28 Luther, like Bunyan, agonized in the fear that God's righteousness meant his condemnation. For both of them the precious teaching of the Scripture on justification by faith alone was the light that broke through the darkness of their hopelessness. Luther wrote about it like this:

At last, by the mercy of God, meditating day and night, I gave heed to the context of the words [Rom. 1:16–17], namely, "In it the righteousness of God is revealed . . . as it is written, 'He who through faith is righteous shall live.'" There I began to understand [that] the righteousness of God is that by which the righteous lives by a gift of God, namely by faith. And this is the meaning: the righteousness of God is revealed by the gospel, namely, the passive righteousness with which [the] merciful God justifies us by faith, as it is written, "He who through faith is righteous shall live." Here I felt that I was altogether born again and had entered paradise itself through open gates. Here a totally other face of the entire Scripture showed itself to me. . . . I extolled my sweetest word with a love as great as the hatred with which I had before hated the word, "righteousness of God." Thus that place in Paul was for me truly the gate to paradise. (John Dillenberger, ed., *Martin Luther: Selections from His Writings* [Garden City, NY: Doubleday, 1961], 11–12)

For a classic statement of this powerful doctrine of justification by faith alone, see James Buchanan, *The Doctrine of Justification* (orig. 1867; Edinburgh: Banner of Truth, 1961), or, in more recent years, R. C. Sproul, *Faith Alone: The Evangelical Doctrine of Justification* (Grand Rapids, MI: Baker, 1995).

29 Bunyan, *Grace Abounding to the Chief of Sinners*, 52–53. Luther's *Commentary on Galatians* has been published in recent times with an introduction by D. Stuart Briscoe: *Martin Luther, Commentary on Galatians* (Old Tappan, NJ: Revell, 1998).

years later. But his popularity as a powerful lay preacher exploded. The extent of his work grew. "When the country understood that . . . the tinker had turned preacher," John Brown tells us, "they came to hear the word by hundreds, and that from all parts."[30] Charles Doe, a comb maker in London, said (later in Bunyan's life), "Mr. Bunyan preached so New Testament-like he made me admire and weep for joy, and give him my affections."[31] In the days of toleration, a day's notice would get a crowd of twelve hundred to hear him preach at 7 o'clock in the morning on a weekday.[32]

Once, while he was in prison, a whole congregation of sixty people was arrested and brought in at night. A witness tells us, "I . . . heard Mr. Bunyan both preach and pray with that mighty spirit of Faith and Plerophory [fullness] of Divine Assistance, that . . . made me stand and wonder.[33] The greatest Puritan theologian and a contemporary of Bunyan, John Owen, when asked by King Charles why he, a great scholar, went to hear an uneducated tinker preach, said, "I would willingly exchange my learning for the tinker's power of touching men's hearts."[34]

The Incredible Elizabeth Bunyan

Ten years after they were married, when Bunyan was thirty, his wife died, leaving him with four children under ten, one of them blind. A year later, in 1659, he married Elizabeth, who was a remarkable woman. The year after their marriage, Bunyan was arrested and put in prison. She was pregnant with their firstborn and miscarried in the crisis. Then she cared for the four children alone as stepmother for twelve years and bore Bunyan two more children, Sarah and Joseph.

She deserves at least one story here—about her valor in going to the authorities in August 1661, a year after John's imprisonment. She had already been to London with one petition. Now she was met with one stiff question:

"Would he stop preaching?"
"My lord, he dares not leave off preaching as long as he can speak."
"What is the need of talking?"

---

[30] John Brown, *John Bunyan*, 105.
[31] Ibid., 369.
[32] Ibid., 370.
[33] Ibid., 160.
[34] Ibid., 366. This is a paraphrase of an indirect quote.

"There is need for this, my lord, for I have four small children that cannot help themselves, of which one is blind, and we have nothing to live upon but the charity of good people."

Matthew Hale, with pity, asks if she really has four children being so young.

"My lord, I am but mother-in-law [stepmother] to them, having not been married to him yet full two years. Indeed, I was with child when my husband was first apprehended; but being young and unaccustomed to such things, I being smayed at the news, fell into labor, and so continued for eight days, and then was delivered; but my child died."

Hale is moved, but other judges are hardened and speak against him. "He is a mere tinker!"

"Yes, and because he is a tinker and a poor man, therefore he is despised and cannot have justice."

One Mr. Chester is enraged and says Bunyan will preach and do as he wishes.

"He preacheth nothing but the word of God!" she says.

Mr. Twisden, in a rage: "He runneth up and down and doeth harm."

"No, my lord, it is not so; God hath owned him and done much good by him."

The angry man continues, "His doctrine is the doctrine of the devil."

She replies, "My lord, when the righteous Judge shall appear, it will be known that his doctrine is not the doctrine of the devil!"[35]

Bunyan's biographer comments, "Elizabeth Bunyan was simply an English peasant woman: could she have spoken with more dignity had she been a crowned queen?"[36]

Imprisoned from "My Poor Blind Child"

So for twelve years, Bunyan chooses prison and a clear conscience over freedom and a conscience soiled by the agreement not to preach. He could have had his freedom when he wanted it. But he and Elizabeth were made of the same stuff. When asked to recant and not to preach, he said,

If nothing will do unless I make of my conscience a continual butchery and slaughtershop, unless putting out my own eyes, I commit me to the blind to lead me, as I doubt not is desired by some, I have determined, the Almighty

---

[35] Ibid., 149–50.
[36] Ibid.

God being my help and shield, yet to suffer, if frail life might continue so long, even till the moss shall grow on mine eyebrows, rather than thus to violate my faith and principles.[37]

Nevertheless he was sometime tormented that he might not be making the right decision in regard to his family.

The parting with my Wife and poor children hath often been to me in this place as the pulling of the Flesh from my bones; and that not only because I am somewhat too fond of these great Mercies, but also because I should have often brought to my mind the many hardships, miseries and wants that my poor Family was like to meet with should I be taken from them, especially my poor blind child, who lay nearer my heart than all I had besides; O the thoughts of the hardship I thought my Blind one might go under, would break my heart to pieces.[38]

Persevering in Bedford, Not London

Yet he stayed. In 1672, he was released from prison because of the Declaration of Religious Indulgence. Immediately he was licensed as the pastor of the church in Bedford, which he had been serving all along, even from within prison, by writings and periodic visits. A barn was purchased and renovated as their first building, and this was where Bunyan ministered as pastor for the next sixteen years until his death. He never was wooed away from this little parish by the larger opportunities in London. The estimate is that, in 1676, there were perhaps 120 nonconformist parishioners in Bedford, with others no doubt coming to hear him from the surrounding villages.

There was one more imprisonment in the winter and spring of 1675–76. John Brown thinks that this was the time when *The Pilgrim's Progress* was written. But even though Bunyan wasn't in prison again during his ministry, the tension of the days was extraordinary. Ten years after his last imprisonment in the mid-1680s, persecution was heavy again. "Richard Baxter [for example] though an old man now, was shut up in gaol, where he remained for two years more, and where he had innumerable companions in distress."[39]

---

[37] Ibid., 224.
[38] Bunyan, *Grace Abounding to the Chief of Sinners*, 123.
[39] Brown, *John Bunyan*, 336. Baxter was a Puritan pastor whose books are famous for their practical helpfulness even today. He was born in 1615 and died in 1691. His main parish was Kidderminster, where

Meetings were broken in upon, worshipers hurried to prison; "separatists changed the place of gathering from time to time, set their sentinels on the watch, left off singing hymns in their services, and for the sake of greater security worshiped again and again at the dead of night. Ministers were introduced to their pulpits through trap-doors in floor or ceiling, or through doorways extemporized in walls."[40] Bunyan expected to be taken away again. He deeded over all his possessions to his wife Elizabeth so that she would not be ruined by his fines or imprisonment.[41]

A Pilgrim Dies away from Home

But God spared him. Until August 1688. In that month, he traveled the fifty miles to London to preach and to help make peace between a man in his church and his alienated father. He was successful in both missions. But after a trip to an outlying district, he returned to London on horseback through excessive rains. He fell sick of a violent fever, and on August 31, 1688, at age sixty, followed his famous fictional Pilgrim from the "City of Destruction" across the river into the "New Jerusalem."

His last sermon had been on August 19 in London at Whitechapel on John 1:13. His last words from the pulpit were, "Live like the children of God, that you may look your Father in the face with comfort another day."[42] His wife and children were probably unaware of the crisis until it was too late. So Bunyan, in all likelihood, died without the comfort of family—just as he had spent so much of his life without the comforts of home. "The inventory of Bunyan's property after his death added up to a total of 42 pounds and 19 shillings. This is more than the average tinker would leave, but it suggests that most of the profits from *The Pilgrim's Progress* had gone to printers of pirated editions."[43] He was born poor and never let himself become wealthy in this life. He is buried in London at Bunhill Fields.

So, in sum, we can include in Bunyan's sufferings the early, almost

---

he preached and cared and catechized for twenty years. His most notable works include *The Reformed Pastor* and *The Saints' Everlasting Rest.*
[40] Ibid., 336.
[41] Ibid., 340.
[42] Ibid., 372.
[43] Christopher Hill, *A Tinker and a Poor Man: John Bunyan and His Church, 1628–1688* (New York: Alfred A. Knopf, 1989), 367.

simultaneous, death of his mother and sister; the immediate remarriage of his father; the military draft in the midst of his teenage grief; the discovery that his first child was blind; the spiritual depression and darkness during the early years of his marriage; the death of his first wife, which left him with four small children; a twelve-year imprisonment, cutting him off from his family and church; the constant stress and uncertainty of imminent persecution, including one more imprisonment; and the final sickness and death far from those he loved most on earth. And this summary doesn't include any of the normal pressures and pains of ministry and marriage and parenting and controversy and criticism and sickness along the way.

Writing for the Afflicted Church

The question, then, that I bring to Bunyan's suffering is: What was its fruit? What did it bring about in his own life and, through him, in the lives of others? Knowing that I am leaving out many important things, I would answer that with five observations.

Bunyan's suffering confirmed him in his calling as a writer, especially for the afflicted church. Probably the greatest distortion of Bunyan's life in the portrait I have given so far in this chapter is that it passes over one of the major labors of his life, his writing. Books had awakened his own spiritual quest and guided him in it.[44] Books would be his main legacy to the church and the world.

Of course he is famous for *The Pilgrim's Progress*—"next to the Bible, perhaps the world's best-selling book . . . translated into over 200 languages."[45] It was immediately successful, with three editions in 1678, the first year it was published. It was despised at first by the intellectual elite, but as Lord Macaulay points out, *"The Pilgrim's Progress* is perhaps the only book about which, after the lapse of a hundred years, the educated minority has come over to the opinion of the common people."[46]

But most people don't know that Bunyan was a prolific writer before and after *The Pilgrim's Progress*. Christopher Hill's index of "Bun-

---

[44] See notes 17 and 28 and recall the role of *The Plain Man's Pathway to Heaven* and *The Practice of Piety* and Luther's *Commentary on Galatians.*
[45] Hill, *A Tinker and a Poor Man,* 375.
[46] Quoted in Barry Horner, *The Pilgrim's Progress by John Bunyan, Themes and Issues: An Evangelical Apologetic* (Lindenhurst, NY: Reformation Press, 1998), 7–8.

yan's Writings" lists fifty-eight books.[47] The variety in these books was remarkable: books dealing with controversies (like those concerning the Quakers and concerning justification and baptism), collections of poems, children's literature, and allegory (like *The Holy War* and *The Life and Death of Mr. Badman*). But the vast majority were practical doctrinal expositions of Scripture built from sermons for the sake of strengthening and warning and helping Christian pilgrims make their way successfully to heaven.

He was a writer from beginning to end. He had written four books before he went to prison at thirty-two, and in one year alone—1688, the year he died—five books were published. This is extraordinary for a man with no formal education. He knew neither Greek nor Hebrew and had no theological degrees. This was such an offense in his own day that his pastor, John Burton, came to his defense, writing a foreword for his first book in 1656 (when Bunyan was twenty-eight):

> This man is not chosen out of an earthly but out of the heavenly university, the Church of Christ. . . . He hath, through grace, taken these three heavenly degrees, to wit, union with Christ, the anointing of the Spirit, and experiences of the temptations of Satan, which do more fit a man for that mighty work of preaching the Gospel than all university learning and degrees that can be had.[48]

Bunyan's suffering left its mark on all his written work. George Whitefield said of *The Pilgrim's Progress*, "It smells of the prison. It was written when the author was confined in Bedford jail. And ministers never write or preach so well as when under the cross: the Spirit of Christ and of Glory then rests upon them."[49]

The smell of affliction was on most of what Bunyan wrote. In fact, I suspect that one of the reasons the Puritans are still being read today with so much profit is that their entire experience, unlike ours, was one of persecution and suffering. To our chipper culture this may seem somber at times, but the day you hear that you have cancer, or that your child is blind, or that a mob is coming, you turn away from the light books to the weighty ones that were written on the precipice of

---

[47] Hill, *A Tinker and a Poor Man*, xv–xvii. Christopher Hill, "Bunyan's Writings," in *The Works of John Bunyan*, ed. George Offor (Edinburgh: Banner of Truth, 1991), 3:763 (list 60).
[48] John Bunyan, *Some Gospel Truths Opened* in *The Works of John Bunyan*, ed. Offor, 2:141.
[49] Quoted in Horner, *The Pilgrim's Progress by John Bunyan, Themes and Issues*, iii.

eternity where the fragrance of heaven and the stench of hell are both in the air.

Bunyan's writings were an extension of his pastoral ministry, mainly to his flock in Bedford, who lived in constant danger of harassment and prison. His suffering fit him well for the task. Which leads to the second effect of Bunyan's suffering I want to mention.

Bunyan's suffering deepened his love for his flock and gave his pastoral labor the fragrance of eternity. His writings were filled with love to his people. For example, three years into his imprisonment, he wrote a book for his own flock called *Christian Behavior*, which he ended like this:

> Thus have I, in a few words, written to you before I die, a word to provoke you to faith and holiness, because I desire that you may have the life that is laid up for all them that believe in the Lord Jesus, and love one another, when I am deceased. Though then I shall rest from my labors, and be in paradise, as through grace I comfortably believe, yet it is not there, but here, I must do you good. Wherefore, I, not knowing the shortness of my life, nor the hindrance that hereafter I may have of serving my God and you, I have taken this opportunity to present these few lines unto you for your edification.[50]

In his autobiography, written about halfway through his imprisonment, he spoke of his church and the effect he hoped his possible martyrdom would have on them: "I did often say before the Lord, that if to be hanged up presently before their eyes would be means to awake in them and confirm them in the truth, I gladly should consent to it."[51] In fact, many of his flock joined him in jail, and he ministered to them there. He echoed the words of Paul when he described his longings for them: "In my preaching I have really been in pain, I have, as it were, travailed to bring forth Children to God."[52]

He gloried in the privilege of the gospel ministry. This too flowed from his suffering. If all is well and this world is all that matters, a pastor may become jealous of prosperous people who spend their time in leisure. But suffering abounds, and if prosperity is a cloak for the true

---

[50] John Bunyan, *Christian Behavior Being the Fruits of True Christianity*, in *The Works of John Bunyan*, ed. Offor, 2:574.
[51] Ibid., 110.
[52] Ibid.

condition of frisky, fun-loving, perishing Americans, then being a pastor may be the most important and glorious of all work. Bunyan thought it was: "My heart hath been so wrapped up in the glory of this excellent work, that I counted myself more blessed and honored of God by this, than if I had made me the emperor of the Christian world, or the lord of all the glory of the earth without it."[53]

He loved his people, he loved the work, and he stayed with it and with them to the end of his life. He served them and he served the world from a village parish with perhaps 120 members.

Bunyan's suffering opened his understanding to the truth that the Christian life is hard and that following Jesus means having the wind in your face. In 1682, six years before his death, he wrote a book called *The Greatness of the Soul* based on Mark 8:36–37, "What does it profit a man to gain the whole world, and forfeit his soul? For what will a man give in exchange for his soul?" He says that his aim is to "awaken you, rouse you off of your beds of ease, security, and pleasure, and fetch you down upon your knees before him, to beg of him grace to be concerned about the salvation of your souls."[54] And he does not mean the point of conversion, but the process of perseverance. "The one who endures to the end, he will be saved" (Mark 13:13). He hears Jesus warning us that life with him is hard:

> Following of me is not like following . . . some other masters. The wind sits always on my face and the foaming rage of the sea of this world, and the proud and lofty waves thereof do continually beat upon the sides of the bark or ship that myself, my cause, and my followers are in; he therefore that will not run hazards, and that is afraid to venture a drowning, let him not set foot into this vessel.[55]

Two years later, commenting on John 15:2 ("Every branch that bears fruit, He prunes"), he says, "It is the will of God, that they that go to heaven should go thither hardly or with difficulty. The righteous shall scarcely be saved. That is, they shall, but yet with great difficulty, that it may be the sweeter."[56]

---

[53] Ibid., 111.
[54] John Bunyan, *The Greatness of the Soul and Unspeakableness of the Loss Thereof*, in *The Works of John Bunyan*, ed. Offor, 1:105.
[55] Ibid.
[56] John Bunyan, *Seasonable Counsel, Advice to Sufferers*, in *The Works of John Bunyan*, ed. Offor, 2:725.

He had tasted this at the beginning of his Christian life and at every point along the way. In the beginning:

> My soul was perplexed with unbelief, blasphemy, hardness of heart, questions about the being of God, Christ, the truth of the word, and certainty of the world to come: I say, then I was greatly assaulted and tormented with atheism.[57]

> Of all the temptations that ever I met with in my life, to question the being of God and the truth of his gospel is the worst, and the worst to be borne.[58]

In *The Excellency of a Broken Heart* (the last book he took to the publisher) he says,

> Conversion is not the smooth, easy-going process some men seem to think. . . . It is wounding work, of course, this breaking of the hearts, but without wounding there is no saving. . . . Where there is grafting there is a cutting, the scion must be let in with a wound; to stick it on to the outside or to tie it on with a string would be of no use. Heart must be set to heart and back to back, or there will be no sap from root to branch, and this I say, must be done by a wound.[59]

Bunyan's suffering made him passionate about these things—and patient. You can hear his empathy with strugglers in these typically earthy words in a book from 1678 called *Come and Welcome to Jesus Christ*:

> He that comes to Christ cannot, it is true, always get on as fast as he would. Poor coming soul, thou art like the man that would ride full gallop whose horse will hardly trot. Now the desire of his mind is not to be judged of by the slow pace of the dull jade he rides on, but by the hitching and kicking and spurring as he sits on his back. Thy flesh is like this dull jade, it will not gallop after Christ, it will be backward though thy soul and heaven lie at stake.[60]

It seems to me that Bunyan knew the balance of Philippians 2:12–13, "So then, my beloved . . . work out your salvation with fear and trembling; for it is God who is at work in you, both to will and to work for His good pleasure." First, he publishes a book called *Saved By Grace*[61]

[57] Bunyan, *Grace Abounding to the Chief of Sinners*, 96.
[58] Ibid., 128.
[59] Quoted in Brown, *John Bunyan*, 373. See the fuller original in John Bunyan, *The Acceptable Sacrifice: The Excellency of a Broken Heart*, in *The Works of John Bunyan*, ed. Offor, 1:720.
[60] John Bunyan, *Come and Welcome to Jesus Christ*, in *The Works of John Bunyan*, ed. Offor, 1:252.
[61] John Bunyan, *Saved by Grace*, in *The Works of John Bunyan*, ed. Offor, 1:335–61.

based on Ephesians 2:5, "By grace you have been saved." And then in the same year he follows it with a book called *The Strait Gate*,[62] based on Luke 13:24, "Strive to enter at the strait gate: for many, I say unto you, will seek to enter in, and shall not be able" (KJV).

Bunyan's sufferings had taught him the words of Jesus firsthand: "The way is hard that leads to life, and those who find it are few" (Matt. 7:14 ESV).[63]

Bunyan's sufferings strengthened his assurance that God is sovereign over all the afflictions of his people and will bring them safely home. There have always been, as there are today, people who try to solve the problem of suffering by denying the sovereignty of God—that is, the all-ruling providence of God over Satan and over nature and over human hearts. But it is remarkable how many of those who stand by the doctrine of God's sovereignty over suffering have been those who suffered most and who found in the doctrine the most comfort and help.[64]

Bunyan was among that number. In 1684, he wrote an exposition for his suffering people based on 1 Peter 4:19, "Let them that suffer according to the will of God commit the keeping of their souls to him in well doing, as unto a faithful Creator" (KJV). The book was called *Seasonable Counsel, or Advice to Sufferers*. He takes the phrase "according to the will of God" and unfolds the sovereignty of God in it for the comfort of his people.

> It is not what enemies will, nor what they are resolved upon, but what God will, and what God appoints; that shall be done. . . . No enemy can bring suffering upon a man when the will of God is otherwise, so no man can save himself out of their hands when God will deliver him up for his glory . . . [just as Jesus showed Peter "by what death he would glorify God," John 21:19]. We shall or shall not suffer, even as it pleaseth him.[65]

Thus God has appointed the persons who will suffer, the time of their suffering, the place of their suffering, and how they will suffer.

---

[62] John Bunyan, *The Strait Gate*, in *The Works of John Bunyan*, ed. Offor, 1:362–90.

[63] For a serious meditation on this passage, see B. B. Warfield, "Are They Few That Be Saved?" *Biblical and Theological Studies*, ed. Samuel G. Craig (Philadelphia: P&R, 1952), 334–50.

[64] For examples, see Faith Cook, *Singing in the Fire* (Edinburgh: Banner of Truth, 1995), and John Piper, "Suffering: The Sacrifice of Christian Hedonism," in *Desiring God* (Colorado Springs: Multnomah, 2011), 253–88; and Piper, "The Supremacy of God in Missions through Suffering," in *Let the Nations Be Glad* (Grand Rapids, MI: Baker Academic, 2010), 93–130.

[65] Bunyan, *Seasonable Counsel*, 722. For a meditation on the theological problems involved with this biblical view, see John Piper, "The Pleasure of God in All That He Does," in *The Pleasures of God* (Colorado Springs: Multnomah, 2012), 33–59.

God Appoints Who Will Suffer

In the first case, "God has appointed *who* shall suffer. Suffering comes not by chance, or by the will of man, but by the will and appointment of God." Thus Bunyan cites 1 Thessalonians 3:3, "that no man should be moved by these afflictions: for yourselves know that we are appointed thereunto" (KJV). We must not think that suffering is a strange thing for those who fear God (1 Pet. 4:12). He reminds us and appeals to Revelation 6:11, where the martyrs under the altar in heaven are told "that they should rest for a little while longer, until the number of their fellow servants and their brethren who were to be killed ['mark that,' Bunyan says] even as they had been, would be completed also." An appointed number of martyrs! From which Bunyan concludes, "Suffering for righteousness and for righteousness' sake, is by the will of God. God has appointed who shall suffer."[66]

"My Times Are in Thy Hands"

Second, "God has appointed . . . *when* they shall suffer for his truth in the world. Sufferings for such and such a man are timed, as to when he shall be tried for his faith." Hence when Paul was afraid in Corinth, the Lord strengthened him in a dream by saying, "Do not be afraid any longer, but go on speaking and do not be silent; for I am with you, and no man will attack you in order to harm you, for I have many people in this city" (Acts 18:9–10). "His time of suffering," Bunyan says, "was not yet come there." In the same way it was said of Jesus, "They sought to take him: but no man laid hands on him, because his hour was not yet come" (John 7:30 KJV). Bunyan concludes, "The times, then, and the seasons, even for the sufferings of the people of God, are not in the hands of their enemies, but in the hand of God; as David said, 'My times are in thy hand'" (Ps. 31:15 KJV).[67]

Suffering Saints Are Sprinkled on the Earth to Keep It from Stinking

Third, "God has appointed *where* this, that or the other good man shall suffer. Moses and Elias [Elijah], when they appeared on the holy mount, told Jesus of the sufferings which he should accomplish at Jerusalem" (Luke 9:30–31). "The saints are sprinkled by the hand of God here

---

[66] Bunyan, *Seasonable Counsel*, 723.
[67] Ibid.

and there, as salt is sprinkled upon meat to keep it from stinking. And as they are sprinkled, that they may season the earth; so accordingly, where they must suffer is also appointed for the better confirming of the truth. Christ said, it could not be that a prophet should 'perish out of Jerusalem' (Luke 13:33). But why . . . ? God has appointed that they should suffer there. So then, who, when, and where, is at the will of God, and they, accordingly, are ordered by that will."[68]

"By What Death He Should Glorify God"

Fourth, "God has appointed . . . *what kind of sufferings* this or that saint shall undergo. . . . God said that he would show Paul beforehand how great things he should suffer for his sake (Acts 9:16). And it is said that Christ did signify to Peter beforehand 'by what kind of death he should glorify God' (John 21:19)." As with the time and place and persons, so it is with the kind of sufferings we endure: They "are all writ down in God's book; and though the writing seem as unknown characters to us, yet God understands them very well. . . . It is appointed who of them should die of hunger, who with the sword, who should go into captivity, and who should be eaten up of beasts. Let it then be concluded, that hitherto it appears, that the sufferings of saints are ordered and disposed by the will of God."[69]

We could go even further with Bunyan as he shows "for what truth" his saints will suffer, and "by whose hand" and "how long." But let us ask, What is Bunyan's aim in this exposition of the sovereignty of God in suffering? He tells us plainly: "I have, in a few words, handled this . . . to show you that our sufferings are ordered and disposed by him, that you might always, when you come into trouble for this name, not stagger nor be at a loss, but be stayed, composed, and settled in your minds, and say, 'The will of the Lord be done'" (Acts 21:14).[70]

The Mercy That We Suffer Rather Than Torture

He warns against feelings of revenge.

---

[68] Ibid.

[69] Ibid. Compare Jer. 15:2–3: "And it shall be that when they say to you, 'Where should we go?' then you are to tell them, 'Thus says the LORD: "Those destined for death, to death; and those destined for the sword, to the sword; and those destined for famine, to famine; and those destined for captivity, to captivity. I will appoint over them four kinds of doom," declares the LORD: "the sword to slay, the dogs to drag off, and the birds of the sky and the beasts of the earth to devour and destroy."'"

[70] Ibid., 724.

Learn to pity and bewail the condition of the enemy. . . . Never grudge them their present advantages. "Fret not thyself because of evil men. Neither be thou envious at the workers of iniquity" (Prov. 24:19). Fret not, though they spoil thy resting place. It is God that hath bidden them do it, to try thy faith and patience thereby. Wish them no ill with what they get of thine; it is their wages for their work, and it will appear to them ere long that they have earned it dearly. . . . Bless God that thy lot did fall on the other side. . . . [71] How kindly, therefore, doth God deal with us, when he chooses to afflict us but for a little, that with everlasting kindness he may have mercy upon us (Isa. 54:7–8). [72]

"No Fruit, Because There Is No Winter There"

The key to suffering rightly is to see in all things the hand of a merciful and good and sovereign God and "to live upon God that is invisible." [73] There is more of God to be had in times of suffering than at any other time.

There is that of God to be seen in such a day as cannot be seen in another. His power in holding up some, his wrath in leaving of others; his making of shrubs to stand, and his suffering of cedars to fall; his infatuating of the counsel of men, and his making of the devil to outwit himself; his giving of his presence to his people, and his leaving of his foes in the dark; his discovering [disclosing] the uprightness of the hearts of his sanctified ones, and laying open the hypocrisy of others, is a working of spiritual wonders in the day of his wrath, and of the whirlwind and storm. . . . We are apt to overshoot, in the days that are calm, and to think ourselves far higher, and more strong than we find we be, when the trying day is upon us. . . . We could not live without such turnings of the hand of God upon us. We should be overgrown with flesh, if we had not our seasonable winters. It is said that in some countries trees will grow, but will bear no fruit, because there is no winter there. [74]

So Bunyan begs his people to humble themselves under the mighty hand of God and to trust that all will be for their good. "Let me beg of thee, that thou wilt not be offended either with God, or men, if

---

[71] Ibid., 725.

[72] Ibid., 737. If one asks whether God is sovereign over the temptations of soul as well as sufferings of body, Bunyan answers yes. Looking back on his own dark seasons of doubt and despair, he writes, "Now I saw that as God had his hand in all the providences and dispensations that overtook his elect, so he had his hand in all the temptations that they had to sin against him, not to animate them to wickedness, but to choose their temptations and troubles for them, and also to leave them for a time to such things only as might not destroy, but humble them—as might not put them beyond, but lay them in the way of the renewing of his mercy." Bunyan, *Grace Abounding to the Chief of Sinners*, 61.

[73] Bunyan, *Grace Abounding to the Chief of Sinners*, 109.

[74] Bunyan, *Seasonable Counsel*, 694.

the cross is laid heavy upon thee. Not with God, for he doth nothing without a cause, nor with men, for . . . they are the servants of God to thee for good. Take therefore what comes to thee from God by them, thankfully."[75]

"If It Is in Thy Heart to Fly, Fly"

If one should ask, may we ever, then, avail ourselves of opportunities to escape suffering, Bunyan answers,

> Thou mayest do in this as it is in thy heart. If it is in thy heart to fly, fly; if it be in thy heart to stand, stand. Anything but a denial of the truth. He that flies, has warrant to do so; he that stands, has warrant to do so. Yea, the same man may both fly and stand, as the call and working of God with his heart may be. Moses fled, Exodus 2:15; Moses stood, Hebrews 11:27. David fled, 1 Samuel 19:12; David stood, 1 Samuel 24:8. Jeremiah fled, Jeremiah 37:11–12; Jeremiah stood, 38:17. Christ withdrew himself, Luke 19:10; Christ stood, John 18:1–8. Paul fled, 2 Cor. 11:33; Paul stood, Acts 20:22–23. . . .
>
> There are few rules in this case. The man himself is best able to judge concerning his present strength, and what weight this or that argument has upon his heart to stand or fly. . . . Do not fly out of a slavish fear, but rather because flying is an ordinance of God, opening a door for the escape of some, which door is opened by God's providence, and the escape countenanced by God's Word. Matthew 10:23. . . . If, therefore, when thou hast fled, thou art taken, be not offended at God or man: not at God, for thou art his servant, thy life and thy all are his; not at man, for he is but God's rod, and is ordained, in this, to do thee good. Hast thou escaped? Laugh. Art thou taken? Laugh. I mean, be pleased which way soever things shall go, for that the scales are still in God's hand.[76]

This is what Bunyan means by "living upon God that is invisible." This is the faith that makes a person radically free and bold and undaunted in the cause of God and truth. Bunyan's life did not arise out of sand. It grew like a great tree in the rock of granite truth about the sovereignty of God over all his suffering.

Bunyan's suffering deepened in him a confidence in the Bible as the Word of God and a passion for biblical exposition as the key to perseverance. If "living upon God that is invisible" is the key to suffering

---

[75] Ibid.
[76] Ibid., 726.

rightly, what is the key to living upon God? Bunyan's answer is: Lay hold on Christ through the Word of God, the Bible. He doesn't mean this, of course, to the exclusion of prayer. In fact, he pleaded for his people to pray for him and confessed his utter dependence on God in prayer:

> Christians, pray for me to our God with much earnestness, fervency, and frequently in all your knockings at our Father's door, because I do very much stand in need thereof, for my work is great, my heart is vile, and the devil lieth at watch, the world would fain be saying, Aha, aha, thus would we have it! And of myself, keep myself I cannot, trust myself I dare not; if God do not help me I am sure it will not be long before my heart deceive, and the world have their advantage of me.[77]

Prison as an Inlet into the Word of God

But what we need most to hear from Bunyan is how his suffering drove him into the Word and opened the Word to him. Prison proved for Bunyan to be a hallowed place of communion with God because his suffering unlocked the Word and the deepest fellowship with Christ he had ever known. Martin Luther said the same thing, and even made it into a rule that suffering is essential to know the Word of God as we ought, basing it on Psalm 119:71, "It is good for me that I was afflicted, that I may learn Your statutes." Luther had his own scandalous way of saying it:

> As soon as God's Word becomes known through you, the devil will afflict you, will make a real doctor [theologian or teacher] of you, and will teach you by his temptations to seek and to love God's Word. For I myself . . . owe my papists many thanks for so beating, pressing, and frightening me through the devil's raging that they have turned me into a fairly good theologian, driving me to a goal I should never have reached.[78]

Bunyan made the same discovery, as have so many others.[79]

---

[77] Brown, *John Bunyan*, 119.

[78] Ewald M. Plass, comp., *What Luther Says: An Anthology* (St. Louis, MO: Concordia, 1959), 3:1360. The reader may be interested in seeing more about how Luther came to this conviction and how it affected his life; see John Piper, "Sacred Study: Martin Luther and the External Word" (pages 67–91 of this volume).

[79] For example, John Paton, the Scottish missionary to the New Hebrides (Vanuatu) one hundred years ago, described one of his most harrowing escapes from danger as he hid in a tree with cannibals raging around him:

> Never, in all my sorrows, did my Lord draw nearer to me, and speak more soothingly in my soul, than when the moonlight flickered among these chestnut leaves, and the night air played on my throbbing brow, as I told all my heart to Jesus. Alone, yet not alone! If it be to glorify my God, I will not grudge to spend many nights alone in such a tree, to feel again my Savior's spiritual presence, to enjoy His consoling fellowship. If thus thrown back upon your own soul, alone, all alone, in the midnight, in

I never had in all my life so great an inlet into the Word of God as now [in prison]. Those scriptures that I saw nothing in before were made in this place and state to shine upon me. Jesus Christ also was never more real and apparent than now. Here I have seen him and felt him indeed. . . . I have had sweet sights of the forgiveness of my sins in this place, and of my being with Jesus in another world. . . . I have seen *that* here that I am persuaded I shall never, while in this world, be able to express. . . . I never knew what it was for God to stand by me at all times and at every offer of Satan to afflict me, as I have found Him since I came in hither.[80]

"In My Chest Pocket I Have a Key"

Bunyan especially cherished the promises of God as the key for opening the door of heaven. "I tell thee, friend, there are some promises that the Lord hath helped me to lay hold of Jesus Christ through and by, that I would not have out of the Bible for as much gold and silver as can lie between York and London piled up to the stars."[81]

One of the greatest scenes in *The Pilgrim's Progress* is when Christian recalls, in the dungeon of Doubting Castle, that he has a key to the door. Very significant is not only what the key is, but where it is:

"What a fool I have been, to lie like this in a stinking dungeon, when I could have just as well walked free. In my chest pocket I have a key called Promise that will, I am thoroughly persuaded, open any lock in Doubting-Castle." "Then," said Hopeful, "that is good news. My good brother, do immediately take it out of your chest pocket and try it." Then Christian took the key from his chest and began to try the lock of the dungeon door; and as he turned the key, the bolt unlocked and the door flew open with ease, so that Christian and Hopeful immediately came out.[82]

Three times Bunyan says that the key was in Christian's "*chest* pocket" or simply his "chest." I take this to mean that Christian had hidden it in his heart by memorization and that it was now accessible in prison (though he had no Bible available) for precisely this reason. This is how the Word sustained and strengthened Bunyan.

---

the bush, in the very embrace of death itself, have you a Friend that will not fail you then? (*John G. Paton: Missionary to the New Hebrides, An Autobiography Edited by His Brother* [orig. 1889; Edinburgh: Banner of Truth, 1965], 200)

[80] Bunyan, *Grace Abounding to the Chief of Sinners*, 121.

[81] John Bunyan, *Sighs from Hell*, in *The Works of John Bunyan*, ed. Offor, 3:721.

[82] Bunyan, *The Pilgrim's Progress*, 172.

"Prick Him Anywhere . . . His Blood Is Bibline"

Everything he wrote was saturated with the Bible. He pored over his English Bible, which was all he had most of the time. Which is why he can say of his writings, "I have not for these things fished in other men's waters; my Bible and Concordance are my only library in my writings."[83] The great London preacher Charles Spurgeon, who read *The Pilgrim's Progress* every year, put it like this:

> He had studied our Authorized Version . . . till his whole being was saturated with Scripture; and though his writings are charmingly full of poetry, yet he cannot give us his *Pilgrim's Progress*—that sweetest of all prose poems—without continually making us feel and say, "Why, this man is a living Bible!" Prick him anywhere; and you will find that his blood is Bibline, the very essence of the Bible flows from him. He cannot speak without quoting a text, for his soul is full of the Word of God.[84]

Bunyan reverenced the Word of God and trembled at the prospect of dishonoring it. "'Let me die with the Philistines' (Judg. 16:30) rather than deal corruptly with the blessed word of God."[85] This, in the end, is why Bunyan is still with us today rather than disappearing into the mist of history. He is with us and ministering to us because he reverenced the Word of God and was so permeated by it that his blood is "Bibline"—the essence of the Bible flows from him.

And this is what he has to show us. That "to live upon God that is invisible" is to live upon the Word of God. To serve and suffer rooted in God is to serve and suffer saturated with the Word of God. This is how we shall live, this is how we shall suffer. And, if we are called to be leaders among the people of God, this is how we shall help our people get safely to the Celestial City. We will woo them with the Word. We will say to them what Bunyan said to his people—and I say to you, dear reader:

> God hath strewed all the way from the gate of hell, where thou wast, to the gate of heaven, whither thou art going, with flowers out of his own garden. Behold how the promises, invitations, calls, and encouragements, like lilies, lie round about thee! Take heed that thou dost not tread them under thy foot.[86]

---

[83] Brown, *John Bunyan*, 364.

[84] Charles Spurgeon, *Autobiography*, 2 vols. (Edinburgh: Banner of Truth, 1973), 2:159.

[85] Bunyan, *Grace Abounding to the Chief of Sinners*, 114.

[86] Bunyan, *Come and Welcome to Jesus Christ* (1678), quoted in Brown, *John Bunyan*, 300.

God moves in a mysterious way
His wonders to perform;
He plants his footsteps in the sea,
And rides upon the storm.

Ye fearful saints, fresh courage take,
The clouds ye so much dread
Are big with mercy, and shall break
In blessings on your head.

Judge not the Lord by feeble sense,
But trust him for his grace;
Behind a frowning providence
He hides a smiling face.

His purposes will ripen fast,
Unfolding every hour;
The bud may have a bitter taste,
But sweet will be the flower.
William Cowper
"God Moves in a Mysterious Way"

2

"The Clouds Ye So Much
Dread Are Big with Mercy"

Insanity and Spiritual Songs in the Life of William Cowper

A Love Affair with Poetry

There are at least three reasons why I am drawn to the life story of the eighteenth-century poet William Cowper (pronounced "Cooper"). One is that ever since I was seventeen—probably before—I have felt the power of poetry.

I went to my file recently and found an old copy of *Leaves of Grass*, the student literary magazine from Wade Hampton High School, Greenville, South Carolina. It was the 1964 edition—the year I graduated. I read the poems that I wrote for it more than thirty-five years ago. Then I took out *Kodon*, the literary magazine from my Wheaton College days, and remembered the poem "One of Many Lands," which I wrote in one of my bleak moments as a college freshman. Next, from the musty folder of memorabilia came a copy of *The Opinion* (1969) from Fuller Seminary with its poem "For Perfect Eve" (to whom I have now been married thirty-two years). Then, when I was teaching came the Bethel College *Coeval* from 1976 with the poem "Dusk." It struck me again what a longtime friend poetry has been. And still is. I write poems for my children's birthdays and for my wife on birthdays and anniversaries and Mother's Day. For almost twenty years I have written four Advent poems each year and read them from the pulpit to my much-loved flock at Bethlehem Baptist Church.

One of the reasons for this is that I live with an almost constant awareness of the breach between the low intensity of my own passion and the staggering realities of the universe around me—heaven, hell, creation, eternity, life, Jesus Christ, justification by faith, God. All of us (whether we know it or not) try to close this breach between the weakness of our emotions and the wonder of the world. Some of us do it with poetry.

William Cowper did it with poetry. I think I understand something of what he means, for example, when he writes a poem about seeing his mother's portrait after fifty-three years. She had died when he was six.

> And, while that face renews my filial grief,
> Fancy shall weave a charm for my relief.[1]

Fancy—the imaginative effort to put his emotion in a poem—will bring him some pleasant, painful satisfaction. There is a deep relief that comes when we find a way of seeing and savoring some precious reality, then saying it in a way that comes a little closer to closing the breach between what we've glimpsed with our mind and what we've grasped with our heart. It shouldn't be surprising that probably more than three hundred pages of the Bible were written as poetry, because one great aim of the Bible is to build a bridge between the prosaic deadness of the human heart and the inexpressible reality of the living God.

The Man Who Wrote the Hymn above Our Mantel

The second reason I am drawn to William Cowper is that I want to know the man behind the hymn "God Moves in a Mysterious Way," one of the last poems Cowper ever wrote. It appeared in the collection of *Olney Hymns* under the title "Conflict: Light Shining Out of Darkness." Over the years it has become very precious to me and many in our church. It has carried us through fire.

> God moves in a mysterious way
> His wonders to perform;
> He plants his footsteps in the sea,
> And rides upon the storm.

---

[1] William Cowper, "On the Receipt of My Mother's Picture out of Norfolk," *The Poetical Works of William Cowper*, ed. William Michael Rossetti (London: William Collins, n.d.), 407.

Deep in unfathomable mines
Of never-failing skill,
He treasures up his bright designs
And works his sovereign will.

Ye fearful saints, fresh courage take,
The clouds ye so much dread
Are big with mercy, and shall break
In blessings on your head.

Judge not the Lord by feeble sense,
But trust him for his grace;
Behind a frowning providence
He hides a smiling face.

His purposes will ripen fast,
Unfolding every hour;
The bud may have a bitter taste,
But sweet will be the flower.

Blind unbelief is sure to err,
And scan his work in vain:
God is his own interpreter,
And He will make it plain.[2]

For fourteen years an embroidered version of this hymn has hung in our living room. It was created and given to us by a young mother who was sustained by it through great sadness. It expresses the foundation of my theology and my life so well that I long to know the man who wrote it.

In the third place, I want to know why William Cowper struggled with depression and despair almost all his life. I want to try to come to terms with insanity and spiritual songs in the same heart of one whom I believe was a genuine Christian.

An Uneventful Life—On the Outside

Cowper was born in 1731 and died in 1800. That makes him a contemporary of John Wesley and George Whitefield, the leaders of the Evangelical Revival in England. He embraced Whitefield's Calvinistic

---

[2] Ibid., 292.

theology rather than Wesley's Arminianism. But it was a warm, evangelical brand of Calvinism, shaped (in Cowper's case) largely by one of the healthiest men in the eighteenth century, the "old African blasphemer," John Newton. Cowper said he could remember how, as a child, he would see the people at four o'clock in the morning coming to hear Whitefield preach in the open air. "Moorfields [was] as full of the lanterns of the worshipers before daylight as the Haymarket was full of flambeaux on opera nights."[3]

Cowper was twenty-seven years old when Jonathan Edwards died in America. He lived through the American and French Revolutions. His poetry was known by Benjamin Franklin, who gave Cowper's first volume a good review.[4] But, though he was known internationally, he was not a man of affairs or travel. He was a recluse who spent virtually all his adult life in the rural English countryside near Olney and Weston.

From the standpoint of adventure or politics or public engagement, his life was utterly uneventful—the kind of life no child would ever choose to read about. But those of us who are older have come to see that the events of the soul are probably the most important events in life. And the battles in this man's soul were of epic proportions.

Consider, then, this seemingly uneventful life with a view to seeing the battles of the soul. He was born on November 15, 1731, at Great Berkhampstead, a town of about fifteen hundred, near London. His father was rector of the village church and one of King George II's chaplains. So the family was well-to-do but not evangelical,[5] and William grew up without any saving relation to Christ.

His mother died when he was six, and his father sent him to Pitman's, a boarding school in Bedfordshire. It was a tragic mistake, as we will see from his own testimony later in life. From the age of ten until he was seventeen, he attended Westminster School and learned his French and Latin and Greek well enough to spend the last years of his

---

[3] Gilbert Thomas, *William Cowper and the Eighteenth Century* (London: Ivor Nicholson and Watson, 1935), 204.
[4] Ibid., 267.
[5] By this term I simply mean that the form of Christianity he imbibed at home did not highlight the "evangel," that is, the gospel of Christ crucified and risen for sinners, which is recorded for us in the infallible Bible and preached in the power of the Holy Spirit, and believed in a very personal way that issues in a life of conscious devotion to Christ as the eternal Son of God, with disciplines of Bible reading and prayer and the pursuit of holiness and a concern for unbelievers to hear the gospel and be saved from everlasting torment. Those would be the typical marks of an "evangelical" as I am using the term.

life, fifty years later, translating the Greek of Homer and the French of Madam Guyon.

From 1749 he was apprenticed to a solicitor with a view to practicing law. At least this was his father's view. He never really applied himself and had no heart for the public life of a lawyer or a politician. For ten years he did not take his legal career seriously but lived a life of leisure with token involvement in his supposed career.

"Day and Night I Was upon the Rack"

In 1752, he sank into his first paralyzing depression—the first of four major battles with mental breakdown so severe as to set him to staring out of windows for weeks at a time. Struggle with despair came to be the theme of his life. He was twenty-one years old and not yet a believer. He wrote about the attack of 1752 like this:

> [I was struck] with such a dejection of spirits, as none but they who have felt the same, can have the least conception of. Day and night I was upon the rack, lying down in horror, and rising up in despair. I presently lost all relish for those studies, to which before I had been closely attached; the classics had no longer any charms for me; I had need of something more salutary than amusement, but I had no one to direct me where to find it.[6]

He came through this depression with the help of the poems of George Herbert (who had lived 150 years earlier, 1593–1633). "He found the hymns 'uncouth' and 'Gothic,' yet they spoke to his soul."[7] We are not told which of Herbert's poems broke through to Cowper with light, but there is one that has done so for me, and I like to think it did the same for Cowper. It is called "The Pulley." What makes it so relevant for Cowper's condition is Herbert's insight into how God, at times, withholds rest from our soul, not to make us miserable, but that restlessness may toss us to his breast.

> Having a glass of blessings standing by,
> "Let us," said he, "pour on him all we can;
> Let the world's riches, which dispersed lie,
> Contract into a span."

---

[6] Thomas, *William Cowper and the Eighteenth Century*, 94.
[7] George Melvyn Ella, *William Cowper: Poet of Paradise* (Durham: Evangelical Press, 1993), 60.

So strength first made a way;
Then beauty flow'd, then wisdom, honour, pleasure;
When almost all was out, God made a stay,
Perceiving that alone of all his treasure,
    Rest in the bottom lay.

"For if I should," said he,
"Bestow this jewel also on my creature,
He would adore my gifts instead of me,
And rest in Nature, not the God of Nature:
    So both should losers be.

"Yet let him keep the rest,
But keep them with repining restlessness;
Let him be rich and weary, that at least,
If goodness lead him not, yet weariness
    May toss him to my breast."[8]

A Change of Scenery Does Not Heal

Throughout Cowper's life, God would have his strange means of toss-
ing this stormy soul again and again back to his breast. In 1752, there
was enough grace in the truth and beauty in the poems of George Herbert that Cowper felt hope and got the strength to take several months
away from London by the sea in Southampton. What happened there
was both merciful and sad. He wrote in his *Memoir*:

> The morning was calm and clear; the sun shone bright upon the sea; and the
> country on the borders of it was the most beautiful I had ever seen. . . . Here
> it was, that on a sudden, as if another sun had been kindled that instant in
> the heavens, on purpose to dispel sorrow and vexation of spirit, I felt the
> weight of all my weariness taken off; my heart became light and joyful in a
> moment; I could have wept with transport had I been alone.[9]

That was the mercy. The sadness of it was that even though he said,
at the time, that "nothing less than the Almighty fiat could have filled
me with such inexpressible delight,"[10] nevertheless he confessed later
that instead of giving God the credit for this mercy, he formed the habit

---

[8] George Herbert, "The Pulley," in *Eerdmans Book of Christian Poetry*, comp. Pat Alexander (Grand
Rapids, MI: Eerdmans, 1981), 28.
[9] Thomas, *William Cowper and the Eighteenth Century*, 94.
[10] Ella, *William Cowper: Poet of Paradise*, 62.

merely of battling his depression, if at all, by seeking changes of scenery. It was the merciful hand of God in nature. But he did not see him or give him glory. Not yet.

Theodora Lost

Between 1749 and 1756, Cowper was falling in love with his cousin Theodora, whose home he visited regularly on the weekends. They were engaged, but for some mysterious reason her father, Ashley Cowper, forbade the marriage. His apparent reason was the inappropriateness of consanguinity—a man marrying his own cousin. But it seems strange that the relation was allowed to develop for seven years, as well as to move into an engagement, if it was to be shattered at the last minute. It is probably true that her father knew things about William that convinced him he would not have been a good husband for his daughter.

But it didn't turn out the way her father hoped. Though the pair never saw each other again after 1756, Theodora outlived William but never married. She followed his poetic career from a distance and sent him money anonymously when he was in need, even a regular stipend at one point. We know of nineteen poems that he wrote to her as "Delia." One of them, written some years after their parting, shows the abiding pain:

> But now, sole partner in my Delia's heart,
> Yet doomed far off in exile to complain,
> Eternal absence cannot ease my smart,
> And hope subsists but to prolong my pain.[11]

What we will find is that William Cowper's life seems to be one long accumulation of pain.

As "at the Place of Execution"

In 1759, when he was twenty-eight years old, he was appointed, through the influence of his father, to be a commissioner of bankrupts in London. Four years later he was about to be made Clerk of Journals in Parliament. What would have been a great career advancement to most men struck fear into William Cowper—so much so that he had a

---

[11] Cowper, *The Poetical Works*, ed. Rossetti, 253.

total mental breakdown, tried three different ways to commit suicide, and was put into an asylum.

His father had arranged for the position. But his enemies in Parliament decided to require a public interrogation for his son as a prerequisite. Cowper wrote about the dreadful attack of 1863:

> All the horrors of my fears and perplexities now returned. A thunderbolt would have been as welcome to me as this [interrogation]. . . . Those whose spirits are formed like mine, to whom a public exhibition of themselves, on any occasion, is mortal poison, may have some idea of the horror of my situation; others can have none.[12]

For more than half a year, his feelings were those "of a man when he arrives at the place of execution."[13]

At that point something dreadful returned to his memory that causes us to wonder about what kind of father William Cowper had. The thirty-two-year-old clerk suddenly recalled a "treatise on self-murder" that he read when he was eleven years old.

> I well recollect when I was about eleven years of age, my father desired me to read a vindication of self-murder, and give him my sentiments upon the question: I did so, and argued against it. My father heard my reasons, and was silent, neither approving nor disapproving; from whence I inferred that he sided with the author against me.[14]

In the week before his examination (October 1763), he bought laudanum to use as a poison. He pondered escaping to France to enter a monastery. He had illusions of seeing himself slandered in the newspaper anonymously. He was losing his hold on reality almost entirely. The day before the Parliamentary examination, he set out to drown himself and took a cab to Tower Wharf. But at Custom House Quay he found the water too low and "a porter seated upon some goods" as if "a message to prevent" him.[15]

When he got home that evening, he tried to take the laudanum but found his fingers "closely contracted" and "entirely useless." The next morning he tried three times to hang himself with a garter. The third

---

12 Thomas, *William Cowper and the Eighteenth Century*, 114.
13 Ibid.
14 Ibid., 118.
15 Ibid.

time he became unconscious, but the garter broke. The laundress found him in bed and called his uncle, who canceled the examination immediately. And that was the end of Cowper's brush with public life—but not the end of his brush with death.

Now came the horrible conviction of sin, as Cowper contemplated that he was as guilty as if he had succeeded with self-murder because he attempted and simply failed:

> Conviction of sin took place, especially of that just committed; the meanness of it, as well as its atrocity, were exhibited to me in colors so inconceivably strong that I despised myself, with a contempt not to be imagined or expressed. . . . This sense of it secured me from the repetition of a crime which I could not now reflect on without abhorrence. Before I rose from bed, it was suggested to me that there was nothing wanted but murder, to fill up the measures of my iniquities; and that, though I had failed in my design, yet I had all the guilt of that crime to answer for. A sense of God's wrath, and a deep despair of escaping it, instantly succeeded. The fear of death became much more prevalent in me than ever the desire of it had been.[16]

Now everything he read condemned him. Sleep would not come, and when it did, it brought him terrifying dreams. When he awoke, he "reeled and staggered like a drunken man."[17]

Bless You, Insane Asylum, for My Life

So in December 1763, he was committed to St. Albans Insane Asylum, where the fifty-eight-year-old Dr. Nathaniel Cotton tended the patients. Cotton was somewhat of a poet, but most of all, by God's wonderful design, an evangelical believer and a lover of God and the gospel. He loved Cowper and held out hope to him repeatedly in spite of his insistence that he was damned and beyond hope. Six months into his stay, Cowper found a Bible lying (not by accident) on a bench.

> Having found a Bible on the bench in the garden, I opened upon the 11th of St. John, where Lazarus is raised from the dead; and saw so much benevolence, mercy, goodness, and sympathy with miserable men, in our Saviour's conduct, that I almost shed tears upon the revelation; little thinking that it

---

[16] Ibid., 119.
[17] Ibid., 120.

was an exact type of the mercy which Jesus was on the point of extending towards myself. I sighed, and said, "Oh, that I had not rejected so good a Redeemer, that I had not forfeited all his favours." Thus was my heart softened, though not yet enlightened.[18]

Increasingly, he felt he was not utterly forsaken. Again he felt led to turn to the Bible. The first verse Cowper saw was Romans 3:25: "Whom God hath set forth to be a propitiation through faith in his blood, to declare his righteousness for the remission of sins that are past, through the forbearance of God" (KJV).

Immediately I received the strength to believe it, and the full beams of the Sun of Righteousness shone upon me. I saw the sufficiency of the atonement He had made, my pardon sealed in His blood, and all the fullness and completeness of His justification. In a moment I believed, and received the gospel. . . . Whatever my friend Madan[19] had said to me, long before, revived in all its clearness, with demonstration of the spirit and with power. Unless the Almighty arm had been under me, I think I should have died with gratitude and joy. My eyes filled with tears, and my voice choked with transport; I could only look up to heaven in silent fear, overwhelmed with love and wonder.[20]

He had come to love St. Albans and Dr. Cotton so much that he stayed on another twelve months after his conversion. One might wish the story were one of emotional triumph after his conversion. But it did not turn out that way. Far from it.

The Sweet Mercy of a Slave-Trading Seaman

In June 1765, Cowper left St. Albans and moved in with the Unwin family in Huntingdon. Mary Unwin was only eight years older than Cowper, but she was to become to him like a mother for almost thirty years. In 1767, Mr. Morley Unwin, Mary's husband, died in a tragic fall from his horse. Cowper lived in Mary Unwin's house for the rest of her life. This was significant not only because she was so caring of Cowper,

---

[18] Ibid., 131–32.

[19] His cousin, Martin Madan, was an evangelical pastor. He had tried to encourage Cowper before his entering St. Albans, speaking to him earnestly of original sin, which gave him some hope, putting him more on a level with the rest of mankind rather than singled out for disfavor. Madan spoke to him of the all-atoning blood of Christ and the necessity of a lively faith in Christ. Cowper had only cried out that he wished God would work in his life. Ella, *William Cowper: Poet of Paradise*, 87.

[20] Thomas, *William Cowper and the Eighteenth Century*, 132.

but also because it set the stage for the most important relationship in Cowper's life—his friendship with John Newton.

John Newton was the curate at the church in Olney, not far from the Unwins' home. He had lost his mother when he was six, just like Cowper. But after being sent to school for a few years, he traveled with his father on the high seas, eventually becoming a slave-trading seaman himself. He was powerfully converted, and God called him to the ministry. He had been at Olney since 1764 and would be there till 1780.

We know him mainly as the author of "Amazing Grace." But we should also know him as one of the healthiest, happiest pastors in the eighteenth century. Some said that other pastors were respected by their people, but Newton was loved. To illustrate the kind of spirit he had, here is a quote that gets at the heart of how he approached the ministry:

> Two heaps of human happiness and misery; now if I can take but the smallest bit from one heap and add to the other, I carry a point. If, as I go home, a child has dropped a halfpenny, and if, by giving it another, I can wipe away its tears, I feel I have done something. I should be glad to do greater things, but I will not neglect this. When I hear a knock on my study door, I hear a message from God; it may be a lesson of instruction, perhaps a lesson of penitence; but, since it is *his* message, it must be interesting.[21]

John Newton was told that a family near his parish had lost their father and husband—the Unwins. He made the trip to them and was such a help to them that they decided to move to Olney and sit under his ministry. So in September 1767, they moved from Huntingdon to Olney and lived in a place called Orchard Side for almost twenty years. For thirteen of those years, Newton was Cowper's pastor and counselor and friend. Cowper said, "A sincerer or more affectionate friend no man ever had."[22]

The Olney Hymns as Therapy

Newton saw Cowper's bent to melancholy and reclusiveness and drew him into the ministry of visitation as much as he could. They would take long walks together between homes and talk of God and his purposes for the church. Then, in 1769, Newton got the idea of collaborating

---

[21] Ibid., 202.
[22] Ibid., 192.

with Cowper on a book of hymns to be sung by their church. He thought it would be good for Cowper's poetic bent to be engaged.

In the end, Newton wrote about two hundred of the hymns, and Cowper wrote sixty-eight. The hymnal was published in 1779. Besides "Amazing Grace," Newton wrote "How Sweet the Name of Jesus Sounds" and "Glorious Things of Thee Are Spoken" and "Come, My Soul, Thy Suit Prepare." Cowper wrote "God Moves in a Mysterious Way" and "There Is a Fountain Filled with Blood" and "O for a Closer Walk with God."

Nature "Became a Universal Blank"

But before Cowper could complete his share, he had what he called "the fatal dream." January had come again. His breakdowns had always been at their worst in January. And it was now ten years since "the dreadful '63." They came virtually every ten years in their most intense form. He does not say precisely what the dream was, but only that a "word" was spoken that reduced him to spiritual despair, something to the effect of "It is all over with you, you are lost."[23]

Twelve years later, he still shuddered at the dream. He wrote to Newton in 1785, "I had a dream twelve years ago before the recollection of which all consolation vanishes, and, it seems to me, must always vanish." Not long before his death he told Lady Hesketh, "In one day, in one *minute* I should rather have said, [Nature] became a universal blank to me; and though from a different cause, yet with an effect as difficult to remove, as blindness itself."[24]

Again there were repeated attempts at suicide, and each time God providentially prevented him. Newton stood by him all the way through this, even sacrificing at least one vacation so as not to leave Cowper alone.

In 1780, Newton left Olney for a new pastorate in Lombard Street, London, where he served for the next twenty-seven years. It is a great tribute to him that he did not abandon his friendship with Cowper, though this would, no doubt, have been emotionally easy to do. Instead there was an earnest exchange of letters for twenty years. Cowper poured out his soul to Newton as to no one else.

---

[23] Ibid., 225.
[24] Ibid., 226.

"Truths . . . Couched in Prose, They Would Not Hear"

Perhaps it was good for Newton to go away, because when he left, Cowper poured himself into his major poetic projects (between 1780 and 1786). Most of us today have never heard of any of these poems. His most famous and lengthy was called *The Task*, a hundred-page poem in blank verse. Even though he saw himself, in his blackest moods, as reprobate and hopeless, he never stopped believing in the truth of the Evangelical Awakening. All his poems are meant to teach as well as to entertain.

He wrote about himself:

> . . . I, who scribble rhyme
> To catch the triflers of the time,
> And tell them truths divine and clear
> Which, couched in prose, they would not hear.[25]

His first volume of poems was published in 1782, when he was fifty-one. Three years later came *The Task*, which established his fame. The great usefulness of these poems is that they "helped to spread [the Awakening's] ideas among the educated of all classes. . . . Because of his formal alliance with the [evangelical] movement and the practical effects of his work, [Cowper] remains its [poet] laureate."[26]

Perhaps the productivity staved off the threatened breakdown of 1783, the next ten-year interval. But the reprieve did not last. In 1786, Cowper entered his fourth deep depression and again tried unsuccessfully to commit suicide. He and Mary moved from Olney to Weston that year, and the long decline of both of them began. He cared for her as for a dying mother from 1790 to 1796—filling what moments he could with work on his translations of Homer and other Greek (and French) works. He wrote his last original poem in 1799, called "The Castaway," and then died, apparently in utter despair, in 1800.

Reflections on His Depression

William Cowper's melancholy is disturbing. We need to come to terms with it in the framework of God's sovereign power and grace to save and sanctify his people. What are we to make of this man's lifelong

---

[25] Ibid., 265.
[26] Ibid., 183.

battle with depression, and indeed his apparent surrender to despair and hopelessness in his own life?

One thing to notice is that there is some inconsistency in the way he reports his misery and hopelessness. For example, in a letter to John Newton on January 13, 1784, he wrote,

> Loaded as my life is with despair, I have no such comfort as would result from a supposed probability of better things to come, were it once ended. . . . You will tell me that this cold gloom will be succeeded by a cheerful spring, and endeavour to encourage me to hope for a spiritual change resembling it—but it will be lost labour. Nature revives again; but a soul once slain lives no more. . . . My friends, I know, expect that I shall see yet again. They think it necessary to the existence of divine truth, that he who once had possession of it should never finally lose it. I admit the solidity of this reasoning in every case but my own. And why not in my own? . . . I forestall the answer: God's ways are mysterious, and He giveth no account of His matters—an answer that would serve my purpose as well as theirs that use it. There is a mystery in my destruction, and in time it shall be explained.[27]

Notice that he affirms the truth of the doctrine of the perseverance of God's saints and does not even quarrel with the reality of his own conversion at St. Albans. What he disputes is that the general truth applies to him. He is the lone exception in the universe. He is reprobate, though once he was elect. Ask not why. God gives no account. This is the bleakest way possible of talking. It cuts off all reasoning and exhortation.

All Is Not Night

But notice something else. In that same year, he was writing *The Task*. In it, he recounts what Christ meant to him in a way that makes it very hard to believe there are no times now when this is still real for him:

> I was a stricken deer, that left the herd
> Long since; with many an arrow deep infixt
> My panting side was charg'd, when I withdrew
> To seek a tranquil death in distant shades.
> There was I found by one who had himself

---

[27] Ibid., 281–82.

Been hurt by th' archers. In his side he bore,
And in his hands and feet, the cruel scars.
With gentle force soliciting the darts,
He drew them forth, and heal'd, and bade me live.
Since then, with few associates, in remote
And silent woods I wander, far from those
My former partners of the peopled scene;
With few associates, and not wishing more.[28]

What would he mean in 1784, twelve years after the "fatal dream," that Jesus had drawn the arrows out and healed him and bade him live? Were there not moments when he truly felt this and affirmed it against the constitutional gloom of his own mind?

Even in the 1790s there were expressions of hope. From time to time he gave evidence, for example, that he was permitted by God "once more to approach Him in prayer." His earliest biographer and friend said that in the days of that last decade, God had once more opened a passage for him, but that "spiritual hounds" haunted him at night.[29]

And there was horrible blackness for him much of the time. He wrote to John Newton (friend to the end!) in 1792 that he always seemed to be "scrambling in the dark, among rocks and precipices, without a guide. Thus I have spent twenty years, but thus I shall not spend twenty years more. Long ere that period arrives, the grand question concerning my everlasting weal or woe will be decided."[30] This is bleak, but it is not the settled reprobation we read about in 1786.

A Castaway?

Three years later, on March 20, 1799, he wrote his last original poem, with the seemingly hopeless title "The Castaway." It tells the story of a sailor washed overboard in a storm. His comrades desperately try to throw him something to hold on to. But the ship cannot be stopped in the wind and leaves the castaway behind, treading water in the darkness. He survives for an hour calling out in vain. Then "by toil subdued, he drank / The stifling wave, and then he sank."

This is clearly meant by Cowper to be a parable of his own forsaken

---

[28] Ibid., 302.
[29] Ibid., 368, 374.
[30] Ibid., 376.

and doomed condition. The last two verses make the application to himself:

> I therefore purpose not, or dream
> Descanting on his fate,
> To give the melancholy theme
> A more enduring date:
> But misery still delights to trace
> Its semblance in another's case.
>
> No voice divine the storm allayed,
> No light propitious shone,
> When, snatched from all effectual aid,
> We perished, each alone:
> But I beneath a rougher sea,
> And whelmed in deeper gulfs than he.[31]

There is something paradoxical about this statement of despair. The fact that he wrote it at all shows that his spirit was not wholly paralyzed with meaninglessness and emptiness. He is still strangely alert and responsive to the world. A man cannot write a beautiful poem who has lost all his joy in beauty. What kind of "misery" is it that "still delights"?

> But misery still delights to trace
> Its semblance in another's case.

This remnant of delight and this alertness to spiritual reality and poetic form seem to point to something less than absolute desolation. Moreover, there is another pointer. The title of the poem is significant. At least once before he had used the word "castaway" in a poem—Olney Hymn 36, "Welcome Cross." The poem magnifies the mercy and goodness of God in the trials he designs for us here. It ends,

> Did I meet no trials here,
> No chastisement by the way,
> Might I not with reason fear
> I should prove a castaway?
> Bastards may escape the rod,
> Sunk in earthly vain delight;

---

[31] Cowper, *The Poetical Works*, 426.

But the true-born child of God
Must not—would not, if he might.

Here the word "castaway" is taken from 1 Corinthians 9:27, "But I keep under my body, and bring it into subjection: lest that by any means, when I have preached to others, I myself should be a castaway" (KJV). Here the inescapable trials and chastisements are made an argument not that he is a castaway, but that he is not. He is, rather, a true-born child of God. We do well, therefore, to put a question mark of doubt over the darkness with which Cowper cloaks his final days.

The last days of his life seemed to bring no relief in his sense of forsakenness. No happy ending. In March of 1800, he said to visiting Dr. Lubbock, "I feel unutterable despair." On April 24, Miss Perowne offered some refreshment to him, to which he replied, "What can it signify?" He never spoke again and died the next afternoon.[32]

The Roots of Gloom

What were the roots of such overwhelming and intractable gloom? No doubt there are secrets that God only knows. But we can see some reasons why he may have struggled the way he did.

Consider the home into which he was born. His father, John, married his mother, Ann, in 1728. Between the wedding in 1728 and his birth in 1731, three children had already been born and lost. He lives. But between 1731 and 1736, when his brother John was born, two more children enter the family and then die. Then his mother dies a few days after John's birth. William is six years old. The marriage is one sustained heartache.

The pain and emotional trauma of the death of his mother can probably not be calculated. It's true that the happy, healthy, well-adjusted John Newton also lost his mother at the age of six, the very year Cowper was born. But there is a difference, as we will see in a moment.

"Dupe of To-morrow Even from a Child"

In 1790, at the age of fifty-nine, Cowper received in the mail a portrait of his mother that swept him away with the emotion of years. He had not laid eyes on her face for fifty-three years. He wrote a poem to

---

[32] Thomas, *William Cowper and the Eighteenth Century*, 384.

capture and release the pain and the pleasure of that "meeting." We
catch a glimpse of what it was for him at age six to have lost his mother.
And perhaps why he took so to Mrs. Mary Unwin.

> Oh that those lips had language! Life has passed
> With me but roughly since I heard thee last.
>
> My mother! when I learned that thou wast dead,
> Say, wast thou conscious of the tears I shed?
> Hovered thy spirit o'er thy sorrowing son,
> Wretch even then, life's journey just begun?
>
> I heard the bell tolled on thy burial day,
> I saw the hearse that bore thee slow away,
> And turning from my nursery window, drew
> A long, long sigh, and wept a last adieu!
>
> Thy maidens, grieved themselves at my concern,
> Oft gave me promise of thy quick return.
> What ardently I wished, I long believed,
> And disappointed still, was still deceived;
> By expectation every day beguiled,
> Dupe of to-morrow even from a child.
>
> But the record fair,
> That memory keeps of all thy kindness there,
> Still outlives many a storm, that has effaced
> A thousand other themes less deeply traced.
> Thy nightly visits to my chamber made
> That thou mightst know me safe and warmly laid;
> Thy morning bounties ere I left my home,
> Thy biscuit, or confectionery plum;
> The fragrant waters on my cheeks bestowed
> By thy own hand, till fresh they shone and glowed:
> All this, and more endearing still than all,
> Thy constant flow of love, that knew no fall,
> Ne'er roughened by those cataracts and breaks,
> That humour interposed too often makes:
> All this still legible in memory's page,
> And still to be so to my latest age.[33]

---

[33] Cowper, *The Poetical Works*, 406–9.

One begins to ponder the strange relations Cowper had all his life with older women, wanting them in his life, and yet causing them great confusion with the love poems he would write when he had no romantic intentions. Lady Austen in particular was bewildered by the way Cowper wrote to her.[34] This kind of behavior may have had its roots not only in the loss of his mother, but in the virtual loss of his father and his horrible experience in boarding school between the ages of six and eight.

Should Fathers Say, "Go Thither Where the Quicksands Lay"?

He hated boarding school and longed for his father:

> But my chief affliction consisted in my being singled out from all the other boys, by a lad about fifteen years of age as a proper object upon which he might let loose the cruelty of his temper. I choose to forbear a particular recital of the many acts of barbarity, with which he made it his business continually to persecute me: it will be sufficient to say, that he had, by his savage treatment of me, impressed such a dread of his figure upon my mind, that I well remember being afraid to lift up my eyes upon him, higher than his knees; and that I knew him by his shoe-buckles, better than any other part of his dress. May the Lord pardon him, and may we meet in glory![35]

One would never have said it in the eighteenth century. But knowing what we know today about its effects and what we know about boys at that age, it is hard not to raise the specter of sexual abuse. What horrors a little six-year-old boy may have experienced, combined with the loss of his mother and the virtual loss of his father!

Perhaps the most poignant lines Cowper ever wrote are hidden away in a poem called "Tirocinium" (Latin for the state of a new recruit—inexperienced, raw) in which he pleads for a private education rather than one at boarding school. What comes through here is a loud cry for his father to have been there for him, and a powerful plea to fathers even in the twenty-first century to be there for our children:

---

[34] One writer says that his attitudes toward women were "simple as an infant." I would call them insensitive and unhealthy. In the summer of 1781, Cowper was introduced to the widow of Sir Robert Austen. She soon became "sister Ann" and more. She probably fell in love with him and cannot be blamed for thinking that he reciprocated. After two months, he wrote her not to think it romance. Later she came to Olney, and even stayed in Orchard Side because of an illness. She and Cowper had much time together in those days, and he wrote at least one very gallant poem for her that would have given any woman the thought of romance. But he had to write her again in the spring of 1784 to "renounce her society." There was no reconciliation this time. Cowper never met her again after 1784. She had inspired *John Gilpin* and *The Task*, but now she was gone. See Thomas, *William Cowper and the Eighteenth Century*, 289–90.
[35] Ibid., 69–70.

Would you your son should be a sot or dunce,
Lascivious, headstrong, or all these at once,
That in good time, the stripling's finished taste
For loose expense and fashionable waste
Should prove your ruin, and his own at last,
Train him in public with a mob of boys,
Childish in mischief only and in noise,
Else of a mannish growth, and five in ten
In infidelity and lewdness, men.
There shall he learn, ere sixteen winters old,
That authors are most useful, pawned or sold,
That pedantry is all that schools impart,
But taverns teach the knowledge of the heart.[36]

And seems it nothing in a father's eye
That unimproved those many moments fly?
And is he well content, his son should find
No nourishment to feed his growing mind
But conjugated verbs, and nouns declined?
For such is all the mental food purveyed
By public hackneys in the schooling trade.
Who feed a pupil's intellect with store
Of syntax truly, but with little more,
Dismiss their cares when they dismiss their flock,
Machines themselves, and governed by a clock.
Perhaps a father blest with any brains
Would deem it no abuse or waste of pains,
To improve this diet at no great expense,
With savoury truth and wholesome common sense,
To lead his son for prospects of delight
To some not steep though philosophic height,
Thence to exhibit to his wondering eyes
Yon circling worlds, their distance, and their size.[37]

To show him in an insect or a flower
Such microscopic proofs of skill and power,
As hid from ages past, God now displays
To combat atheists with in modern days.[38]

---

[36] Cowper, *The Poetical Works*, 223.
[37] Ibid., 231.
[38] Ibid., 232.

[O Father] Nature pulling at thine heart,
Condemns the unfatherly, the imprudent part.
Thou wouldst not, deaf to nature's tenderest plea,
Turn him adrift upon a rolling sea,
Nor say, go thither, conscious that there lay
A brood of asps, or quicksands in his way;
Then only governed by the self-same rule
Of natural pity, send him not to school.
No—Guard him better: Is he not thine own,
Thyself in miniature, thy flesh, thy bone?
And hopest thou not ('tis every father's hope)
That since thy strength must with thy years elope,
And thou wilt need some comfort to assuage
Health's last farewell, as staff of thine old age,
That then, in recompense of all thy cares
Thy child shall show respect to thy gray hairs.[39]

He never wrote a tribute to his father that we know of. He says almost nothing about him. But this is a powerful plea for fathers to love their children and give them special attention in their education. This is what he missed from the age of six onward.

Distrust the Certainties of Despair

What shall we learn from the life of William Cowper? The first lesson is this: We fortify ourselves against the dark hours of depression by cultivating a deep distrust of the certainties of despair. Despair is relentless in the certainties of his pessimism. But we have seen that Cowper is not consistent. Some years after his absolute statements of being cut off from God, he is again expressing some hope in being heard. His certainties were not sureties. So it will always be with the deceptions of darkness. Let us now, while we have the light, cultivate distrust of the certainties of despair.

Love Your Children Dearly

The second lesson I see is that we should love our children deeply and keep communicating that love to them. And, unless some extraordinary call of God prevents it, let us keep them close to us and secure with us.

---

[39] Ibid., 236.

John Newton, like William Cowper, lost his mother when he was six. But he did not lose his father in the same way. In spite of all the sin and misery of those early years of Newton's life, there was a father—even on the high seas, even setting a bad example in many ways. And who can say what deep roots of later health were preserved because of that one solid rock: a present father? But for Cowper the legacy of his father, who died when he was twenty-five, is marked by Cowper's total silence. Almost everything in his life that he valued, he wrote poems about. But none for his father. Let us be there for our sons and daughters. We are a crucial link in their normal sexual and emotional development.

Despair Not of the Despairing

Third, may the Lord raise up many John Newtons among us, for the joy of our churches and for the survival of the William Cowpers in our midst. Newton remained Cowper's pastor and friend the rest of his life, writing and visiting again and again. He did not despair of the despairing. After one of these visits in 1788, Cowper wrote:

> I found those comforts in your visit, which have formerly sweetened all our interviews, in part restored. I knew you; knew you for the same shepherd who was sent to lead me out of the wilderness into the pasture where the Chief Shepherd feeds His flock, and felt my sentiments of affectionate friendship for you the same as ever. But one thing was still wanting, and that the crown of all. I shall find it in God's time, if it be not lost for ever.[40]

That is not utter hopelessness. And the reason it is not is because the shepherd had drawn near again. Those were the times when Cowper felt a ray of hope.

The Healthy Gift of Self-Forgetfulness

Fourth, in the very research and writing of this chapter, I experienced something that may be a crucial lesson for those of us who are given to too much introspection and analysis. I devoted about three days—from waking until sleeping—to William Cowper, besides leisurely reading of his life and poetry before those three days. These days I was almost entirely outside myself as it were. Now and then I "came to" and became

---

[40] Thomas, *William Cowper and the Eighteenth Century*, 356.

aware that I had been absorbed wholly in the life of another. But most of the time I was not self-conscious. I was not thinking about me at all. I was the one thinking, not the one thought about. This experience, when I "came to" and thought about it, seemed to me extremely healthy. That is the way I experienced it. In other words, I felt best when I was not aware of being one who feels. I was feeling and thinking of something outside myself—the life of William Cowper.

I think this is the way most of life should be. Periodic self-examination is needed and wise and biblical. But for the most part, mental health is the use of the mind to focus on worthy reality outside ourselves. While I was a student at Wheaton College, a very wise and deep and happy teacher of literature, Clyde Kilby, showed us and taught us this path to health. Once he said, "I shall not demean my own uniqueness by envy of others. I shall stop boring into myself to discover what psychological or social categories I might belong to. Mostly I shall simply forget about myself and do my work."[41]

He had learned the deep significance of this outward-oriented self-forgetfulness from C. S. Lewis and drew our attention to it often. Mental health is, in great measure, the gift of self-forgetfulness. The reason is that introspection destroys what matters most to us—the authentic experience of great things outside ourselves. Lewis grasped this as well as anyone in the twentieth century:

> The enjoyment and the contemplation of our inner activities are incompatible. You cannot hope and also think about hoping at the same moment; for in hope we look to hope's object and we interrupt this by (so to speak) turning round to look at the hope itself. Of course the two activities can and do alternate with great rapidity. . . . The surest means of disarming an anger or a lust was to turn your attention from the girl or the insult and start examining the passion itself. The surest way of spoiling a pleasure was to start examining your satisfaction. But if so, it followed that all introspection is in one respect misleading. In introspection we try to look "inside ourselves" and see what is going on. But nearly everything that was going on a moment before is stopped by the very act of our turning to look at it. Unfortunately this does not mean that introspection finds nothing. On the contrary, it finds precisely what is left behind by the suspension of all our normal activities; and what is left behind is mainly mental images and physical sensations.

---

[41] For this and other resolutions of Dr. Kilby, see John Piper, *The Pleasures of God* (Colorado Springs: Multnomah, 2012), 78–79.

The great error is to mistake this mere sediment or track or byproduct for the activities themselves.[42]

Oh, the danger of too much pondering of our inner states! It distorts the bad and it suspends, or even destroys, the good.

You cannot study pleasure in the moment of the nuptial embrace, nor re-pentance while repenting, nor analyze the nature of humour while roaring with laughter. But when else can you really know these things? "If only my toothache would stop, I could write another chapter about pain." But once it stops, what do I know about pain?[43]

Self-forgetfulness in the contemplation of something great or the doing of something good is a gift from God. In the end, the harder you try to forget yourself, the more impossible it is. It must be pursued indirectly. One great antidote to depression is simply to see what is really there in the world. Which is why Clyde Kilby resolved:

I shall open my eyes and ears. Once every day I shall simply stare at a tree, a flower, a cloud, or a person. I shall not then be concerned at all to ask what they are, but simply be glad that they are. I shall joyfully allow them the mystery of what Lewis calls their "divine, magical, terrifying, and ecstatic" existence.[44]

Escape: The Path to Suicide

A fifth lesson I speak with some hesitation. We should be slow to judge the needs and possibilities of another person's mental health. But at least I suggest that Cowper would have benefited by less retreat and ease and contemplation and more engagement with suffering people who needed help. Gilbert Thomas says of Cowper's major poem *The Task* (more than one hundred pages), "The whole has one tendency: to discountenance the modern enthusiasm after a London life, and to recommend rural ease and leisure, as friendly to the cause of piety and virtue."[45] This is a remarkable contrast to what was brewing in William Carey's much healthier mind not far away. The last thing Carey wanted to do was to recommend rural ease and leisure! What was

---

[42] C. S. Lewis, *Surprised by Joy: The Shape of My Early Life* (New York: Harcourt, Brace and World, 1955), 218–19.
[43] C. S. Lewis, "Myth Became Fact," in *God in the Dock* (Grand Rapids, MI: Eerdmans, 1970), 65–66.
[44] Piper, *The Pleasures of God*, 79n11.
[45] Thomas, *William Cowper and the Eighteenth Century*, 197.

needed in the world was not people retreating to tea and lakes in order to be more virtuous than they would be in the London pubs. What was needed was people giving their lives away to rescue people from the darkness of London and even more from the utter alienation of places like India.

Was Cowper cutting himself off from greater mental health by living a life of such continual leisure and distance from the world of need? He talks of his constant walks and religious conversations as though that were the aim of life. And his moralizing seems to be done from a safe distance from the London scenes. I cannot overlook the deep strain of escape in his life. I do not condemn him for this, because I simply do not know what a mind so fragile as his could endure.

Gilbert Thomas suggests, "That Cowper was an escapist, in the physical sense, may be true: his supersensitive nervous constitution demanded solitude."[46] Perhaps. But those of us who have the choice still in front of us would do well to ponder that neither health nor holiness are had by escape from perishing people. The path of love, no matter how dirty or dangerous, is the path to wholeness and heaven.

The Hope-Giving Fruit of Feeling Hopelessness

A sixth lesson from the life of William Cowper I have learned from how God seems to use it in the lives of others. Some years ago I presented an early version of this chapter as a Sunday evening message at Bethlehem Baptist Church. It proved to be one of the most encouraging things I had done in a long time. This bleak life was felt by many as hope-giving. There are no doubt different reasons for this in the cases of different people. But the lesson is surely that those of us who teach and preach and want to encourage our people to press on in hope and faith must not limit ourselves to success stories. The tormented life of William Cowper had a hope-giving effect on my people. That is a very important lesson.

There is biblical warrant for this strange strategy of encouragement. For example, David, the king of Israel, speaks in Psalm 40:1–3 about his extended misery in "the pit of destruction" and "the miry clay." "I waited patiently for the LORD; and He inclined to me and heard my cry. He brought me up out of the pit of destruction, out of the miry clay."

---

[46] Ibid., 321.

He does not tell us how long he "waited patiently." Hours? Days? Weeks? Months? The first point is that though he was there for an extended time, he did not curse God, but cried out. But the main point here is that people are helped by the testimony of his deliverance—not in spite of, but because of David's sharing in the miseries they all know. "He set my feet upon a rock making my footsteps firm. He put a new song in my mouth, a song of praise to our God; many will see and fear and will trust in the LORD." People feared God and put their trust in him because the king was in "the pit of destruction" and God heard his cry and delivered him. Who knows but that any misery we meet is not designed for such a painful path toward praise by other people?

Of course, one might object, "Yes, but David was delivered in this life and had a 'new song' put in his mouth. William Cowper didn't." That's probably true. I say "probably" because it may be that Cowper had new songs given to him again and again after repeated times of suicidal blackness. Whether he did in the end is doubtful. But this too is not unforeseen in the Bible.

When David says in Psalm 139:7, "Where can I go from Your Spirit? Or where can I flee from Your presence?" his implied answer is "Nowhere." But his last place of retreat is the darkness of his own soul in a time of distress. "If I say, 'Surely the darkness will overwhelm me, and the light around me will be night,' even the darkness is not dark to You, and the night is as bright as the day. Darkness and light are alike to You" (Ps. 139:11–12). Notice that the issue here is not objective overwhelming darkness; it is David's *saying*, "Surely the darkness will overwhelm me." It is a subjective sense of darkness. It is despairing feelings. This sounds exactly like Cowper in the last days. "The light around me will be night." But to this, the answer is, "Even the darkness is not dark to You." What is dark to God's children—objectively and subjectively—is not dark to God.

The point is, there are stories in the Bible, in history, and in our own lives that do not appear to have happy endings of cheerfulness. These too are not without hope and are designed by God's sovereign and merciful wisdom for the hope of those who fear they are utterly alone in their misery. The principle is expressed by Paul in 1 Timothy 1:16, "For this reason I found mercy, so that in me as the foremost [sinner], Jesus Christ might demonstrate His perfect patience as an example for those who would believe in Him for eternal life." The examples of God's patience in history will not serve their saving and sustaining purposes if we do not tell the stories—like the story of William Cowper.

Never Cease to Sing the Gospel to the Deaf

One final, all-important lesson: Let us rehearse the mercies of Jesus often in the presence of discouraged people. Let us point them again and again to the blood of Jesus. These were the two things that brought Cowper to faith in 1764. Remember how he said that in John 11 he "saw so much benevolence, mercy, goodness, and sympathy with miserable men, in our Saviour's conduct, that I almost shed tears."[47] And remember how on the decisive day of awakening he said, "I saw the sufficiency of the atonement He had made, my pardon sealed in His blood, and all the fullness and completeness of His justification."[48]

In Cowper's most famous hymn, this is what he sings—the preciousness of the blood of Christ to the worst of sinners.

There is a fountain filled with blood
Drawn from Emmanuel's veins;
And sinners, plunged beneath that flood,
Lose all their guilty stains.

The dying thief rejoiced to see
That fountain in his day;
And there have I, as vile as he,
Washed all my sins away.

Dear dying Lamb, thy precious blood
Shall never lose its power;
Till all the ransomed church of God
Be saved to sin no more.

E'er since, by faith, I saw the stream
Thy flowing wounds supply,
Redeeming love has been my theme,
And shall be till I die.[49]

---

[47] See note 18.
[48] See introduction, note 29.
[49] The original title in the *Olney Hymnal* was "Praise for the Fountain Opened." Cowper, *The Poetical Works*, 280. There are three more verses than those cited here.

Don't make your mercy to the downcast contingent on quick results. You cannot persuade a person that he is not reprobate if he is utterly persuaded that he is. He will tell you he is deaf. No matter. Keep soaking him in the "benevolence, mercy, goodness, and sympathy" of Jesus and "the sufficiency of the atonement" and "the fullness and completeness of [Christ's] justification." Yes, he may say that these are all wonderful in themselves, but that they do not belong to him. To this you say, "Doubt your despairing thoughts. Whence this great confidence you have in your damnation? A little skepticism is in order here. Who do you think you are"—perhaps you smile when you say this (but not lightly)—"making final declarations about your soul that lie hidden in the secrets of the Almighty? No. No. Renounce such confidence. If you have no ability for faith in the love of God for you, make no more such great pretenses to have such certainty of faith in your damnation. This is not yours to know. Rather, yours is to listen to Jesus." Then go on telling him the glories of Christ and his all-sufficient sacrifice for sin. Pray that in God's time these truths may yet be given the power to awaken hope and beget a spirit of adoption.

We have good reason to hope that if we make redeeming love our theme until we die, and if we promote the love and patience of John Newton in our own souls and in our churches, then the William Cowpers among us will not be given over to the enemy in the end.

When I really enjoy God, I feel my desires of him the more insatiable, and my thirstings after holiness the more unquenchable. . . . Oh, for holiness! Oh, for more of God in my soul! Oh, this pleasing pain! It makes my soul press after God. . . . Oh, that I may feel this continual hunger, and not be retarded, but rather animated by every "cluster from Canaan," to reach forward in the narrow way, for the full enjoyment and possession of the heavenly inheritance. Oh, that I might never loiter on my heavenly journey!

David Brainerd
The Diary

3

"Oh, That I Might Never Loiter on My Heavenly Journey!"

Misery and Mission in the Life of David Brainerd

A Lineage of Weakness, Suited for Great Use

David Brainerd was born on April 20, 1718, in Haddam, Connecticut. That year, John Wesley and Jonathan Edwards turned fourteen. Benjamin Franklin turned twelve and George Whitefield three. The Great Awakening was just over the horizon, and Brainerd would live through both waves of it in the mid-thirties and early forties of the eighteenth century, then die of tuberculosis in Jonathan Edwards's house at the age of twenty-nine on October 9, 1747.

Brainerd's father, Hezekiah, was a Connecticut legislator and died when David was nine years old. I have four sons of my own, and judging by their warm emotional attachment at that age, I think that might be the hardest year of all to lose a father. Hezekiah had been a rigorous Puritan with strong views of authority and strictness at home; and he pursued a very earnest devotion that included days of private fasting to promote spiritual welfare.[1]

Brainerd was the sixth child and third son born to Hezekiah and Dorothy. After him came three more children. Dorothy had brought

---

[1] Jonathan Edwards, *An Account of the Life of the Reverend Mr. David Brainerd*, in *The Life of David Brainerd*, ed. Norman Pettit, vol. 7 of *The Works of Jonathan Edwards* (New Haven, CT: Yale University Press, 1985), 33. All page numbers in the text refer to this volume, which contains not only Edwards's edition of Brainerd's *Diaries*, but also some journal extracts and an extensive introduction by Norman Pettit and related correspondence.

one little boy from a previous marriage, and so there were twelve of them in the home—but not for long. Five years after his father died at the age of forty-six, David's mother died just before he turned fourteen.

It seems there was an unusual strain of weakness and depression in the family. Not only did the parents die early, but also David's brother Nehemiah died at thirty-two, his brother Israel died at twenty-three, his sister Jerusha died at thirty-four, and he died at twenty-nine. In 1865 a descendant, Thomas Brainerd (in a biography of John Brainerd), said, "In the whole Brainerd family for two hundred years there has been a tendency to a morbid depression, akin to hypochondria" (p. 64).

So on top of having an austere father and suffering the loss of both parents as a sensitive child, David probably inherited some kind of physical tendency to depression. Whatever the cause, he suffered from the blackest dejection off and on throughout his short life. He says at the very beginning of his diary, "I was, I think, from my youth something sober and inclined rather to melancholy than the other extreme" (p. 101).

Religion with No True Grace in the Soul

When his mother died, he moved from Haddam across the Connecticut River to East Haddam to live with his married sister, Jerusha. He described his religion during these years as very careful and serious, but having no true grace—in other words, in the language of eighteenth-century Puritanism, unconverted, not a true Christian. When he turned nineteen, he inherited a farm and moved for a year a few miles west to Durham to try his hand at farming. But his heart was not in it. He longed for "a liberal education" (p. 103). In fact, Brainerd was a contemplative and a scholar from head to toe. If he hadn't been expelled from Yale, he may well have pursued a teaching or pastoral ministry instead of becoming a missionary to the Indians.

After a year on the farm, he came back to East Haddam and began to prepare himself to enter Yale. This was the summer of 1738. He was twenty years old. During the year on the farm, he had made a commitment to God to enter the ministry. But still he was not converted. He read the whole Bible twice that year and began to see more clearly that all his religion was legalistic and simply based on his own efforts. He had great quarreling with God within his soul. He rebelled against original sin and against the strictness of the divine law and against the sovereignty of God. He quarreled with the fact that there was nothing he could do in his own strength to commend himself to God (pp. 113–24).

He came to see that "all my good frames [i.e., devotional states] were but self-righteousness, not bottomed on a desire for the glory of God" (p. 103). "There was no more goodness in my praying than there would be in my paddling with my hands in the water . . . because [my prayers] were not performed from any love or regard to God. . . . I never once prayed for the glory of God" (p. 134). "I never once intended his honor and glory. . . . I had never once acted for God in all my devotions. . . . I used to charge them with sin . . . [because] of wanderings and vain thoughts . . . and not because I never had any regard in them to the glory of God" (p. 136).

"I Felt Myself in a New World"

But then the miracle happened, the day of his new birth. Half an hour before sunset at the age of twenty-one, he was in a lonely place trying to pray.

> As I was walking in a dark thick grove, "unspeakable glory" seemed to open to the view and apprehension of my soul. . . . It was a new inward apprehension or view that I had of God; such as I never had before, nor anything that I had the least remembrance of it. So that I stood still and wondered and admired. . . . I had now no particular apprehension of any one person of the Trinity, either the Father, Son, or Holy Spirit, but it appeared to be divine glory and splendor that I then beheld. And my soul "rejoiced with joy unspeakable" to see such a God, such a glorious divine being, and I was inwardly pleased and satisfied that he should be God over all forever and ever. My soul was so captivated and delighted with the excellency, the loveliness and the greatness and other perfections of God that I was even swallowed up in him, at least to that degree that I had no thought, as I remember at first, about my own salvation or scarce that there was such a creature as I.
>
> Thus the Lord, I trust, brought me to a hearty desire to exalt him, to set him on the throne and to "seek first his Kingdom," i.e. principally and ultimately to aim at his honor and glory as the King and sovereign of the universe, which is the foundation of the religion Jesus Christ has taught. . . . I felt myself in a new world. . . . I wondered that all the world did not comply with this way of salvation entirely by the "righteousness of Christ." (pp. 138–40)

Jonathan Edwards wrote at the top of the manuscript of Brainerd's diary at this point, "Lord's Day, July 12th 1739 forever to be remembered by D. B." (p. 140). Brainerd was twenty-one years old. He had entered into an experience of God's grace that would ruin his educational career but rescue him again and again from despair.

Whittelsey "Has No More Grace Than a Chair"

Two months later he entered Yale to prepare for the ministry. It was a hard beginning. There was hazing by the upperclassmen, little spirituality, difficult studies, and he got measles and had to go home for several weeks during that first year.

The next year he was sent home because he was so sick he was spitting blood. So even at this early age he already had the tuberculosis he would die of seven years later. The amazing thing may not be that he died so early and accomplished so little, but that, being as sick as he was, he lived as long as he did and accomplished so much.

When he came back to Yale in November 1740, the spiritual climate was radically changed. George Whitefield had been there, and now many students were very serious about their faith, which suited Brainerd well. In fact, tensions were emerging between the awakened students and the seemingly less spiritual faculty and staff. In 1741, pastor-evangelists Gilbert Tennent, Ebenezer Pemberton, and James Davenport fanned the flames of discontent among the students with their fiery preaching.

Jonathan Edwards was invited to preach the commencement address in 1741 in the hopes that he would pour a little water on the fire and stand up for the faculty against the enthusiasm of the students. Some faculty had even been criticized as being unconverted. Edwards preached a sermon called "The Distinguishing Marks of a Work of the Spirit of God" and totally disappointed the faculty and staff. He argued that the work going on in the awakening of those days, and specifically among the students, was a real spiritual work in spite of the excesses.

That very morning it had been voted by the college trustees that "if any student of this College shall directly or indirectly say, that the Rector, either of the Trustees or tutors are hypocrites, carnal or unconverted men, he shall for the first offense make a public confession in the hall, and for the second offense be expelled" (p. 41). Edwards was clearly more sympathetic with the students than the college was. He even went so far as to say in his commencement address that afternoon, "It is no evidence that a work is not the work of God, if many that are subjects of it . . . are guilty of [so] great forwardness to censure others as un-converted" (p. 42).

Brainerd was in the crowd as Edwards spoke. One can't help but wonder whether Edwards later felt some responsibility for what hap-pened to Brainerd in the next term. He was at the top of his class aca-demically but was summarily expelled in early 1742 during his third year. He was overheard to say that one of the tutors, Chauncey Whit-telsey, "has no more grace than a chair" and that he wondered why the Rector "did not drop down dead" for fining students for their evangeli-cal zeal (pp. 42, 155).

The Lasting Fruit of Eight Wrong Words

This expulsion wounded Brainerd very deeply. He tried again and again in the next several years to make things right. Numerous people came to his aid, but all to no avail. God had another plan for Brainerd. Instead of a quiet six years in the pastorate or lecture hall followed by death and little historical impact for Christ's kingdom, God meant to drive him into the wilderness that he might suffer for his sake and have an incalculable influence on the history of missions.

Before the way was cut off for him to the pastorate, Brainerd had no thought of being a missionary to the Indians. But now he had to rethink his whole life. There was a law, recently passed, that no established minister could be installed in Connecticut who had not graduated from Harvard, Yale, or a European university (p. 52). So Brainerd felt cut off from his life calling.

There is a tremendous lesson here. God is at work for the glory of his name and the good of his church even when the good intentions of his servants fail—even when that failing is owing to sin or carelessness. One careless word, spoken in haste, and Brainerd's life seemed to fall apart before his eyes. But God knew better, and Brainerd came to accept it. In fact, I am tempted to speculate whether the modern missionary movement, which was so repeatedly inspired by Brainerd's missionary life, would have happened if David Brainerd had not been expelled from Yale and cut off from his hopes to serve God in the pastorate! But God alone knows the "would have been's" of history (Matt. 11:21).

Lose the Good and Gain the Best

In the summer of 1742, a group of ministers (called New Lights) sympathetic to the Great Awakening licensed Brainerd to preach. Jonathan Dickinson, the leading Presbyterian in New Jersey, took an interest in Brainerd and tried to get him reinstated in Yale. When that failed, the suggestion was made that Brainerd become a missionary to the Indians under the sponsorship of the Commissioners of the Society in Scotland for Propagating Christian Knowledge. Dickinson was one of those commissioners. On November 25, 1742, Brainerd was examined for his fitness for the work and was appointed as a missionary to the Indians (p. 188).

He spent the winter serving a church on Long Island so that he could enter the wilderness in the spring. His first assignment was to the Housatonic Indians at Kaunaumeek, about twenty miles northwest of Stockbridge, Massachusetts, where Jonathan Edwards would eventually serve as a missionary to the Indians. Brainerd arrived on April 1, 1743, and preached for one year, using an interpreter and trying to learn the language from John Sergeant, the veteran missionary at Stockbridge (p. 228). While here he was able to start a school for Indian children and translate some of the Psalms (p. 61).

Then came a reassignment to go to the Indians along the Delaware River in Pennsylvania. On May 1, 1744, he left Kaunaumeek and settled in the Forks of the Delaware River, northeast of Bethlehem, Pennsylvania. At the end of the month he rode to Newark, New Jersey, to be examined by the Newark Presbytery and was ordained on June 11, 1744 (pp. 251–52).

At Last God Moved with Amazing Power

He preached to the Indians at the Forks of the Delaware for one year. But on June 19, 1745, he made his first preaching tour to the Indians at Crossweeksung, New Jersey. This was the place where God moved in amazing power and brought awakening and blessing to the Indians. Within a year there were 130 persons in his growing assembly of believers (p. 376). The whole, newly converted Christian community moved from Crossweeksung to Cranberry in May, 1746, to have their own land and village. Brainerd stayed with these Indians until he was too sick to minister, and in November 1746, he left Cranberry to spend four months trying to recuperate in Elizabethtown at the house of Jonathan Dickinson.

On March 20, 1747, he made one last visit to his Indian friends and then rode to the house of Jonathan Edwards in Northampton, Massachusetts, arriving May 28, 1747. He made one trip to Boston during the summer and then returned and died of tuberculosis in Edwards's house on October 9, 1747.

One Short Life

It was a short life—twenty-nine years, five months, and nineteen days. And only eight of those years as a believer. Only four as a missionary. Why has Brainerd's life made the impact that it has? One obvious reason is that Jonathan Edwards took the *Diaries* and published them as a *Life of Brainerd* in 1749. But why has this book never been out of print? Why did John Wesley say, "Let every preacher read carefully over the *Life of David Brainerd*" (p. 3)? Why was it written of Henry Martyn (missionary to India and Persia) that "perusing the life of David Brainerd, his soul was filled with a holy emulation of that extraordinary man; and after deep consideration and fervent prayer, he was at length fixed in a resolution to imitate his example"?[2] Why did William Carey regard Edwards's *Life of Brainerd* as precious and holy? Why did Robert Morrison and Robert McCheyne of Scotland and John Mills of America and Fredrick Schwartz of Germany and David Livingstone of England and Andrew Murray of South Africa and Jim Elliot of twentieth-century America look upon Brainerd with a kind of awe and draw power from him as countless others have (p. 4)?

Gideon Hawley, another missionary protégé of Jonathan Edwards, spoke for hundreds when he wrote in 1753 about his struggles as a missionary: "I need, greatly need, something more than humane [human or natural] to support me. I read my Bible and Mr. Brainerd's *Life*, the only books I brought with me, and from them have a little support" (p. 3).

Why has this life had such a remarkable influence? Or perhaps I should pose a more modest and manageable question: Why does it have such an impact on me? How has it helped me to press on in the ministry and to strive for holiness and divine power and fruitfulness in my life?

---

[2] "Brainerd, David," *Religious Encyclopaedia*, vol. 1, ed. Philip Schaff (New York: Christian Literature, 1888), 320.

The answer is that Brainerd's life is a vivid, powerful testimony to the truth that God can and does use weak, sick, discouraged, beat-down, lonely, struggling saints who cry to him day and night to accomplish amazing things for his glory. There is great fruit in their afflictions. To illustrate this, we will look first at Brainerd's struggles, then at how he responded to them, and finally at how God used him with all his weaknesses.

Brainerd Struggled with Almost-Constant Sickness

He had to drop out of college for some weeks because he had begun to cough up blood in 1740. In May 1744 he wrote, "Rode several hours in the rain through the howling wilderness, although I was so disordered in body that little or nothing but blood came from me" (p. 247).

Now and again he would write something like, "In the afternoon my pain increased exceedingly; and was obliged to betake myself to bed. . . . Was sometimes almost bereaved of the exercise of my reason by the extremity of pain" (p. 253). In August of 1746 he wrote, "Having lain in cold sweat all night, I coughed much bloody matter this morning, and was under great disorder of body, and not a little melancholy" (p. 420). In September he wrote, "Exercised with a violent cough and a considerable fever; had no appetite to any kind of food; and frequently brought up what I ate, as soon as it was down; and oftentimes had little rest in my bed, by reason of pains in my breast and back: was able, however, to ride over to my people, about two miles, every day, and take some care of those who were then at work upon a small house for me to reside in amongst the Indians" (p. 430).

In May 1747 at Jonathan Edwards's house, the doctors told him that he had incurable consumption and did not have long to live (p. 447). In the last couple of months of his life, the suffering was incredible. September 24: "In the greatest distress that ever I endured having an uncommon kind of hiccough; which either strangled me or threw me into a straining to vomit" (p. 469). Edwards comments that in the week before Brainerd died, "He told me it was impossible for any to conceive of the distress he felt in his breast. He manifested much concern lest he should dishonor God by impatience under his extreme agony; which was such that he said the thought of enduring it one minute longer was almost insupportable." The night before he died, he said to those around him that "it was another thing to die than people imagined" (pp. 475–76).

What strikes the reader of these diaries is not just the severity of Brainerd's suffering in the days before antibiotics and painkillers, but especially how relentless the sickness was. It was almost always there. And yet he pressed on with his work.

Brainerd Struggled with Recurring Depression

Brainerd came to understand more fully from his own experience the difference between spiritual desertion and the disease of melancholy. So his later judgments about his own spiritual condition are probably more careful than the earlier ones. But however one assesses his psychological condition, he was tormented again and again with the most desperate discouragements. And the marvel is that he survived and kept going at all.

Brainerd said he had been this way from his youth (p. 101). But he said that there was a difference between the depression he suffered before and after his conversion. After his conversion there seemed to be a rock of electing love under him that supported him, so that in his darkest times he could still affirm the truth and goodness of God, even though he couldn't sense it for a season (pp. 93, 141, 165, 278).

But even so, it was bad enough. Often his distress was owing to the hatred of his own remaining sinfulness. Thursday, November 4, 1942: "'Tis distressing to feel in my soul that hell of corruption which still remains in me" (p. 185). Sometimes this sense of unworthiness was so intense that he felt cut off from the presence of God. January 23, 1743: "Scarce ever felt myself so unfit to exist, as now: I saw I was not worthy of a place among the Indians, where I am going. . . . None knows, but those that feel it, what the soul endures that is sensibly shut out from the presence of God: Alas, 'tis more bitter than death!" (pp. 195–96).

He often called his depression a kind of death. There are at least twenty-two places in the diary where he longed for death as a freedom from his misery. For example, Sunday, February 3, 1745: "My soul remembered 'the wormwood and the gall' (I might almost say hell) of Friday last; and I was greatly afraid I should be obliged again to drink of that 'cup of trembling,' which was inconceivably more bitter than death, and made me long for the grave more, unspeakably more, than for hid treasures" (p. 285). Sunday, December 16, 1744: "Was so overwhelmed with dejection that I knew not how to live: I longed for death exceedingly: My soul was 'sunk in deep waters,' and 'the floods' were ready to 'drown me': I was so much oppressed that my soul was in a kind of horror" (p. 278).

Perhaps the worst mental condition of all was the disappearance of all capacity to fear or to love at all. Some passages that reveal these times are so bleak that Jonathan Edwards left them out of his *Life*. We know this because there are thirty-six pages of Brainerd's diary in his own hand preserved at the Beineke Library at Yale University that can be compared with the way Edwards edited these pages (pp. 79, 100–53). Here is one such section that shows an aspect of Brainerd's depression that is classic in its numbness against any feeling at all.

> I felt something like a criminal at the bar waiting for his sentence, excepting this, I felt but little concern which way my case went, for the fear of hell was almost, if not entirely, taken away from me. I had the greatest certainty that my state was forever unalterable by anything that I could do, and wondered and was almost astonished that I had never been sensible of it before because it [*sic*, I] had now the clearest demonstration of it. And in this case I felt neither love to God, or desire of heaven as I used to think I did. Neither fear of hell, or love to the present world. Indeed I had rather be, or suffer anything than return to my former course of carelessness. I thought my convictions were all gone and that seemed dreadful. But I thought I could but go to hell, and that I had no sense of, nor could make it appear dreadful as formerly. Indeed I seemed to feel wholly destitute of any happiness or hopes and expectations of happiness either in the present or coming world, and yet felt no considerable degree of misery sensibly though I felt indeed something so far bordering on despair of any satisfying good that it appeared almost as comfortable to think of being annihilated as anything that I then knew of, though I can truly say I was not willing for that neither. My whole soul was unspeakably bewildered and lost in myself and I knew of nothing that seemed likely to make me happy, in case I could with the greatest ease have obtained the best good that I had any conception of. And being that lost I became a suitable object for the compassion of Jesus Christ to be set upon, since he came "to seek and to save that which is lost" (Luke 19:10). (pp.131–33)

Only in retrospect did he see himself as a "suitable object for the compassion of Jesus Christ." But in the hour of darkness there was no sense of hope or love or fear. This is the most fearful side of depression, since the natural restraints on suicide begin to vanish. But, unlike William Cowper, Brainerd was spared the suicidal drive. His wishes for death were all restrained within the bounds of the biblical truth, "The Lord gave and the Lord has taken away" (Job 1:21). He wishes for death many times, but only that God would take him (pp. 172, 183, 187, 215, 249 for example).

It caused him compounded misery when he thought how much his mental distress hindered his ministry and his devotion. Wednesday, March 9, 1743: "Rode 16 miles to Montauk, and had some inward sweetness on the road, but something of flatness and deadness after I came there and had seen the Indians: I withdrew and endeavored to pray, but found myself awfully deserted and left, and had an afflicting sense of my vileness and meanness" (p. 199).

At times he was simply immobilized by the distresses and couldn't function anymore. Tuesday, September 2, 1746: "Was scarce ever more confounded with a sense of my own unfruitfulness and unfitness of my work, than now. Oh, what a dead, heartless, barren, unprofitable wretch did I now see myself to be! My spirits were so low, and my bodily strength so wasted, that I could do nothing at all. At length, being much overdone, lay down on a buffalo skin; but sweat much of the whole night" (pp. 423ff.).

It is simply amazing how often Brainerd pressed on with the practical necessities of his work in the face of these waves of discouragement. This has no doubt endeared him to many missionaries who know first-hand the kinds of pain he endured.

Brainerd Struggled with Loneliness

He tells of having to endure the profane talk of two strangers one night in April 1743 and says, "Oh, I longed that some dear Christian knew my distress!" (p. 204). A month later he says, "Most of the talk I hear is either Highland Scotch or Indian. I have no fellow Christian to whom I might unbosom myself and lay open my spiritual sorrows, and with whom I might take sweet counsel in conversation about heavenly things, and join in social prayer" (p. 207). This misery made him sometimes shrink back from going off on another venture. Tuesday, May 8, 1744: "My heart sometimes was ready to sink with the thoughts of my work, and going alone in the wilderness, I knew not where" (p. 248).

In December 1745, he wrote a letter to his friend Eleazar Wheelock and said, "I doubt not by that time you have read my journal through you'll be more sensible of the need I stand in of a companion in travel than ever you was [sic] before" (p. 584). But he didn't just want any kind of person, of course. He wanted a soul companion. Many of us can empathize with him when he says, "There are many with whom I can talk about religion: but alas, I find few with whom I can talk religion itself: But, blessed be the Lord, there are some that love to feed on the kernel rather than the shell" (p. 292).

But Brainerd was alone in his ministry to the end. During the last nineteen weeks of his life, Jerusha Edwards, Jonathan Edwards's seventeen-year-old daughter, was his nurse, and many speculate that there was deep (even romantic) love between them. But in the wilderness and in the ministry he was alone and could only pour out his soul to God. And God bore him and kept him going.

Brainerd Struggled with Immense External Hardships

He describes his first mission station at Kaunaumeek in May 1743: "I live poorly with regard to the comforts of life: most of my diet consists of boiled corn, hasty pudding, etc. I lodge on a bundle of straw, and my labor is hard and extremely difficult; and I have little experience of success to comfort me" (p. 207). In August he says, "In this weak state of body, [I] was not a little distressed for want of suitable food. Had no bread, nor could I get any. I am forced to go or send ten or fifteen miles for all the bread I eat; and sometimes 'tis moldy and sour before I eat it, if I get any considerable quantity. . . . But through divine goodness I had some Indian meal, of which I made little cakes and fried them. Yet felt contented with my circumstances, and sweetly resigned to God" (pp. 213–14).

He says that he was frequently lost in the woods and was exposed to cold and hunger (p. 222). He speaks of his horse being stolen or being poisoned or having a broken leg (pp. 294, 339). He tells about how the smoke from a fireplace would often make the room intolerable to his lungs and he would have to go out into the cold to get his breath, and then could not sleep through the night (p. 422).

But the battle with external hardships, as great as they were, was not his worst struggle. He had an amazing resignation and even rest, it seems, in many of these circumstances. He knew where they fit in his biblical approach to life:

> Such fatigues and hardship as these serve to wean me more from the earth; and, I trust, will make heaven the sweeter. Formerly, when I was thus exposed to cold, rain, etc., I was ready to please myself with the thoughts of enjoying a comfortable house, a warm fire, and other outward comforts; but now these have less place in my heart (through the grace of God) and my eye is more to God for comfort. In this world I expect tribulation; and it does not now, as formerly, appear strange to me; I don't in such seasons of difficulty flatter myself that it will be better hereafter; but rather think how much worse it might be; how much greater trials others of God's children have endured; and how much greater are yet perhaps reserved for me. Blessed be God that he makes [is] the comfort to me, under my sharpest trials; and scarce ever lets these thoughts be attended with terror or melancholy; but they are attended frequently with great joy. (p. 274)

So in spite of the terrible external hardships that Brainerd knew, he pressed on and even flourished under these tribulations that led to the weight of glory in the kingdom of God.

Brainerd Struggled with a Bleak Outlook on Nature

We will forgive him for this quickly because few of us have suffered physically what he suffered or endured the hardships he did in the wilderness. It is hard to relish the beauty of a rose when you are coughing up blood.

But we have to see this as part of Brainerd's struggle, because an eye for beauty instead of bleakness might have lightened some of his load. Edwards extolled Brainerd for not being a person of "warm imagination" (p. 93). This was a virtue for Edwards because it meant that Brainerd was free from what he called religious "enthusiasm"—the intensity of religious emotion based on sudden impressions and sights in the imagination rather than on spiritual apprehension of God's moral perfections. So Edwards applauded Brainerd for not having "strong and lively images formed in his imagination" (p. 93).

But there is a costly downside to an unimaginative mind. In Brainerd's case, it meant that he seemed to see nothing in nature but a "howling wilderness" and a bleak enemy. There was nothing in his diaries like the transports of Jonathan Edwards as he walked in the woods and saw images of divine glory and echoes of God's excellence everywhere. In his *Personal Narrative*, Edwards tells us of several early experiences not long after his teenage awakening that reveal the kind of seeing heart he had in regard to the beauties of nature.

> I walked abroad alone, in a solitary place in my father's pasture, for contemplation. And as I was walking there, and looking up on the sky and clouds, there came into my mind so sweet a sense of the glorious *majesty* and *grace* of God, that I know not how to express. I seemed to see them both in a sweet conjunction; majesty and meekness joined together: it was a sweet and gentle, and holy majesty; and also a majestic meekness; an awful sweetness; a high, and great, and holy gentleness.
>
> The appearance of everything was altered; there seemed to be, as it were, a calm, sweet cast, or appearance of divine glory, in almost everything. God's excellency, his wisdom, his purity and love, seemed to appear in everything; in the sun, and moon, and stars; in the clouds and blue sky; in the grass, flowers, trees; in the water, and all nature; which used greatly to fix my mind. I often used to sit and view the moon for a long time; and in the day, spent much time in viewing the clouds and sky, to behold the sweet glory of God in these things; in the meantime, singing forth, with a low voice, my contemplations of the Creator and Redeemer.[3]

Norman Pettit is right, it seems to me, when he says,

> Where Edwards saw mountains and waste places as the setting for divine disclosure, Brainerd saw only a "howling desert." Where Edwards could take spiritual delight "in the sun, moon, and stars; in the clouds, and blue sky; in the grass, flowers, trees," Brainerd never mentioned natural beauty. In contrast to Edwards' joy in summer is Brainerd's fear of winter. (p. 23)

Brainerd never mentioned an attractive landscape or sunset. He did at one place say he had discovered the need for diversions in his labor for the sake of maximizing his usefulness (p. 292). But he never once described such a diversion or any impact that it had on him.

It is a sad thing that Brainerd was blinded (perhaps by his own suffering[4]) to one of God's antidotes to depression. Charles Spurgeon, the

---

[3] Jonathan Edwards, *Personal Narrative*, in *Jonathan Edwards: Selections*, ed. Clarence H. Faust and Thomas H. Johnson (New York: Hill and Wang, 1962), 60–61.

[4] Clyde Kilby laments Brainerd's "defection from Scripture itself" in his seeming total disregard of the heavens and the earth as the handiwork of God. In the more than six hundred pages of the *Diary* and *Journal* there are fewer than a half-dozen instances in which the very suggestion of any regard for natural beauty occurs. . . . So far as the record shows, never once did a bird's song pierce his ear as it did King Solomon's,

great British preacher and pastor from the late 1800s who knew his own share of discouragement and depression, described this God-given remedy for melancholy that Brainerd seemed unable to taste:

> Nature . . . is calling him to health and beckoning him to joy. He who forgets the humming of the bees among the heather, the cooing of the wood-pigeons in the forest, the song of birds in the woods, the rippling of rills among the rushes, and the sighing of the wind among the pines, needs not wonder if his heart forgets to sing and his soul grows heavy. A day's breathing of fresh air upon the hills, or a few hours' ramble in the beech woods' umbrageous calm, would sweep the cobwebs out of the brain of scores of our toiling ministers who are not but half alive. A mouthful of sea air, or a stiff walk in the wind's face, would not give grace to the soul, but it would yield oxygen to the body, which is next best. . . . For lack of opportunity, or inclination, these great remedies are neglected, and the student becomes a self-immolated victim.[5]

I say again, we will forgive Brainerd quickly for not drawing strength and refreshment from God's gallery of joy, because his suffering made it so hard for him to see. But we must make every effort not to succumb with him here. Spurgeon and Edwards are the models for us on spiritual uses of nature. And, of course, an even greater authority said, "Consider the lilies" (Matt. 6:28 KJV).

Brainerd Struggled to Love the Indians

If love is known by sacrifice, then Brainerd loved immensely. But if it is also known by heartfelt compassion, then Brainerd struggled to love more than he did. Sometimes he was melted with love. September 18, 1742: "Felt some compassion for souls, and mourned I had no more. I feel much more kindness, meekness, gentleness and love towards all mankind, than ever" (p. 181). December 26, 1742: "Felt much

---

and never once did Brainerd feel, like King David, the tenderness of still waters and green pastures. Never once is it evident that, like Christ, he observed the lilies of the field.

And Kilby will not allow that Brainerd's ill health is a sufficient explanation for this defect:

> To be sure, Brainerd's experience was not that of a man who goes for an outing in nature. He knew what it meant to be lost at night in the forest (but for that matter so did John Wesley) and to hear the wolves howling around him. The wilderness was for him an enemy to be overcome. Brainerd's antipathy to mountains cannot be accounted for on the ground of his ill health, for he had unusually good health on his first visit to the frontier over the Blue Mountains and through the lovely Lehigh Gap, yet it was nothing more than "a hideous and howling wilderness" to him. (Clyde Kilby, "David Brainerd: Knight of the Grail," in *Heroic Colonial Christians*, ed. Russell T. Hitt [Philadelphia: Lippincott, 1966], 182–83)

[5] Charles Spurgeon, *Lectures to My Students* (Grand Rapids, MI: Zondervan, 1972), 158.

sweetness and tenderness in prayer, especially my whole soul seemed to love my worst enemies, and was enabled to pray for those that are strangers and enemies to God with a great degree of softness and pathetic fervor" (p. 193). Tuesday, July 2, 1745: "Felt my heart drawn out after God in prayer, almost all the forenoon; especially while riding. And in the evening, could not help crying to God for those poor Indians; and after I went to bed my heart continued to go out to God for them, till I dropped asleep. Oh, 'Blessed be God that I may pray!'" (p. 302).

But other times he seemed empty of affection or compassion for their souls. He expresses guilt that he should preach to immortal souls with no more ardency and so little desire for their salvation (p. 235). His compassion could simply go flat. November 2, 1744: "About noon, rode up to the Indians; and while going, could feel no desires for them, and even dreaded to say anything to 'em" (p. 272). So Brainerd struggled with the rise and fall of love in his own heart. He loved, but longed to love so much more.

Brainerd Struggled to Stay True to His Calling

Even though Brainerd's expulsion from Yale initially hindered his entering the pastorate and turned him to consider the missionary career, the missionary call he felt from the Lord in this was not abandoned when other opportunities for the pastorate finally did come along. There were several opportunities for him to have a much easier life in the settled life of the parish minister.

The church at Millington, near his hometown of Haddam, called him in March 1744, and he describes the call as a great care and burden. He turned it down and prayed that the Lord would send laborers to his vineyard (p. 244). The church at East Hampton on Long Island called him too. Jonathan Edwards called this "the fairest, pleasantest town on the whole island, and one of its largest and most wealthy parishes" (p. 245n8). Brainerd wrote on Thursday, April 5: "Resolved to go on still with the Indian affair, if divine providence permitted; although before felt some inclination to go to East Hampton, where I was solicited to go" (p. 245).

There were other opportunities too. But each time the struggle was resolved with this sense of burden and call: "[I] could have no freedom in the thought of any other circumstances or business in life: All my desire was the conversion of the heathen, and all my hope was in God: God does not suffer me to please or comfort myself with hopes of seeing friends, returning to my dear acquaintance, and enjoying worldly comforts" (p. 263). So the struggle was obviously there, but he was held to his post by a readiness to suffer and a passion to see the kingdom of Christ spread among the Indians.

A Passion to Finish Well

We turn now to how Brainerd responded to these struggles. What we are struck with immediately is that he pressed on. One of the main reasons Brainerd's life has such powerful effects on people is that in spite of all his struggles he never gave up his faith or his ministry. He was consumed with a passion to finish his race, and honor his Master, and spread the kingdom, and advance in personal holiness. It was this unswerving allegiance to the cause of Christ that makes the bleakness of his life glow with glory so that we can understand Henry Martyn when he wrote, as a student in Cambridge in 1802, "I long to be like him!" (p. 4).

There is something that captures the soul when we see a man of single-minded passion persevering against all odds, finishing his course no matter the cost. The spirit of Jesus, when he set his face like flint to go to Jerusalem (Luke 9:51, 53), runs through the generations of all his most inspiring followers. Does not our spine tingle with longing to be radically devoted to Christ when we read, for example, Paul's determined purpose that puts submission above security: "I do not account my life of any value nor as precious to myself, if only I may accomplish my course and the ministry which I received from the Lord Jesus, to testify to the gospel of the grace of God!" (Acts 20:24 RSV). Single-minded devotion, which makes all else die away, captures the heart and makes us long, with Thomas, to follow no matter what: "Let us also go, so that we may die with Him" (John 11:16).

Clyde Kilby attributed Brainerd's influence to this kind of inspiration.

> It is not Brainerd's accomplishments as a missionary, significant as they were, that have perpetuated his influence. It certainly is not his perturbations of spirit or his sense of vileness or his flagellation "complex" or his morbidity. I venture to say that it is not even his diary so much as the *idea*

back of all which eventuated in molding the man. In our timidity and our shoddy opportunism we are always stirred when a man appears on the horizon willing to stake his all on a conviction.[6]

A Kind of "Pleasing Pain"

Brainerd's conviction was that no aspiration on earth surpassed the supreme purpose to savor and spread the reign of Christ in his own personal holiness and the conversion of the Indians for the glory of God. He called his passion for more holiness and more usefulness a kind of "pleasing pain." "When I really enjoy God, I feel my desires of him the more insatiable, and my thirstings after holiness the more unquenchable. . . . Oh, for holiness! Oh, for more of God in my soul! Oh, this pleasing pain! It makes my soul press after God. . . . Oh, that I might never loiter on my heavenly journey!" (p. 186).

He was gripped by the apostolic admonition: "Walk circumspectly . . . redeeming the time, because the days are evil" (Eph. 5:15–16 KJV). He embodied the counsel: "Let us not be weary in well doing, for in due season we shall reap, if we faint not" (Gal. 6:9 KJV). He strove to be, as Paul says, "abounding in the work of the Lord" (1 Cor. 15:58). April 17, 1747: "O I longed to fill the remaining moments all for God! Though my body was so feeble, and wearied with preaching and much private conversation, yet I wanted to sit up all night to do something for God. To God the giver of these refreshments, be glory forever and ever; Amen" (p. 246). February 21, 1746: "My soul was refreshed and comforted, and I could not but bless God, who had enabled me in some good measure to be faithful in the day past. Oh, how sweet it is to be spent and worn out for God!" (p. 366).

"In Prayer . . . Ineffable Comforts into My Soul"

Among all the means that Brainerd used for pursuing greater and greater holiness and usefulness, prayer and fasting stand out above all. We read of him spending whole days in prayer. Wednesday, June 30, 1742: "Spent almost the whole day in prayer incessantly" (p. 172). Sometimes he set aside as many as six periods in the day to pray: "Blessed be God, I had much freedom five or six times in the day, in prayer and praise, and felt a weighty concern upon my spirit for the salvation of those

---

[6] Kilby, "David Brainerd: Knight of the Grail," 202.

precious souls and the enlargement of the Redeemer's kingdom among them" (p. 280).

Sometimes he would seek out a family or friend to pray with. He prayed for his own sanctification. He prayed for the conversion and purity of his Indians. He prayed for the advancement of the kingdom of Christ around the world and especially in America. Sometimes the spirit of prayer would hold him so deeply that he could scarcely stop.

These were some of the sweetest times for Brainerd, and he writes of them in ways that make the saint's heart hunger for God:

> Retired pretty early for secret devotions; and in prayer God was pleased to pour such ineffable comforts into my soul that I could do nothing for some time but say over and over, "O my sweet Saviour! O my sweet Saviour!" "Whom have I in heaven but thee? and there is none upon earth, that I desire beside thee" [Ps. 73:25]. If I had a thousand lives my soul would gladly have laid 'em all down at once to have been with Christ. My soul never enjoyed so much of heaven before. 'Twas the most refined and most spiritual season of communion with God I ever yet felt. I never felt so great a degree of resignation in my life. (pp. 164–65)

Once, visiting in a home with friends in May 1746, he got alone to pray:

> I continued wrestling with God in prayer for my dear little flock here; and more especially for the Indians elsewhere; as well as for dear friends in one place and another; till it was bed time and I feared I should hinder the family, etc. But oh, with what reluctancy did I find myself obliged to consume time in sleep! (p. 402)

A Birthday with No Cake, No Food

And along with prayer, Brainerd pursued holiness and usefulness with fasting. Again and again in his diary he tells of days spent in fasting. One of the most remarkable, in view of how most of us celebrate our birthdays, is the fast on his twenty-fifth birthday:

> Wednesday, April 20. Set apart this day for fasting and prayer, to bow my soul before God for the bestowment of divine grace; especially that all my spiritual afflictions and inward distresses might be sanctified to my soul. And endeavored also to remember the goodness of God to me the year past, this day being my birthday. Having obtained help of God, I have hitherto lived and am now arrived at the age of twenty-five years. My soul was pained

to think of my barrenness and deadness; that I have lived so little to the glory of the eternal God. I spent the day in the woods alone, and there poured out my complaint to God. Oh, that God would enable me to live to His glory for the future! (p. 205)

He fasted for guidance when he was perplexed about the next steps of his ministry. Monday, April 19, 1742: "I set apart this day for fasting and prayer to God for his grace, especially to prepare me for the work of the ministry, to give me divine aid and direction in my preparations for that great work, and in his own time to 'Send me into his harvest' [Matt. 9:38; Luke 10:2]" (p. 162). And he fasted simply with the hope of making greater advances in his own spiritual life and holiness. Thursday, February 9, 1744: "Observed this day as a day of fasting and prayer, entreating of God to bestow upon me his blessing and grace; especially to enable me to live a life of mortification to the world, as well as of resignation and patience" (p. 238).

When he was dying in Jonathan Edwards's house, he urged young ministers who came to see him to engage in frequent days of private prayer and fasting because of how useful it was (p. 473). Edwards himself said, "Among all the many days [Brainerd] spent in secret fasting and prayer and that he gives an account of in his diary, there is scarce an instance of one but what was either attended or soon followed with apparent success and a remarkable blessing in special incomes and consolations of God's Spirit; and very often before the day was ended" (p. 531).

"Studied Closely, till I Felt My Bodily Strength Fail"

Along with prayer and fasting, Brainerd bought up the time with study and mingled all three of these together. December 20, 1745: "I spent much of the day in writing; but was enabled to intermix prayer with my studies" (p. 280). January 7, 1744: "Spent this day in seriousness, with steadfast resolutions for God and a life of mortification. Studied closely, till I felt my bodily strength fail" (p. 234). December 20, 1742: "Spent this day in prayer, reading and writing; and enjoyed some assistance, especially in correcting some thoughts on a certain subject" (p. 192).

He was constantly writing and thinking about theological things. That's why we have the *Diaries* and *Journal*! But there was more. We frequently read things like, "Was most of the day employed in writing on a divine subject. Was frequent in prayer" (p. 240). "I spent most of the time in writing on a sweet divine subject" (p. 284). "Was engaged in writing again almost the whole day" (p. 287). "Rose early and wrote by candlelight some considerable time; spent most of the day in writing" (p. 344). "Towards night, enjoyed some of the clearest thoughts on a divine subject . . . that ever I remember to have had upon any subject whatsoever; and spent two or three hours in writing them" (p. 359).

Writing on a "Divine Subject . . . So Sweet an Entertainment"

Why all this writing? There are at least two reasons why Brainerd and why I and many others count writing an essential part of our spiritual life—not just ministerial life, but spiritual life. First, it brings clarity to the mind about great matters that we are reading or thinking about. Second, it intensifies the affections that are kindled by the clear and solid sight of great truth. Brainerd mentions both of these motivations in the entry from February 1, 1746:

> Towards night, enjoyed some of the clearest thoughts on a divine subject (viz., that treated of 1 Cor. 15:13–16) that ever I remember to have had upon any subject whatsoever; and spent two or three hours in writing them. I was refreshed with the intenseness: My mind was so engaged in these medita-tions I could scarcely turn it to anything else; and indeed I could not be willing to part with so sweet an entertainment. (p. 359)

"An Habitual Vision of Greatness"

Just at this point Brainerd is so needed by our breezy culture. His meditations and writing were continually about "divine subjects." His thought and writing were marked by what he called "intenseness." Our day is marked, on the contrary, by small subjects and casual treatments. Richard Foster lamented this in 1996 with these words:

> I am concerned that our reading and our writing is gravitating to the lowest common denominator so completely that the great themes of majesty and nobility and felicity are made to seem trite, puny, pedestrian. . . . In reality I am concerned about the state of the soul in the midst of all the cheap sen-sory overload going on today. You see, without what Alfred North Whitehead called "an habitual vision of greatness," our soul will shrivel up and lose the capacity for beauty and mystery and transcendence. . . . In this day and age having nothing at all to say does not disqualify a person from writing a

book. The sad truth is that many authors simply have never learned to reflect substantively on anything.[7]

Brainerd's prayer, his meditation, his writing, and his whole life are one sustained indictment of our trivial time and culture—even much Christian culture. So much was at stake for Brainerd! He exemplified what Foster exhorted: "Give sustained attention to the great themes of the human spirit—life and death, transcendence, the problem of evil, the human predicament, the greatness of rightness, and much more."[8] Brainerd did this, not out of concern for sustaining the greatness of his own soul, but out of passion for the greatness of God in Christ and the tragedy of unreached Indians entering eternity without a saving knowledge of this God. Therefore his life was one long, agonizing strain to be "redeeming the time" (Eph. 5:16 KJV) and "not be weary in well doing" (Gal. 6:9 KJV) and "abounding in the work of the Lord" (1 Cor. 15:58). And what makes his life so powerful is that he pressed on in this passion under the immense struggles and hardships that he faced.

The Fruit of Brainerd's Affliction

We turn finally to the question, What was the fruit of Brainerd's affliction? First, I would mention the effect of Brainerd's life on Jonathan Edwards, the great pastor and theologian of Northampton, Massachusetts, in whose house Brainerd died at the age of twenty-nine. Edwards bears his own testimony:

> I would not conclude my observations on the merciful circumstances of Mr. Brainerd's death without acknowledging with thankfulness the gracious dispensation of Providence to me and my family in so ordering that he . . . should be cast hither to my house, in his last sickness, and should die here: So that we had opportunity for much acquaintance and conversation with him, and to show him kindness in such circumstances, and to see his dying behavior, to hear his dying speeches, to receive his dying counsel, and to have the benefit of his dying prayers. (p. 541)

Edwards said this even though he must have known it probably cost him the life of his eighteen-year-old daughter to have had Brainerd in

---

[7] Richard Foster, "Heart to Heart: A Pastoral Letter from Richard J. Foster, November, 1996," *Renovaré* (1996): 1.
[8] Ibid.

his house with that terrible disease. Jerusha had tended to Brainerd as a nurse for the last nineteen weeks of his life, and four months after he died, she died of the same affliction on February 14, 1748. Edwards wrote:

> It has pleased a holy and sovereign God, to take away this my dear child by death, on the 14th of February . . . after a short illness of five days, in the 18th year of her age. She was a person of much the same spirit with Brainerd. She had constantly taken care of and attended him in this sickness, for nineteen weeks before his death; devoting herself to it with great delight, because she looked on him as an eminent servant of Jesus Christ.[9]

So Edwards really meant what he said, that it was a "gracious dispensation of Providence" that Brainerd came to his house to die. He said it with full awareness of the cost.

A Pebble Dropped in the Sea of History

As a result of the immense impact of Brainerd's devotion on his life, Jonathan Edwards wrote, in the next two years, *The Life of David Brainerd*, which has been reprinted more often than any of his other books. And through this *Life*, the impact of Brainerd on the church has been incalculable. Beyond all the famous missionaries who tell us that they have been sustained and inspired by Brainerd's *Life*,[10] how many countless other unknown faithful servants must there be who have found from Brainerd's testimony the encouragement and strength to press on!

It is an inspiring thought that one small pebble dropped in the sea of history can produce waves of grace that break on distant shores hundreds of years later and thousands of miles away. Robert Glover ponders this thought with wonder when he writes,

> It was Brainerd's holy life that influenced Henry Martyn to become a missionary and was a prime factor in William Carey's inspiration. Carey in turn moved Adoniram Judson. And so we trace the spiritual lineage from step to step—Hus, Wycliffe, Francke, Zinzendorf, the Wesleys and Whitefield,

---

[9] Sereno Dwight, *Memoirs of Jonathan Edwards*, in *The Works of Jonathan Edwards*, ed. Edward Hickman, 2 vols. (Edinburgh: Banner of Truth, 1974), 1:xciv.
[10] For extended lists, see Kilby, "David Brainerd: Knight of the Grail," 197–203; John Thornbury, *David Brainerd: Pioneer Missionary to the American Indians* (Durham: Evangelical Press, 1996), 298–300; and Norman Pettit, editor's introduction to Edwards, *The Life of David Brainerd*, 3–4.

Brainerd, Edwards, Carey, Judson, and ever onward in the true apostolic
succession of spiritual grace and power and world-wide ministry.[11]

The Ironic Fruit of Failure

A lesser-known effect of Brainerd's life, and one that owes far more
to the gracious providence of God than to any intention on Brainerd's
part, was the founding of Princeton College and Dartmouth College.
Jonathan Dickinson and Aaron Burr, who were Princeton's first leaders
and among its founders, took direct interest in Brainerd's case at Yale
and were extremely upset that the school would not readmit him. This
event brought to a head the dissatisfaction that the New York and New
Jersey Presbyterian Synods had with Yale and solidified the resolve to
found their own school. The College of New Jersey (later Princeton)
was chartered in October 1746. Dickinson was made the first president,
and when the classes began in his house in May 1747 in Elizabethtown,
Brainerd was there trying to recover his health in his last months. Thus
he is considered to be the first student enrolled. David Field and Archibald Alexander and others testify that in a real sense "Princeton
college was founded because of Brainerd's expulsion from Yale" (p. 55).

Another surprising effect of Brainerd's life is the inspiration he provided for the founding of Dartmouth College by Eleazar Wheelock.
Brainerd felt a failure among the Iroquois Indians on the Susquehanna.
He labored among them for a year or so and then moved on. But his
diary of the time kindled the commitment of Wheelock to go to the
Iroquois of Connecticut. And inspired by Brainerd's example in teaching the Indians, he founded in 1748 a school for Indians and whites
at Lebanon. Later it was moved to Hanover, New Hampshire, where
Wheelock founded Dartmouth College (p. 62).

In 1740 Yale, Harvard, and William and Mary were the only Colonial colleges, and they were not sympathetic to the evangelical piety
of the Great Awakening. But the tide of Awakening brought in a zeal
for education as well as piety, and the Presbyterians founded Princeton,
the Baptists founded Brown, the Dutch Reformed founded Rutgers, and
the Congregationalists founded Dartmouth. It is remarkable that David
Brainerd must be reckoned as an essential motivational component in
the founding of two of those schools. If he was a somewhat frustrated

---

[11] Robert Glover, *The Progress of World-Wide Missions* (orig. 1924; New York: Harper and Row, 1952), 56.

scholar, thinking and writing by candlelight in the wilderness,[12] his vision for evangelical higher education had a greater fulfillment probably than if he had given his life to that cause instead of to the missionary passion that he felt.

Who Can Measure the Worth of a Worshiping Soul?

I close by stating that the most lasting and significant effect of Brainerd's ministry is the same as the most lasting and significant effect of every pastor's ministry. There are a few Indians—perhaps several hundred—who, now and for eternity, owe their everlasting life to the direct love and ministry of David Brainerd. Some of their stories would make another chapter—a very inspiring one. Who can describe the value of one soul transferred from the kingdom of darkness, and from the weeping and gnashing of teeth, to the kingdom of God's dear Son! If we live twenty-nine years or if we live ninety-nine years, would not any hardships be worth the saving of one person from the eternal torments of hell for the everlasting enjoyment of the glory of God?

My last word must be the same as Jonathan Edwards's. I thank God for the ministry of David Brainerd in my own life—the passion for prayer, the spiritual feast of fasting, the sweetness of the Word of God, the unremitting perseverance through hardship, the relentless focus on the glory of God, the utter dependence on grace, the final resting in the righteousness of Christ, the pursuit of perishing sinners, the holiness while suffering, the fixing of the mind on what is eternal, and finishing well without cursing the disease that cut him down at twenty-nine. With all his weaknesses and imbalances and sins, I love David Brainerd.

Perhaps his habit of writing is part of the reason I have continued to keep a journal over the past thirty-four years. From that journal—weak and worldly compared to Brainerd's—I recall that on June 28, 1986, my longtime associate and friend Tom Steller and his wife, Julie, and I visited Northampton, Massachusetts, in search of Brainerd's grave. I wrote:

> This afternoon Tom and Julie and I drove to Northampton. We found the gravestone of David Brainerd, a dark stone slab the size of the grave top and a smaller white marble inset in the slab with these words:

---

[12] Saturday, December 14: "Rose early and wrote by candlelight some considerable time" (p. 344).

Sacred to the memory of the
Rev. David Brainerd. A faithful and
laborious missionary to the
Stockbridge, Delaware and Susquehanna
Tribes of Indians who
died in this town. October 10, 1747 AE 32[13]

Tom and Julie (and their daughters Ruth and Hannah) and I took hands
and stood around the grave and prayed to thank God for Brainerd and Jonathan Edwards and to dedicate ourselves to their work and their God. It was
a memorable, and I hope, powerful and lasting moment.

Our prayer was then, and is now, that God would grant us a persevering grace to spread a passion for the supremacy of God in all
things for the joy of all peoples. Life is too precious to squander on
trivial things. Grant us, Lord, the unswerving resolve to pray and live
with David Brainerd's urgency: "Oh, that I might never loiter on my
heavenly journey!"

---

[13] Both these final facts are inaccurate: he died October 9 at the age of 29.

Jesus also suffered outside the gate in order to sanctify the people through his own blood. Therefore let us go forth to him outside the camp, and bear the abuse he endured. For here we have no lasting city, but we seek the city which is to come.

Hebrews 13:12–14 RSV

Conclusion

A Plea to Follow in the Fruitful Wake of the Suffering Swans

Ten thousand effects follow from every motion of your hand. The hidden mysteries of the chain of causation in the physical world is enough to hold us with amazement. How much more the ripple effect in the realm of persons and spirits! Clyde Kilby, who taught English literature at Wheaton College, pondered this in relation to David Brainerd and marveled:

> The pebble falling into the pond sends its waves onward until they are invisible, and yet in the mystery of the physical world, never end. If William Carey is stirred by David Brainerd, and if then John Newton, the great hymn writer, says that Carey is more to him than "bishop or archbishop: he is an apostle!" it is obvious that the waves are in motion. Or again if Adoniram Judson is inspired toward missionary labors in Burma through Carey, it is evident that the waves go onward.[1]

If William Cowper creates a cadence and a rhyme and a vision of reality on some dark day two hundred years ago, and then a broken-hearted church today sings "God Moves in a Mysterious Way" and hope awakens, the waves go on. If John Bunyan bends down and kisses his blind daughter, then walks back to his prison cell and writes a story that three centuries later, in Chinese, gives courage to an underground house-church pastor, the waves go on. How great are the wonders laid up for us in the God-wrought, sovereign sequences of history! "How

---

[1] Clyde Kilby, "David Brainerd: Knight of the Grail," *Heroic Colonial Christians*, ed. Russell T. Hitt (Philadelphia: Lippincott, 1966), 201–2.

unsearchable are his judgments and how inscrutable his ways!" (Rom. 11:33 ESV).

The afflictions of John Bunyan and William Cowper and David Brainerd were not for naught. The pebbles did not drop in vain—neither in their own lifetimes, nor in the centuries to follow. God has breathed on the waters and made their ripples into waves. And now the parched places of our lives are watered with the memories of sustaining grace.

The Christian Life Is Hill Difficulty

Bunyan's life and labor call us to live like Pilgrim on the way to the Celestial City. His suffering and his story summon us, in the prosperous and pleasure-addicted West, to see the Christian life in a radically different way than we ordinarily do. There is a great gulf between the Christianity that wrestles with whether to worship at the cost of imprisonment and death, and the Christianity that wrestles with whether the kids should play soccer on Sunday morning. The full title of *The Pilgrim's Progress* shows the essence of the pilgrim path: "The Pilgrim's Progress from this World, to that Which is to Come: Delivered under the Similitude of a Dream wherein Is Discovered, the Manner of His Setting out, his Dangerous Journey, and Safe Arrival at the Desired Country." For Bunyan, in fact and fiction, the Christian life is a "Dangerous Journey."

The narrow way leads from the Wicket Gate to the Hill Difficulty.

> The narrow way lay right up the hill, and the name of the going up the side of the hill is called *Difficulty*. Christian now went to the Spring, and drank thereof, to refresh himself (Isaiah 49:10), and then began to go up the Hill, saying,
>
> > The Hill, though high, I covet to ascend,
> > The Difficulty will not me offend;
> > For I perceive the Way to life lies here.
> > Come, pluck up Heart, let's neither faint nor fear;
> > Better, though difficult, the Right Way to go,
> > Than wrong, though easy, where the End is Woe.[2]

This is the Christian life for Bunyan—experienced in prison and explained in parables. But we modern, Western Christians have come

---

[2] John Bunyan, *The Pilgrim's Progress* (Uhrichsville, OH: Barbour and Company, 1990), 40.

to see safety and ease as a right. We move away from bad neighborhoods. We leave hard relationships. We don't go to dangerous, unreached people groups.

Bunyan beckons us to listen to Jesus and his apostles again. Jesus never called us to a life of safety, nor even to a fair fight. "Lambs in the midst of wolves" is the way he describes our sending (Luke 10:3). "If they have called the head of the house Beelzebul, how much more will they malign the members of his household!" (Matt. 10:25). "He who loves his life loses it, and he who hates his life in this world will keep it to life eternal" (John 12:25). "Whoever of you does not renounce all that he has cannot be my disciple" (Luke 14:33 RSV).

The apostle Paul continues the same call: "Through many tribulations we must enter the kingdom of God" (Acts 14:22). We are "heirs of God and fellow heirs with Christ, if indeed we suffer with Him" (Rom. 8:17). We should not be "moved by . . . afflictions . . . [since] this is to be our lot" (1 Thess. 3:3 RSV). Faith and suffering are two great gifts of God: "To you it has been granted for Christ's sake, not only to believe in Him, but also to suffer for His sake" (Phil. 1:29). The apostle Peter confirms the theme: "Do not be surprised at the fiery ordeal among you, which comes upon you for your testing, as though some strange thing were happening to you" (1 Pet. 4:12). It isn't strange. It's normal. That is the message of *The Pilgrim's Progress*. The Hill Difficulty is the only path to heaven. There is no other. Suffering is as normal as a father disciplining a son. That is how the writer to the Hebrews describes the suffering of the saints: "God deals with you as with sons; for what son is there whom his father does not discipline? But if you are without discipline, of which all have become partakers, then you are illegitimate children and not sons" (Heb. 12:7–8). The pattern is rooted in the Old Testament itself. So the psalmist says, "Many are the afflictions of the righteous" (Ps. 34:19; see Gal. 4:29).

Oh, how we need Bunyan! We are soft and thin-skinned. We are worldly; we fit far too well into our God-ignoring culture. We are fearful and anxious and easily discouraged. We have taken our eyes off the Celestial City and the deep pleasures of knowing God and of denying ourselves the lesser things that titillate for a moment but then shrink our capacities for great joy. Bunyan's *Seasonable Counsel* for us is: Take up your cross daily and follow Jesus. "For whoever wishes to save his life will lose it; but whoever loses his life for My sake will find it" (Matt. 16:25).

Come, Wounded William Cowper, Teach Us How to Sing

The fruit of William Cowper's affliction is a call to free ourselves from trite and chipper worship. If the Christian life has become the path of ease and fun in the modern West, then corporate worship is the place of increasing entertainment. The problem is not a battle between contemporary worship music and hymns; the problem is that there aren't enough martyrs during the week. If no soldiers are perishing, what you want on Sunday is Bob Hope and some pretty girls, not the army chaplain and a surgeon.

Cowper was sick. But in his sickness he saw things that we so desperately need to see. He saw hell. And sometimes he saw heaven. He knew terror. And sometimes he knew ecstasy. When I stand to welcome the people to worship on Sunday morning, I know that there are William Cowpers in the congregation. There are spouses who can barely talk. There are sullen teenagers living double lives at home and school. There are widows who still feel the amputation of a fifty-year partner. There are single people who have not been hugged for twenty years. There are men in the prime of their lives with cancer. There are moms who have carried two tiny caskets. There are soldiers of the cross who have risked all for Jesus and bear the scars. There are tired and discouraged and lonely strugglers. Shall we come to them with a joke?

They can read the comics every day. What they need from me is not more bouncy, frisky smiles and stories. What they need is a kind of joyful earnestness that makes the broken heart feel hopeful and helps the ones who are drunk with trifles sober up for greater joys.

What William Cowper gives us from his suffering is a vision that sustains the suffering church. Until we suffer, we will not be interested. But that day is coming for all of us. And we do well not to wait until it comes before we learn the lessons of Cowper's great hymn "God Moves in a Mysterious Way":

> Ye fearful saints, fresh courage take,
> The clouds ye so much dread
> Are big with mercy, and shall break
> In blessings on your head.

Blind unbelief is sure to err,
And scan his work in vain:
God is his own interpreter,
And He will make it plain.

There is an entire theology of suffering in Cowper's hymns. It is sturdy and sound and redwood-like in the midst of our sapling sermonettes. Oh, how our people need to study and savor and sing the great God-centered truth of these verses! (For the entire hymn, see chapter 2.) How shall entertaining worship services—with the aim of feeling lighthearted and friendly—help a person prepare to suffer, let alone prepare to die? If we know how to suffer well, and if we feel that "to die is gain" because of Jesus, then we will know how to live well. We will know how to laugh—not mainly at jokes (which takes no more grace than a chair has) but at the future. "Strength and dignity are her clothing, and she laughs at the time to come" (Prov. 31:25 ESV).

Worship is the display of the surpassing worth of God revealed in Jesus Christ. Suffering in the path of Christian obedience, with joy— because the steadfast love of the Lord is better than life (Ps. 63:3)—is the clearest display of the worth of God in our lives. Therefore, faith-filled suffering is essential in this world for the most intense, authentic worship. When we are most satisfied with God in suffering, he will be most glorified in us in worship. Our problem is not styles of music. Our problem is styles of life. When we embrace more affliction for the worth of Christ, there will be more fruit in the worship of Christ.

Oh, come, wounded William Cowper, and feed us on the fruit of your affliction. Teach us to study, savor, and sing your sacred songs of suffering joy.

One Passion: The Salvation of Sinners for the Glory of God

When we have learned from John Bunyan that the path to life leads up Hill Difficulty, and from William Cowper that earnest, joyful worship is the fruit of affliction, then let us learn from David Brainerd that a life devoted to the glory of Christ is a life devoted to the Great Commission. The fruit of Brainerd's affliction was the salvation of hundreds of Indians and the inspiration of thousands of missionaries. His suffering is the sound of a trumpet over all the unreached peoples of the world, pealing out the word of Christ: "All authority in heaven and on earth has been given to me. Go therefore and make disciples of all nations" (Matt. 28:18–19 ESV).

His suffering extends the shadow of the cross into our lives and bids us ask if we can say with Paul, "I am crucified with Christ" (Gal. 2:20 KJV). It echoes the single-minded passion of the apostle when he said, "I do not account my life of any value nor as precious to myself, if only I may accomplish my course and the ministry which I received from the Lord Jesus, to testify to the gospel of the grace of God" (Acts 20:24 RSV). It summons us from Calvary with the words of Hebrews 13:12–14, "Jesus also suffered outside the gate in order to sanctify the people through his own blood. Therefore let us go forth to him outside the camp, and bear the abuse he endured. For here we have no lasting city, but we seek the city which is to come" (RSV).

When you spend the last seven years of your life spitting up blood and die at age twenty-nine, you don't just say those words—"here we have no lasting city"—you feel them the way you feel the wind on a cliff's edge. Oh, how many feel the wind and run inland! The call of Christ and the call of Brainerd are exactly the opposite of such a retreat: Since we have no lasting city here, stop working so hard trying to make it lasting and luxurious, and "go forth to him outside the camp"— outside the safe place, outside the comfortable place. Yes, Golgotha is a bleak hill—a skull with a frown of affliction on its face. But remember: "Behind a frowning providence he hides a smiling face." Let go of what holds you back from full and radical service—be ready to suffer for finishing the Great Commission. Don't forget "that you have for yourselves a better possession and a lasting one" (Heb. 10:34). You have God—and all that he is for you in Jesus.

"You will make known to me the path of life; in Your presence is fullness of joy; in Your right hand there are pleasures forever" (Ps. 16:11). The path to everlasting joy in God leads up Hill Difficulty, with deep and joyful worship, into an unreached world of perishing sinners, where the repentance of one soul sets the angels of God to singing. This is a fruit of affliction that will last forever and multiply all your joys in Christ.

The Swans Are Not Silent

Book 3

The Roots of Endurance

*Invincible Perseverance in the Lives of
John Newton, Charles Simeon,
and William Wilberforce*

To
my grandfather
Elmer Albert Piper

who said,
when he was almost dead
and Daddy prayed for faith,
one word:
"Amen"

The Roots of Endurance

Book 3

Contents

A book by Richard Sibbes, one of the choicest of the Puritan writers, was read by Richard Baxter, who was greatly blessed by it. Baxter then wrote his *Call to the Unconverted* which deeply influenced Philip Doddridge, who in turn wrote *The Rise and Progress of Religion in the Soul*. This brought the young William Wilberforce, subsequent English statesman and foe of slavery, to serious thoughts of eternity. Wilberforce wrote his *Practical Book of Christianity* which fired the soul of Leigh Richmond. Richmond, in turn, wrote *The Dairyman's Daughter*, a book that brought thousands to the Lord, helping Thomas Chalmers the great preacher, among others.

Ernest Reisinger

"Every Christian a Publisher"

Preface

One reason "the swans are not silent" is that they all knew "the roots of endurance." Charles Simeon (1759–1836) endured as a faithful, evangelical, Anglican vicar for fifty-four years in one parish through opposition so severe that his "pewholding" parishioners boycotted his services during the first twelve years. William Wilberforce (1759–1833) endured as a faithful evangelical member of the British House of Commons, battling relentlessly for thirty years for the first triumph over the African slave trade in 1807, and another twenty-six years (three days before he died) to see slavery itself declared illegal. John Newton (1725–1807) was himself one of those African slave-trading captains, but was saved by "Amazing Grace"—to which he wrote the hymn—and became one of the roots of endurance that nourished both Simeon and Wilberforce in their trials.

Even if you have never heard of them, I urge you to get to know them. Together they are three of the healthiest, happiest, most influential[1] Christians of the latter eighteenth and early nineteenth centuries. My overwhelming impression, after seeing their lives woven together in preparation for this book, is the remarkable mental health they shared. Not that they were perfect or without dark seasons. But on the whole, they are extraordinary examples of deep and joyful maturity. Their

---

[1] The influence of Newton is symbolized by the almost universal use of the hymn "Amazing Grace," which he wrote. Wilberforce's influence is summed up in the glorious triumph over the African slave trade in England. Simeon is less known. But consider these two testimonies. Lord Macaulay, who had graduated from Cambridge in 1822 when Simeon was in his prime at Trinity Church in Cambridge, wrote in 1844, looking back on Simeon's entire influence, "As to Simeon, if you knew what his authority and influence were, and how they extended from Cambridge to the most remote corners of England, you would allow that his real sway over the Church was far greater than that of any Primate [bishop]" (Arthur J. Tait, *Charles Simeon and His Trust* [London: Society for Promoting Christian Knowledge, 1936], 58). And Charles Smyth wrote, "[Simeon,] more than any other, inspired and promoted the 'Evangelical Revival in the second and third generation of its course'" (quoted in Arthur Pollard, "The Influence and Significance of Simeon's Work," in *Charles Simeon (1759–1833): Essays Written in Commemoration of His Bi-Centenary by Members of the Evangelical Fellowship for Theological Literature*, ed. Arthur Pollard and Michael Hennell [London: SPCK, 1959], 181).

lives—as one person said of Wilberforce—were fatal not only to immorality but to dullness.[2] There was an invincible perseverance because there was invincible joy.

So the song of these three swans is worthy of the story that I tell here for the third time to explain the title of this series, The Swans Are Not Silent. St. Augustine, the bishop of Hippo in North Africa, retired in AD 430. He handed over his duties to his humble successor, Eraclius. At the ceremony, Eraclius stood to preach as the aged Augustine sat on his bishop's throne behind him. Overwhelmed by a sense of inadequacy in Augustine's presence, Eraclius said, "The cricket chirps, the swan is silent."[3] The assumption of this series of books is that he was wrong.

You are now reading Book Three in the series. Book One is *The Legacy of Sovereign Joy: God's Triumphant Grace in the Lives of Augustine, Luther, and Calvin* (Crossway, 2000), and Book Two is *The Hidden Smile of God: The Fruit of Affliction in the Lives of John Bunyan, William Cowper, and David Brainerd* (Crossway, 2001).

As in the first two books, each chapter here is based on a message that I gave at the annual Bethlehem Conference for Pastors, which this year (2002) marked its fifteenth anniversary. I choose the word "message" intentionally—not "sermons," since they are not expositions of Scripture, and not "lectures," because they are passionately personal and, at times, will taste like preaching. There is no attempt here at dispassionate distance from my subject matter. I have a goal, and it is not hidden. I long to endure to the end for the glory of Christ, and I want to help others do the same. I believe God has ordained the history of sustaining grace in the lives of his living and long-dead people as a means to that end. God-centered, Christ-exalting, Bible-saturated saints who have endured to the end are one of the roots of our own endurance.[4]

As I write this preface I have just preached to my people several

---

[2] See page 350.

[3] Peter Brown, *Augustine of Hippo* (Berkeley, CA: University of California Press, 1969), 408.

[4] There are enough academic remnants left in me to include even more of a disclaimer, and enough of the pastor in me to restrict it to a footnote and be unashamed: My historical efforts in these biographies lay claim to no comprehensiveness or originality of research. I lean heavily, but not totally, on secondary sources that I cite generously as a tribute and for verification. In search of God's providence and grace, I ransack the sources for evidences of what makes a person tick spiritually. So there are huge Christian assumptions that I bring to the task: for instance, that God exists and is involved in the lives of these men, and that the Bible is true and gives valid interpretations of experience, and so on. I do not give deep and broad attention to the wider historical setting and culture in which they lived. And the list of limitations could go on. The point is: I am a pastor reading and writing between sermon preparation, staff leadership, prayer meetings, building programs, church-planting efforts, and so forth. If academic historians say, "Farewell," I don't blame them. I only hope that what I write is true and helps people endure to the end.

messages in which I pleaded with them to be "coronary Christians," not "adrenal Christians." Not that adrenaline is bad, I said; it gets me through lots of Sundays. But it lets you down on Mondays. The heart is another kind of friend. It just keeps on serving—very quietly, through good days and bad days, happy and sad, high and low, appreciated and unappreciated. It never says, "I don't like your attitude, Piper; I'm taking a day off." It just keeps humbly lub-dubbing along. It endures the way adrenaline doesn't.

Coronary Christians are like the heart in the causes they serve. Adrenal Christians are like adrenaline—a spurt of energy and then fatigue. What we need in the cause of social justice (for example, against racism and abortion), and the cause of world missions (to plant churches among the unreached peoples of the world), and the cause of personal holiness and evangelism (to lead people to Christ and love them no matter what) is not spurts of energy but people who endure for the long haul. Marathoners, not sprinters.

I believe that reading about the lives of these three "coronary Christians" will help us endure to the end and finish well. Perhaps we will learn and experience what William Wilberforce discovered in his unwavering battle against the African slave trade: "I daily become more sensible that my work must be affected by constant and regular exertions rather than by sudden and violent ones."[5] May God be merciful in our day to multiply such coronary Christians for the cause of Christ and his kingdom.

---

[5] John Pollock, *Wilberforce* (London: Constable, 1977), 116.

Acknowledgments

For all the elders and ministers and support staff of Bethlehem Baptist Church, I give public thanks. What a gift they are to me! Carried on the wings of prayer day by day, I do my happy work. Yes, there are hard days and low seasons. But I say with Paul, "sorrowful, yet always rejoicing" (2 Cor. 6:10). And largely because of these praying, hard-working, ever-encouraging friends. I could not be a pastor at Bethlehem *and* write if it were not for them.

At Desiring God Ministries, Justin Taylor is the kind of theological assistant who comes into a life like Halley's comet, once every seventy-six years or so. I thank God that Justin's orbit passed through my solar system at such a time as this. Vicki Anderson absorbs a hundred things that would land on me weekly and make my writing impossible. I thank God for her administrative excellence to be there for me in relation to so many good people. And special thanks to Carol Steinbach and Tamika Burns for the text and person indexes. I know, Carol, that preparing indexes is not *special* after doing so many, but it was, for you, a special year. Life is hard and God is good.

The backbone of this book was formed in preparation for the Bethlehem Conference for Pastors. The human key to that conference is Jon Bloom. Without him, no conference. Without a conference, no book. So thanks again, Jon, for all the years of loving pastors with me.

Believing in this series and encouraging me along the way has been Lane Dennis, president of Crossway. Your friendship, Lane, is a precious gift to Noël and me. And speaking of Noël, she just read the whole manuscript in the last two days and made dozens of wise suggestions. So I do not tire of singing your praises, my good wife.

Finally, I thank God for my grandfather, Pastor Elmer Albert

Piper. I have dedicated the book to him. With no formal theological education, he could quote most of the New Testament by heart. "One generation shall commend your works to another, and shall declare your mighty acts" (Ps. 145:4). By grace, utter grace, I have good roots.

For you have need of endurance, so that when you have done the will of God you may receive what is promised.
Hebrews 10:36

Here is a call for the endurance of the saints, those who keep the commandments of God and their faith in Jesus.
Revelation 14:12

Have the full assurance of hope until the end, so that you may not be sluggish, but imitators of those who through faith and patience inherit the promises.
Hebrews 6:11–12

Introduction

The Biblical Roots of Endurance

Perhaps it's because I am in my mid-fifties as I write this, but whatever the reason, my mind defaults to thoughts about endurance these days. I want to finish well for the glory of Christ. I want to die well. But I have seen too much quitting and falling and failing to take anything for granted. "Let anyone who thinks that he stands take heed lest he fall" (1 Cor. 10:12).

But I don't think that's the main reason endurance returns so often to my mind. I think it is a combination of global anxiety and biblical urgency. We are unsettled by the world. It does not feel safe. It seems fragile and insecure. The twentieth century was a sequence of bloody nightmares from which we could not wake up—because we were not asleep.[1] The twenty-first century has begun with the shattering realization that there is no safe place on earth. Slowly, perhaps, many are wakening to the biblical view that "here we have no lasting city, but we seek the city that is to come" (Heb. 13:14); that this world does not offer a "kingdom that cannot be shaken" (Heb. 12:28); that we are "sojourners and exiles" (1 Pet. 2:11); that we should "not be surprised at the fiery trial . . . as though something strange were happening" to us (1 Pet. 4:12); that "there will be great earthquakes, and in various places famines and pestilences . . . [and] terrors" (Luke 21:11); that "there will come times of difficulty . . . people will be . . . abusive . . . heartless . . . brutal . . . treacherous, reckless" (2 Tim. 3:1–4).

---

[1] One way to sober yourself with the horrific reality of evil in the twentieth century is to consult a website like "Freedom, Democracy, Peace; Power, Democide, and War," accessed February 22, 2002, www.hawaii.edu/powerkills/welcome.html, where the evidence is given for about 170,000,000 people being murdered by their own governments in the twentieth century, not counting the world wars and other lesser conflicts.

The Unbiblical Absolutes of Self-Protection

There is a mind-set in the prosperous West that we deserve pain-free, trouble-free existence. When life deals us the opposite, we have a right not only to blame somebody or some system and to feel sorry for ourselves, but also to devote most of our time to coping, so that we have no time or energy left over for serving others.

This mind-set gives a trajectory to life that is almost universal—namely, away from stress and toward comfort and safety and relief. Then within that very natural trajectory some people begin to think of ministry and find ways of serving God inside the boundaries set by the aims of self-protection. Then churches grow up in this mind-set, and it never occurs to anyone in such a community of believers that choosing discomfort, stress, and danger might be the right thing—even the normal, biblical thing—to do.

I have found myself in conversation with Christians for whom it is simply a given that you do not put yourself or your family at risk. The commitment to safety and comfort is an unquestioned absolute. The demands of being a Christian in the twenty-first century will probably prove to be a rude awakening for such folks. Since we have not embraced the Calvary road voluntarily, God may simply catapult us onto it as he did the home-loving saints in Acts 11:19: "Those who were scattered *because of the persecution* that arose over Stephen traveled as far as Phoenicia and Cyprus and Antioch, speaking the word."

Stress and Danger Are Normal

One way or the other, Christ will bring his church to realize that "in the world you will have tribulation" (John 16:33); that "all who desire to live a godly life in Christ Jesus will be persecuted" (2 Tim. 3:12); that we are called to "share in suffering for the gospel by the power of God" (2 Tim. 1:8); that "we . . . groan inwardly as we wait eagerly for adoption as sons, the redemption of our bodies" (Rom. 8:23); that "whoever would save his life will lose it, but whoever loses his life for [Christ's] sake and the gospel's will save it" (Mark 8:35); and that "through many tribulations we must enter the kingdom of God" (Acts 14:22).

If we will not freely take our cross and follow Jesus (Mark 8:34) on the Calvary road, it may be thrust on us. It would be better to hear the warnings now and wake up to biblical reality. Existence in this fallen world will not be pain-free and trouble-free. There will be groaning because of our finitude and fallenness, and many afflictions because of our calling (Rom. 8:23; Ps. 34:19). Frustration is normal, disappointment is normal, sickness is normal. Conflict, persecution, danger, stress—they are all normal. The mind-set that moves away from these will move away from reality and away from Christ. Golgotha was not a suburb of Jerusalem.

Christians Move toward Need, Not Comfort

For the apostle Paul, following Christ meant bearing the marks of his suffering. "We are treated as impostors, and yet are true; as unknown, and yet well known; as dying, and behold, we live; as punished, and yet not killed; as sorrowful, yet always rejoicing; as poor, yet making many rich; as having nothing, yet possessing everything" (2 Cor. 6:8–10). Being a Christian should mean that our trajectory is toward need, regardless of danger and discomfort and stress. In other words, Christians characteristically will make life choices that involve putting themselves and their families at temporal risk while enjoying eternal security. "Sorrowful, yet always rejoicing . . . having nothing, yet possessing everything."

The Biblical Urgency of the Call for Endurance

All of this raises the question of endurance. How can we keep on loving and serving people when life has so much pain and disappointment? What are the roots of endurance? The magnitude of this question in the real world is one reason endurance has such a prominent place in the New Testament. One of the great themes of the Bible could be summed up in the words "You have need of endurance" (Heb. 10:36).[2] Or the banner flying over the whole Book could be, "Here is a call for the endurance of the saints" (Rev. 14:12).

It is not a small consideration, since Jesus said, "The one who endures to the end will be *saved*" (Matt. 24:13). And Paul said, "If we endure, we will also *reign* with him" (2 Tim. 2:12). And the writer to

---

[2] For an extended treatment of the doctrine of perseverance, see Thomas R. Schreiner and Ardel B. Caneday, *The Race Set before Us: A Biblical Theology of Perseverance and Assurance* (Downers Grove, IL: InterVarsity Press, 2001). For an old and standard classic, see John Owen, *The Doctrine of the Saint's Perseverance Explained and Confirmed*, in *The Works of John Owen*, vol. 11 (orig. 1654; Edinburgh: Banner of Truth, 1965).

the Hebrews said, "We . . . *share in Christ,* if indeed we hold our original confidence firm to the end" (Heb. 3:14).

Repeatedly we are commanded to "stand" in the face of opposition that would knock us down or lure us to fall down or bow down. "Take up the whole armor of God, that you may be able to with*stand* in the evil day, and having done all, to *stand firm*" (Eph. 6:13). "*Stand firm* thus in the Lord, my beloved" (Phil. 4:1). "Brothers, *stand firm* and hold to the traditions that you were taught by us" (2 Thess. 2:15).

We are admonished, "Do not grow weary in doing good" (2 Thess. 3:13). "Continue in what you have learned and have firmly believed" (2 Tim. 3:14). "Let us hold fast the confession of our hope without wavering" (Heb.10:23). "Hold fast what you have until I come" (Rev. 2:25). A blessing is pronounced on those who endure under trial. "Blessed is the man who remains steadfast under trial, for when he has stood the test he will receive the crown of life, which God has promised to those who love him" (James 1:12).

The assumption behind all these biblical texts is that the Christian life is hard. "The gate is narrow and the way is hard that leads to life" (Matt. 7:14); the Word of God can be "choked by the cares and riches and pleasures of life" (Luke 8:14); "your adversary the devil prowls around like a roaring lion, seeking someone to devour" (1 Pet. 5:8); and "there are many adversaries" (1 Cor. 16:9).

Therefore the danger is real that professing Christians will simply grow weary in well doing (Gal. 6:9); that we will fail to take heed to ourselves (1 Tim. 4:16) and each other (Heb. 3:13; 10:24–25); and that we will just drift through life (Heb. 2:1) and fail to see that there is a fight to be fought and a race to be won (1 Tim. 6:12; 2 Tim. 4:7).

How My Mind Has Changed

As I complete my fiftieth year as a professing Christian, I feel the urgency of endurance more than ever. I used to think differently. I used to think, when I was in my twenties and thirties, that sanctification had a kind of cumulative effect and that at fifty, the likelihood of apostasy would be far smaller than at thirty or forty. In one sense this is true. Surely growth in grace and knowledge and faith helps us "no longer be children, tossed to and fro by the waves and carried about by every wind of doctrine" (Eph. 4:14). I see more clearly now that even after years of such growth and stability, shocking coldness and even apostasies are possible. And I have known moments of horrifying blankness that made me realize my utter dependence on the mercies of God being new every morning.

Perseverance is a gift. That I will wake up and be a believer tomorrow morning is not finally and decisively owing to my will, but to God. I have known too many mornings on the precipice to think otherwise. That I have been snatched back every time is sheer mercy. The human will cannot be depended on, because in the crisis of faith it is precisely the will that is weak and falling. The question is: Who will seize it and bring it back to God in faith? More and more I love the candor and truth of the old hymn by Robert Robinson:

> O to grace how great a debtor
> Daily I'm constrained to be!
> Let thy goodness like a fetter
> Bind my wandering heart to thee:
> Prone to wander, Lord, I feel it,
> Prone to leave the God I love;
> Here's my heart, O, take and seal it;
> Seal it for thy courts above.[3]

Desperate Praying for Endurance

That is my cry: "Let your goodness, O God, bind my heart with a chain to you! Seal my will to yours with an unbreakable application of your eternal covenant." Is this the way Christians should pray? "Keep me! Preserve me! Defeat every rising rebellion! Overcome every niggling doubt! Deliver from every destructive temptation! Nullify every fatal allurement! Expose every demonic deception! Tear down every arrogant argument! Shape me! Incline me! Hold me! Master me! Do whatever you must do to keep me trusting you and fearing you till Jesus comes or calls." Should we pray for endurance like this?

Yes. It is the way the Lord taught us to pray. It's the way the psalmist prayed, and the way the apostle Paul prayed. When we pray, "Hallowed be your name . . . your will be done, on earth as it is in heaven" (Matt. 6:9–10), we are asking that God would cause his name to be reverenced

---

[3] Robert Robinson, "Come, Thou Fount of Every Blessing," in *The Worshipping Church* (Carol Stream, IL: Hope, 1990), 45.

and his will to be done.[4] We are asking for divine influence to move our hearts and the hearts of others from irreverence to reverence and from rebellion to joyful submission. We are admitting that without divine help, our hearts do not endure in reverence and obedience.

The psalmists prayed in the same way. They pleaded that God would overcome their failing wills: "*Incline* my heart to your testimonies, and not to selfish gain!" (Ps. 119:36). In other words, the psalmist saw that he was "prone to wander" away from endurance and faithfulness, and pleaded with God to intervene and change his will when he started to love money more than truth. Similarly he prayed that God would *open* his eyes to see the compelling beauty of what was there in the Word (Ps. 119:18), and that God would *unite* his heart from all its divided allegiances (Ps. 86:11), and that God would *satisfy*[5] him with divine love, and so wean him off the world (Ps. 90:14). Without this kind of divine help, nobody will endure to the end in love to Christ. That is why the apostle Paul prays this way for his people: "May the Lord *direct your hearts* to the love of God and to the steadfastness of Christ" (2 Thess. 3:5). If we are going to endure in faith and obedience, God must "direct our hearts" to Christ.

The Foundation of Prayer in Promised Grace

That kind of praying is rooted in the new-covenant promise of sovereign, sustaining grace—the hope that God himself has promised to keep his people. In other words, the command that we endure to the end is not only a command, but a creation of God. God commands it, and God gives it. That is the foundation of our asking for it. One of the most magnificent expressions of God's promise to help us endure is in Jeremiah 32:38–41.

> And they shall be my people, and I will be their God. I will give them one
> heart and one way, that they may fear me forever, for their own good and

---

[4] I stress this because for years I prayed the Lord's Prayer as if the first three petitions were a kind of acclamation of praise, and not a desperate plea for God to act. The Greek verb form used for the three verbs—your name "hallowed," your kingdom "come," your will "be done"—is called a third person imperative. We don't have such a thing in English. But you can see the significance of it by comparing the use of this construction in other places; for example, in the form of the verb for "be baptized" in Acts 2:38: "Repent and be baptized every one of you." It is clearly an exhortation here: "be baptized." Similarly in the Lord's Prayer, we are "exhorting" God urgently to be hallowed. We want him to cause this to come about in the world and, for starters, in our own hearts.

[5] Notice that the four italicized words ("incline," "open," "unite," and "satisfy") from these four texts (Ps. 119:36; 119:18; 86:11; 90:14) form an acronym: "IOU'S." I use this regularly as a reminder of how to pray for my own soul and for others.

the good of their children after them. I will make with them an everlasting covenant, that I will not turn away from doing good to them. And I will put the fear of me in their hearts, that they may not turn from me. I will rejoice in doing them good, and I will plant them in this land in faithfulness, with all my heart and all my soul.

Here is one of the most stunning and precious promises of sustaining grace in the Bible. This is the new-covenant promise of God's initiative to do for us what under the old covenant the Jewish people, by and large, were not enabled to do.[6] Must we endure to the end to be saved? Yes. And in this new covenant, God promises, "I will put the fear of me in their hearts, that they may not turn from me" (Jer. 32:40). He promises to do *for* us what he commands *from* us. This is what marks the Christian pursuit of endurance from all others. It has been purchased by the blood of Jesus Christ and promised to those who are his.

A Peculiar Kind of Striving

So the form of our endurance has a peculiar energy: we put out great effort to endure to the end, but we do it in a peculiar way, namely, in the strength that God supplies. Paul said it like this in Philippians 2:12–13, "Work out your own salvation with fear and trembling, for it is God who works in you, both to will and to work for his good pleasure." We work and we tremble at the magnitude of what is at stake in our

---

[6] Here are some other places where promises of the new covenant are found: Deut. 30:6, "And the Lord your God will circumcise your heart and the heart of your offspring, so that you will love the Lord your God with all your heart and with all your soul, that you may live." Jer. 31:31–33:

Behold, the days are coming, declares the Lord, when I will make a new covenant with the house of Israel and the house of Judah, not like the covenant that I made with their fathers on the day when I took them by the hand to bring them out of the land of Egypt, my covenant that they broke, though I was their husband, declares the Lord. For this is the covenant that I will make with the house of Israel after those days, declares the Lord: I will put my law within them, and I will write it on their hearts. And I will be their God, and they shall be my people.

Ezek. 11:19–20, "And I will give them one heart, and a new spirit I will put within them. I will remove the heart of stone from their flesh and give them a heart of flesh, that they may walk in my statutes and keep my rules and obey them. And they shall be my people, and I will be their God." Ezek. 36:26–27, "And I will give you a new heart, and a new spirit I will put within you. And I will remove the heart of stone from your flesh and give you a heart of flesh. And I will put my Spirit within you, and cause you to walk in my statutes and be careful to obey my rules." The fulfillment of the new covenant is in the work of Jesus Christ in dying for our sins and purchasing the benefits of the promises of the new covenant: "This cup that is poured out for you is the *new covenant* in my blood" (Luke 22:20; 1 Cor. 11:26). Heb. 9:15, "Therefore he is the mediator of a *new covenant*, so that those who are called may receive the promised eternal inheritance, since a death has occurred that redeems them from the transgressions committed under the first covenant." Along with this redemption comes the blessing promised in the new covenant of divine enabling for the endurance in faith that God commands. Heb. 13:20–21, "Now may the God of peace who brought again from the dead our Lord Jesus, the great shepherd of the sheep, *by the blood of the eternal covenant*, equip you with everything good that you may do his will, *working in us that which is pleasing in his sight*, through Jesus Christ, to whom be glory forever and ever. Amen."

endurance and what great obstacles there are in ourselves and in the world and in the Devil. But we do not tremble with the anxiety of the abandoned. We are not abandoned. In all our striving, there is a deep restfulness of confidence, for we are striving not in our strength but God's. "Finally, be strong in the Lord and in the strength of his might" (Eph. 6:10). Not our might, *his* might.

Yes, there is a fight to be fought and a race to be run. Paul leaves us no question about that:

> Do you not know that in a race all the runners run, but only one receives the prize? So run that you may obtain it. Every athlete exercises self-control in all things. They do it to receive a perishable wreath, but we an imperishable. So I do not run aimlessly; I do not box as one beating the air. But I discipline my body and keep it under control, lest after preaching to others I myself should be disqualified. (1 Cor. 9:24–27)

But be careful in reading such texts. Oh, how easy it would be to simply turn them into moral self-improvement programs that have nothing to do with the blood-bought, Spirit-wrought new-covenant promises of divine enabling received by faith in Christ.

The crucial Christian difference for Paul was that he believed all his running and fighting and body disciplining was a gift of grace purchased by Jesus Christ and received by faith in him so that Jesus would get the glory and not Paul himself. For example, Paul said, "By the grace of God I am what I am, and his grace toward me was not in vain. On the contrary, I worked harder than any of them, though it was not I, but the grace of God that is with me" (1 Cor. 15:10). Yes, he worked to endure, but no, it was not finally and decisively dependent on him, but on the grace of God. "It depends not [finally and decisively] on human will or exertion, but on God, who has mercy" (Rom. 9:16).

Enduring by Grace through Faith So God Gets the Glory

The biblical call to endure in faith and obedience is a call to trust the Christ-purchased, empowering grace of God.[7] God's grace is first the gift of pardon and imputed righteousness;[8] then it is the gift of power

---

[7] I have tried to spell this kind of living out in great biblical and practical detail in the book, *Future Grace* (Colorado Springs: Multnomah, 2012).

[8] This term will become clearer in what follows, but in advance, it refers to the divine righteousness that God credits to our account on the basis of Christ's life and death. It is not what we do, but what God is and did

to fight the good fight and to overflow in good deeds. Christ died to purchase both redeeming pardon *and* transforming power: "[Christ] gave himself for us to *redeem* us from all lawlessness and to *purify* for himself a people for his own possession who are zealous for good works" (Titus 2:14). Therefore, all our ability to endure to the end in good works is a gift of grace. This is what Paul says in 2 Corinthians 9:8: "God is able to make all grace abound to you, so that having all sufficiency in all things at all times, you may abound in every good work." Grace abounds to us so that we may abound in good works. It is our work, yes, but enabled by his grace.

That is why he gets the glory for our good works. Jesus called us to a life of good works, but in a peculiar way: namely, so that our Father, not ourselves, would get the glory: "Let your light shine before others, so that they may see your good works and give glory to your Father who is in heaven" (Matt. 5:16). This is exactly the way the apostle Peter reasoned in 1 Peter 4:11, "[Serve] by the strength that God supplies—in order that in everything God may be glorified through Jesus Christ. To him belong glory and dominion forever and ever. Amen."

The aim of all our endurance is that Christ be seen and savored in the world as our glorious God. Paul makes this plain in 2 Thessalonians 1:11–12, where he prays for us "that our God may make you worthy of his calling and may fulfill every resolve for good and every work of faith by his power, *so that the name of our Lord Jesus may be glorified in you*, and you in him, *according to the grace of our God* and the Lord Jesus Christ." Paul asks that God would energize all our resolves so that we would endure by the grace of God and for the glory of Christ, the image of God. Similarly, in Philippians 1:11 he prays that we would be "filled with the fruit of righteousness that comes through Jesus Christ, to the glory and praise of God." He asks God to fill us with the fruit of righteousness because of the work of Jesus Christ, and that in this way God would see to it that he himself gets the glory.

This is what we pray for, and this is what we trust in as we take up the biblical command to endure to the end. We trust in the

---

in Jesus Christ. It is the basis of our acceptance with God. It is the foundation, not the effect, of our moral transformation that necessarily follows. As our sins were imputed to Christ who knew no sin, so God's righteousness is imputed to us who had no righteousness. 2 Cor. 5:21, "For our sake he made him to be sin who knew no sin, so that in him we might become the righteousness of God." I have recently written a book defending and explaining the doctrine of imputed righteousness: *Counted Righteous in Christ* (Wheaton, IL: Crossway, 2002).

new-covenant promises of sustaining, enabling grace that were obtained for us infallibly and irrevocably by Jesus Christ in his death and resurrection. Therefore our fight and our race and endurance is a radically God-centered, Christ-exalting, Spirit-dependent, promise-supported life. It is not a "just do it" ethic. It is not a moral self-improvement program. It is not a "Judeo-Christian ethic" shared by a vaguely spiritual culture with a fading biblical memory. It is a deeply cross-embracing life that knows the Christ of the Bible as the Son of God who was crucified first as our substitute and then as our model of endurance.

Pardon before Power

Nothing was more important for John Newton, Charles Simeon, and William Wilberforce than the centrality of the cross as the root of endurance. They did exactly what Hebrews 12:1–2 calls us to do: "Let us run with *endurance* the race that is set before us, *looking to Jesus*, the founder and perfecter of our faith, who for the joy that was set before him *endured the cross*." They endured . . . looking to Jesus . . . who endured the cross.

But oh how jealous they were—as I am jealous—that we embrace the cross of Christ first and decisively as the ground of our acceptance with God, through faith alone, *before* we experience the cross as the price and inspiration of our own labors to endure in the battle for justice in the world. That is, they were careful to savor the cross first as the basis of justification before they experienced its purchased power for sanctification. *Before* the power of endurance came the pardon of guilt. *Before* the blood-bought enabling of righteous living came the free gift of perfect righteousness credited to our account because of Christ alone through faith alone.

The Politician Who Cared Deeply about Doctrine

Astonishingly William Wilberforce, the politician who had no formal theological training at all, was more explicit and urgent about this matter than either of the two pastors, Newton or Simeon. As he endured decade after decade in the battle against the African slave trade, he came to an amazing diagnosis of the problem. His nominally Christian, British countrymen did not understand justification by faith in its proper, foundational relation to sanctification. They were confusing the two.

First, they considered doctrine as ethically unimportant. They had what he called "the fatal habit"—and surely we in the prosperous, pragmatic West would have to admit that it is even more habitual today—"of considering Christian morals as distinct from Christian doctrines. . . . Thus the peculiar doctrines of Christianity went more and more out of sight, and as might naturally have been expected, the moral system itself also began to wither and decay, being robbed of that which should have supplied it with life and nutriment."[9] The central "peculiar doctrine" that went out of sight with worst effect was a true understanding of justification by faith.

What was it particularly that was lost? Here is how he put it in 1797: The errors and moral failures of the mass of nominal Christians

> RESULT FROM THE MISTAKEN CONCEPTION ENTERTAINED OF THE FUNDAMENTAL PRINCIPLES OF CHRISTIANITY. They consider not that Christianity is a scheme "for justifying *the ungodly*" [Rom. 4:5], by Christ's dying for them "*when yet sinners*" [Rom. 5:6–8], a scheme "for reconciling us to God—*when enemies*" [Rom. 5:10]; and for making the fruits of holiness *the effects, not the cause,* of our being justified and reconciled.[10]

This is the root of endurance in true godliness that was lost. And the effect in the culture was devastating. Nominal Christians were confusing and reversing sanctification and justification. They were making the fruits of holiness the cause and not the effects of being justified.

In other words, they were cutting themselves off from the very power of justification by faith that was the deepest root of life and power that the Bible offers for defeating sin and freeing us for lifelong endurance in the cause of righteousness. Wilberforce returns again to this theme with these clear and powerful words: "The true Christian . . . knows therefore that this holiness is not to PRECEDE his reconciliation to God, and be its CAUSE; but to FOLLOW it, and be its EFFECT. That, in short, it is by FAITH IN CHRIST only that he is to be justified in the sight of God."[11] In this way alone does a person become "entitled to all the privileges which belong to this high relation," which include in this

---

[9] William Wilberforce, *A Practical View of Christianity* (Peabody, MA: Hendrickson, 1996), 198.
[10] Ibid., 64. The capitalization and italics are his.
[11] Ibid., 166.

earthly life a "partial renewal after the image of his Creator," and in the life to come "the more perfect possession of the Divine likeness."[12]

The deepest root of endurance for Wilberforce—and Newton and Simeon shared this view entirely—was the precious and powerful experience of the justification of the *ungodly* by faith alone (Rom. 4:5)—leading necessarily to a life of glorious freedom in the never-ending battle against sin and injustice. Any effort to short-circuit this process of faith in Christ for his imputed righteousness first, and transformed morality second, would in the end be the undoing of morality and of a nation.

The Surprising Place of Cross-Focused Doctrine

This discovery in William Wilberforce and Charles Simeon surprised me. I did not expect to find a politician decrying the decay of doctrinal knowledge as the root of failed endurance in righteous living. All I knew when I took up the study of Wilberforce was that he had an unparalleled reputation for Christian endurance in the cause of justice for African slaves. That is what I wanted to understand.[13] And all I knew of Charles Simeon when I began to study his life was that he had served in one university church for fifty-four years, and in the first twelve years there was such vigorous opposition to his ministry from his people that the "pewholders" (as they were called in those days) would not let anyone sit in the pews, so that he had to preach to an audience standing in the space that was left. I wanted to understand how one endures so long under such relentless opposition.

I did not realize that both of these men would make the cross of Christ so vital to the root of their endurance, and that Wilberforce in particular would focus on the very nature of justification as the linchpin of endurance in righteous living. I knew Newton somewhat better before I began a more thorough study of his life. Everyone knows his tribute to "Amazing Grace" that saved a "wretch" like me. So I expected what I found in Newton—overflowing grace for the worst of sinners grounded in the finished and perfect work of Jesus Christ on the cross. So there is a continuity in these three men at the deepest level, not just at the experiential level of lifelong endurance against all obstacles.

---

[12] Ibid.

[13] The 2002 Bethlehem Conference for Pastors was built around this issue of racial justice and the foundation for it in God-centered thinking. Messages from that conference are available at www.desiringGod.org.

They are united in their delight in and devotion to the cross of Christ as the ground of God's righteousness freely imputed to them through faith alone as the root of all righteous endurance.

And the Surprising Place of Cross-Focused Delight

The word "delight" is chosen carefully. This was another surprise in studying the lives of these three men. I did not expect the aggressive way that they made joy essential to Christian living and long endurance through pain. It was not a general, vague joy, but a specific, focused joy in the cross and in the Christ who died for us there. For example, Simeon said, "By this then, my brethren, you may judge whether you are Christians in deed and in truth, or such in name only. For a nominal Christian is content with *proving* the way of salvation by a crucified Redeemer. But the true Christian loves it, *delights* in it, glories in it, and shudders at the very thought of glorying in anything else."[14] Delight in the Christ of the cross, not just dutiful endurance, was essential for all three of these men. It is—as we will see—one of the essential roots of endurance.

The Linking of Three Lives

There are several ways to think about the interrelatedness of Newton (1725–1807), Simeon (1759–1836), and Wilberforce (1759–1833). They were contemporaries who knew and respected each other. Their lives were interwoven in a common cause of evangelical reformation. The first two were local church pastors and the third a member of the House of Commons all his life. All had drunk deeply at the wells of George Whitefield and John Wesley. Simeon and Wilberforce were the same age and Newton their senior by thirty-four years. Therefore, the role of Newton in these relationships was of father and counselor and encourager—which was his well-known and cherished gift. In a sense, then, Newton *was* a root of their renowned endurance.

Newton's Wise Nurture of William Wilberforce

Already as a boy, Wilberforce knew John Newton. The aunt and uncle with whom he stayed for long periods after his father died when he was eight were friends of Newton and listened to him often. Therefore

---

[14] Charles Simeon, *Evangelical Preaching: An Anthology of Sermons by Charles Simeon* (Sisters, OR: Multnomah, 1986), 71, emphasis added.

Newton watched Wilberforce's career from the time he was a boy and grieved over his worldly wanderings before his conversion at age twenty-six. But when Wilberforce was powerfully converted—a great story of God's surprising providence that we will see in chapter 3—it was John Newton to whom he turned for counsel about whether he could remain in public political life as an evangelical. In the history of the world, more hung on that private meeting of December 7, 1785, than we know.

Wilberforce reported, "He told me he always had hopes and confidence that God would sometime bring me to Him. . . . When I came away I found my mind in a calm, tranquil state, more humbled, and looking more devoutly up to God."[15] But more important historically than the peace of Wilberforce's soul that day was the counsel he received about political life as an evangelical. Newton told him to stay in politics. "It is hoped and believed that the Lord has raised you up for the good of His church and for the good of the nation."[16]

And till the day Newton died in 1807, he was Wilberforce's cheerleader. Or, more biblically, he was like a Moses on the mountain to Joshua on the field doing battle with Amalek. Wilberforce wrote him in 1788:

> I believe I can truly declare, that not a single day has passed in which you have not been in my thoughts. . . . O my dear Sir, let not your hands cease to be lifted up, lest Amalek prevail—entreat for me that I may be enabled by divine grace to resist and subdue all the numerous enemies of my salvation. My path is peculiarly steep and difficult and dangerous, but the prize is a crown of glory and "celestial panoply" is offered me and the God of Hosts for my ally.[17]

The Blessing Returned on Newton's Head

Though Newton was older and more seasoned and the one Wilberforce looked to for wise counsel,[18] Newton learned from and honored his

---

[15] Robert Isaac Wilberforce and Samuel Wilberforce, *The Life of William Wilberforce*, abridged ed. (London, 1843), 48.

[16] Ibid. This quote is from a letter Newton wrote two years later, but it sums up what Wilberforce said he received from Newton that day. Similarly Newton wrote to Wilberforce in 1799 concerning the entire "Clapham Sect"—the like-minded group of friends who lived near each other and fought the same battles, "But when I think of you, Mr. Thornton and a few of your friends, I am ready to address you in the words of Mordecai—who knoweth but God raised you up for such a time as this!" Richard Cecil, *The Life of John Newton*, ed. Marylynn Rouse (Fearn: Christian Focus, 2000), 177.

[17] Ibid., 176–77.

[18] Newton nurtured and sustained Wilberforce's endurance with regular letters (at least four a year by his own telling). A taste of this nurture: "My heart is with you, my dear sir. I see, though from a distance, the importance and difficulties of your situation. May the wisdom that influenced Joseph and Moses and

younger "Joshua." In 1797, when Wilberforce published his one main, nation-shaping book—the one that diagnosed Britain's ills as rooted in the doctrinal failure to grasp justification by faith—Newton told him that he read it three times in the first two months after it came out. "I have been nearly fifty years in the Lord's school . . . but still I had something to learn from your book."[19] He was not slack in honoring the accomplishments of Wilberforce far and near. He once said that he believed Britain owed to Wilberforce the "pleasing prospect of an opening for the gospel in the southern Hemisphere." In fact, six years after Newton's death, because of Wilberforce's relentless advocacy, liberty to preach the gospel finally came to the British colonies as far away as India.[20]

Another Young Beneficiary of Newton's Amazing Grace

The relation between Newton and Charles Simeon was not as close, but they knew each other, and Newton admired the young vicar of Trinity Church, Cambridge. He knew of his long endurance and wrote of him, "There is good going on at Cambridge. Mr. Simeon is much beloved and very useful; his conduct has almost suppressed the spirit of opposition which was once very fierce against him."[21] The ordeal that Simeon had endured at Trinity Church was known far and wide. Even Wilberforce, years after the battles had been won in Cambridge, wrote to Simeon in 1829, "The degree in which, without any sacrifice of principle, you have been enabled to live down the prejudices of many of our high ecclesiastical authorities, is certainly a phenomenon I never expected to witness."[22]

Tribute to the Little-Known Emissaries of Sustaining Grace

Typical of the interweaving of these men's lives was one other brief but all-important link between Simeon and Wilberforce. Isaac Milner,

---

Daniel rest upon you. Not only to guide and animate you in the line of Political Duty—but especially to keep you in the habit of dependence upon God, and communion with him, in the midst of all the changes and bustle around you." Ibid., 176.

[19] Wilberforce, *A Practical View of Christianity*, 263.

[20] The British citizen and missionary William Carey, who went to India in 1793, had to live in a Danish enclave in Serampore, India, until Wilberforce finally triumphed in 1813 (six years after Newton died). The prohibition of evangelism in British areas of India was lifted by the East India Company Charter, and liberty was granted to propagate the Christian Faith. "Parliament had opened a fast-locked door and it was Wilberforce who had turned the key, in a speech which Lord Erskine said 'deserves a place in the library of every man of letters, even if he were an atheist.'" John Pollock, *Wilberforce* (London: Constable, 1977), 238.

[21] Cecil, *Life of John Newton*, 173.

[22] Handley C. G. Moule, *Charles Simeon* (orig. 1892; London: InterVarsity Press, 1948), 152.

the man who led Wilberforce to Christ during several months of travel together in France, was a close friend of Simeon in Cambridge. First as a tutor and then principal of Queens' College in the university, Milner became a strong supporter of Simeon in his trials. Thus a relatively unknown person in history may have played a role in the lives of Simeon and Wilberforce beyond anything we know. It is fitting that such a one be mentioned here as a kind of tribute to all the unknown emissaries of grace God sends to us in time of need.

Gratitude That These Three Swans Are Still Not Silent

This book and this whole series of books, The Swans Are Not Silent, is a kind of debt I owe to people living and dead whom God mercifully sends my way to strengthen my hand in the fight of faith. I said at the start of this introduction that I want to finish life well for the glory of Christ. One of the "roots of endurance" that I depend on is the life and ministry of men and women whose God-centered, Christ-exalting, cross-focused perseverance inspires me to press on through hardship. The Bible encourages me in this: "[Do] not be sluggish, but imitators of those who through faith and patience inherit the promises" (Heb. 6:12). "As an example of suffering and patience . . . take the prophets. . . . You have heard of the steadfastness of Job, and you have seen the purpose of the Lord, how the Lord is compassionate and merciful" (James 5:10–11).

The twenty-first century will not be an easy time to be a Christian. It is not meant to be easy. But we are not left without help. The Bible centers on a crucified, risen, and reigning Christ and is full of promises for every crisis. And the history of God's church is full of empowering examples of those who proved that the grace of God is sufficient to enable us to endure to the end and be saved.

Amazing grace!—how sweet the sound
That saved a wretch like me,
I once was lost, but now am found,
Was blind, but now I see.
John Newton

By faith he triumphs over . . . smiles and enticements: he sees that
all that is in the world, suited to gratify the desires of the flesh or
the eye, is not only to be avoided as sinful, but as incompatible with
his best pleasures.
John Newton

He believes and feels his own weakness and unworthiness, and lives
upon the grace and pardoning love of his Lord. This gives him an
habitual tenderness and gentleness of spirit. Humble under a sense
of much forgiveness to himself, he finds it easy to forgive others.
John Newton

1

John Newton

The Tough Roots of His Habitual Tenderness

John Newton was born July 24, 1725, in London to a godly mother and an irreligious, seafaring father. His mother died when he was six. Left mainly to himself, Newton became a debauched sailor—a miserable outcast on the coast of West Africa for two years; a slave-trading sea captain until an epileptic seizure ended his career; a well-paid "surveyor of tides" in Liverpool; a loved pastor of two congregations in Olney and London for forty-three years; a devoted husband to Mary for forty years until she died in 1790; a personal friend to William Wilberforce, Charles Simeon, Henry Martyn, William Carey, John Wesley, and George Whitefield; and, finally, the author of the most famous hymn in the English language, "Amazing Grace."[1] He died on December 21, 1807, at the age of eighty-two.

Durable as Redwoods, Tender as Clover

Why am I interested in this man? Because one of my great desires is to see Christians be as strong and durable as redwood trees, and as tender and

---

[1] Besides appearing in almost all church hymnals, "'Amazing Grace' has been adapted by scores of performers, from country music to gospel to folk singers. . . . Judy Collins sings in St. Paul's Chapel at Columbia University, and talks about how this song carried her through the depths of her alcoholism. Jessye Norman sends 'Amazing Grace' soaring across the footlights at Manhattan Center stage. While in Nashville, Johnny Cash visits a prison and talks about the hymn's impact on prisoners. The folk singer, Jean Ritchie, shares a reunion of her extended family in Kentucky where everyone rejoices together. 'Amazing Grace' is also featured in the repertory of the Boys Choir of Harlem, which performs the hymn in both New York and Japan" ("Amazing Grace: The Story of a Song That Makes a Difference," Films Media Group, accessed February 2, 2016, http://films.com/ecTitleDetail.aspx?TitleID=7557&r=FFHCollections.aspx).

fragrant as a field of clover—unshakably rugged in the "defense and confirmation" of the truth (Phil. 1:7) and relentlessly humble and patient and merciful in dealing with people. Ever since I came to Bethlehem Baptist Church as preaching pastor in 1980, this vision of ministry has beckoned me because, soon after I came, I read through Matthew and Mark and put in the margin of my Greek New Testament a "to" (for tough) and a "te" (for tender) beside Jesus's words and deeds that fit one category or the other. The impact on me was significant in shaping the course of my work. What a mixture he was! No one ever spoke like this man.

It seems to me that we are always falling off the horse on one side or the other in this matter of being tough and tender, durable and delightful, courageous and compassionate—wimping out on truth when we ought to be lionhearted, or wrangling when we ought to be weeping. I know it's a risk to take up this topic and John Newton in a cultural situation like ours where some readers need a good (tender!) kick in the pants to be more courageous and others confuse courage with what William Cowper called "a furious and abusive zeal."[2] Oh, how rare are the Christians who speak with a tender heart and have a theological backbone of steel.

I dream of being one someday, and I long to be used by God in the ministry to produce such fruit. Oh, for Christians and pastors whose might in the truth is matched by their meekness. Whose theological acumen is matched by their manifest contrition. Whose heights of intellect are matched by their depths of humility. Yes, and the other way around!— whose relational warmth is matched by their rigor of study, whose bent toward mercy is matched by the vigilance of their biblical discernment, and whose sense of humor is exceeded by the seriousness of their calling.

I dream of durable, never-say-die defenders of true doctrine who are mainly known for the delight they have in God and the joy in God that they bring to the people of God—who enter controversy when necessary, not because they love ideas and arguments, but because they love Christ and the church.

Lovers of Doctrine Who Spread Joy

There's a picture of this in Acts 15. Have you ever noticed the amazing unity of things here that we tend to tear apart? A false doctrine arises

---

[2] Richard Cecil, *Memoirs of the Rev. John Newton*, in *The Works of the Rev. John Newton*, 6 vols. (Edinburgh: Banner of Truth, 1985), 1:123.

in Antioch; some begin to teach, "Unless you are circumcised . . . you cannot be saved" (v. 1). Paul and Barnabas weigh in with what Luke calls "no small dissension and debate" (v. 2). So the church decides to send them off to Jerusalem to get the matter settled. And amazingly, verse 3 says that on their way to the great debate they were "describing in detail the conversion of the Gentiles, and brought *great joy* to all the brothers" (v. 3).

This is my vision: the great debaters on their way to a life-and-death showdown of doctrinal controversy, so thrilled by the mercy and power of God in the gospel that they are spreading joy everywhere they go. Oh, how many there are today who tell us that controversy only kills joy and ruins the church; and how many others there are who, on their way to the controversy, feel no joy and spread no joy in the preciousness of Christ and his salvation. One of the aims of my life and this book is to declare that it is possible and necessary to be as strong and rugged for truth as a redwood and as tender and fragrant for Christ as a field of clover.

No Perfect Pastors

So now, with the help of the life of John Newton, I want to say it again. And make no mistake—our heroes have feet of clay. There are no perfect Christians—laypeople or pastors. Newton himself warns us:

> In my imagination, I sometimes fancy I could [create] a perfect minister. I take the eloquence of ____, the knowledge of ____, the zeal of ____, and the pastoral meekness, tenderness, and piety of ____. Then, putting them all together into one man, I say to myself, "This would be a perfect minister." Now there is One, who, if he chose to, could actually do this; but he never did it. He has seen fit to do otherwise, and to divide these gifts to every man severally as he will.[3]

So neither Newton nor we will ever be all that we should be in this life. But oh, how much more like the Great Shepherd we should long to be. Newton had his strengths, and I want us to learn from them. At times his strengths were his weakness, but that too will be instructive. The theme of this chapter is "the tough roots of John Newton's habitual tenderness." His great strength was "speaking the truth in love" (Eph.

---

[3] Ibid., 107.

4:15). As you read, read for what *you* need, not for what so-and-so across town needs. On which side of the horse are *you* falling off?

I begin with a brief telling of his life, because for Newton, his life was the clearest testimony to the heart-breaking mercy of God he ever saw. Even at the end of his life he was still marveling that he was saved and called to preach the gospel of grace. From his last will and testament we read:

> I commit my soul to my gracious God and Savior, who mercifully spared and preserved me, when I was an apostate, a blasphemer, and an infidel, and delivered me from the state of misery on the coast of Africa into which my obstinate wickedness had plunged me; and who has been pleased to admit me (though most unworthy) to preach his glorious gospel.[4]

This was one of the deepest roots of his habitual tenderness. He could not get over the wonder of his own rescue by sheer, triumphant grace.

His Childhood and Youth

Newton's mother was a devout Congregationalist and taught her only child, John, the Westminster Catechism and the hymns of Isaac Watts. But she died in 1732 when John was six, and his father's second wife had no spiritual interest. Newton wrote in his *Narrative* that he was in school only two of all his growing-up years, from ages eight to ten, at a boarding school in Stratford. So he was mainly self-taught, and that remained true all his life. He never had any formal theological education.[5]

At the age of eleven he began to sail the high seas with his father. He made five voyages to the Mediterranean before he was eighteen. He wrote about his relationship to his father: "I am persuaded he loved me, but he seemed not willing that I should know it. I was with him in a state of fear and bondage. His sternness . . . broke and overawed my spirit."[6]

---

[4] Ibid., 90.
[5] In view of the fact that two of the three "Swans" in this book (Newton and Wilberforce) had no formal theological education, this might be a good place to encourage readers who, like these two great saints, have not been trained formally but who have drunk deeply at the wells of God's Word. Don't feel paralyzed in ministry and evangelism and eldership if you have not gone to seminary. Give yourself to reading and thinking and praying. There are many such lovers of God's truth who understand things and speak things as well as many seminary-trained pastors and teachers. I don't say this with any desire to diminish the value of formal training. I only want to say it is not essential for fruitful ministry if other ways of study and experience are seriously pursued.
[6] Ibid., 2.

A Durable Romance

When he was seventeen, he met Mary Catlett and fell in love with her. She was thirteen. For the next seven years of traveling and wretchedness, he dreamed about her. "None of the scenes of misery and wickedness I afterwards experienced ever banished her a single hour together from my waking thoughts for the seven following years."[7] They did eventually marry when he was twenty-four, and were married for forty years until she died in 1790. His love for her was extraordinary before and after the marriage. Three years after she died, he published a collection of letters he had written to her on three voyages to Africa after they were married.

Moral Ruin and Misery

He was pressed into naval service against his will when he was eighteen and sailed away bitterly on the *Harwich* as a midshipman. His friend and biographer Richard Cecil says, "The companions he met with here completed the ruin of his principles."[8] Of himself he wrote, "I was capable of anything; I had not the least fear of God before my eyes, nor (so far as I remember) the least sensibility of conscience. . . . My love to [Mary] was now the only restraint I had left."[9] On one of his visits home, he deserted the ship and was caught, "confined two days in the guard-house . . . kept a while in irons . . . publicly stripped and whipt, degraded from his office."[10]

When he was twenty years old, he was put off his ship on some small islands just southeast of Sierra Leone, West Africa, and for about a year and a half he lived as a virtual slave in almost destitute circumstances. The wife of his master despised him and treated him cruelly. He wrote that even the African slaves would try to smuggle him food from their own slim rations.[11] Later in life he marveled at the seemingly accidental way a ship put anchor on his island after seeing some smoke, and just happened to be a ship with a captain who knew Newton's father and managed to free him from his bondage.[12] That was February 1747. He was not quite twenty-one, and God was about to close in.

---

[7] Ibid., 6.
[8] Ibid., 9.
[9] Ibid., 12.
[10] Ibid., 10.
[11] Ibid., 16.
[12] Ibid., 78.

The Precious Storm at Sea

The ship had business on the seas for over a year. Then on March 21, 1748, on his way home to England in the North Atlantic, God acted to rescue the "African blasphemer."[13] On this day fifty-seven years later, in 1805, when Newton was eighty years old, he wrote in his diary, "March 21, 1805. Not well able to write. But I endeavor to observe the return of this day with Humiliation, Prayer and Praise."[14] He had marked the day as sacred and precious for over half a century.

He awoke that night to a violent storm as his room began to fill with water. As he ran for the deck, the captain stopped him and had him fetch a knife. The man who went up in his place was immediately washed overboard.[15] He was assigned to the pumps and heard himself say, "If this will not do, the Lord have mercy upon us."[16] It was the first time he had expressed the need for mercy in many years.

He worked the pumps from 3 in the morning until noon, slept for an hour, and then took the helm and steered the ship till midnight. At the wheel he had time to think back over his life and his spiritual condition. At about six o'clock the next evening it seemed as though there might be hope. "I thought I saw the hand of God displayed in our favor. I began to pray: I could not utter the prayer of faith; I could not draw near to a reconciled God, and call him *Father* . . . the comfortless principles of infidelity were deeply riveted. . . . The great question now was, how to obtain *faith*."[17]

He found a Bible and got help from Luke 11:13, which promises the Holy Spirit to those who ask. He reasoned, "If this book be true, the promise in this passage must be true likewise. I have need of that very Spirit, by which the whole was written, in order to understand it aright. He has engaged here to give that Spirit to those who ask: I must therefore pray for it; and, if it be of God, he will make good on his own word."[18]

He spent all the rest of the voyage in deep seriousness as he read and prayed over the Scriptures. On April 8, they anchored off Ireland,

---

[13] Ibid., 88.

[14] D. Bruce Hindmarsh, *John Newton and the English Evangelical Tradition* (Grand Rapids, MI: Eerdmans, 2001), 13.

[15] Cecil, *Memoirs of the Rev. John Newton*, 25.

[16] Ibid., 26.

[17] Ibid., 28.

[18] Ibid.

and the next day the storm was so violent they would have surely been sunk had they still been at sea. Newton described what God had done in those two weeks:

> Thus far I was answered, that before we arrived in Ireland, I had a satisfactory evidence in my own mind of the truth of the Gospel, as considered in itself, and of its exact suitableness to answer all my needs. . . . I stood in need of an Almighty Savior; and such a one I found described in the New Testament. Thus far the Lord had wrought a marvelous thing: I was no longer an infidel: I heartily renounced my former profaneness, and had taken up some right notions; was seriously disposed, and sincerely touched with a sense of the undeserved mercy I had received, in being brought safe through so many dangers. I was sorry for my past misspent life, and purposed an immediate reformation. I was quite freed from the habit of swearing, which seemed to have been as deeply rooted in me as a second nature. Thus, to all appearance, I was a new man.[19]

It was a remarkable change, but from his later mature standpoint, Newton did not view it as full conversion.

> I was greatly deficient in many respects. I was in some degree affected with a sense of my enormous sins, but I was little aware of the innate evils of my heart. I had no apprehension of . . . the hidden life of a Christian, as it consists in communion with God by Jesus Christ: a continual dependence on him. . . . I acknowledged the Lord's mercy in pardoning what was past, but depended chiefly upon my own resolution to do better for the time to come. . . . I cannot consider myself to have been a believer (in the full sense of the word) till a considerable time afterwards.[20]

Captain, Epileptic, and Surveyor

For six years after this time he said he had no "Christian friend or faithful minister to advise me."[21] He became the captain of a slave-trading ship and went to sea again until December 1749. In his mature years he came to feel intense remorse for his participation in the slave trade and joined William Wilberforce in opposing it. Thirty years after leaving the sea, he wrote an essay, "Thoughts upon the African Slave Trade," which closed with a reference to "a commerce

---

[19] Ibid., 32.
[20] Ibid., 32–33.
[21] Ibid., 33.

so iniquitous, so cruel, so oppressive, so destructive, as the African Slave Trade!"[22]

On February 1, 1750, he married Mary. That June his father drowned while swimming in the Hudson Bay. John went on three long voyages after the marriage and left Mary alone for ten to thirteen months each time. Then in November 1754, he had an epileptic seizure and never sailed again.

Self-Taught

In the years between his seafaring and his pastorate at Olney, he was a surveyor of tides in Liverpool and a very active ministerial layperson. He interacted with evangelicals from both the Anglican and Independent wings of the Awakening. He was especially taken by George Whitefield and "was even tagged with the epithet 'Little Whitefield' for his constant attendance upon the evangelist."[23] He devoted himself to a rigorous program of self-study and applied himself to Greek and Hebrew and Syriac. He said, "I was in some hopes that perhaps, sooner or later, [Christ] might call me into his service. I believe it was a distant hope of this that determined me to study the original Scriptures."[24]

Along with these he was reading "the best writers in divinity" in Latin and English and French (which he taught himself while at sea), but gave himself mainly to the Scriptures.[25] The upshot theologically of this study, together with his personal experience of grace, is summed up by Bruce Hindmarsh: "By the early 1760's Newton's theological formation was complete, and there would be few significant realignments of his essential beliefs. He was a five-point Calvinist."[26] But the spirit of his Calvinism was sweet and tender—as it should be!

---

[22] John Newton, "Thoughts upon the African Slave Trade," in *The Works of the Rev. John Newton,* 6:123.

[23] D. Bruce Hindmarsh, "'I Am a Sort of Middle-Man': The Politically Correct Evangelicalism of John Newton," in *Amazing Grace: Evangelicalism in Australia, Britain, Canada, and the United States,* ed. George Rawlyk and Mark Noll (Grand Rapids, MI: Baker, 1993), 32.

[24] Cecil, *Memoirs of the Rev. John Newton,* 50. Later in his ministry, Newton counseled a younger minister, "The original Scriptures well deserve your pains, and will richly repay them" (*The Works of the Rev. John Newton,* 1:143). Concerning the early years of studying the languages, he says, "You must not think that I have attained, or ever aimed at, a critical skill in any of these. . . . In the Hebrew, I can read the Historical Books and Psalms with tolerable ease; but, in the Prophetical and difficult parts, I am frequently obliged to have recourse to lexicons, etc. However, I know so much as to be able, with such helps as are at hand, to judge for myself the meaning of any passage I have occasion to consult" (Cecil, *Memoirs of the Rev. John Newton,* 49–50).

[25] Ibid., 50.

[26] Hindmarsh, "I Am a Sort of Middle-Man," 42.

Two Pastorates, No Children, and Heaven

In 1764, he accepted the call to the pastorate of the Church of England parish in Olney and served there for almost sixteen years. Then he accepted the call at age fifty-four to St. Mary's Woolnoth in London, where he began his twenty-seven-year ministry on December 8, 1779. His eyes and ears were failing, and his good friend Richard Cecil suggested he cease preaching when he turned eighty, to which Newton responded, "What! Shall the old African blasphemer stop while he can speak?"[27] The last time he was in the pulpit of St. Mary's was in October 1806, when he was eighty-one years old.

John and Mary had no children of their own, but adopted two nieces. When Mary died seventeen years before John, he lived with the family of one of these nieces and was cared for by her as if he were her own father. He died on December 21, 1807, at the age of eighty-two. A month before he died, he expressed his settled faith:

> It is a great thing to die; and, when flesh and heart fail, to have God for the strength of our heart, and our portion forever. I know whom I have believed, and he is able to keep that which I have committed against that great day. Henceforth there is laid up for me a crown of righteousness, which the Lord, the righteous Judge, shall give me that day.[28]

Newton's Habitual Tenderness

We turn now to the theme of this chapter, namely, "The Tough Roots of John Newton's Habitual Tenderness." This tenderness and these roots are seen in his remarkable pastoral ministry for over forty years.

The phrase "habitual tenderness" is Newton's own phrase to describe the way a believer should live. In writing to a friend, he describes the believer's life: "He believes and feels his own weakness and unworthiness, and lives upon the grace and pardoning love of his Lord. This gives him an habitual tenderness and gentleness of spirit."[29] In that sentence, it is plain already what some of the roots of tenderness are, but before we look at them more closely, let's get some snapshots of this man's "habitual tenderness."

---

[27] Cecil, *Memoirs of the Rev. John Newton*, 88.
[28] Ibid., 89.
[29] *The Works of the Rev. John Newton*, 1:170.

It will be helpful to speak of persons and patterns. That is, to whom was he tender, and what form did his tenderness take?

Loving People at First Sight

Richard Cecil said, "Mr. Newton could live no longer than he could *love*."[30] His love to people was the signature of his life. This was true of groups of people and individual people. He loved perishing people, and he loved his own flock of redeemed people.

> Whoever . . . has tasted of the love of Christ, and has known, by his own experience, the need and the worth of redemption, is enabled, Yea, he is constrained, to love his fellow creatures. *He loves them at first sight*; and, if the providence of God commits a dispensation of the gospel, and care of souls to him, he will feel the warmest emotions of friendship and tenderness, while he beseeches them by the tender mercies of God, and even while he warns them by his terrors.[31]

It's the phrase "at first sight" that stands out in this quote. Newton's first reflex was to love lost people. When he spoke to unbelievers, he spoke like this:

> A well-wisher to your soul assures you, that whether you know these things or not, they are important realities. . . . Oh hear the warning voice! *Flee from the wrath to come*. Pray thee that the eyes of your mind may be opened, then you will see your danger, and gladly follow the shining light of the Word.[32]

Suffer the Little Children to Come

One clear mark of Christlike tenderness is love for children. "Let the little children come to me; do not hinder them" (Mark 10:14) is the badge of tenderness that Jesus wore. When Newton came to Olney, one of the first things he did was begin a meeting for children on Thursday afternoons. He met with them himself, gave them assignments, and spoke to them from the Bible. At one point he said, "I suppose I have

---

[30] Cecil, *Memoirs of the Rev. John Newton*, 95.

[31] *The Works of the Rev. John Newton*, 5:132, emphasis added.

[32] Richard Cecil, *The Life of John Newton*, ed. Marylynn Rouse (Fearn: Christian Focus, 2000), 351, emphasis added. He had a special concern for sailors and lamented their neglect in evangelism and Christian publishing. He eventually wrote a preface for a devotional book designed especially for sailors. See Cecil, *The Life of John Newton*, 76–77, 347–48. Note: Marylynn Rouse's name is misspelled on the cover of this book as Rousse, but is correct on the inside title page.

200 that will constantly attend."[33] And what made it more remarkable to his parishioners was that the meetings were open to all the children, not just the members of his church.

Josiah Bull said, "The *young* especially had a warm place in his affectionate heart. . . . Mr. Jay . . . relates that once a little sailor-boy with his father called on Mr. Newton. He took the boy between his knees, told him that he had been much at sea himself, and then sang him part of a naval song."[34]

The Flocks

For forty-three years his two flocks had an especially tender place in his heart. Richard Cecil said that Newton's preaching was often not well prepared, nor careful or "graceful" in delivery. But, he said, "He possessed . . . so much affection for his people, and so much zeal for their best interests, that the defect of his manner was little consideration with his constant hearers."[35] Once Newton complained in a letter of his busyness: "I have seldom one-hour free from interruption. Letters that must be answered, visitants that must be received, business that must be attended to. I have a good many sheep and lambs to look after, sick and afflicted souls dear to the Lord; and *therefore, whatever stands still, these must not be neglected.*"[36]

Minister to the Depressed

Newton's tenderness touched individuals as well as groups. The most remarkable instance of this was, of course, William Cowper, the mentally ill poet and hymn-writer who came to live in Olney during twelve of Newton's sixteen years there. Newton took Cowper into his home for five months during one season and fourteen months during another, when he was so depressed it was hard for him to function alone. In fact, Richard Cecil said that over Newton's whole lifetime, "His house was an asylum for the perplexed or afflicted."[37] Newton says of Cowper's stay: "For nearly 12 years we were seldom separated for seven hours

---

[33] Ibid., 143.
[34] Josiah Bull, *"But Now I See": The Life of John Newton* (orig. 1868; Edinburgh: Banner of Truth, 1998), 366–67.
[35] Cecil, *Memoirs of the Rev. John Newton*, 92.
[36] Cecil, *The Life of John Newton*, 139, emphasis added.
[37] Cecil, *Memoirs of the Rev. John Newton*, 95.

at a time when we were awake and at home: the first six I passed daily admiring and aiming to imitate him: during the second six, I walked pensively with him in the valley of the shadow of death."[38]

When Cowper's brother died in 1770, Newton resolved to help Cowper by collaborating with him in writing hymns for the church. These came to be known as "The Olney Hymns." But soon Cowper was emotionally unable to carry through his part of the plan. Newton pressed on, writing one hymn a week without Cowper until there were well over three hundred. Sixty-seven are attributed to William Cowper.[39] The last hymn that Cowper composed for *The Olney Hymns* was "God Moves in a Mysterious Way," which he entitled "Light Shining out of Darkness." The next day, in January 1773, he sank into the blackest depression and never went to hear Newton preach again. Newton preached his funeral sermon seven years later and explained what happened and how he responded.

> He drank tea with me in the afternoon. The next morning a violent storm overtook him. . . . I used to visit him often but no argument could prevail with him to come and see me. He used to point with his finger to the church and say: "You know the comfort I have had there and how I have seen the glory of the Lord in His house, and until I go there I'll not go anywhere else." He was one of those who came out of great tribulations. He suffered much here for twenty-seven years, but eternity is long enough to make amends for all. For what is all he endured in this life, when compared with the rest which remaineth for the children of God.[40]

What would most of us have done with a depressed person who could scarcely move out of his house? William Jay summed up Newton's response: "He had the tenderest disposition; and always judiciously regarded his friend's depression and despondency as a physical effect, for the removal of which he prayed, but never reasoned or argued with him concerning it."[41]

Satan Will Not Love You for This

Another example of his tenderness toward an individual is the case of the missionary, Henry Martyn. The young Martyn was very discour-

---

[38] Cecil, *The Life of John Newton*, 125.
[39] Ibid.
[40] Ibid., 129–30.
[41] Ibid., 282.

aged from some criticism he had received of his "insipid and inanimate manner in the pulpit." He came to Newton, who blocked every one of Martyn's discouragements with hope. Martyn wrote in his journal (April 25, 1805) that when Newton heard of the criticism he had received,

> he said he had heard of a clever gardener, who would sow seeds when the meat was put down to roast, and engage to produce a salad by the time it was ready, but the Lord did not sow oaks in this way. On my saying that perhaps I should never live to see much fruit; he answered I should have the bird's-eye view of it, which would be much better. When I spoke of the opposition that I should be likely to meet with, he said, he supposed Satan would not love me for what I was about to do. The old man prayed afterwards with sweet simplicity.[42]

From Liberal to Lover of the Truth

Another instance of remarkable patience and tenderness was toward Thomas Scott, who was a liberal, "nearly . . . Socinian" clergyman in Ravenstone, a neighboring parish. Scott made jest of Newton's evangelical convictions. He looked upon Newton's religious sentiments as "rank fanaticism" and found his theology unintelligible. "Once I had the curiosity to hear [Newton] preach; and, not understanding his sermon, I made a very great jest of it, where I could do it without giving offense. I had also read one of his publications; but, for the same reason, I thought the greater part of it whimsical, paradoxical, and unintelligible."[43]

But things were soon to change. Gospel-driven love triumphed over liberalism and turned Scott into a strong evangelical preacher. The turning point came when Scott was shamed by Newton's pastoral care for two of his own parishioners whom he had neglected.

> In January, 1774 two of my parishioners, a man and his wife, lay at the point of death. I had heard of the circumstance; but, according to my general custom, not being sent for, I took no notice of it: till, one evening, the woman being now dead, and the man dying, I heard that my neighbor Mr. Newton had been several times to visit them. Immediately my conscience reproached me with being shamefully negligent, in sitting at home within a

[42] Ibid., 184.
[43] Ibid., 65.

few doors of dying persons, my general hearers, and never going to visit them. Directly it occurred to me, that, whatever contempt I might have for Mr. Newton's doctrines, I must acknowledge his practice to be more consistent with the ministerial character than my own.[44]

Scott and Newton exchanged about ten letters between May and December 1775. Scott was impressed with how friendly Newton was, even when Scott was very provocative. Newton "shunned everything controversial as much as possible, and filled his letters with the most useful and least offensive instructions."[45] After a lull in their correspondence from December 1775 to April 1777, Scott came into "discouraging circumstances" and chose to call on the tenderhearted evangelical. "His discourse so comforted and edified me, that my heart, being by this means relieved from its burden, became susceptible of affection for him."[46] This affectionate relationship led Scott into the full experience of saving grace and evangelical truth. He became the pastor at Olney when Newton was called to London and wrote a distinctly evangelical book, *The Force of Truth*,[47] and was among William Wilberforce's favorite preachers. Such were the persons and fruit of Newton's habitual tenderness.

Consider now the patterns of Newton's tenderness.

Not Driven Away or Carried Away

One way to describe the pattern of Newton's tenderness is to say that it was patient and perceptive. He captures this balance when he says, "Apollos met with two candid people in the church: they neither ran away because he was *legal*, nor were carried away because he was *eloquent*."[48] In other words, Newton was not driven away by people's imperfections, and he was not overly impressed by their gifts. He was patient and perceptive. He saw beneath the surface that repelled and the surface that attracted. He once wrote to a friend, "Beware, my friend, of mistaking the ready exercise of gifts for the exercise of grace."[49] Being gracious to people did not mean being gullible.

---

[44] Ibid., 64.
[45] Ibid., 66.
[46] Ibid., 67.
[47] Thomas Scott, *The Force of Truth* (orig. 1779; Edinburgh: Banner of Truth, 1979).
[48] Cecil, *Memoirs of the Rev. John Newton*, 101.
[49] *The Works of the Rev. John Newton*, 1:164.

Defeating Heresy by Establishing Truth

The most illuminating way I know to illustrate Newton's deeply rooted habitual tenderness is in the way he handled doctrinal and moral truth that he cherished deeply. Here we see the very *roots* of the tenderness (truth) at work in the *fruit* of tenderness (love). Patience and perception guided him between doctrinaire intellectualism on the one side and doctrinal indifference and carelessness on the other side.

With respect to patience Newton said:

> I have been thirty years forming my own views; and, in the course of this time, some of my hills have sunk, and some of my valleys have risen: but, how unreasonable within me to expect all this should take place in another person; and that, in the course of a year or two.[50]

He had a passion for propagating the truth, even the whole Reformed vision of God as he saw it. But he did not believe controversy served the purpose. "I see the unprofitableness of controversy in the case of Job and his friends: for, if God had not interposed, had they lived to this day they would have continued the dispute."[51] So he labored to avoid controversy and to replace it with positive demonstrations of biblical truth. "My principal method of defeating heresy is by establishing truth. One proposes to fill a bushel with *tares*: now, if I can fill it first with *wheat*, I shall defy his attempts."[52] He knew that receiving the greatest truths required supernatural illumination. From this he inferred that his approach should be patient and unobtrusive:

> I am a friend of peace; and being deeply convinced that no one can profitably understand the great truths and doctrines of the gospel any farther than he is taught of God, I have not a wish to obtrude my own tenets upon others, in a way of controversy; yet I do not think myself bound to conceal them.[53]

The Temper of Tenderness in Telling Truth

Newton had a strong, clear, Calvinistic theology. He loved the vision of God in true biblical Calvinism. In the preface to *The Olney Hymns*, he

---

[50] Cecil, *Memoirs of the Rev. John Newton*, 101.
[51] Ibid., 106. In a letter to a friend he warned that if we do not look continually to the Lord, controversy will obstruct communion with God. "Though you set out in defense of the cause of God, if you are not continually looking to the Lord to keep you, it may become your own cause and awaken in you those tempers which are inconsistent with true peace of mind and will surely obstruct communion with God" (*The Works of the Rev. John Newton*, 1:273–74).
[52] Cecil, *Memoirs of the Rev. John Newton*, 100.
[53] *The Works of the Rev. John Newton*, 3:303.

wrote, "The views I have received of the doctrines of grace are essential to my peace; I could not live comfortably a day, or an hour, without them. I likewise believe . . . them to be friendly to holiness, and to have a direct influence in producing and maintaining a gospel conversation; and therefore I must not be ashamed of them."[54] But he believed "that the cause of truth itself may be discredited by an improper management." Therefore, he says, "The Scripture, which . . . teaches us *what* we are to say, is equally explicit as to the *temper* and Spirit in which we are to speak. Though I had knowledge of all mysteries, and the tongue of an angel to declare them, I could hope for little acceptance or usefulness, unless I was to speak 'in love.'"[55]

> Of all people who engage in controversy, we, who are called Calvinists, are most expressly bound by our own principles to the exercise of gentleness and moderation. . . . The Scriptural maximum, that "The wrath of man worketh not the righteousness of God," is verified by daily observation. If our zeal is embittered by expressions of anger, invective, or scorn, we may think we are doing service to the cause of truth, when in reality we shall only bring it into discredit.[56]

He had noticed that one of the most "Calvinistic" texts in the New Testament called for tenderness and patience with opponents, because the decisive work is God's:

> And the Lord's servant must not be quarrelsome but kind to everyone, able to teach, patiently enduring evil, correcting his opponents with gentleness. God may perhaps grant them repentance leading to a knowledge of the truth, and they may escape from the snare of the devil, after being captured by him to do his will. (2 Tim. 2:24–26)

So, for the sake of repentance and knowledge of truth, Newton's pattern of tenderness in doctrinal matters was to shun controversy.

---

[54] Ibid.

[55] *The Works of the Rev. John Newton*, 5:131. Newton took Eph. 4:15 ("speaking the truth in love") as his inaugural text when he came to St. Mary's (*The Works of the Rev. John Newton*, 5:126–36). Richard Cecil describes how this text was fleshed out in Newton's ministry:

> His zeal in propagating the truth . . . was not more conspicuous, than the tenderness of the spirit as to the manner of his maintaining and delivering it. He was found constantly *speaking the truth in love; and in meekness instructing those that oppose themselves, if God peradventure would give them repentance to the acknowledging of the truth.* There was a gentleness, a candour, and a forbearance in him, that I do not recollect to have seen in an equal degree among his brethren. (Cecil, *Memoirs of the Rev. John Newton*, 122).

[56] *The Works of the Rev. John Newton*, 1:271.

Commending Opponents to God in Prayer

The sovereignty of God in freeing people from error or from unbelief also made prayer central to Newton's pattern of tenderness. In a letter about controversy, he wrote a friend:

> As to your opponent, I wish, that, before you set pen to paper against him, and during the whole time you are preparing your answer, you may commend him by earnest prayer to the Lord's teaching and blessing. This practice will have a direct tendency to conciliate your heart to love and pity him; and such a disposition will have a good influence upon every page you write. . . . [If he is a believer,] in a little while you will meet in heaven; he will then be dearer to you than the nearest friend you have upon earth is to you now. Anticipate that period in your thoughts. . . . [If he is an unconverted person,] he is a more proper object of your compassion than your anger. Alas! "He knows not what he does." But you know who has made you to differ [1 Cor. 4:7].[57]

His Calvinism Is like Sugar in His Tea

Newton cared more about influencing people with truth for their good than winning debates. William Jay recounts how Newton described the place of his Calvinism. He was having tea one day with Newton. Newton said, "'I am more of a Calvinist than anything else; but I use my Calvinism in my writings and my preaching as I use this sugar'—taking a lump, and putting it into his tea-cup, and stirring it, adding, 'I do not give it alone, and whole; but mixed and diluted.'"[58] In other words, his Calvinism permeated all that he wrote and taught and served to sweeten everything. Few people like to eat sugar cubes, but they like the effect of sugar when it permeates in right proportion.

So Newton did not serve up the "five points" by themselves but blended them in with everything he taught. This way of flavoring life was essential to his pattern of tenderness that developed in dealing with people's doctrinal differences. Bruce Hindmarsh remarks, "It is not surprising, therefore, that he wrote principally biographies, sermons, letters, and hymnody—not treatises or polemical tracts, much less a 'body of divinity.'"[59]

---

[57] Ibid., 269.
[58] Hindmarsh, "I Am a Sort of Middle-Man," 52.
[59] Ibid.

Misgivings about Newton's Approach

Did Newton strike the right balance of a patient, tenderhearted, non-controversial pattern of ministry and a serious vigilance against harmful error? Perhaps rather than indict Newton in particular, we should speak generally about the possible weakness in his approach. For example, William Plummer has misgivings:

> The pious and amiable John Newton made it a rule never to attack error, nor warn his people against it. He said: "The best method of defeating heresy is by establishing the truth. One proposes to fill a bushel with tares; now if I can fill it first with wheat, I shall defeat his attempts." Surely the truth ought to be abundantly set forth. But this is not sufficient. The human mind is not like a bushel. It may learn much truth and yet go after folly. The effect of Mr. Newton's practice was unhappy. He was hardly dead till many of his people went far astray. Paul says: "Preach the word; be instant in season, out of season; reprove, rebuke, exhort with all long-suffering and doctrine" (2 Tim. 4:2). The more subtle, bitter, and numerous the foes of the truth are the more fearless and decided should its friends be. The life of truth is more important than the life of any man or any theories.[60]

Bruce Hindmarsh has misgivings at another level. "While it is no disgrace that Newton was more a pastor than a theologian, it is one of the most serious indictments of the English Evangelical Revival that it produced so few theologians of stature."[61] In other words, if our zeal for peace and conciliation and heartfelt affection for God and for people creates a milieu in which rigorous, critical thinking and theology will not flourish, we may hurt the cause of Christ in generations to come while seeming to make the cause more pleasing now.

He Could Draw a Line

I am not sure that Newton is to be faulted on these counts, even if the general concern is legitimate. It is true that John Wesley wrote to him, "You appear to be designed by divine providence for an healer of breaches, a reconciler of honest but prejudiced men, and an uniter (happy work!) of the children of God."[62] But it is also true that the

---

[60] William S. Plummer, THE CHRISTIAN, to which is added, FALSE DOCTRINES AND FALSE TEACHERS: How to Know Them and How to Treat Them (Harrisonburg, VA: Sprinkle, 1997), 22.
[61] Hindmarsh, "I Am a Sort of Middle-Man," 53.
[62] Ibid., 31.

relationship with Wesley was broken off in 1762 because of the controversy, not over election or perseverance, but over perfectionism.[63]

It is true that Richard Cecil criticized his hero, saying "that he did not always administer consolation . . . with sufficient discrimination. His talent," he said, "did not lie in *discerning of spirits*."[64] But it is also true that Newton was unwavering in his commitment to holiness and doctrinal fidelity and was used by God to bring Thomas Scott from the brink of Socinianism to solid Reformed Christianity.

Most pastors and laypeople cannot devote much of their time to blowing the trumpet for rigorous intellectual theology. They should see its usefulness and necessity and encourage its proper place. But they cannot be faulted that they mainly have flocks to love and hearts to change. Defending the truth is a crucial part of that, but it is not the main part. *Holding* the truth and *permeating* all our ministry with the greatness and sweetness of truth for the transformation of our people's lives is the main part of our ministry.

The Eye and Tongue of a Poet

One other aspect of the pattern of Newton's tenderness calls for attention. It is the language he used in making the truth winsome and healing. Newton had the eye and heart and tongue of a spiritual poet, and this gave his speech a penetrating power that many Reformed preachers desperately need. He wrote hymns and poems for his people and for special occasions. Instead of excessive abstraction in his preaching, there was the concrete word and illustration. Instead of generalizing, there was the specific bird or flower or apple or shabby old man.

---

[63] Ibid., 43. In Liverpool, fifty-one Methodists claimed instantaneous and entire sanctification. Hindmarsh writes, "While Newton had been able to suppress his differences with Wesley over predestination, the extent of the atonement, and final perseverance, he was not able to accept the behavior of Wesley's followers in the wake of the perfectionism revival. The claim to perfection, however hedged about by talk of grace, seemed in many cases no more than an enthusiastic self-righteousness that belied trusting wholly in the merits of Christ for redemption. Newton had earlier worked out a formula that would maintain evangelical solidarity with Arminians by saying, 'Though a man does not accord with my view of election, yet if he gives me good evidence, that *he is effectually called of God*, he is my brother' [Hindmarsh, *The Works of the Rev. John Newton*, 6:199]. He could not, however, make any rapprochement with Wesley's growing stress upon perfectionism. The behavior of his followers raised the specter of a Pelagianism that lay outside his understanding of evangelical theology, unduly stressing human agency in salvation."

[64] Cecil writes, "I never saw him so much moved, as when any friend endeavored to correct his errors in this respect. His credulity seemed to arise from the consciousness he had of his own integrity; and from the sort of parental fondness which he bore to all his friends, real or pretended. I knew one, since dead, whom he thus described, while living: 'He is certainly an odd man, and has his failings; but he has great integrity, and I hope is going to heaven:' whereas, almost all who knew him thought the man should go first into the pillory!" (Cecil, *Memoirs of the Rev. John Newton*, 94–95).

He had an eye that saw everything as full of divine light for ministry to people. For example, in his diary for July 30, 1776, Newton describes his reactions while watching an eclipse of the moon.

> Tonight I attended an eclipse of the moon. How great, O Lord, are thy works! With what punctuality do the heavenly bodies fulfill their courses. . . . I thought, my Lord, of Thine eclipse. The horrible darkness which overwhelmed Thy mind when Thou saidst, "Why hast thou forsaken me?" Ah, sin was the cause—my sins—yet I do not hate sin or loathe myself as I ought.[65]

Oh, how we need Christians—especially preachers—with eyes like this. Seeing God and his ways everywhere in nature and life, then making our communications full of concreteness from daily life.

Newton's language was permeated by this concreteness. Most of us tend to gravitate to abstractions. We say, "Men tend to choose lesser pleasures and reject greater ones." But Newton says, "The men of this world are children. Offer a child an apple and bank note, he will doubtless choose the apple."[66] We say, "Men are foolish to fret so much over material things when they will inherit eternal riches." But Newton says:

> Suppose a man was going to New York to take possession of a large estate, and his [carriage] should break down a mile before he got to the city, which obliged him to *walk* the rest of the way; what a fool we should think him, if we saw him wringing his hands, and blubbering out all the remaining mile, "My [carriage] is broken! My [carriage] is broken!"[67]

This is not merely a matter of style. It is a matter of life and vitality. It is a sign to people that your mind is healthy, and it may be a means to their health. Unhealthy minds can only deal in abstractions and cannot get outside themselves to be moved by concrete, external wonders. We will never be tender toward our people if we merely communicate the heaviness of general concepts and theories rather than the specific stuff of the world in which they live. This kind of communication was part and parcel of his winsome, humble, compelling tenderness.

---

[65] Cecil, *The Life of John Newton*, 134.
[66] Cecil, *Memoirs of the Rev. John Newton*, 107.
[67] Ibid., 108.

The Health of Natural Humor

And yes, there is a crucial place for humor in this pattern of tenderness—not the contrived levity of a "communicator" who knows how to work an audience—but the balanced, earthy experience of the way the world really is in its horror and humor. There would be more real laughter if there were more real tears.

"One day by a strong sneeze he shook off a fly which had perched upon his gnomon, and immediately said: 'Now if this fly keeps a diary, he'll write Today a terrible earthquake.'" At another time, when asked how he slept, he instantly replied, "I'm like a beef-steak—once turned, and I am done."[68] What these quips indicate is a healthy mind awake to the world and free from bondage to morose speculations or introspection. This kind of mental health is essential for a Christian to be a tender and winsome minister to the whole range of human experience.

I turn now to the roots of John Newton's habitual tenderness.

Realism about the Limits of This Life

Few things will tend to make you more tender than to be much in the presence of suffering and death. "My course of study," Newton said, "like that of a surgeon, has principally consisted in walking the hospital."[69] His biblical assessment of the misery that he saw was that some, but not much, of it can be removed in this life. He would give his life to bring as much relief and peace for time and eternity as he could. But he would not be made hard and cynical by irremediable miseries like Cowper's mental illness.[70] "I endeavor to walk through the world

---

[68] Bull, *"But Now I See,"* 370. The meaning of "gnomon" in 1803, according to the *Shorter Oxford Dictionary*, included "nose." That is probably Newton's reference. "Striking illustrations, happy turns of thought, racy and telling expressions, often enriched Mr. Newton's extempore discourses" (Bull, *"But Now I See,"* 369). Another instance of Newton's humor is seen in a letter to Thomas Scott, who became the vicar in Olney when Newton left. Newton wrote to him, "Methinks I see you sitting in my old corner in the study. I will warn you of one thing. That room—(do not start)—used to be haunted. I cannot say I ever saw or heard anything with my bodily organs, but I have been sure there were evil spirits in it and very near me—a spirit of folly, a spirit of indolence, a spirit of unbelief, and many others—indeed their name is legion. But why should I say they are in your study when they followed me to London, and still pester me here?" (Cecil, *The Life of John Newton*, 145).

[69] Cecil, *Memoirs of the Rev. John Newton*, 100.

[70] See pages 283–84. Another case of constitutional depression (as he judged it) besides Cowper's was that of Hannah Wilberforce. Newton wrote to her in a letter dated July 1764:

> Things which abate the comfort and alacrity of our Christian profession are rather impediments than properly sinful, and will not be imputed to us by him who knows our frame, and remembers that we are but dust. Thus, to have an infirm memory, to be subject to disordered, irregular, or low spirits, are faults of the constitution, in which the will has no share, though they are all burdensome and oppressive, and sometimes needlessly so by our charging ourselves with guilt on their account. The same may be observed of the unspeakable and fierce suggestions of Satan, with which some people

as a physician goes through Bedlam [the famous insane asylum]: the patients make a noise, pester him with impertinence, and hinder him in his business; but he does the best he can, and so gets through."[71] In other words, his tender patience and persistence in caring for difficult people came, in part, from a very sober and realistic view of what to expect from this world. Life is hard, and God is good.

Just as we saw at the beginning, there are no perfect pastors or laypeople. This must not discourage us but only make us patient as we wait for the day when all things will be new. Newton gives beautiful, concrete expression to this conviction as he watches the dawn outside his window.

> The day is now breaking: how beautiful its appearance! how welcome the expectation of the approaching sun! It is this thought makes the dawn agreeable, that it is the presage of a brighter light; otherwise, if we expect no more day than it is this minute, we should rather complain of darkness, than rejoice in the early beauties of the morning. Thus the Life of grace is the dawn of immortality: beautiful beyond expression, if compared with the night and thick darkness which formerly covered us; yet faint, indistinct, and unsatisfying, in comparison of the glory which shall be revealed.[72]

This sober realism about what we can expect from this fallen world is a crucial root of habitual tenderness in the life of John Newton.

All-Pervasive Humility and Gratitude at Having Been Saved

This he comes back to more than anything as the source of tenderness. Till the day he died, he never ceased to be amazed that, as he said at age seventy-two, "such a wretch should not only be spared and par-

---

are pestered, but which shall be laid to him from whom they proceed, and not to them who are troubled and terrified, because they are forced to feel them. (Cecil, *The Life of John Newton*, 126)

[71] Ibid., 103.

[72] *The Works of the Rev. John Newton*, 1:319. Another example of the limits of this age that make us patient with people's failings is the God-ordained necessity of temptations. Newton asks "why the Lord permits some of his people to suffer such violent assaults from the powers of darkness" (ibid., 226). "Though the Lord sets such bounds to [Satan's] rage as he cannot pass, and limits him both as to manner and time, he is often pleased to suffer him to discover his malice to a considerable degree; not to gratify Satan, but to humble and prove *them*; to shew them what is in their hearts, to make them truly sensible of their immediate and absolute dependence upon himself, and to quicken them to watchfulness and prayer" (p. 227). He goes on to suggest that another design of temptation is "for the manifestation of his power, and wisdom, and grace, in supporting the soul under such pressures as are evidently beyond its own strength to sustain" (p. 228). He gives Job as an illustration. "The experiment answered many good purposes: Job was humbled, yet approved; his friends were instructed; Satan was confuted, and disappointed; and the wisdom and mercy of the Lord, in his darkest dispensations toward his people, were gloriously illustrated" (p. 228). "If the Lord has any children who are not exercised with spiritual temptations, I am sure they are but poorly qualified to 'speak a word in season to them that are weary'" (p. 231).

doned, but reserved to the honor of preaching thy Gospel, which he had blasphemed and renounced . . . this is wonderful indeed! The more thou hast exalted me, the more I ought to abase myself."[73] He wrote his own epitaph:

JOHN NEWTON,
Clerk,
Once an Infidel and Libertine,
A Servant of Slaves in Africa,
Was,
by the rich mercy of our Lord and Savior
JESUS CHRIST,
Preserved, restored, pardoned,
And appointed to preach the Faith
He had long laboured to destroy.
He ministered
Near 16 years as curate and vicar
of Olney in Bucks,
And 28
as rector of these united parishes.

When he wrote his *Narrative* in the early 1760s he said, "I know not that I have ever since met so daring a blasphemer."[74] The hymn we know as "Amazing Grace" was written to accompany a New Year's sermon based on 1 Chronicles 17:16, "Then King David went in and sat before the LORD, and said, 'Who am I, O LORD God, and what is my house, that you have brought me thus far?'"[75]

Amazing grace!—how sweet the sound—
That saved a wretch like me,
I once was lost, but now am found,
Was blind, but now I see.

The effect of this amazement is tenderness toward others. "[The 'wretch' who has been saved by grace] believes and feels his own weakness and unworthiness, and lives upon the grace and pardoning love of his Lord. This gives him an habitual tenderness and gentleness of spirit.

---

[73] Cecil, *Memoirs of the Rev. John Newton*, 86.
[74] Ibid., 22.
[75] Cecil, *The Life of John Newton*, 365–68.

Humble under a sense of much forgiveness to himself, he finds it easy to forgive others."[76]

He puts it in a picture:

> A company of travelers fall into a pit: one of them gets a passenger to draw him out. Now he should not be angry with the rest for falling in; nor because they are not yet out, as he is. He did not pull himself out: instead, therefore, of reproaching them, he should show them pity. . . . A man, truly illuminated, will no more despise others, than Bartimaeus, after his own eyes were opened, would take a stick, and beat every blind man he met.[77]

Glad-hearted, grateful lowliness and brokenness as a saved "wretch" was probably the most prominent root of Newton's habitual tenderness with people.

Peaceful Confidence in the Pervasive, Loving Providence of God

In order to maintain love and tenderness that thinks more about the other person's need than our own comforts, we must have an unshakable hope that the sadness of our lives will work for our everlasting good. Otherwise we will give in, turn a deaf ear to need, and say, "Let us eat, drink, and be merry, for tomorrow we die." Newton found this peace and confidence in the all-governing providence of God over good and evil. He describes his own experience when he describes the believer:

> And his faith upholds him under all trials, by assuring him that every dispensation is under the direction of his Lord; that chastisements are a token of his love; that the season, measure, and continuance of his sufferings, are appointed by Infinite Wisdom, and designed to work for his everlasting good; and that grace and strength shall be afforded him, according to his day.[78]

This keeps him from being overwhelmed with anger and bitterness and resentment when he is assaulted with pressures and disappointments. It is as practical as pastoral interruptions. "When I hear a knock at my study door, I hear a message from God. It may be a lesson of instruction; perhaps a lesson of patience: but, since it is *his* message, it

---

[76] *The Works of the Rev. John Newton*, 1:170.
[77] Cecil, *Memoirs of the Rev. John Newton*, 105.
[78] *The Works of the Rev. John Newton*, 1:169.

must be interesting."[79] He knew that even his temptations were ordered by the sovereign goodness of God and that not to have any was dangerous for the soul. He approved of Samuel Rutherford's comment that "there is no temptation like being without temptation."[80]

And this same faith in God's gracious providence to help him profit from the painful things in life also spared him from the pleasant things in life that would deceive him and choke off the superior pleasures he has in God. If the world triumphs in this way, we will lose our joy in Christ and his mercy, and that will be the end of all Christ-exalting tenderness. So it is a crucial root of his habitual tenderness when he says, "By faith [the believer] triumphs over [the world's] smiles and enticements: he sees that all that is in the world, suited to gratify the desires of the flesh or the eye, is not only to be avoided as sinful, but as incompatible with his best pleasures."[81]

John Newton's habitual tenderness is rooted in the sober realism of the limits of redemption in this fallen world where we "groan inwardly as we wait eagerly for . . . the redemption of our bodies" (Rom. 8:23), the all-pervasive humility and gratitude for having been a blasphemer of the gospel and now being a heaven-bound preacher of it, and the unshakable confidence that the all-governing providence of God will make every experience turn for his good, so that he doesn't spend his life murmuring, "My carriage is broken, my carriage is broken," but sings, "'Tis grace has brought me safe thus far, and grace will lead me home."

---

[79] Cecil, *Memoirs of the Rev. John Newton*, 76.
[80] *The Works of the Rev. John Newton*, 1:259.
[81] Ibid., 171–72.

My dear brother, we must not mind a little suffering for Christ's sake.
Charles Simeon

I have continually had such a sense of my sinfulness as would sink me into utter despair, if I had not an assured view of the sufficiency and willingness of Christ to save me to the uttermost. And at the same time I had such a sense of my acceptance through Christ as would overset my little bark, if I had not ballast at the bottom sufficient to sink a vessel of no ordinary size.
Charles Simeon

A nominal Christian is content with proving the way of salvation by a crucified Redeemer. But the true Christian loves it, delights in it, glories in it, and shudders at the very thought of glorying in anything else. . . . Let all your joys flow from the contemplation of his cross.
Charles Simeon

Charles Simeon

*The Ballast of Humiliation
and the Sails of Adoration*

In April 1831, Charles Simeon was seventy-one years old. He had been the pastor of Trinity Church in Cambridge, England, for forty-nine years. One afternoon his friend Joseph Gurney asked him how he had surmounted persecution and outlasted all the great prejudice against him in his many years of ministry. He said to Gurney:

> My dear brother, we must not mind a little suffering for Christ's sake. When I am getting through a hedge, if my head and shoulders are safely through, I can bear the pricking of my legs. Let us rejoice in the remembrance that our holy Head has surmounted all His suffering and triumphed over death. Let us follow Him patiently; we shall soon be partakers of His victory.[1]

When I set myself to meditate on the life of Charles Simeon, that is the achievement I wanted to understand. I had heard that he stayed in the same church as pastor for fifty-four years and that in the first twelve there was so much opposition from his congregation that "pewholders" locked their pews, stayed away, and forced him to preach to a standing congregation who fit in the building where they could. I wanted to verify this and understand how a man endures that kind of opposition without giving up and leaving for a more cordial reception elsewhere. My aim was to grow, and help others grow, in the biblical experience

---
[1] H. C. G. Moule, *Charles Simeon* (London: InterVarsity, 1948), 155–56.

of James 1:2–3: "Count it all joy, my brothers, when you meet trials of various kinds, for you know that the testing of your faith produces steadfastness."[2]

Patience in Tribulation

So I confess at the outset that I have a spiritual and pastoral aim in this chapter, as in the whole book. I want to encourage you—as I pursue this myself—to receive and obey Romans 12:12, "Be patient in tribulation." May Simeon's life and ministry help us see persecution, opposition, slander, misunderstanding, disappointment, self-recrimination, weakness, and danger as the normal portion of faithful Christian living and ministry. I want us to see a beleaguered triumph in the life of a man who was a sinner like us and who, year after year in his trials, "grew downward" in humility and upward in his adoration of Christ and who did not yield to bitterness or to the temptation to leave his charge—for fifty-four years.

Escaping Emotional Fragility

What I have found is that in my pastoral disappointments and discouragements there is a great power for perseverance in keeping before me the life of a person who surmounted great obstacles in obedience to God's call by the power of God's grace. I need this inspiration from another century, because I know that I am, in great measure, a child of my times. And one of the pervasive marks of our times is emotional fragility. It hangs in the air we breathe. We are easily hurt. We pout and mope easily. We blame easily. We break easily. Our marriages break easily. Our faith breaks easily. Our happiness breaks easily. And our commitment to the church breaks easily. We are easily disheartened, and it seems we have little capacity for surviving and thriving in the face of criticism and opposition.

A typical emotional response to trouble in the church is to think, *If that's the way they feel about me, then I'll just find another church.* We see very few healthy, happy examples today whose lives spell out in flesh and blood the rugged words, "Count it all joy, my brothers,

---

[2] The Greek word translated "steadfastness" is ὑπομονήν (*hupomonēn*) and means "patient endurance, perseverance, steadfastness." It is clearly one of the great gifts and goals of the Christian life, as numerous texts show. Rom. 2:7; 5:3; Col. 1:11; 1 Tim. 6:11; James 5:11; 2 Pet. 1:6; Rev. 2:2–3, 19.

when you meet trials of various kinds" (James 1:2). When historians list the character traits of America in the last third of the twentieth century, commitment, constancy, tenacity, endurance, patience, resolve, and perseverance will not be on the list. The list will begin with an all-consuming interest in self-esteem. It will be followed by the subheadings of self-assertiveness, self-enhancement, and self-realization. And if we think that we are not children of our times, let us simply test ourselves to see how we respond when people reject our ideas or spurn our good efforts or misconstrue our best intentions.

We all need help here. We are surrounded by, and are part of, a society of emotionally fragile quitters. The spirit of the age is too much in us. We need to spend time with the kind of people—whether dead or alive—whose lives prove there is another way to live. Scripture says, be "imitators of those who through faith and *patience* inherit the promises" (Heb. 6:12). So I want to hold up for us the faith and the patient endurance of Charles Simeon for our inspiration and imitation.

Simeon's Life and Times

Let's orient ourselves with some facts about his life and times. When Simeon was born on September 24, 1759, Jonathan Edwards had died just the year before. John and Charles Wesley and George Whitefield were still alive, and the "Methodist" Awakening was in full swing. Simeon would live for seventy-seven years, from 1759 to 1836—through the American Revolution, the French Revolution, and not quite into the decade of the telegraph and the railroad.

His father was a wealthy attorney, but no believer. We know nothing of his mother. She probably died early, so that he never knew her. At seven he went to England's premier boarding school, the Royal College of Eton. He was there for twelve years and was known as a homely, fancy-dressing, athletic show-off. The atmosphere was irreligious and degenerate in many ways. Looking back late in life, he said that he would be tempted to take the life of his son rather than let him see the vice he himself had seen at Eton.[3]

He said he only knew one religious book besides the Bible in those twelve years—namely, *The Whole Duty of Man*, a devotional book of the seventeenth century. Whitefield thought the book so bad that

[3] Moule, *Charles Simeon*, 18.

once, when he caught an orphan in Georgia with a copy of it, he made him throw it in the fire. William Cowper said it was a "repository of self-righteous and pharisaical lumber."[4] That, in fact, would be a good description of Simeon's life to that point.

How God Saved Him

At nineteen he went to King's College in the University of Cambridge. In the first four months, God brought him from darkness to light. The amazing thing about his conversion to Christ is that God did it against the remarkable odds of having no other Christian around. Cambridge was so destitute of evangelical faith that, even after he was converted, Simeon did not meet another believer on campus for almost three years. "The waves of the great Methodist revival appear to have left Cambridge almost or quite untouched."[5]

Three days after he arrived at Cambridge on January 29, 1779, the provost, William Cooke, announced that Simeon had to attend the Lord's Supper. Simeon was terrified. We can see, in retrospect, that this was the work of God in his life. He knew enough to fear that it was very dangerous to eat the Lord's Supper as an unbeliever or a hypocrite. So he began desperately to read and to try to repent and make himself better. He began with *The Whole Duty of Man* but got no help. He passed through that first Communion unchanged. But he knew it wasn't the last. He turned to a book by a Bishop Wilson on the Lord's Supper. As Easter Sunday approached, a wonderful thing happened.

Keep in mind that this young man had almost no preparation of the kind we count so important. He had no mother to nurture him. His father was an unbeliever. His boarding school was a godless and corrupt place. And his university was destitute, as far as he knew, of other evangelical believers. He was nineteen years old, sitting in his dormitory room as Passion Week began at the end of March 1779.

Here is his own account of what happened.

In Passion Week, as I was reading Bishop Wilson on the Lord's Supper, I met with an expression to this effect—"That the Jews knew what they did, when they transferred their sin to the head of their offering." The thought

---

[4] R. Southey, *The Life of William Cowper*, 2 vols. (1854), 1:81, quoted in Hugh Evan Hopkins, *Charles Simeon of Cambridge* (Grand Rapids, MI: Eerdmans, 1977), 27.
[5] Moule, *Charles Simeon*, 21.

came into my mind, What, may I transfer all my guilt to another? Has God provided an Offering for me, that I may lay my sins on His head? Then, God willing, I will not bear them on my own soul one moment longer. Accordingly I sought to lay my sins upon the sacred head of Jesus; and on the Wednesday began to have a hope of mercy; on the Thursday that hope increased; on the Friday and Saturday it became more strong; and on the Sunday morning, Easter-day, April 4, I awoke early with those words upon my heart and lips, "Jesus Christ is risen to-day! Hallelujah! Hallelujah!" From that hour peace flowed in rich abundance into my soul; and at the Lord's Table in our Chapel I had the sweetest access to God through my blessed Savior.[6]

Bearing Fruit Worthy of Repentance

The effect was immediate and dramatic. His well-known extravagance gave way to a life of simplicity. This is the very same effect we will see in the twenty-six-year-old William Wilberforce in the next chapter. All the rest of his life, Simeon lived in simple rooms on the university campus, moving only once to larger quarters so that he could have more students for his conversation gatherings. When his brother left him a fortune, he turned it down and channeled all his extra income to religious and charitable goals. He began at once to teach his new biblical faith to his servant girl at the college. When he went home for holidays, he called the family together for devotions. His father never came, but his two brothers were both eventually converted. And in his private life he began to practice what in those days was known as "Methodism"—strict discipline in prayer and meditation.

We can catch a glimpse of his zeal from this anecdote about his early rising for Bible study and prayer.

Early rising did not appeal to his natural tendency to self-indulgence, however, especially on dark winter mornings. . . . On several occasions he overslept, to his considerable chagrin. So he determined that if ever he did it again, he would pay a fine of half a crown to his "bedmaker" (college servant). A few days later, as he lay comfortably in his warm bed, he found himself reflecting that the good woman was poor and could probably do with half a crown. So, to overcome such rationalizations, he vowed that next time he would throw a guinea[7] into the river. This (the story goes) he duly did, but

---

[6] Ibid., 25–26
[7] A "guinea" was a gold coin issued in England from 1663 to 1813 and worth one pound and one shilling.

only once, for guineas were scarce; he could not afford to use them to pave the river bed with gold.[8]

In spite of this disciplined approach to spiritual growth, Simeon's native pride and impetuousness did not disappear overnight. We will see shortly that this was one of the thorns he would be plucking at for some time.

The Call to Trinity Church, Cambridge

After three years, in January 1782, Simeon received a fellowship at the university. This gave him a stipend and certain rights in the university. For example, over the next fifty years he was three times dean for a total of nine years, and once vice provost. But that was not his main calling. In May that year, he was ordained a deacon in the Anglican Church, and after a summer preaching interim in St. Edward's Church in Cambridge, he was called to Trinity Church as vicar (pastor). He preached his first sermon there on November 10, 1782. And there he stayed for fifty-four years until his death on November 13, 1836.

Celibacy

Simeon never married. I have read only one sentence about this fact. H. C. G. Moule said he "had deliberately and resolutely chosen the then necessary celibacy of a Fellowship that he might the better work for God at Cambridge."[9] This too requires a special kind of endurance. Not many have it, and it is a beautiful thing when one finds it. Who knows how many men and women Simeon inspired with the possibility of celibacy and chastity because of his lifelong commitment to Christ and his church as an unmarried man. One such person in our day who counts Simeon as a hero in this and other regards is John Stott, a kind of latter-day Simeon in more ways than most realize. Not only did neither marry, but both were evangelical and Anglican, Cambridge graduates, long-time pastors in one church, celibate, committed to social concern, and engaged in world evangelization.[10]

---

[8] Ibid., 66.

[9] Ibid., 111.

[10] John Stott's great admiration for Simeon is unconcealed. He wrote the introduction for a collection of Simeon's sermons, *Evangelical Preaching: An Anthology of Sermons by Charles Simeon* (Sisters, OR: Multnomah, 1986), and confessed to a friend, "Charles Simeon of Cambridge remains something of a guru

A Long Global Impact

In his fifty-four years at Trinity Church, Simeon became a powerful force for evangelicalism in the Anglican church. His position at the university, with his constant influence on students preparing for the ministry, made him a great recruiter of young evangelicals for pulpits around the land. But not only around the land. He became the trusted adviser of the East India Company and recommended most of the men who went out as chaplains, which is the way Anglicans could be missionaries to the East in those days.

Simeon had a great heart for missions. He was the spiritual father and mentor of the great Henry Martyn, who when he died in 1813 at the age of thirty-one, had been a chaplain in the East India Company and had in less than five years translated the New Testament into Urdu (then called Hindoostani) and Persian and supervised its translation into Arabic. Simeon was the key spiritual influence in the founding of the Church Missionary Society and was zealous in his labors for the British and Foreign Bible Society and the Society for Promoting Christianity among the Jews. In fact, on his deathbed he was dictating a message to be given to the Society about his deep humiliation that the church had not done more to gather in the Jewish people.

A Preacher without Labels

Simeon probably exerted his greatest influence through sustained biblical preaching year after year. This was the central labor of his life. He lived long enough to place into the hands of King William IV in 1833 the completed twenty-one volumes of his collected sermons. This is the best place to go to research Simeon's theology. One can find his views on almost every key text in the Bible. That is what he wanted to be above all theological labels, biblical.

---

to me." Timothy Dudley-Smith, *John Stott: A Global Ministry, A Biography, the Latter Years* (Downers Grove, IL: InterVarsity Press, 2001), 428. The author of that biography says,

> The parallels between the two men are certainly striking. Both were privileged sons of comparatively affluent parents, educated at public schools, undergraduates at Cambridge. They shared a transforming experience of conversion to Christ, early and severe trials and testing, and virtually a lifetime's ministry in a single church. Each cultivated habits well beyond the norm for early rising, disciplined prayer and the study of Scripture. Each became a mentor to students, and a leader to younger clergy as well as among his contemporaries. They shared a call to the single life, and to the rediscovery (and subsequent teaching) of the art of expository preaching. Like John Stott, Simeon had a world vision (as one of the founders of the Church Missionary Society) and a grasp of strategic organization, as in the patronage trust which he founded and which still bears his name. Each was a believer in the power of the printed word, and published many volumes of Bible exposition. (Ibid., 428–29)

He did not want to be labeled a Calvinist or an Arminian. He wanted to be faithful to Scripture through and through and give every text its due proportion, whether it sounded Arminian or Calvinistic. But he was known as an evangelical Calvinist, and rightly so. As I have read portions of his sermons on texts concerning election, effectual calling, and perseverance, I have found him uninhibited in his affirmation of what the Puritans called "the doctrines of grace." In fact, he uses that phrase approvingly in his sermon on Romans 9:19–24.[11]

But he had little sympathy for uncharitable Calvinists. In a sermon on Romans 9:16, he said:

> Many there are who cannot see these truths [the doctrines of God's sovereignty], who yet are in a state truly pleasing to God; yea many, at whose feet the best of us may be glad to be found in heaven. It is a great evil, when these doctrines are made a ground of separation one from another, and when the advocates of different systems anathematize each other. . . . In reference to truths which are involved in so much obscurity as those which relate to the sovereignty of God, mutual kindness and concession are far better than vehement argumentation and uncharitable discussion.[12]

A Conversation with John Wesley

An example of how he lived out this counsel is seen in the way he conversed with the elderly John Wesley. He tells the story himself:

> Sir, I understand that you are called an Arminian; and I have been sometimes called a Calvinist; and therefore I suppose we are to draw daggers. But before I consent to begin the combat, with your permission I will ask you a few questions. Pray, Sir, do you feel yourself a depraved creature, so depraved that you would never have thought of turning to God, if God had not first put it into your heart?
>
> Yes, I do indeed.
>
> And do you utterly despair of recommending yourself to God by anything you can do; and look for salvation solely through the blood and righteousness of Christ?
>
> Yes, solely through Christ.
>
> But, Sir, supposing you were at first saved by Christ, are you not somehow or other to save yourself afterwards by your own works?

---

[11] Charles Simeon, *Horae Homileticae*, 21 vols. (1832), 15:358.
[12] Ibid., 357.

No, I must be saved by Christ from first to last.

Allowing, then, that you were first turned by the grace of God, are you not in some way or other to keep yourself by your own power?

No.

What then, are you to be upheld every hour and every moment by God, as much as an infant in its mother's arms?

Yes, altogether.

And is all your hope in the grace and mercy of God to preserve you unto His heavenly kingdom?

Yes, I have no hope but in Him.

Then, Sir, with your leave I will put up my dagger again; for this is all my Calvinism; this is my election, my justification by faith, my final perseverance: it is in substance all that I hold, and as I hold it; and therefore, if you please, instead of searching out terms and phrases to be a ground of contention between us, we will cordially unite in those things wherein we agree.[13]

But don't take this to mean that Simeon pulled any punches when expounding biblical texts. He was very forthright in teaching what the Bible teaches and calling error by its real name. But he was jealous of not getting things out of balance.

Christ, the Center of All Subjects

Hugh Evan Hopkins, a biographer of Simeon, explains the essence of his preaching:

His matter was never trivial, and he never for a moment wandered into idle rhetoric. To expound the Scripture before him as closely and clearly as he could, and then to bring its message to bear full on the conscience and will of the hearers, was his settled aim from the first, kept in view intelligently with great pains. And what was his doctrine? In two words, it was Jesus Christ. Everything in Simeon's preaching radiated from Jesus Christ, and returned upon Him. Not that he forced texts away from their surroundings, and forgot the literal in the mystical. But he was sure that Christ is the burden of the words of the Prophets and the Apostles; and he knew that He was everything for Charles Simeon. . . . For him Christ was the centre of all subjects for sinful man; and all his hearers were for him sinful men, for whom the Gospel was the one remedy. Christ was the Gospel; and personal faith in Him, a living Person, was the Gospel secret. . . . Simeon himself thus describes

---

13 Moule, *Charles Simeon*, 79–80.

the three great aims of all his preaching: *"To humble the sinner, To exalt the Saviour, To promote holiness."*[14]

Let the Bible Speak

He said that his invariable rule was "to endeavor to give to every portion of the Word of God its full and proper force, without considering what scheme it favors, or whose system it is likely to advance."[15] "My endeavor is to bring out of Scripture what is there, and not to thrust in what I think might be there. I have a great jealousy on this head; never to speak more or less than I believe to be the mind of the Spirit in the passage I am expounding."[16]

He makes an observation that is true enough to sting every person who has ever been tempted to adjust Scripture to fit a system.

> Of this he [speaking of himself in the third person] is sure, that there is not a decided Calvinist or Arminian in the world who equally approves of the whole of Scripture . . . who, if he had been in the company of St. Paul whilst he was writing his Epistles, would not have recommended him to alter one or other of his expressions.
>
> But the author would not wish one of them altered; he finds as much satisfaction in one class of passages as in another; and employs the one, he believes, as freely as the other. Where the inspired Writers speak in unqualified terms, he thinks himself at liberty to do the same; judging that they needed no instruction from *him* how to propagate the truth. He is content to sit as a learner at the feet of the holy Apostles and has no ambition to teach them how they ought to have spoken.[17]

With that remarkable devotion to Scripture, Simeon preached in the same pulpit for fifty-four years with a global impact. It was this combination of deep and fruitful devotion to Scripture and fifty-four years of endurance in one place of ministry, in spite of opposition and difficulty, that drew me to Simeon. That is what I turn to now. First his trials, and then finally the roots of his endurance that enabled him to press on to the end and not give up. How was he able to be so "patient in tribulation"?

---

[14] Ibid., 52.
[15] Ibid., 79.
[16] Ibid., 77.
[17] Ibid., 79.

The Unripe Self

The most fundamental trial that Simeon had—and that we all have—was himself. He had a somewhat harsh and self-assertive air about him. One day early in Simeon's ministry, he was visiting Henry Venn, who was pastor twelve miles from Cambridge at Yelling. When he left to go home, Venn's daughters complained to their father about his manner. Venn took the girls to the backyard and said, "Pick me one of those peaches." But it was early summer, and "the time of peaches was not yet." They asked why he would want the green, unripe fruit. Venn replied, "Well, my dears, it is green now, and we must wait; but a little more sun, and a few more showers, and the peach will be ripe and sweet. So it is with Mr. Simeon."[18]

Simeon came to know himself and his sin very deeply. He described his maturing in the ministry as a growing downward. We will come back to this as the key to his great perseverance and success.

The Unwanted Vicar

The previous vicar of Trinity Church died in October 1782, just as Charles Simeon was about to leave the university to live in his father's home. Simeon had often walked by the church, he tells us, and said to himself, "How should I rejoice if God were to give me that church, that I might preach the Gospel there and be a herald for Him in the University."[19] His dream came true when Bishop Yorke appointed him "curate-in-charge" (being only ordained a deacon at the time). His wealthy father had nudged the bishop to prefer his son; and the pastor at St. Edward's, where Simeon preached that summer, gave him an endorsement. So he received the assignment and preached his first sermon at Trinity Church on November 10, 1782.

But the parishioners did not want Simeon. They wanted the assistant curate, Mr. Hammond. Simeon was willing to step out, but then the bishop told him that even if he did decline the appointment, Hammond would not be appointed. So Simeon stayed—for fifty-four years! And gradually—very gradually—overcame the opposition.

The first thing the congregation did in rebellion against Simeon was to refuse to let him be the Sunday afternoon lecturer. This second Sunday

---

[18] Ibid., 44.
[19] Ibid., 37.

service was in their charge. For five years they assigned the lecture to Mr. Hammond. Then when he left, instead of turning it over to their pastor of five years, they gave it to another independent man for seven more years! Finally, in 1794, Simeon was chosen lecturer.[20] Thus for twelve years he served a church who was so resistant to his leadership they would not let him preach Sunday afternoons but hired an assistant to keep him out.

Simeon tried to start a later Sunday evening service, and many towns-people came. But the churchwardens locked the doors while the people stood waiting in the street. Once Simeon had the doors opened by a lock-smith, but when it happened again, he relented and dropped the service.

The second thing the church did was to lock the pew doors on Sun-day mornings. The pewholders refused to come and refused to let others sit in their personal pews. Simeon set up seats in the aisles and nooks and corners at his own expense. But the churchwardens took them out and threw them into the churchyard. When he tried to visit from house to house, hardly a door would open to him. This situation lasted at least ten years. The records show that in 1792 Simeon got a legal decision that the pewholders could not lock their pews.[21] But he didn't use it. He let his steady, relentless ministry of the Word and prayer and com-munity witness gradually overcome the resistance.

But I mustn't give the impression that all the troubles were finished after the first twelve years. There were, to be sure, years of peace, but in 1812 (after he had been there thirty years!) there were again opponents in the congregation making the waters rough. He wrote to a friend, "I used to sail in the Pacific; I am now learning to navigate the Red Sea that is full of shoals and rocks." Who of us would not have concluded that at age fifty-three, after thirty years in one church, an upsurge of opposition is surely a sign to move on? But again he endured patiently, and in 1815 he writes that peace had come to the church and that he had "the joy of ministering to an united and affectionate flock."[22]

Despised in His Own University

As the students made their way to Trinity Church, they were prejudiced against the pastor by the hostile congregation, and for years he was

---

[20] Ibid., 39.
[21] Ibid., 45.
[22] William Carus, *Memoirs of the Life of the Rev. Charles Simeon* (London, 1847), 245.

smeared with all kinds of rumors. "From the very first, and for many years after, he was personally slandered as a bad man who had a high profession of goodness; a terrible dagger-thrust at any time, but never more so than when, as then, the outward practice of religion has fallen into general neglect."[23] The students at Cambridge held Simeon in derision for his biblical preaching and his uncompromising stand as an evangelical.

They repeatedly disrupted his services and caused a carousing in the streets. One observer wrote from personal experience, "For many years Trinity Church and the streets leading to it were the scenes of the most disgraceful tumults."[24] Simeon himself tells of "several occasions [when] stones were thrown in at the windows."[25] On one occasion a band of undergraduates determined to assault Simeon personally as he left the church after service. They waited by the usual exit for him, but providentially he took another way home that day.[26] Students who were converted and wakened by Simeon's preaching were soon ostracized and ridiculed. They were called "Sims"—a term that lasted all the way to the 1860s—and their way of thinking was called derisively "Simeonism."

But harder to bear than the insults of the students was the ostracism and coldness of his peers in the university. One of the Fellows scheduled Greek classes on Sunday night to prevent students from going to Simeon's service. In another instance, one of the students who looked up to Simeon was denied an academic prize because of his "Simeonism."[27] Sometimes Simeon felt utterly alone at the university where he lived. He looked back on those early years and wrote, "I remember the time that I was quite surprised that a Fellow of my own College ventured to walk with me for a quarter of an hour on the grass-plot before Clare Hall; and for many years after I began my ministry I was 'as a man wondered at,' by reason of the paucity of those who showed any regard for true religion."[28]

Even after he had won the respect of many, there could be grave mistreatment. For example, even as late as 1816 (thirty-four years into his

---

[23] Moule, *Charles Simeon*, 53.
[24] Ibid., 58.
[25] Ibid., 56.
[26] Ibid., 59.
[27] Ibid., 55.
[28] Ibid., 59.

ministry), he wrote to a missionary friend, "Such conduct is observed towards me at this very hour by one of the Fellows of the College as, if practiced by *me*, would set not the College only but the whole town and University in a flame."[29]

Broken and Restored for Ministry in Old Age

In 1807, after twenty-five years of ministry, his health failed suddenly. His voice gave way so that preaching was very difficult, and at times he could only speak in a whisper. After a sermon he would feel "more like one dead than alive."[30] This broken condition lasted for thirteen years, till he was sixty years old. In all this time, Simeon pressed on in his work.

The way this weakness came to an end is remarkable and shows the amazing hand of God on Simeon's life. "It passed away quite suddenly and without any evident physical cause."[31] He tells the story that in 1819 he was on his last visit to Scotland. As he crossed the border, he says he was "almost as perceptibly revived in strength as the woman was after she had touched the hem of our Lord's garment."[32] His interpretation of God's providence in this begins back before the weakness had befallen him in 1807. Up till then he had promised himself a very active life up to age sixty, and then a Sabbath evening. Now he seemed to hear his Master saying:

> I laid you aside, because you entertained with satisfaction the thought of resting from your labor; but now you have arrived at the very period when you had promised yourself that satisfaction, and have determined instead to spend your strength for me to the latest hour of your life, I have doubled, trebled, quadrupled your strength, that you may execute your desire on a more extended plan.[33]

So at sixty years of age, Simeon renewed his commitment to his pulpit and the local and global mission of the church and preached vigorously for seventeen more years, until two months before his death. Surely there is a lesson for us here concerning retirement. Is there any biblical warrant for the modern, Western assumption that old age or

---

[29] Ibid., 127.
[30] Ibid., 125.
[31] Ibid.
[32] Ibid.
[33] Ibid.

retirement years are to be years of coasting or easing up or playing? I am not aware of such a principle in the Bible. In fact, it is a great sadness to see so many older Christians adapting to this cultural norm and wasting the last decades of their lives in innocent lounging around. Who knows but that greater strength and health would be given if there were resolves to move toward need and not comfort in our old age? Who knows whether God would give awakening and renewal if we would renew our dreams of ministry to the perishing world and not just the "ministry" of playing with our grandchildren?

The Roots of His Endurance

How did Simeon endure his trials for so long without giving up or being driven out of his church? There were numerous biblical strategies of endurance. But there was also a root that was deeper than the particular forms and strategies of endurance. First we will look at the forms and strategies of endurance, and finally focus on the root that sustained them all.

A Strong Sense of His Accountability before God for the Souls of His Flock

In his first year in the pulpit he preached a sermon about his accountability before God and said to the people standing in the aisles:

> Remember the nature of my office, and the care incumbent on me for the welfare of your immortal souls. . . . Consider whatever may appear in my discourses harsh, earnest or alarming, not as the effects of enthusiasm, but as the rational dictates of a heart impressed with a sense both of the value of the soul and the importance of eternity. . . . By recollecting the awful consequences of my neglect, you will be more inclined to receive favorably any well-meant admonitions.[34]

Fifteen years later he preached on the subject again. Years after this sermon, one of his friends told of how its power was still being felt. Simeon said the pastor is like the keeper of a lighthouse. He painted a vivid picture of a rocky coast strewn with dead and mangled bodies with the wailing of widows and orphans. He pictured the delinquent

---

[34] Ibid., 46.

keeper being brought out and at last the answer given: "Asleep!"[35] The way he made this word burst on the ears of the hearers never let at least one of them ever forget what is at stake in the pastoral ministry. Wakeful endurance was a life-and-death matter for Simeon. He dared not have a casual, sleepy-eyed approach to ministry.

It did not matter that his people were often against him. He was not commissioned by them, but by the Lord. And they were his responsibility. He believed Hebrews 13:17—that he would one day have to give an account for the souls of his church.

Free from the Scolding Tone Even through Controversy

How many times have we heard a pastor's wounded pride or his personal anger at parishioners sleeping through his preaching! This is deadly for the ministry. Moule, Simeon's biographer, said of him that his style of address in those early years of intense opposition was "totally free from that easy but fatal mistake of troubled pastors, the scolding accent."[36]

Years after his conversion he said that his security in God gave him the capacity to be hopeful in the presence of other people even when burdened within: "With this sweet hope of ultimate acceptance with God, I have always enjoyed much cheerfulness before men; but I have at the same time labored incessantly to cultivate the deepest humiliation before God."[37]

Joseph Gurney saw the same thing in Simeon for years and wrote, that in spite of Simeon's private weeping, "it was one of his grand principles of action, to endeavor at all times to honor his Master by maintaining a cheerful happy demeanor in the presence of his friends."[38] He had evidently learned the lesson of Matthew 6:17–18, "But when you fast, anoint your head and wash your face, that your fasting may not be seen by others but by your Father who is in secret."

Simeon's joyful, life-giving demeanor can perhaps best be seen in the descriptions of him by William Cowper and William Wilberforce. Cowper wrote:

> . . . with a smile
> Gentle and affable, and full of grace,

---

[35] Hopkins, *Charles Simeon of Cambridge*, 64–65.
[36] Moule, *Charles Simeon*, 46.
[37] Hopkins, *Charles Simeon of Cambridge*, 156.
[38] Moule, *Charles Simeon*, 157.

As fearful of offending whom he wish'd
Much to persuade, he plied his ear with truths
Not harshly thunder'd forth or rudely press'd
But, like his purpose, gracious, kind and sweet.[39]

And Wilberforce recorded in his journal: "Simeon with us—his heart glowing with love of Christ. How full he is of love, and of desire to promote the spiritual benefit of others. Oh! that I might copy him as he Christ."[40]

Not a Rumor-Tracker

He was like Charles Spurgeon, who gave a lecture to his students titled "The Blind Eye and the Deaf Ear."[41] The pastor must have one blind eye and one deaf ear, and turn that eye and that ear to the rumors that would incense him.

Simeon was deeply wronged in 1821. We are not given the details. But when he was asked about his response (which had evidently been nonretaliatory), he said, "My rule is—never to hear, or see, or know, what if heard, or seen, or known, would call for animadversion from me. Hence it is that I dwell in peace in the midst of lions."[42] In other words, we would all do well not to be curious about what others are saying about us. There is little good that can come of it: pride, if the comments are good; discouragement, if they are critical; anger, if they are false. These are not the emotions we need to cultivate. Trusted counsel from reliable people, not rumors, is the stuff of good self-assessment.

Not a Heresy-Hunter

A pastor wrote to Simeon, wanting him to "answer and knock down" a certain preacher whom he suspected of doctrinal error. But Simeon was more exercised by the manner in which this informing pastor sought to go about this controversy. He wrote back to him:

> I know you will forgive me if I say that the very account you give of yourself in relation to controversy is a dissuasive from embarking in it. Let a man once engage in it, and it is surprising how the love of it will grow upon him;

---

[39] Hopkins, *Charles Simeon of Cambridge*, 66.
[40] Ibid., 166.
[41] Charles Spurgeon, *Lectures to My Students* (Grand Rapids, MI: Zondervan, 1972), 321–35.
[42] Moule, *Charles Simeon*, 191.

and he will find both a hare in every bush, and will follow it with something of a huntsman's feelings.[43]

Controversy and doctrinal accountability are tasks we must engage in until the Lord returns. It is not a happy business, but it is a necessary one. And in so doing, we must all heed Simeon's words to examine our motives lest we love controversy more than the truth itself.

Dealing with Opponents in a Forthright, Face-to-Face Way

In 1810, a man named Edward Pearson accused Simeon of setting too high a standard of holiness in his preaching. This criticism was made public in pamphlets. Simeon wrote to Pearson and said:

> Persons who have the same general design, but differ in some particular modes of carrying it into execution, often stand more aloof from each other than they do from persons whose principles and conduct they entirely disapprove. Hence prejudice arises and a tendency to mutual crimination; whereas, if they occasionally conversed for half an hour with each other, they would soon rectify their mutual misapprehensions, and concur in aiding, rather than undermining, the efforts of each other for the public good.[44]

It is remarkable, as Simeon said, how much evil can be averted by doing things face to face. We attempt far too much fence mending today by letter or e-mail or phone. There is something mysteriously powerful about the peacemaking potentials of personal, face-to-face conversation. It did not spare Simeon years of criticism, but it was surely one of the means God used to overcome the opposition in the long run.

Receiving Rebuke and Growing from It

Receiving and benefiting from criticism is utterly essential to survive and thrive in Christian life and ministry. We need to absorb and profit from reproof—from the Lord and from man. Recall how Simeon interpreted his thirteen-year weakness from age forty-seven to sixty as a rebuke from the Lord for his intention to retire at sixty. He took it well and gave himself with all his might to the ministry of the Word until he died. At seventy-six he wrote, "Through mercy I am, for min-

---

[43] Hopkins, *Charles Simeon of Cambridge*, 171.
[44] Ibid., 126–27.

isterial service, stronger than I have been at any time this thirty years
. . . preaching at seventy-six with all the exuberance of youth . . . but
looking for my dismission [death] daily."[45] He was not embittered by a
thirteen-year rebuke. He was impelled by it.

It was the same with rebukes from men. If these rebukes came from
his enemies, his sentiment was the sentiment of Genesis 50:20: "As for
you, you meant evil against me, but God meant it for good." Simeon
said, "If I suffer with a becoming spirit, my enemies, though unwit-
tingly, must of necessity do me good."[46]

But his friends rebuked him as well. For example, he had the bad
habit of speaking as if he were very angry about mere trifles. One day
at a Mr. Hankinson's house, he became so irritated at how the servant
was stoking the fire that he gave him a swat on the back to get him to
stop. Then when he was leaving, the servant got a bridle mixed up, and
Simeon's temper broke out violently against the man. Mr. Hankinson
wrote a letter as if from his servant and put it in Simeon's bag to be
found later. In it he said that he did not see how a man who preached
and prayed so well could be in such a passion about nothing and wear
no *bridle* on his tongue. He signed it "John Softly."

Simeon responded (on April 12, 1804) directly to the servant with
the words, "To John Softly, from Charles, Proud and Irritable: I most
cordially thank you, my dear friend, for your kind and seasonable reproof." Then he wrote to his friend Mr. Hankinson, "I hope, my dearest
brother, that when you find your soul nigh to God, you will remember
one who so greatly needs all the help he can get."[47] We will see the root
of this willingness to be humbled in just a moment.

Unimpeachable in His Finances with No Love of Money

He gave his enemies no foothold when it came to lifestyle and wealth.
He lived as a single man simply in his rooms at the university and
gave all his excess income to the poor of the community. He turned
down the inheritance of his rich brother.[48] Moule said he had "a noble

---

[45] Ibid., 162.

[46] Ibid., 39.

[47] Ibid., 147.

[48] In a memorandum Simeon wrote to explain why, with his resources, he did not abandon his role and
dependence on the modest living of a University Fellow:

> My brother was extremely liberal. . . . . At his death an exceeding great void would have been made,
> if I had not determined to accept a part of his property and to appropriate it to the Lord's service

indifference to money."[49] And his active involvement with the relief for the poor in the area went a long way toward overcoming the prejudices against him. It is hard to be the enemy of a person who is full of practical good deeds. In this way he put into practice the counsel of the apostle Peter: "This is the will of God, that by doing good you should put to silence the ignorance of foolish men" (1 Pet. 2:15).

Seeing Discouraging Things Hopefully

When the members of his congregation locked their pews and kept them locked for over ten years, Simeon said:

> In this state of things I saw no remedy but faith and patience. The passage of Scripture which subdued and controlled my mind was this, "The servant of the Lord must not strive" [2 Tim. 2:24]. It was painful indeed to see the church, with the exception of the aisles, almost forsaken; but I thought that if God would only give a double blessing to the congregation that did attend, there would on the whole be as much good done as if the congregation were doubled and the blessing limited to only half the amount. This comforted me many, many times, when, without such a reflection, I should have sunk under my burden.[50]

One illustration of the truth of Simeon's confidence is the story of one of his preaching trips to Scotland. He happened to visit the home of a minister named Stewart who was not truly converted and was quite miserable. Through the personal life and witness of Simeon, Mr. Stewart was transformed, and for fifteen years afterward was powerful for the gospel.

One of the couples who said later that they "owed their own selves" to the new preaching of Mr. Stewart were the parents of Alexander Duff. They brought up their son in the full faith of the gospel and with a special sense of dedication to the service of Christ. Duff, in turn, became one of the great Scottish missionaries to India for over fifty years. So it

---

and the service of the poor. The loss they would have sustained being about £700 or £800 a year, I suffered my brother to leave me £15,000, and have regularly consecrated the interest of it to the Lord; and shall (D.V.) continue to do so to my dying hour. Had I wished for money for my own use, I might have had half his fortune; but I wanted nothing for myself, being determined (as far as such a thing could be at any time said to be determined) to live and die in the College, where the income which I previously enjoyed (though moderate in itself) sufficed not only for all my own wants, but for liberal supplies to the poor also. . . . The fact is, I have not increased my own expenditure above £50 a year; nor do I consider myself as anything but a steward of my deceased brother for the poor. (Quoted in Arthur J. Tait, *Charles Simeon and His Trust* [London: Society for Promoting Christian Knowledge, 1936], 51–52)

[49] Moule, *Charles Simeon*, 129.

[50] Ibid., 39.

is true that you never know when the Lord may give a double blessing on your ministry to a small number and multiply it thirty-, sixty-, or a hundredfold even after you are dead and gone. This confidence kept Simeon going more than once.

Suffering as a Privilege of Bearing the Cross with Christ

One striking witness to this was during a time when the university was especially cold and hostile to him.

> I was an object of much contempt and derision in the University. I strolled forth one day, buffeted and afflicted with my little Testament in my hand, I prayed earnestly to my God that He would comfort me with some cordial from His Word, and that, on opening the book, I might find some text which should sustain me. It was not for direction I was looking, for I am no friend to such superstitions . . . but only for support. The first text which caught my eye was this: *"They found a man of Cyrene, Simon by name; him they compelled to bear His cross."* You know Simon is the same name as Simeon. What a word of instruction was there—what a blessed hint of my encouragement! To have the cross laid upon me, that I might bear it after Jesus—what a privilege! It was enough. Now I could leap and sing for joy as one whom Jesus was honoring with a participation of His sufferings.[51]

We recall his words when he was seventy-one and Joseph Gurney asked him how he had surmounted his persecution for forty-nine years. He said, "My dear brother, we must not mind a little suffering for Christ's sake."

The Deepest Root of Simeon's Endurance

But where now did this remarkable power and all these forms and strategies of endurance come from? Simeon did not respond to trial and suffering the way ordinary humans respond. Something else was at work here than a mere man. Beneath the forms of his endurance was a life of prayer and meditation that drew up resources for the battle from some deeper place. Both prayer and meditation were essential to tap the grace of God. "Meditation is the grand means of our growth in grace; without it, prayer itself is an empty service."[52] A friend of Simeon's

---

[51] Ibid., 59–60.
[52] Ibid., 137–38.

named Housman lived with him for a few months and tells us about this discipline of prayer and the Word.

> Simeon invariably arose every morning, though it was the winter season, at four o'clock; and, after lighting his fire, he devoted the first four hours of the day to private prayer and the devotional study of the Scriptures. . . . Here was the secret of his great grace and spiritual strength. Deriving instruction from such a source, and seeking it with such diligence, he was comforted in all his trials and prepared for every duty.[53]

Yes, it was a secret of his strength. But it was not the deepest secret. *What* Simeon experienced in the Word and prayer was extraordinary. It is so utterly different from the counsel we receive today that it is worth looking at carefully.

Growing Downward in Humiliation before God, Upward in Adoration of Christ

Handley Moule captures the essence of Simeon's secret of longevity in this sentence: "'Before honor is humility,' and he had been '*growing downwards*' year by year under the stern discipline of difficulty met in the right way, the way of *close and adoring communion with God.*"[54] Those two things were the heartbeat of Simeon's inner life: growing downward in humility and growing upward in adoring communion with God.

But the remarkable thing about humiliation and adoration in the heart of Charles Simeon is that they were inseparable. Simeon was utterly unlike most of us today who think that we should get rid once and for all of feelings of vileness and unworthiness as soon as we can. For him, adoration only grew in the freshly plowed soil of humiliation for sin. So he actually labored to know his true sinfulness and his remaining corruption as a Christian.

> I have continually had such a sense of my sinfulness as would sink me into utter despair, if I had not an assured view of the sufficiency and willingness of Christ to save me to the uttermost. And at the same time I had such a sense of my acceptance through Christ as would overset my little bark, if I had not ballast at the bottom sufficient to sink a vessel of no ordinary size.[55]

---

[53] Ibid., 66.
[54] Ibid., 64, emphasis added.
[55] Ibid., 134.

The Ballast of Humiliation

He never lost sight of the need for the heavy ballast of his own humiliation. After he had been a Christian forty years he wrote:

> With this sweet hope of ultimate acceptance with God, I have always enjoyed much cheerfulness before men; but I have at the same time labored incessantly to cultivate the deepest humiliation before God. I have never thought that the circumstance of God's having forgiven me, was any reason why I should forgive myself; on the contrary, I have always judged it better to loathe myself the more, in proportion as I was assured that God was pacified towards me (Ezek. 16:63). . . . There are but two objects that I have ever desired for these forty years to behold; the one, is my own vileness; and the other is, the glory of God in the face of Jesus Christ: and I have always thought that they should be viewed together; just as Aaron confessed all the sins of all Israel whilst he put them on the head of the scapegoat. The disease did not keep him from applying to the remedy, nor did the remedy keep him from feeling the disease. By this I seek to be, not only *humble and thankful* but *humbled in thankfulness*, before my God and Savior continually.[56]

If Simeon is right, vast portions of contemporary Christianity are wrong. And I can't help wondering whether one of the reasons we are emotionally capsized so easily today—so vulnerable to winds of criticism or opposition—is that in the name of forgiveness and grace, we have thrown the ballast overboard. Simeon's boat drew a lot of water. But it was steady and on course and the mastheads were higher and the sails bigger and more full of the Spirit than most people's today who talk more of self-esteem than self-humbling.

Ballast Below, Full Sails Above—at the Same Time

One of Simeon's missionary friends wrote about a time in 1794 when a certain Mr. Marsden entered Simeon's room and found him "so absorbed in the contemplation of the Son of God, and so overpowered with a display of His mercy to his soul, that he was incapable of pronouncing a single word," till at length he exclaimed, "Glory, glory." Only a few days later, the missionary friend found Simeon at the hour

---

[56] Carus, *Memoirs of the Life of the Rev. Charles Simeon*, 303–4.

of the private lecture on Sunday scarcely able to speak, "from a deep humiliation and contrition."[57]

Moule comments that these two experiences are not the alternating excesses of an ill-balanced mind. Rather, they are "the two poles of a sphere of profound experience."[58] For Simeon, adoration of God grew best in the plowed soil of his own contrition. He had no fear of turning up every sin in his life and looking upon it with great grief and hatred, because he had such a vision of Christ's sufficiency that this would always result in deeper cleansing and adoration.

Humiliation and adoration were inseparable. He wrote to Mary Elliott, the sister of the writer of the hymn "Just as I Am":

> I would have the whole of my experience one continued sense—first, of my nothingness, and dependence on God; second, of my guiltiness and desert before Him; third, of my obligations to redeeming love, as utterly over-whelming me with its incomprehensible extent and grandeur. Now I do not see why any one of these should swallow up another.[59]

As an old man he said, "I have had deep and abundant cause for humiliation, [but] I have never ceased to wash in that fountain that was opened for sin and uncleanness, or to cast myself upon the tender mercy of my reconciled God."[60] He was convinced that biblical doctrines "at once most abase and most gladden the soul."[61] He spoke once to the Duchess de Broglie when he made a visit to the Continent. He commented later, "[I] opened to her my views of the Scripture system . . . and showed her that brokenness of heart is the key to the whole."[62]

"My Proper Place"

He actually fled for refuge to the place that many today try so hard to escape.

> Repentance is in every view so desirable, so necessary, so suited to honor God, that I seek that above all. The tender heart, the broken and contrite

---

[57] Moule, *Charles Simeon*, 135.
[58] Ibid.
[59] Ibid., 160–61.
[60] Carus, *Memoirs of the Life of the Rev. Charles Simeon*, 518–19.
[61] Moule, *Charles Simeon*, 67.
[62] Ibid., 96.

spirit, are to me far above all the joys that I could ever hope for in this vale of tears. I long to be in my proper place, my hand on my mouth, and my mouth in the dust. . . . I feel this to be safe ground. Here I cannot err. . . . I am sure that whatever God may despise . . . He will not despise the broken and contrite heart.[63]

On the occasion of the fiftieth anniversary of his work at Trinity Church, looking back over his many successes, he said, "I love the valley of humiliation. I there feel that I am in my proper place."[64]

In the last months of his life he wrote, "In truth, I love to see the creature annihilated in the apprehension, and swallowed up in God; I am then safe, happy, triumphant."[65] Why? Why is this evangelical humiliation a place of happiness for Simeon? Listen to the benefits he sees in this kind of experience:

By constantly meditating on the goodness of God and on our great deliverance from that punishment which our sins have deserved, we are brought to feel our vileness and utter unworthiness; and while we continue in this spirit of self-degradation, everything else will go on easily. We shall find ourselves advancing in our course; we shall feel the presence of God; we shall experience His love; we shall live in the enjoyment of His favor and in the hope of His glory. . . . You often feel that your prayers scarcely reach the ceiling; but, oh, get into this humble spirit by considering how good the Lord is, and how evil you all are, and then prayer will mount on wings of faith to heaven. The sigh, the groan of a broken heart, will soon go through the ceiling up to heaven, aye, into the very bosom of God.[66]

A Focus on God, Not on Self

Simeon saw that the pathway to genuine humility could not be had by looking inward—either in thinking little of his gifts or in thinking much about his sins. The key was to look away from himself and toward *God.* Hopkins writes:

Self-humiliation for Simeon consisted not of belittling the gifts that God had given him or pretending that he was a man of no account, or exaggerating the sins of which he was very conscious. He went about it by consciously

---

[63] Ibid., 133–34.
[64] Ibid., 159–60.
[65] Ibid., 162.
[66] Ibid., 137–38.

bringing himself into the presence of God, dwelling thoughtfully on his majesty and glory, magnifying the mercy of his forgiveness and the wonder of his love. These were the things that humbled him—not so much his own sinfulness but God's incredible love.[67]

All the way to the end of his life, Simeon was focused upon the centrality of God as the root of his acceptance and endurance. He found his assurance, he said, "in the *sovereignty* of God in choosing such a one—and the *mercy* of God in pardoning such a one—and the *patience* of God in bearing with such a one—and the *faithfulness* of God in perfecting his work and performing all his promises to such a one."[68]

"I Am Enjoying" . . . the Cross

My conclusion is that the secret of Charles Simeon's perseverance was that he never threw overboard the heavy ballast of his own humiliation for sin and that this helped keep his masts erect and his sails full of the spirit of adoration. "I love simplicity; I love contrition. . . . I love the religion of heaven; to fall on our faces while we adore the Lamb is the kind of religion which my soul affects."[69] He once said that "there are but two lessons for Christians to learn: the one is, to enjoy God in everything; the other is, to enjoy everything in God."[70] As he lay dying in October 1836, a friend sat by his bed and asked what he was thinking of just then. He answered, "I don't think now; I am *enjoying*."[71]

He grew downward in the pain of contrition, and he grew upward in the joy of adoration. And the weaving together of these two experiences into one is the achievement of the cross of Christ and the root of Simeon's great endurance. He loved to contemplate the cross of Christ not only because it signified "salvation through a crucified Redeemer," but also because by this cross he had died to the pleasures, riches, and honors of this world. Man's admiration could not lure him; man's condemnation could not lame him. He was dead to all that now, because "by [the cross] the world has been crucified to me, and I to the world" (Gal. 6:14). The cross was the place of his greatest humiliation and the place of his greatest adoration. It was death-dealing and life-giving.

---

[67] Hopkins, *Charles Simeon of Cambridge*, 156.
[68] Ibid., 180–81.
[69] Ibid., 83–84.
[70] Ibid., 203.
[71] Moule, *Charles Simeon*, 172.

Therefore Simeon said that he, like Paul, "would 'know nothing' else (1 Cor. 2:2) and 'glory in nothing else' (Gal. 6:14 AT)."[72]

Christ was crucified for him. He was crucified with Christ. This was the key to life and endurance. This was "the power of God and the wisdom of God" (1 Cor. 1:24).

> So unfathomable are the counsels of divine wisdom contained in it, that all the angels of heaven are searching into it with a thirst that is insatiable. Such is its efficacy, that nothing can withstand its influence. By this then, my brethren, you may judge whether you are Christians in deed and in truth, or whether you are only such in name. . . . For a nominal Christian is content with *proving* the way of salvation by a crucified Redeemer. But the true Christian *loves* it, *delights* in it, *glories* in it, and *shudders* at the very thought of glorying in anything else.[73]

Here is the root of Simeon's endurance: the cross of Christ giving rise to a "shuddering delight"—shuddering at his own remaining corruption that may betray his soul by fear of man and the love of the world; delight that rises higher than all that man can take or give, and therefore triumphs over all threats and allurements. Christ is all. "Let all your joys flow from the contemplation of his cross."[74]

---

[72] Simeon, *Evangelical Preaching*, 68.
[73] Ibid., 71, emphasis added.
[74] Ibid.

The fatal habit of considering Christian morals as distinct from Christian doctrines insensibly gained strength. Thus the peculiar doctrines of Christianity went more and more out of sight, and as might naturally have been expected, the moral system itself also began to wither and decay, being robbed of that which should have supplied it with life and nutriment.
William Wilberforce

We can scarcely indeed look into any part of the sacred volume without meeting abundant proofs that it is the religion of the Affections which God particularly requires. . . . Joy . . . is enjoined on us as our bounden duty and commended to us as our acceptable worship. . . . A cold . . . unfeeling heart is represented as highly criminal.
William Wilberforce

If we would . . . rejoice in [Christ] as triumphantly as the first Christians did; we must learn, like them to repose our entire trust in him and to adopt the language of the apostle, "God forbid that I should glory, save in the cross of Jesus Christ." "Who of God is made unto us wisdom and righteousness and sanctification, and redemption."
William Wilberforce

His presence was as fatal to dullness as to immorality. His mirth was as irresistible as the first laughter of childhood.
James Stephen

3

William Wilberforce

"Peculiar Doctrines," Spiritual Delight,
and the Politics of Slavery

Against great obstacles William Wilberforce, an evangelical member of Parliament, fought for the abolition of the African slave trade and against slavery itself until they were both illegal in the British Empire. The battle consumed almost forty-six years of his life (from 1787 to 1833). The defeats and setbacks along the way would have caused the ordinary politician to embrace a more popular cause. Though he never lost a parliamentary election from age twenty-one to seventy-four, the cause of abolishing the slave trade was defeated eleven times before its passage in 1807. And the battle for abolishing slavery itself did not gain the decisive victory until three days before he died in 1833. What were the roots of this man's endurance in the cause of public righteousness?

What Made Him Tick?

To understand and appreciate the life and labor of William Wilberforce, one of the wisest things to do is to read his own book, *A Practical View of Christianity*, first and then read biographies. The book was published in 1797, when Wilberforce was thirty-seven years old and had been a member of the British Parliament already for sixteen years. It proved incredibly popular for the time, going through five printings in six months and being translated into five foreign languages. The book makes crystal clear what drives Wilberforce as a person and a politician. Hearing it from his own mouth, as it were, will make the reading of all the biographies more fruitful. They don't always put a premium on what he does. So it can easily be missed, if we don't read Wilberforce first.

What made Wilberforce tick was a profound biblical allegiance to what he called the "peculiar doctrines" of Christianity. These, he said, give rise in turn to true "affections" for spiritual things, which then break the power of pride and greed and fear and lead to transformed morals, which lead to the political welfare of the nation. No true Christian can endure in battling unrighteousness unless his heart is aflame with new spiritual affections, or passions. "Mere knowledge is confessedly too weak. The affections alone remain to supply the deficiency."[1] This is the key to public and political morality. "If . . . a principle of true Religion [the Spirit-given new affections] should . . . gain ground, there is no estimating the effects on public morals, and the consequent influence on our political welfare."[2]

The Great Doer

But he was no ordinary pragmatist or political utilitarian, even though he was one of the most practical men of his day. Yes, he was a great doer. One of his biographers said, "He lacked time for half the good works in his mind."[3] James Stephen, who knew him well, remarked, "Factories did not spring up more rapidly in Leeds and Manchester than schemes of benevolence beneath his roof."[4] "No man," Wilberforce wrote, "has a right to be idle." "Where is it," he asked, "that in such a world as this, [that] health, and leisure, and affluence may not find some ignorance to instruct, some wrong to redress, some want to supply, some misery to alleviate?"[5] In other words, he lived to do good—or as Jesus said, to let his light shine before men that they might see his good deeds and give glory to his Father in heaven (Matt. 5:16).

There is little doubt that Wilberforce changed the moral outlook of Great Britain. . . . The reformation of manners [morals] grew into Victorian virtues and Wilberforce touched the world when he made goodness fashion-

---

[1] William Wilberforce, *A Practical View of Christianity*, ed. Kevin Charles Belmonte (Peabody, MA: Hendrickson, 1996), 51.
[2] Ibid., 211.
[3] John Pollock, *Wilberforce* (London: Constable, 1977), 223.
[4] Ibid.
[5] Wilberforce, *A Practical View of Christianity*, 90.

able. . . . Contrast the late eighteenth century . . . with its loose morals and corrupt public life, with the mid-nineteenth century. Whatever its faults, nineteenth-century British public life became famous for its emphasis on character, morals, and justice and the British business world famous for integrity.[6]

But he was practical with a difference. He believed with all his heart that new affections for God were the key to new morals and lasting political reformation. And these new affections and this reformation did not come from mere ethical systems. They came from what he called the "peculiar doctrines" of Christianity. For Wilberforce, practical deeds were born in "peculiar doctrines." By that term he simply meant the central distinguishing doctrines of human depravity, divine judgment, the substitutionary work of Christ on the cross, justification by faith alone, regeneration by the Holy Spirit, and the practical necessity of fruit in a life devoted to good deeds.[7]

The Fatal Habit of Nominal Christians

He wrote his book to show that the "bulk"[8] of Christians in England were merely nominal because they had abandoned these doctrines in favor of a system of ethics and had thus lost the power of ethical life and the political welfare. He wrote:

> The fatal habit of considering Christian morals as distinct from Christian doctrines insensibly gained strength. Thus the peculiar doctrines of Christianity went more and more out of sight, and as might naturally have been expected, the moral system itself also began to wither and decay, being robbed of that which should have supplied it with life and nutriment.[9]

He pled with nominal Christians of England not to turn "their eyes from the grand peculiarities of Christianity, [but] to keep these ever in view, as the pregnant principles whence all the rest must derive their origin, and receive their best support."[10]

---

[6] John Pollock, "A Man Who Changed His Times," in *Character Counts: Leadership Qualities in Washington, Wilberforce, Lincoln, and Solzhenitsyn*, ed. Os Guinness (Grand Rapids, MI: Baker, 1999), 87.
[7] "The grand radical defect in the practical system of these nominal Christians, is their forgetfulness of all the peculiar doctrines of the Religion which they profess—the corruption of human nature—the atonement of the Savior—the sanctifying influence of the Holy Spirit." Ibid., 162–63.
[8] This is his favorite word for the majority of nominal Christians in Britain in his day.
[9] Wilberforce, *A Practical View of Christianity*, 198.
[10] Ibid., 70.

Knowing that Wilberforce was a politician all his adult life who never lost an election from the time he was twenty-one years old, we might be tempted to think that his motives were purely pragmatic—as if he should say, "If Christianity works to produce the political welfare, then use it." But that is not the spirit of his mind or his life. In fact, he believed that such pragmatism would ruin the very thing it sought, the reformation of culture.

The Decisive Direction of Sin: Vertical

Take the example of how people define sin. When considering the nature of sin, Wilberforce said, the vast bulk of Christians in England estimated the guilt of an action "not by the proportion in which, according to Scripture, [actions] are offensive to God, but by that in which they are injurious to society."[11] Now, on the face of it that sounds noble, loving, and practical. Sin hurts people, so don't sin.

Wouldn't that definition of sin be good for society? But Wilberforce says, "Their slight notions of the guilt and evil of sin [reveal] an utter [lack] of all suitable reverence for the Divine Majesty. This principle [reverence for the Divine Majesty] is justly termed in Scripture, 'The beginning of wisdom' [Ps. 111:10]."[12] And without this wisdom, there will be no deep and lasting good done for man, spiritually or politically. Therefore, the supremacy of God's glory in all things is what he calls "the grand governing maxim" in all of life.[13] The good of society may never be put ahead of this. That would dishonor God and, paradoxically, defeat the good of society. For the good of society, the good of society must not be the primary good.

What's Wrong with Dueling?

A practical example of how his mind worked is shown in his approach to the practice of dueling. Wilberforce hated this folly—the practice that demanded that a man of honor accept a challenge to a duel when another felt insulted. Wilberforce's close friend, the prime minister William Pitt, actually fought a duel with George Tierney in 1798, and Wilberforce was shocked that the prime minister would risk his life and the

---

[11] Ibid., 147.
[12] Ibid., 149.
[13] Ibid., 81.

nation in this way.[14] Many opposed it on its human unreasonableness. But Wilberforce wrote:

> It seems hardly to have been enough noticed in what chiefly consists its *essential* guilt; that it is a deliberate preference of the favour of man, before the favour and approbation of God, *in articulo mortis* ["at the point of death"], in an instance, wherein our own life, and that of a fellow creature are at stake, and wherein we run the risk of rushing into the presence of our Maker in the very act of offending him.[15]

In other words, offending God is the essential consideration, not killing a man or imperiling a nation. That is what made Wilberforce tick. He was not a political pragmatist. He was a radically God-centered Christian who was a politician. And his true affections for God based on the "peculiar doctrines" of Christianity were the roots of his endurance in the cause of justice.

His Early Life

Wilberforce was born August 24, 1759, in Hull, England. His father died just before Wilberforce turned nine years old. He was sent to live with his uncle and aunt, William and Hannah, where he came under evangelical influences. His mother was more high church and was concerned her son was "turning Methodist." So she took him out of the boarding school where they had sent him and put him in another.[16] He had admired George Whitefield, John Wesley, and John Newton as a child. But soon he left all the influence of the evangelicals behind. At his new school, he said later, "I did nothing at all." That lifestyle continued through his years in St. John's College at Cambridge. He was able to live off his parents' wealth and get by with little work. He lost any interest in biblical religion and loved circulating among the social elite.

He became friends with his contemporary William Pitt, who in just a few years, at the age of twenty-four in 1783, became the prime minister of England. On a lark, Wilberforce stood for the seat in the House of Commons for his hometown of Hull in 1780 when he was twenty-one. He spent £8,000 on the election. The money and his incredible gift for speaking triumphed over both his opponents. Pitt said

---

[14] Pollock, *Wilberforce*, 162.
[15] Wilberforce, *A Practical View of Christianity*, 115–16.
[16] Pollock, *Wilberforce*, 5.

Wilberforce possessed "the greatest natural eloquence of all the men I ever knew."[17] Wilberforce never lost an election during his lifelong political career.

Thus began a fifty-year investment in the politics of England. He began it as a late-night, party-loving, upper-class unbeliever. He was single and would stay that way happily until he was thirty-seven years old. Then he met Barbara on April 15, 1797. He fell immediately in love. Within eight days he proposed to her, and on May 30 they were married, about six weeks after they met—and stayed married until William died thirty-six years later. In the first eight years of their marriage they had four sons and two daughters. We will come back to William as a family man, because it sheds light on his character and how he endured the political battles of the day.

"The Great Change": The Story of His Conversion

I have skipped over the most important thing, his conversion to a deep, Christian, evangelical faith. It is a great story of the providence of God pursuing a person through seemingly casual choices. On the long holidays when Parliament was not in session, Wilberforce would sometimes travel with friends or family. In the winter of 1784, when he was twenty-five, he invited on an impulse Isaac Milner, his former schoolmaster and friend from grammar school, who was now a tutor in Queens College, Cambridge, to go with him and his mother and sister to the French Riviera. To his amazement, Milner turned out to be a convinced Christian without any of the stereotypes that Wilberforce had built up against evangelicals. They talked for hours about the Christian faith.

In another seemingly accidental turn, Wilberforce saw lying in the house where they were staying a copy of Philip Doddridge's *The Rise and Progress of Religion in the Soul* (1745). He asked Milner about it, and Milner said that it was "one of the best books ever written" and suggested they take it along and read it on the way home.[18] Wilberforce later ascribes a huge influence in his conversion to this book. When he arrived home in February 1785, he "had reached intellectual assent to the Biblical view of man, God and Christ." But he would not yet have

---

[17] Pollock, "A Man Who Changed His Times," 78.
[18] Ibid., 34.

claimed what he later described as true Christianity. It was all intellectual. He pushed it to the back of his mind and went on with political and social life.

That summer Wilberforce traveled again with Milner, and they discussed the Greek New Testament for hours. Slowly his "intellectual assent became profound conviction."[19] One of the first manifestations of what he called "the great change"—the conversion—was the contempt he felt for his wealth and the luxury he lived in, especially on these trips between parliamentary sessions. Seeds were sown almost immediately at the beginning of his Christian life, it seems, of the later passion to help the poor and to turn all his inherited wealth and his naturally high station into a means of blessing the oppressed.

"Highly Dangerous Possessions"

Simplicity and generosity were the mark of his life. Much later, after he was married, he wrote, "By careful management, I should be able to give at least one-quarter of my income to the poor."[20] His sons reported that before he married he was giving away well over a fourth of his income, one year actually giving away £3000 more than he made. He wrote that riches were, "considering them as in themselves, acceptable, but, from the infirmity of [our] nature, as highly dangerous possessions; and [we are to value] them chiefly not as instruments of luxury or splendor, but as affording the means of honoring [our] heavenly Benefactor, and lessening the miseries of mankind."[21] This was the way his mind worked: Everything in politics was for the alleviation of misery and the spread of happiness.

The Regret That Leads to Life

By October he was bemoaning the "shapeless idleness" of his past. He was thinking particularly of his time at Cambridge—"the most valuable years of life wasted, and opportunities lost, which can never be recovered."[22] He had squandered his early years in Parliament as well:

---

[19] Ibid., 37.
[20] Betty Steele Everett, *Freedom Fighter: The Story of William Wilberforce* (Fort Washington, PA: Christian Literature Crusade, 1994), 68.
[21] Wilberforce, *A Practical View of Christianity*, 113.
[22] Robert Isaac Wilberforce and Samuel Wilberforce, *The Life of William Wilberforce* (London: John Murray, 1838), 1:107.

"The first years I was in Parliament I did nothing—nothing that is to any purpose. My own distinction was my darling object."[23] He was so ashamed of his prior life that he wrote with apparent overstatement, "I was filled with sorrow. I am sure that no human creature could suffer more than I did for some months. It seems indeed it quite affected my reason."[24] He was tormented about what his new Christianity meant for his public life. William Pitt tried to talk him out of becoming an evangelical and argued that this change would "render your talents useless both to yourself and mankind."[25]

Ten Thousand Doubts and Good Counsel

To resolve the anguish he felt over what to do with his life as a Christian, he resolved to risk seeing John Newton on December 7, 1785—a risk because Newton was an evangelical and not admired or esteemed by Wilberforce's colleagues in Parliament. He wrote to Newton on December 2:

> I wish to have some serious conversation with you. . . . I have had ten thousand doubts within myself, whether or not I should discover myself to you; but every argument against it has its foundation in pride. I am sure you will hold yourself bound to let no one living know of this application, or of my visit, till I release you from the obligation. . . . PS Remember that I must be secret, and that the gallery of the House is now so universally attended, that the face of a member of parliament is pretty well known.[26]

It was a historically significant visit. Not only did Newton give encouragement to Wilberforce's faith, but he also urged him not to cut himself off from public life. Wilberforce wrote about the visit:

> After walking about the Square once or twice before I could persuade myself, I called upon old Newton—was much affected in conversing with him—something very pleasing and unaffected in him. He told me he always had hopes and confidence that God would sometime bring me to Him. . . . When I came away I found my mind in a calm, tranquil state, more humbled, and looking more devoutly up to God.[27]

---

[23] Pollock, "A Man Who Changed His Times," 80.
[24] Pollock, *Wilberforce*, 37.
[25] Ibid., 38.
[26] Robert Isaac Wilberforce and Samuel Wilberforce, *The Life of William Wilberforce*, abridged ed. (London, 1843), 47.
[27] Ibid., 48.

Wilberforce was relieved that the sixty-year-old Newton urged him not to cut himself off from public life. Newton wrote to Wilberforce two years later: "It is hoped and believed that the Lord has raised you up for the good of His church and for the good of the nation."[28] One marvels at the magnitude of some small occasions when one thinks what hung in the balance in that moment of counsel, in view of what Wilberforce would accomplish for the cause of abolition.

The battle and uncertainties lasted on into the new year, but finally a more settled serenity came over him, and on Easter Day 1786, the politician for Yorkshire took to the fields to pray and give thanks, as he said in a letter to his sister Sally, "amidst the general chorus with which all nature seems on such a morning to be swelling the song of praise and thanksgiving."[29] It was, he said almost ten years later, as if "to have awakened . . . from a dream, to have recovered, as it were, the use of my reason after a delirium."[30]

With this change came a whole new regimen for the use of his months of recess from Parliament. Beginning not long after his conversion and lasting until he was married eleven years later, he would now spend his days studying "about nine or ten hours a day," typically "breakfasting alone, taking walks alone, dining with the host family and other guests but not joining them in the evening until he 'came down about three-quarters of an hour before bedtime for what supper I wanted.'"[31] "The Bible became his best-loved book and he learned stretches by heart."[32] He was setting out to recover a lot of ground lost to laziness in college.

"God Has Set before Me Two Great Objects"

Now we turn to what makes Wilberforce so relevant to the cause of racial justice in our day—namely, his lifelong devotion to the cause of abolishing the African slave trade, and then slavery itself. In 1787, Wilberforce wrote a letter in which he estimated that the annual export of slaves from the western coast of Africa for all nations exceeded £100,000.[33] Seventeen years later, in 1804, he estimated that for the

---

[28] Ibid.
[29] Ibid., 39.
[30] Wilberforce and Wilberforce, *The Life of William Wilberforce*, 1:107–8.
[31] Ibid., 43.
[32] Ibid., 44.
[33] Ibid., 72

Guiana importation alone, 12,000–15,000 human beings were enslaved every year the trade continued. One year after his conversion, God's apparent calling on his life had become clear to him. On October 28, 1787, he wrote in his diary, "God Almighty has set before me two great objects, the suppression of the Slave Trade and the Reformation of Manners [morals]."[34]

Soon after Christmas 1787, a few days before the parliamentary recess, Wilberforce gave notice in the House of Commons that early in the new session he would bring a motion for the abolition of the slave trade. It would be twenty years before he could carry the House of Commons and the House of Lords in putting abolition into law. But the more he studied the matter and the more he heard of the atrocities, the more resolved he became. In May 1789, he spoke to the House about how he came to his conviction: "I confess to you, so enormous, so dreadful, so irremediable did its wickedness appear that my own mind was completely made up for Abolition. . . . Let the consequences be what they would, I from this time determined that I would never rest until I had effected its abolition."[35]

He embraced the guilt for himself when he said in that same year, "I mean not to accuse anyone but to take the shame upon myself, in common indeed with the whole Parliament of Great Britain, for having suffered this horrid trade to be carried on under their authority. We are all guilty—we ought all to plead guilty, and not to exculpate ourselves by throwing the blame on others."[36]

In 1793 he wrote to a supporter who thought he was growing soft and cautious in the cause, "If I thought the immediate Abolition of the Slave Trade would cause an insurrection in our islands, I should not for an instant remit my most strenuous endeavors. Be persuaded then, I shall still less ever make this grand cause the sport of the caprice, or sacrifice it to motives of political convenience or personal feeling."[37] Three years later, almost ten years after the battle was begun, he wrote:

> The grand object of my parliamentary existence [is the abolition of the slave trade]. . . . Before this great cause all others dwindle in my eyes, and I must

---

[34] Ibid., 69.
[35] Ibid., 56.
[36] Ibid., 89.
[37] Ibid., 123.

say that the *certainty* that I am right *here*, adds greatly to the complacency with which I exert myself in asserting it. If it please God to honor me so far, may I be the instrument of stopping such a course of wickedness and cruelty as never before disgraced a Christian country.[38]

Triumph over All Opposition

Of course the opposition that raged for these twenty years was because of the financial benefits of slavery to the traders and to the British economy, because of what the plantations in the West Indies produced. They could not conceive of any way to produce without slave labor. This meant that Wilberforce's life was threatened more than once. When he criticized the credibility of a slave-ship captain, Robert Norris, the man was enraged, and Wilberforce feared for his life. Short of physical harm, there was the painful loss of friends. Some would no longer fight with him, and they were estranged. Then there was the huge political pressure to back down because of the international political ramifications. For example, if Britain really outlawed slavery, the West Indian colonial assemblies threatened to declare independence from Britain and to federate with the United States. These kinds of financial and political arguments held Parliament captive for decades.

But the night—or I should say early morning—of victory came in 1807. The moral vision and the political momentum for abolition had finally become irresistible. At one point "the House rose almost to a man and turned towards Wilberforce in a burst of Parliamentary cheers. Suddenly, above the roar of 'Hear, hear,' and quite out of order, three hurrahs echoed and echoed while he sat, head bowed, tears streaming down his face."[39] At 4:00 a.m., February 24, 1807, the House divided— Ayes, 283; Noes, 16; Majority for the Abolition, 267. And on March 25, 1807, the royal assent was declared. One of Wilberforce's friends wrote, "[Wilberforce] attributes it to the immediate interposition of Providence."[40] In that early morning hour, Wilberforce turned to his best friend and colleague, Henry Thornton, and said, "Well, Henry, what shall we abolish next?"[41]

---

[38] Pollock, *Wilberforce*, 143.
[39] Wilberforce and Wilberforce, *The Life of William Wilberforce*, 1:211.
[40] Ibid., 212.
[41] Ibid.

The Battle Was Not Over

Of course the battle wasn't over. And Wilberforce fought on[42] until his death twenty-six years later in 1833. Not only was the *implementation* of the abolition law controversial and difficult, but all it did was abolish the slave *trade*, not slavery itself. That became the next major cause. In 1821, Wilberforce recruited Thomas Fowell Buxton to carry on the fight, and from the sidelines, aged and fragile, he cheered him on. Three months before his death in 1833, he was persuaded to propose a last petition against slavery. "I had never thought to appear in public again, but it shall never be said that William Wilberforce is silent while the slaves require his help."[43]

The decisive vote of victory for that one came on July 26, 1833, only three days before Wilberforce died. Slavery itself was outlawed in the British colonies. Minor work on the legislation took several more days. "It is a singular fact," Buxton said, "that on the very night on which we were successfully engaged in the House of Commons, in passing the clause of the Act of Emancipation—one of the most important clauses ever enacted . . . the spirit of our friend left the world. The day which was the termination of his labors was the termination of his life."[44]

William Cowper wrote a sonnet[45] to celebrate Wilberforce's labor for the slaves, which begins with the lines,

> Thy country, Wilberforce, with just disdain,
> Hears thee by cruel men and impious call'd
> Fanatic, for thy zeal to loose the enthrall'd
> From exile, public sale, and slavery's chain.

---

[42] In 1823, Wilberforce wrote a fifty-six-page booklet, *Appeal to the Religion, Justice and Humanity of the Inhabitants of the British Empire in Behalf of the Negro Slaves in the West Indies.* Ibid., 285.

[43] Pollock, "A Man Who Changed His Times," 90.

[44] Ibid., 91.

[45] Thy country, Wilberforce, with just disdain
Hears thee by cruel men and impious call'd
Fanatic, for thy zeal to loose the enthrall'd
From exile, public sale, and slavery's chain.
Friend of the poor, the wrong'd, the fetter-gall'd,
Fear not lest labor such as thine be vain.
Thou hast achieved a part: hast gained the ear
Of Britain's senate to thy glorious cause;
Hope smiles, joy springs; and though cold Caution pause,
And weave delay, the better hour is near
That shall remunerate thy toils severe,
By peace for Afric, fenced with British laws.
Enjoy what thou has won, esteem and love
From all the Just on earth, and all the Blest above.

Friend of the poor, the wrong'd, the fetter-gall'd,
Fear not lest labor such as thine be vain.

Wilberforce's friend and sometimes pastor, William Jay, wrote a tribute with this accurate prophecy, "His disinterested, self-denying, laborious, undeclining efforts in this cause of justice and humanity . . . will call down the blessings of millions; and ages yet to come will glory in his memory."[46]

But He Was Not a Single-Issue Candidate

I must not give the impression that all Wilberforce cared about or worked for was the abolition of slavery. In fact, the diversity of the evangelistic and benevolent causes he labored to advance makes his devotion to abolition all the more wonderful. Most of us make the multiplicity of demands an excuse for not giving ourselves to any one great cause over the long haul. Not so with Wilberforce.[47] There was a steady stream of action to alleviate pain and bring the greater social (and eternal!) good. "At one stage he was active in sixty-nine different initiatives."[48]

His involvements ranged widely. He was involved with the British Foreign Bible Society, the Church Missionary Society, the Society for the Manufacturing Poor, and the Society for the Better Observance of Sunday. He worked for the alleviation of harsh child labor conditions (like the use of small boys by chimney sweeps to climb up chimneys), for agricultural reform that supplied affordable food to the poor, for prison reform and the restriction of capital punishment from cavalier use, and for the prevention of cruelty to animals.[49] On and on the list could go. In fact, it was the very diversity of the needs and crimes and injustices that confirmed his evangelical conviction that one must finally

---

[46] William Jay, *The Autobiography of William Jay*, ed. George Redford and John Angell James (orig. 1854; Edinburgh: Banner of Truth, 1974), 315.

[47] See pages 328–29.

[48] Pollock, "A Man Who Changed His Times," 89.

[49] Of course, concern for animals is not the apex of the moral life. But it may be indicative of a character that supports far more significant mercies. As the Scripture says, "Whoever is righteous has regard for the life of his beast, but the mercy of the wicked is cruel" (Prov. 12:10). So the following personal recollection of Wilberforce's grandson is not insignificant.

Wilberforce was also a great lover of animals and a founder of the Royal Society for the Prevention of Cruelty to Animals, which led me to a lovely story. His last surviving grandson told me how his father as a small boy was walking with Wilberforce on a hill near Bath when they saw a poor carthorse being cruelly whipped by the carter as he struggled to pull a load of stone up the hill. The little liberator expostulated with the carter who began to swear at him and tell him to mind his own business, and so forth. Suddenly the carter stopped and said, "Are you Mr. Wilberforce? . . . Then I will never beat my horse again!" (Pollock, "A Man Who Changed His Times," 90)

deal with the *root* of all these ills if one is to have a lasting and broad influence for good. That is why, as we have seen, he wrote his book, *A Practical View of Christianity*.

The Personal Evangelism of a Politician

Alongside all his social engagements, Wilberforce carried on a steady relational ministry, as we might call it, seeking to win his unbelieving colleagues to personal faith in Jesus Christ. Even though he said, "The grand business of [clergymen's] lives should be winning souls from the power of Satan unto God, and compared with it all other pursuits are mean and contemptible,"[50] he did not believe that this was the responsibility *only* of the clergy. In a chance meeting with James Boswell, Samuel Johnson's biographer, he spent time into the night dealing with him about his soul, but seemed not to be able to get beyond some serious feelings.[51] He grieved for his longtime unbelieving parliamentary friend Charles Fox and longed "that I might be the instrument of bringing him to the knowledge of Christ!"[52]

He anonymously visited in prison a famous infidel named Richard Carlile, who was imprisoned for his blasphemous writings. When Wilberforce took out a small Bible, Carlile said, "I wish to have nothing to do with that book; and you cannot wonder at this, for if that book be true, I am damned forever!" To which Wilberforce replied, "No, no, Mr. Carlile, according to that book, there is hope for all who will seek for mercy and forgiveness; for it assures us that God hath no pleasure in the death of him that dieth."[53]

Missions and Mercy across the Miles

His zeal for the gospel and his compassion for perishing people were extended from personal relationships at home to places as far away as India. On April 14, 1806, he wrote, "Next to the Slave Trade, I have long thought our making no effort to introduce the blessings of religious and moral improvement among our subjects in the East, the greatest of our *national* crimes."[54] Seven years later, "Wilberforce . . . enthralled

---

[50] Pollock, *Wilberforce*, 148.
[51] Ibid., 119.
[52] Ibid., 205.
[53] Ibid., 258.
[54] Ibid., 235–36.

the House . . . with the cause of Christian missions in India."[55] The Englishman William Carey had to live in Serampore, a Danish enclave in India, until Wilberforce triumphed in 1813 when the prohibition of evangelism in British colonies in India was lifted by the East India Company Charter, which now guaranteed liberty to propagate the Christian faith. "Parliament had opened a fast-locked door and it was Wilberforce who had turned the key, in a speech which Lord Erskine said 'deserves a place in the library of every man of letters, even if he were an atheist.'"[56] Even at this huge distance, Wilberforce brought together evangelistic zeal and concern for social justice. He bemoaned the practice of *suttee* and would read out at his supper table the names of women who had been killed on the funeral fires of their husbands; he knew something of the tyrannies of the caste system.[57]

The link that Wilberforce saw between social good and eternal good is seen in the case of the remote English people of Mendip Hills. In 1789, when Wilberforce saw the terrible plight of these backward, poor, unpastored people, he urged the philanthropist Hannah More to conceive a plan that he would pay for. She worked out a plan to establish a school and teach them to read. She wrote to Wilberforce, "What a comfort I feel in looking around on these starving and half-naked multitudes, to think that by your liberality many of them may be fed and clothed; and O if but one soul is rescued from eternal misery how we may rejoice over it in another state!"[58]

The breadth of his heart and the diversity of his action beckons us all the more to ponder the source of his constancy, especially in a cause that was at first unpopular and easily defeated—the economically advantageous slave trade.

Extraordinary Endurance

Consider now the remarkable perseverance of this man in the cause of justice. I admit, this is what drew me to Wilberforce in the first place—his reputation as a man who simply would not give up when the cause was just.

There was a ray of hope in 1804 that things might be moving to

---

[55] Ibid., 235–36.
[56] Ibid., 238.
[57] Ibid., 236.
[58] Ibid., 92–93.

a success (three years before it actually came), but Wilberforce wrote, "I have been so often disappointed, that I rejoice with trembling and shall scarcely dare to be confident till I actually see the Order in the Gazette."[59] But these repeated defeats of his plans did not defeat *him*. His adversaries complained that "Wilberforce jumped up whenever they knocked him down."[60] One of them in particular put it like this: "It is necessary to watch him as he is blessed with a very sufficient quantity of that Enthusiastic spirit, which is so far from yielding that it grows more vigorous from blows."[61]

When John Wesley was eighty-seven years old (in 1790), he wrote to Wilberforce and said, "Unless God has raised you up for this very thing, you will be worn out by the opposition of man and devils. But if God be for you, who can be against you."[62] Two years later, Wilberforce wrote in a letter, "I daily become more sensible that my work must be affected by constant and regular exertions rather than by sudden and violent ones."[63] In other words, with fifteen years to go in the first phase of the battle, he knew that only a marathon mentality, rather than a sprint mentality, would prevail in this cause.

Six years later, in 1800, on his forty-first birthday, as he rededicated himself to his calling, he prayed, "Oh Lord, purify my soul from all its stains. Warm my heart with the love of thee, animate my sluggish nature and fix my inconstancy, and volatility, that I may not be weary in well doing."[64] God answered that prayer, and the entire Western world may be glad that Wilberforce was granted constancy and perseverance in his labors, especially his endurance in the cause of justice against the sin of slavery and racism.

Obstacles

What makes Wilberforce's perseverance through four decades of political action in the single-minded cause of justice so remarkable is not only the length of it but the obstacles he had to surmount in the battle for abolition of the slave trade and then of slavery itself. I have mentioned the massive financial interests on the other side, both personal and na-

---

[59] Ibid., 189.
[60] Ibid., 123.
[61] Ibid., 105.
[62] Ibid.
[63] Ibid., 116.
[64] Ibid., 179.

tional. It seemed utterly unthinkable to Parliament that Britain could prosper without what the plantations of the West Indies provided. Then there were the international politics and how Britain was positioned in relation to France, Portugal, Brazil, and the new nation, the United States of America. If one nation, like Britain, unilaterally abolished the slave trade but the others did not, it would simply mean—so the argument ran—that power and wealth would be transmitted to the other nations and Britain would be weakened internationally.

Slander

In February 1807, when Wilberforce, at forty-seven, led the first victory over the slave trade, it was true that, as John Pollock says, "his achievement brought him a personal moral authority with public and Parliament above any living man."[65] But as every public person knows, and as Jesus promised,[66] the best of men will be maligned for the best of actions.

On one occasion in 1820, thirteen years after the first victory, he took a very controversial position with regard to Queen Caroline's marital unfaithfulness and experienced a dramatic public outrage against him. He wrote in his diary on July 20, 1820, "What a lesson it is to a man not to set his heart on low popularity when after 40 years [of] disinterested public service, I am believed by the Bulk to be a Hypocritical Rascal. O what a comfort it is to have to fly for refuge to a God of unchangeable truth and love."[67]

Probably the severest criticism he ever received was from a slavery-defending adversary named William Cobett, in August 1823, who turned Wilberforce's commitment to abolition into a moral liability by claiming that Wilberforce pretended to care for slaves from Africa but cared nothing about the "wage slaves"—the wretched poor of England.

> You seem to have a great affection for the fat and lazy and laughing and singing and dancing Negroes. . . . [But] Never have you done one single act in favor of the laborers of this country [a statement Cobett knew to be false]. . . . You make your appeal in Picadilly, London, amongst those who

---

[65] Ibid., 215. Wilberforce's own assessment of the resulting moral authority was this (written in a letter, March 3, 1807): "The authority which the great principles of justice and humanity have received will be productive of benefit in all shapes and directions."

[66] Matt. 10:25, "If they have called the master of the house Beelzebul, how much more will they malign those of his household."

[67] Pollock, *Wilberforce*, 276.

are wallowing in luxuries, proceeding from the labor of the people. You should have gone to the gravel-pits, and made your appeal to the wretched creatures with bits of sacks around their shoulders, and with hay-bands round their legs; you should have gone to the roadside, and made your appeal to the emaciated, half-dead things who are there cracking stones to make the roads as level as a die for the tax eaters to ride on. What an insult it is, and what an unfeeling, what a cold-blooded hypocrite must he be that can send it forth; what an insult to call upon people under the name of free British laborers; to appeal to them in behalf of Black slaves, when these free British laborers; these poor, mocked, degraded wretches, would be happy to lick the dishes and bowls, out of which the Black slaves have breakfasted, dined, or supped.[68]

A Father's Pain

But far more painful than any of these criticisms were the heartaches of family life. Every leader knows that almost any external burden is bearable if the family is whole and happy. But when the family is torn, all burdens are doubled. Wilberforce and his wife, Barbara, were very different. "While he was always cheerful, Barbara was often depressed and pessimistic. She finally worried herself into very bad health which lasted the rest of her life." And other women who knew her said she "whined when William was not right beside her."[69]

When their oldest, William, was at Trinity College, Cambridge, he fell away from the Christian faith and gave no evidence of the precious experience his father called "the great change." Wilberforce wrote on January 10, 1819, "O that my poor dear William might be led by thy grace, O God." On March 11, he poured out his grief:

> Oh my poor Willm. How strange he can make so miserable those who love him best and whom really he loves. His soft nature makes him the sport of his companions, and the wicked and idle naturally attach themselves like dust and cleave like burrs. I go to pray for him. Alas, could I love my Savior more and serve him, God would hear my prayer and turn his heart.[70]

He got word from Henry Venn that William was not reading for his classes at Cambridge but was spending his father's allowance foolishly.

---

[68] Ibid., 287.
[69] Everett, *Freedom Fighter*, 64–65.
[70] Pollock, *Wilberforce*, 267.

Wilberforce agonized and decided to cut off his allowance, have him suspended from school, put him with another family, and not allow him to come home. "Alas my poor Willm! How sad to be compelled to banish my eldest son."[71] Even when William finally came back to faith, it grieved Wilberforce that three of his sons became very high-church Anglicans with little respect for the dissenting church that Wilberforce, even as an Anglican, loved so much for its evangelical truth and life.[72]

On top of this family burden came the death of his daughter Barbara. In the autumn of 1821, at thirty-two, she was diagnosed with consumption (tuberculosis). She died five days after Christmas. Wilberforce wrote to a friend, "Oh my dear Friend, it is in such seasons as these that the value of the promises of the Word of God are ascertained both by the dying and the attendant relatives. . . . The assured persuasion of Barbara's happiness has taken away the sting of death."[73] He sounds strong, but the blow shook his remaining strength, and in March 1822, he wrote to his son, "I am confined by a new malady, the Gout."[74]

His Bad Eyes, Ulcerated Bowels, Opium, and Curved Spine

The word "new" in that letter signals that Wilberforce labored under some other extraordinary physical handicaps that made his long perseverance in political life all the more remarkable. He wrote in 1788 that his eyes were so bad "[I can scarcely] see how to direct my pen." The humorous side to this was that "he was often shabbily dressed, according to one friend, and his clothes sometimes were put on crookedly because he never looked into a mirror. Since his eyes were too bad to let him see his image clearly, he didn't bother to look at all!"[75] But in fact, there was little humor in his eye disease. In later years he frequently mentioned the "peculiar complaint of my eyes," that he could not see well enough to read or write during the first hours of the day. "This was a symptom of a slow buildup of morphine poisoning."[76]

This ominous assessment was owing to the fact that from 1788, doctors prescribed daily opium pills to Wilberforce to control the debility

---

[71] Ibid., 268. From his diary, April 11, 1819.
[72] The official biography written by his sons is defective in portraying Wilberforce in a false light as opposed to dissenters, when in fact some of his best friends and spiritual counselors were among their number. After Wilberforce's death, three of his sons became Roman Catholic.
[73] Ibid., 280.
[74] Ibid.
[75] Everett, *Freedom Fighter*, 69.
[76] Pollock, *Wilberforce*, 81.

of his ulcerative colitis. The medicine was viewed in his day as a "pure drug," and it never occurred to any of his enemies to reproach him for his dependence on opium to control his illness.[77] "Yet effects there must have been," Pollock observes. "Wilberforce certainly grew more untidy, indolent (as he often bemoaned) and absent-minded as his years went on though not yet in old age; it is proof of the strength of his will that he achieved so much under a burden which neither he nor his doctors understood."[78]

In 1812, Wilberforce decided to resign his seat in Yorkshire—not to leave politics, but to take a less demanding seat from a smaller county. He gave his reason as the desire to spend more time with his family. The timing was good, because in the next two years, on top of his colon problem and eye problem and emerging lung problem, he developed a curvature of the spine. "One shoulder began to slope; and his head fell forward, a little more each year until it rested on his chest unless lifted by conscious movement: he could have looked grotesque were it not for the charm of his face and the smile which hovered about his mouth."[79] For the rest of his life he wore a brace beneath his clothes that most people knew nothing about.[80]

He Did Not Fight Alone

What were the roots of Wilberforce's perseverance under these kinds of burdens and obstacles? Before we focus on the decisive root, we must pay due respect to the power of camaraderie in the cause of righteousness. Many people associate Wilberforce's name with the term *Clapham Sect*. That term was not used during his lifetime. But the band that it referred to were "tagged 'the Saints' by their contemporaries in Parliament—uttered by some with contempt, while by others with deep

---

[77] Ibid., 79–81, for a full discussion of the place of opium in his life and culture. "Wilberforce resisted the craving and only raised his dosage suddenly when there were severe bowel complaints." In April 1818, thirty years after the first prescription, "Wilberforce noted in his diary that his dose 'is still as it has long been,' a pill three times a day (after breakfast, after tea, and bedtime) each of four grains. Twelve grains daily is a good but not outstanding dose and very far from addiction after such a length of time."

[78] Ibid., 81.

[79] Ibid., 234.

[80] "He was obliged to wear 'a steel girdle cased in leather and an additional part to support the arms. . . . It must be handled carefully, the steel being so elastic as to be easily broken.' He took a spare one ('wrapped up for decency's sake in a towel') wherever he stayed; the fact that he lived in a steel frame for his last 15 or 18 years might have remained unknown had he not left behind at the Lord Calthorpe's Suffolk home, Ampton Hall, the more comfortable of the two. 'How gracious is God,' Wilberforce remarked in the letter asking for its return, 'in giving us such mitigations and helps for our infirmities.'" Ibid., 233–34.

admiration."[81] The group centered around the church of John Venn, rector of Clapham, a suburb of London. It included Wilberforce, Henry Thornton, James Stephen, Zachary Macaulay, Granville Sharp, John Shore (Lord Teignmouth), and Charles Grant.

Henry Thornton, banker and economist, was Wilberforce's "dearest friend"[82] and cousin. In the spring of 1792, he "suggested to Wilberforce that they set up a 'chummery' at Battersea Rise, the small estate that Thornton had bought in Clapham. Each would pay his share of the housekeeping, and this became Wilberforce's home for the next five years."[83]

> At certain points these friends . . . resided in adjoining homes in a suburb of London called Clapham Common, functioning as one. In fact, their *esprit de corps* was so evident and contagious that whether geographically together or not, they operated like "a meeting which never adjourned." The achievement of Wilberforce's vision is largely attributable to the value he and his colleagues placed on harnessing their diverse skills while submitting their egos for the greater public good.[84]

Wilberforce did not set out to gather a strategic band of comrades to strengthen his cause. It came together because of the kind of man he was and the compelling vision he had of what a public Christian life should be. He had a deep "love of conversation and could hardly resist prolonging a chat and kept many late hours leaving the mornings to less important things."[85] This love of company and great capacity for friendship combined with the power of his vision for public righteousness to attract "the Saints." Together they accomplished more than any could have done on his own. "William Wilberforce is proof that a man can change his times, though he cannot do it alone."[86]

The Deeper Root of Childlike Joy

But there is a deeper root of Wilberforce's endurance than camaraderie. It is the root of childlike, child-loving, self-forgetting joy in Christ. The testimonies and evidence of this in Wilberforce's life are many. A certain

[81] J. Douglas Holladay, "A Life of Significance," in Guinness, *Character Counts*, 72.
[82] Pollock, *Wilberforce*, 102.
[83] Ibid., 117.
[84] Holladay, "A Life of Significance," 72.
[85] Pollock, *Wilberforce*, 118–19.
[86] Pollock, "A Man Who Changed His Times," 88.

Miss Sullivan wrote to a friend about Wilberforce around 1815: "By the tones of his voice and expression of his countenance he showed that *joy* was the prevailing feature of his own mind, joy springing from entireness of trust in the Savior's merits and from love to God and man. . . . His joy was quite penetrating."[87]

On the occasion of Wilberforce's death, Joseph Brown spoke in St. Paul's Church in Middlesex. He focused on this attribute of the man.

> He was also a most cheerful Christian. His harp appeared to be always in tune; no "gloomy atmosphere of a melancholy moroseness" surrounded him; his sun appeared to be always shining: hence he was remarkably fond of singing hymns, both in family prayer and when alone. He would say, "A Christian should have joy and peace in believing [Rom. 15:13]: It is his duty to abound in praise."[88]

The poet Robert Southey said, "I never saw any other man who seemed to enjoy such a perpetual serenity and sunshine of spirit. In conversing with him, you feel assured that there is no guile in him; that if ever there was a good man and happy man on earth, he was one."[89] In 1881 Dorothy Wordsworth, sister of the famous romantic poet, wrote, "Though shattered in constitution and feeble in body he is as lively and animated as in the days of his youth."[90] His sense of humor and delight in all that was good was vigorous and unmistakable. In 1824, John Russell gave a speech in the Commons with such wit that Wilberforce "collapsed in helpless laughter."[91]

This playful side made him a favorite of children, as they were favorites of his. His best friend's daughter, Marianne Thornton, said that often "Wilberforce would interrupt his serious talks with her father and romp with her in the lawn. 'His love for and enjoyment in all children was remarkable.'"[92] Once, when his own children were playing upstairs and he was frustrated at having misplaced a letter, he heard a great din of children shouting. His guest thought he would be perturbed. Instead he smiled and said, "What a blessing to have these dear children! Only

---

[87] Ibid., 152.
[88] Joseph Brown quoted in *The Christian Observer* (London), January 1834: 63.
[89] Jay, *The Autobiography of William Jay*, 317.
[90] Pollock, *Wilberforce*, 267.
[91] Ibid., 289.
[92] Ibid., 183.

think what a relief, amidst other hurries, to hear their voices and know they are well."[93]

> He was an unusual father for his day. Most fathers who had the wealth and position he did rarely saw their children. Servants and a governess took care of the children, and they were to be out of sight most of the time. Instead, William insisted on eating as many meals as possible with the children, and he joined in their games. He played marbles and Blindman's Bluff and ran races with them. In the games, the children treated him like one of them.[94]

Southey once visited the house when all the children were there and wrote that he marveled at "the pell-mell, topsy-turvy and chaotic confusion" of the Wilberforce apartments in which the wife sat like Patience on a monument while her husband "frisks about as if every vein in his body were filled with quicksilver."[95] Another visitor in 1816, Joseph John Gurney, a Quaker, stayed a week with Wilberforce and recalled later, "As he walked about the house he was generally humming the tune of a hymn or Psalm as if he could not contain his pleasurable feelings of thankfulness and devotion."[96]

Interested in All and Interesting to All

There was, in this childlike love of children and joyful freedom from care, a deeply healthy self-forgetfulness. Richard Wellesley, Duke of Wellington, wrote after a meeting with Wilberforce, "You have made me so entirely forget you are a great man by seeming to forget it yourself in all our intercourse."[97] The effect of this self-forgetting joy was another mark of mental and spiritual health, namely, a joyful ability to see all the good in the world instead of being consumed by one's own problems (even when those problems were huge).

Wilberforce's friend James Mackintosh spoke of that remarkable trait of healthy, adult childlikeness, namely, the freedom from self-absorption that is interested in the simplest and most ordinary things:

> If I were called upon to describe Wilberforce in one word, I should say that he was the most "amusable" man I ever met in my life. Instead of having to

---

[93] Ibid., 232.
[94] Everett, *Freedom Fighter*, 70.
[95] Pollock, *Wilberforce*, 267.
[96] Ibid., 261.
[97] Ibid., 236.

think of what subjects will interest him it is perfectly impossible to hit one that does not. I never saw anyone who touched life at so many points and this is the more remarkable in a man who is supposed to live absorbed in the contemplation of a future state. When he was in the House of Commons he seemed to have the freshest mind of any man there. There was all the charm of youth about him.[98]

His Presence Fatal to Dullness

This must have been the way many viewed him, for another of his contemporaries, James Stephen, recalled after Wilberforce's death, "Being himself amused and interested by everything, whatever he said became amusing or interesting. . . . His presence was as fatal to dullness as to immorality. His mirth was as irresistible as the first laughter of childhood."[99]

Here is a great key to his perseverance and effectiveness. His presence was "fatal to dullness . . . [and] immorality." In other words, his indomitable joy moved others to be happy and good. He remarked in his book *A Practical View of Christianity*, "The path of virtue is that also of real interest and of solid enjoyment."[100] In other words, "It is more blessed to give than to receive" (Acts 20:35). He sustained himself and swayed others by his joy. If a man can rob you of your joy, he can rob you of your usefulness. Wilberforce's joy was indomitable, and therefore he was a compelling Christian and politician all his life. This was the strong root of his endurance.

Hannah More, his wealthy friend and a patron of many of his schemes for doing good, said to him, "I declare I think you are serving God by being yourself agreeable . . . to worldly but well-disposed people, who would never be attracted to religion by grave and severe divines, even if such fell in their way."[101] In fact, I think one of the reasons Wilberforce did not like to use the word "Calvinist,"[102] although

---

[98] Holladay, "A Life of Significance," 74.

[99] Pollock, *Wilberforce*, 185.

[100] Wilberforce, *A Practical View of Christianity*, 12.

[101] Ibid., 119.

[102] He disliked anything that "produced hard and sour divinity." He wrote in a letter on May 26, 1814, "There are no names or party distinctions in heaven." Though he wrote in 1821, "I myself am no Calvinist," he "urged the claims of Calvinist clergy for bishoprics." In 1799 he had written, "God knows, I say it solemnly, that it has been (particularly of late) and shall be more and more my endeavor to promote the cordial and vigorous and systematical exertions of all friends of the essentials of Christianity, softening prejudices, healing divisions and striving to substitute a rational and an honest zeal for fundamentals, in place of a hot party spirit." Pollock, *Wilberforce*, 153. More than once he was heard to say, "Though I am an Episcopalian by education and conviction, I yet feel such a oneness and sympathy with the cause of God

the faith and doctrines he expresses seem to line up with the Calvinism of Whitefield and Newton,[103] was this very thing: Calvinists had the reputation of being joyless.

A certain Lord Carrington apparently expressed to Wilberforce his mistrust of joy. Wilberforce responded:

> My grand objection to the religious system still held by many who declare themselves orthodox Churchmen . . . is, that it tends to render Christianity so much a system of prohibitions rather than of privilege and hopes, and thus the injunction to rejoice, so strongly enforced in the New Testament, is practically neglected, and Religion is made to wear a forbidding and gloomy air and not one of peace and hope and joy.[104]

Joy Is Our "Bounden Duty"

Here is a clear statement of Wilberforce's conviction that joy is not optional. It is an "injunction . . . strongly enforced in the New Testament." Or as he says elsewhere, "We can scarcely indeed look into any part of the sacred volume without meeting abundant proofs, that it is the religion of the Affections which God particularly requires. . . . Joy . . . is enjoined on us as our bounden duty and commended to us as our acceptable worship. . . . A cold . . . unfeeling heart is represented as highly criminal."[105]

So for Wilberforce, joy was both a means of survival and perseverance on the one hand, and a deep act of submission, obedience, and worship on the other hand. Joy in Christ was commanded. And joy in Christ was the only way to flourish fruitfully through decades of

---

at large, that nothing would be more delightful than my communing, once every year, with every church that holds the Head, even Christ." Jay, *The Autobiography of William Jay*, 298–99.

[103] Many of his closest and most admired friends were Calvinists—for example, Hannah More and William Jay. He used his influence to promote Calvinists to bishoprics. When he sought out a church to attend, he often chose to sit under the ministry of Calvinists—for example, Thomas Scott, "one of the most determined Calvinists in England" (Pollock, *Wilberforce*, 153), and William Jay. He believed in the absolute sovereignty of God over all the pleasures and pain of the world ("It has pleased God to visit my dearest wife with a very dangerous fever." Ibid., 179). He knew that his own repentance was a gift of God ("May I, Oh God, be enabled to repent and turn to thee with my whole heart. I am now flying from thee." Ibid., 150). He loved the essay on regeneration by the Calvinist John Witherspoon and wrote a preface for it (Jay, *The Autobiography of William Jay*, 298). As I completed his book, *A Practical View of Christianity*, I could not recall a single sentence that a Calvinist like John Newton or George Whitefield or Charles Spurgeon could not agree with.

[104] Pollock, *Wilberforce*, 46.

[105] Wilberforce, *A Practical View of Christianity*, 45–46. I cannot let these sentences pass without pointing out the poetic power of Wilberforce's diction. Did you notice how he put parallel consonant sounds together? "Joy . . . enjoined. Commended . . . as acceptable. Cold . . . criminal." This kind of thing runs through all his writing and signals a passion to make his words pleasing and effective even as they instruct.

temporary defeat. It was a deep root of endurance. "Never were there times," he wrote, "which inculcated more forcibly than those in which we live, the wisdom of seeking happiness beyond the reach of human vicissitudes."[106]

But What about the Hard Times?

The word "seeking" is important. It is not as though Wilberforce succeeded perfectly in "attaining" the fullest measure of joy. There were great battles in the soul as well as in Parliament. For example, in March 1788, after a serious struggle with colitis, he seemed to enter into a "dark night of the soul." "Corrupt imaginations are perpetually rising in my mind and innumerable fears close me in on every side."[107] We get a glimpse of how he fought for joy in these times from what he wrote in his notebook of prayers:

> Lord, thou knowest that no strength, wisdom or contrivance of human power can signify, or relieve me. It is in thy power alone to deliver me. I fly to thee for succor and support, O Lord let it come speedily; give me full proof of thy Almighty power; I am in great troubles, insurmountable by me; but to thee slight and inconsiderable; look upon me O Lord with compassion and mercy, and restore me to rest, quietness, and comfort, in the world, or in another by removing me hence into a state of peace and happiness. Amen.[108]

Less devastating than "the dark night" were the recurrent disappointments with his own failures. But even as we read his self-indictments, we hear the hope of victory that sustained him and restored him to joy again and again. For example, in January 13, 1798, he wrote in his diary:

> Three or four times have I most grievously broke my resolutions since I last took up my pen. Alas! alas! how miserable a wretch am I! How infatuated, how dead to every better feeling yet—yet—yet—may I, Oh God, be enabled to repent and turn to thee with my whole heart, I am now flying from thee. Thou hast been above all measure gracious and forgiving.[109]

---

[106] Ibid., 239.
[107] Pollock, *Wilberforce*, 82.
[108] Ibid., 81–82.
[109] Ibid., 150. He confesses again, after a sarcastic rejoinder in the Commons, "In what a fermentation of spirits was I on the night of answering Courtenay. How jealous of character and greedy of applause. Alas, alas! Create in me a clean heart, O God, and renew a right spirit within me" (p. 167).

Unwearied Endeavor to Relish God

When Wilberforce pressed his readers to "unwearied endeavor" for more "relish" of heavenly things—that is, when he urged them to fight for joy—he was doing what he had learned from long experience. He wrote:

> [The true Christian] walks in the ways of Religion, not by constraint, but willingly; they are to him not only safe, but comfortable, "ways of pleasantness as well as of peace" [Prov. 3:17]. . . . With earnest prayers, therefore, for the Divine Help, with jealous circumspection and resolute self-denial, he guards against, and abstains from, whatever might be likely again to darken his enlightened judgment, or to vitiate his reformed taste; thus making it his unwearied endeavor to grow in the knowledge and love of heavenly things, and to obtain a warmer admiration, and a more cordial relish of their excellence.[110]

There was in Wilberforce, as in all the most passionate saints, a holy dread of losing his "reformed taste"[111] for spiritual reality. This dread gave rise to "earnest prayers . . . resolute self-denial" and rigorous abstinence from anything that would rob him of the greater joys. He illustrated this dread with the earthly pleasure of "honor." "[The] Christian . . . dreads, lest his supreme affections being thereby gratified [with human praise], it should be hereafter said to him 'remember that thou in thy life-time receivedst thy good things'" (Luke 16:25).[112]

He speaks of "self-denial" exactly the way Jesus did, not as an end in itself, but as a means to the highest pleasures. The mass of nominal Christians of his day did not understand this. And it was the root of their worldliness. "Pleasure and Religion are contradictory terms with the bulk of nominal Christians."[113] But for Wilberforce it was the opposite. The heart and power of true religion—and the root of righteous political endurance—was spiritual pleasure. "O! little do they know of the true measure of enjoyment, who can compare these delightful complacencies with the frivolous pleasures of dissipation, or the coarse gratifications of sensuality. . . . The nominal Christian . . . knows not the sweetness of the delights with which true Christianity repays those

---

[110] Ibid., 102–3.
[111] The word "reformed" does not refer here to "Calvinistic," but simply to a spiritual taste that was once worldly and now has been "re-formed" into a spiritual taste for spiritual things.
[112] Pollock, *Wilberforce*, 122.
[113] Ibid., 103.

trifling sacrifices."[114] That is what he calls true self-denial—"trifling sacrifices"—just as the apostle Paul called all his earthly treasures "rubbish, in order that I may gain Christ" (Phil. 3:8).

Joy in Christ was so crucial to living the Christian life and persevering in political justice that Wilberforce fought for it with relentless vigilance. "[The Christian's] watch must thus during life know no termination, because the enemy will ever be at hand; so it must be the more close and vigilant, because he is nowhere free from danger, but is on every side open to attack."[115] Therefore, when we say that Wilberforce's happiness was unshakable and undefeatable because it was beyond the reach of human vicissitudes, we don't mean it was beyond struggle; we mean he had learned the secret of "the good fight" (1 Tim. 6:12), and that his embattled joy reasserted itself in and after every tumult in society and in the soul.

Rooting Joy in Truth in the "Retired Hours"

The durable delights in God and the desires for the fullness of Christ that sustained Wilberforce's life did not just happen. He speaks of "the cultivation of . . . desire."[116] There were roots in doctrine. And the link between life and doctrine was prayer. He spoke in his book on Christianity of descending to the world from the "retired hours":

> Thus, at chosen seasons, the Christian exercises himself, and when, from this elevated region he descends into the plain below, and mixes in the bustle of life, he still retains the impressions of his retired hours. By these he realizes to himself the unseen world: he accustoms himself to speak and act as in the presence of "an innumerable company of angels, and of the spirits of just men made perfect, and of God the Judge of all" [Heb. 12:22–23].[117]

He was writing here out of his own experience. He could not conceal from others his commitment to personal prayer and private devotion. This was one of the main focuses in the funeral sermon by Joseph Brown:

> Persons of the highest distinction were frequently at his breakfast-table, but he never made his appearance till he had concluded his own meditations,

---

[114] Ibid., 237.
[115] Ibid., 123.
[116] Wilberforce, *A Practical View of Christianity*, 122.
[117] Ibid., 123.

reading his Bible, and prayer; always securing, as it were, to God, or rather to his own soul, I believe, the first hour of the morning. Whoever surrounded his breakfast-table, however distinguished the individuals, they were invited to join the family circle in family prayer. In reference to his own soul, I am informed, he set apart days, or a part of them, on which he had received particular mercies, for especial prayer. Not only did he pray in his closet, and with his family but if his domestics were ill, at their bed-side—there was their valued master praying with them—praying for them.[118]

He counseled his readers to "rise on the wings of contemplation, until the praises and censures of men die away upon the ear, and the still small voice of conscience is no longer drowned by the din of this nether world."[119] So the question is: Contemplation on what? Where did Wilberforce go to replenish his soul? If his childlike, child-loving, self-forgetting, indomitable joy was a life-giving root for his endurance in the lifelong fight for abolition, what, we might say, is the root of the root? Or what was the solid ground where the root was planted?

The Gigantic Truths of the Gospel

The main burden of Wilberforce's book, *A Practical View of Christianity*, is to show that true Christianity, which consists in these new, indomitable spiritual affections for Christ, is rooted in the great doctrines of the Bible about sin and Christ and faith.[120] "Let him then who would abound and grow in this Christian principle, be much conversant with the great doctrines of the Gospel."[121] "From the neglect of these peculiar doctrines arise the main practical errors of the bulk of professed Christians. These gigantic truths retained in view, would put to shame the littleness of their dwarfish morality. . . . The whole superstructure of Christian morals is grounded on their deep and ample basis."[122] There is a "perfect harmony between the leading doctrines and the practical precepts of Christianity."[123] And thus it is a "fatal habit"—so common in his day and ours—"to consider Christian morals as distinct from Christian doctrines."[124]

---

[118] Joseph Brown, quoted in *The Christian Observer* (London), January 1834: 63.
[119] Wilberforce, *A Practical View of Christianity*, 122.
[120] See page 328.
[121] Wilberforce, *A Practical View of Christianity*, 170.
[122] Ibid., 166–67.
[123] Ibid., 182.
[124] Ibid., 198.

Christ Our Righteousness

More specifically, it is the achievement of God through the death of Christ that is at the center of "these gigantic truths" leading to the personal and political reformation of morals. The indomitable joy that carries the day in time of temptation and trial is rooted in the cross of Christ. If we would fight for joy and endure to the end in our struggle with sin, we must know and embrace the full meaning of the cross.

> If we would . . . rejoice in [Christ] as triumphantly as the first Christians did; we must learn, like them to repose our entire trust in him and to adopt the language of the apostle, "God forbid that I should glory, save in the cross of Jesus Christ" [Gal. 6:14], "who of God is made unto us wisdom and righteousness, and sanctification, and redemption" [1 Cor. 1:30].[125]

In other words, the joy that triumphs over all obstacles and perseveres to the end in the battle for justice is rooted most centrally in the doctrine of justification by faith. Wilberforce says that all the spiritual and practical errors of the nominal Christians of his age—the lack of true religious affections and moral reformation—

> RESULT FROM THE MISTAKEN CONCEPTION ENTERTAINED OF THE FUNDAMENTAL PRINCIPLES OF CHRISTIANITY. They consider not that Christianity is a scheme "for justifying *the ungodly*" [Rom. 4:5], by Christ's dying for them "*when yet sinners*" [Rom. 5:6–8], a scheme "for reconciling us to God—*when enemies* [Rom. 5:10]; and for making the fruits of holiness *the effects, not the cause*, of our being justified and reconciled.[126]

Politician with a Passion for Pure Doctrine

It is a stunning thing that a politician and a man with no formal theological education should not only *know* the workings of God in justification and sanctification but *consider them so utterly essential* for Christian living and public virtue. Many public people *say* that changing society requires changing people, but few show the depth of understanding Wilberforce did concerning *how* that comes about. For him, the right grasp of the central doctrine of justification and its relation to sanctification—an emerging Christlikeness in private and public—were

---

[125] Ibid., 66.
[126] Ibid., 64, emphasis added, but the capitalization is his original emphasis.

essential to his own endurance and for the reformation of the morals of England.

This was why he wrote *A Practical View of Christianity*. The "bulk" of Christians in his day were "nominal," he observed, and what was the root difference between the nominal and the real? It was this: the nominal pursued morality (holiness, sanctification) without first relying utterly on the free gift of justification and reconciliation by faith alone based on Christ's blood and righteousness. "The grand distinction which subsists between the true Christian and all other Religionists (the class of persons in particular whom it is our object to address) is concerning the *nature* of holiness, and the *way in which it is to be obtained*."[127] What they do not see is that there must be a reconciliation with God and an imputed righteousness from him *before* we can live holy and righteous lives in the world. This was all-important to Wilberforce.

He saw that the nominal Christians of his day had the idea that "[morality] is to be *obtained* by their own natural unassisted efforts: or if they admit some vague indistinct notion of the assistance of the Holy Spirit, it is unquestionably obvious on conversing with them that this does not constitute the *main practical* ground of their dependence."[128] They don't recognize what constitutes a true Christian—namely, his renouncing "with indignation every idea of attaining it by his own strength. All his hopes of possessing it rest altogether on the divine assurances of the operation of the Holy Spirit, in those who cordially embrace the Gospel of Christ."[129]

This gospel that must be "cordially" embraced (that is, with the heart and affections, not just the head) is the good news that reconciliation and a righteous standing with God precede and ground even the Spirit-given enabling for practical holiness. "The true Christian . . . knows therefore that this holiness is not to PRECEDE his reconciliation to God, and be its CAUSE; but to FOLLOW it, and be its EFFECT. That, in short, it is by FAITH IN CHRIST only that he is to be justified in the sight of God."[130] In this way alone does a person become "entitled to all the privileges which belong to this high relation," which include in

---

[127] Ibid., 166.
[128] Ibid.
[129] Ibid.
[130] Ibid.

this earthly life a "partial renewal after the image of his Creator," and in the life to come "the more perfect possession of the Divine likeness."[131]

Perhaps Our Greatest Need

Is it not remarkable that one of the greatest politicians of Britain and one of the most persevering public warriors for social justice should elevate doctrine so highly? Perhaps this is why the impact of the church today is as weak as it is. Those who are most passionate about being practical for the public good are often the least doctrinally interested or informed. Wilberforce would say: you can't endure in bearing fruit if you sever the root.

From the beginning of his Christian life in 1785 until he died in 1833, Wilberforce lived off the "great doctrines of the gospel," especially the doctrine of justification by faith alone based on the blood and righteousness of Jesus Christ. This is where he fed his joy. Because of these truths, "when all around him is dark and stormy, he can lift up an eye to Heaven, radiant with hope and glistening with gratitude."[132] The joy of the Lord became his strength (Neh. 8:10). And in this strength he pressed on in the cause of abolishing the slave trade until he had the victory.

Therefore, in all our zeal today for racial harmony, or the sanctity of human life, or the building of a moral culture, let us not forget these lessons: never minimize the central place of God-centered, Christ-exalting doctrine; labor to be indomitably joyful in all that God is for us in Christ by trusting his great finished work; and never be idle in doing good—that men may see our good deeds and give glory to our Father who is in heaven (Matt. 5:16).

---

[131] Ibid.
[132] Ibid., 173.

Whatever was written in former days was written for our instruction, that through endurance and through the encouragement of the Scriptures we might have hope.
Romans 15:4

Let us run with endurance the race that is set before us, looking to Jesus.
Hebrews 12:1–2

Conclusion

The Imperfection and All-Importance of History

As I look back over what I have written, I feel ambivalent about it. On the one hand, it seems utterly provincial in view of the breadth and horror of the obstacles to endurance in many parts of the world today and in other cultures of that day. Here were three British men (how different some of the demands on women!), well-fed, well-clothed, living in the secure, comfortable, fast-developing, prosperously emerging modern world. The threats to their endurance were not beheading, burning at the stake, imprisonment, poisoning, starvation, torture, exile.

Not only that, when I consider the boundless resources in the Scriptures for our endurance, the scope of these chapters and these lives is very narrow. For example, consider the stupendous scope of Romans 15:4: "Whatever was written in former days was written for our instruction, that through *endurance* and through the encouragement of the Scriptures we might have hope." What this verse says is that *everything* written in the Bible was put there by God for the sake of our endurance—that no matter what our suffering, we might not lose *hope* but be encouraged to press on in faith.

So on the one hand, what I have written is historically and culturally narrow, and a mere fragment of the wealth of what God offers us for our endurance in the Bible. It is right and fitting for an author to say this and a reader to hear it. How finite and limited and fallible we are as humans! Banish all thoughts of finality or comprehensiveness or perfection. Finitude and fallenness will yield no final and comprehensive books or sermons. Those who claim otherwise simply have not counted the languages and cultures in the world and do not see how deeply we are corrupted by sin.

And consider also how little I have said about the *goal* of endurance! Endurance implies endurance *for* something. This is the main thing. We want to get there! Those who write poems and say memorable things about how the journey, not the destination, is the main thing simply have not tasted what Christians have tasted.

When you have tasted the Christian hope, you don't say clever things about the glory of striving over arriving. You say that striving and enduring are worth it because they lead to "eternal life" (Matt. 19:29; John 12:25; Rom. 2:7; Gal. 6:8) . . . that enduring is worth it because it produces a "weight of glory" (2 Cor. 4:17) . . . that it's worth it because those who hold fast "inherit the promises" (Heb. 6:12) . . . that those who endure persecution will receive a "great . . . reward" (Matt. 5:12) . . . that those who don't grow weary will "reap . . . in due season" (Gal. 6:9) . . . that those who make sacrifices "will be repaid at the resurrection of the just" (Luke 14:14) . . . that those who conquer will "eat of the tree of life" (Rev. 2:7) . . . and that "if in this life only we have hoped in Christ, we are of all people most to be pitied" (1 Cor. 15:19 AT).

Christians know that that there is joy on the journey. The Calvary road is not a joyless road. But we also know that this embattled joy flows from the hope we have in the future, and that if that future is cut off, the present taste of it is cut off. We are able to rejoice in the tribulations of this life for one reason: they work *hope* (Rom. 5:3–4). If the hope is vain, the joy vanishes. Sufferings are sufferable in joy because they are suffered in hope: "I consider that the sufferings of this present time are not worth comparing with the glory that is to be revealed to us" (Rom. 8:18). Those who exalt striving over arriving have not suffered enough agony or seen enough of God. Christians endure not because life is good, but because death is gain.

How is it gain? What is the "life" and "glory" and "promise" and "reward" and "harvest" and "repayment at the resurrection" when we "eat of the tree of life"? The Bible leaves no doubt: It is Christ. Paul said, "To die is gain," and then said, "My desire is to depart and be with Christ." Christ was the gain. He "would rather be away from the body" because that would mean being "at home with the Lord" (2 Cor. 5:8). But the decisive word is given by Jesus when he brought his prayer for all the saints to a climax with this petition: "Father, I desire that they also, whom you have given me, may be with me where I am, to see my glory" (John 17:24). Christ is the life and the glory and the promise and the reward and the harvest and the repayment at the resurrection and the tree of life.

Which is why the Bible says, "Let us run with endurance the race that is set before us, looking to *Jesus*" (Heb. 12:1–2). Jesus Christ is the deepest root of endurance. Seeing and savoring him is the source of strength that keeps us striving against sin and Satan and sickness and sabotage.[1] And the place he is seen most clearly and most powerfully and most mercifully is in his massive achievement for us on the cross.

This brings me now to the other side of my ambivalence about the present book. I said I feel ambivalent about what I have written because it is culturally and historically limited, and because it is biblically fragmentary compared to what God has provided for our endurance in his Word. But now, on the other hand, I say with joy and confidence that with all these limitations, what we have seen and heard from the lives of John Newton, Charles Simeon, and William Wilberforce brings us finally, in each case, to the one main root of endurance. And I would venture the bold claim that this root transcends all cultures and all centuries, and that it sums up the whole Bible—namely, Christ crucified, risen, and reigning as the ground and goal of all our endurance.

If these witnesses, by their Christ-exalting endurance, help us see the glory of God in the face of the crucified Christ, then they will have served us well. These swans will not have sung in vain if we, by seeing and savoring Jesus Christ more clearly, do justice, pursue world missions, love our neighbors, care for the poor, seek the lost, and finish well.

---

[1] This is so important for our survival as Christians that I wrote a book called *Seeing and Savoring Jesus Christ*, with thirteen portraits of the Lord to help us see him for who he is and savor him for all he's worth (Wheaton, IL: Crossway, 2004). We can't endure without "looking to Jesus."

The Swans Are Not Silent

Book 4

Contending for Our All

*Defending Truth and Treasuring Christ
in the Lives of Athanasius, John Owen,
and J. Gresham Machen*

To
R. C. Sproul

Faithful Contender for
the Supreme Greatness
of the Holiness of God

Contending for Our All

Book 4

Contents

Our upbringing and the whole atmosphere of the world we live in make it certain that our main temptation will be that of yielding to winds of doctrine, not that of ignoring them. We are not at all likely to be hidebound: we are very likely indeed to be the slaves of fashion. If one has to choose between reading the new books and reading the old, one must choose the old: not because they are necessarily better but because they contain precisely those truths of which our own age is neglectful. The standard of permanent Christianity must be kept clear in our minds and it is against that standard that we must test all contemporary thought. In fact, we must at all costs *not* move with the times. We serve One who said, "Heaven and Earth shall move with the times, but my words shall not move with the times" (Matt. 24:35; Mark 13:31; Luke 21:33).
C. S. Lewis
"Christian Apologetics"

Preface

The title of this series of books, The Swans Are Not Silent, comes from a story about St. Augustine. When he handed over his duties as the bishop of Hippo in North Africa in AD 426, his humble replacement, Eraclius, rose to speak and said, "The cricket chirps, the swan is silent."[1] Therefore, in titling this series The Swans Are *Not* Silent, I mean to say that great voices like Augustine's have been heard all through church history, and we will do well to listen.

I am deeply thankful to God that the swans are not silent and that the list of faith-inspiring heroes in Hebrews 11 did not end with the New Testament. God has worked through the lives of countless saints of whom we should say, "Though they died, they still speak" (cf. Heb. 11:4).

Some swans are alive and sing in our own day. But not many. And only time will tell if their song will survive the centuries. But time has already rendered that judgment for hundreds of swans. They have died, and their work has stood the test of time. Their song is, therefore, especially valuable for us to hear. You can hear them by studying what they wrote and by reading good biographies about them. This use of your time is probably wiser than staying up-to-date with news that will be forgotten in a fortnight and with ideas that will prove powerless in ten years.

I know of no one who has made a case for the old authors and the old books better than C. S. Lewis (1898–1963). When he neared sixty, he confessed with humility and wisdom: "I have lived nearly sixty years with myself and my own century and am not so enamored of either as to desire no glimpse of a world beyond them."[2] The "world

---

[1] Peter Brown, *Augustine of Hippo* (Berkeley: University of California Press, 1969), 408.
[2] C. S. Lewis, *Studies in Medieval and Renaissance Literature*, quoted in *The Quotable Lewis*, ed. Jerry Root and Wayne Martindale (Wheaton, IL: Tyndale, 1989), 509.

beyond them" was not future or make-believe. It was the world of the past.

He practiced what he preached by writing an introduction for Athanasius's *The Incarnation of the Word of God*, written probably in AD 318. At the risk of tempting you to put down the book in your hands and read only old books, I will nevertheless tell you what Lewis said about the reading of old books like the classic by Athanasius.

> There is a strange idea abroad that in every subject the ancient books should be read only by the professionals, and that the amateur should content himself with the modern books. . . . [Students are directed not to Plato but to books on Plato]—all about "isms" and influences and only once in twelve pages telling him what Plato actually said. . . . But if he only knew, the great man, just because of his greatness, is much more intelligible than his modern commentator. . . .
>
> Now this seems to me topsy-turvy. Naturally, since I myself am a writer, I do not wish the ordinary reader to read no modern books. But if he must read only the new or only the old, I would advise him to read the old. And I would give him this advice precisely because he is an amateur and therefore much less protected than the expert against the dangers of an exclusive contemporary diet. A new book is still on its trial and the amateur is not in a position to judge it. It has to be tested against the great body of Christian thought down the ages, and all its hidden implications (often unsuspected by the author himself) have to be brought to light. . . .
>
> It is a good rule, after reading a new book, never to allow yourself another new one till you have read an old one in between. If that is too much for you, you should at least read one old one to every three new ones. . . .
>
> We all, therefore, need the books that will correct the characteristic mistakes of our own period. And that means the old books. . . . We may be sure that the characteristic blindness of the twentieth century—the blindness about which posterity will ask, "But how *could* they have thought that?"—lies where we have never suspected it, and concerns something about which there is untroubled agreement between Hitler and President Roosevelt or between Mr. H. G. Wells and Karl Barth. None of us can fully escape this blindness. . . . The only palliative is to keep the clean sea breeze of the centuries blowing through our minds, and this can be done only by reading old books.[3]

---

[3] C. S. Lewis, "On The Reading of Old Books," in *C. S. Lewis: Essay Collection and Other Short Pieces*, ed. Lesley Walmsley (London: HarperCollins, 2000), 438–40.

In this book I invite you to feel the "clean sea breeze" blowing from the fourth, seventeenth, and early twentieth centuries. Perhaps this will lure you to read what Athanasius, John Owen, and J. Gresham Machen wrote. Their lives are not only pleasant as refreshing breezes from distant times but are also needed as exemplary contenders for the purity and preciousness of biblical truth. I will try to explain why in the introduction. For now, I thank God again that these three swans are not silent and that they were willing to suffer for the sake of safeguarding the gospel for us. They would have all said with Athanasius, "We are contending for our all."[4]

---

[4] "Wherefore . . . considering that *this struggle is for our all* . . . let us also make it our earnest care and aim to guard what we have received." Athanasius, *Athanasius: Select Works and Letters*, in *Nicene and Post-Nicene Fathers*, ed. Philip Schaff and Henry Wace (1892; repr., Peabody, MA: Hendricksen, 1999), 4:234, emphasis added.

Acknowledgments

I am surrounded by minds and hands that make my own mind and hands fruitful. I cannot thank God adequately that he has made the lines fall for me in these pleasant places. Being a pastor at Bethlehem Baptist Church is like being planted in rich soil with daily watering and ample sunshine and the addition of ever-fresh nutriment. I bless the day that God called me to the ministry of the Word and set me as an elder in this church.

Justin Taylor has served as an ever-competent, willing editor and research assistant who regularly goes beyond what would be required. I thank God for his partnership over these last six years. Carol Steinbach—with assistance from Greg Sweet, Catherine Tong, and Molly Piper—extends her camaraderie in this cause into a third decade and provides again the useful person and Scripture indexes—and weekly encouragements to me in her role at Desiring God.

My wife, Noël, has read more Piper books more times than anyone in the world. As I write this, she is sitting in our living room with the manuscript of this book spread out on her lap with a red pen in hand and lots of pink Post-Its appearing on the edges of the proofs. She has an eagle eye for spelling, dates, grammar, style, and logic. Not much gets by her. Her probing questions don't have the effect of making me feel better. They just make the book better. It is all part of our uncommon union, for which I am deeply thankful to God.

These chapters took their first shape as messages in the Bethlehem Conference for Pastors. There would be no Swan books without that conference. So I feel an indebtedness to the brothers who have come to worship and to learn. These conferences would not happen as they do without the extraordinary gifts and grace of Scott Anderson, the Director for Conferences at Desiring God.

I have dedicated the book to R. C. Sproul, founder of Ligonier Ministries. Dr. Sproul is one of the clearest and most compelling contenders for the fullness of the biblical faith with all its magnificent contours. I rejoice in the centrality and supremacy of God he has so relentlessly and faithfully kept before the church for these last three decades.

Finally, I thank Jesus Christ who loved me and gave himself for me. He is the same yesterday, today, and forever. May we learn from Athanasius, Owen, and Machen to contend well for his cause until he comes.

Men tell us that our preaching should be positive and not negative, that we can preach the truth without attacking error.

But if we follow that advice we shall have to close our Bible and desert its teachings. The New Testament is a polemic book almost from beginning to end.

Some years ago I was in a company of teachers of the Bible in the colleges and other educational institutions of America. One of the most eminent theological professors in the country made an address. In it he admitted that there are unfortunate controversies about doctrine in the Epistles of Paul; but, said he in effect, the real essence of Paul's teaching is found in the hymn to Christian love in the thirteenth chapter of 1 Corinthians; and we can avoid controversy today, if we will only devote the chief attention to that inspiring hymn.

In reply, I am bound to say that the example was singularly ill-chosen. That hymn to Christian love is in the midst of a great polemic passage; it would never have been written if Paul had been opposed to controversy with error in the Church. It was because his soul was stirred within him by a wrong use of the spiritual gifts that he was able to write that glorious hymn. So it is always in the Church. Every really great Christian utterance, it may almost be said, is born in controversy. It is when men have felt compelled to take a stand against error that they have risen to the really great heights in the celebration of truth.

J. Gresham Machen
"Christian Scholarship and the Defense of the Faith"

Sacred Controversy in Scripture, History, and the Lives of the Swans

Controversy, Cowardice, and Pride

Some controversy is crucial for the sake of life-giving truth. Running from it is a sign of cowardice. But enjoying it is usually a sign of pride. Some necessary tasks are sad, and even victory is not without tears—unless there is pride. The reason enjoying controversy is a sign of pride is that humility loves truth-based unity more than truth-based victory. Humility loves Christ-exalting exultation more than Christ-defending confrontation—even more than Christ-defending vindication. Humility delights to worship Christ in spirit and truth. If it must fight for worship-sustaining truth, it will, but that is not because the fight is pleasant. It's not even because victory is pleasant. It's because knowing and loving and proclaiming Christ for who he really is and what he really did is pleasant.

Indeed knowing and loving the truth of Christ is not only pleasant now, it is the only path to everlasting life and joy. That's why Athanasius (298–373), John Owen (1616–1683), and J. Gresham Machen (1881–1937) took so seriously the controversies of their time. It was not what they liked, but it was what love required—love for Christ and his church and his world.

Controversy Less Crucial, but Necessary

There are more immediately crucial tasks than controversy about the truth and meaning of the gospel. For example, it is more immediately crucial that we believe the gospel, and proclaim it to the unreached, and pray for power to attend the preaching of the gospel. But this is like saying that flying food to starving people is more immediately crucial than the science of aeronautics. True. But the food will not be flown to the needy if someone is not doing aeronautics. It is like saying that giving penicillin shots to children dying of fever is more immediately crucial than the work of biology and chemistry. True. But there would be no penicillin without such work.

In every age there is a kind of person who tries to minimize the importance of truth-defining and truth-defending controversy by saying that prayer, worship, evangelism, missions, and dependence on the Holy Spirit are more important. Who has not heard such rejoinders to controversy: "Let's stop arguing about the gospel and get out there and share it with a dying world." Or: "Prayer is more powerful than argument." Or: "We should rely on the Holy Spirit and not on our reasoning." Or: "God wants to be worshiped, not discussed."

I love the passion for faith and prayer and evangelism and worship behind those statements. But when they are used to belittle gospel-defining, gospel-defending controversy, they bite the hand that feeds them. Christ-exalting prayer will not survive in an atmosphere where the preservation and explanation and vindication of the teaching of the Bible about the prayer-hearing God are devalued. Evangelism and world missions must feed on the solid food of well-grounded, unambiguous, rich gospel truth in order to sustain courage and confidence in the face of afflictions and false religions. And corporate worship will be diluted with cultural substitutes where the deep, clear, biblical contours of God's glory are not seen and guarded from ever-encroaching error.

It is not valid to contrast dependence on the Holy Spirit with the defense of his Word in controversy. The reason is that the Holy Spirit uses means—including the preaching and defending of the gospel. J. Gresham Machen put it like this:

> It is perfectly true, of course, that argument alone is quite insufficient to make a man a Christian. You may argue with him from now until the end of the world; you may bring forth the most magnificent arguments—but all will be in vain unless there is one other thing: the mysterious, creative power of the Holy Spirit in the new birth. But because argument is insufficient, it does not follow that it is unnecessary. Sometimes it is used directly

by the Holy Spirit to bring a man to Christ. But more frequently it is used indirectly.[1]

This is why Athanasius, John Owen, and J. Gresham Machen engaged their minds and hearts and lives in the Christ-defining and Christ-defending controversies of their day. It was not because the Holy Spirit and prayer were inadequate. It was because the Holy Spirit works through the Word preached and explained and defended. It was because biblical prayer aims not just at the heart of the person who needs persuading, but also at the persuader.[2] The Holy Spirit makes a biblical argument compelling in the mouth of the teacher and in the heart of the student.

And Athanasius, Owen, and Machen believed that what they were contending for was of infinite worth. It was indeed not a distraction from the work of love. It was love—love to Christ, his church, and his world.

Controversy When "Our All" Is at Stake

In Athanasius's lifelong battle for the deity of Christ against the Arians, who said that Christ was created, Athanasius said, "Considering that *this struggle is for our all* . . . let us also make it our earnest care and aim to guard what we have received."[3] When *all* is at stake, it is worth contending. This is what love does.

Machen, in his twentieth-century American situation, put it like this: "Controversy of the right sort is good; for out of such controversy, as Church history and Scripture alike teach, there comes the salvation of souls."[4] When you believe that *soul-saving* truth (our *all*) is at stake in a controversy, running away is not only cowardly but cruel. These men never ran.

John Owen, the greatest Puritan intellect, took up more controversies than Machen and Athanasius combined, but was driven by an even

---

[1] J. Gresham Machen, "Christian Scholarship and the Defense of the Faith," in *J. Gresham Machen: Selected Shorter Writings*, ed. D. G. Hart (Phillipsburg, NJ: P&R, 2004), 144–45. One should also recall how Paul "reasoned" in the synagogues in order to win converts by the power of the Holy Spirit (Acts 17:2, 17; 18:4, 19; 24:25).

[2] Second Thess. 3:1, "Finally, brothers, pray for us, that the word of the Lord may speed ahead and be honored." Col. 4:3, "Pray also for us, that God may open to us a door for the word." Eph. 6:19, "[Pray] for me, that words may be given to me in opening my mouth boldly to proclaim the mystery of the gospel."

[3] Athanasius, *Athanasius: Select Works and Letters*, in *Nicene and Post-Nicene Fathers* (*NPNF*), ed. Philip Schaff and Henry Wace (1892; repr., Peabody, MA: Hendricksen, 1999), 4:234, emphasis added.

[4] J. Gresham Machen, *What Is Faith?* (1925; repr., Edinburgh: Banner of Truth, 1991), 42–43.

more manifest love for Christ. Not that he loved Christ more (only God can know that), but he articulated the battle for communion with Christ more explicitly than they. For Owen, virtually every confrontation with error was for the sake of the contemplation of Christ. Communion with Christ was his constant theme and goal. He held the view that such contemplation and communion were only possible by means of true views of Christ. Truth about Christ was necessary for communion with Christ.

Therefore all controversy in the defense of this truth was for the sake of worship.

> What soul that hath any acquaintance with these things falls not down with reverence and astonishment? How glorious is he that is the Beloved of our souls! . . . When . . . our life, our peace, our joy, our inheritance, our eternity, *our all,* lies herein, shall not the thoughts of it always dwell in our hearts, always refresh and delight our souls?[5]

As with Athanasius, Owen said that "our all" is at stake in contending for the truth of Christ. Then he brings the battle into the closest connection with the blessing of communion with God. Even *in* the battle, not just *after* it, we must commune with God. "When we have *communion with God in the doctrine we contend for*—then shall we be garrisoned by the grace of God against all the assaults of men."[6] The aim of contending for Christ is also essential to the means. If we do not delight in Christ through the truth that we defend, our defense is not for the sake of the preciousness of Christ. The end and the means of Christ-exalting controversy is worship.

A Mistaken Notion about Controversy and Church Vitality

There is a mistaken notion about the relationship between the health of the church and the presence of controversy. For example, some say that spiritual awakening and power and growth will not come to the church of Christ until church leaders lay aside doctrinal differences and come together in prayer. Indeed there should be much corporate prayer for God's mercy on us. And indeed there are some doctrinal differences that

---

[5] John Owen, *Of Communion with God,* in *The Works of John Owen,* ed. William Goold, 24 vols. (1850–1853; repr., Edinburgh: Banner of Truth, 1965), 2:69, emphasis added.
[6] Owen, *Works,* ed. Goold, 1:lxiii–lxiv, emphasis added.

should not be elevated to a place of prominence. Machen explained his own passion for doctrine with this caution: "We do not mean, in insisting upon the doctrinal basis of Christianity, that all points of doctrine are equally important. It is perfectly possible for Christian fellowship to be maintained despite differences of opinion."[7]

But there is a historical and biblical error in the assumption that the church will not grow and prosper in times of controversy. Machen said, as we saw above, that church history and Scripture teach the value of right controversy. This is important to see, because if we do not see it, we will yield to the massive pragmatic pressure of our time to minimize doctrine. We will cave in to the pressure that a truth-driven ministry cannot be a people-loving, soul-saving, church-reviving, justice-advancing, missions-mobilizing, worship-intensifying, Christ-exalting ministry. But, in fact, it is truth—biblical truth, doctrinal truth—that gives foundation and duration to all these things.

The Witness of Church History to the Place of Controversy

The witness of church history is that seasons of controversy have often been seasons of growth and strength. This was the case in the first centuries of the church. Most Christians today would be stunned if they knew that the battle for the deity of Christ was not a battle between the great force of orthodoxy on the one hand, and marginal heretics on the other. It was a battle in which at times the majority of the church leaders in the world were unorthodox.[8] Yet the church grew in spite of controversy and persecution. Indeed I believe we must say that the growth of the true church in those days was *because of* leaders like Athanasius, who took a stand for the sake of truth. Without controversy there would have been no gospel, and therefore no church.

The Protestant Reformation

The time of the Protestant Reformation was a time of great controversy both between the Protestants and Roman Catholics and between the Reformers themselves. Yet the fullness of the gospel was preserved in

---

[7] J. Gresham Machen, *Christianity and Liberalism* (1923; repr., Grand Rapids, MI: Eerdmans, 1992), 48.
[8] The Council of Nicaea did not settle the issue of Christ's deity—it drew the battle lines. The majority of bishops who signed it (all but two) were politically motivated. "In the years immediately following, we find a large majority of the Eastern bishops, especially of Syria and Asia Minor, the very regions whence the numerical strength of the council was drawn, in full reaction against the council." *NPNF*, 4:xxi.

these great doctrinal battles, and true faith spread and was strengthened. In fact, the spread and vitality of the Reformed faith in the century after John Calvin's death in 1564 was astonishing[9] and produced some of the greatest pastors and theologians the world has ever known[10]—all of this born in the controversies of Wittenberg and Geneva.

The First Great Awakening

The First Great Awakening in Britain and America in the eighteenth century was a time of tremendous growth for the church and of profound awakening of thousands of individuals. But it is common knowledge that the two greatest itinerant preachers in this movement were opposed to each other's understanding of God's work in salvation. George Whitefield was a Calvinist, and John Wesley was an Arminian.

J. I. Packer explains the five points of Calvinism in this way:

> (1) Fallen man in his natural state lacks all power to believe the gospel, just as he lacks all power to believe the law, despite all external inducements that may be extended to him. (2) God's election is a free, sovereign, unconditional choice of sinners, as sinners, to be redeemed by Christ, given faith, and brought to glory. (3) The redeeming work of Christ had as its end and goal the salvation of the elect. (4) The work of the Holy Spirit in bringing men to faith never fails to achieve its object. (5) Believers are kept in faith and grace by the unconquerable power of God till they come to glory. These five points are conveniently denoted by the mnemonic TULIP: Total depravity, Unconditional election, Limited atonement, Irresistible grace, Preservation of the saints.

And here is how Packer unpacks the five points of Arminianism:

---

[9] German Calvinist Abraham Scultetus (1566–1624) described the spread of Reformed influence thirty years after Calvin's death.

> I cannot fail to recall the optimistic mood which I and many others felt when we considered the condition of the Reformed churches in 1591. In France there ruled the valiant King Henri IV, in England the mighty Queen Elizabeth, in Scotland the learned King James, in the Palatinate the bold hero John Casimir, in Saxony the courageous and powerful Elector Christian I, in Hesse the clever and prudent Landgrave William, who were all inclined to Reformed religion. In the Netherlands everything went as Prince Maurice of Orange wished, when he took Breda, Zutphen, Hulst, and Nijmegen. . . . We imagined that *aureum seculum*, a golden age, had dawned. (Scultetus, quoted in Alister E. McGrath, *A Life of John Calvin* [Grand Rapids, MI: Baker, 1990], 199)

[10] When I speak of notable pastors and theologians, I am thinking mainly of the pastoral theologians called Puritans who flourished in Great Britain in the century following John Calvin's death. J. I. Packer called these pastor-theologians the "Redwoods" of church history. "California's Redwoods make me think of England's Puritans, another breed of giants who in our time have begun to be newly appreciated. Between 1550 and 1700 they too lived unfrilled lives in which, speaking spiritually, strong growth and resistance to fire and storm were what counted." *A Quest For Godliness: The Puritan Vision of the Christian Life* (Wheaton, IL: Crossway, 1990), 11.

(1) Man is never so completely corrupted by sin that he cannot savingly be-lieve the gospel when it is put before him, nor (2) is he ever so completely controlled by God that he cannot reject it. (3) God's election of those who shall be saved is prompted by his foreseeing that they will of their own accord believe. (4) Christ's death did not ensure the salvation of anyone, for it did not secure the gift of faith to anyone (there is no such gift): what it did was rather to create a possibility of salvation for everyone if they believe. (5) It rests with believers to keep themselves in a state of grace by keeping up their faith; those who fail here fall away and are lost. Thus, Arminianism made man's salvation depend ultimately on man himself, saving faith being viewed throughout as man's own work and, because his own, not God's in him.[11]

At the human center of the Great Awakening was controversy.

Wesley's disagreement with Calvinism "burst forth in a sermon from 1740 titled 'Free Grace.' . . . For Wesley the Calvinist insistence that God's electing power was the basic element in the sinner's conversion verged dangerously close to antinomianism. . . . Wesley could not be persuaded that the Bible taught Calvinist doctrines."[12]

Whitefield responded to Wesley's criticism with a published letter from Bethesda, Georgia, dated December 24, 1740. He knew that controversy between evangelicals would be frowned upon by some and savored by others. Yet he felt compelled to engage in the controversy:

> I am very apprehensive that our common adversaries will rejoice to see us differing among ourselves. But what can I say? The children of God are in danger of falling into error. . . . When I remember how Paul reproved Peter for his dissimulation, I fear I have been sinfully silent too long. Oh! then, be not angry with me, dear and honored sir, if now I deliver my soul, by telling you that I think, in this you greatly err.[13]

Mark Noll says that Whitefield's response to Wesley "inaugurated the most enduring theological conflict among evangelicals, the conflict between Arminian and Calvinist interpretations of Scripture on the nature, motive powers and implications of salvation."[14] Nevertheless, with

---

[11] Ibid., 128.

[12] Mark A. Noll, *The Rise of Evangelicalism: The Age of Edwards, Whitefield, and the Wesleys* (Downers Grove, IL: InterVarsity Press, 2003), 122.

[13] George Whitefield, "A Letter From George Whitefield to the Rev. Mr. John Wesley, in Answer to Mr. Wesley's Sermon Entitled 'Free Grace,'" (December 24, 1740), in *George Whitefield's Journals* (Edinburgh: Banner of Truth, 1960), 569ff.

[14] Noll, *The Rise of Evangelicalism*, 122.

controversy at the center, the Great Awakening brought unprecedented life and growth to churches in the American colonies and Britain. Take the Baptists, for example. They were the "primary beneficiaries of the Great Awakening"[15] in America. "In the colonies of North America there were less than one hundred Baptist churches in 1740, but almost five hundred by the outbreak of the war with Britain in 1776."[16] Similarly the Presbyterian churches rose from about 160 in 1740 to nearly six hundred by 1776.[17] The point is that controversy was prominent in the Great Awakening, and God blessed the movement with spiritual life and growth.

The Second Great Awakening

The same thing can be said of the Second Great Awakening. It was "the most influential revival of Christianity in the history of the United States. Its very size and its many expressions have led some historians to question whether a *single* Second Great Awakening can be identified as such. Yet from about 1795 to about 1810 there was a broad and general rekindling of interest in Christianity through the country."[18] Francis Asbury and Charles Finney were the main leaders of this Awakening. Both were controversial, and both saw amazing growth.

When Francis Asbury came to America in 1771, four Methodist ministers were caring for about three hundred laypeople. When he died in 1816, there were two thousand ministers and over two hundred thousand Methodists in the States and several thousand more in Canada.[19] But his attachment to the Englishman John Wesley and his unorthodox methods of ministry brought Asbury into controversy with American patriots and church leaders. For example, he was banished from Maryland because he would not sign an oath of loyalty to the new state government.[20] The blessing of God on his ministry for forty-five years was unbroken by the controversy that swirled around it.

Finney, who broke with his Presbyterian background, was unorthodox both in method and theology. He took over the use of the contro-

---

[15] Ibid., 183.
[16] Ibid.
[17] Ibid., 185.
[18] Mark A. Noll, *A History of Christianity in the United States and Canada* (Grand Rapids, MI: Eerdmans, 1992), 166.
[19] Ibid., 173.
[20] Ibid., 171.

versial "anxious bench" and made it into a norm of later revivalism.[21]
He was more Arminian than John Wesley:

> Wesley maintained that the human will is incapable of choosing God apart
> from God's preparatory grace, but Finney rejected this requirement. He
> was a perfectionist who believed that a permanent stage of higher spiritual
> life was possible for anyone who sought it wholeheartedly. Following the
> theologians of New England, he held a governmental view of the atonement
> whereby Christ's death was a public demonstration of God's willingness to
> forgive sins rather than payment for sin itself.[22]

This kind of theology was bound to meet opposition. One example of that controversy can be seen by observing Finney's relationship with his contemporaries Asahel Nettleton and Lyman Beecher.
"Finney was the spokesman for the surging frontier religion which
was both speculative and emotional. Nettleton was the defender of
the old New England orthodoxy which refused to be shaken from the
moorings of the past."[23] Lyman Beecher was a Congregational pastor
in Boston and shared Nettleton's historic Calvinist views. Both these
men had fruitful ministries, and Nettleton's itinerant evangelism was
blessed with so many conversions that Francis Wayland (1796–1865),
an early president of Brown University, said, "I suppose no minister
of his time was the means of so many conversions. . . . He . . . would
sway an audience as the trees of the forest are moved by a mighty
wind."[24]

But the controversy between Finney on the one hand, and Nettleton and Beecher on the other, was so intense that a meeting was called
in New Lebanon, New York, in 1827 to work out the differences.

---

[21] Ibid., 176.

[22] Ibid., 177. Finney also rejected the doctrine of original sin and the imputation of Christ's righteousness. "I insisted that our reason was given for the very purpose of enabling us to justify the ways of God; and that no such fiction of imputation could by any possibility be true." Finney, quoted in J. F. Thornbury, *God Sent Revival: The Story of Asahel Nettleton and the Second Great Awakening* (Grand Rapids, MI: Evangelical Press, 1977), 160.

[23] Thornbury, *God Sent Revival*, 168.

[24] Ibid., 55. The reason Wayland could say this, in spite of Finney's amazing success, was that Nettleton's converts had a remarkable reputation of remaining faithful over time and proving themselves true converts, while Finney's were more like the converts of mass evangelism in our own day—a large percentage fell away.

> Given the extent of his exposure, and the permanence of his converts, he may well have been, next to George Whitefield, the most effective evangelist in the history of the United States. The ratio of his converts to the population of America in his day [about nine million] is very revealing. Although there is no way of knowing how many were brought to salvation through his preaching, a conservative estimate would be twenty-five thousand. Based on the reports of firsthand witnesses, and pastors who labored in the communities where his revivals took place, sometimes examining the situation thirty years later, only a small fraction of these converts were spurious. (Ibid., 233)

Numerous concerned clergy came from both the Finney and the Beecher side. It ended without reconciliation, and Beecher said to Finney, "Finney, I know your plan, and you know I do; you mean to come to Connecticut and carry a streak of fire to Boston. But if you attempt it, as the Lord liveth, I'll meet you at the State line, and call out all the artillery men, and fight every inch of the way to Boston, and then I'll fight you there."[25]

Controversy and Vitality and Growth Are Compatible

The point of these illustrations from church history is to lay to rest the notion that powerful spiritual awakening can only come when controversy is put aside. Though I would not want to press it as a strategy, history seems to suggest the opposite. When there is a great movement of God to bring revival and reformation to his church, controversy becomes part of the human process. It would not be far off to say with Parker Williamson that at least in some instances the controversy was not just a result but a means of the revitalization of the church.

> Historically, controversies that have swirled around the meaning and implications of the Gospel, far from damaging the Church, have contributed to its vitality. Like a refiner's fire, intense theological debate has resulted in clarified belief, common vision, and invigorated ministry.[26]

J. Gresham Machen came to the same conclusion as he looked over the history of the church and the nature of Christ's mission in the world:

> Every true revival is born in controversy, and leads to more controversy. That has been true ever since our Lord said that he came not to bring peace upon the earth but a sword. And do you know what I think will happen when God sends a new reformation upon the church? We cannot tell when that blessed day will come. But when the blessed day does come, I think we can say at least one result that it will bring. We shall hear nothing on that day about the evils of controversy in the church. All that will be swept away as with a mighty flood. A man who is on fire with a message never talks in that wretched, feeble way, but proclaims the truth joyously and

---

[25] Ibid., 178.
[26] Parker T. Williamson, *Standing Firm: Reclaiming Christian Faith in Times of Controversy* (Springfield, PA: PLC, 1996), 2.

fearlessly, in the presence of every high thing that is lifted up against the gospel of Christ.[27]

Probably the regular presence of controversy in times of revival and reformation is owing to several factors. In these seasons of emerging spiritual life, passions run higher. And when passions are higher, controversy is more likely. Satan too can see the dangers of revival to his cause and will surely work to bring disunity and disrepute on the leaders if he can. But more essentially, awakening and reformation are caused and carried by more clear perception of the glories of Christ and the repugnance of sin, and when these are seen more clearly and spoken of more precisely, division is more likely than when Christ is spoken of in vague terms and people care little for his name. Add to this that in times of revival people see more clearly that eternity is at stake in what we believe, and this gives a cutting edge to doctrine. It really matters when you see that "our all" is at stake.

The Witness of Scripture to the Place of Controversy

In addition to church history, the Bible itself testifies that there is a body of doctrine about God and his ways that exists objectively outside ourselves, and that this truth is so important that preserving it is worth controversy if necessary. The apostle Paul calls this body of doctrine "the standard of teaching to which you were committed" (Rom. 6:17). That's the way it functions. It is a standard, a yardstick, a pattern. You measure all other truth by it. Elsewhere he calls it "the whole counsel of God" (Acts 20:27) and the "pattern of the sound words" and "the good deposit entrusted to you" (2 Tim. 1:13–14). In other words, it doesn't change.

The importance of this revealed truth about God and his ways can hardly be overemphasized. It awakens and sustains faith;[28] it is the source of obedience;[29] it frees from sin;[30] it liberates from Satan's

---

[27] Ned B. Stonehouse, *J. Gresham Machen: A Biographical Memoir* (1954; repr., Edinburgh: Banner of Truth, 1987), 148.

[28] Rom. 10:17, "So faith comes from hearing, and hearing through the word of Christ."

[29] John 17:17, "Sanctify them in the truth; your word is truth." 2 Pet. 1:3–4, "His divine power has granted to us everything pertaining to life and godliness, through the true knowledge of Him who called us by His own glory and excellence. For by these He has granted to us His precious and magnificent promises, so that by them you may become partakers of *the* divine nature, having escaped the corruption that is in the world by lust" (NASB).

[30] John 8:32, "And you will know the truth, and the truth will set you free."

bondage;[31] it awakens and sustains love;[32] it saves;[33] it sustains joy.[34] And most of all—as the sum of all the rest—this body of biblical truth is the means of having God the Father and God the Son: "Whoever abides in the teaching has both the Father and the Son" (2 John 9).

The reason Christianity has been so uncongenial to the pragmatic mind-set that resists controversy at all costs is that at the core of Christian faith are history and doctrine that do not change. Machen states with characteristic clarity:

> From the beginning, the Christian gospel, as indeed the name "gospel" or "good news" implies, consisted in an account of something that had happened. And from the beginning, the meaning of the happening was set forth; and when the meaning of the happening was set forth then there was Christian doctrine. "Christ died"—that is history; "Christ died for our sins"—that is doctrine. Without these two elements joined in an absolutely indissoluble union, there is no Christianity.[35]

This is why controversy comes. Attempts to "reinterpret" the biblical happening or the biblical interpretation of the happening—the history or the doctrine—are a threat to the heart of Christianity. Christianity is not merely a life or a morality. It is God acting once for all in history, and God interpreting the meaning of those actions in Scripture.

The magnitude of what is at stake in preserving the true meaning of Scripture is so great that controversy is a price faithful teachers have been willing to pay from the very beginning. It is fair to say that we would not have the New Testament if there had been no controversy in the early church. If you remove the documents from the New Testament that were not addressing controversy you will, at most, have a tiny handful from the twenty-seven books.[36]

---

[31] 2 Tim. 2:24–26, "The Lord's bond-servant must not be quarrelsome, but be kind to all, able to teach, patient when wronged, with gentleness correcting those who are in opposition, if perhaps God may grant them repentance leading to the knowledge of the truth, and they may come to their senses *and escape* from the snare of the devil, having been held captive by him to do his will" (NASB).

[32] Phil. 1:9, "And this I pray, that your love may abound still more and more in real knowledge and all discernment" (NASB).

[33] 1 Tim. 4:16, "Pay close attention to yourself and to your teaching; persevere in these things, for as you do this you will ensure salvation both for yourself and for those who hear you" (NASB). Acts 20:26–27, "I testify to you this day that I am innocent of the blood of all men. For I did not shrink from declaring to you the whole purpose of God" (NASB). 2 Thess. 2:9–10, "The coming of the lawless one is . . . and with all wicked deception for those who are perishing, because they refused to love the truth and so be saved."

[34] John 15:11, "These things I have spoken to you, that my joy may be in you, and that your joy may be full."

[35] Machen, *Christianity and Liberalism*, 27.

[36] Here is a sampling of the controversies we find in the New Testament: Jesus's controversy over paying taxes to Caesar (Mark 12:14–17), whether there is marriage in the resurrection (Matt. 22:23–32), what

The New Testament Summons to Controversy

Not only is the New Testament an *example* of controversy, it is also a *summons* to controversy, when controversy is necessary. Jude, the brother of the Lord, says, "I found it necessary to write appealing to you *to contend* for the faith that was once for all delivered to the saints" (Jude 3).

The apostle Paul rejoices that the Philippians are his partners in "the *defense* and confirmation of the gospel" (Phil. 1:7). He charges Timothy to "preach the word. . . . For the time is coming when people will not endure sound teaching, but having itching ears they will accumulate for themselves teachers to suit their own passions, and will turn away from listening to the truth and wander off into myths" (2 Tim. 4:2–4).

Notice that these are church members, not people in the world, who will depart from sound teaching. "*From among your own selves*," Paul warns the elders of Ephesus, "will arise men speaking twisted things, to draw away the disciples after them" (Acts 20:30). And, as the apostle Peter says, "There will be false teachers *among you*, who will secretly bring in destructive heresies" (2 Pet. 2:1). Therefore, Paul concludes soberly, "There must be factions among you in order that those who are genuine among you may be recognized" (1 Cor. 11:19).

So Let Us Learn from Those Who Have Contended Well

In view of the witness of church history and Scripture to the necessity of controversy in this imperfect world, and the compatibility of controversy and revitalization, we will do well to learn as much as we can from those who have walked through controversy and blessed

---

the greatest commandment is (Matt. 22:36–40), when divorce is permitted (Matt. 5:31–32; 19:9), who the Son of Man is (Matt. 16:13). The controversy in Acts over the feeding of the Hellenistic widows (Acts 6:1–6) and over whether circumcision is required for salvation (Acts 15). The controversies of Paul over whether we should do evil, that good may come (Rom. 3:8), and why God still finds fault when he is the ruler of human wills (Rom. 9:19), and whether all days should be esteemed alike (Rom. 14:5), and how to handle immorality in the church (1 Corinthians 5), and whether to go to court before unbelieving judges (1 Corinthians 6), and whether singleness is better than marriage, or whether a believer should marry an unbeliever (1 Corinthians 7), and whether meat offered to idols should be eaten by believers (1 Corinthians 8), and whether women may pray and prophesy in public services (1 Cor. 14:34–35), and how the gift of tongues and prophecy should be used (1 Corinthians 12–14), and whether the dead are raised bodily from the dead (1 Corinthians 15), and whether one should add works to faith as an instrument of justification (Galatians 3–5), and with those professing Christians who want to make his imprisonment harder and worship their bellies (Philippians 1, 3), and with those who accused him of flattery (1 Thess. 2:5), and with those who said that the day of the Lord had already come (2 Thessalonians 2), and with those who demanded that food and marriage be avoided (1 Tim. 4:3), and with those who say godliness is a means of gain (1 Tim. 6:5). And then there are all the controversies referred to in the letters of John and Peter and the book of Revelation. But this is enough to show how the earliest church was riddled with controversy.

the church in doing so. Athanasius and Owen and Machen have done that. The lessons they have to teach us are many. Their lives instruct us in the subtleties of how language is manipulated in controversy, and how personal holiness and communion with God are essential in the battle, and how love and patience with our adversaries can sometimes conquer better than argument, and how perseverance through suffering is essential to long-term faithfulness to truth, and how larger cultural issues shape church disputes, and how important it is to out-rejoice the adversary if we claim to contend for good news.

I hope that you will come to love these three brothers who have gone before. I pray that you will count them among the number referred to in Hebrews 13:7, "Remember your leaders, those who spoke to you the word of God. Consider the outcome of their way of life, and imitate their faith." They are worthy in their own right to be emulated—not without reservation; they are mere men. But time has tested them and their work. And it is worth our attention. It is a bonus—a very large one—that all three are from outside our own century (the fourth, seventeenth, and early twentieth). In this way we see reality through the eyes of a different time. That is a great advantage. It serves to liberate us from the dangers of chronological snobbery that assumes ours is the wisest of times.

And as we learn from the heroes of our faith, let us resolve to renounce all controversy-loving pride and all controversy-fearing cowardice. And with humility and courage (that is, with faith in the sovereign Christ) let us heed Martin Luther's warning not to proclaim only what is safe while the battle rages around what is necessary:

> If I profess with the loudest voice and clearest exposition every portion of the truth of God except precisely that little point which the world and the devil are at that moment attacking, I am not confessing Christ, however boldly I may be professing Christ. Where the battle rages there the loyalty of the soldier is proved, and to be steady on all the battlefield besides is mere flight and disgrace if he flinches at that point.[37]

---

[37] Martin Luther, quoted in Williamson, *Standing Firm*, 5. Denny Burk argues that the quotation may not in fact be from Luther: http://www.dennyburk.com/the-apocryphal-martin-luther.

And, in a word, the achievements of the Savior, resulting from His becoming man, are of such kind and number, that if one should wish to enumerate them, he may be compared to men who gaze at the expanse of the sea and wish to count its waves.

For as one cannot take in the whole of the waves with his eyes, for those which are coming on baffle the sense of him that attempts it; so for him that would take in all the achievements of Christ in the body, it is impossible to take in the whole, even by reckoning them up, as those which go beyond his thought are more than those he thinks he has taken in.

Better is it, then, not to aim at speaking of the whole, where one cannot do justice even to a part, but, after mentioning one more, to leave the whole for you to marvel at. For all alike are marvelous, and wherever a man turns his glance, he may behold on that side the divinity of the Word, and be struck with exceeding great awe.

Athanasius
On the Incarnation of the Word

1

Contending for Christ
Contra Mundum

Exile and Incarnation in the Life of Athanasius

Best-Loved Bishop

Athanasius was born in AD 298 in Egypt and became the bishop of
Alexandria on June 8, 328, at the age of thirty. The people of Egypt
viewed him as their bishop until he died on May 2, 373, at the age of
seventy-five.[1] I say he was "viewed" by the people as their bishop during these years because Athanasius was driven out of his church and
office five times by the powers of the Roman Empire. Seventeen of his
forty-five years as bishop were spent in exile. But the people never acknowledged the validity of the other bishops sent to take his place. He
was always bishop in exile as far as his flock was concerned.

Gregory of Nazianzus (330–389) gave a memorial sermon in Constantinople seven years after the death of Athanasius and described the
affections of the Egyptian people for their bishop. Gregory tells us that
when Athanasius returned from his third exile in 364, having been gone
for six years, he arrived "amid such delight of the people of the city and
of almost all Egypt, that they ran together from every side, from the
furthest limits of the country, simply to hear the voice of Athanasius,
or feast their eyes upon the sight of him."[2]

---

[1] Timothy D. Barnes, *Athanasius and Constantius: Theology and Politics in the Constantinian Empire*
(Cambridge, MA: Harvard University Press, 1993), 19.
[2] Gregory of Nazianzus, *Oration 21: On Athanasius of Alexandria*, in *Select Orations, Sermons, Letters;
Dogmatic Treatises*, in *Nicene and Post-Nicene Fathers* (NPNF), ed. Philip Shaff and Henry Wace, 2nd
series (Grand Rapids, MI: Eerdmans, 1955), 7:277 ¶27.

From their standpoint, none of the foreign appointments to the office of bishop in Alexandria for forty-five years was valid but one, Athanasius. This devotion was owing to the kind of man Athanasius was. Gregory remembered him like this:

> Let one praise him in his fastings and prayers . . . another his unwearied-ness and zeal for vigils and psalmody, another his patronage of the needy, another his dauntlessness towards the powerful, or his condescension to the lowly. . . . [He was to] the unfortunate their consolation, the hoary-headed their staff, youths their instructor, the poor their resource, the wealthy their steward. Even the widows will . . . praise their protector, even the orphans their father, even the poor their benefactor, strangers their entertainer, brethren the man of brotherly love, the sick their physician.[3]

One of the things that makes that kind of praise from a contemporary the more credible is that, unlike many ancient saints, Athanasius is not recorded as having done any miracles. Archibald Robertson, who edited Athanasius's works for *Nicene and Post-Nicene Fathers*, said, "He is . . . surrounded by an atmosphere of truth. Not a single miracle of any kind is related of him. . . . The saintly reputation of Athanasius rested on his life and character alone, without the aid of any reputation for miraculous power."[4] Then he goes on with his own praise of Athanasius:

> In the whole of our minute knowledge of his life there is a total lack of self-interest. The glory of God and the welfare of the Church absorbed him fully at all times. . . . The Emperors recognized him as a political force of the first order . . . but on no occasion does he yield to the temptation of using the arm of flesh. Almost unconscious of his own power . . . his humility is the more real for never being conspicuously paraded. . . . Courage, self-sacrifice, steadiness of purpose, versatility and resourcefulness, width of ready sympathy, were all harmonized by deep reverence and the discipline of a single-minded lover of Christ.[5]

Athanasius: Father of Orthodoxy *Contra Mundum*

This single-minded love for Jesus Christ expressed itself in a lifelong battle to explain and defend Christ's deity and to worship Christ

---

[3] Ibid., 272 ¶10.
[4] *NPNF*, 4:lxvii.
[5] Ibid.

as Lord and God. This is what Athanasius is best known for. There were times when it seemed the whole world had abandoned orthodoxy. That is why the phrase *Athanasius contra mundum* (against the world) arose. He stood steadfast against overwhelming defection from orthodoxy, and only at the end of his life could he see the dawn of triumph.

But in a sense it is anachronistic to use the word *orthodoxy* this way—to say that the world *abandoned* orthodoxy. Was it already there to abandon? Of course, biblical truth is always there to abandon. But *orthodoxy* generally refers to a historic or official or universally held view of what is true to Scripture. Was *that* there to abandon? The answer is suggested in the other great name given to Athanasius, namely, "Father of Orthodoxy."[6] That phrase seems to say that orthodoxy came to be because of Athanasius. And in one sense that is true in regard to the doctrine of the Trinity. The relationships between the Father and the Son and the Holy Spirit had not received formal statement in any representative council before the time of Athanasius.

R. P. C. Hanson wrote, "There was not as yet any orthodox doctrine [of the Trinity], for if there had been, the controversy could hardly have lasted sixty years before resolution."[7] The sixty years he has in mind is the time between the Council of Nicaea in 325 and the Council of Constantinople[8] in 381. The Council of Nicaea established the battle lines and staked out the deity of Christ, and the Council of Constantinople confirmed and refined the Nicene Creed. In the intervening sixty years there was doctrinal war over whether the Nicene formulation would stand and become "orthodoxy."

This was the war Athanasius fought for forty-five years. It lasted all his life, but the orthodox outcome was just over the horizon when he died in 373. And under God this outcome was owing to the courage and constancy and work and writing of Athanasius. No one comes close to his influence in the cause of biblical truth during his lifetime.[9]

---

[6] Ibid., lviii.

[7] R. P. C. Hanson, *The Search for the Christian Doctrine of God: The Arian Controversy* (Edinburgh: T&T Clark, 1988), xviii–xix.

[8] See the chapter on "The Council of Constantinople" in Robert Letham, *The Holy Trinity: In Scripture, History, Theology, and Worship* (Phillipsburg, NJ: P&R, 2004), 167–83.

[9] "The Nicene formula found in Athanasius a mind predisposed to enter into its spirit, to employ in its defense the richest resources of theological and biblical training, of spiritual depth and vigor, of self-sacrificing but sober and tactful enthusiasm; *its victory in the East is due under God to him alone.*" *NPNF*, 4:lxix.

Arius Fires the Shot Heard 'round the Roman World

The war was sparked in AD 319. A deacon in Alexandria named Arius, who had been born in 256 in Libya, presented a letter to Bishop Alexander arguing that if the Son of God were truly a Son, he must have had a beginning. There must have been a time, therefore, when he did not exist. Most of what we know of Arius is from others. All we have from Arius's own pen are three letters, a fragment of a fourth, and a scrap of a song, the *Thalia*.[10] In fact, he proved to be a very minor character in the controversy he unleashed. He died in 336.[11]

Athanasius was a little over twenty when the controversy broke out—over forty years younger than Arius (a lesson in how the younger generation may be more biblically faithful than the older[12]). Athanasius was in the service of Alexander, the bishop of Alexandria. Almost nothing is known of his youth. Gregory of Nazianzus celebrates the fact that Athanasius was brought up mainly in biblical rather than philosophical training.

> He was brought up, from the first, in religious habits and practices, after a brief study of literature and philosophy, so that he might not be utterly unskilled in such subjects, or ignorant of matters which he had determined to despise. For his generous and eager soul could not brook being occupied in vanities, like unskilled athletes, who beat the air instead of their antagonists and lose the prize. From meditating on every book of the Old and New

---

[10] Letham, *The Holy Trinity*, 109.

[11] Archibald Robertson recounts the death of Arius like this:

> From Jerusalem Arius had gone to Alexandria, but had not succeeded in obtaining admission to the Communion of the Church there. Accordingly he repaired to the capital about the time of the Council [of Tyre]. The Eusebians resolved that here at any rate he should not be repelled. Arius appeared before the Emperor and satisfied him by a sworn profession of orthodoxy, and a day was fixed for his reception to communion. The story of the distress caused to the aged bishop Alexander [Bishop of Constantinople] is well known. He was heard to pray in the church that either Arius or himself might be taken away before such an outrage to the faith should be permitted. As a matter of fact Arius died suddenly [AD 336] the day before his intended reception. His friends ascribed his death to magic, those of Alexander to the judgment of God, the public generally to the effect of excitement on a diseased heart. Athanasius, while taking the second view, describes the occurrence with becoming sobriety and reserve. (*NPNF* 4:xli)

[12] The Bible encourages us to hold older people in honor. "You shall stand up before the gray head and honor the face of an old man, and you shall fear your God: I am the LORD" (Lev. 19:32). In general, wisdom is found with age and experience (1 Kings 12:8), but not always. Timothy is exhorted in 1 Timothy 4:12, "Let no one despise you for your youth." There are situations when he would have to correct the elderly (1 Tim. 5:1). And in the book of Job the young Elihu proved to be wiser than Job's three older friends.

> Now Elihu had waited to speak to Job because they were older than he. And when Elihu saw that there was no answer in the mouth of these three men, he burned with anger. And Elihu the son of Barachel the Buzite answered and said: "I am young in years, and you are aged; therefore I was timid and afraid to declare my opinion to you. I said, 'Let days speak, and many years teach wisdom.' But it is the spirit in man, the breath of the Almighty, that makes him understand. It is not the old who are wise, nor the aged who understand what is right." (Job 32:4–9)

Testament, with a depth such as none else has applied even to one of them, he grew rich in contemplation, rich in splendor of life.[13]

This was the service he was to render for forty-five years: biblical blow after blow against the fortresses of the Arian heresy. Robert Letham confirms the outcome of Gregory's observation: "Athanasius' contribution to the theology of the Trinity can scarcely be overestimated. . . . He turned discussion away from philosophical speculation and back to a biblical and theological basis."[14]

In 321, a synod was convened in Alexandria, and Arius was deposed from his office and his views declared heresy. Athanasius at age twenty-three wrote the deposition for Alexander. This was to be his role now for the next fifty-two years—writing to declare the glories of the incarnate Son of God. The deposition of Arius unleashed sixty years of ecclesiastical and empire-wide political conflict.

Eusebius of Nicomedia (modern-day Izmit in Turkey) took up Arius's theology and became "the head and center of the Arian cause."[15] For the next forty years, the eastern part of the Roman Empire (measured from the modern Istanbul eastward) was mainly Arian. That is true in spite of the fact that the great Council of Nicaea decided in favor of the full deity of Christ. Hundreds of bishops signed it and then twisted the language to say that Arianism really fit into the wording of Nicaea.

The Council of Nicaea (325)

Emperor Constantine had seen the sign of the cross during a decisive battle thirteen years before the Council of Nicaea and was converted to Christianity. He was concerned with the deeply divisive effect of the Arian controversy in the empire. Bishops had tremendous influence, and when they were at odds (as they were over this issue), it made the unity and harmony of the empire more fragile. Constantine's Christian advisor, Hosius, had tried to mediate the Arian conflict in Alexandria, but failed. So in 325, Constantine called the Council at Nicaea across the Bosporus from Constantinople (today's Istanbul). He pulled together, according to tradition,[16] 318 bishops plus other attenders like Arius and

---

[13] Gregory of Nazianzus, *Oration 21*, 270–71 ¶6.
[14] Letham, *The Holy Trinity*, 145.
[15] *NPNF*, 4:xvi.
[16] Archibald Robertson estimates the bishops at something over 250, and attributes the number 318 to the symbolic significance it had. "According to Athanasius, who again, toward the end of his life (*ad Afr.* 2)

Athanasius, neither of whom was a bishop. He fixed the order of the Council and enforced its decisions with civil penalties.

The Council lasted from May through August and ended with a statement of orthodoxy that has defined Christianity to this day. The wording today that we call the Nicene Creed is really the slightly altered language of the Council of Constantinople in 381. But the decisive work was done in 325. The anathema at the end of the Creed of Nicaea shows most clearly what the issue was. The original Creed of Nicaea was written in Greek, but here it is in English:

> We believe in one God, the Father Almighty, Maker of all things visible, and invisible.
>
> And in one Lord Jesus Christ, the Son of God, begotten of the Father the only-begotten, that is, of the essence of the Father [ἐκ τῆς οὐσίας τοῦ πατρὸς], God of God [Θεὸν ἐκ Θεοῦ], and Light of Light [καὶ Φῶς ἐκ Φωτὸς], very God of very God [Θεὸν ἀληθινὸν ἐκ Θεου ἀληθινοῦ], begotten, not made [γεννηθέντα, οὐ ποιηθέντα], being of one substance with the Father [ὁμοούσιον τῷ πατρὶ]; by whom all things were made in heaven and on earth; who for us men, and for our salvation, came down and was incarnate and was made man; he suffered, and the third day he rose again, ascended into heaven; from thence he cometh to judge the quick and the dead.
>
> And in the Holy Ghost.
>
> And those who say: there was a time when he was not; and: he was not before he was made; and: he was made out of nothing, or out of another substance or thing [ἢ ἐξ ἑτέρας ὑποστάσεως ἢ οὐσίας], or the Son of God is created, or changeable, or alterable; they are condemned by the holy catholic and apostolic Church.

The key phrase, ὁμοούσιον τῷ πατρί (one being with the Father), was added later due to the insistence of the emperor. It made the issue crystal clear. The Son of God could not have been created, because he did not have merely a *similar* being to the Father (ὁμοιούσιον τῷ πατρὶ) but was of the very being of the Father (ὁμοούσιον τῷ πατρὶ). He was not brought into existence with similar being but was eternally one with divine being.

---

acquiesces in the precise figure 318 (Gen xiv. 14; the Greek numeral τιη combines the Cross [τ] with the initial letters of the Sacred Name [ιη]) which a later generation adopted (it first occurs in the alleged Coptic acts of the Council of Alexandria, 362, then in the Letter of Liberius to the bishops of Asia in 365), on grounds perhaps symbolical rather than historical." *NPNF*, 4:xvii n. 1.κ

Astonishingly all but two bishops signed the creed, some, as Robertson says, "with total duplicity."[17] Bishops Secundus and Theonas, along with Arius (who was not a bishop), were sent into exile. Eusebius of Nicomedia squeaked by with what he called a "mental reservation" and within four years would persuade the emperor that Arius held substantially to the Creed of Nicaea—which was pure politics.[18]

When Athanasius's mentor, Alexander, Bishop of Alexandria, died on April 17, 328, three years after the Council of Nicaea, the mantel of Egypt and of the cause of orthodoxy fell to Athanasius. He was ordained as bishop on June 8 that year. This bishopric was the second in Christendom after Rome. It had jurisdiction over all the bishops of Egypt and Libya. Under Athanasius, Arianism died out entirely in Egypt. And from Egypt, Athanasius wielded his empire-wide influence in the battle for the deity of Christ.

Athanasius, the Desert Monks, and Antony

We've passed over one crucial and decisive event in his role as Alexander's assistant. He made a visit with Alexander to the Thebaid, the desert district in southern Egypt where he came in contact with the early desert monks—the ascetics who lived lives of celibacy, solitude, discipline, prayer, simplicity, and service to the poor. Athanasius was deeply affected by this visit and was "set on fire by the holiness of their lives."[19]

For the rest of his life there was an unusual bond between the city bishop and the desert monks. They held him in awe, and he admired them and blessed them. Robinson says, "He treats . . . the monks as equals or superiors, begging them to correct and alter anything amiss in his writings."[20] The relationship became a matter of life and death because when Athanasius was driven out of his office by the forces of the empire, there was one group he knew he could trust with his protection. "The solitaries of the desert, to a man, would be faithful to Athanasius during the years of trial."[21]

One in particular captured Athanasius's attention, affection, and admiration: Antony. He was born in 251. At twenty he sold all his

---

[17] *NPNF*, 4:xx.
[18] Ibid., xx. "In 329 we find Eusebius once more in high favor with Constantine, discharging his episcopal functions, persuading Constantine that he and Arius held substantially the Creed of Nicaea."
[19] F. A. Forbes, *Saint Athanasius* (1919; repr., Rockford, IL: Tan, 1989), 8.
[20] *NPNF*, 4:lxvii.
[21] Forbes, *Saint Athanasius*, 36.

possessions and moved to the desert but served the poor nearby. At thirty-five he withdrew for twenty years into total solitude, and no one knew if he was alive or dead. Then at fifty-five he returned and ministered to the monks and the people who came to him for prayer and counsel in the desert until he died at 105. Athanasius wrote the biography of Antony. This was Athanasius's ideal: the combination of solitude and compassion for the poor based on rock-solid orthodoxy.

Antony made one rare appearance in Alexandria that we hear about, namely, to dispel the rumor that the desert monks were on the Arian side. He denounced Arianism "as the worst of heresies, and was solemnly escorted out of town by the bishop [Athanasius] in person."[22] Orthodoxy, rigorous asceticism for the sake of purity, and compassion for the poor—these were the virtues Athanasius loved in Antony and the monks. And he believed their lives were just as strong an argument for orthodox Christology as his books were.

> Now these arguments of ours do not amount merely to words, but have in actual experience a witness to their truth. For let him that will, go up and behold the proof of virtue in the virgins of Christ and in the young men that practice holy chastity, and the assurance of immortality in so great a band of His martyrs.[23]

Athanasius's biography of Antony is significant for another reason. It was translated from Greek to Latin and found its way into the hands of Ponticianus, a friend of St. Augustine, sometime after 380. Ponticianus told St. Augustine the story of Antony. As he spoke, Augustine says, he was "violently overcome by a fearful sense of shame." This led to Augustine's final struggles in the garden in Milan and his eventual conversion. "Athanasius' purpose in writing Antony's *Life* had gained its greatest success: Augustine would become the most influential theologian in the church for the next 1,000 years."[24]

Athanasius Embroiled in Controversy

Within two years after taking office as Bishop of Alexandria, Athanasius became the flash point of controversy. Most of the bishops who had

---

[22] *NPNF*, 4:xlii (July 27, 338).
[23] Ibid., 62.
[24] David Wright, "The Life Changing 'Life of Antony,'" in *Christian History* 28 (1999): 17.

signed the Creed of Nicaea did not like calling people heretics, even if they disagreed with this basic affirmation of Christ's deity. They wanted to get rid of Athanasius and his passion for this cause. Athanasius was accused of levying illegal taxes. There were accusations that he was too young when ordained, that he used magic, that he subsidized treasonable persons, and more. Constantine did not like Athanasius's hard line either and called him to Rome in 331 to face the charges the bishops were bringing. The facts acquitted him, but his defense of the Nicene formulation of Christ's deity was increasingly in the minority.

The First Exile of Athanasius (336–337)

Finally his enemies resorted to intrigue. They bribed Arsenius, a bishop in Hypsele (on the Nile in southern Egypt), to disappear so that the rumor could be started that Athanasius had arranged his murder and cut off one of his hands to use for magic. Constantine was told and asked for a trial to be held in Tyre. Meanwhile one of Athanasius's trusted deacons had found Arsenius hiding in a monastery and had taken him captive and brought him secretly to Tyre.

At the trial the accusers produced a human hand to confirm the indictment. But Athanasius was ready. "Did you know Arsenius personally?" he asked. "Yes" was the eager reply from many sides. So Arsenius was ushered in alive, wrapped up in a cloak. When he was revealed to them, they were surprised but demanded an explanation of how he had lost his hand. Athanasius turned up his cloak and showed that one hand at least was there. There was a moment of suspense, artfully managed by Athanasius. Then the other hand was exposed, and the accusers were requested to point out whence the third had been cut off.[25]

As clear as this seemed, Athanasius was condemned at this council and fled in a boat with four bishops and came to Constantinople. The accusers threw aside the Arsenius indictment and created another with false witnesses: Athanasius had tried to starve Constantine's capitol by preventing wheat shipments from Alexandria. That was too much for Constantine, and even without condemning evidence, he ordered Athanasius banished to Treveri (Trier, near today's Luxembourg). Athanasius left for exile on February 8, 336.

Constantine died the next year, and the empire was divided among

---

[25] *NPNF*, 4:xl.

his three sons, Constantius (taking the East), Constans (taking Italy and Illyricum), and Constantine II (taking the Gauls and Africa). One of Constantine II's first acts was to restore Athanasius to his office in Alexandria on November 23, 337.

The Second Exile of Athanasius (339–346)

Two years later Eusebius, the leader of the Arians, had persuaded Constantius to get rid of Athanasius. He took the ecclesiastical power into his hands, declared Gregory the bishop of Alexandria, put his own secular governor in charge of the city, and used force to take the bishop's quarters and the churches. Athanasius was forced to leave the city to spare more bloodshed.

This was the beginning of his second exile—the longest time away from his flock. He left on April 16, 339, and didn't return until October 21, 346, over seven years in exile. Constantine's other two sons supported Athanasius and called the Council of Sardica (now Sophia in Bulgaria), which vindicated him in August 343. But it took three years until the political factors fell into place for his return. Constans threatened Constantius with war if he did not reinstate Athanasius. In the meantime the Arians had fallen out of favor with Constantius and the substitute bishop Gregory had died. So Athanasius was restored to his people with rejoicing after seven years away.

During the following season of peace, Alexandria and the surrounding districts seemed to have experienced something of a revival, with a strong ascetic flavor. Athanasius wrote:

> How many unmarried women, who were before ready to enter upon marriage, now remained virgins to Christ![26] How many young men, seeing the examples of others, embraced the monastic life! . . . How many wid-

---

[26] It is partly paradoxical that Athanasius, the great defender of the incarnation and of the honor God paid to the physical world by taking it on himself, would also be such a strong defender of celibacy as a great virtue. In fact, he sees the incarnation not so much an endorsement of the good of marriage as an empowerment to abstain from the imperfect sexual impulses that inevitably accompany marriage. "Let him that will, go up and behold the proof of virtue in the virgins of Christ and in the young men that practice holy chastity, and the assurance of immortality in so great a band of His martyrs" (*NPNF*, 4:62). "Is this, then, a slight proof of the weakness of death? Or is it a slight demonstration of the victory won over him by the Savior, when the youths and young maidens that are in Christ despise this life and *practice to die?*" (*NPNF*, 4:51). The ascetic influence of Origen is seen here (*NPNF*, 4:xv). Thus Athanasius, with most Christians of his day, saw the body not only as a gift for experiencing God's creation, but as a fallen hindrance to rising to intellectual and spiritual enjoyment of God. For a different assessment of the function of creation in the spiritual life, see John Piper, "How to Wield the World in the Fight for Joy: Using All Five Senses to See the Glory of God," in *When I Don't Desire God* (Wheaton, IL: Crossway, 2004), 115–35.

ows and how many orphans, who were before hungry and naked, now through the great zeal of the people, were no longer hungry, and went forth clothed! In a word, so great was their emulation in virtue, that you would have thought every family and every house a Church, by reason of the goodness of its inmates, and the prayers which were offered to God. And in the Churches there was a profound and wonderful peace, while the Bishops wrote from all quarters, and received from Athanasius the customary letters of peace.[27]

The Third Exile of Athanasius (356–362)

On January 18, 350, Constans was murdered. This freed Constantius to solidify his power and to attack Athanasius and the Nicene theology unopposed. The people of Alexandria held off one armed assault on the city by the emperor's secretary Diogenes in 355, but the next year Constantius sent Syrianus, his military commander, to exert the emperor's control in Alexandria.

> On Thursday night, Feb. 8 [356], Athanasius was presiding at a crowded service of preparation for a Communion on the following morning . . . in the Church of Theonas . . . the largest in the city. Suddenly the church was surrounded and the doors broken in, and just after midnight Syrianus . . . "entered with an infinite force of soldiers." Athanasius . . . calmly took his seat upon the throne (in the recess of the apse), and ordered the deacon to begin the 136th psalm, the people responding at each verse "for His mercy endureth for ever." Meanwhile the soldiers crowded up to the chancel, and in spite of entreaties the bishop refused to escape until the congregation were in safety. He ordered the prayers to proceed, and only at the last moment a crowd of monks and clergy seized the Archbishop and managed to convey him in the confusion out of the church in a half-fainting state . . . but thankful that he had been able to secure the escape of his people before his own. . . . From that moment Athanasius was lost to public view for "six years and fourteen days."[28]

He had spared his people briefly. But in June the supporters of Athanasius were attacked with a viciousness unlike anything before.

> In the early hours of Thursday, June 13 [356], after a service (which had begun overnight . . .), just as all the congregation except a few women had

---

[27] *NPNF*, 4:278.
[28] Ibid., l.

left, the church of Theonas was stormed and violences perpetrated which left far behind anything that Syrianus had done. Women were murdered, the church wrecked and polluted with the very worst orgies of heathenism, houses and even tombs were ransacked throughout the city and suburbs on pretence of "seeking for Athanasius."[29]

The secular authorities forced a new bishop on the people. It proved to be a disaster. Bishop George instigated violent persecution of any who sided with Athanasius and did not support the Arian cause. Many were killed and others banished. At last, in December 361, the people's patience was exhausted, and George was lynched.

Such was the mingling of secular and ecclesiastical forces in those days. But at the darkest hour for Athanasius and for the cause of orthodoxy, the dawn was about to break. This third exile proved to be the most fruitful. Protected by an absolutely faithful army of desert monks, no one could find him, and he produced his most significant written works: *The Arian History*, the four *Tracts against Arians*, the four dogmatic letters *To Serapion*, and *On the Councils of Ariminum and Seleucia*.

This last work was a response to the two councils called by Constantius in 359 to settle the conflict between the Arians and the supporters of Nicaea. Four hundred bishops assembled in Ariminum in Italy, and 160 assembled in Seleucia in Asia Minor. The aim was a unifying creed for Christianity. The upshot of these councils was a compromise, sometimes called semi-Arian, that said the Son is "like the Father" but did not say how. It basically avoided the issue. For Athanasius this was totally unacceptable. The nature of Christ was too important to obscure with vague language.

The Triumph of God's Fugitive

It is one of the typical ironies of God's providence that the triumph over Arianism would happen largely through the ministry of a fugitive living and writing within inches of his death. Here is the way Archibald Robertson described the triumph of the third exile:

> The third exile of Athanasius marks the summit of his achievement. Its commencement is the triumph, its conclusion the collapse of Arianism.

---

[29] Ibid., lii.

It is true that after the death of Constantius [November 3, 361] the battle went on with variations of fortune for twenty years, mostly under the reign of an ardently Arian Emperor [Valens] (364–378). But by 362 the utter lack of inner coherence in the Arian ranks was manifest to all; the issue of the fight might be postponed by circumstances but could not be in doubt. The break-up of the Arian power was due to its own lack of reality: as soon as it had a free hand, it began to go to pieces. But the watchful eye of Athanasius followed each step in the process from his hiding-place, and the event was greatly due to his powerful personality and ready pen, knowing whom to overwhelm and whom to conciliate, where to strike and where to spare. This period then of forced abstention from affairs was the most stirring in spiritual and literary activity in the whole life of Athanasius. It produced more than half of . . . his entire extant works. . . . Let it be noted once for all how completely the amazing power wielded by the wandering fugitive was based upon the devoted fidelity of Egypt to its pastor. Towns and villages, deserts and monasteries, the very tombs were scoured by the Imperial inquisitors in the search for Athanasius; but all in vain; not once do we hear of any suspicion of betrayal. The work of the golden decade [the period of revival before the third exile] was bearing its fruit.[30]

Athanasius returned to Alexandria on February 21, 362, by another irony. The new and openly pagan emperor, Julian, reversed all the banishments of Constantius. The favor lasted only eight months. But during these months Athanasius called a synod at Alexandria and gave a more formal consolidation and reconciliation to the gains he had accomplished in the last six years of his writing. It had a tremendous impact on the growing consensus of the church in favor of Nicene orthodoxy. Jerome says that this synod "snatched the whole world from the jaws of Satan."[31] And Robertson calls it "the crown of the career of Athanasius."[32] The rallying point that it gave for orthodoxy in 362 enabled the reuniting forces of Eastern Christendom to withstand the political Arianism under Emperor Valens, who reigned from 364 to 378.

The Fourth Exile of Athanasius (362–364)

But in October 362 Athanasius was again driven from his office by Julian's wrath when he realized that Athanasius took his Christianity

---

[30] Ibid., li.
[31] Ibid., lviii.
[32] Ibid.

seriously enough to reject the pagan gods. Again he spent the next fifteen months among the desert monks. The story goes that he was freed to return by a prophecy by one of the monks that Julian had that very day fallen in battle in Persia. It proved true, and Athanasius was restored to his ministry on February 14, 364.

The Fifth Exile of Athanasius (365–366)

A year and a half later, Emperor Valens ordered that all the bishops earlier expelled under Julian should be removed once again by the civil authorities. On October 5, 365, the Roman prefect broke into the church in Alexandria and searched the apartments of the clergy, but the sixty-seven-year-old Athanasius had been warned and escaped one last time—his fifth exile. It was short because a dangerous revolt led by Procopius had to be put down by Valens, so he judged it was not time to allow popular discontent to smolder in Athanasius-loving Alexandria. Athanasius was brought back on February 1, 366.

He spent the last years of his life fulfilling his calling as a pastor and overseer of pastors. He carried on extensive correspondence and gave great encouragement and support to the cause of orthodoxy around the empire. He died on May 2, 373.

Lessons from Athanasius's Calling to Controversy

What then may we learn about the sacred calling of controversy from the life of Athanasius?

1. Defending and explaining doctrine is for the sake of the gospel and our everlasting joy.

When Athanasius was driven into his third exile, he wrote an open letter, "To the Bishops of Egypt." In it he referred to the martyrs who had died defending the deity of Christ. Then he said, "Wherefore . . . considering that *this struggle is for our all* . . . let us also make it our earnest care and aim to guard what we have received."[33] "The Arian controversy was to him no battle for ecclesiastical power, nor for theological triumph. It was a religious crisis involving the reality of revelation and redemption."[34] He said in essence, "We are contending for our all."

What was at stake was everything. Oh, how thankful we should be

---

[33] Ibid., 234.
[34] Ibid., lxvii.

that Athanasius saw things so clearly. The incarnation has to do with the gospel. It has to do with salvation. It has to do with whether there is any hope or eternal life. The creed that Athanasius helped craft, and that he embraced and spent his life defending and explaining, says this plainly:

> We believe . . . in one Lord Jesus Christ, the Son of God, begotten of the Father . . . very God of very God . . . being of one substance with the Father . . . *who for us men, and for our salvation, came down and was incarnate* and was made man; he suffered, and the third day he rose again.

In other words, the deity of the incarnate Son of God is essential for the truth and validity of the gospel of our salvation. There is no salvation if Jesus Christ is not God. It's true that Athanasius deals with salvation mainly in terms of restoring the image of God in man by Christ's taking human nature into union with the divine nature.[35] But Athanasius does not emphasize this to the exclusion of the death of Christ and the atonement. You hear both of these in this passage from *On the Incarnation of the Word*:

> For the Word, perceiving that no otherwise could the corruption of men be undone save by death as a necessary condition, while it was impossible for the Word to suffer death, being immortal, and Son of the Father; to this end He takes to Himself a body capable of death, that it, by partaking of the Word Who is above all, might be worthy to die in the stead of all, and might, because of the Word which was come to dwell in it, remain incorruptible, and that thenceforth corruption might be stayed from all by the Grace of the Resurrection. Whence, by offering unto death the body He Himself had taken, as an offering and sacrifice free from any stain, straightway He put away death from all His peers by the offering of an equivalent. For being over all, the Word of God naturally by offering His own temple and corporeal instrument for the life of all satisfied the debt by His death. And thus He, the incorruptible Son of God, being conjoined with all by a like nature, naturally clothed all with incorruption, by the promise of the resurrection.[36]

---

[35] I think Robert Letham's judgment is too sweeping when he says, "For Athanasius the decisive fulcrum is the Incarnation. As a result, the Cross has diminished significance. [R. P. C.] Hanson likens his theory of salvation to a sacred blood transfusion that almost does away with a doctrine of the Atonement. Athanasius lacks reasons why Christ should have died. For him, corruption consists in fallenness, rather than in sin." Letham, *The Holy Trinity*, 133. More balanced and fair is the observation of Archibald Robertson: "Athanasius felt . . . the supremacy of the Cross as the purpose of the Savior's coming, but he does not in fact give to it the central place in his system of thought which it occupies in his instincts" (*NPNF*, 4:lxix).
[36] *NPNF* 4:40–41.

Substitutionary Atonement for Our Debt

Yes, Christ was incarnate that "the corruption of men be undone," and that the "corruption might be stayed." But the human condition is not viewed only as a physical problem of corrupt nature. It is also viewed as a moral shortfall that creates a "debt" before God. Thus a substitutionary death is required. No man could pay this debt. Only a God-man could pay it. This is seen even more clearly when Athanasius, in commenting on Luke 10:22, speaks of Christ's taking the curse of God in our place:

> For man, being in Him, was quickened: for this was why the Word was united to man, namely, that against man the curse might no longer prevail. This is the reason why they record the request made on behalf of mankind in the seventy-first Psalm [*sic*]: "Give the King Thy judgment, O God" (Ps. lxxii. I): asking that both the judgment of death which hung over us may be delivered to the Son, and that He may then, by dying for us, abolish it for us in Himself. This was what He signified, saying Himself, in the eighty-seventh Psalm [*sic*]: "Thine indignation lieth hard upon me" (Ps. lxxxviii. 7). For He bore the indignation which lay upon us, as also He says in the hundred and thirty-seventh [*sic*]: "Lord, Thou shalt do vengeance for me" (Ps. cxxxviii. 8, LXX).[37]

Beyond merely mentioning the substitutionary sacrifice of Christ, Athanasius, in at least one place, refers to the wrath-bearing substitutionary sacrifice as the "especial cause" of the incarnation to rescue us from sin.

> Since it was necessary also that the debt owing from all should be paid again: for, as I have already said, it was owing that all should die, for which *especial cause*, indeed, He came among us: to this intent, after the proofs of His Godhead from His works, He next offered up His sacrifice also on behalf of all, yielding His Temple to death in the stead of all, in order firstly to make men quit and free of their old trespass, and further to show Himself more powerful even than death, displaying His own body incorruptible, as first-fruits of the resurrection of all.[38]

Athanasius is willing to make the death of Christ for our debt, owing to our trespasses, the "special cause" of the incarnation. But he returns

---

[37] Ibid., 88. (The psalms are off by one because of a different numbering system being used.)
[38] Ibid., 47, emphasis added.

quickly to his more common way of seeing things, namely, restoration of the image of God.

We may admit that Athanasius did not see the fullness of what Christ achieved on the cross in terms of law and guilt and justification. But what he saw we may be blind to. The implications of the incarnation are vast, and one reads Athanasius with the sense that we are paupers in our perception of what he saw. However lopsided his view of the cross may have been, he saw clearly that the incarnation of the divine Son of God was essential. Without it the gospel is lost. There are doctrines in the Bible that are worth dying for and living for. They are the ground of our life. They are the heart of our worship. The divine and human nature of Christ in one Person is one of those doctrines. He was contending for our all.

2. Joyful courage is the calling of a faithful shepherd.

Athanasius stared down murderous intruders into his church. He stood before emperors who could have killed him as easily as exiling him. He risked the wrath of parents and other clergy by consciously training young people to give their all for Christ, including martyrdom. He celebrated the fruit of his ministry with these words: "In youth they are self-restrained, in temptations endure, in labors persevere, when insulted are patient, when robbed make light of it: and, wonderful as it is, they despise even death and become martyrs of Christ"[39]—martyrs not who kill as they die, but who love as they die.

Athanasius contra mundum should inspire every pastor to stand his ground meekly and humbly and courageously whenever a biblical truth is at stake. But be sure that you always out-rejoice your adversaries. If something is worth fighting for, it is worth rejoicing over. And the joy is essential in the battle, for nothing is worth fighting for that will not increase our everlasting joy in God.

Courage in conflict must mingle with joy in Christ. This is what Athanasius loved about Antony and what he sought to be himself. This was part of his battle strategy with his adversaries:

> Let us be *courageous* and *rejoice* always. . . . Let us consider and lay to heart that while the Lord is with us, our foes can do us no hurt. . . . But if they see us *rejoicing in the Lord*, contemplating the bliss of the future, mindful of the

---

[39] Ibid., 65.

> Lord, deeming all things in His hand . . . —they are discomfited and turned backwards.[40]

So, Athanasius would have us learn from his life and the life of his heroes this lesson: even if at times it may feel as though we are alone *contra mundum*, let us stand courageous and out-rejoice our adversaries.

3. Loving Christ includes loving true propositions about Christ.

What was clear to Athanasius was that propositions about Christ carried convictions that could send you to heaven or to hell. Propositions like "There was a time when the Son of God was not," and "He was not before he was made," and "The Son of God is created" were damnable. If they were spread abroad and believed, they would damn the souls who embraced them. And therefore Athanasius labored with all his might to formulate propositions that would conform to reality and lead the soul to faith and worship and heaven.

I believe Athanasius would have abominated, with tears, the contemporary call for "depropositionalizing" that we hear among many of the so-called "reformists" and "the emerging church," "younger evangelicals," "postfundamentalists," "postfoundationalists," "postpropositionalists," and "postevangelicals."[41] I think he would have said, "Our young people in Alexandria die for the truth of propositions about Christ. What do your young people die for?" And if the answer came back, "We die for Christ, not propositions about Christ," I think he would have said, "That's what the heretic Arius said. So which Christ will you die for?" To answer that question requires propositions about him. To refuse to answer implies that it doesn't matter what we believe or die for as long as it has the label *Christ* attached to it.

Athanasius would have grieved over sentences like "It is Christ who unites us; it is doctrine that divides." And sentences like: "We should ask, Whom do you trust? rather than what do you believe?"[42] He would have grieved because he knew this is the very tactic used by the Arian bishops to cover the councils with fog so that the word *Christ* could mean anything. Those who talk like this—"Christ unites,

---

[40] Ibid., 207.

[41] See the critical interaction with these movements in Millard J. Erickson, Paul Kjoss Helseth, Justin Taylor, eds., *Reclaiming the Center: Confronting Evangelical Accommodation in Postmodern Times* (Wheaton, IL: Crossway, 2004).

[42] These sentences are from E. Stanley Jones, *The Christ of the Indian Road* (New York: Abingdon, 1925), 155–57. I cite this older book because it is being used with enthusiasm by some today to buttress a vision that beclouds the importance of doctrine.

doctrine divides"—have simply replaced propositions about Christ with the word *Christ*. It carries no meaning until one says something about him. They think they have done something profound and fresh when they call us away from the propositions of doctrine to the word *Christ*. In fact, they have done something very old and worn and deadly.

This leads to a related lesson . . .

4. *The truth of biblical language must be vigorously protected with nonbiblical language.*

Bible language can be used to affirm falsehood. Athanasius's experience has proved to be illuminating and helpful in dealing with this fact. Over the years I have seen this misuse of the Bible especially in liberally minded baptistic and pietistic traditions. They use the slogan, "The Bible is our only creed." But in refusing to let explanatory, confessional language clarify what the Bible means, the slogan can be used as a cloak to conceal the fact that Bible language is being used to affirm what is not biblical. This is what Athanasius encountered so insidiously at the Council of Nicaea. The Arians affirmed biblical sentences while denying biblical meaning. Listen to this description of the proceedings:

> The Alexandrians . . . confronted the Arians with the traditional Scriptural phrases which appeared to leave no doubt as to the eternal Godhead of the Son. But to their surprise they were met with perfect acquiescence. Only as each test was propounded, it was observed that the suspected party whispered and gesticulated to one another, evidently hinting that each could be safely accepted, since it admitted of evasion. If their assent was asked to the formula "like to the Father in all things," it was given with the reservation that man as such is "the image and glory of God." The "power of God" elicited the whispered explanation that the host of Israel was spoken of as δυναμις κυριου, and that even the locust and caterpillar are called the "power of God." The "eternity" of the Son was countered by the text, "We that live are always" (2 Cor. 4:11)! The fathers were baffled, and the test of ομοουσιον, with which the minority had been ready from the first, was being forced upon the majority by the evasions of the Arians.[43]

R. P. C. Hanson explained the process like this: "Theologians of the Christian Church were slowly driven to a realization that the deepest questions which face Christianity cannot be answered in purely biblical

---

[43] *NPNF*, 2nd series, 4:xix.

language, *because the questions are about the meaning of biblical language itself.*"[44] The Arians railed against the unbiblical language being forced on them. They tried to seize the biblical high ground and claim to be the truly biblical people—the pietists, the simple Bible-believers—because they wanted to stay with biblical language only—and by it smuggle in their nonbiblical meanings.

But Athanasius saw through this "postmodern," "post-conservative," "post-propositional" strategy and saved for us not just Bible words, but Bible truth. May God grant us the discernment of Athanasius for our day. Very precious things are at stake.[45]

5. A widespread and long-held doctrinal difference among Christians does not mean that the difference is insignificant or that we should not seek to persuade toward the truth and seek agreement.

What if someone had said to Athanasius, "Athanasius, people have disagreed on this issue of Christ's deity for three hundred years, and there has never been an official position taken in the church to establish one side as orthodox and the other as heresy. So who do you think you are? Half the bishops in the world [an understatement] disagree with you, and they read the same Bible you do. So stop fighting this battle and let different views exist side by side."

We may thank God that Athanasius did not think that way. He did not regard the amount of time that has elapsed or the number of Christians who disagreed to determine which doctrines are important and which we should strive to teach and spread and make normative in the church.

And so today we should not conclude that the absence of consensus in the church means doctrinal stalemate or doctrinal insignificance. God may be pleased to give the blessing of unity on some crucial areas of doctrine that are not yet resolved in the Christian church. I think, for example of the issue of manhood and womanhood, the issue of justification by faith, the issue of how the death of Christ saves sinners,

---

[44] Hanson, *The Search for the Christian Doctrine of God*, xxi.

[45] Another way that Athanasius and the orthodox bishops at Nicaea protected the truth was to include denials as well as affirmations. In their case they were called anathemas. The point here is this: When mistaken teachers are looking for a way to have their views accepted in the mainstream, they are often willing to agree with affirmations and give them a different meaning. Or sometimes the affirmations are broad and general and so do not make clear what is being excluded as false. But if a denial is included, which explicitly names what is being rejected as false, then the mistaken person cannot as easily weasel around the denial. For example, an open theist may affirm the statement "We believe in the full omniscience of God." But he would have a difficult time making the denial, "We deny that God is ignorant of anything that shall come to pass."

and the issue of the sovereignty of God's grace in converting the soul. I don't think we should assume that, because much time has gone by and many people disagree, it must always be this way. Who knows but that, by God's amazing grace, wrong views on these things could become as marginal as the Arianism of the Jehovah's Witnesses is today. I don't mean that all these issues are as essential as the deity of Christ, but only that a much greater consensus may be reached on the true interpretation of Scripture than is often thought. I think that would be a good thing for the church and the world and the glory of Christ.

6. Pastors should not aim to preach only in categories of thought that can be readily understood by this generation. Rather, we should also aim at creating biblical categories of thought that are not present.

Another way to put it is to use the terminology of Andrew Walls: Don't embrace the indigenous principle of Christianity at the expense of the pilgrim principle.[46] The indigenous principle says, "I have become all things to all people, that by all means I might save some" (1 Cor. 9:22). The pilgrim principle says, "Do not be conformed to this world, but be transformed by the renewal of your mind" (Rom. 12:2).

Some of the most crucial and precious truths of the Scripture are counterintuitive to the fallen human mind. They don't fit easily into our sin-soaked heads. The orthodox understanding of the Trinity is one of those. If the indigenous principle had triumphed in the fourth century, we might all be Arians. It is far easier for the human mind to say that the Son of God, like all other sons, once was not, and then came into being, than it is to say that he has always been God with the Father, and there is only one God. But the Bible will not let its message be fitted into the categories we bring with our fallen, finite minds. It presses us relentlessly to create new categories of thought to contain the mysteries of the gospel.

The Danger of Adapting to the "Seekers"

Archibald Robertson points out that with the conversion of Constantine and the Edict of Milan (313), which gave legal status to Christianity, "the inevitable influx of heathen into the Church, now that the empire had become Christian, brought with it multitudes to whom Arianism

---

[46] Andrew Walls, *Missionary Movement in Christian History* (Mary Knoll, NY: Orbis, 2001), 7–9.

was a more intelligible creed than that of Nicaea."[47] And if you want to grow a church, the temptation is to give the people what they already have categories to understand and enjoy. But once that church is grown, it thinks so much like the world that the difference is not decisive. The radical, biblical gospel is blunted, and the glory of Christ is obscured.

Rather, alongside the indigenous principle of accommodation and contextualization, Athanasius would plead with us to have a deep commitment to the pilgrim principle of confrontation and transformation—and brain-boggling, mind-altering, recategorization of the way people think about reality.

And we must not treat these two principles as merely sequential. They start and continue together. We must not assume that the first and basic truths of Christianity fit into the fallen mind of unbelievers, and that later we transform their minds with more advanced truths. That's not the case. From the very beginning, we are speaking to them God-centered, Christ-exalting truths that shatter fallen, human categories of thought. We must not shy away from this. We must do all we can to advance it and to help people, by the grace of God, to see what is happening to them (the shattering of their categories) as the best news in all the world.

From the very beginning, in the most winsome way possible, we must labor to create categories like these (to mention a few):

- God rules the world of bliss and suffering and sin, right down to the roll of the dice and the fall of a bird and the driving of the nail into the hand of his Son; yet, though God wills that such sin and suffering exist, he does not sin, but is perfectly holy.
- God governs all the steps of all people, both good and bad, at all times and in all places, yet such that all are accountable before him and will bear the just consequences of his wrath if they do not believe in Christ.
- All are dead in their trespasses and sin and are not morally able to come to Christ because of their rebellion, yet they are responsible to come and will be justly punished if they don't.
- Jesus Christ is one person with two natures, divine and human, such that he upheld the world by the word of his power while living in his mother's womb.

---

[47] NPNF, 4:xxxv.

- Sin, though committed by a finite person and in the confines of finite time, is nevertheless deserving of an infinitely long punishment because it is a sin against an infinitely worthy God.
- The death of the one God-man, Jesus Christ, so displayed and glorified the righteousness of God that God is not unrighteous to declare righteous ungodly people who simply believe in Christ.

These kinds of mind-boggling, category-shattering truths demand our best thought and our most creative labors. We must aim to speak them in a way that, by the power of God's Word and Spirit, a place for them would be created in the minds of those who hear. We must not preach only in the categories that are already present in our listeners' fallen minds, or we will betray the gospel and conceal the glory of God. Athanasius's lifelong struggle is a sobering witness to this truth.

7. Finally, we must not assume that old books, which say some startling things, are necessarily wrong, but that they may in fact have something glorious to teach us that we never dreamed.[48]

For example, Athanasius says some startling things about human deification that we would probably never say. Is that because one of us is wrong? Or is it because the language and the categories of thought that he uses are so different from ours that we have to get inside his head before we make judgments about the truth of what he says? And might we discover something great by this effort to see what he saw?

For example, he says, "[The Son] was made man that we might be made God ($\theta\epsilon o\pi o\iota\eta\theta\hat\omega\mu\epsilon v$)."[49] Or: "He was not man, and then became God, but He was God, and then became man, and that to deify us."[50] The issue here is whether the word "made God" or "deify" ($\theta\epsilon o\pi o\iota\epsilon\omega$) means something unbiblical or whether it means what 2 Peter 1:4 means when it says, "that you may become partakers of the divine nature" ($\H i\nu\alpha\ldots\gamma\epsilon\nu\eta\sigma\theta\epsilon\ \theta\epsilon i\alpha\varsigma\ \kappa o\iota\nu\omega\nu o\H i\ \phi\H v\sigma\epsilon\omega\varsigma$). Athanasius explains it like this:

> John then thus writes; 'Hereby know we that we dwell in Him and He in us, because He hath given us of His Spirit. . . . And the Son is in the Father, as His own Word and Radiance; but we, apart from the Spirit, are strange and distant from God, and by the participation of the Spirit we are knit into

---

[48] See the quotes from C. S. Lewis in the preface.
[49] *NPNF*, 2nd series, 4:65.
[50] Ibid., 329.

the Godhead; so that our being in the Father is not ours, but is the Spirit's which is in us and abides in us. . . . What then is our likeness and equality to the Son? . . . The Son is in the Father in one way, and we become in Him in another, and that neither we shall ever be as He, nor is the Word as we.[51]

What becomes clear when all is taken into account is that Athanasius is pressing a reality in the Scriptures that we today usually call glorification. But he is using the terminology of 2 Peter 1:4 and Romans 8:29. "He has granted to us his precious and very great promises, so that through them you may become partakers of the divine nature." "Those whom he foreknew he also predestined to be conformed to the image of his Son, in order that he might be the firstborn among many brothers." Athanasius is pressing the destiny and the glory of being a brother of the second Person of the Trinity and "sharing in his nature."[52]

Are We Created Finally to See or to Be?

And thus Athanasius raises for me in a fresh way one of the most crucial questions of all: What is the ultimate end of creation—the ultimate goal of God in creation and redemption? Is it being or seeing? Is it our being like Christ or our seeing the glory of Christ? How does Romans 8:29 ("predestined to be conformed to the image of his Son") relate to John 17:24 ("Father, I desire that they also, whom you have given me, may be with me where I am, to see my glory")? Is the beatific vision of the glory of the Son of God the aim of human creation? Or is likeness to that glory the aim of creation?

Athanasius has helped me go deeper here by unsettling me. (This is one of the great values of reading the old books.) I am inclined to stress *seeing* as the goal rather than *being*. The reason is that it seems to me that putting the stress on *seeing* the glory of Christ makes him the focus, but putting the stress on *being* like Christ makes me the focus. But Athanasius will not let me run away from the biblical texts. His language of deification forces me to think more deeply and worship more profoundly.

---

[51] Ibid., 406–7.

[52] "Glorification (in Western terminology), or deification (according to the East), is brought to fruition at the eschaton and lasts for eternity, and so is the final goal of salvation. . . . According to the Eastern church, the goal of salvation is to be made like God. This the Holy Spirit effects in us. It involves no blurring of the Creator-creature distinction, but rather focuses on the union and communion that we are given by God, in which we are made partakers of the divine nature (2 Pet. 1:3–4)." Letham, *The Holy Trinity*, 474, 498.

Created for Delighting in and Displaying the Glory of God

My present understanding would go like this: the ultimate end of creation is neither being nor seeing, but *delighting* and *displaying*. Delighting in and displaying "the glory of God in the face of Jesus Christ" (2 Cor. 4:6). And the displaying happens both in the *delighting*, since we glorify most what we enjoy most, and in the *deeds* of the resurrection body that flow from this enjoyment on the new earth in the age to come. The display of God's glory will be both internal and external. It will be both spiritual and physical. We will display the glory of God by the Christ-exalting joy of our heart and by the Christ-exalting deeds of our resurrection bodies.

How then should we speak of our future *being* and *seeing* if they are not the ultimate end? How shall we speak of "sharing God's nature" and being "conformed to his Son"? The way I would speak of our future *being* and *seeing* is this: by the Spirit of God who dwells in us, our final destiny is not self-admiration or self-exaltation, but *being* able to see the glory of God without disintegrating, and *being* able to delight in the glory of Christ with the very delight of God the Father for his own Son (John 17:26),[53] and *being* able to do visible Christ-exalting deeds that flow from this delight. So *being* like God is the ground of *seeing* God for who he is, and this seeing is the ground of *delighting in* the glory of God with the very delight of God, which then overflows with *visible displays* of God's glory.

An Ever-Growing Wave of Revelation of God through Man

In this way a wave of revelation of divine glory in the saints is set in motion that goes on and grows for all eternity. As each of us sees Christ and delights in Christ with the delight of the Father, mediated by the Spirit, we will overflow with visible actions of love and creativity on the new earth. In this way we will see the revelation of God's glory in each other's lives in ever-new ways. New dimensions of the riches of the glory of God in Christ will shine forth every day from our new delights and new deeds. And these in turn will become new seeings of Christ that will elicit new delights and new doings. And so the ever-growing wave of the revelation of the riches of the glory of God will roll on forever and ever.

---

[53] John 17:26, "I made known to them your name, and I will continue to make it known, that the love with which you have loved me may be in them, and I in them."

And we will discover that this was possible only because the infinite Son of God took on himself human nature so that we in our human nature might be united to him and display more and more of his glory. We will find in our eternal experience of glorification that God's infinite beauty took on human form so that our human form might increasingly display his infinite beauty.

I am thankful to God that I did not run away from the ancient and strange word "deification" in Athanasius. There is here "a grace the magnitude of which our minds can never fully grasp."[54] Thank you, Athanasius. Thank you, not only for pressing the meaning of 2 Peter 1:4 (partakers of the divine nature), but even more for a lifetime of exile and suffering for the glory of Christ. Thank you for not backing down when you were almost alone. Thank you for seeing the truth so clearly and for standing firm. You were a gift of God to the church and the world. I join Parker Williamson in one final accolade to the glory of Christ:

> Athanasius set his name to the creed which expressed his belief, and for fifty years he stood unswervingly by that confession. Every argument that ingenuity could invent was used to prove it false. Bishops met together in great numbers, condemned his views, and invoked upon him the curse of God. Emperors took sides against him, banished him time and time again, and chased him from place to place, setting a reward on his head. At one time all bishops of the church were persuaded or coerced into pronouncing sentence against him, so that the phrase originated, "Athanasius against the world." But with all this pressure bearing on him, he changed his ground not one inch. His clear eye saw the truth once, and he did not permit his conscience to tamper with temptations to deny it. His loyalty to the truth made him a great power for good, and a great blessing to the churches of his own, and of all times.[55]

---

[54] John Calvin, quoted in Letham, *The Holy Trinity*, 472.
[55] Parker T. Williamson, *Standing Firm: Reclaiming Christian Faith in Times of Controversy* (Springfield, PA: PLC, 1996), 38.

[More important than all is] a diligent endeavor to have the power of the truths professed and contended for abiding upon our hearts, that we may not contend for notions, but that we have a practical acquaintance within our own souls. When the heart is cast indeed into the mould of the doctrine that the mind embraceth—when the evidence and necessity of the truth abides in us—when not the sense of the words only is in our heads, but the sense of the thing abides in our hearts—when we have communion with God in the doctrine we contend for—then shall we be garrisoned by the grace of God against all the assaults of men.

John Owen
The Mystery of the Gospel Vindicated

2

Communing with God
in the Things for
Which We Contend

How John Owen Killed His Own Sin
While Contending for Truth

Standing on Owen's Shoulders

Some of us stand on the shoulders of men who have stood on the shoulders of John Owen. J. I. Packer, Roger Nicole, and Sinclair Ferguson, for example, are three contemporary pillars in the house of my thinking, and each has testified publicly that John Owen is the most influential Christian writer in his life. That is amazing for a man who has been dead for over three hundred years, and who wrote in a style so difficult to read that even he saw his work as immensely demanding in his own generation.

One example of a difficult but compelling book is *The Death of Death in the Death of Christ*, probably his most famous and most influential book. It was published in 1647 when Owen was thirty-one years old. It is the fullest and probably the most persuasive book ever written on the doctrine sometimes called "limited atonement," or better called "definite atonement" or "particular redemption."

The point of the book is that when Paul says, "Christ loved *the church* and gave himself up *for her*" (Eph. 5:25), he means that Christ really did something decisive and unique for the church when he died for her—something that is particular and sovereign, and different from what he does for people who experience his final judgment and wrath. The book argues that the particular love that Christ has for his bride is something more wonderful than the general love he has for his enemies. It is a *covenant* love. It pursues and overtakes and subdues and forgives and transforms and overcomes every resistance in the beloved. *The Death of Death* is a great and powerful book—it kept me up for many evenings several decades ago as I was trying to decide what I really believed about the third point of Calvinism (limited atonement).[1]

But back to the point: it is amazing that Owen can have such remarkable impact *today* when he has been dead over three hundred years. And it is all the more amazing when you realize that his style of writing is extremely difficult. Even he knows his work is difficult. In the preface ("To the Reader") of *The Death of Death*, Owen does what no good marketing agent would allow today. He begins like this: "READER, . . . If thou art, as many in this pretending age, *a sign or title gazer*, and comest into books as Cato into the theatre, to go out again—thou hast had thy entertainment; farewell!"[2]

Nevertheless, J. I. Packer and Roger Nicole and Sinclair Ferguson did not bid Owen farewell. They lingered. And they learned. And today all three of them say that no Christian writer has had a greater impact on them than John Owen.

---

[1] The claim of this doctrine is commonly misunderstood. It does not mean that not all who come to Christ can be saved. They can. Nor does it mean that John 3:16 isn't true—that "God so loved the world, that he gave his only Son, that whoever believes in him should not perish but have eternal life." Indeed the giving of the Son and his death have purchased a *bona fide* offer of salvation for all people. *Whoever* believes will not perish but have eternal life. This universal offer of the gospel purchased by the blood of Christ is not denied by the doctrine of particular redemption. Rather, this doctrine asserts that, and more. It goes beyond these truths to make another biblical truth clear, namely, that in the death of Christ, God really paid the debt for all the sins of all the elect (all who would believe on him). Christ really and effectively absorbed all the wrath that was owing to his bride. He did not absorb all the wrath that would one day be poured out on those who do not believe. No sin is punished twice, once in Jesus and once in hell. The punishment of sin in the cross was "definite" or "particular." That is, it was the particular, definite, effective punishment owing to the elect—those who would believe. The blood of Christ purchased the new-covenant promises (Luke 22:20). And these promises are not simply offers of salvation. They are effective causes of salvation: "I will put the fear of me in their hearts, that they may not turn from me" (Jer. 32:40). The power and efficacy of the atonement is greater than most Christians have seriously considered. It does not just offer salvation to all. It does that *and* accomplishes the propitiation of God's elect. To know yourself loved by the Christ of Calvary in a saving way is not merely to know the love of one who *offers* you life and watches to see what you will do with it, but rather, one who purchases you particularly, pursues you particularly, conquers you, wakens your faith, and gives you life with him forever. This is what he bought at Calvary, not just the possibility for you to pursue him. If you want the best statement on this doctrine, go to Owen himself, *The Death of Death in the Death of Christ.*

[2] John Owen, *The Death of Death in the Death of Christ*, in *The Works of John Owen*, ed. William Goold, 16 vols. (Edinburgh: Banner of Truth, 1965), 10:149.

Owen Saved Packer's Life

Packer says that Owen is the hero of his book *A Quest for Godliness*, a book about *The Puritan Vision of the Christian Life*. That is saying a lot, because for Packer the Puritans are the redwoods in the forest of theology.[3] And John Owen is "the greatest among the Puritan theologians." In other words, he is the tallest of the redwoods. "For solidity, profundity, massiveness and majesty in exhibiting from Scripture God's ways with sinful mankind there is no one to touch him."[4]

But Packer has a very personal reason for loving John Owen. I've heard him tell the story of the crisis he came into soon after his conversion. He was in danger in his student days of despairing under a perfectionistic teaching that did not take indwelling sin seriously. The discovery of John Owen brought him back to reality. "Suffice it to say," Packer recalls, "that without Owen I might well have gone off my head or got bogged down in mystical fanaticism."[5]

So Packer virtually says he owes his life, and not just his theology, to John Owen. It's not surprising then that Packer would say with regard to Owen's style that, while laborious and difficult, "the reward to be reaped from studying Owen is worth all the labour involved."[6]

Nicole Puts Owen over Edwards

Roger Nicole, who taught at Gordon-Conwell Seminary for over forty years, said when he was at the Bethlehem Conference for Pastors that John Owen is the greatest theologian who has ever written in the English language. He paused and added, "Even greater than the great Jonathan Edwards!" That really caught my attention, because others have considered Edwards peerless in America,[7] if not the English-speaking world, or even more widely.[8]

---

[3] J. I. Packer, *A Quest for Godliness: The Puritan Vision of the Christian Life* (Wheaton, IL: Crossway, 1990), 11.

[4] Ibid., 81.

[5] Ibid., 12. The story is told more fully in the introduction to John Owen, *Sin and Temptation*, ed. James M. Houston, abridged ed. (Portland: Multnomah, 1983), xxv–xxix.

[6] Packer, *A Quest for Godliness*, 147.

[7] "Jonathan Edwards has proven to be the most influential religious thinker in American history." Douglas Sweeney, "Edwards' Legacy," Jonathan Edwards Center at Yale University, http://edwards.yale.edu/research /about-edwards/legacy. Paul Ramsey called him "the greatest philosopher-theologian yet to grace the American scene." Perry Miller, "General Editor's Note," in *Freedom of the Will*, ed. Paul Ramsey, vol. 1 of *The Works of Jonathan Edwards* (New Haven, CT: Yale University Press, 1957), viii.

[8] Martyn Lloyd-Jones said, "I am tempted, perhaps foolishly, to compare the Puritans to the Alps, Luther and Calvin to the Himalayas, and Jonathan Edwards to Mount Everest! He has always seemed to me the man most like the Apostle Paul." Quoted by Samuel T. Logan in the foreword to Stephen Nichols, *Jonathan*

Owen's Impact on a Teenager

Sinclair Ferguson wrote an entire book on Owen, *John Owen on the Christian Life*, and tells us about his debt that began, if you can believe it, when he was still a teenager:

> My personal interest in [Owen] as a teacher and theologian began in my late teenage years when I first read some of his writing. Like others, before and since, I found that they dealt with issues which contemporary evangelical literature rarely, if ever, touched. Owen's penetrating exposition opened up areas of need in my own heart, but also correspondingly profound assurances of grace in Jesus Christ.... Ever since those first encounters with his *Works*, I have remained in his debt.... To have known the pastoral ministry of John Owen during these years (albeit in written form) has been a rich privilege; to have known Owen's God an even greater one.[9]

The Atlas of Independency

Of course, the magnitude of John Owen's influence goes well beyond these three men. To Ambrose Barnes he was "the Calvin of England." To Anthony Wood he was "the Atlas and Patriarch of Independency."[10] Charles Bridges, in *The Christian Ministry* (1830), said,

> Indeed upon the whole—for luminous exposition, and powerful defense of Scriptural doctrine—for determined enforcement of practical obligation— for skillful anatomy of the self-deceitfulness of the heart—and for a detailed and wise treatment of the diversified exercises of the Christian's heart, he stands probably unrivalled.[11]

If Nicole and Bridges are right—that John Owen is unrivaled in the English-speaking world—then Jonathan Edwards is not too far behind, and Edwards pays his respect to Owen not only by quoting him substantially in *Religious Affections*, but also by recording in his "Catalogue" of readings the recommendation of Hallyburton to his students at St. Andrews University that the writings of John Owen are to be

---

Edwards: A Guided Tour of His Life and Thought (Phillipsburg, NJ: P&R, 2001), 9. Other superlative descriptions of Edwards can be found in Iain Murray, *Jonathan Edwards: A New Biography* (Edinburgh: Banner of Truth, 1987), xv–xvii.

[9] Sinclair B. Ferguson, *John Owen on the Christian Life* (Edinburgh: Banner of Truth, 1987), x–xi.

[10] Both quotes are from Peter Toon, *God's Statesman: The Life and Work of John Owen* (Exeter: Paternoster, 1971), 173.

[11] Charles Bridges, *The Christian Ministry* (orig. 1830; Edinburgh: Banner of Truth, 1967), 41.

valued "above all human writings for a true view of the mystery of the gospel."[12]

One of the reasons I linger over these tributes so long is that I want you to feel drawn not just to Owen, but to the value of having some great heroes in the Christian ministry. There are not many around today. And God wills that we have heroes. Hebrews 13:7 says, "Remember your leaders, those who spoke to you the word of God. *Consider the outcome of their way of life, and imitate their faith.*" It seems to me that the Christian leaders today who come closest to *being* heroes are the ones who *had* great heroes. I hope you have one or two, living or dead. Maybe Owen will become one. He would be a good choice.[13]

How We Know of Owen's Life

Most people—even pastors and theologians—don't know much about John Owen. One of the reasons is that his writings are not popular today.[14] But another reason is that not much is known about him—at least not much about his personal life. Peter Toon, in his 1971 biography, says, "Not one of Owen's diaries has been preserved; and . . . the extant letters in which he lays bare his soul are very few, and recorded, personal reactions of others to him are brief and scarce."[15] "We have to rely on a few letters and a few remarks of others to seek to understand him as a man. And these are insufficient to probe the depths of his character. So Owen must remain hidden as it were behind a veil . . . his secret thoughts remain his own."[16]

I think this may be a little misleading because when you read the more practical works of Owen, the man shines through in a way that I think reveals the deep places of his heart. But still, the details of his personal life are frustratingly few. You will see this—and perhaps share my frustration—in what follows.

---

[12] Jonathan Edwards, *Treatise Concerning the Religious Affections*, in *Religious Affections*, ed. John E. Smith, vol. 2 of The *Works of Jonathan Edwards* (New Haven, CT: Yale University Press, 1959), 69. The quotes of Owen in Edwards are on 250ff., 372ff.

[13] For a complete bibliography of writings by and about Owen, see www.johnowen.org. A helpful overview of Owen's theology can be found in Sinclair Ferguson, *John Owen on the Christian Life* (Edinburgh: Banner of Truth, 1987). Two significant academic works on Owen are: Carl R. Trueman, *John Owen: Reformed Catholic, Renaissance Man* (Aldershot: Ashgate, 2007); and Kelly M. Kapic, *Communion with God: The Divine and the Human in the Theology of John Owen* (Grand Rapids, MI: Baker Academic, 2007).

[14] The Banner of Truth Trust has caused a little renaissance of interest by publishing his collected works in twenty-three volumes (seven of them the massive *Hebrews* commentary) plus a number of abridged paperbacks. Owen's writings are also available digitally from Logos.

[15] Toon, *God's Statesman*, vii.

[16] Ibid., 177.

What Is Puritanism?

Owen was born in England in 1616, the same year that William Shakespeare died and four years before the Pilgrims set sail for New England. This is virtually in the middle of the great Puritan century (roughly 1560—1660).

> Puritanism was at heart a spiritual movement, passionately concerned with God and godliness. It began in England with William Tyndale the Bible translator, Luther's contemporary, a generation before the word "Puritan" was coined, and it continued till the latter years of the seventeenth century, some decades after "Puritan" had fallen out of use. . . . Puritanism was essentially a movement for church reform, pastoral renewal and evangelism, and spiritual revival. . . . The Puritan goal was to complete what England's Reformation began: to finish reshaping Anglican worship, to introduce effective church discipline into Anglican parishes, to establish righteousness in the political, domestic, and socio-economic fields, and to convert all Englishmen to a vigorous evangelical faith.[17]

Birth and Boyhood

Owen was born in the middle of this movement and became its greatest pastor-theologian, as the movement ended almost simultaneously with his death in 1683.[18] His father was a pastor in Stadham, five miles north of Oxford. He had three brothers and a sister. In all his writings he does not mention his mother or his siblings. There is one brief reference to his father that says, "I was bred up from my infancy under the care of my father, who was a Nonconformist all his days, and a painful laborer in the vineyard of the Lord."[19]

At the age of ten he was sent to the grammar school run by Edward Sylvester in Oxford, where he prepared for the university. He entered Queens College, Oxford, at twelve, took his Bachelor of Arts at sixteen and his MA three years later at nineteen. We can get a flavor of what the boy was like from the observation by Peter Toon that Owen's zeal for knowledge was so great at this time that "he often allowed himself only four hours of sleep each night. His health was affected, and in later

---

[17] Packer, *A Quest for Godliness*, 28.
[18] J. I. Packer says that Puritanism developed under Elizabeth, James, and Charles, and blossomed in the Interregnum (1640s and 1650s) before it withered in the dark tunnel of persecution between 1660 (Restoration) and 1689 (Toleration). Packer, *A Quest for Godliness*, 28ff.
[19] Owen, *The Works of John Owen*, ed. Goold, 12:224.

life, when he was often on a sick-bed, he regretted these hours of rest that he had missed as a youth."[20]

Owen began his work for the BD but could not stand the high-church Arminianism and the formalism of Oxford, and finally dropped out to become a personal tutor and chaplain to some wealthy families near London.

Five Events That Shaped His Life

In 1642, the civil war began between Parliament and King Charles (between the high-church religion of William Laud and the Puritan religion of the Presbyterians and Independents in the House of Commons). Owen was sympathetic with Parliament against the king and Bishop Laud, and so he was pushed out of his chaplaincy and moved to London, where five major events of his life happened in the next four years that stamped the rest of his life.

Owen's Conversion

The first is his conversion—or possibly the awakening of the assurance of salvation and the deepening of his personal communion with God. It is remarkable that it happened in a way almost identical to Charles Spurgeon's conversion two centuries later. On January 6, 1850, Spurgeon was driven by a snowstorm into a Primitive Methodist chapel where a layman stood in for the pastor and took the text from Isaiah, "Look to me and be saved, all the ends of the earth." Spurgeon looked and was saved.[21]

Owen was a convinced Calvinist with large doctrinal knowledge, but he lacked the sense of the reality of his own salvation. That sense of personal reality in all that he wrote was going to make all the difference in the world for Owen in the years to come. So what happened one Sunday in 1642 is very important.

When Owen was twenty-six years old, he went with his cousin to hear the famous Presbyterian Edmund Calamy at St. Mary's Church Aldermanbury. But it turned out Calamy could not preach and a country preacher took his place. Owen's cousin wanted to leave. But something held Owen to his seat. The simple preacher took as his text Matthew

---

[20] Toon, *God's Statesman*, 6.
[21] Charles Spurgeon, *C. H. Spurgeon: Autobiography*, 2 vols. (Edinburgh: Banner of Truth, 1962), 1:87.

8:26, "Why are you fearful, O you of little faith?" It was God's appointed word and appointed time for Owen's awakening. His doubts and fears and worries as to whether he was truly born anew by the Holy Spirit were gone. He felt himself liberated and adopted as a son of God. When you read the penetrating, practical works of Owen on the work of the Spirit and the nature of true communion with God, it is hard to doubt the reality of what God did on this Sunday in 1642.[22]

Owen's Marriage and Dying Children

The second crucial event in those early years in London was Owen's marriage to a young woman named Mary Rooke. He was married to her for thirty-one years, from 1644 to 1675. We know virtually nothing about her. But we do know one absolutely stunning fact that must have colored all of Owen's ministry for the rest of his life (he died eight years after she died). We know that she bore him eleven children, and all but one died as a child, and that one daughter died as a young adult. In other words, Owen experienced the death of eleven children and the death of his wife! That's one child born and lost on average every three years of Owen's adult life.[23]

We don't have one reference to Mary or to the children or to his pain in all his books. But just knowing that the man walked in the valley of the shadow of death most of his life gives me a clue to the depth of dealing with God that we find in his works. God has his strange and painful ways of making his ministers the kind of pastors and theologians he wants them to be.

His First Book: Displaying Arminianism

The third event in these early London years is the publishing of his first book. He had read thoroughly about the recent controversy in Holland between the Remonstrants (whom he called Arminians) and the Calvinists. The Remonstrance was written in 1610, and the Calvinist response

---

[22] Toon, *God's Statesman*, 12ff.

[23] Andrew Thomson wrote, "Nearly all the information that has descended to us regarding this union [with Mary], from the earlier biographies amounts to this,—that the lady bore to him eleven children, all of whom, except one daughter, died in early youth. This only daughter became the wife of a Welsh gentleman; but the union proving unhappy, she 'returned to her kindred and to her father's house,' and soon after died of consumption." *The Works of John Owen*, ed. Goold, 1:xxxiii. "When [Mary] died in 1676 [Owen] remained a widower for about 18 months and married Dorothy D'Oyley. His exercises by affliction were very great in respect of his children, none of whom he much enjoyed while living, and saw them all go off the stage before him" (p. xcv).

was the Synod of Dordt in 1618. In spite of all its differences, Owen saw the English High Church of William Laud and the Dutch Remonstrants as essentially one in their rejection of predestination, which for Owen had become utterly crucial, especially since his conversion that he so thoroughly attributed to God.

So he published his first book in April 1643 with the polemical, preface-like title *A Display of Arminianism: being a discovery of the old Pelagian idol, free-will, with the new goddess, contingency, advancing themselves into the throne of God in heaven to the prejudice of His grace, providence and supreme dominion over the children of men.*[24] This is important not only because it set his direction as a Calvinist, but as a public, controversial writer whose whole life would be swallowed up by writing to the final month of his life in 1683.

Owen Becomes a Pastor

The fourth crucial event in these years was Owen's becoming a pastor of a small parish in Fordham, Essex, on July 16, 1643. He didn't stay long in this church. But I mention it because it set the course of his life as a pastor. He was always essentially a pastor, even when involved with administration at the University of Oxford and even when involved with the political events of his day. He was anything but a cloistered academic. All of his writing was done in the press of pastoral duties. There are points in his life where this will seem utterly amazing—that he could keep on studying and writing with the kind of involvements and burdens that he carried.

Owen Catapulted into Political Life

The fifth event of these early years in London was the invitation in 1646 to speak to the Parliament. In those days there were fast days during the year when the government asked certain pastors to preach to the House of Commons. It was a great honor. This message catapulted Owen into political affairs for the next fourteen years.

Owen came to the attention of Oliver Cromwell, the governmental leader ("Protector") in the absence of a king, and Cromwell is reputed to have said to Owen, "Sir, you are a person I must be acquainted

---

[24] This treatise is found in volume 10 of *The Works of John Owen*.

with"; to which Owen replied, "That will be much more to my advantage than yours."[25]

Well, maybe and maybe not. With that acquaintance, Owen was thrown into the turmoil of the civil war. Cromwell made him his chaplain and carried him off to Ireland and Scotland to preach to his troops and to assess the religious situation in those countries and to give the theological justification for Cromwell's politics.

Vice Chancellor of Oxford University

Not only that, Cromwell in 1651 appointed Owen to the deanship at Christ Church College in Oxford and then the next year made him also the vice chancellor. He was involved with Oxford for nine years until 1660 when Charles II returned and things began to go very badly for the Puritans.

It is astonishing how Owen was able to keep on studying and writing in spite of how public and how administratively laden his life was. At Oxford, Owen was responsible for the services of worship because Christ Church was a cathedral as well as a college and he was the preacher. He was responsible for the choice of students, the appointment of chaplains, the provision of tutorial facilities, the administration of discipline, the oversight of property, the collection of rents and tithes, the gift of livings, and the care of almsmen for the church hospital. His whole aim in all his duties, Peter Toon says, was "to establish the whole life of the College on the Word of God."[26]

His life was pervaded with pressure. It is hard to imagine what kind of family life he had. And we should keep in mind that during this time his children were dying. We know that at least two sons died in the plague of 1655. When he finished his duties as vice chancellor, he said in his closing address,

> Labors have been numberless; besides submitting to enormous expense, often when brought to the brink of death on your account, I have hated these limbs and this feeble body which was ready to desert my mind; the reproaches of the vulgar have been disregarded; the envy of others has been overcome: in these circumstances I wish you all prosperity and bid you farewell.[27]

---

[25] *A Religious Encyclopedia*, ed. Philip Schaff (New York: Christian Literature, 1888), 3:1711.
[26] Toon, *God's Statesman*, 54.
[27] Ibid., 77ff.

Owen Ever Studying, Ever Writing

In spite of all this administrative pressure, and even hostility because of his commitment to godliness and to the Puritan cause, he was constantly studying and writing, probably late at night instead of sleeping. That's how concerned he was with doctrinal faithfulness to Scripture. Peter Toon lists twenty-two published works during those years. For example, he published his defense of the *Saints' Perseverance* in 1654. He saw a man named John Goodwin spreading error on this doctrine and he felt constrained, despite all his other duties, to answer him—with over six hundred pages! It fills all of volume 11 in his *Works*. And he wasn't writing fluff that would vanish overnight. One biographer said that this book is "the most masterly vindication of the perseverance of the saints in the English tongue."[28]

During these administrative years he also wrote *Of the Mortification of Sin in Believers* (1656), *Of Communion with God* (1657), and *Of Temptation: The Nature and Power of It* (1658). What is so remarkable about these books is that they are what I would call intensely personal, and in many places, very sweet. So he wasn't just fighting doctrinal battles—he was fighting sin and temptation. And he wasn't just fighting—he was fostering heartfelt communion with God in the students.

Fugitive Pastor to the End

He was relieved of his duties of the deanship in 1660 (having laid down the vice chancellorship in 1657). Cromwell had died in 1658. The monarchy with Charles II was back. The Act of Uniformity, which put two thousand Puritans out of their pulpits, was just around the corner (1662). The days ahead for Owen now were not the great political, academic days of the last fourteen years. He was now, from 1660 until his death in 1683, a kind of fugitive pastor in London.

During these years he became what some have called the "Atlas and Patriarch of Independency." He had begun his ministry as a Puritan of Presbyterian persuasion. But he became persuaded that the Congregational form of government is more biblical. He was the main spokesman for this wing of Nonconformity and wrote extensively to defend the view.[29]

---

[28] Owen, *Works*, ed. Goold, 1:lvii.
[29] *A Discourse Concerning Evangelical Love, Church Peace and Unity* (1672); *An Inquiry into the Original Nature . . . and Communion of Evangelical Churches* (1681); and the classic text, *True Nature of a Gospel Church* (1689, posthumously).

A Defender of Tolerance against State Oppression

But even more significant, he was the main spokesman for *tolerance* of both Presbyterian and Episcopal forms. Even while at Oxford he had the authority to quash Anglican worship, but he allowed a group of Episcopalians to worship in rooms across from his own quarters.[30] He wrote numerous tracts and books to call for tolerance within Orthodoxy. For example, in 1667 he wrote (in *Indulgence and Toleration Considered*):

> It seems that we are some of the first who ever anywhere in the world, from the foundation of it, thought of ruining and destroying persons of the same religion with ourselves, merely upon the choice of some peculiar ways of worship in that religion.[31]

His ideas on tolerance were so significant that they had a large influence on William Penn, the Quaker and founder of Pennsylvania, who was a student of Owen. And it is significant to me as a Baptist that in 1669 he wrote, with several other pastors, a letter of concern to the governor and Congregationalists of Massachusetts, pleading with them not to persecute the Baptists.[32]

Caring for His Flock, Even When Absent

During these twenty-three years after 1660, Owen was a pastor. Because of the political situation he was not always able to stay in one place and be with his people, but he seemed to carry them on his heart even when he was moving around. Near the end of his life he wrote to his flock, "Although I am absent from you in body, I am in mind and affection and spirit present with you, and in your assemblies; for I hope you will be found my crown and rejoicing in the day of the Lord."[33]

Not only that, he actively counseled and made plans for their care in his absence. He exhorted them in one letter with words that are amazingly relevant to pastoral care struggles in our churches today:

> I beseech you to hear a word of advice in case the persecution increases, which it is like to do for a season. I could wish that because you have no

---

[30] Owen, *Works*, ed. Goold, 1:li.
[31] Toon, *God's Statesman*, 132.
[32] Ibid., 162. See the letter in Peter Toon, ed., *The Correspondence of John Owen (1616–1683)* (Cambridge: James Clarke, 1970), 145–46.
[33] Toon, *God's Statesman*, 157.

ruling elders, and your teachers cannot walk about publicly with safety, that you would appoint some among yourselves, who may continually as their occasions will admit, go up and down from house to house and apply themselves peculiarly to the weak, the tempted, the fearful, those who are ready to despond, or to halt, and to encourage them in the Lord. Choose out those unto this end who are endued with a spirit of courage and fortitude; and let them know that they are happy whom Christ will honor with His blessed work. And I desire the persons may be of this number who are faithful men, and know the state of the church; by this means you will know what is the frame of the members of the church, which will be a great direction to you, even in your prayers.[34]

Under normal circumstances Owen believed and taught that "The first and principal duty of a pastor is to feed the flock by diligent preaching of the word."[35] He pointed to Jeremiah 3:15 and the purpose of God to "give to his [church pastors] according to his own heart, who should feed them with knowledge and understanding" (AT). He showed that the care of preaching the gospel was committed to Peter, and in him to all true pastors of the church under the name of "feeding" (John 21:15–17). He cited Acts 6 and the apostles' decision to free themselves from all encumbrances that they may give themselves wholly to the Word and prayer. He referred to 1 Timothy 5:17—it is the pastor's duty to "labor in the word and doctrine" (NKJV)—and to Acts 20:28 where the overseers of the flock are to feed them with the Word. Then he says,

> Nor is it required only that he preach now and then at his leisure; but that he lay aside all other employments, though lawful, all other duties in the church, as unto such a constant attendance on them as would divert him from this work, that he give himself unto it. . . . Without this, no man will be able to give a comfortable account of his pastoral office at the last day.[36]

I think it would be fair to say that this is the way Owen fulfilled his charge during these years whenever the political situation allowed him.

Owen and Bunyan, the Patriarch and the Prisoner

During these last years of Owen's life some Puritans were in prison, and others, like Owen, were not. Part of the explanation was how openly

---

[34] Toon, *Correspondence of John Owen*, 171.
[35] Owen, *Works*, ed. Goold, 16:74.
[36] Ibid., 74–75.

they preached. Part of it was that Owen was a national figure with connections in high places. Part of it was that the persecution was not nationally uniform, but some local officials were more rigorous than others.

But whatever the explanation for Owen's freedom while others were in prison, the kind of relationship that he had in these years with John Bunyan, who spent too many of them in prison, was remarkable. One story says that King Charles II asked Owen one time why he bothered going to hear an uneducated tinker like Bunyan preach. Owen replied, "Could I possess the tinker's abilities for preaching, please your majesty, I would gladly relinquish all my learning."[37]

One of the best illustrations of God's mercy in a frowning providence is the story of how Owen failed to help Bunyan get out of prison. Repeatedly when Bunyan was in prison, Owen worked for his release with all the strings he could pull. But to no avail. But when John Bunyan came out in 1676, he brought with him a manuscript "the worth and importance of which can scarcely be comprehended"—*Pilgrim's Progress*.[38] In fact, Owen met with Bunyan and recommended his own publisher, Nathaniel Ponder. The partnership succeeded, and the book that has probably done more good than any book besides the Bible was released to the world—all because Owen failed in his good attempts to get Bunyan released.

> Judge not the Lord by feeble sense,
> But trust him for his grace;
> Behind a frowning providence
> He hides a smiling face.[39]

Buried Together

Owen died on August 24, 1683. He was buried on September 4 in Bunhill Fields, London, where five years later the tinker and immortal dreamer of Bedford Jail was buried with him. It was fitting for the two to lie down together when the Congregational giant had labored so long in the cause of toleration for lowly Baptists in England and New England.

---

[37] Toon, *God's Statesman*, 162.
[38] Ibid., 161.
[39] William Cowper, "God Moves in a Mysterious Way" (1774).

His All-Encompassing Aim: Holiness—His Own and Others'

Let's stand back now and try to get close to the heart of what made this man tick and what made him great. Let us be inspired by this man in some deeply personal and spiritual ways. That seems to be the way he has touched people most—people like J. I. Packer and Sinclair Ferguson.

I think the words that come closest to giving us the heart and aim of his life are found in the preface to the little book *Of the Mortification of Sin in Believers*, which was based on sermons that he preached to the students and academic community at Oxford:

> I hope I may own in sincerity that my heart's desire unto God, and the chief design of my life . . . are, that mortification and universal holiness may be promoted in my own and in the hearts and ways of others, to the glory of God, that so the Gospel of our Lord and Savior Jesus Christ may be adorned in all things.[40]

"Mortification" means warfare on our own sin with a view to killing it. Owen's book was an exposition of Romans 8:13 ("If you live according to the flesh you will die, but if by the Spirit you put to death the deeds of the body, you will live"). He paraphrased this truth in the memorable phrase, "Be killing sin or it will be killing you."[41]

That book was written in 1656. Twenty-five years later he was still sounding the same note in his preaching and writing. In 1681, he published *The Grace and Duty of Being Spiritually Minded*. Sinclair Ferguson is probably right when he says, "*Everything* he wrote for his contemporaries had a practical and pastoral aim in view—the promotion of true Christian living"[42]—in other words, the mortification of sin and the advancement of holiness.

This was his burden not only for the churches but also for the university when he was there. Peter Toon says, "Owen's special emphasis was to insist that the whole academic curriculum be submerged in preaching and catechizing and prayer. He wanted the graduates of Oxford not only to be proficient in the Arts and Sciences but also to aspire after godliness."[43]

---

[40] Owen, *The Works of John Owen*, ed. Goold, 6:4.
[41] Ibid., 9.
[42] Ferguson, *John Owen on the Christian Life*, xi, emphasis added. See note 58.
[43] Toon, *God's Statesman*, 78.

Calling Parliament to Personal Holiness

Even in his political messages—the sermons to Parliament—the theme was repeatedly personal holiness. He based this on the Old Testament pattern—"the people of Israel were at the height of their fortunes when their leaders were godly."[44] So the key issue for him was that the legislature be made up of holy people.

His concern that the gospel spread and be adorned with holiness was not just a burden for his English homeland. When he came back from Ireland in 1650, where he had seen the English forces under Cromwell decimate the Irish, he preached to Parliament and pleaded for another kind of warfare:

> How is it that Jesus Christ is in Ireland only as a lion staining all his garments with the blood of his enemies; and none to hold him out as a Lamb sprinkled with his own blood to his friends? . . . Is this to deal fairly with the Lord Jesus?—call him out to do battle and then keep away his crown? God hath been faithful in doing great things for you; be faithful in this one—do your utmost for the preaching of the Gospel in Ireland.[45]

From his writings and from the testimony of others, it seems fair to say that the aim of personal holiness in all of life, and the mortifying of all known sin, really was the labor not only of his teaching but of his own personal life.

The Divine Luster of All His Accomplishments

David Clarkson, his pastoral associate in the later years of Owen's ministry, gave his funeral address. In it he said:

> A great light is fallen; one of eminency for holiness, learning, parts and abilities; a pastor, a scholar, a divine of the first magnitude; holiness gave a divine luster to his other accomplishments, it shined in his whole course, and was diffused through his whole conversation.[46]

John Stoughton said, "His piety equaled his erudition."[47] Thomas Chalmers of Scotland commented on Owen's book *On the Nature, Power, Deceit, and Prevalence of Indwelling Sin in Believers*, "It is most

---

44 Ibid., 120.
45 Ibid., 41.
46 Ibid., 173.
47 *A Religious Encyclopedia*, 2:1712.

important to be instructed on this subject by one who had reached such lofty attainments in holiness, and whose profound and experimental [experiential] acquaintance with the spiritual life so well fitted him for expounding its nature and operations."[48]

Why We Need to Listen to John Owen

The reason this question of personal holiness is so urgent for us today is not only because there is a "holiness without which no one will see the Lord" (Heb. 12:14), but also because there seems to be a shortage of political and ecclesiastical leaders today who make the quest for holiness as central as the quest for church growth or academic achievement or political success. In recent years, even a president of the United States has communicated clearly that he did not think his personal morality was a significant factor in his leadership of the nation. The cavalier way that many church leaders treat sexual propriety is an echo of the same disease. John Owen would have been astonished at both the national and the ecclesiastical scene in America.

John Owen is a good counselor and model for us on this matter of holiness because he was not a hermit. We often think that some people have the monkish luxury of just staying out of the mess of public life and becoming holy people. Not so the Puritans of Owen's day. J. I. Packer said that Puritanism was "a reformed monasticism outside the cloister and away from monkish vows."[49] This is especially true of Owen.

The Great Doer

His contemporary, Richard Baxter, called Owen "the great doer."[50] He lived in the public eye. He was involved in academic administration; he was in politics up to his ears; he was entangled with the leading military officers of the country; he was embroiled in controversies over all kinds of matters from the authenticity of the Hebrew vowel points and the Epistle of Ignatius to the national laws of toleration and the nature of justification. He was looked to by thousands of congregational independent ministers as their spokesman at the national level; he was all

---

[48] Owen, *Works*, ed. Goold, 1:lxxxiv.
[49] Packer, *A Quest for Godliness*, 28.
[50] Toon, *God's Statesman*, 95.

the while pastoring people—and, we must not forget, losing a child in death every three years.

The Cost of Public Faithfulness: Criticism

We all know that a life like this is shot through with criticism that can break the spirit and make the quest for personal holiness doubly difficult. When Owen's adversaries could not better him in argument, they resorted to character assassination. He was called "the great bellwether of disturbance and sedition . . . a person who would have vied with Mahomet himself both for boldness and imposture . . . a viper, so swollen with venom that it must either burst or spit its poison."[51]

And even more painful and disheartening was the criticism of friends. He once got a critical letter from John Eliot, the missionary to the Indians in America, that wounded him more deeply, he said, than any of his adversaries. Owen wrote to Eliot:

> What I have received from you . . . hath printed deeper, and left a greater impression upon my mind, than all the virulent revilings and false accusations I have met withal from my professed adversaries. . . . That I should now be apprehended to have given a wound unto *holiness* in the churches, it is one of the saddest frowns in the cloudy brows of Divine Providence.[52]

Add to this the daily burdens of living in a pre-technological world with no modern conveniences and passing through two major plagues, one of which in 1665 killed seventy thousand of the half-million people in London,[53] plus the twenty years of living outside the protection of the law—then we know that John Owen's holiness was not worked out in the comforts of peace and leisure and safety. When a man like this, under these circumstances, is remembered and extolled for centuries for his personal holiness, we should listen.

How Owen Pursued Private and Public Holiness

Owen's personal holiness and public fruitfulness did not just happen to him. He pursued them. There were strategies of personal discipline and public authenticity that God used to make him what he was. In all our

---

[51] Owen, *The Works of John Owen*, ed. Goold, 1:lxxxix.
[52] Toon, *Correspondence of John Owen*, 154, emphasis added.
[53] Toon, *God's Statesman*, 131.

life and ministry, as we care for people and contend for the faith, we can learn much from Owen's pursuit of holiness in private and public.

Owen Humbled Himself under the Mighty Hand of God

Though he was one of the most influential and well-known men of his day, his own view of his place in God's economy was sober and humble. Two days before he died, he wrote in a letter to Charles Fleetwood, "I am leaving the ship of the Church in a storm, but while the great Pilot is in it the loss of a poor under-rower will be inconsiderable."[54]

Packer says that "Owen, [though] a proud man by nature, had been brought low in and by his conversion, and thereafter he kept himself low by recurring contemplation of his inbred sinfulness."[55] Owen illustrates this:

> To keep our souls in a constant state of mourning and self-abasement is the most necessary part of our wisdom . . . and it is so far from having any inconsistency with those consolations and joys, which the gospel tenders unto us in believing, as that it is the only way to let them into the soul in a due manner.[56]

With regard to his immense learning and the tremendous insight he had into the things of God, he seems to have a humbler attitude toward his achievement because he had climbed high enough to see over the first ridge of revelation into the endless mysteries of God.

> I make no pretence of searching into the bottom or depths of any part of this "great mystery of godliness, God manifest in the flesh." They are altogether unsearchable, unto the [limit] of the most enlightened minds, in this life. What we shall farther comprehend of them in the other world, God only knows.[57]

This humility opened Owen's soul to the greatest visions of Christ in the Scriptures. And he believed with all his heart the truth of 2 Corinthians 3:18, that by contemplating the glory of Christ "we may be gradually transformed into the same glory."[58] And that is nothing other than holiness.

---

[54] Toon, *The Correspondence of John Owen*, 174.
[55] Packer, *A Quest for Godliness*, 193.
[56] Owen, *The Works of John Owen*, ed. Goold, 7:532.
[57] Ibid., 1:44; cf. 6:64, 68.
[58] Toon, *God's Statesman*, 175; Owen, *The Works of John Owen*, ed. Goold, 1:275.

Owen Grew in Knowledge by Obeying What He Knew

Owen recognized that holiness is not merely the goal of all true learning; it is also one crucial means of more true learning. This elevated holiness even higher in his life: it was the aim of his life *and*, in large measure, the means of getting there.

> The true notion of *holy evangelical truths* will not *live*, at least not *flourish*, where they are divided from a holy conversation [= life]. As we learn all to practise, so we learn much by practice. . . .
>
> And hereby alone can we come unto the *assurance* that what we know and learn is indeed the truth [cf. John 7:17]. . . . And hereby will they be led continually into farther degrees of knowledge; for the mind of man is capable of receiving *continual supplies* in the increase of light and knowledge . . . if . . . they are improved unto their proper end in obedience unto God. But without this the mind will be quickly stuffed with notions, so that no streams can descend into it from the fountain of truth.[59]

Thus Owen kept the streams of the fountain of truth open by making personal obedience the effect of all that he learned.

Owen Passionately Pursued a Personal Communion with God

It is incredible that Owen was able, under the pressures of his life, to keep writing books that were both weighty and edifying. Andrew Thomson, one of his biographers, wrote,

> It is interesting to find the ample evidence which [his work on *Mortification*] affords, that amid the din of theological controversy, the engrossing and perplexing activities of a high public station, and the chilling damps of a university, he was yet living near God, and like Jacob amid the stones of the wilderness, maintaining secret intercourse with the eternal and invisible.[60]

Packer says that the Puritans differ from evangelicals today because with them

> communion with God was a *great* thing, to evangelicals today it is a comparatively *small* thing. The Puritans were concerned about communion with God in a way that we are not. The measure of our unconcern is the little that we say about it. When Christians meet, they talk to each other about their

---

[59] Owen, *Works*, ed. Goold, 4:206, italics original.
[60] Ibid., 1:lxiv–lxv.

Christian work and Christian interests, their Christian acquaintances, the state of the churches, and the problems of theology—but rarely of their daily experience of God.[61]

But God was seeing to it that Owen and the suffering Puritans of his day lived closer to God and sought after communion with God more earnestly than we. Writing a letter during an illness in 1674, Owen said to a friend, "Christ is our best friend, and ere long will be our only friend. I pray God with all my heart that I may be weary of everything else but converse and communion with Him."[62] God was using illness and all the other pressures of Owen's life to drive him into communion with God and not away from it.

Severest Thought for the Contemplation of Christ

But Owen was also very intentional about his communion with God. He said, "Friendship is most maintained and kept up by visits; and these, the more free and less occasioned by urgent business."[63] In other words, in the midst of all his academic and political and ecclesiastical labors, he made many visits to his Friend, Jesus Christ.

And when he went, he did not just go with petitions for things or even for deliverance in his many hardships. He went to see his glorious Friend and to contemplate his greatness. The last book he wrote—he was finishing it as he died—is called *Meditations on the Glory of Christ*. That says a great deal about the focus and outcome of Owen's life. In it he said:

> The revelation ... of Christ ... deserves the severest of our thoughts, the best of our meditations and our utmost diligence in them. ... What better preparation can there be for [our future enjoyment of the glory of Christ] than in a constant previous contemplation of that glory in the revelation that is made in the Gospel.[64]

The contemplation Owen has in mind is made up of at least two things: on the one hand there is what he called his "severest thoughts" and "best meditations," or in another place "assiduous meditations," and,

---

[61] Packer, *A Quest for Godliness*, 215.
[62] Toon, *God's Statesman*, 153.
[63] Owen, *Works*, ed. Goold, 7:197ff.
[64] Ibid., 1:275.

on the other hand, relentless prayer. The two are illustrated in his work on Hebrews.

Assiduous Meditation, Constant Prayer

One of his greatest achievements was his seven-volume commentary on Hebrews. When he finished it near the end of his life, he said, "Now my work is done: it is time for me to die."[65] How did he do it? We get a glimpse from the preface:

> I must now say, that, after all my searching and reading, *prayer and assiduous meditation* have been my only resort, and by far the most useful means of light and assistance. By these have my thoughts been freed from many an entanglement.[66]

Whether it is for the sake of the holiness of our own soul or the ability to discern and answer the "madness" of false teachers, Owen repeatedly commended serious study of the Scriptures combined with "continual attendance on the throne of grace."

> Diligent, constant, serious reading, studying, meditating on the Scriptures, with the assistance and direction of all the rules and advantages for the right understanding of them . . . accompanied with continual attendance on the throne of grace for the presence of the Spirit of truth with us, to lead us into all truth, and to increase his anointing of us day by day, "shining into our hearts to give us the knowledge of the glory of God in the face of Jesus Christ," is . . . for our preservation against these abominations, and the enabling of us to discover their madness and answer their objections, of indispensable necessity.[67]

His aim in all he did was to grasp the mind of Christ and reflect it in his behavior. This means that the quest for holiness was always bound up with a quest for true knowledge of God. That's why prayer and study and meditation always went together.

> I suppose . . . this may be fixed on as a common principle of Christianity; namely, that constant and fervent prayer for the divine assistance of the Holy Spirit, is such an indispensable means for . . . attaining the knowledge of the mind of God in the Scripture, as that without it all others will not [avail].[68]

---

[65] Toon, *God's Statesman*, 168.
[66] Owen, *Works*, ed. Goold, 1:lxxxv, emphasis added.
[67] Ibid., 12:50.
[68] Ibid., 4:203.

Owen gives us a glimpse into the struggle that we all have in this regard, lest anyone think he was above the battle. He wrote to John Eliot in New England,

> I do acknowledge unto you that I have a dry and barren spirit, and I do heartily beg your prayers that the Holy One would, notwithstanding all my sinful provocations, water me from above.[69]

In other words, the prayers of others, not just his own, were essential for his holiness.

The source of all that Owen preached and wrote was this "assiduous meditation" on Scripture and prayer. Which leads us to the fourth way that Owen achieved such holiness in his immensely busy and productive life.

Commending in Public Only What He Experienced in Private

One great hindrance to holiness in the ministry of the Word is that we are prone to preach and write without pressing into the things we say and making them real to our own souls. Over the years words begin to come easy, and we find we can speak of mysteries without standing in awe; we can speak of purity without feeling pure; we can speak of zeal without spiritual passion; we can speak of God's holiness without trembling; we can speak of sin without sorrow; we can speak of heaven without eagerness. And the result is an increasing hardening of the spiritual life.

Words came easy for Owen, but he set himself against this terrible disease of inauthenticity and secured his growth in holiness. He began with the premise: "Our happiness consisteth not in the *knowing* the things of the gospel, but in the *doing* of them."[70] Doing, not just knowing, was the goal of all his studies.

As a means to this authentic doing, he labored to experience every truth he preached. He said,

> I hold myself bound in conscience and in honor, not even to imagine that I have attained a proper knowledge of any one article of truth, much less to publish it, unless through the Holy Spirit I have had such a taste of it, in its

---

[69] Toon, *Correspondence of John Owen*, 154.
[70] Owen, *Works*, ed. Goold, 14:311.

spiritual sense, that I may be able, from the heart, to say with the psalmist, "I have believed, and therefore I have spoken."[71]

So, for example, his *Exposition of Psalm 130* (320 pages on eight verses) is the laying open not only of the Psalm but of his own heart. Andrew Thomson says,

> When Owen . . . laid open the book of God, he laid open at the same time the book of his own heart and of his own history, and produced a book which . . . is rich in golden thoughts, and instinct with the living experience of "one who spake what he knew, and testified what he had seen."[72]

The same biographer said of Owen's *On The Grace and Duty of Being Spiritually Minded* (1681) that he "first preached [it] to his own heart, and then to a private congregation; and which reveals to us the almost untouched and untrodden eminences on which Owen walked in the last years of his pilgrimage."[73]

Communing with God in the Doctrine We Contend For

The conviction that controlled Owen in this was the following:

> A man preacheth that sermon only well unto others which preacheth itself in his own soul. And he that doth not feed on and thrive in the digestion of the food which he provides for others will scarce make it savory unto them; yea, he knows not but the food he hath provided may be poison, unless he have really tasted of it himself. If the word do not dwell with power *in* us, it will not pass with power *from* us.[74]

It was this conviction that sustained Owen in his immensely busy public life of controversy and conflict. Whenever he undertook to defend a truth, he sought first of all to take that truth deeply into his heart and gain a real spiritual experience of it so that there would be no artificiality in the debate and no mere posturing or gamesmanship. He was made steady in the battle because he had come to experience the truth at the personal level of the fruits of holiness and knew that God was in it. Here is the way he put it in the Preface to *The Mystery of the Gospel Vindicated* (1655):

---

[71] Ibid., 10:488.
[72] Ibid., 1:lxxxiv.
[73] Ibid., 1:xcix–c.
[74] Ibid., 16:76.

> When the heart is cast indeed into the mould of the doctrine that the mind
> embraceth—when the evidence and necessity of the truth abides in us—when
> not the sense of the words only is in our heads, but the sense of the thing
> abides in our hearts—when we have communion with God in the doctrine
> we contend for—then shall we be garrisoned by the grace of God against all
> the assaults of men.[75]

That, I think, was the key to Owen's life and ministry, so renowned for holiness—"when we have *communion* with God in the *doctrine* we contend for—then shall we be garrisoned by the grace of God against all the assaults of men."

Preparing to Meet Christ

The last thing Owen was doing, as the end of his life approached, was communing with Christ in a work that was later published as *Meditations on the Glory of Christ*. His friend William Payne was helping him edit the work. Near the end Owen said, "O, brother Payne, the long-wished for day is come at last, in which I shall see the glory in another manner than I have ever done or was capable of doing in this world."[76]

John Owen contended for the fullness of biblical faith because he wanted generations after him to enjoy that same "long-wished for day" when we will see the glory of Christ "in another manner" than we have ever seen it here. He knew that our final salvation depends on our present seeing of the glory of Christ in the gospel (2 Cor. 4:4). And he knew that it is the pure in heart who see this glory (Matt. 5:8). The purifying work of the Holy Spirit opens us to see and savor the glory of God in the face of Christ. This spiritual sight, in turn, enables us to be more and more conformed to Christ (2 Cor. 3:18). Therefore Owen saw the intimate connection between contending for the gospel and being consecrated by the gospel. He never made controversy, nor its victory, an end in itself.[77] The end was to see Jesus Christ, be satisfied with him, and be transformed into his likeness. For this great spiritual transaction, there must be Spirit and truth. And that meant, in his day,

---

[75] Ibid., 12:52.

[76] Toon, *God's Statesman*, 171.

[77] "It is the direction, satisfaction, and peace of the consciences of men, and not the curiosity of notions or subtlety of deputations, which it is our duty to design." John Owen, *The Works of John Owen*, ed. Goold, 5:8.

consecration and controversy. Prayer and study. Faith and a fight to preserve its foundation for others.

I thank God for John Owen's unwavering passion for communion with God. I thank God that this passion motivated his fierce attack on his own unholiness, and that it proved to be the "key to Owen's own steadfastness amid all those winds of doctrine which unsettled" his century.[78] We are debtors to his mighty pen and to the passion for God's glory and his own holiness that drove it.

---

[78] Andrew Thomson wrote: "This secret communion with God in the doctrines contended for was the true key to Owen's own steadfastness amid all those winds of doctrine which unsettled everything but what was rooted in the soil." Ibid., 1:lxiv.

As for me, I believe that a great opportunity has been opened to Christian people by the "controversy" that is so much decried. Conventions have been broken down; men are trying to penetrate beneath pious words to the thing that these words designate; it is becoming increasingly necessary for a man to choose whether he will stand with Christ or against Him. Such a condition, I for my part believe, has been brought about by the Spirit of God; already there has been genuine spiritual advance. It has been signally manifested at the institution which I have the honor to serve [Princeton Seminary]. . . .

During the academic year, 1924–25, there has been something like an awakening, Youth has begun to think for itself; the evil of compromising associations has been discovered; Christian heroism in the face of opposition has come again to its rights; a new interest has been aroused in the historical and philosophical questions that underlie the Christian religion; true and independent convictions have been formed.

Controversy, in other words, has resulted in a striking intellectual and spiritual advance. Some of us discern in all this the work of the Spirit of God. . . . Controversy of the right sort is good; for out of such controversy, as Church history and Scripture alike teach, there comes the salvation of souls.

J. Gresham Machen
What Is Faith?

Contending for Facts
for the Sake of Faith

J. Gresham Machen's Constructive
Controversy with Modernism

The Tragic End in Midlife

On New Year's Eve 1936, in a Roman Catholic hospital in Bismarck, North Dakota, J. Gresham Machen was one day away from death at the age of fifty-five. It was Christmas break at Westminster Seminary in Philadelphia where he taught New Testament. His colleagues had said he looked "deadly tired" at the end of the term. But instead of resting, he had taken the train from Philadelphia to the 20-below-zero winds of North Dakota to preach in a few Presbyterian churches at the request of pastor Samuel Allen.

Ned Stonehouse, his New Testament assistant, said, "There was no one of sufficient influence to constrain him to curtail his program to any significant degree."[1] He was the acknowledged leader of the conservative movement in Presbyterianism with no one to watch over him. His heroes and mentors, Warfield and Patton, were dead. He had never married, and so had no wife to restrain him with reality. His mother and father, who gave him so much wise counsel over the years, were dead. His two brothers lived fifteen hundred miles east of where he lay dying. "He had

---

[1] Ned B. Stonehouse, *J. Gresham Machen: A Biographical Memoir* (1954; repr., Edinburgh: Banner of Truth, 1987), 506. This volume was published seventeen years after Machen's death.

a personality that only his good friends found appealing."[2] And so he was remarkably alone and isolated for a man of international stature.

He had pneumonia and could scarcely breathe. Pastor Allen came to pray for him that last day of 1936, and Machen told him of a vision that he had had of being in heaven. "Sam, it was glorious, it was glorious," he said. And a little later he added, "Sam, isn't the Reformed Faith grand?"

The following day—New Year's Day 1937—he mustered the strength to send a telegram to John Murray, his friend and colleague at Westminster. It was his last recorded word: "I'm so thankful for [the] active obedience of Christ. No hope without it." He died about 7:30 p.m.

So much of the man is here in this tragic scene. The stubbornness of going his own way when friends urged him not to take this extra preaching trip. His isolation far from the mainline centers of church life and thought. His suffering for the cause he believed in. His utter allegiance to, and exaltation of, the Reformed faith of the Westminster Confession. And his taking comfort not just from a general truth about Christ, but from a doctrinally precise understanding of the *active* obedience of Christ—which he believed was credited to his account and would make him a suitable heir of eternal life, for Christ's sake.

The Institutional Fruit of His Life

And so Machen was cut off in the midst of a great work—the establishment of Westminster Seminary and the Orthodox Presbyterian Church. He hadn't set out to found a seminary or a new church. But given who he was and what he stood for and what was happening at Princeton, where he had taught for twenty-three years, and in the Presbyterian Church in the USA, it was almost inevitable.

Westminster Seminary was seven years old when Machen died. The Presbyterian Church in America (which was forced under law to change its name and became the Orthodox Presbyterian Church) was six months old, and Machen had been elected the first Moderator on June 11, 1936.

The Fateful Charge of Insubordination

The occasion for starting a new Presbyterian church over against the huge Presbyterian Church in the USA was that on March 29, 1935,

---

[2] George Marsden, "Understanding J. Gresham Machen," in *Understanding Fundamentalism and Evangelicalism* (Grand Rapids, MI: Eerdmans, 1991), 200.

Machen's Presbytery in Trenton, New Jersey, found him guilty of insubordination to church authorities[3] and stripped him of his ordination. An appeal was taken to the General Assembly at Syracuse in the summer of 1936 but failed.

The reason for the charge of insubordination was that Machen had founded an independent board of foreign missions in June 1933 to protest the fact that the Presbyterian Board of Foreign Missions endorsed a laymen's report (called *Rethinking Missions*) that Machen said, was "from beginning to end an attack upon the historic Christian faith."[4]

He pointed out that the board supported missionaries like Pearl Buck in China, who represented the kind of evasive, noncommittal attitude toward Christian truth that Machen thought was destroying the church and its witness. She said, for example, that if someone existed who could create a person like Christ and portray him for us, "then Christ lived and lives, whether He was once one body and one soul, or whether He is the essence of men's highest dreams."[5]

How serious was it that Machen could not give or endorse giving to this board? The General Assembly gave answer in Cleveland in 1934 with this astonishing sentence:

> A church member . . . that will not give to promote the officially authorized missionary program of the Presbyterian Church is in exactly the same position with reference to the Constitution of the Church as a church member . . . that would refuse to take part in the celebration of the Lord's Supper or any other prescribed ordinance of the denomination.[6]

Thus Machen was forced by his own conscience into what the church viewed as the gravest insubordination and disobedience to his ordination vows and removed him from the ministry. Hence the beginning of the Orthodox Presbyterian Church.

"Princeton Seminary Is Dead"

A few years earlier Machen had left Princeton Seminary to found Westminster Seminary. This time he wasn't forced out, but chose freely to leave when the governing boards of the seminary were reorganized so

---

[3] See Stonehouse, *J. Gresham Machen*, 489, for the list of grievances.
[4] Ibid., 475.
[5] Ibid., 474.
[6] Ibid., 485.

that the conservative Board of Directors could be diluted by liberals[7] more in tune with President Stevensen and with the denomination as a whole.[8] Machen said,

> If the proposed . . . dissolution of the present Board of Directors is finally carried out . . . [and] the control of the Seminary passes into entirely different hands—then Princeton Theological Seminary as it has been so long and so honorably known, will be dead, and we shall have at Princeton a new institution of radically different type.[9]

Well, Princeton Seminary did die, in Machen's eyes, and out of the ashes he meant to preserve the tradition of Charles Hodge and Benjamin Warfield. So when he gave the inaugural address of Westminster Seminary on September 25, 1929, to the first class of fifty students and guests, he said,

> No, my friends, though Princeton Seminary is dead, the noble tradition of Princeton Seminary is alive. Westminster Seminary will endeavor by God's grace to continue that tradition unimpaired.[10]

Machen's most enduring response to modernism was the founding of these two institutions: Westminster Seminary (which today is a major influence in American evangelicalism) and the Orthodox Presbyterian Church (which now, over six decades later, bears a witness disproportionate to its small size).[11]

Where Did This Warrior Come From?

Who was J. Gresham Machen? Where did he come from? What shaped and drove him? More important than the mere fact of founding institutions is the question of the worldview that carried him through that achievement. And what was this thing called "modernism" that engaged his amazingly energetic opposition? And what can we learn from his response today?

---

[7] To prove the doctrinal drift of the action to reorganize the seminary, two signers of the liberal "Auburn Affirmation" were appointed to the new board. Ibid., 441.

[8] Ibid., 422.

[9] Ibid., 427.

[10] Ibid., 458.

[11] For a testimony to the life and witness of the Orthodox Presbyterian Church, see Charles Dennison and Richard Gamble, eds., *Pressing toward the Mark: Essays Commemorating Fifty Years of the Orthodox Presbyterian Church* (Philadelphia: The Committee for the Historian of the Orthodox Presbyterian Church, 1986).

John Gresham Machen was born in Baltimore, Maryland, on July 28, 1881, sixteen years after the Civil War. His mother was from Macon, Georgia, and was educated and cultured enough that she published a book in 1903 entitled *The Bible in Browning*. His father was a very successful lawyer from Baltimore. The family hobnobbed with the cultural elite in Baltimore; had a vacation home in Seal Harbor, Maine; and traveled often. Machen sailed to Europe and back some six times. In a word, Machen was a well-to-do Southern aristocrat.

He went to the private University School for Boys where classics (especially Latin) were stressed from the time he was eleven. The family were devoted members of Franklin Street Presbyterian Church, which was a part of the Southern Presbyterian Church.

A Son of Southern Culture for Better or Worse

This cultural atmosphere shaped Machen's views and sentiments in various ways. For example, he shared the Southern paternalistic attitudes toward African-Americans. In an essay for his first year at Johns Hopkins University when he was seventeen, he wrote of his home: "The servants are the real, old-fashioned kind-hearted Southern darkies."[12] His view of the Southern cause in the Civil War, still fresh in everyone's mind, was the same as his favorite professor's at Johns Hopkins:

> That the cause we fought for and our brothers died for was the cause of civil liberty and not the cause of human slavery. . . . It was a point of grammatical concord that was at the bottom of the Civil War—"United States are," said one, "United States is," said another.[13]

Being a Southerner—or part of any other culture for that matter—has its advantages and disadvantages in creating our blind spots and opening our eyes. George Marsden suggests that some of Machen's insight into the cultural movements of his day may be owing to his Southern roots: "Machen as a Southerner may have something to offer us. As a Southerner Machen was an outsider to the mainline Protestant establishment and hence may again have been alert to important trends that others were not seeing."[14]

---

[12] Stonehouse, *J. Gresham Machen*, 46.
[13] Ibid., 50. The professor was B. L. Gildersleeve, whose specialty was the history of American classical scholarship.
[14] Marsden, "Understanding J. Gresham Machen," 199.

Machen Was Wealthy

When he was twenty-one he inherited $50,000 from his maternal grandfather. To put that in perspective, his first *annual* salary at Princeton was $2,000. So he inherited twenty-five times an annual salary when he was twenty-one, and when he was thirty-five he inherited a similar amount when his father died. When he died, his assets totaled $250,000 dollars.[15] This explains why we can read time after time of Machen's funding ministry and publishing efforts with his own money.

As with most of us, therefore, the level at which Machen engaged the culture of his day was being powerfully shaped by the level of his upbringing and education. He went to Johns Hopkins University and majored in classics and then, with the urging of his pastor, went on to Princeton Seminary, even though he was not at all sure he would enter the ministry. And after seminary he spent a year in Germany studying New Testament with well-known German scholars.

The Threats and Blessings of the German University

Here Machen met modernism face to face and was shaken profoundly in his faith. Almost overpowering was the influence of Wilhelm Herrmann, the systematic theologian at Marburg who represented the best of what Machen would later oppose with all his might. Machen was not casting stones over a wall when he criticized modernism. He had been over the wall and was almost lured into the camp.

In 1905 he wrote home:

> The first time that I heard Herrmann may almost be described as an epoch in my life. Such an overpowering personality I think I almost never before encountered—overpowering in the sincerity of religious devotion. . . .
>
> My chief feeling with reference to him is already one of the deepest reverence. . . . I have been thrown all into confusion by what he says—so much deeper is his devotion to Christ than anything I have known in myself during the past few years. . . . Herrmann affirms very little of that which I have been accustomed to regard as essential to Christianity; yet there is no doubt in my mind but that he is a Christian, and a Christian of a peculiarly earnest type. He is a Christian not because he follows Christ as a moral teacher; but because his trust in Christ is (practically, if anything even more truly than theoretically) unbounded. . . .

---

[15] Stonehouse, *J. Gresham Machen*, 393.

Herrmann represents the dominant Ritschlian school. . . . Herrmann has shown me something of the *religious* power which lies back of this great movement, which is now making a fight even for the control of the Northern Presbyterian Church in America. In New England those who do not believe in the bodily Resurrection of Jesus are, generally speaking, religiously dead; in Germany, Herrmann has taught me that is by no means the case. He believes that Jesus is the one thing in all the world that inspires *absolute* confidence, and an *absolute*, joyful subjection; that through Jesus we come into communion with the living God and are made free from the world. It is the faith that is a real experience, a real revelation of God that saves us, not the faith that consists in accepting as true a lot of dogmas on the basis merely of what others have said. . . . *Das Verkehr des Christen mit Gott* is one of the greatest religious books I ever read. Perhaps Herrmann does not give the whole truth—I certainly hope he does not—at any rate he has gotten hold of something that has been sadly neglected in the church and in the orthodox theology. Perhaps he is something like the devout mystics of the middle ages—they were one-sided enough, but they raised a mighty protest against the coldness and deadness of the church and were forerunners of the Reformation.[16]

The Lasting Impact of His German Experience

What Machen seemed to find in Herrmann was what he had apparently not found either in his home or at Princeton, namely, passion and joy and exuberant trust in Christ. At Princeton he had found solid learning and civil, formal, careful, aristocratic presentations of a fairly cool Christianity. He eventually came to see that the truth of the Princeton theology was a firmer ground for life and joy. But at this stage the spirit in which it came, compared to Herrmann's spirit, almost cost evangelicalism one of its greatest defenders. There is a great lesson here for teachers and preachers: to hold young minds, there should be both intellectual credibility *and* joyful, passionate zeal for Christ.

This experience in Germany made a lasting impact on the way Machen carried on controversy. He said again and again that he had respect and sympathy for the modernist who could honestly no longer believe in the bodily resurrection or the virgin birth or the second coming, but it was the rejection of these things without openly admitting one's unbelief that angered Machen.

---

[16] Ibid., 106–8. This quote is a composite of excerpts from letters that year to his parents and brother.

For example, he said once that his problem with certain teachers at Union Seminary was their duplicity:

> There is my real quarrel with them. As for their difficulties with the Christian faith, I have profound sympathy for them, but not with their contemptuous treatment of the conscientious men who believe that a creed solemnly subscribed to is more than a scrap of paper.[17]

He wanted to deal with people in a straightforward manner, and take his opponents' arguments seriously if they would only be honest and open with their constituents and readers.

The Fruit of Doubt

His struggle with doubt gave him patience and empathy with others in the same situation. Twenty years later he wrote,

> Some of us have been through such struggle ourselves; some of us have known the blankness of doubt, the deadly discouragement, the perplexity of indecision, the vacillation between "faith diversified by doubt," and "doubt diversified by faith."[18]

Machen came through this time without losing his evangelical faith and was called to Princeton to teach New Testament, which he did from 1906 until he left to form Westminster in 1929. During that time he became a pillar of conservative, reformed orthodoxy and a strong apologist for biblical Christianity and an internationally acclaimed New Testament scholar with his book, *The Origin of Paul's Religion*, published in 1921 (still used as a text at Fuller Seminary when I went there in 1968), and then his most famous book, *The Virgin Birth of Christ* in 1930.

Was Machen a Fundamentalist?

Machen's years at Princeton were the two decades that are known for the ongoing modernist-fundamentalist controversy. We will see Machen's distinctive response to modernism if we contrast it with what was known most widely as fundamentalism. In the process of defining his response, the meaning of modernism will become clear.

---

[17] Ibid., 221–22.
[18] Ibid., 432.

He was seen as an ally by the fundamentalists, and his ecclesiastical opponents liked to make him "guilty" by association with them. But he did not accept the term for himself. In one sense, fundamentalists were simply those who "[singled] out certain great facts and doctrines [i.e., fundamentals] that had come under particular attack, [and] were concerned to emphasize their truth and to defend them."[19] But there was more attached to the term than that. And Machen didn't like it. He said:

> Do you suppose that I do regret my being called by a term that I greatly dislike, a "Fundamentalist"? Most certainly I do. But in the presence of a great common foe, I have little time to be attacking my brethren who stand with me in defense of the Word of God.[20]

What he didn't like was:

- the absence of historical perspective;
- the lack of appreciation of scholarship;
- the substitution of brief, skeletal creeds for the historic confessions;
- the lack of concern with precise formulation of Christian doctrine;
- the pietistic, perfectionist tendencies (i.e., hang-ups with smoking,[21] etc.);
- one-sided otherworldliness (i.e., a lack of effort to transform culture); and
- a penchant for futuristic chiliasm (or: premillennialism).

Machen was on the other side on all these issues. And so "he never spoke of himself as a Fundamentalist."[22]

Calvinism Is Christianity in Full Flower

But none of those issues goes to the heart of why he did not see himself as a fundamentalist. The issue is deeper and broader and gets at the root of how he fought modernism. The deepest difference goes back to Machen's profound indebtedness to Benjamin Warfield, who died

---

[19] Ibid., 336.

[20] Ibid., 337.

[21] In 1905, as his seminary days were coming to an end, he wrote, "The fellows are in my room now on the last Sunday night, smoking the cigars and eating the oranges which it has been the greatest delight I ever had to provide whenever possible. My idea of delight is a Princeton room full of fellows smoking. When I think what a wonderful aid tobacco is to friendship and Christian patience, I have sometimes regretted that I never began to smoke." Ibid., 85.

[22] Ibid., 337. See J. Gresham Machen, "Does Fundamentalism Obstruct Social Progress?" and Machen, "What Fundamentalism Stands For Now," in *J. Gresham Machen: Selected Shorter Writings*, ed. D. G. Hart (Phillipsburg, NJ: P&R, 2004), 109–22.

February 16, 1921. Machen wrote to his mother, "With all his glaring faults he was the greatest man I have known."[23]

In 1909, at the four hundredth anniversary of John Calvin's birth, Warfield gave an address that stirred Machen to the depths. Warfield made a plea that the Reformed Faith—Calvinism—is not a species of Christian theism alongside others but *is* Christianity come to full flower.

> Calvinism is not a specific variety of theistic thought, religious experience, [or] evangelical faith; but just the perfect expression of these things. The difference between it and other forms of Theism, religion, [and] evangelicalism is a difference not of kind but of degree. . . . It does not take its position then by the side of other types of things; it takes its place over them, as what they ought to be.[24]

So he says Lutheranism is "its sister type of Protestantism" and Arminianism is "its own rebellious daughter."[25] Calvinism's grasp of the supremacy of God in all of life enabled Machen to see that other forms of evangelicalism were all stages of grasping God that are yet in process of coming to a full and pure appreciation of his total God-centeredness.

What this came to mean for Machen was that his mission in defense of supernaturalistic Calvinism was nothing more or less than the defense of the Christian faith in its purest form. So his biggest problem with the term *fundamentalist* was that "it seems to suggest that we are adherents of some strange new sect, whereas in point of fact we are conscious simply of maintaining the historic Christian faith and of moving in the great central current of Christian life."[26]

He was invited to the presidency of Bryan Memorial University in 1927—a move that would have aligned him with fundamentalism outside the Reformed tradition. He answered:

> Thoroughly consistent Christianity, to my mind, is found only in the Reformed or Calvinist Faith; and consistent Christianity, I think, is the Christianity easiest to defend. Hence I never call myself a "Fundamentalist." . . .

---

[23] Stonehouse, *J. Gresham Machen*, 310. George Marsden quotes a letter from Machen on October 5, 1913, in which he said that Warfield was "himself, despite some very good qualities, a very heartless, selfish, domineering sort of man." Marsden, "Understanding J. Gresham Machen," 187. My interpretation of this is that there were things about Warfield that irritated Machen, but Warfield's strengths were such that they made these things pale in comparison.

[24] B. B. Warfield, "Calvinism," in *The Works of Benjamin B. Warfield* (Grand Rapids, MI: Baker, 2000), 9:355–56.

[25] Ibid., 177.

[26] Ibid., 337.

What I prefer to call myself is not a "Fundamentalist" but a "Calvinist"—that is, an adherent of the Reformed Faith. As such I regard myself as standing in the great central current of the Church's life—the current that flows down from the Word of God through Augustine and Calvin, and which has found noteworthy expression in America in the great tradition represented by Charles Hodge and Benjamin Breckinridge Warfield and the other representatives of the "Princeton School."[27]

Liberalism (Modernism) Is Another Religion

So Machen moved in a different world from most fundamentalists. And when he took on modernism, he took it on as a challenge to the whole of Reformed Christianity. His most important book in the debate was *Christianity and Liberalism*, published in 1923.

The title almost says it all: liberalism is not vying with fundamentalism as a species of Christianity. The book is not entitled *Fundamentalism and Liberalism*. Instead liberalism is vying with *Christianity* as a separate religion. He wrote the blurb for the book:

Liberalism on the one hand and the religion of the historic church on the other are not two varieties of the same religion, but two distinct religions proceeding from altogether separate roots.[28]

Stonehouse tells us that Machen's only regret is that he had not used the term *modernism* rather than *liberalism* in the book, since the word *liberalism* seemed to give too much credit to the phenomenon.[29] In Machen's vocabulary, these words refer to the same thing.

Now what was that?

Here again Machen did not move quickly with the fundamentalists to show that the modernists were people who denied certain fundamental Christian doctrines. That was true. But his analysis was wider and deeper. He approached the phenomenon of modernism first through an analysis of modern culture and the spirit of the age. He tried to think through the relationship between modernism and modernity.[30] He wanted to understand it from the inside as it were, on its own terms.

---

[27] Ibid., 428.
[28] Ibid., 342.
[29] Ibid., 343.
[30] Notice the difference in these two terms. *Modernism* is the technical word referring to the theological response to modernity, while *modernity* refers to what Machen calls "modern culture" with its technology, science, communications, transportation, inventions, pace, and dozens of other modern phenomena.

The Roots of Modernism in Modernity

Machen admits from the outset that "modern culture is a tremendous force."[31]

> Modern inventions and the industrialism that has been built upon them have given us in many respects a new world to live in . . . [and these material conditions] have been produced by mighty changes in the human mind. . . . The industrial world of today has been produced not by blind forces of nature but by the conscious activity of the human spirit; it has been produced by the achievements of science.[32]

The problem of modernity is that it has bred forces that are hostile to biblical faith and yet produced a world that believers readily embrace. Machen is exactly right to skewer us in this dilemma when he says,

> We cannot without inconsistency employ the printing-press, the railroad, the telegraph [we in the twenty-first century would say computers, jets, and cell phones] in the propagation of our gospel, and at the same time denounce as evil those activities of the human mind that produced these things.[33]

The Impulses of Modernity

So he calls for a critical assessment of modernity.[34] The negative impulses he sees that all lead to modernism are (1) a suspicion of the past that is natural in view of the stunning advances of recent decades; it does seem as if the past is of relatively little value; (2) skepticism about truth and a replacement of the category of true with the category of useful (pragmatism, utilitarianism); the question of what works seems to be more scientifically productive; (3) the denial that the supernatural, if there is any such thing, can break into the world.

Machen credits modernism—the theological response to this challenge of modernity—with trying to come to terms with the real problem of the age. "What is the relation between Christianity and modern

---

[31] J. Gresham Machen, "Christianity and Culture," in *What Is Christianity? and Other Addresses*, ed. Ned Stonehouse (Grand Rapids, MI: Eerdmans, 1951), 166.

[32] J. Gresham Machen, *Christianity and Liberalism* (1923; repr., Grand Rapids, MI: Eerdmans, 1992), 3.

[33] Machen, "Christianity and Culture," 159.

[34] "Modern culture is a mighty force; it is either helpful to the gospel or else it is a deadly enemy of the gospel. For making it helpful neither wholesale denunciation nor wholesale acceptance is in place; careful discrimination is required, and such discrimination requires intellectual effort. Here lies a supreme duty of the modern Church." J. Gresham Machen, *The New Testament: An Introduction to Its Literature and History* (Edinburgh: Banner of Truth, 1976), 377–78.

culture; may Christianity be maintained in a scientific age? It is this problem which modern liberalism attempts to solve."[35]

In trying to solve the problem, liberalism, that is, modernism, has joined modernity in minimizing the significance of the past in favor of newer impulses, has accepted the utilitarian view of truth, and has surrendered supernaturalism. All three compromises with the spirit of modernity work together to produce the modernist spirit in religion.

Modernism Is Not Ideas but an Atmosphere of Accommodation

And it is a spirit more than a set of doctrines or denials. This is why Machen never tired of pointing out the dangers of what he called "indifferentism" and "latitudinarianism"[36] as well as the outright denials of the resurrection or the virgin birth or the inspiration of Scripture. The spirit of modernism is not a set of ideas but an atmosphere that shifts with what is useful from time to time.

One of their own number, John A. MacCallum, an outspoken modernist minister in Philadelphia, said in a newspaper article in 1923,

> [The liberals] have accepted the enlarged view of the universe which has been established by modern astronomy, geology and biology. Instead of blindly denying scientific facts as the obscurantists have always done, they have adjusted themselves to them, and in so doing have increased their faith and urbanity and consequently extended their influence, particularly with the educated classes. . . . Liberalism is an atmosphere rather than a series of formulas.[37]

When the preference for what is new combines with a naturalistic bias and a skepticism about finding abiding truth, the stage is set for the worst abuses of religious language and the worst manipulations of historic confessions. In essence, what the modernists do is not throw out Christianity but reinterpret the creeds and give old words new meanings. That is, they make them into symbols for ever-changing meanings.

Thus the virgin birth is one theory of the incarnation, the bodily resurrection is one theory of the resurrection, and so on. The old "facts"

---

[35] Machen, *Christianity and Liberalism*, 6.
[36] For example, he says that in German universities you find "those forces which underlie all the doctrinal indifferentism in Great Britain and in this country which really presents the serious danger of the life of our Church." Stonehouse, *J. Gresham Machen*, 241.
[37] Ibid., 347.

don't correspond to anything permanent. They symbolize general principles of religion. And those symbols are arrived at by what is useful or helpful, not by what is true. If they are useful for one generation, good; and if not for another, then they may be exchanged.

Denying Truth by Affirming It Only as Useful

This meant that in the Presbyterian Church of Machen's day, there were hundreds who would not deny the Confession of Faith but by virtue of this modernistic spirit had given it up even though they'd signed it. One of the most jolting and penetrating statements of Machen on this issue is found in his book *What Is Faith?*:

> It makes very little difference how much or how little of the creeds of the Church the Modernist preacher affirms, or how much or how little of the Biblical teaching from which the creeds are derived. He might affirm every jot and tittle of the Westminster Confession, for example, and yet be separated by a great gulf from the Reformed Faith. It is not that part is denied and the rest affirmed; but all is denied, because all is affirmed merely as useful or symbolic and not as true.[38]

Modernistic Hostility to Definitions

This utilitarian view of history and language leads to evasive, vague language that enables the modernist to mislead people into thinking he is still orthodox.

> This temper of mind is hostile to precise definitions. Indeed nothing makes a man more unpopular in the controversies of the present day than an insistence upon definition of terms. . . . Men discourse very eloquently today upon such subjects as God, religion, Christianity, atonement, redemption, faith; but are greatly incensed when they are asked to tell in simple language what they mean by these terms.[39]

Machen's critique of the spirit of modernism that flows from its marriage to modernity comes from two sides. First, internally—does this modern culture really commend itself? Second, externally—does the history of Christ and the apostles really allow for such a modernistic Christianity? Or is it an alien religion?

---

[38] Machen, *What Is Faith?* (orig. 1925; Edinburgh: Banner of Truth, 1991), 34.
[39] Ibid., 13–14.

Is Modernity as Wonderful as We Think?

Machen asks: Granted, we are better off in material things because of modernity, but are we better off in the realm of the spirit and the distinctly human aspects of life?

> The improvement appears in the physical conditions of life, but in the spiritual realm there is a corresponding loss. The loss is clearest, perhaps, in the realm of art. Despite the mighty revolution which has been produced in the external condition of life, no great poet is now living to celebrate the change; humanity has suddenly become dumb. Gone, too, are the great painters and the great musicians and the great sculptors. The art that still subsists is largely imitative, and where it is not imitative it is usually bizarre.[40]

He argues that a "drab utilitarianism" destroys the higher aspirations of the soul and results in an unparalleled impoverishment of human life.[41] When you take away any objective norm of truth, you take away the only means of measuring movement from lesser to greater or worse to better. One doctrine is as good as any contradictory doctrine "provided it suits a particular generation or a particular group of persons." All that's left without truth are the "meaningless changes of a kaleidoscope."[42] Without a sense of progress in view of an objective truth, life becomes less and less, not more and more.

In view of these and other observations about the effects of modernity and modernism, Machen asks modern man if he can be so sure that the past and the truth and the supernatural are really as cheap and expendable as he thought.

> In view of the lamentable defects of modern life, a type of religion certainly should not be commended simply because it is modern or condemned simply because it is old. On the contrary, the condition of mankind is such that one may well ask what it is that made the men of past generations so great and the men of the present generations so small.[43]

Thus Machen seeks to understand and critique modernity and modernism from the inside—and this set him off by and large from the fundamentalists of his day.

---

[40] Machen, *Christianity and Liberalism*, 10.
[41] Ibid., 11–12.
[42] Machen, *What Is Faith?*, 32.
[43] Machen, *Christianity and Liberalism*, 15.

Facts Matter

Then from the outside Machen wields his powers as a historian and a student of the New Testament. He argues on historical grounds that from the beginning, the church was a witnessing church (Acts 1:8) and a church devoted to the apostles' teaching. In other words, her life was built on events without which there would be no Christianity. These events demand faithful witnesses who tell the objective truth about the events since they are essential. And the life of the church was built on the apostles' teaching (Acts 2:42), the authoritative interpretation of the events.

He argues powerfully in the chapter on "Doctrine" in *Christianity and Liberalism* that Paul made much of the truth of his message and the need to get it exactly right, even if the messenger was not exactly right. For example, in Philippians he was tolerant of those who with bad motives preached in order to make his imprisonment worse—because they were saying the objective truth about Christ.

In Galatians, however, he was not tolerant but pronounced a curse on his opponents—because they were getting the message objectively wrong. They were telling Gentiles that works of the flesh would complete God's justifying action in their lives that had begun by faith and the Spirit. It may seem like a triviality since both the Judaizers and Paul would have agreed on dozens of precious things including the necessity of faith for salvation. But it was not trivial. And with this kind of historical observation and argument from the New Testament, Machen shows that truth and objectivity and doctrine are not optional in grasping and spreading Christianity.

> As over against . . . [the pragmatist, modernist] attitude, we believers in historic Christianity maintain the objectivity of truth. . . . Theology, we hold, is not an attempt to express in merely symbolic terms an inner experience which must be expressed in different terms in subsequent generations; but it is a setting forth of those facts upon which experience is based.[44]

Therefore his response to modernism stands: It is not a different kind of Christianity. It is not Christianity at all. "The chief modern rival of Christianity is 'liberalism' . . . at every point the two movements are in

---

[44] Machen, *What Is Faith?*, 32.

direct opposition."[45] The foundational truths have been surrendered; or worse, the concept of truth has been surrendered to pragmatism, so that even affirmations are denials, because they are affirmed as useful but not as true.

What Machen Saw Is Still with Us . . . So Is God

I don't think the structure of the modernism of Machen's day is too different from the postmodernism of our day. In some churches the triumph of modernism is complete. It is still a menace at the door of all our churches and schools and agencies. One of our great protections will be the awareness of stories like Machen's—the enemy he faced, the battle he fought, the weapons he used (and failed to use), the losses he sustained, the price he paid, and the triumphs he wrought. If we do not know history, we will be weak and poor in our efforts to be faithful in our day.

Our hope for the church and for the spread of the true gospel lies not ultimately in our strategies but in God. And there is every hope that he will triumph.

> That Church is still alive; an unbroken spiritual descent connects us with those whom Jesus commissioned. Times have changed in many respects, new problems must be faced and new difficulties overcome, but the same message must still be proclaimed to a lost world. Today we have need of all our faith; unbelief and error have perplexed us sore; strife and hatred have set the world aflame. There is only one hope, but that hope is sure. God has never deserted his church; his promise never fails.[46]

Lessons for Our Day

When we step back now and look at Machen's life and work, what can we learn for our day?

1. Machen's life and thought issues a call for all of us to be honest, open, clear, straightforward, and guileless in our use of language. He challenges us, as does the apostle Paul (2 Cor. 2:17; 4:2; Eph. 4:25; 1 Thess. 2:3–4), to say what we mean and mean what we say, and to repudiate duplicity, trickery, sham, verbal manipulating, sidestepping, and evasion.

[45] Machen, *Christianity and Liberalism*, 53.
[46] Stonehouse, *J. Gresham Machen*, 386.

Machen alerts us to the dangers of the utilitarian uses of moral and religious language. They are still around in our day. For example, Roy Beck quoted Gregory King, spokesman for the Human Rights Campaign Fund, the nation's largest homosexual advocacy group, who told the *Washington Times*, "I personally think that most lesbian and gay Americans support traditional family and American values," which he defined as "tolerance, concern, support, and a sense of community."[47]

This is an example of how words with moral connotations have been co-opted by special-interest groups to gain the moral high ground without moral content. They sound like values, but they are empty. "Tolerance" for what? All things? Which things? The standards are not defined. "Concern" for what? Expressed in what way? Redemptive opposition or sympathetic endorsement? The standard is not defined. "Support" for what? For the behavior that is destructive and wrong? Or for the person who admits the behavior is wrong and is struggling valiantly to overcome it? The object is not defined. "Community" with what standards of unification? Common endorsements of behavior? Common vision of what is right and wrong? Common indifference to what is right and wrong? Again, the standards are not defined.

Yet the opposite of each of these four "family values" (intolerant, unconcerned, oppressive, self-centered) all carry such negative connotations that it is difficult to show in sound bites why the four "values" asserted by the homosexual community are inadequate and even may be wrong as they use them.

All you have is words driven by a utilitarian view of language where honesty and truth are not paramount. Machen shows us that this is not new and that it is destructive to the church and the cause of Christ.

2. Machen alerts us to the doctrinal "indifferentism" of our day and to the fact that we almost take it for granted that utilitarian thinking is the only hope for success and that preaching or teaching doctrine is a prescription for failure. This skepticism about the value of doctrine is owing to bad preaching that is not passionate and clear and interesting and suspenseful and authentic about the glories of God, his way of salvation, and how it all connects with real life. "The dogma is the drama,"[48] as Dorothy Sayers said, and the reason

---

[47] *Christianity Today* 36 (November 9, 1992): 21.
[48] "Official Christianity, of late years, has been having what is known as 'a bad press.' We are constantly assured that the churches are empty because preachers insist too much upon   doctrine—dull dogma as

we don't show this to people in our preaching and teaching and writing is that we have not seen and felt the greatness of the glory of God and all his teachings. Preaching doctrine should not be confusing or boring. Machen says:

> That error, unquestionably, should be avoided. But it should be avoided not by the abandonment of doctrinal preaching, but by our making doctrinal preaching real *preaching*. The preacher should present to his congregation the doctrine that the Holy Scripture contains; but he should fire the presentation of that doctrine with the devotion of the heart, and he should show how it can be made fruitful for Christian life.[49]

3. Machen's life teaches us the importance of founding and maintaining institutions in the preservation and spreading of the true gospel.

Visions of truth and worldview like Machen's are preserved not just in the minds of a few disciples but in charters and covenants and enclaves and books and journals and durable organizations and long-term official commitments. Mark Noll observes, "The genius of Old Princeton had been its embodiment of confessional Calvinism in great institutions: the school itself, the *Princeton Review*, Hodge's *Systematic Theology*, and the Old School party among the northern Presbyterians."[50]

Founding and maintaining institutions are, of course, not the only way of spreading the truth of Christ in the world. And in the name of preserving the truth, they often come to stand in the way of spreading the truth. Nevertheless they are not necessarily bad and are probably a good tension with the more charismatic, spontaneous focus on individualism in ministry.

I personally give God thanks with all my heart for the institutions of the family that I grew up in, and for Wheaton College, and for Fuller Seminary, and for the church that I now serve. By God's grace these institutions preserved and embodied for me the forces of truth and righteousness in such a way that I have been deeply shaped by them. I

---

people call it. The fact is the precise opposite. It is the neglect of dogma that makes for dullness. The Christian faith is the most exciting drama that ever staggered the imagination of man—and the dogma is the drama." Dorothy L. Sayers, "The Greatest Story Ever Staged," in *Creed or Chaos? Why Christians Must Choose Either Dogma or Disaster (Or, Why It Really Does Matter What You Believe)* (repr., Bedford, NH: Sophia Institute Press, 1995).

[49] J. Gresham Machen, "Christian Scholarship and the Building Up of the Church," in *What Is Christianity?*, 139.

[50] Mark Noll, "The Spirit of Old Princeton and the OPC," in *Pressing toward the Mark*, ed. Dennison and Gamble, 245.

think if each person gives serious thought to how he came to have the convictions and values and dreams that he has, he will see that virtually all of us owe much of what we are to institutions, without denying or minimizing that it has been individual teachers, friends, and authors in and around those institutions who have been the immediate mediators of truths and goodness and beauty.

4. Machen's experience calls us to have patience with young strugglers who are having doubts about Christianity. Machen was saved for the kingdom and the church by faculty and parents who gave him room to work it all through. Machen says that he finally found victory and tranquility of spirit "because of the profound and constant sympathy of others."[51]

This is illustrated especially from his mother and father, who responded with love and patience to his fears that he could not enter the ministry because of his doubts. His mother wrote on January 21, 1906, while Machen was in Germany,

> But one thing I can assure you of—that *nothing* that you could do could keep me from loving you—*nothing*. It is easy enough to grieve me. Perhaps I worry too much. But my love for my boy is absolutely indestructible. Rely on that whatever comes. And I have faith in you too and believe that the strength will come to you for your work whatever it may be, and that the way will be opened.[52]

His father wrote on January 26, 1906, "None of the years of study you have had can ever be properly considered as 'wasted' no matter what field of work you may ultimately enter upon. . . . The pecuniary question you need not bother about. I can assure you on that point."[53]

Machen credits the power of his parents in his life in a letter to his father, dated February 4, 1906:

> Without what I got from you and Mother I should long since have given up all thoughts of religion or of a moral life. . . . The only thing that enables me to get any benefit out of my opportunities here is the continual presence with me in spirit of you and Mother and the Christian teaching which you have given me.[54]

---

[51] Ibid., 129.
[52] Ibid., 113.
[53] Ibid., 114.
[54] Ibid., 116–17.

Not only his parents but also his colleagues at Princeton in the first several years steadied his hand and preserved his orthodox faith. He gives amazing tribute to his closest colleague, William Armstrong, in his installation address as Assistant Professor of New Testament on May 3, 1915: "The assistance that he has given me in the establishment of my Christian faith has been simply incalculable."[55]

On July 14, 1906, Armstrong wrote to Machen with an offer to teach that was flexible enough to allow him to begin at Princeton on a trial basis even with some of his doubts unsettled.

> You do not have to be licensed, or ordained or even come under the care of a presbytery. You can start upon the work just as you are. And in regard to your theological opinions you do not have to make any pledge. You are not expected to have reached final conclusion on all matters in this field. Only in your teaching will you be expected to stand on the broad principles of Reformed Theology and in particular on the authority of the Scriptures in religious matters—not that your teaching should be different from your personal convictions—but simply that in matters not finally settled you would await decision before departing from the position occupied by the Seminary. The whole matter reduces itself in simple good faith. Should you find after trying it that you could not teach in the Seminary because you had reached conclusions in your study which made it impossible for you to uphold its position you would simply say so.[56]

Machen would not have been allowed to stay at Princeton if he had come out on the wrong side or stayed indefinitely on the fence. The compromise of an institution's fidelity and the misuse of academic freedom happens when doctrinal and ethical doubts are kept secret, or worse, when lurking denials are put forward as affirmations. Honest, humble struggles can be sustained for some season. But the duplicity that hides secret denials will destroy an institution and a soul.

5. Machen's interaction with modernism shows the value of a God-centered vision of all reality—a worldview, a theology, that is driven by the supremacy of God in all of life. A God-centered worldview gives balance and stability in dealing with error. It enables us to see how an error relates to the larger issues of life and thought. Machen was set off

---

[55] Ibid., 209.
[56] Stonehouse, *J. Gresham Machen*, 133.

from the fundamentalists by this consistently God-centered view of all things. His critique of modernism went deeper and farther because his vision of God caused him to see the problem in a deeper and broader context. The sovereignty of God and his supremacy over all of life causes one to see everything in relation to more things because they all relate to God and God relates to all things.

6. *Machen's engagement in the debates of his day points us to the value and necessity of controversy.* In a lecture delivered in London on June 17, 1932, Machen defended engagement in controversy:

> Men tell us that our preaching should be positive and not negative, that we can preach the truth without attacking error. But if we follow that advice we shall have to close our Bible and desert its teachings. The New Testament is a polemic book almost from beginning to end.
>
> Some years ago I was in a company of teachers of the Bible in the colleges and other educational institutions of America. One of the most eminent theological professors in the country made an address. In it he admitted that there are unfortunate controversies about doctrine in the Epistles of Paul; but, said he in effect, the real essence of Paul's teaching is found in the hymn to Christian love in the thirteenth chapter of I Corinthians; and we can avoid controversy today, if we will only devote the chief attention to that inspiring hymn.
>
> In reply, I am bound to say that the example was singularly ill-chosen. That hymn to Christian love is in the midst of a great polemic passage; it would never have been written if Paul had been opposed to controversy with error in the Church. It was because his soul was stirred within him by a wrong use of the spiritual gifts that he was able to write that glorious hymn. So it is always in the Church. Every really great Christian utterance, it may almost be said, is born in controversy. It is when men have felt compelled to take a stand against error that they have risen to the really great heights in the celebration of truth.[57]

7. *We learn from Machen the inevitability and pain of criticism, even from our brothers.* His colleague, Charles Erdman, publicly accused Machen of "unkindness, suspicion, bitterness and intolerance."[58] When he voted against a church resolution in favor of national Pro-

---

[57] J. Gresham Machen, "Christian Scholarship and the Defense of the New Testament," in *What Is Christianity?*, 132–33. See on this same point Machen, *What Is Faith?*, 41–42; and Machen, *Christianity and Liberalism*, 17.

[58] Stonehouse, *J. Gresham Machen*, 375.

hibition and the Eighteenth Amendment, he was criticized as a secret drunkard and promoter of vice.[59] Since he was single, he was criticized as being naïve and unaware of the responsibilities of the family.[60]

There is in all of us the desire to be liked by others. If it is strong enough, we may go to unwise lengths to avoid criticism. We may even think that we can be kind enough to everyone to avoid criticism. This will not work, especially if we have any public role. It is true that the Bible says that we are to let our light shine that men might see our good deeds and give glory to God (Matt. 5:16). And it is true that we are to silence the ignorance of foolish men by our good deeds (1 Pet. 2:15). But there is also the truth that the world called the most loving Master of the house Beelzebul (Matt. 10:25).

You cannot be kind enough and merciful enough that no one will criticize you. For example, whatever one may think of the spirituality or theology of Mother Teresa (1910–1997), it takes one's breath away to hear feminist Germain Greer criticize her by saying she is a "religious imperialist."

> At my convent school, the pious nuns who always spoke softly and inclined their heads with a small, patient smile were the ones to fear. They became the mother superiors. Mother Teresa is not content with running a convent; she runs an order of Mother Teresa clones, which operates world-wide. In anyone less holy, this would be seen as an obscene ego trip. . . . Mother Teresa epitomizes for me the blinkered charitableness upon which we pride ourselves and for which we expect reward in this world and the next. There is very little on earth that I hate more than I hate that.[61]

In other words, let us forsake all notions that a life devoted to compassion will be spared criticism.

8. His early death at the age of fifty-five reminds us to find the pace to finish the race. God is sovereign and works all our foolishness together for his glory. But our duty and biblical responsibility is to work in such a way as to not allow less important demands of the present to steal our strength—and our life—that might serve some greater demand in the years to come. It is hard to believe that Machen made a wise decision to go to North Dakota during the Christmas break of 1936–1937

---

[59] Ibid., 387.

[60] Ibid., 413.

[61] Germain Greer, quoted in *First Things* 29 (January 1993): 65.

when he was "deadly tired" and needed rest so badly. It is also a rebuke that he was about thirty pounds overweight.[62]

Charles Spurgeon, the London pastor in the nineteenth century, had his own struggles with pace and health. He died at the age of fifty-seven. But he gives wonderful counsel to those who are prone to neglect the body for the sake of mental labor:

> Sedentary habits have tendency to create despondency. . . . To sit long in one posture, poring over a book, or driving a quill, is in itself a taxing of nature; but add to this a badly ventilated chamber, a body which has long been without muscular exercise, and a heart burdened with many cares, and we have all the elements for preparing a seething cauldron of despair, especially in the months of fog. . . . He who forgets the humming of the bees among the heather, the cooing of the wood-pigeons in the forest, the song of birds in the woods, the rippling of rills among the rushes, the sighing of the wind among the pines, needs not wonder if his heart forgets to sing and his soul grows heavy. A day's breathing of fresh air upon the hills, or a few hours' ramble in the beech woods' umbrageous calm, would sweep the cobwebs out of the brain of scores of our toiling ministers who are not but half alive. A mouthful of sea air, or a stiff walk in the wind's face would not give grace to the soul, but it would yield oxygen to the body, which is next best.[63]

One lesson we should learn is to be accountable to a group of friends who will have the courage and the authority to tell us, if necessary, to work and eat more wisely. Machen was not accountable in this way. Ned Stonehouse, his fellow teacher at Westminster at the end, said, "There was no one of sufficient influence to constrain him to curtail his program to any significant degree."[64] Who knows what a great difference it would have made for the whole cause of evangelicalism if Machen had lived and worked another twenty years?

9. *Machen's approach to apologetics raises the question whether our labors for the sake of the lost should not only involve direct attempts to present the gospel, but also indirect attempts to remove obstacles in the culture that make faith more difficult.* Machen certainly saw the intellectual challenge of his day and rose to meet it with his

---

[62] He was 5' 8" tall and for most of his life weighed about 150 pounds. But in the last ten years he allowed himself to reach 180. Stonehouse, *J. Gresham Machen*, 506.

[63] Charles Spurgeon, *Lectures to My Students* (Grand Rapids, MI: Zondervan, 1972), 158.

[64] Stonehouse, *J. Gresham Machen*, 506.

remarkable intellectual powers. He saw that an intellectual cultural atmosphere uncongenial to the categories of truth will make the spread of the gospel all the harder. One of the most provocative aspects of Machen's thought is his contention that apologetics involves preparing a culture more congenial to the gospel.

> It is true that the decisive thing is the regenerative power of God. That can overcome all lack of preparation, and the absence of that makes even the best preparation useless. but as a matter of fact God usually exerts that power in connection with certain prior conditions of the human mind, and it should be ours to create, so far as we can, with the help of God, those favorable conditions for the reception of the gospel. False ideas are the greatest obstacles to the reception of the gospel. We may preach with all the fervor of a reformer and yet succeed only in winning a straggler here and there, if we permit the whole collective thought of the nation or of the world to be controlled by ideas which, by the resistless force of logic, prevent Christianity from being regarded as anything more than a harmless delusion. Under such circumstances, what God desires us to do is to destroy the obstacle at its root. . . . What is today a matter of academic speculation begins tomorrow to move armies and pull down empires. In that second stage, it has gone too far to be combated; the time to stop it was when it was still a matter of impassionate debate. So as Christians we should try to mould the thought of the world in such a way as to make the acceptance of Christianity something more than a logical absurdity. . . . What more pressing duty than for those who have received the mighty experience of regeneration, who, therefore, do not, like the world, neglect that whole series of vitally relevant facts which is embraced in Christian experience— what more pressing duty than for these men to make themselves masters of the thought of the world in order to make it an instrument of truth instead of error?[65]

Is there biblical warrant for this goal in 1 Peter 2:15? "This is the will of God, that by doing good you should put to silence the ignorance of foolish people." We are to silence the ignorance of foolish people by our good deeds; that is, we are to stop the spread of falsehood by powerful evidence to the contrary. Or is there evidence for Machen's view in Ephesians 5:11? "Take no part in the unfruitful works of darkness, but instead expose them." Or should we find support in Matthew 5:14–16?

---

[65] Machen, "Christianity and Culture," 162–63.

> You are the light of the world. A city set on a hill cannot be hidden. Nor do people light a lamp and put it under a basket, but on a stand, and it gives light to all in the house. In the same way, let your light shine before others, so that they may see your good works and give glory to your Father who is in heaven.

Does this light and salt include spreading the preservative idea that there is truth and beauty and valid knowing? Or perhaps most plainly, we should find support for Machen's view in 2 Corinthians 10:4–5. "The weapons of our warfare are not of the flesh but have divine power to destroy strongholds. We destroy arguments and every lofty opinion raised against the knowledge of God, and take every thought captive to obey Christ."

Is Machen's Idea Backward?

In one sense this idea of transforming culture so that the gospel is more readily believed may sound backward. In world missions the gospel comes first, before the culture is transformed. Only then, after the gospel is received, is there set in motion a culture-shaping power that in several generations may result in changing some worldview issues in the culture that make Christianity less foreign even to the nonbeliever, so that there are fewer obstacles to overcome.

But this process is not a straight line to glory on earth (some saved → culture altered → more saved → culture more altered, etc.). The process seems to ebb and flow as generations come and go. Being born and living in that ebb and flow, one must ask: Is it a crucial ministry to engage in debate at foundational levels in order to slow the process of deterioration of gospel-friendly assumptions, and perhaps hasten the reestablishing of assumptions that would make Christianity objectively conceivable and thus more capable of embracing?

The New Testament is a first-generation document. It was not written into a situation where the gospel had been known and believed for centuries and where the culture may have been partially transformed, then had degenerated, and was now in need of another movement of transformation. But there is an analogy to this kind of cultural situation in the Old Testament. The people of God did indeed experience the ebb and flow of being changed by the Word of God, and then drifting away from it, and coming back. So we might see in some of the reforming actions of the Old Testament an analogy to what Machen meant by preparing the culture to make it more receptive to the truth of God. For example, one might think of the removal of the high places by the kings (2 Kings 18:4), or the putting away of foreign wives by the post-exilic Jews (Ezra 10:11).

Machen may have put too much hope in the intellectual power of the church to transform the mind-set of a nation and make evangelism easier. In his speaking of renaissance and revival coming together,[66] he may have put "renaissance" in too prominent a position. I only say this as a caution that others have seen too,[67] not as a final judgment. However, it may be that in our even more anti-intellectual world of the twenty-first century, we would do well to listen to Machen here rather than criticize him.

10. Should we learn, indirectly from the story of Machen's life, that prayer must be foundational to the use of intellectual power? I ask it as a question because I am perplexed. It is strange that Machen's friend and close associate, Ned Stonehouse, in five hundred pages of sympathetic *Memoir*, said nothing about Machen's prayer life. And in the complete twenty-four-page list of Machen's writings in *Pressing toward the Mark: Essays Commemorating Fifty Years of the Orthodox Presbyterian Church*, I found no essay or book on the subject of prayer, though there is a section on prayer in *The New Testament: An Introduction to Its Literature and History*.[68]

Nor is there any reference to his devotional life—meditating on the Word for his own encouragement and strength. Nor is there any reference to personal worship and rarely to corporate worship as a driving force in his life. It seems as though all was swallowed up in the intellectual defense of faith. One wonders whether some ground may have been lost by fighting instead of praying. Of course, he may have had a vital personal prayer life—hidden in accord with the words of the Lord, "When you pray, go into your room and shut the door and pray to your Father who is in secret" (Matt. 6:6).

---

[66] Machen, "Christianity and Culture," 200; Machen, *What Is Christianity?*, 118; and Machen, *What Is Faith?*, 18.

[67] George Marsden observes, "Regarding Common Sense philosophy: as I have argued elsewhere, I believe it led Machen to overestimate the prowess of rational argument and underestimate the importance of point of view. Nonetheless, I also think that it helped Machen recognize some trends that few other mainline Protestant thinkers seemed worried about at the time. . . . Probably he overestimated the degree to which the task of the church in the twentieth century should be an intellectual one. On the other hand, I am convinced that he was right that many of his Christian contemporaries were underestimating the intellectual crisis they faced." Marsden, "Understanding J. Gresham Machen," 198–99.

[68] Machen, *The New Testament*, 319–29.

But that in all his writings he would not take up that topic, and that Stonehouse would not consider it worthy of highlighting as one of the powerful nerve centers of his life and thought, is disconcerting in view of Machen's being a biblically saturated warrior for the Word that commands "watch and pray" as the heart of the warfare. Whether from silence about his prayer life or absence of its centrality, let us learn that without vital prayer, the fruitfulness of our labors will be less and our spiritual vision will be impaired.

11. We learn that God uses men who are persistently flawed. Machen seemed to have a personality that alienated people too easily. The committee that did not recommend him to the chair of Apologetics at Princeton referred to his "temperamental idiosyncrasies."[69] He seems to have had "a flaring temper and a propensity to make strong remarks about individuals with whom he disagreed."[70]

François de Fénelon, the seventeenth-century French bishop, spoke soberly and perceptively on the imperfections of the saints: "It should be remembered that even the best of people leave much to be desired, and we must not expect too much. . . . Do not allow yourself to turn away from people because of their imperfections. . . . I have found that God leaves, even in the most spiritual people, certain weaknesses which seem to be entirely out of place."[71]

12. We should learn from Machen the dangers of bringing blind spots with us from our cultural background. Machen may have lived at a level of cultural wealth and comfort that made it hard for him to see and feel the painful side of being poor and living without the freedom and luxury to travel to Europe repeatedly and go to hotels in order to have quiet for writing. The privations and pressures of the urban poor were so far from Machen's experience that the issue of how to minister more immediately did not press him as hard as it might have others, and so left him perhaps to develop his apologetic in a world cut off in significant measure from the questions of how it relates to the poor and uneducated.

Again I say this with some hesitancy, because all of us are limited by the cultural level at which we live. We see only so many hurts and problems. There are a hundred blind spots for every clear insight.

---

[69] Stonehouse, *J. Gresham Machen*, 389.
[70] Marsden, "Understanding J. Gresham Machen," 186. See note 23.
[71] Quoted in Clay Sterrett, "Hanging Tough," *Faith and Renewal* 16 (January/February 1992): 21.

Machen did give significant thought to the whole issue of education for children,[72] whether or not he faced the complexities of how to tackle the problems of the cities.

Hope in God's Sovereignty through Human Shortcomings

The overarching lesson to be learned from Machen's mixture of weaknesses and strengths is that God reigns over his church and over the world in such a way that he weaves the weaknesses and the strengths of his people with infinite wisdom into a fabric history that displays the full range of his glories. His all-inclusive plan is always more hopeful than we think in the darkest hours of history, and it is always more intermixed with human sin and weakness than we can see in its brightest hours. This means that we should renounce all triumphalism in the bright seasons and renounce all despair in the dark seasons.

When all seems to be going our way, we should hear the words of James 4:14–15, "You do not know what tomorrow will bring. What is your life? For you are a mist that appears for a little time and then vanishes. Instead you ought to say, 'If the Lord wills, we will live and do this or that.'" And when all seems to be going against us, we should hear the words of 1 Corinthians 15:58, "Be steadfast, immovable, always abounding in the work of the Lord, knowing that in the Lord your labor is not in vain."

---

[72] His essay "The Necessity of the Christian School" is a politically engaged and culturally sensitive plea for the national benefit of such schools as well as the benefit to the advance of the gospel. Machen, *Selected Shorter Writings*, ed. Hart, 161–73.

Both these extremes he avoided; he was sublime in action, lowly in mind; inaccessible in virtue, most accessible in intercourse; gentle, free from anger, sympathetic, sweet in words, sweeter in disposition; angelic in appearance, more angelic in mind; calm in rebuke, persuasive in praise, without spoiling the good effect of either by excess, but rebuking with the tenderness of a father, praising with the dignity of a ruler, his tenderness was not dissipated, nor his severity sour; for the one was reasonable, the other prudent, and both truly wise; his disposition sufficed for the training of his spiritual children, with very little need of words; his words with very little need of the rod, and his moderate use of the rod with still less for the knife.

Gregory of Nazianzus
Oration 21: On Athanasius of Alexandria

Conclusion

Contending for Our All:
A Golden Opportunity for Love

Contending for our all cannot be done in a way that contradicts the character of our all—namely, Jesus Christ. This means that when we contend for the fullness of Christ with our lips, we must confirm the love of Christ with our lives. All three of our swans knew this and labored to practice it.

How Athanasius "Snatched the Whole World from the Jaws of Satan"

Athanasius did not gloat over his emerging triumph in the doctrinal battle for the deity of Christ. He had not loved controversy. Victory was not his first delight. The worship of the divine Christ by the unified people of Christ was Athanasius's great joy. Not long after Athanasius died, Gregory of Nazianzus described how merciful Athanasius was with those who had opposed him. On his return to Alexandria from the third exile, he enjoyed the full authority of a beloved bishop. Nevertheless, "those who had been wronged he set free from oppression, making no distinction as to whether they were of his own or of the opposite party. . . . He treated so mildly and gently those who had injured him, that even they themselves, if I may say so, did not find his restoration distasteful."[1]

As the tide turned his way, Athanasius aimed at reconciliation, not retaliation. In the months of peace (February 362–October 23, 362)

---

[1] Gregory of Nazianzus, *Oration 21: On Athanasius of Alexandria*, in *Select Orations, Sermons, Letters; Dogmatic Treatises*, in *Nicene and Post-Nicene Fathers* (NPNF), ed. Philip Shaff and Henry Wace, 2nd series (Grand Rapids, MI: Eerdmans, 1955), 7:278 ¶¶30–31.

before his final brief exiles, he called a crucial council in Alexandria. The conciliatory spirit of this council was decisive in its redemptive effect on the entire movement toward orthodoxy.

> The importance of the Council is out of all proportion either to the number of bishops who took part in it or to the scale of its documentary records. Jerome (*adv. Lucif.* 20) goes so far as to say that by its judicious conciliation it "snatched the whole world from the jaws of Satan." . . . He saw that victory was not to be won by smiting men who were ready for peace, that the cause of Christ was not to be furthered by breaking the bruised reed and quenching the smoking flax. . . . The Council then is justly recognized as the crown of the career of Athanasius, for its resolutions and its Letter unmistakably proceed from him alone, and none but he could have tempered the fiery zeal of the confessors and taught them to distinguish friend from foe.[2]

All over the empire the exiles were returning, and councils were being held repudiating Arianism and affirming the orthodoxy of Nicaea. Archibald Robertson tells us that these councils followed the lead of Athanasius in dealing with those who had formerly compromised themselves with Arianism. The love that Athanasius showed in this controversy had the effect of "obviating countless schisms and attaching to the Church many who might otherwise have been driven back into Arianism."[3]

Owen's Remedy for Farther Evils That Come from Disputes

Similarly, John Owen knew that in contending for our all, the path of love must not be forsaken. But he made a crucial distinction between backing down from conviction on the one hand, and loving the adversary on the other:

> I can freely say, that I know not that man in England who is willing to go farther in forbearance, love, and communion with all that fear God and hold the foundation, than I am; but that this is to be done upon other grounds, principles, and ways, by other means and expedients, than by a condescension from the exactness of the least apex of gospel truth, or by an accommodation of doctrines by loose and general terms, I have elsewhere sufficiently

---

[2] Athanasius, *Athanasius: Select Works and Letters*, in *NPNF*, ed. Philip Schaff and Henry Wace (1892; repr., Peabody, MA: Hendricksen, 1999), 4:lviii.
[3] Ibid., lix.

declared. Let no man deceive you with vain pretences; hold fast the truth as it is in Jesus, part not with one iota, and contend for it when called thereunto.[4]

For Owen the discipline to kill his own sin[5] in the midst of controversy, and to pursue radical, personal holiness while "contending for his all," and to commune with God in the very truths for which he fought,[6] made love essential to controversy. In fact, he wrote a book titled *Evangelical Love, Church Peace, and Unity*. He admitted there that

> it is granted that they [the visible church] may fall into divisions, and schisms, and mutual exasperations among themselves, through the remainders of darkness in their minds and the infirmity of the flesh, Romans 14:3 ["Let not the one who eats despise the one who abstains, and let not the one who abstains pass judgment on the one who eats, for God has welcomed him"]; and in such cases mutual judgings and despisings are apt to ensue, and that to the prejudice and great disadvantage of that common faith which they do profess.[7]

But even though he granted that such "divisions and differences are . . . unavoidable," yet the "remedy of farther evils proceeding from them is plainly and frequently expressed in Scripture. It is love, meekness, forbearance, bowels of compassion."[8] Therefore he made it his aim to deal in his many controversies "without anger, bitterness, clamor, evil speaking, or any other thing that may be irregular in ourselves or give just cause of offence unto others."[9]

Machen on Christian Courage and the Heresy Hunt for Sin in Our Own Soul

J. Gresham Machen did not talk much about the condition of the heart in controversy. He was not given to describing the states of his own soul. His passion—and it was a great passion—was to restore objectivity to the Christian faith.[10] This had an interesting effect on his thought about virtue in controversy: he saw it in reverse. That is, he saw that courage

---

[4] John Owen, *The Mystery of the Gospel Vindicated and Socinianism Examined*, in *The Works of John Owen*, ed. William Goold (Edinburgh: Banner of Truth, 1965), 10:49.
[5] See chapter 2, note 40.
[6] See chapter 2, note 75.
[7] John Owen, *Evangelical Love, Church Peace, and Unity*, in *The Works of John Owen*, ed. Goold, 15:80.
[8] Ibid.
[9] Ibid., 81.
[10] "In *What Is Faith?*, 1925, I tried to combat the anti-intellectualism of the Modernist church—the false separation which is set up between faith and knowledge." J. Gresham Machen, "Christianity in Conflict," in *J. Gresham Machen: Selected Shorter Writings*, ed. D. G. Hart (Phillipsburg, NJ: P&R, 2004), 564.

in controversy is the test of a contrite heart. It works both ways. He said, "A man cannot successfully go heresy-hunting against the sin in his own life if he is willing to deny his Lord in the presence of the enemies outside." In other words, Machen saw the chief shortcoming of controversy not in the lack of humble love in the heart, but in the lack of humble courage in debate. Modernists were betraying their Lord while protesting their love. Therefore Machen made public confession the test of private love, not vice versa. "The two battles are intimately connected. A man cannot fight successfully in one unless he fights also in the other."[11]

Nevertheless he was explicit in speaking of his own aim to debate by the golden rule of Jesus. "I believe in controversy. But in controversy I do try to observe the Golden Rule; I do try to do unto others as I would have others do unto me. And the kind of controversy that pleases me in an opponent is a controversy that is altogether frank."[12]

Francis Schaeffer: Sweet-Singing Twentieth-Century Swan

One of the swans who sang most sweetly in the twentieth century was Francis Schaeffer (1912–1984), the founder of L'Abri Fellowship. He was a wise and humble apologist for the Christian faith, and a model for many of us. In 1970 he wrote an essay called "The Mark of the Christian." The mark, of course, is love. He based the essay on John 13:34–35 where Jesus said, "A new commandment I give to you, that you love one another: just as I have loved you, you also are to love one another. By this all people will know that you are my disciples, if you have love for one another."

Schaeffer spent most of this essay exhorting the church to disagree, when it must, lovingly. Schaeffer's view of biblical truth, like the swans in this book, was so high that he would not let the value of truth be minimized in the name of a unity that was not truth-based. Therefore, he dealt realistically with two biblical demands: the demand for purity and holiness on the one hand, and the demand for visible love and unity on the other hand.

> The Christian really has a double task. He has to practice both God's holiness and God's love. The Christian is to exhibit that God exists as the infinite-personal God; and then he is to exhibit simultaneously God's character of

---

[11] J. Gresham Machen, "Christian Scholarship and Evangelism," in ibid., 147.
[12] Ibid., 149.

holiness and love. Not His holiness without His love: this is only harshness. Not His love without His holiness: that is only compromise. Anything that an individual Christian or Christian group does that fails to show the simultaneous balance of the holiness of God and the love of God presents to a watching world not a demonstration of the God who exists but a caricature of the God who exists.[13]

Schaeffer knew that, in general, the necessary controversies and differences among Christians would not be understood by the watching world.

> You cannot expect the world to understand doctrinal differences, especially in our day when the existence of truth and absolutes are considered unthinkable even as concepts.
>
> We cannot expect the world to understand that on the basis of the holiness of God we are having a different kind of difference, because we are dealing with God's absolutes.[14]

This is why observable love becomes so crucial.

> Before a watching world, an observable love in the midst of difference will show a difference between Christians' differences and other people's differences. The world may not understand what the Christians are disagreeing about, but they will very quickly understand the difference of our differences from the world's differences if they see us having our differences in an open and observable love on a practical level.[15]

Therefore, Schaeffer called controversy among Christians "our golden opportunity" before a watching world. In other words, the aim of love, in view of God's truth and holiness, is not to avoid controversy, but to carry it through with observable practical love between the disagreeing groups. This is our golden opportunity.

> As a matter of fact, we have a greater possibility of showing what Jesus is speaking about here, in the midst of our differences, than we do if we are not differing. Obviously we ought not to go out looking for differences among Christians; there are enough without looking for more. But even so, it is in the midst of a difference that we have *our golden opportunity*. When

---

[13] Francis Schaeffer, *The Mark of Love*, in *A Christian View of the Church*, vol. 4 of *The Complete Works of Francis Schaeffer* (Wheaton, IL: Crossway, 1982), 193–94.
[14] Ibid., 201.
[15] Ibid.

everything is going well and we are all standing around in a nice little circle, there is not much to be seen by the world. But when we come to the place where there is a real difference, and we exhibit uncompromised principles but at the same time observable love, then there is something that the world can see, something they can use to judge that these really are Christians, and that Jesus has indeed been sent by the Father.[16]

The Final Victory Belongs to the Lord

The heart-wrenching truth of our day, and every day, is that Christians not only disagree with the world about the fundamental meaning of life, but also with each other about serious matters. Therefore, we rejoice that it is God himself who will fulfill his plan for the church: "My counsel shall stand, and I will accomplish all my purpose" (Isa. 46:10). We take heart that, in spite of all our blind spots and bungling and disobedience, God will triumph in the earth: "All the ends of the earth shall remember and turn to the LORD, and all the families of the nations shall worship before you. For kingship belongs to the LORD, and he rules over the nations" (Ps. 22:27–28).

Longing for the Day of Unity in the Truth

Yet one of the groanings of this fallen age is controversy, and most painful of all, controversy with brothers and sisters in Christ. We resonate with the apostle Paul—our joy would be full if we could all be "of the same mind, having the same love, being in full accord and of one mind" (Phil. 2:2). But for all his love of harmony and unity and peace, it is remarkable how many of Paul's letters were written to correct fellow Christians. One thinks of 1 Corinthians. It begins with Paul's thanks (1:4) and ends with his love (16:24). But between those verses he labors to set the Corinthians straight in their thinking and behavior.[17]

The assumption of the entire New Testament is that we should strive for peace. Peace and unity in the body of Christ are exceedingly precious. "Behold, how good and pleasant it is when brothers [and sisters] dwell in unity" (Ps. 133:1)! "Seek peace and pursue it" (1 Pet. 3:11).

---

[16] Ibid., 201–2, emphasis added.

[17] He addresses the danger of boasting in leaders (1:10–3:23), the limits of sexual freedom (5:1–8), the extent of true separation (5:9–13), the proper handling of lawsuits (6:1–8), the goodness of sexual relations in marriages (7:1–16), the nature of Christian freedom (8:1–13), the proper demeanor for men and women in worship (11:2–16), how to behave at the Lord's Supper (11:17–34), the use of spiritual gifts (12–14), and the nature and the reality of the resurrection (15).

"Let us then pursue what makes for peace and for mutual upbuilding" (Rom. 14:19). But just as clear is that we are to pursue peace by striving to come to agreement in the truth. "The wisdom from above is first pure, then peaceable" (James 3:17). It is *first* pure. Peace is not a first thing. It is derivative. It comes from hearty agreement in truth.

For example, Paul tells us to set our minds on what is true, and honorable, and just; then the God of peace will be with us (Phil. 4:8–9). Peace is a wonderful by-product of heartfelt commitments to what is true and right. Hebrews speaks of the "peaceful fruit of righteousness" (12:11). Paul tells Timothy to "pursue *righteousness* . . . and peace" (2 Tim. 2:22). The unity we strive for in the church is a unity in knowledge and truth and righteousness. We grow up into the one body "joined and held together" as we "attain to the unity of the faith and *of the knowledge of the Son of God*" (Eph. 4:13, 16). "Grace and peace" are "multiplied" to us "*in the knowledge of God* and of Jesus our Lord" (2 Pet. 1:2). And paradoxically, the weaponry with which we wage war for "the gospel of peace" begins with the belt of *truth* (Eph. 6:14–15) and ends with the sword of the Spirit, the *Word of God* (v. 17).

Why True Unity Flows from Truth

The reason for this is that truth frees us from the control of Satan, the great deceiver and destroyer of unity: "You will know the truth, and the truth will set you free" (John 8:32; cf. 2 Tim. 2:24–26). Truth serves love, the bond of perfection. Paul prays for the Philippians that their "love may abound more and more, with knowledge and all discernment" (Phil. 1:9). Truth sanctifies, and so yields the righteousness whose fruit is peace: "Sanctify them in the truth; your word is truth" (John 17:17; cf. 2 Pet. 1:3, 5, 12).

For the sake of unity and peace, therefore, Paul labors to set the churches straight on numerous issues—including quite a few that do not in themselves involve heresy. He does not exclude controversy from his pastoral writing. And he does not limit his engagement in controversy to first-order doctrines, where heresy threatens. He is like a parent to his churches. Parents do not correct and discipline their children only for felonies. Good parents long for their children to grow up into all the kindness and courtesy of mature adulthood. And since the fabric of truth is seamless, Paul knows that letting minor strands go on unraveling can eventually rend the whole garment.

Thus Paul teaches that elders serve the church on the one hand by caring for the church without being pugnacious (1 Tim. 3:3, 5), and, on the other hand, by rebuking and correcting false teaching. "He must hold firm to the trustworthy word as taught, so that he may be able to give instruction in sound doctrine and also to rebuke those who contradict it" (Titus 1:9; cf. 1:13; 2:15; 1 Tim. 5:20). This is one of the main reasons we have the Scriptures: they are "profitable for teaching, for reproof, for correction, and for training in righteousness" (2 Tim. 3:16).

"By the Open Statement of the Truth We Commend Ourselves"

Faithful Christians do not love controversy; they love peace. They love their brothers and sisters who disagree with them. They long for a common mind for the cause of Christ. But they are bound by their conscience and by the Word of God, for this very reason, to try to persuade the church concerning the fullness of the truth and beauty of God's Word.

We live in a day of politicized discourse that puts no premium on clear assertions. Many use language to conceal where they stand rather than to make clear where they stand. One reason this happens is that clear and open statements usually result in more criticism than ambiguous statements do. Vagueness will win more votes in a hostile atmosphere than forthrightness will.

But we want nothing to do with that attitude. Jesus refused to converse with religious leaders who crafted their answers so as to conceal what they thought (Mark 11:33). Our aim (if not our achievement) is always to be like Paul when he said, "But we have renounced disgraceful, underhanded ways. We refuse to practice cunning or to tamper with God's word, but by the open statement of the truth we would commend ourselves to everyone's conscience in the sight of God" (2 Cor. 4:2).[18]

This is the stance that the swans have always taken. This is the only stance worthy of those who are contending for their all—the truth of Jesus Christ.

---

[18] These final paragraphs are based on what I wrote in "Charity, Clarity, and Hope" in *Recovering Biblical Manhood and Womanhood*, ed. John Piper and Wayne Grudem (Wheaton, IL: Crossway, 1991), 403–22.

Our Prayer in a Time
of Controversy

Gracious Father, have mercy on your children in disputes. We are sorry for any root of pride or fear of man or lack of insight that influences our stance in the controversy before us. We confess that we are not pure in ourselves. Even as we strive to persuade one another, we stand in need of a merciful Advocate. We are sinners. We are finite and fallible.

We take refuge in the glorious gospel of justification by faith alone through grace. We magnify Jesus Christ, our Savior and King, for all he has done to make us his own. We are a thankful people even in this conflict. We are broken and humble to think that we would be loved and forgiven and accepted by an infinitely holy God.

Forbid, O Lord, that our spirit in this struggle would be one of hostility or ill will toward anyone. Deliver us from every form of debate that departs from love or diminishes truth. Grant, Father, as Francis Schaeffer pleaded, that our disagreements would prove to be golden opportunities to show the world how to love—not by avoiding conflicts, but by how we act in them.

Show us, O God, the relationship between doctrine and devotion, between truth and tenderness, between biblical faithfulness and biblical unity, between standing on the truth and standing together. Let none of us be unteachable or beyond correction. May the outcome of our disputes be clearer vision of your glory and grace and truth and wisdom and power and knowledge.

By your Spirit, grant that the result of all our arguments be deeper humility, more dependence on mercy, sweeter fellowship with Jesus, stronger love in our common life, more radical obedience to the commands of our King, more authentic worship, and a greater readiness and eagerness to lay down our lives to finish the Great Commission.

In all this, Father, our passion is that you would be glorified through Jesus Christ. Amen.

The Swans Are Not Silent

Book 5

Filling Up the Afflictions of Christ

The Cost of Bringing the Gospel to the Nations in the Lives of William Tyndale, John Paton, and Adoniram Judson

To those who suffer
to spread the gospel
"Remember those who are in prison,
as though in prison with them,
and those who are mistreated,
since you also are in the body."
Hebrews 13:3

Filling Up the Afflictions of Christ

Book 5

Contents

A letter from John Calvin to five young Frenchmen about to be martyred in 1553 for carrying the gospel into France:

We who are here shall do our duty in praying that [God] would glorify Himself more and more by your constancy, and that He may, by the comfort of His Spirit, sweeten and endear all that is bitter to the flesh, and so absorb your spirits in Himself, that in contemplating that heavenly crown, you may be ready without regret to leave all that belongs to this world.

Now, at this present hour, necessity itself exhorts you more than ever to turn your whole mind heavenward. As yet, we know not what will be the event. But, since it appears as though God would use your blood to seal His truth, there is nothing better for you than to prepare yourselves for that end, beseeching Him so to subdue you to His good pleasure, that nothing may hinder you from following whithersoever He shall call. . . . Since it pleases Him to employ you to the death in maintaining His quarrel, He will strengthen your hands in the fight and will not suffer a single drop of your blood to be shed in vain.

Your humble brother, John Calvin

Preface

This is the fifth book in a collection called The Swans Are Not Silent. By *swans* I mean the inspiring lives of faithful Christians in history. They are *not silent* in the sense that their lives still speak powerfully for our encouragement and guidance.

The terminology of *swans not being silent* comes from the story of St. Augustine's retirement as the bishop of Hippo in North Africa in AD 430. He was one of the greatest voices for biblical truth in the history of the Christian church. When Eraclius, his humble successor, preached at the retirement celebration, he said, "The cricket chirps, the swan is silent."

When I first read that years ago, I said, *No, Eraclius, the swans are not silent.* They go on speaking. That is, they continue speaking, *if* someone tells their story and gives them a voice. That is what I am trying to do with these stories—fifteen of them now (three in each book).

One of the most sobering discoveries of my life is that God spreads the life-giving news about Jesus Christ by means of suffering and martyrdom. That's what the lives of William Tyndale, Adoniram Judson, and John Paton illustrate. They were living—and dying—examples of Colossians 1:24: "I rejoice in my sufferings for your sake, and in my flesh I am filling up what is lacking in Christ's afflictions for the sake of his body, that is, the church."

Afflictions are not merely the *result* of missionary fruitfulness but also the *means*. God has appointed our pain to be part of his powerful display of the glory of Christ. The worth of Jesus in the world shines more brightly in the lives of those who say by their sacrificial lives, "I have suffered the loss of all things and count them as rubbish, in order that I may gain Christ" (Phil. 3:8).

Few things inspire me to live radically for Christ more than the story of those who did. I pray that this will be the effect on you as well. The nations are in desperate need. And Christ is a great Savior.

Acknowledgments

I am thankful to Lane Dennis and the team at Crossway for the beautiful work they have done in publishing this series of books called The Swans Are Not Silent. This is Book Five, and the fruit and fellowship of each volume has been pleasant.

My executive pastoral assistant, David Mathis, encourages and assists and frees me for this work in a way that not only makes it possible but makes it joyful. I thank God for David's proactive thoughtfulness, his theological depth, his biblical faithfulness, his rigorous editing, and his personal friendship.

The elders and staff at Bethlehem Baptist Church continue to support me in ways I don't deserve, encouraging me and covering for me in a hundred ways when I am away finishing a project like this. The church is in good hands. One of these days I will go to heaven instead of going back to the pulpit. They will do just fine. They lean on the One who cannot fail.

Noël and Talitha give me the space and seclusion and prayer I need to work at home. The bond we enjoy is deep. I am who I am because of those I am bound to—especially Jesus and my family. Oh, how thankful I am that this bond is life-sustaining, not life-destroying.

Finally, in this book especially, I thank God that he is "near to the brokenhearted and saves the crushed in spirit." Where would we be if we could not say of him, "Many are the afflictions of the righteous, but the LORD delivers him out of them all" (Ps. 34:18–19)?

Introduction

Tears of Blood to Bless the World

The Lord Jesus said to us in very sobering words, "Truly, truly, I say to you, unless a grain of wheat falls into the earth and dies, it remains alone; but if it dies, it bears much fruit" (John 12:24). Then he added this: "Whoever loves his life loses it, and whoever hates his life in this world will keep it for eternal life" (John 12:25).

In other words, a fruitful life and an eternal life come from dying like a seed and hating your life in this world. What overwhelms me as I ponder this and trace the lives of William Tyndale, John Paton, and Adoniram Judson is how strategic it was that they died so many times and in so many ways before their lives on earth ended. This is no rhetorical flourish. The Bible speaks this way, and these followers of Christ knew it.

For example, when John Paton was celebrating the triumphs of the gospel on the island of Tanna in the New Hebrides, after long missionary labor and suffering, he traced this victory back to the fact that "seeds of faith and hope were planted not only in tears, but tears of blood."[1] Then, to give biblical force to what he had just said, he simply cited the amazing phrase from 2 Corinthians 11:23 where Paul described his sufferings with the words "in deaths oft." That is the old King James Version and is exactly literal.

Paul said in 1 Corinthians 15:31, "I die every day!" The seed falls into the ground and dies not just once in martyrdom but over and over as we obey the command to take up our cross "daily" and follow Jesus (Luke 9:23).

---

[1] John G. Paton, *Missionary to the New Hebrides: An Autobiography Edited by His Brother* (1889; repr., Edinburgh: Banner of Truth, 1965), 221.

God's Painful Path to Reach All Peoples

More and more I am persuaded from Scripture and from the history of missions that God's design for the evangelization of the world and the consummation of his purposes includes the suffering of his ministers and missionaries. To put it more plainly and specifically, God designs that the suffering of his ambassadors is one essential means in the triumphant spread of the good news among all the peoples of the world.

I am saying more than the obvious fact that suffering is a *result* of faithful obedience in spreading the gospel. That is true. Jesus said suffering will result from this faithfulness. "You will be hated by all for my name's sake" (Luke 21:17). "If they persecuted me, they will also persecute you" (John 15:20). I am saying that this suffering is part of God's strategy for making known to the world who Christ is, how he loves, and how much he is worth.

This is both frightening and encouraging. It frightens us because we know that we may very likely be called to suffer in some way in order to get the breakthrough we long to see in a hard frontline missions situation. But it also encourages us because we can know that our suffering is not in vain and that the very pain that tends to dishearten us is the path to triumph, even when we can't see it. Many have gone before us on the Calvary Road of suffering and proved by their perseverance that fruit follows the death of humble seeds.

Jesus came into the world to suffer and die for the salvation of a countless number of believers from all the peoples of the world. "The Son of Man came not to be served but to serve, and to give his life as a ransom for many" (Mark 10:45). "By your blood you ransomed people for God from every tribe and language and people and nation" (Rev. 5:9).

Suffering and death in the place of sinners was the way that Christ accomplished salvation. "Christ redeemed us from the curse of the law by becoming a curse for us" (Gal. 3:13). "He was pierced for our transgressions; he was crushed for our iniquities" (Isa. 53:5). We preach that. It is the heart of the gospel.

But this voluntary suffering and death to save others is not only the *content* but it is also the *method* of our mission. We proclaim the good news of what he accomplished, and we join him in the Calvary method. We embrace his sufferings *for* us, and we spread the gospel by our suffering *with* him. As Josef Tson puts it in his own case: "I am an extension of Jesus Christ. When I was beaten in Romania, He suffered in my body. It is not my suffering: I only had the honor to share His sufferings."[2] Pastor Tson goes on to say that Christ's suffering is for *propitiation*; our suffering is for *propagation*. In other words, when we suffer with him in the cause of missions, we display the way Christ loved the world and in our own sufferings extend his to the world. This is what it means to fill up the afflictions of Christ (Col. 1:24).

First Bible, Then Biography

The plan of this book is to focus first on some of the Scriptures that support these claims (the introduction) and then to let the lives of Tyndale, Paton, and Judson give these Scriptures a flesh-and-blood reality. Among thousands of devoted and faithful missionaries in the history of world missions, Tyndale, Judson, and Paton are not the only ones who display this truth.

In fact, we will, no doubt, find out in heaven that many of the most faithful and fruitful missionaries are almost completely unknown, except in the all-important books of heaven. But the lives of some have been recorded on earth. I am thankful for this. They are a source of great strength to me. That's why I read about their lives. Among those whose lives are recorded for us, few are more heartbreakingly inspiring than the lives of Tyndale, Paton, and Judson. With the thousands of others, these three show how the advance of the gospel of Christ comes about not only through the faithful proclamation of the truth but also through filling up the afflictions of Christ.

God's Plan for the Nations of the World

The invincible purpose of God in history is that "the gospel of the glory of Christ" (2 Cor. 4:4) spread to all the peoples of the world and take root in God-centered, Christ-exalting churches. This was the promise of the Old Testament:

> All the ends of the earth shall remember
> and turn to the Lord,
> and all the families of the nations

---

[2] Josef Tson, *A Theology of Martyrdom* (Wheaton, IL: The Romanian Missionary Society, n.d.), 4.

> shall worship before you.
> For kingship belongs to the LORD,
>   and he rules over the nations. (Ps. 22:27–28)

It was the promise of Jesus to his disciples:

> And this gospel of the kingdom will be proclaimed throughout the whole world as a testimony to all nations, and then the end will come. (Matt. 24:14)

It was the design of God in the cross, as heaven's worship proclaims:

> You were slain, and by your blood you ransomed people for God from every tribe and language and people and nation. (Rev. 5:9)

It was the final command of the risen, all-authoritative Christ:

> All authority in heaven and on earth has been given to me. Go therefore and make disciples of all nations, baptizing them in the name of the Father and of the Son and of the Holy Spirit, teaching them to observe all that I have commanded you. And behold, I am with you always, to the end of the age. (Matt. 28:18–20)

It was the divine aim of Paul's apostleship:

> Through [Christ] we have received grace and apostleship to bring about the obedience of faith for the sake of his name among all the nations. (Rom. 1:5)

It was Paul's holy ambition, rooted not just in a unique apostolic call but also in the Old Testament promise that is still valid today:

> I make it my ambition to preach the gospel, not where Christ has already been named, lest I build on someone else's foundation, but as it is written,
>
> > "Those who have never been told of him will see,
> > and those who have never heard will understand."
> >   (Rom. 15:20–21; cf. Isa. 52:15)
>
> So the Lord has commanded us, saying,
>
> > "I have made you a light for the Gentiles,
> > that you may bring salvation to the ends of the earth."
> >   (Acts 13:47; cf. Isa. 42:6)

It was the divine purpose of the sending and filling of the Holy Spirit:

> You will receive power when the Holy Spirit has come upon you, and you will
> be my witnesses in Jerusalem and in all Judea and Samaria, and to the end
> of the earth. (Acts 1:8)

The invincible purpose of God is that "the gospel of the glory of Christ" spread to all the peoples of the world and take root in God-centered, Christ-exalting churches. This great global vision of the Christian movement becomes clear and powerful and compelling in the church whenever there is a deep biblical awakening in Christ's people.

This was true in the time of William Tyndale (b. 1494), who was captivated by the fervor of the Reformation as God awakened his church to the truth of justification by faith alone. It was true of the generation later when John Paton (b. 1824) was part of the great stir-rings in Scotland that Iain Murray calls "the missionary awakening."[3] And it was true of the time of Adoniram Judson (b. 1788) as the Second Great Awakening stirred in America.

Your Persecution Is "for a Witness"

The truth that is especially illustrated by the lives of these servants is that God's strategy for breaking through Satan's authority in the world, and spreading the gospel, and planting the church includes the sacrificial suffering of his frontline heralds. Again I emphasize, since it so easily missed, that I am not referring only to the fact that suffering *results* from frontline proclamation. I am referring also to the fact that this suffering is one of God's intended strategies for the success of his mission. Jesus said to his disciples as he sent them out:

> Behold, I am sending you out as sheep in the midst of wolves, so be wise as
> serpents and innocent as doves. (Matt. 10:16)

There is no doubt what usually happens to a sheep in the midst of wolves. And Paul confirmed the reality in Romans 8:36, quoting Psalm 44:22:

> As it is written, "For your sake we are being killed all the day long; we are
> regarded as sheep to be slaughtered."

---

[3] Iain Murray, *A Scottish Christian Heritage* (Edinburgh: Banner of Truth, 2006), 218. In chapters 6 and 7, Murray documents the relationship between true gospel awakening and the missionary effect in Scotland.

Jesus knew this would be the portion of his darkness-penetrating, mission-advancing, church-planting missionaries. Tribulation, distress, persecution, famine, nakedness, danger, sword (Rom. 8:35)— that is what Paul expected, because that is what Jesus promised. Jesus continued:

> Beware of men, for they will deliver you over to courts and flog you in their synagogues, and you will be dragged before governors and kings for my sake, *to bear witness before them* and the Gentiles. (Matt. 10:17–18)

Notice that the "witness" before governors and kings is not a mere *result* or consequence but a *design*. Literally: "You will be dragged before . . . kings *for a witness to them* [*eis marturion autois*]." God's design for reaching some governors and kings is the persecution of his people. Why this design for missions? One answer from the Lord Jesus goes like this:

> A disciple is not above his teacher, nor a servant above his master. . . . If they have called the master of the house Beelzebul, how much more will they malign those of his household. (Matt. 10:24–25)

Suffering was not just a *consequence* of the Master's obedience and mission. It was the central *strategy* of his mission. It was the way he accomplished our salvation. Jesus calls us to join him on the Calvary Road, to take up our cross daily, to hate our lives in this world, and to fall into the ground like a seed and die, that others might live.

We are not above our Master. To be sure, our suffering does not atone for anyone's sins, but it is a deeper way of doing missions than we often realize. When the martyrs cry out to Christ from under the altar in heaven, "How long before you will judge and avenge our blood?" they are told "to rest a little longer, until the number of their fellow servants and their brothers should be complete, who were to be killed as they themselves had been" (Rev. 6:10–11).

Martyrdom is not the mere consequence of radical love and obedience; it is the keeping of an appointment set in heaven for a certain number: "Wait till the number of martyrs is complete who are to be killed." Just as Christ died to save the unreached peoples of the world, so some missionaries are to die to save the people of the world.

Filling Up the Afflictions of Christ[4]

We would be warranted at this point to be concerned that this way of talking might connect our suffering and Christ's suffering too closely—as though we were fellow redeemers. There is only one Redeemer. Only one death atones for sin—Christ's death. Only one act of voluntary suffering takes away sin. Jesus did this "once for all when he offered up himself" (Heb. 7:27). "He has appeared once for all at the end of the ages to put away sin by the sacrifice of himself" (Heb. 9:26). "By a single offering [Christ] *has perfected for all time* those who are being sanctified" (Heb. 10:14). When he shed his blood, he did it "*once for all*," having obtained "*eternal* redemption" (Heb. 9:12). "There is one God, and there is one mediator between God and men, the man Christ Jesus" (1 Tim. 2:5). So there is no doubt that our sufferings add nothing to the atoning worth and sufficiency of Christ's sufferings.

However, there is one verse in the Bible that sounds to many people as if our sufferings are part of Christ's redeeming sufferings. As it turns out, that is not what it means. On the contrary, it is one of the most important verses explaining the thesis of this book—that missionary sufferings are a strategic part of God's plan to reach the nations. The text is Colossians 1:24 where Paul says,

> Now I rejoice in my sufferings for your sake, and in my flesh I am filling up what is lacking in Christ's afflictions for the sake of his body, that is, the church.

In his sufferings Paul is "filling up what is lacking in Christ's afflictions for . . . the church." What does that mean? It means that Paul's sufferings fill up Christ's afflictions *not* by adding anything to their worth, but by extending them to the people they were meant to save.

What is lacking in the afflictions of Christ is not that they are deficient in worth, as though they could not sufficiently cover the sins of all who believe. What is lacking is that the infinite value of Christ's afflictions is not known and trusted in the world. These afflictions and what they mean are still hidden to most peoples. And God's intention is that the mystery be revealed to all the nations. So the afflictions of Christ are "lacking" in the sense that they are not seen and known and loved

---

[4] The following exposition of Col. 1:24 depends heavily on the thought and words of my book *Desiring God* (Colorado Springs: Multnomah, 2011), 267–70.

among the nations. They must be carried by missionaries. And those missionaries "complete" what is lacking in the afflictions of Christ by extending them to others.

Epaphroditus Gives the Explanation

There is a strong confirmation of this interpretation in the use of similar words in Philippians 2:30. There was a man named Epaphroditus in the church at Philippi. When the church there gathered support for Paul (perhaps money or supplies or books), they decided to send them to Paul in Rome by the hand of Epaphroditus. In his travels with this supply, Epaphroditus almost lost his life. He was sick to the point of death, but God spared him (Phil. 2:27).

So Paul tells the church in Philippi to honor Epaphroditus when he comes back (v. 29), and he explains his reason with words very similar to Colossians 1:24. He says, "For he nearly died for the work of Christ, risking his life to *complete* [similar word to the one in Col. 1:24] *what was lacking* [same word as in Col. 1:24] in your service to me" (Phil. 2:30). In the Greek original, the phrase *"complete what was lacking in your service to me"* is almost identical with *"filling up what is lacking in Christ's afflictions"* in Colossians 1:24.

In what sense, then, was the service of the Philippians to Paul "lacking," and in what sense did Epaphroditus "complete" or "fill up" what was lacking in their service? A hundred years ago, Marvin Vincent explained it like this:

> The gift to Paul was a gift of the church as a body. It was a sacrificial offering of love. What was lacking, and what would have been grateful to Paul and to the church alike, was the church's presentation of this offering in person. This was impossible, and Paul represents Epaphroditus as supplying this lack by his affectionate and zealous ministry.[5]

I think that is exactly what the same words mean in Colossians 1:24. Christ has prepared a love offering for the world by suffering and dying for sinners. It is full and lacking in nothing—except one thing, a personal presentation by Christ himself to the nations of the world. God's answer to this lack is to call the people of Christ (people like Paul) to make a personal presentation of the afflictions of Christ to the world.

---

[5] Marvin Vincent, I.C.C., *Epistle to the Philippians and to Philemon* (Edinburgh: T&T Clark, 1897), 78.

In doing this, we "complete what is lacking in the afflictions of Christ." We finish what they were designed for, namely, a personal presentation to the people who do not know about their infinite worth.

Filling Up His Afflictions with Our Afflictions

But the most amazing thing about Colossians 1:24 is *how* Paul fills up Christ's afflictions. He says that it is *his own sufferings* that fill up Christ's afflictions. "I rejoice in my sufferings for your sake, and in my flesh I am filling up what is lacking in Christ's afflictions." This means, then, that Paul exhibits the sufferings of Christ by suffering *himself* for those he is trying to win. In *his* sufferings they see Christ's sufferings.

Here is the astounding upshot: *God intends for the afflictions of Christ to be presented to the world through the afflictions of his people.* God really means for the body of Christ, the church, to experience some of the suffering he experienced so that when we proclaim the cross as the way to life, people will see the marks of the cross in us and feel the love of the cross from us. Our calling is to make the afflictions of Christ real for people by the afflictions we experience in bringing them the message of salvation.

The Blood of the Martyrs Is Seed

This is why Paul spoke of his scars as "the marks of Jesus." In his wounds people could see Christ's wounds. "I bear on my body the marks of Jesus" (Gal. 6:17). The point of bearing the marks of Jesus is that Jesus might be seen and that his love might work powerfully in those who see.

> [We] always carr[y] in the body the death of Jesus, so that the life of Jesus may also be manifested in our bodies. For we who live are always being given over to death for Jesus' sake, so that the life of Jesus also may be manifested in our mortal flesh. So death is at work in us, but life in you. (2 Cor. 4:10–12)

The history of the expansion of Christianity has proved that "the blood of the martyrs is seed," the seed of new life in Christ spreading through the world. That famous quote comes from Tertullian, who lived from about AD 160 to AD 225. What he actually wrote was: "The oftener we are mown down by you [Romans], the more in number we

[Christians] grow; the blood of Christians is seed."[6] For almost three hundred years, Christianity grew in soil that was wet with the blood of the martyrs. In his *History of Christian Missions*, Stephen Neil mentions the sufferings of the early Christians as one of the six main reasons the church grew so rapidly.

> Because of their dangerous situation vis-à-vis the law, Christians were almost bound to meet in secret. . . . Every Christian knew that sooner or later he might have to testify to his faith at the cost of his life. . . . When persecution did break out, martyrdom could be attended by the utmost possible publicity. The Roman public was hard and cruel, but it was not altogether without compassion; and there is no doubt that the attitude of the martyrs, and particularly of the young women who suffered along with the men, made a deep impression. . . . In the earlier records what we find is calm, dignified, decorous behaviour; cool courage in the face of torment, courtesy towards enemies, and a joyful acceptance of suffering as the way appointed by the Lord to lead to his heavenly kingdom. There are a number of well-authenticated cases of conversion of pagans in the very moment of witnessing the condemnation and death of Christians; there must have been far more who received impressions that in the course of time would be turned into a living faith.[7]

May the Lord of the Nations Give Us His Passion

When Paul shares in Christ's sufferings with joy and love, he delivers, as it were, those very sufferings to the ones for whom Christ died. Paul's missionary suffering is God's design to complete the sufferings of Christ, by making them more visible and personal and precious to those for whom he died.

So I say this very sobering word: God's plan is that his saving purpose for the nations will triumph through the suffering of his people, especially his frontline forces who break through the darkness of Satan's blinding hold on an unreached people. That is what the lives of William Tyndale, John Paton, and Adoniram Judson illustrate so dramatically. My prayer is that their stories here will awaken in you a passion for Christ's fame among the nations and sympathy for those who will perish for their sin without having heard the good news of Christ.

---

[6] Tertullian, *The Apology*, trans. Rev. S. Thelwell in Ante-Nicene Fathers, ed. Alexander Roberts and James Donaldson (orig. 1885; Peabody, MA: Hendrickson, 2004), 3:55.
[7] Stephen Neil, *A History of Christian Missions* (London: Penguin, 1964), 43–44.

1

William Tyndale

*"Always Singing One Note"—A Vernacular Bible:
The Cost of Bringing the Bible to England*

Stephen Vaughan was an English merchant commissioned by Thomas Cromwell, the king's adviser, to find William Tyndale and inform him that King Henry VIII desired him to come back to England out of hiding on the continent. In a letter to Cromwell from Vaughan dated June 19, 1531, Vaughan wrote about Tyndale (1494–1536) these simple words: "I find him always singing one note."[1] That one note was this: Will the King of England give his official endorsement to a vernacular Bible for all his English subjects? If not, Tyndale would not come. If so, Tyndale would give himself up to the king and never write another book.

This was the driving passion of his life—to see the Bible translated from the Greek and Hebrew into ordinary English available for every person in England to read.

Whatever It Costs

Henry VIII was angry with Tyndale for believing and promoting Martin Luther's Reformation teachings. In particular, he was angry because of Tyndale's book *An Answer unto Sir Thomas More's Dialogue*. Thomas More (famous today for his book *Utopia* and as portrayed in the movie *A Man for All Seasons*) was the lord chancellor who helped Henry VIII write his repudiation of Luther called *Defense of the Seven Sacraments*.

---

[1] David Daniell, *William Tyndale: A Biography* (New Haven, CT: Yale University Press, 1994), 217.

Thomas More was thoroughly Roman Catholic and radically anti-Reformation, anti-Luther, and anti-Tyndale. So Tyndale had come under excoriating criticism by Thomas More.[2] In fact, More had a "near-rabid hatred"[3] for Tyndale and published three long responses to him totaling nearly three-quarters of a million words.[4]

But in spite of this high-court anger against Tyndale, the king's message to Tyndale, carried by Vaughan, was mercy: "The king's royal majesty is . . . inclined to mercy, pity, and compassion."[5]

The thirty-seven-year-old Tyndale was moved to tears by this offer of mercy. He had been in exile away from his homeland for seven years. But then he sounded his "one note" again: Will the king authorize a vernacular English Bible from the original languages? Vaughan gives us Tyndale's words from May 1531:

> I assure you, if it would stand with the King's most gracious pleasure to grant only a bare text of the Scripture [that is, without explanatory notes] to be put forth among his people, like as is put forth among the subjects of the emperor in these parts, and of other Christian princes, be it of the translation of what person soever shall please his Majesty, I shall immediately make faithful promise never to write more, nor abide two days in these parts after the same: but immediately to repair unto his realm, and there most humbly submit myself at the feet of his royal majesty, offering my body to suffer what pain or torture, yea, what death his grace will, so this be obtained. Until that time, I will abide the asperity of all chances, whatsoever shall come, and endure my life in as many pains as it is able to bear and suffer.[6]

In other words, Tyndale would give himself up to the king on one condition—that the king authorize an English Bible translated from the Greek and Hebrew in the common language of the people.

The king refused. And Tyndale never went to his homeland again. Instead, if the king and the Roman Catholic Church would not provide a printed Bible in English for the common man to read, Tyndale would, even if it cost him his life—which it did five years later.

---

[2] For example, in More's 1529 book, *Dialogue Concerning Heresies.*
[3] Daniell, *Tyndale*, 4.
[4] Thomas More wrote vastly more to condemn Tyndale than Tyndale wrote in defense. After one book called *An Answer unto Sir Thomas More's Dialogue* (1531), Tyndale was done. For Thomas More, however, there were "close on three quarters of a million words against Tyndale . . . [compared to] Tyndale's eighty thousand in his *Answer.*" Ibid., 277.
[5] Ibid., 216.
[6] Ibid.

As I Live, the Plowboy Will Know His Bible

When he was twenty-eight years old in 1522, he was serving as a tutor in the home of John Walsh in Gloucestershire, England, spending most of his time studying Erasmus's Greek New Testament that had been printed just six years before in 1516.

We should pause here and make clear what an incendiary thing this Greek New Testament was in history. David Daniell describes the magnitude of this event:

> This was the first time that the Greek New Testament had been printed. It is no exaggeration to say that it set fire to Europe. Luther [1483–1546] translated it into his famous German version of 1522. In a few years there appeared translations from the Greek into most European vernaculars. They were the true basis of the popular reformation.[7]

Every day William Tyndale was seeing these Reformation truths more clearly in the Greek New Testament as an ordained Catholic priest. Increasingly, he was making himself suspect in this Catholic house of John Walsh. Learned men would come for dinner, and Tyndale would discuss the things he was seeing in the New Testament. John Foxe tells us that one day an exasperated Catholic scholar at dinner with Tyndale said, "We were better be without God's law than the pope's."

In response, Tyndale spoke his famous words, "I defy the Pope and all his laws. . . . If God spare my life ere many years, I will cause a boy that driveth the plow, shall know more of the Scripture than thou dost."[8]

The One-Note Crescendo

Four years later Tyndale finished the English translation of the Greek New Testament in Worms, Germany, and began to smuggle it into England in

---

[7] William Tyndale, *Selected Writings*, ed. David Daniell (New York: Routledge, 2003), ix.

Modern champions of the Catholic position like to support a view of the Reformation, that it was entirely a political imposition by a ruthless minority in power against both the traditions and the wishes of the pious people of England. . . . The energy which affected every human life in northern Europe, however, came from a different place. It was not the result of political imposition. It came from the discovery of the Word of God as originally written . . . in the language of the people. Moreover, it could be read and understood, without censorship by the Church or mediation through the Church. . . . Such reading produced a totally different view of everyday Christianity: the weekly, daily, even hourly ceremonies so lovingly catalogued by some Catholic revisionists are not there; purgatory is not there; there is no aural confession and penance. Two supports of the Church's wealth and power collapsed. Instead there was simply individual faith in Christ the Saviour, found in Scripture. That and only that "justified" the sinner, whose root failings were now in the face of God, not the bishops or the pope. (Daniell, *Tyndale*, 58)

[8] Daniell, *Tyndale*, 79.

bales of cloth. He had grown up in Gloucestershire, the cloth-working county, and now we see what that turn of providence was about.[9] By October 1526, the book had been banned by Bishop Tunstall in London, but the print run had been at least three thousand. And the books were getting to the people. Over the next eight years, five pirated editions were printed as well.[10]

In 1534, Tyndale published a revised New Testament, having learned Hebrew in the meantime, probably in Germany, which helped him better understand the connections between the Old and New Testaments. Daniell calls this 1534 New Testament "the glory of his life's work."[11] If Tyndale was "always singing one note," this was the crescendo of the song of his life—the finished and refined New Testament in English.

The Very First New Testament in English from the Greek

For the first time ever in history, the Greek New Testament was translated into English. And for the first time ever, the New Testament in English was available in a printed form. Before Tyndale, there were only handwritten manuscripts of the Bible in English. These manuscripts we owe to the work and inspiration of John Wycliffe and the Lollards[12] from a hundred and thirty years earlier.[13] For a thousand years, the only translation of the Greek and Hebrew Bible was the Latin Vulgate, and few people could understand it, even if they had access to it.

Before he was martyred in 1536, Tyndale had translated into clear, common English[14] not only the New Testament[15] but also the Pentateuch, Joshua to 2 Chronicles, and Jonah.[16] All this material became the basis of

---

[9] "Not for nothing did William Tyndale, exiled in Cologne, Worms and Antwerp use the international trade routes of the cloth merchants to get his books into England, smuggled in bales of cloth." Ibid., 15.

[10] Ibid., 188.

[11] Ibid., 316.

[12] "In the summer of 1382, Wyclif was attacked in a sermon preached at St. Mary's, Oxford, and his followers were for the first time denounced as 'Lollards'—a loose and suitably meaningless term of abuse ('mutterers') current in the Low Countries for Bible students, and thus heretics." David Daniell, *The Bible in English: Its History and Influence* (New Haven, CT: Yale University Press, 2003), 73.

[13] Gutenberg's printing press came in 1450.

[14] "Tyndale transmitted an English strength which is the opposite of Latin, seen in the difference between 'high' and 'elevated,' 'gift' and 'donation,' 'many' and 'multitudinous.'" Daniell, *Tyndale*, 3.

[15] Tyndale did not follow Luther in putting Hebrews, James, Jude, and Revelation in a special section of the New Testament set apart as inferior. "Tyndale, as shown later by his preface to James in his 1534 New Testament, is not only wiser and more generous—he is more true to the New Testament." Ibid., 120.

[16] This is available in print with all its original notes and introductions: *Tyndale's Old Testament*, trans. William Tyndale (New Haven, CT: Yale University Press, 1992). Also available is *Tyndale's New Testament*, trans. William Tyndale (New Haven, CT: Yale University Press, 1989).

the *Great Bible* issued by Miles Coverdale in England in 1539[17] and the basis for the *Geneva Bible* published in 1557—"the Bible of the nation,"[18] which sold over a million copies between 1560 and 1640.

Under God, Tyndale Gave Us Our English Bible

We do not get a clear sense of Tyndale's achievement without some comparisons. We think of the dominant King James Version as giving us the pervasive language of the English Bible. But Daniell clarifies the situation:

> William Tyndale gave us our English Bible. The sages assembled by King James to prepare the Authorized Version of 1611, so often praised for un-likely corporate inspiration, took over Tyndale's work. Nine-tenths of the Authorized Version's New Testament is Tyndale's. The same is true of the first half of the Old Testament, which was as far as he was able to get before he was executed outside Brussels in 1536.[19]

Here is a sampling of the English phrases we owe to Tyndale:

Let there be light. (Gen. 1:3)

Am I my brother's keeper? (Gen. 4:9)

The LORD bless thee and keep thee. The LORD make his face to shine upon thee and be merciful unto thee. The LORD lift up his countenance upon thee, and give thee peace. (Num. 6:24–26)

There were shepherds abiding in the field. (Luke 2:8)

---

[17] How could it be that Tyndale was martyred in 1536 for translating the Bible into English, and that his New Testament could be burned in London by Bishop Tunstall, and yet an entire printed Bible, es-sentially Tyndale's, *The Great Bible*, could be published in England three years later, officially endorsed by this Bible-burning bishop? Daniell explains: "Tunstall, whose name would shortly appear on the title pages approving two editions of the Great Bible, was playing politics, being a puppet of the Pope through Wolsey and the king, betraying his Christian humanist learning at the direction of the church, needing to be receiving [Thomas] Wolsey's favor. . . . To burn God's word for politics was to Tyndale barbarous." Daniell, *Tyndale*, 93.

[18] Tyndale, *Selected Writings*, xi.

[19] Daniell, *William Tyndale*, 1. Daniell speaks with more precision elsewhere and says that the Authorized Version is 83 percent Tyndale's (Tyndale, *Selected Writings*, vii). Brian Moynahan, *God's Bestseller: William Tyndale, Thomas More, and the Writing of the English Bible—A Story of Martyrdom and Betrayal* (New York: St. Martin's, 2002), 1, confirms this with his estimates: Tyndale's words "account for 84 percent of the [King James Version] New Testament and 75.8 percent of the Old Testament books that he translated." Daniell also points out how remarkable the Old Testament translations were: "These opening chapters of Genesis are the first translations—not just the first printed, but the first translations—from Hebrew into English. This needs to be emphasized. Not only was the Hebrew language only known in England in 1529 and 1530 by, at the most, a tiny handful of scholars in Oxford and Cambridge, and quite possibly by none; that there was a language called Hebrew at all, or that it had any connection whatsoever with the Bible, would have been news to most of the ordinary population." Daniell, *William Tyndale*, 287.

Blessed are they that mourn for they shall be comforted. (Matt. 5:4)

Our Father, which art in heaven, hallowed be thy name. (Matt. 6:9)

. . . the signs of the times. (Matt. 16:3)

The spirit is willing but the flesh is weak. (Matt. 26:41)

He went out . . . and wept bitterly. (Matt. 26:75)[20]

In the beginning was the Word and the Word was with God and the Word was God. (John 1:1)

In him we live, move and have our being. (Acts 17:28)

. . . a law unto themselves. (Rom. 2:14)

Though I speak with the tongues of men and of angels (1 Cor. 13:1)

Fight the good fight. (1 Tim. 6:12)

According to Daniell, "The list of such near-proverbial phrases is endless."[21] Five hundred years after his great work, "newspaper headlines still quote Tyndale, though unknowingly, and he has reached more people than even Shakespeare."[22]

He Gave Us New Prose—and a Reformation

Luther's translation of 1522 is often praised for "having given a language to the emerging German nation." Daniell claims the same for Tyndale in English:

In his Bible translations, Tyndale's conscious use of everyday words, without inversions, in a neutral word-order, and his wonderful ear for rhythmic patterns, gave to English not only a Bible language, but a new prose. England was blessed as a nation in that the language of its principal book, as the Bible in English rapidly became, was the fountain from

---

[20] "Wept bitterly" is still used by almost all modern translations (NIV, NASB, ESV, NKJV). It has not been improved on for five hundred years in spite of weak efforts like one recent translation: "cried hard." Unlike that phrase, "the rhythm of his two words carries the experience." Tyndale, *Selected Writings*, xv.
[21] Daniell, *William Tyndale*, 142.
[22] Ibid., 2.

which flowed the lucidity, suppleness and expressive range of the great-est prose thereafter.[23]

His craftsmanship with the English language amounted to genius.[24]

He translated two-thirds of the Bible so well that his translations endured until today.[25]

This was not merely a literary phenomenon; it was a spiritual explosion. Tyndale's Bible and writings were the kindling that set the Reformation on fire in England.

Two Ways to Die to Bear Fruit for God

The question arises: How did William Tyndale accomplish this historic achievement? We can answer this in Tyndale's case by remembering two ways that a pastor or any spiritual leader must die in order to bear fruit for God (John 12:24; Rom. 7:4). On the one hand, we must die to the notion that we do not have to think hard or work hard to achieve spiritual goals. On the other hand, we must die to the notion that our thinking and our working are decisive in achieving spiritual goals.

Paul said in 2 Timothy 2:7, "Think over what I say, for the Lord will give you understanding in everything." First, think. Work. Don't bypass the hard work of thinking about apostolic truth. But second, remember this: "*The Lord* will give you understanding." You work. He gives. If he withholds, all our working is in vain. But he ordains that we use our minds and that we work in achieving spiritual ends. So Paul says in 1 Corinthians 15:10, "I worked harder than any of them, though it was not I, but the grace of God that is with me." The key to spiritual achievement is to work hard, and to know and believe and be happy that God's sovereign grace is the decisive cause of all the good that comes.

How Erasmus and Tyndale Were Alike

The way these two truths come together in Tyndale's life explains how he could accomplish what he did. And one of the best ways to see it is

---

[23] Ibid., 116.

[24] Tyndale, *Selected Writings*, xv.

[25] Daniell, *William Tyndale*, 121. "Tyndale gave the nation a Bible language that was English in words, word-order and lilt. He invented some words (for example, 'scapegoat') and the great Oxford English Dictionary has misattributed, and thus also misdated a number of his first uses." Ibid., 3.

to compare him with Erasmus, the Roman Catholic humanist scholar who was famous for his books *Enchiridion* and *The Praise of Folly* and for his printed Greek New Testament.

Erasmus was twenty-eight years older than Tyndale, but they both died in 1536—Tyndale martyred by the Roman Catholic Church, Erasmus a respected member of that church. Erasmus had spent time in Oxford and Cambridge, but we don't know if he and Tyndale ever met.

On the surface, one sees remarkable similarities between Tyndale and Erasmus. Both were great linguists. Erasmus was a Latin scholar and produced the first printed Greek New Testament. Tyndale knew eight languages: Latin, Greek, German, French, Hebrew, Spanish, Italian, and English. Both men loved the natural power of language and were part of a rebirth of interest in the way language works.

For example, Erasmus wrote a book called *De copia* that Tyndale no doubt used as a student at Oxford.[26] It helped students increase their abilities to exploit the "copious" potential of language. This was hugely influential in the early 1500s in England and was used to train students in the infinite possibilities of varied verbal expression. The aim was to keep language from sinking down to mere jargon and worn-out slang and uncreative, unimaginative, prosaic, colorless, boring speech.

One practice lesson for students from *De copia* was to give "no fewer than one hundred fifty ways of saying 'Your letter has delighted me very much.'" The point was to force students to "use of all the verbal muscles in order to avoid any hint of flabbiness."[27] It is not surprising that this is the kind of educational world that gave rise to William Shakespeare (who was born in 1564). Shakespeare is renowned for his unparalleled use of copiousness in language. One critic wrote, "Without Erasmus, no Shakespeare."[28]

So both Erasmus and Tyndale were educated in an atmosphere of conscious craftsmanship.[29] That is, they both believed in hard work to say things clearly and creatively and compellingly when they spoke for Christ.

---

[26] "Tyndale could hardly have missed *De copia*." Daniell, *William Tyndale*, 43. This book went through 150 additions by 1572.

[27] Ibid., 42.

[28] Emrys Jones, *The Origins of Shakespeare* (New York: Oxford University Press, 1977), 13.

[29] "Tyndale as conscious craftsman has been not just neglected, but denied: yet the evidence of the book that follows makes it beyond challenge that he used, as a master, the skill in the selection and arrangement of words which he partly learned at school and university, and partly developed from pioneering work by Erasmus." Daniell, *William Tyndale*, 2.

Not only that, but they both believed the Bible should be translated into the vernacular of every language. Erasmus wrote in the preface to his Greek New Testament,

> Christ wishes his mysteries to be published as widely as possible. I would wish even all women to read the gospel and the epistles of St. Paul, and I wish that they were translated into all languages of all Christian people, that they might be read and known, not merely by the Scotch and the Irish, but even by the Turks and the Saracens. I wish that the husbandman may sing parts of them at his plow, that the weaver may warble them at his shuttle, that the traveler may with their narratives beguile the weariness of the way.[30]

Tyndale could not have said it better.

Both were concerned with the corruption and abuses in the Catholic Church, and both wrote about Christ and the Christian life. Tyndale even translated Erasmus's *Enchiridion*, a kind of spiritual handbook for the Christian life—what Erasmus called *philosophia Christi.*

From a Lightning Bug to a Lightning Bolt

But there was a massive difference between these men, and it had directly to do with the other half of the paradox mentioned above, namely, that we must die not just to intellectual and linguistic laziness, but also to human presumption—human self-exaltation and self-sufficiency. Erasmus and Luther had clashed in the 1520s over the freedom of the will—Erasmus defending human self-determination and Luther arguing for the depravity and bondage of the will.[31] Tyndale was firmly with Luther here.

> Our will is locked and knit faster under the will of the devil than could an hundred thousand chains bind a man unto a post.[32]

> Because . . . [by] nature we are evil, therefore we both think and do evil, and are under vengeance under the law, convict to eternal damnation by the law, and are contrary to the will of God in all our will and in all things consent to the will of the fiend.[33]

---

[30] Ibid., 67.
[31] Erasmus's book was titled *On the Freedom of the Will*, and Luther's was *The Bondage of the Will*.
[32] Tyndale, *Selected Writings*, 39.
[33] Ibid., 37.

It is not possible for a natural man to consent to the law, that it should be good, or that God should be righteous which maketh the law.[34]

This view of human sinfulness set the stage for Tyndale's grasp of the glory of God's sovereign grace in the gospel. Erasmus—and Thomas More with him—did not see the depth of the human condition (their own condition) and so did not see the glory and explosive power of what the reformers saw in the New Testament. What the reformers like Tyndale and Luther saw was not a *philosophia Christi* but the massive work of God in the death and resurrection of Christ to save hopelessly enslaved and hell-bound sinners.

Erasmus does not live or write in this realm of horrible condition and gracious blood-bought salvation. He has the appearance of reform in the *Enchiridion*, but something is missing. To walk from Erasmus into Tyndale is to move (to paraphrase Mark Twain) from a lightning bug to a lightning bolt.

Daniell puts it like this:

> Something in the *Enchiridion* is missing. . . . It is a master-piece of human-ist piety. . . . [But] the activity of Christ in the Gospels, his special work of salvation so strongly detailed there and in the epistles of Paul, is largely missing. Christologically, where Luther thunders, Erasmus makes a sweet sound: what to Tyndale was an impregnable stronghold feels in the *Enchiridion* like a summer pavilion.[35]

Where Luther and Tyndale were blood-earnest about our dreadful human condition and the glory of salvation in Christ, Erasmus and Thomas More joked and bantered. When Luther published his Ninety-Five Theses in 1517, Erasmus sent a copy of them to More—along with a "jocular letter including the anti-papal games, and witty satirical diatribes against abuses within the church, which both of them loved to make."[36]

The Difference: Clarity and Seriousness about the Gospel

I linger here with this difference between Tyndale and Erasmus because I am trying to penetrate to how Tyndale accomplished what he did

---

[34] Ibid., 40.
[35] Daniell, *William Tyndale*, 68–69.
[36] Ibid., 254.

through translating the New Testament. Explosive Reformation is what he accomplished in England. This was not the effect of Erasmus's highbrow, elitist, layered nuancing of Christ and church tradition. Erasmus and Thomas More may have satirized the monasteries and clerical abuses, but they were always playing games compared to Tyndale.

And in this they were very much like notable Christian writers in our own day. Listen to this remarkable assessment from Daniell, and see if you do not hear a description of certain writers in our day who belittle doctrine and extol ambiguity as the humble and mature mind-set:

> Not only is there no fully realized Christ or Devil in Erasmus's book . . . there is a touch of irony about it all, with a feeling of the writer cultivating a faintly superior ambiguity: as if to be dogmatic, for example about the full theology of the work of Christ, was to be rather distasteful, below the best, elite, humanist heights. . . . By contrast Tyndale . . . is ferociously single-minded ["always singing one note"]; the matter in hand, the immediate access of the soul to God without intermediary, is far too important for hints of faintly ironic superiority. . . . Tyndale is as four-square as a carpenter's tool. But in Erasmus's account of the origins of his book there is a touch of the sort of layering of ironies found in the games with *personae*.[37]

It is ironic and sad that today supposedly avant-garde Christian writers can strike this cool, evasive, imprecise, artistic, superficially reformist pose of Erasmus and call it *"post*modern" and capture a generation of unwitting, historically naive people who don't know they are being duped by the same old verbal tactics used by the elitist, humanist writers in past generations. We see them in the controversies between the slippery Arians and Athanasius,[38] and we see them now in Tyndale's day. It's not postmodern. It's pre-modern—because it's perpetual.

At Root: A Passion for Justification by Faith

What drove Tyndale to sing "one note" all his life was the rock-solid conviction that all humans were in bondage to sin, blind, dead, damned, and helpless, and that God had acted in Christ to provide salvation by grace through faith. This is what lay hidden in the Latin Scriptures and

---

[37] Ibid., 69–70.
[38] See, for example, the chapter on Athanasius that starts on page 395 of this volume.

the church system of penance and merit. The Bible must be translated for the sake of the liberating, life-giving gospel.[39]

There is only one hope for our liberation from the bonds of sin and eternal condemnation, Tyndale said: "Neither can any creature loose the bonds, save the blood of Christ only."[40]

> By grace . . . we are plucked out of Adam the ground of all evil and graffed [sic] in Christ, the root of all goodness. In Christ God loved us, his elect and chosen, before the world began and reserved us unto the knowledge of his Son and of his holy gospel: and when the gospel[41] is preached to us [it] openeth our hearts and giveth us grace to believe, and putteth the spirit of Christ in us: and we know him as our Father most merciful, and consent to the law and love it inwardly in our heart and desire to fulfill it and sorrow because we do not.[42]

This massive dose of bondage to sin and deliverance by blood-bought sovereign grace[43] is missing in Erasmus. This is why there is an elitist lightness to his religion—just like there is to so much of evangelicalism today. Hell and sin and atonement and sovereign grace were not weighty realities for Erasmus. But for Tyndale they were everything. And in the middle of these great realities was the doctrine of justification by faith alone. This is why the Bible had to be translated, and ultimately this is why Tyndale was martyred.

> By faith are we saved only in believing the promises. And though faith be never without love and good works, yet is our saving imputed neither to love nor unto good works but unto faith only.[44]

---

[39] "Central to Tyndale's insistence on the need for the Scriptures in English was his grasp that Paul had to be understood in relation to each reader's salvation, and he needed there, above all, to be clear." Daniell, *William Tyndale*, 139.

[40] Tyndale, *Selected Writings*, 40.

[41] Here is Tyndale's definition of the "gospel" that rings with exuberant joy:

> *Evangelion* (that we call the gospel) is a Greek word and signifieth good, merry, glad and joyful tidings, that maketh a man's heart glad and maketh him sing, dance, and leap for joy. . . . [This gospel is] all of Christ the right David, how that he hath fought with sin, with death, and the devil, and overcome them: whereby all men that were in bondage to sin, wounded with death, overcome of the devil are without their own merits or deservings loosed, justified, restored to life and saved, brought to liberty and reconciled unto the favor of God and set at one with him again: which tidings as many as believe laud, praise and thank God, are glad, sing and dance for joy. (Ibid., 33)

[42] Ibid., 37.

[43] "Tyndale was more than a mildly theological thinker. He is at last being understood as, theologically as well as linguistically, well ahead of his time. For him, as several decades later for Calvin (and in the 20th century Karl Barth) the overriding message of the New Testament is the sovereignty of God. Everything is contained in that. It must never, as he wrote, be lost from sight. . . . Tyndale, we are now being shown, was original and new—except that he was also old, demonstrating the understanding of God as revealed in the whole New Testament. For Tyndale, God is, above all, sovereign, active in the individual and in history. He is the one as he put it, in whom alone is found salvation and flourishing." Ibid., viii–ix.

[44] Ibid., 38.

Faith the mother of all good works justifieth us, before we can bring forth any good work: as the husband marryeth his wife before he can have any lawful children by her.[45]

This is the answer to how William Tyndale accomplished what he did in translating the New Testament and writing books that set England on fire with the Reformed faith. He worked assiduously, like the most skilled artist, in the craft of compelling translation, and he was deeply passionate about the great doctrinal truths of the gospel of sovereign grace.

Man is lost, spiritually dead, condemned. God is sovereign; Christ is sufficient. Faith is all. Bible translation and Bible truth were inseparable for Tyndale, and in the end it was the truth—especially the truth of justification by faith alone—that ignited Britain with Reformed fire and then brought the death sentence to this Bible translator.

Blood-Serious Opposition to Bible Translation

It is almost incomprehensible to us today how viciously the Roman Catholic Church opposed the translation of the Scriptures into English. John Wycliffe and his followers called "Lollards"[46] had spread written manuscripts of English translations from the Latin in the late 1300s. In 1401, Parliament passed the law *de Haeretico Comburendo*—"on the burning of heretics"—to make heresy punishable by burning people alive at the stake. The Bible translators were in view.

Then in 1408, the archbishop of Canterbury, Thomas Arundell, created the *Constitutions of Oxford*, which said,

It is a dangerous thing, as witnesseth blessed St. Jerome, to translate the text of the Holy Scripture out of one tongue into another, for in the translation the same sense is not always easily kept. . . . We therefore decree and ordain, that no man, hereafter, by his own authority translate any text of the Scripture into English or any other tongue . . . and that no man can read any such book . . . in part or in whole.[47]

Together these statutes meant that you could be burned alive by the Catholic Church for simply reading the Bible in English. Let that sink in. The dramatist John Bale (1495–1563) "as a boy of 11 watched the

---

[45] Daniell, *William Tyndale*, 156–57.
[46] See note 12.
[47] Moynahan, *God's Bestseller*, xxii.

burning of a young man in Norwich for possessing the Lord's Prayer in English. . . . John Foxe records . . . seven Lollards burned at Coventry in 1519 for teaching their children the Lord's Prayer in English."[48]

The Burning Fury of More

Tyndale hoped to escape this condemnation by getting official authorization for his translation in 1524. But he found just the opposite and had to escape from London to the European continent where he did all his translating and writing for the next twelve years. He lived as a fugitive the entire time until his death near Brussels in 1536.

He watched a rising tide of persecution and felt the pain of seeing young men burned alive who were converted by reading his translation and his books. His closest friend, John Frith, was arrested in London and tried by Thomas More and burned alive July 4, 1531, at the age of twenty-eight. Richard Bayfield ran the ships that took Tyndale's books to England. He was betrayed and arrested, and Thomas More wrote on December 4, 1531, that Bayfield "the monk and apostate [was] well and worthily burned in Smythfelde."[49]

Three weeks later, the same end came to John Tewkesbury. He was converted by reading Tyndale's *Parable of the Wicked Mammon*, which defended justification by faith alone. He was whipped in Thomas More's garden and had his brow squeezed with small ropes until blood came out of his eyes. Then he was sent to the Tower where he was racked till he was lame. Then at last they burned him alive. Thomas More "rejoiced that his victim was now in hell, where Tyndale 'is like to find him when they come together.'"[50]

Four months later, James Bainham followed in the flames in April 1532. He had stood up during the mass at St. Augustine's Church in London and lifted a copy of Tyndale's New Testament and pleaded with the people to die rather than deny the Word of God. That virtually was to sign his own death warrant. Add to these Thomas Bilney, Thomas Dusgate, John Bent, Thomas Harding, Andrew Hewet, Elizabeth Barton, and others—all burned alive for sharing the views of William Tyndale about the Scriptures and the Reformed faith.[51]

---

[48] William Tyndale, *The Obedience of a Christian Man*, ed. David Daniell (London: Penguin, 2000), 202.
[49] Moynahan, *God's Bestseller*, 260.
[50] Ibid., 261.
[51] The list and details are given in Daniell, *William Tyndale*, 183–84.

Why So Much Hatred?

Why this extraordinary hostility against the English New Testament, especially from Thomas More who vilified Tyndale repeatedly in his denunciation of the Reformers he burned? Some would say that the New Testament in English was rejected because it was accompanied with Reformation notes that the church regarded as heretical. That was true of later versions, but not of the first 1526 edition. It did not have notes, and this is the edition that Bishop Tunstall burned in London.[52] The church burned the Word of God. They burned the Bible in public. That shocked Tyndale.

There were surface reasons and deeper reasons why the church opposed an English Bible. The surface reasons were the claims that the English language is rude and unworthy of the exalted language of God's Word; and when one translates, errors can creep in, so it is safer not to translate. Moreover, if the Bible is in English, then each man will become his own interpreter, and many will go astray into heresy and be condemned; and it was church tradition that only priests are given the divine grace to understand the Scriptures. What's more, there is a special sacramental value to the Latin service that people cannot understand but through which grace is given. Such were the kinds of things being said on the surface.

But there were deeper reasons why the church opposed the English Bible: one doctrinal (justification, which we will see in the last months of Tyndale's life) and the other ecclesiastical (the papal, sacramental structure of the Roman Catholic Church). The church realized that they would not be able to sustain certain doctrines biblically because the people would see that they are not in the Bible. And the church realized that their power and control over the people, and even over the state, would be lost if certain doctrines were exposed as unbiblical—especially the priesthood and purgatory and penance.

The Bible Must Not Be Available for Interpretation

Thomas More's criticism of Tyndale boils down mainly to the way Tyndale translated five words. He translated *presbuteros* as *elder* instead of *priest*. He translated *ekklesia* as *congregation* instead of *church*. He translated *metanoeo* as *repent* instead of *do penance*. He translated

---

[52] Ibid., 192–93.

exomologeo as *acknowledge* or *admit* instead of *confess*. And he translated *agape* as *love* rather than *charity*.

Daniell comments, "He cannot possibly have been unaware that those words in particular undercut the entire sacramental structure of the thousand year church throughout Europe, Asia and North Africa. It was the Greek New Testament that was doing the undercutting."[53] And with the doctrinal undermining of these ecclesiastical pillars of priesthood and penance and confession, the pervasive power and control of the church collapsed. England would not be a Catholic nation. The Reformed faith would flourish there in due time.

The Sorrows and Sufferings of a Young Fugitive

What did it cost William Tyndale under these hostile circumstances to stay faithful to his calling as a translator of the Bible and a writer of the Reformed faith?

He fled his homeland in 1524 and was burned at the stake in 1536. He gives us some glimpse of those twelve years as a fugitive in Germany and the Netherlands in one of the very few personal descriptions we have, from Stephen Vaughan's letter in 1531. He refers to

> . . . my pains . . . my poverty . . . my exile out of mine natural country, and bitter absence from my friends . . . my hunger, my thirst, my cold, the great danger wherewith I am everywhere encompassed, and finally . . . innumerable other hard and sharp fightings which I endure.[54]

All these sufferings came to a climax on May 21, 1535, in the midst of Tyndale's great Old Testament translation labors. We can feel some of the ugliness of what happened in the words of David Daniell: "Malice, self-pity, villainy and deceit were about to destroy everything. These evils came to the English House [in Antwerp], wholly uninvited, in the form of an egregious Englishman, Henry Philips."[55] Philips won Tyndale's trust over some months and then betrayed him. John Foxe tells how it happened:

> So when it was dinner-time, Master Tyndale went forth with Philips, and at the going forth of Poyntz's house, was a long narrow entry, so that two could

---

[53] Ibid., 149.
[54] Ibid., 213.
[55] Ibid., 361.

not go in a front. Mr. Tyndale would have put Philips before him, but Philips would in no wise, but put Master Tyndale before, for that he pretended to show great humanity. So Master Tyndale, being a man of no great stature, went before, and Philips, a tall comely person, followed behind him: who had set officers on either side of the door upon two seats, who, being there, might see who came in the entry: and coming through the same entry, Philips pointed with his finger over Master Tyndale's head down to him, that the officers who sat at the door might see that it was he whom they should take. . . . Then they took him, and brought him to the emperor's attorney, or procurer-general, where he dined. Then came the procurer-general to the house of Poyntz, and sent away all that was there of Master Tyndale's, as well his books as other things: and from thence Tyndale was had to the castle of Filford, eighteen English miles from Antwerp, and there he remained until he was put to death.[56]

The Cold and Final Castle

Vilvoorde Castle is six miles north of Brussels and about the same distance from Louvain. Here Tyndale stayed for eighteen months. "The charge was heresy, with not agreeing with the holy Roman Emperor—in a nutshell, being Lutheran."[57] A four-man commission from the Catholic center of Louvain was authorized to prove that Tyndale was a heretic. One of them named Latomus filled three books with his interactions with Tyndale and said that Tyndale himself wrote a "book" in prison to defend his chief doctrinal standard: *Sola fides justificat apud Deum—Faith Alone Justifies before God*. This was the key issue in the end. The evil of translating the Bible came down to this: Are we justified by faith alone?

These months in prison were not easy. They were a long dying, leading to death. We get one glimpse into the prison to see Tyndale's condition and his passion. He wrote a letter in September 1535, when there seems to have been a lull in the examinations. It was addressed to an unnamed officer of the castle. Here is a condensed version of Mozley's translation of the Latin:

> I beg your lordship, and that of the Lord Jesus, that if I am to remain here through the winter, you will request the commissary to have the kindness to send me, from the goods of mine which he has, a warmer cap; for I suffer

---

[56] Ibid., 364.
[57] Ibid., 365.

greatly from cold in the head, and am afflicted by a perpetual catarrh, which is much increased in this cell; a warmer coat also, for this which I have is very thin; a piece of cloth too to patch my leggings. My overcoat is worn out; my shirts are also worn out. He has a woolen shirt, if he will be good enough to send it. I have also with him leggings of thicker cloth to put on above; he has also warmer night-caps. And I ask to be allowed to have a lamp in the evening; it is indeed wearisome sitting alone in the dark. But most of all I beg and beseech your clemency to be urgent with the commissary, that he will kindly permit me to have the Hebrew Bible, Hebrew grammar, and Hebrew dictionary, that I may pass the time in that study. In return may you obtain what you most desire, so only that it be for the salvation of your soul. But if any other decision has been taken concerning me, to be carried out before winter, I will be patient, abiding the will of God, to the glory of the grace of my Lord Jesus Christ: whose spirit (I pray) may ever direct your heart. Amen W. Tindalus[58]

We don't know if his requests were granted. He did stay in that prison through the winter. His verdict was sealed in August 1536. He was formally condemned as a heretic and degraded from the priesthood. Then in early October (traditionally October 6), he was tied to the stake and then strangled by the executioner, then afterward consumed in the fire. Foxe reports that his last words were, "Lord! Open the King of England's eyes!"[59] He was forty-two years old, never married, and never buried.

He Will Ease Your Pain or Shorten It

His closing words to us are clear from his life and from his writings. Following God's call in accomplishing the spread of his saving gospel is often very costly. I will let Tyndale speak in his own words from his book *The Obedience of a Christian Man*:

> If God promise riches, the way thereto is poverty. Whom he loveth he chasteneth, whom he exalteth, he casteth down, whom he saveth he damneth first, he bringeth no man to heaven except he send him to hell first. If he promise life he slayeth it first, when he buildeth, he casteth all down first. He is no patcher, he cannot build on another man's foundation. He will not work until all be past remedy and brought unto such a case, that men may

---

[58] Ibid., 379.
[59] Ibid., 382–83. "Contemporaries noted no such words, however, only that the strangling was bungled and that he suffered terribly." Moynahan, *God's Bestseller*, 377.

see how that his hand, his power, his mercy, his goodness and truth hath wrought all together. He will let no man be partaker with him of his praise and glory.[60]

Let us therefore look diligently whereunto we are called, that we deceive not ourselves. We are called, not to dispute as the pope's disciples do, but to die with Christ that we may live with him, and to suffer with him that we may reign with him.[61]

For if God be on our side: what matter maketh it who be against us, be they bishops, cardinals, popes or whatsoever names they will.[62]

So let Tyndale's very last word to us be the last word he sent to his best friend, John Frith, in a letter just before Frith was burned alive for believing and speaking the truth of Scripture:

Your cause is Christ's gospel, a light that must be fed with the blood of faith. . . . If when we be buffeted for well-doing, we suffer patiently and endure, that is acceptable to God; for to that end we are called. For Christ also suffered for us, leaving us an example, that we should follow his steps, who did no sin.

Hereby have we perceived love, that he had lain down his life for us; therefore we ought also to lay down our lives for the brethren. . . . Let not your body faint. . . . If the pain be above your strength, remember, Whatsoever ye shall ask in my name, I will give it you. And pray to our Father in that name, and he will ease your pain, or shorten it. . . . Amen.[63]

---

[60] Tyndale, *The Obedience of a Christian Man*, 6.
[61] Ibid., 8.
[62] Ibid., 6.
[63] From *Foxe's Book of Martyrs*.

2

John G. Paton

"You Will Be Eaten by Cannibals!":
Courage in the Face of Fierce Opposition

In 1606, a chain of eighty islands in the South Pacific was discovered by Fernandez de Quiros of Spain. In 1773, the islands were explored by Captain James Cook and named the New Hebrides because of the similarities with the Hebrides Islands off the northwest coast of Scotland. In 1980, the New Hebrides gained its independence from Britain and France and was named Vanuatu. The chain of islands is about 450 miles long. If you draw a line straight from Honolulu to Sydney, it will cut through Port Vila, the capital of Vanuatu, two-thirds of the way between Hawaii and Australia. The population today is about 215,000.

Baptized with the Blood of Martyrs
To the best of our knowledge, the New Hebrides had no Christian influence before John Williams and James Harris from the London Missionary Society landed in 1839. Both of these missionaries were killed and eaten by cannibals on the island of Erromanga on November 20 of that year, only minutes after going ashore. Forty-eight years later, John Paton wrote, "Thus were the New Hebrides baptized with the blood of martyrs; and Christ thereby told the whole Christian world that he claimed these islands as His own."[1]

---

[1] John G. Paton, *Missionary to the New Hebrides: An Autobiography Edited by His Brother* (1889; repr., Edinburgh: Banner of Truth, 1965), 75.

The London Missionary Society sent another team to the island of Tanna in 1842, and these missionaries were driven off within seven months. But on the island of Aneityum, John Geddie from the Presbyterian Church in Nova Scotia (coming in 1848) and John Inglis from the Reformed Presbyterian Church in Scotland (coming in 1852) saw amazing fruit, so that by 1854 "about 3,500 savages [more than half the population[2]] threw away their idols, renouncing their heathen customs and avowing themselves to be worshippers of the true Jehovah God."[3] When Geddie died in 1872, all the population of Aneityum was said to be Christian.[4]

The Dangerous and Hope-Filled Setting of Paton's Mission

This is part of a great work God was doing in the South Sea Islands in those days. In 1887, the sixty-three-year-old John Paton recorded the wider triumphs of the gospel. When certain people argued that the Aborigines of Australia were subhuman and incapable of conversion or civilization, Paton responded with mission facts as well as biblical truth.

> Recall . . . what the Gospel has done for the near kindred of these same Aborigines. On our own Aneityum, 3,500 Cannibals have been led to renounce their heathenism. . . . In Fiji, 79,000 Cannibals have been brought under the influence of the Gospel; and 13,000 members of the Churches are professing to live and work for Jesus. In Samoa, 34,000 Cannibals have professed Christianity; and in nineteen years, its College has sent forth 206 Native teachers and evangelists. On our New Hebrides, more than 12,000 Cannibals have been brought to sit at the feet of Christ, though I mean not to say that they are all model Christians; and 133 of the Natives have been trained and sent forth as teachers and preachers of the Gospel.[5]

This is the remarkable missionary context for the life and ministry of John G. Paton, who was born near Dumfries, Scotland, on May 24, 1824. He sailed for the New Hebrides (via Australia) with his wife Mary on April 16, 1858, at the age of thirty-three. They reached their appointed island of Tanna on November 5, and in March the next year

---

[2] Kenneth Scott Latourette, *A History of the Expansion of Christianity, The Great Century: The Americas, Australasia and Africa, 1800 AD to 1914 AD* (1943; repr., Grand Rapids, MI: Zondervan, 1970), 228.
[3] Paton, *Autobiography*, 77.
[4] George Patterson, *Missionary Life among the Cannibals: Being the Life of the Rev. John Geddie, D.D., First Missionary to the New Hebrides; with the History of the Nova Scotia Presbyterian Mission on That Group* (Toronto: James Campbell, 1882), 508.
[5] Paton, *Autobiography*, 265.

both his wife and his newborn son died of the fever. He served alone on the island for the next four years under incredible circumstances of constant danger until he was driven off the island in February 1862.

For the next four years, he did extraordinarily effective mobilization work for the Presbyterian mission to the New Hebrides, traveling around Australia and Great Britain. He married again in 1864 and took his wife Margaret back this time to the smaller island of Aniwa ("It measures scarcely seven miles by two"[6]). They labored together for forty-one years until Margaret died in 1905, when John Paton was eighty-one.

When they came to Aniwa in November 1866, they saw the destitution of the islanders. It will help us appreciate the magnitude of their labors and the wonders of their fruitfulness if we see some of what they faced.

The native people were cannibals and occasionally ate the flesh of their defeated foes. They practiced infanticide and widow sacrifice, killing the widows of deceased men so they could serve their husbands in the next world.[7]

> Their worship was entirely a service of fear, its aim being to propitiate this or that evil spirit, to prevent calamity or to secure revenge. They deified their chiefs . . . so that almost every village or tribe had its own Sacred Man. . . . They exercised an extraordinary influence for evil, these village or tribal priests, and were believed to have the disposal of life and death through their sacred ceremonies. . . . They also worshipped the spirits of departed ancestors and heroes, through their material idols of wood and stone. . . . They feared the spirits and sought their aid; especially seeking to propitiate those who presided over war and peace, famine and plenty, health and sickness, destruction and prosperity, life and death. Their whole worship was one of slavish fear; and, so far as ever I could learn, they had no idea of a God of mercy or grace.[8]

Paton admitted that at times his heart wavered as he wondered whether these people could be brought to the point of weaving Christian ideas into the spiritual consciousness of their lives.[9] But he took heart from

---

[6] Ibid., 312.
[7] Ibid., 69, 334.
[8] Ibid., 72. This description was made of the natives on the island of Tanna but applies equally well to the conditions on the nearby island of Aniwa.
[9] Ibid., 74.

the power of the gospel and from the fact that thousands on Aneityum had come to Christ.

So he learned the language and reduced it to writing.[10] He built orphanages ("We trained these young people for Jesus"[11]). "Mrs. Paton taught a class of about fifty women and girls. They became experts at sewing, singing and plaiting hats, and reading."[12] They "trained the Teachers . . . translated and printed and expounded the Scriptures . . . ministered to the sick and dying . . . dispensed medicines every day . . . taught them the use of tools . . ." and more.[13] They held worship services every Lord's Day and sent native teachers to all the villages to preach the gospel.

In the next fifteen years, John and Margaret Paton saw the entire island of Aniwa turn to Christ. Years later he wrote, "I claimed Aniwa for Jesus, and by the grace of God Aniwa now worships at the Savior's feet."[14] When he was seventy-three years old and traveling around the world trumpeting the cause of missions in the South Seas, he was still ministering to his beloved Aniwan people and "published the New Testament in the Aniwan Language" in 1897.[15] Even to his death, he was translating hymns and catechisms[16] and creating a dictionary for his people even when he couldn't be with them anymore.[17]

During his years of labor on the islands, Paton kept a journal and notebooks and letters from which he wrote his *Autobiography* in three parts from 1887 to 1898. Almost all we know of his work comes from that book, which is still in print in one volume from the Banner of Truth Trust.

Paton outlived his wife by two years and died in Australia on January 28, 1907, at the age of eighty-two. Today, over a hundred years after the death of John Paton, about 92 percent of the population of Vanuatu identifies itself as Christian, perhaps 41 percent of the population being evangelical.[18] The sacrifices and the legacy of the missionaries to the New Hebrides are stunning, and John G. Paton stands out as one

---

[10] Ibid., 319.
[11] Ibid., 317.
[12] Ibid., 377.
[13] Ibid., 378.
[14] Ibid., 312.
[15] Ralph Bell, *John G. Paton: Missionary to the New Hebrides* (Butler, IN: Highley, 1957), 238.
[16] Ibid.
[17] Paton, *Autobiography*, 451.
[18] See the Joshua Project, accessed February 15, 2016, http://www.joshuaproject.net/countries/NH.

of the great ones. In telling his story, we will focus on one of the most inspiring aspects of his character: his courage.

Overcoming Criticism

Paton had courage to overcome the criticism he received from respected elders for going to the New Hebrides. A certain Mr. Dickson exploded, "The cannibals! You will be eaten by cannibals!" The memory of Williams and Harris on Erromanga was only nineteen years old. But to this Paton responded:

> Mr. Dickson, you are advanced in years now, and your own prospect is soon to be laid in the grave, there to be eaten by worms; I confess to you, that if I can but live and die serving and honoring the Lord Jesus, it will make no difference to me whether I am eaten by Cannibals or by worms; and in the Great Day my Resurrection body will rise as fair as yours in the likeness of our risen Redeemer.[19]

This is the kind of in-your-face spiritual moxie that would mark Paton's whole life. It's a big part of what makes reading his story so invigorating.

Another kind of criticism for his going was that he would be leaving a very fruitful ministry. Paton had served for ten years as a city missionary in urban Glasgow among lower-income people with tremendous success, and hundreds of unchurched people were attending his classes and services during the week. One of his loved professors of divinity and minister of the congregation where he had served as an elder tried to persuade him to stay in that ministry. He reported that the professor made his case as follows:

> Green Street Church was doubtless the sphere for which God had given me peculiar qualifications, and in which He had so largely blessed my labors; that if I left those now attending my Classes and Meetings, they might be scattered, and many of them would probably fall away; that I was leaving certainty for uncertainty—work in which God had made me greatly useful, for work in which I might fail to be useful, and only throw away my life amongst Cannibals.[20]

Paton said the opposition to his going was deeply troubling:

---

[19] Paton, *Autobiography*, 56.
[20] Ibid., 55.

The opposition was so strong from nearly all, and many of them warm Christian friends, that I was sorely tempted to question whether I was carrying out the Divine will, or only some headstrong wish of my own. This also caused me much anxiety, and drove me close to God in prayer.[21]

We will see shortly how he rose above these temptations to turn away from his missionary calling.

Courage in the Face of Possible and Real Loss

He and his wife arrived on the island of Tanna on November 5, 1858, and Mary was pregnant. The baby was born February 12, 1859. "Our island-exile thrilled with joy! But the greatest of sorrows was treading hard upon the heels of that great joy!"[22] Mary had repeated attacks of ague, fever, pneumonia, and diarrhea with delirium for two weeks.

> Then in a moment, altogether unexpectedly, she died on March third. To crown my sorrows, and complete my loneliness, the dear baby-boy, whom we had named after her father, Peter Robert Robson, was taken from me after one week's sickness, on the 20th of March. Let those who have ever passed through any similar darkness as of midnight feel for me; as for all others, it would be more than vain to try to paint my sorrows![23]

He dug the two graves with his own hands and buried them by the house he had built.

> Stunned by that dreadful loss, in entering upon this field of labor to which the Lord had Himself so evidently led me, my reason seemed for a time almost to give way. The ever-merciful Lord sustained me . . . and that spot became my sacred and much-frequented shrine, during all the following months and years when I labored on for the salvation of the savage Islanders amidst difficulties, dangers, and deaths. . . . But for Jesus, and the fellowship he vouchsafed to me there, I must have gone mad and died beside the lonely grave![24]

The courage to risk the loss was remarkable. But the courage to experience the loss and press on alone was supernatural.

---

[21] Ibid., 56.
[22] Ibid., 79.
[23] Ibid.
[24] Ibid., 80.

I felt her loss beyond all conception or description, in that dark land. It was very difficult to be resigned, left alone, and in sorrowful circumstances; but feeling immovably assured that my God and father was too wise and loving to err in anything that He does or permits, I looked up to the Lord for help, and struggled on in His work.[25]

Here we get a glimpse of the theology that we will see underneath this man's massive courage and toil.

I do not pretend to see through the mystery of such visitations—wherein God calls away the young, the promising, and those sorely needed for his service here; but this I do know and feel, that, in the light of such dispensations, it becomes us all to love and serve our blessed Lord Jesus so that we may be ready at his call for death and eternity.[26]

Courage to Risk His Own Sickness with No Doctors and No Escape

"Fever and ague had attacked me fourteen times severely."[27] In view of his wife's death, Paton never knew when any one of these attacks would mean his own death. Imagine struggling with a life-and-death sickness over and over with only one Christian native friend named Abraham who had come with him to the island to help him.

For example, as he was building a new house to get to higher, healthier ground, he collapsed with the fever on his way up the steep hill from the coast:

When about two-thirds up the hill I became so faint that I concluded I was dying. Lying down on the ground, sloped against the root of a tree to keep me from rolling to the bottom, I took farewell of old Abraham, of my mission work, and of everything around! In this weak state I lay, watched over by my faithful companion, and fell into a quiet sleep.[28]

He revived and was restored. But only great courage could press on month after month, year after year, knowing that the fever that took his wife and son lay at the door.

And it's not as if these dangers were only during one season at the beginning of his missionary life. Fifteen years later, with another wife

---

[25] Ibid., 85.
[26] Ibid.
[27] Ibid., 105.
[28] Ibid., 106.

and another child on another island, he records, "During the hurricanes, from January to April, 1873, when the *Dayspring* [the mission
ship] was wrecked, we lost a darling child by death, my dear wife had
a protracted illness, and I was brought very low with severe rheumatic
fever . . . and was reported as dying."[29]

Courage to Face Mortal Enemies

The most common demand for courage was the almost-constant threat
to his life from the hostilities of the natives. This is what makes his *Autobiography* read like a thriller. In his first four years on Tanna, when
he was all alone, he moved from one savage crisis to the next. One
wonders how his mind kept from snapping, as he never knew when his
house would be surrounded with angry natives or whether he would be
ambushed along the way. How do you survive when there is no time or
place for leisure? No unwinding? No sure refuge on earth?

> Our continuous danger caused me now oftentimes to sleep with my clothes
> on, that I might start at a moment's warning. My faithful dog Clutha would
> give a sharp bark and awake me. . . . God made them fear this precious crea-
> ture, and often used her in saving our lives.[30]

> My enemies seldom slackened their hateful designs against my life, however
> calmed or baffled for the moment. . . . A wild chief followed me around for
> four hours with his loaded musket, and, though often directed towards me,
> God restrained his hand. I spoke kindly to him, and attended to my work as
> if he had not been there, fully persuaded that my God had placed me there,
> and would protect me till my allotted task was finished. Looking up in un-
> ceasing prayer to our dear Lord Jesus, I left all in his hands, and felt im-
> mortal till my work was done. Trials and hairbreadth escapes strengthened
> my faith, and seemed only to nerve me for more to follow; and they did tread
> swiftly upon each other's heels.[31]

One of the most remarkable things about Paton's dealing with danger is
the gutsy forthrightness with which he spoke to his assailants. He often
rebuked them to their faces and scolded them for their bad behavior
even as they held the axe over his head.

---

[29] Ibid., 384.
[30] Ibid., 178.
[31] Ibid., 117.

One morning at daybreak I found my house surrounded by armed men, and a chief intimated that they had assembled to take my life. Seeing that I was entirely in their hands, I knelt down and gave myself away body and soul to the Lord Jesus, for what seemed the last time on earth. Rising, I went out to them, and began calmly talking about their unkind treatment of me and contrasting it with all my conduct towards them. . . . At last some of the Chiefs, who had attended the Worship, rose and said, "Our conduct has been bad; but now we will fight for you, and kill all those who hate you."[32]

[Once] when natives in large numbers were assembled at my house, a man furiously rushed on me with his axe but a Kaserumini Chief snatched a spade with which I had been working, and dexterously defended me from instant death. Life in such circumstances led me to cling very near to the Lord Jesus; I knew not, for one brief hour, when or how attack might be made; and yet, with my trembling hand clasped in the hand once nailed on Calvary, and now swaying the scepter of the universe, calmness and peace and resignation abode in my soul.[33]

As his courage increased and his deliverances were multiplied, he would make it his aim to keep warring factions separated, and he would throw himself between them and argue for peace. "Going amongst them every day, I did my utmost to stop hostilities, setting the evils of war before them, and pleading with the leading men to renounce it."[34] He would go to visit his enemies when they were sick and wanted his help, never knowing what was an ambush and what was not.

Once a native named Ian called Paton to his sickbed, and as Paton leaned over him, he pulled a dagger and held it to Paton's heart.

I durst neither move nor speak, except that my heart kept praying to the Lord to spare me, or if my time was come, to take me home to Glory with Himself. There passed a few moments of awful suspense. My sight went and came. Not a word had been spoken, except to Jesus; and then Ian wheeled the knife around, thrust it into the sugar cane leaf. And [he] cried to me, "Go, go quickly!" . . . I ran for my life a weary four miles till I reached the Mission House, faint, yet praising God for such a deliverance.[35]

---

[32] Ibid., 115.
[33] Ibid., 117.
[34] Ibid., 139.
[35] Ibid., 191.

Courage to Die?

A final kind of courage I will mention is the courage in the face of accusations that he was a coward. After four years, the entire island population rose against Paton, blaming him for an epidemic, and made siege against him and his little band of Christians. There were spectacularly close calls and a miraculous deliverance from fire by wind and rain,[36] and finally a wonderful answer to prayer as a ship arrived just in time to take him off the island.

In response to this, and after four years of risking his life hundreds of times and losing his wife and child, he recounts,

> Conscious that I had, to the last inch of life, tried to do my duty, I left all results in the hands of my only Lord, and all criticisms to His unerring judgment. Hard things also were occasionally spoken to my face. One dear friend, for instance, said, "You should not have left. You should have stood at the post of duty till you fell. It would have been to your honor, and better for the cause of the Mission, had you been killed at the post of duty like the Gordons and others.[37]

Oh, how easy it would have been for him to respond by walking away from the mission at a moment like that. But courage pressed on for another four decades of fruitful ministry on the island of Aniwa and around the world.

And so the next question I ask of Paton's life is, *What did this courage achieve?*

The Outcome of His Courage?

We have already seen one main answer to this question—namely, the entire island of Aniwa turned to Christ. Four years of seemingly fruitless and costly labor on Tanna could have meant the end of Paton's missionary life. He could have remembered that in Glasgow for ten years he had had unprecedented success as an urban missionary. Now for four years he seemed to have accomplished nothing, and he lost his wife and child in the process. But instead of going home, he turned his missionary heart to Aniwa. And this time the story was different. "I claimed Aniwa for Jesus, and by the grace of God, Aniwa now worships at the Savior's feet."[38]

---

[36] Ibid., 215.
[37] Ibid., 223.
[38] Ibid., 312.

Awakening at Home

The courageous endurance on Tanna resulted in a story that awakened thousands to the call of missions and strengthened the home church. The reason Paton wrote the second volume of his *Autobiography*, he says, was to record God's "marvelous goodness in using my humble voice and pen, and the story of my life, for interesting thousands and tens of thousands in the work of Missions."[39] And the influence goes on today—even, I pray, in this book.

> Oftentimes, while passing through the perils and defeats of my first four years in the Mission-field on Tanna, I wondered . . . why God permitted such things. But on looking back now, I already clearly perceive . . . that the Lord was thereby preparing me for doing, and providing me materials wherewith to accomplish, the best work of all my life, namely the kindling of the heart of Australian Presbyterianism with a living affection for these Islanders of their own Southern Seas . . . and in being the instrument under God of sending out Missionary after Missionary to the New Hebrides, to claim another island and still another for Jesus. That work, and all that may spring from it in Time and Eternity, never could have been accomplished by me but for first the sufferings and then the story of my Tanna enterprise![40]

And the awakening was not just in Australia, but in Scotland and around the world. For example, he tells us what the effect of his home tour was on his own small Reformed Presbyterian Church after his four years of pain and seeming fruitlessness on Tanna. "I was . . . filled with a high passion of gratitude to be able to proclaim, at the close of my tour . . . that of all her ordained Ministers, one in every six was a Missionary of the Cross!"[41] Indeed the effects at home were far more widespread than that, and here is a lesson for all churches today.

> Nor did the dear old Church thus cripple herself; on the contrary, her zeal for Missions accompanied, if not caused, unwonted prosperity at home. New waves of liberality passed over the heart of her people. Debts that had burdened many of the Churches and Manses were swept away. Additional Congregations were organized. And in May, 1876, the Reformed Presbyterian Church entered into an honorable and independent Union

---

[39] Ibid., 220.
[40] Ibid., 222–23.
[41] Ibid., 280.

with her larger, wealthier, and more progressive sister, the Free Church of Scotland.[42]

In other words, the courageous perseverance of John Paton on Tanna, in spite of apparent fruitlessness, bore fruit for the mission field and for the church at home in ways he could have never dreamed in the midst of his dangers.

Silencing Skeptics

Another one of those good effects was to vindicate the power of the gospel to convert the hardest people. Paton had an eye to the sophisticated European despisers of the gospel as he wrote the story of his life. He wanted to give evidence to skeptical modern men that the gospel can and does transform the most unlikely people and their societies.

So in his *Autobiography* he tells stories of particular converts like Kowia, a chief on Tanna. When he was dying, he came to say farewell to Paton.

> "Farewell, Missi, I am very near death now; we will meet again in Jesus and with Jesus!" . . . Abraham sustained him, tottering to the place of graves; there he lay down . . . and slept in Jesus; and there the faithful Abraham buried him beside his wife and children. Thus died a man who had been a cannibal chief, but by the grace of God and the love of Jesus changed, transfigured into a character of light and beauty. What think ye of this, ye skeptics as to the reality of conversion? . . . I knew that day, and I know now, that there is one soul at least from Tanna to sing the glories of Jesus in Heaven—and, oh, the rapture when I meet him there![43]

And then, of course, there was old Abraham himself. He was not one of Paton's converts, but he was a converted cannibal from Aneityum and Paton's absolutely trustworthy helper on Tanna during all his time there. So Paton writes again as a witness to European skeptics:

> When I have read or heard the shallow objections of irreligious scribblers and talkers, hinting that there was no reality in conversions, and that mission effort was but waste, oh, how my heart has yearned to plant them just one week on Tanna, with the "natural" man all around in the person of Cannibal and Heathen, and only the one "spiritual" man in the person of the converted

---

[42] Ibid.
[43] Ibid., 160.

Abraham, nursing them, feeding them, saving them "for the love of Jesus"— that I might just learn how many hours it took to convince them that Christ in man was a reality after all! All the skepticism of Europe would hide its head in foolish shame; and all its doubts would dissolve under one glance of the new light that Jesus, and Jesus alone, pours from the converted Cannibal's eye.[44]

The list could go on as to what Paton's courage achieved. But we turn to the question, *Where did this courage come from?* But the two questions overlap, because what the courage achieved was the vindication of its source.

Where Did This Courage Come From?

The answer Paton would want us to give is that it came from God. But he would also want us to see what precious means God used and, if possible, apply them to ourselves and our situations. What was it then that God used to awaken in John Paton such remarkable courage?

His Courage Came from His Father

The tribute Paton pays to his godly father is worth the price of his *Autobiography*, even if you don't read anything else. Maybe it's because I have a daughter and four sons, but I wept as I read this section. It filled me with such longing to be a father like this.

There was a small room, the "closet" where his father would go for prayer, as a rule, after each meal. The eleven children knew it, and they reverenced the spot and learned something profound about God from their father's devotion to prayer. The impact on John Paton was immense.

> Though everything else in religion were by some unthinkable catastrophe to be swept out of memory, were blotted from my understanding, my soul would wander back to those early scenes, and shut itself up once again in that Sanctuary Closet, and, hearing still the echoes of those cries to God, would hurl back all doubt with the victorious appeal, "He walked with God, why may not I?"[45]

> How much my father's prayers at this time impressed me I can never explain, nor could any stranger understand. When, on his knees and all of us kneeling around him in Family Worship, he poured out his whole soul

---

[44] Ibid., 107.
[45] Ibid., 8.

with tears for the conversion of the Heathen world to the service of Jesus, and for every personal and domestic need, we all felt as if in the presence of the living Savior, and learned to know and love him as our Divine friend.[46]

One scene best captures the depth of love between John and his father and the power of the impact on John's life of uncompromising courage and purity. The time came for the young Paton to leave home and go to Glasgow to attend divinity school and become a city missionary in his early twenties. From his hometown of Torthorwald to the train station at Kilmarnock was a forty-mile walk. Forty years later Paton wrote:

> My dear father walked with me the first six miles of the way. His counsels and tears and heavenly conversation on that parting journey are fresh in my heart as if it had been but yesterday; and tears are on my cheeks as freely now as then, whenever memory steals me away to the scene. For the last half mile or so we walked on together in almost unbroken silence—my father, as was often his custom, carrying hat in hand, while his long flowing yellow hair (then yellow, but in later years white as snow) streamed like a girl's down his shoulders. His lips kept moving in silent prayers for me; and his tears fell fast when our eyes met each other in looks for which all speech was vain! We halted on reaching the appointed parting place; he grasped my hand firmly for a minute in silence, and then solemnly and affectionately said: "God bless you, my son! Your father's God prosper you, and keep you from all evil!"
>
> Unable to say more, his lips kept moving in silent prayer; in tears we embraced, and parted. I ran off as fast as I could; and, when about to turn a corner in the road where he would lose sight of me, I looked back and saw him still standing with head uncovered where I had left him—gazing after me. Waving my hat in adieu, I rounded the corner and out of sight in an instant. But my heart was too full and sore to carry me further, so I darted into the side of the road and wept for a time. Then, rising up cautiously, I climbed the dike to see if he yet stood where I had left him; and just at that moment I caught a glimpse of him climbing the dyke and looking out for me! He did not see me, and after he gazed eagerly in my direction for a while, he got down, set his face toward home, and began to return—his head still uncovered, and his heart, I felt sure, still rising in prayers for me. I watched through blinding tears, till his form faded from my gaze; and then, hastening on my way, vowed deeply and oft, by the help of God, to live and act so as never to grieve or dishonor such a father and mother as he had given me.[47]

---

[46] Ibid., 21.
[47] Ibid., 25–26.

The impact of his father's faith and prayer and love and discipline was immeasurable.

His Courage Came from a Deep Sense of Divine Calling

Before he was twelve years old, Paton says, "I had given my soul to God, and was resolved to aim at being a missionary of the cross, or a minister of the gospel."[48] As he came to the end of his studies in divinity in Glasgow at the age of thirty-two, he says, "I continually heard . . . the wail of the perishing Heathen in the South Seas; and I saw that few were caring for them, while I well knew that many would be ready to take up my work in Calton."[49] "The Lord kept saying within me, 'Since none better qualified can be got, rise and offer yourself!'"

When he was criticized for leaving a fruitful ministry, one crucial event sealed his sense of calling, namely, a word from his parents:

> Heretofore we feared to bias you, but now we must tell you why we praise God for the decision to which you have been led. Your father's heart was set upon being a Minister, but other claims forced him to give it up. When you were given to them, your father and mother laid you upon the altar, their first-born, to be consecrated, if God saw fit, as a Missionary of the Cross; and it has been their constant prayer that you might be prepared, qualified, and led to this very decision; and we pray with all our heart that the Lord may accept your offering, long spare you, and give you many souls from the Heathen World for your hire.[50]

In response to that, Paton wrote, "From that moment, every doubt as to my path of duty forever vanished. I saw the hand of God very visibly, not only preparing me before, but now leading me to, the Foreign Mission field."[51] That sense of duty and calling bred in him an undaunted courage that would never look back.

His Courage Came from a Sense of Holy Heritage in His Church

Paton was part of the Reformed Presbyterian Church of Scotland, one of the oldest but smallest Protestant churches. It traced its lineage back to the Scottish Covenanters and had in it a strong sense of valor for

---

[48] Ibid. 21.
[49] Ibid., 52.
[50] Ibid., 57.
[51] Ibid.

the cause of the great truths of the Reformation. Paton once wrote, "I am more proud that the blood of Martyrs is in my veins, and their truths in my heart, than other men can be of noble pedigree or royal names."[52]

The truths he has in mind are the robust doctrines of Calvinism. He said in his *Autobiography*, "I am by conviction a strong Calvinist."[53] For him this meant, as we have seen, a strong confidence that God can and will change the hearts of the most unlikely people. His Reformed doctrine of regeneration was crucial here in maintaining his courage in the face of humanly impossible odds. Commenting on the conversion of one native, he said, "Regeneration is the sole work of the Holy Spirit in the human heart and soul, and is in every case one and the same. Conversion, on the other hand, bringing into play the action also of the human will, is never absolutely the same perhaps in even two souls."[54] "Oh, Jesus! To Thee alone be all the glory. Thou hast the key to unlock every heart that Thou has created."[55]

In other words, Calvinism, contrary to all misrepresentation, was not a hindrance to missions but the hope of missions for John Paton and hundreds of other missionaries like him. So it's not surprising what the next source of courage was for Paton.

His Courage Came from His Confidence in the Sovereignty of God Controlling All Adversities

We have already seen the words he wrote over his wife's and child's grave: "Feeling immovably assured that my God and father was too wise and loving to err in anything that he does or permits, I looked up to the Lord for help, and struggled on in His work."[56]

Over and over this faith sustained him in the most threatening and frightening situations. As he was trying to escape from Tanna at the end of four years of dangers, he and Abraham were surrounded by raging natives who kept urging each other to strike the first blow.

> My heart rose up to the Lord Jesus; I saw Him watching all the scene. My peace came back to me like a wave from God. I realized that I was immortal

---

[52] Ibid., 280.
[53] Ibid., 195.
[54] Ibid., 372.
[55] Ibid., 373.
[56] Ibid., 85.

till my Master's work with me was done. The assurance came to me, as if a voice out of Heaven had spoken, that not a musket would be fired to wound us, not a club prevail to strike us, not a spear leave the hand in which it was held vibrating to be thrown, not an arrow leave the bow, or a killing stone the fingers, without the permission of Jesus Christ, whose is all power in Heaven and on Earth. He rules all Nature, animate and inanimate, and restrains even the Savage of the South Seas.[57]

After getting away with his life and losing everything that he had on earth ("my little earthly All"), instead of despairing or pouting or being paralyzed with self-pity, he moved forward expecting to see God's good purpose in time—which he saw in the ministry that opened to him, first of missions mobilization and then of work on Aniwa. "Often since have I thought that the Lord stripped me thus bare of all these interests, that I might with undistracted mind devote my entire energy to the special work soon to be carved out for me, and of which at this moment neither I nor anyone had ever dreamed."[58]

Year after year, "disappointments and successes were strangely intermingled"[59] in his life. There was no long period of time, it seems, where life was very easy. But we would distort the man if we said there were no low moments. "I felt so disappointed, so miserable," he wrote about one period of his travels, "that I wished I had been in my grave with my dear departed and my brethren on the Islands who had fallen around me."[60] It was not always easy after the words "The Lord has taken away" to add the words "Blessed be the name of the Lord." But the way out was clear, and he used it again and again. When the mission ship *Dayspring* that he had worked so hard to fund was sunk in a storm, he wrote:

> Whatever trials have befallen me in my Earthly Pilgrimage, I have never had the trial of doubting that perhaps, after all, Jesus had made some mistake. No! my blessed Lord Jesus makes no mistakes! When we see all His meaning, we shall then understand, what now we can only trustfully believe that all is well—best for us, best for the cause most dear to us, best for the good of others and the glory of God.[61]

---

[57] Ibid., 207.
[58] Ibid., 220.
[59] Ibid., 247.
[60] Ibid., 232.
[61] Ibid., 488.

Near the end of his life, at age seventy-nine, he was back on his beloved island Aniwa.

> I cannot visit the villages, or go among the people and the sick, as formerly, owing to an increased feebleness in my legs and lumbago. Which is painful for the last fortnight. But all is as our Master sends it, and we submit thankfully, as all is nothing to what we deserve; and adored be our God. We have in our dear Lord Jesus [grace] for peace and joy in all circumstances.[62]

His Courage Came through a Certain Kind of Praying

The prayer that made all the difference was the kind that submitted to God's sovereign wisdom. How do you claim the promises of God for protection when your wife was equally faithful but, rather than being protected, died? How do you bank on God's care when the Gordons on Erromanga were equally trusting in God's care and were martyred?[63] Paton had learned the answer to this question from listening to his mother pray, even before he learned the theology that supports it.

When the potato crop failed in Scotland, Mrs. Paton said to her children, "O my children, love your Heavenly Father, tell Him in faith and prayer all your needs, and He will supply your wants so far as it shall be for your good and His glory."[64] This is what Paton trusted God for in claiming the promises: God would supply all his needs insofar as this would be for Paton's good and for God's glory.

His courage, when he was surrounded by armed natives, came through a kind of praying that claimed the promises under the overarching submission to God's wisdom as to what would work most for God's glory and his good.

---

[62] Bell, *John G. Paton*, 238.

[63] Mr. and Mrs. G. N. Gordon were killed on Erromanga on May 20, 1861. They had labored four years on the island when they walked into an ambush.

> A blow was aimed at him with a tomahawk, which he caught; the other man struck, but his weapon was also caught. One of the tomahawks was then wrenched out of his grasp. Next moment, a blow on the spine laid the dear Missionary low, and a second on the neck almost severed the head from the body. . . . Mrs. Gordon came running to see the noise . . . "Ouben slipped stealthily behind her, sank his tomahawk into her back and with another blow almost severed her head! Such was the fate of those two devoted servants of the Lord; loving in their lives, and in their deaths not divided—their spirits, wearing the crown of martyrdom, entered Glory together, to be welcomed by Williams and Harris, whose blood was shed near the same now hallowed spot for the name and the cause of Jesus. (Paton, *Autobiography*, 166)

[64] Ibid., 22. Compare this way of praying with the way Shadrach, Meshach, and Abednego faced the fiery furnace in Dan. 3:17–18: "If this be so, our God whom we serve is able to deliver us from the burning fiery furnace, and he will deliver us out of your hand, O king. But if not, be it known to you, O king, that we will not serve your gods or worship the golden image that you have set up."

I . . . assured them that I was not afraid to die, for at death my Savior would take me to be with Himself in Heaven, and to be far happier than I had ever been on Earth. I then lifted up my hands and eyes to the Heavens, and prayed aloud for Jesus . . . either to protect me or to take me home to Glory as He saw to be for the best.[65]

That was how he prayed again and again: "Protect me or . . . take me home to Glory as you see to be for the best." He knew that Jesus had promised suffering and martyrdom to some of his servants (Luke 11:49; 21:12–18). So the promises Paton claimed were both: either protect me, or take me home in a way that will glorify you and do good for others.[66]

After one harrowing journey, he wrote, "Had it not been for the assurance that . . . in every path of duty He would carry me through or dispose of me therein for His glory, I could never have undertaken either journey."[67] The peace God gave him in these crises was not the peace of sure escape but the peace that God is good and wise and omnipotent and will do all things well. "We felt that God was near, and omnipotent to do what seemed best in his sight."[68]

Did ever mother run more quickly to protect her crying child in danger's hour, than the Lord Jesus hastens to answer believing prayer and send help to His servants *in His own good time and way, so far as it shall be for His glory and their good?*[69]

---

[65] Paton, *Autobiography*, 164.

[66] This meant that, in one sense, life was not simple. If God may rescue us for his glory or let us be killed for his glory, which way to turn in self-preservation is not an easy question to answer.

> To know what was best to be done, in such trying circumstances, was an abiding perplexity. To have left altogether, when so surrounded by perils and enemies, at first seemed the wisest course, and was the repeated advice of many friends. But again, I had acquired the language, and had gained a considerable influence amongst the Natives, and there were a number warmly attached both to myself and to the Worship. To have left would have been to lose all, which to me was heart-rending; therefore, risking all with Jesus, I held on while the hope of being spared longer had not absolutely and entirely vanished. (Ibid., 173)

[67] Ibid., 148. "Often have I seized the pointed barrel and directed it upwards, or, pleading with my assailant, uncapped his musket in the struggle. At other times, nothing could be said, nothing done, but stand still in silent prayer, asking to protect us or to prepare us for going home to His glory. He fulfilled His own promise—'I will not fail thee nor forsake thee'" (Ibid., 329–30).

[68] Ibid., 197.

[69] Ibid., 164, emphasis added. Paton taught his helpers to pray this way as well, and we hear the same faith and prayer in Abraham, his trustworthy Aneityumese servant:

> O Lord, our Heavenly Father, they have murdered Thy servants on Erromanga. They have banished the Aneityumese from dark Tanna. And now they want to kill Missi Paton and me.
>
> Our great King, protect us, and make their hearts soft and sweet to Thy Worship. Or, if they are permitted to kill us, do not Thou hate us, but wash us in the blood of Thy dear Son Jesus Christ. . . . Make us two and all Thy servants strong for Thee and for Thy Worship; and if they kill us now, let us die together in Thy good work, like Thy servants Missi Gordon the man and Missi Gordon the woman. (Ibid., 171)

His Courage Came from a Certain Kind of Joy

The joy that made all the difference was the joy in God that Paton knew could not be surpassed anywhere in any other ministry.

> Oh that the pleasure-seeking men and women of the world could only taste and feel the real joy of those who know and love the true God—a heritage which the world . . . cannot give to them, but which the poorest and humblest followers of Jesus inherit and enjoy![70]

> My heart often says within itself—when, *when* will men's eyes at home be opened? When will the rich and the learned . . . renounce their shallow frivolities, and go to live amongst the poor, the ignorant, the outcast, and the lost, and write their eternal fame on the souls by them blessed and brought to the Savior? Those who have tasted this highest joy, "The joy of the Lord," will never again ask—*Is Life worth living?*[71]

Near the end of his life, he wrote about the joy that carried him forward, and about his hope that his own children would undertake the same mission and find the same joy:

> Let me record my immovable conviction that this is the noblest service in which any human being can spend or be spent; and that, if God gave me back my life to be lived over again, I would without one quiver of hesitation lay it on the altar to Christ, that He might use it as before in similar ministries of love, especially amongst those who have never yet heard the Name of Jesus. Nothing that has been endured, and nothing that can now befall me, makes me tremble—on the contrary, *I deeply rejoice*—when I breathe the prayer that it may please the blessed Lord to turn the hearts of all my children to the Mission Field and that He may open up their way and make it *their pride and joy* to live and die in carrying Jesus and His Gospel into the heart of the Heathen World![72]

Where did the joy of John G. Paton most deeply repose? The answer, it seems, is that it rested most deeply in the experience of personal communion with Jesus Christ mediated through the promise "Behold, I am

---

[70] Ibid., 78.

[71] He goes on to expand the ground of this joy:

> Life, any life, would be well spent, under any conceivable conditions, in bringing one human soul to know and love and serve God and His Son, and thereby securing for yourself at least one temple where your name and memory would be held for ever and for ever in affectionate praise—a regenerated Heart in heaven. That fame will prove immortal, when all the poems and monuments and pyramids of Earth have gone into dust. (Ibid., 411–12)

[72] Ibid., 444, emphasis added.

with you always" (Matt. 28:20). Therefore, the final source of his courage I would mention is this precious fellowship, especially in danger.

His Courage Came from Personal Fellowship with Jesus

The sweetness of this fellowship reached its highest and deepest point when it was given through the promise of Christ's word to an endangered missionary hovering on the brink of eternity.

The promise had been given precisely in the context of the Great Commission: "Go therefore and make disciples of all nations. . . . And behold, I am with you always, to the end of the age" (Matt. 28:19–20). More than any other promise, this one brought Jesus close and real to John Paton in all his dangers. After the measles epidemic that killed thousands on the islands, and for which the missionaries were blamed, he wrote, "During the crisis, I felt generally calm, and firm of soul, standing erect and with my whole weight on the promise 'Lo! I am with you always.' Precious promise! How often I adore Jesus for it, and rejoice in it! Blessed be his name."[73]

The power this promise had to make Christ real to Paton in hours of crisis was unlike any other Scripture or prayer:

> Without that abiding consciousness of the presence and power of my dear Lord and Savior, nothing else in all the world could have preserved me from losing my reason and perishing miserably. In His words, "Lo, I am with you always, even unto the end of the world," became to me so real that it would not have startled me to behold Him, as Stephen did, gazing down upon the scene. I felt His supporting power. . . . It is the sober truth, and it comes back to me sweetly after 20 years, that I had my nearest and dearest glimpses of the face and smiles of my blessed Lord in those dread moments when musket, club, or spear was being leveled at my life.[74]

> Oh the bliss of living and enduring, as seeing "Him who is invisible"![75]

One of the most powerful paragraphs in his *Autobiography* describes his experience of hiding in a tree, at the mercy of an unreliable chief, as hundreds of angry natives hunted him for his life. What he experienced

---

[73] Ibid., 154.
[74] "My constant custom was, in order to prevent war, to run right in between the contending parties. My faith enabled me to grasp and realize the promise, 'Lo, I am with you always.' In Jesus I felt invulnerable and immortal, so long as I was doing his work. And I can truly say, that these were the moments when I felt my Savior to be most truly and sensibly present, inspiring and empowering me." Ibid., 342.
[75] Ibid., 117.

there was the deepest source of Paton's joy and courage. In fact, I would dare to say that to share this experience and call others to enjoy it was the reason that he wrote the story of his life.[76]

He began his *Autobiography* with the words, "What I write here is for the glory of God."[77] That is true. But God gets glory when his *Son* is exalted. And his Son is exalted when we cherish him above all things, especially when "all things" are about to be snatched from us, including our life on earth. That is what this story is about. Here is the story of Paton in the tree.

> Being entirely at the mercy of such doubtful and vacillating friends, I, though perplexed, felt it best to obey. I climbed into the tree and was left there alone in the bush. The hours I spent there live all before me as if it were but of yesterday. I heard the frequent discharging of muskets, and the yells of the Savages. Yet I sat there among the branches, as safe as in the arms of Jesus. Never, in all my sorrows, did my Lord draw nearer to me, and speak more soothingly in my soul, than when the moonlight flickered among those chestnut leaves, and the night air played on my throbbing brow, as I told all my heart to Jesus. Alone, yet not alone! If it be to glorify my God, I will not grudge to spend many nights alone in such a tree, to feel again my Savior's spiritual presence, to enjoy His consoling fellowship. If thus thrown back upon your own soul, alone, all alone, in the midnight, in the bush, in the very embrace of death itself, have you a Friend that will not fail you then?[78]

"Have You a Friend That Will Not Fail You?"

This is the question that Paton leaves in our ears. Jesus came into the world to befriend sinners. His enemies accused him of this and spoke more truly than they knew. They called him "a glutton and a drunkard, a friend of tax collectors and sinners!" (Matt. 11:19). But Jesus knew who needed the physician—the sick. And if they would have him heal the deep disease of their sin, he would have them as his friend. "No longer do I call you servants, for the servant does not know what his master is doing; but I have called you friends" (John 15:15).

The features of friendship that Jesus focused on in this relationship were, first, that he laid down his life to save his friends. "Greater love

---

[76] "I pity from the depth of my heart every human being, who, from whatever cause, is a stranger to the most ennobling, uplifting, and consoling experience that can come to the soul of man—blessed communion with the Father of our Spirits, through gracious union with the Lord Jesus Christ." Ibid., 359.
[77] Ibid., 2.
[78] Ibid., 200.

has no one than this, that someone lay down his life for his friends" (John 15:13); and, second, friends of the Master know what he is doing (v. 15). They are part of the inner ring of the Great Planner. This means that the friendship of Jesus is woven into his mission. His friends understand what he is up to in the world.

And they not only understand, they agree. They are on board with the plan. Friends don't just sit and look at each other. They link arms and pursue a common cause. "You are my friends if you do what I command you" (v. 14). If Jesus is the Supreme Lord as well as the Best Friend, it cannot be otherwise. Servants do what the master says because they have to. Friends do it because they want to. And they want to because they have been taken into the council chamber. They have been shown the greatness of the plan and the greatness of the victory. They are thrilled to be with Jesus in this great global mission.

It will be a costly mission. There will be afflictions all along the way. That is the appointed path to triumph. So Paton leaves us with his question: "If thus thrown back upon your own soul, alone, all alone, in the midnight, in the bush, in the very embrace of death itself, have you a Friend that will not fail you then?"

3

Adoniram Judson

"How Few There Are Who Die So Hard":
The Cost of Bringing Christ to Burma

The story of Adoniram Judson's losses is almost overwhelming. Just when you think the last one was the worst, and he could endure no more, another comes. In fact, it would be overwhelming if we could not see it all from God's long historical view. The seed that died a thousand times has given life in Myanmar (Burma) to an extraordinary movement to Christ.

The Fruit of His Affliction

When Adoniram Judson entered Burma in July 1813, it was a hostile and utterly unreached place. William Carey had told Judson in India a few months earlier not to go there. Today it probably would be considered a closed country—with anarchic despotism, fierce war with Siam, enemy raids, constant rebellion, and no religious toleration. All the previous missionaries had died or left.[1]

But Judson went there with his twenty-three-year-old wife of seventeen months. He was twenty-four years old, and he worked there for thirty-eight years until his death at age sixty-one, with one trip home to New England after thirty-three years. The price he paid was immense. He was a seed that fell into the ground and died again and

---

[1] Courtney Anderson, *To the Golden Shore: The Life of Adoniram Judson* (Grand Rapids, MI: Zondervan, 1956), 134.

again. And the fruit God gave is celebrated even in scholarly works like David Barrett's *World Christian Encyclopedia*: "The largest Christian force in Burma is the Burma Baptist Convention, which owes its origin to the pioneering activity of the American Baptist missionary Adoniram Judson."[2] At the turn from the second to the third millennium, Patrick Johnstone estimated the Myanmar (Burma's new name) Baptist Convention to be 3,700 congregations with 617,781 members and 1,900,000 affiliates[3]—the fruit of this dead seed.

Of course, there were others besides Adoniram Judson—hundreds of others over time. They too came and gave away their lives. Many of them died much younger than Judson. They only serve to make the point. The astonishing fruit in Myanmar today has grown in the soil of the suffering and death of many missionaries, especially Adoniram Judson.

One question that moves my study and prayer and writing of this book is: If Christ delays his return another two hundred years—a mere fraction of a day in his reckoning—which of us who are alive today will have suffered and died so that the triumphs of grace will be told about one of the 3,500 people groups who are in the same condition today that the Karen, Chin, Kachin, and Burmese were in 1813? Who will labor so long and so hard and so perseveringly that in two hundred years there will be two million Christians in many of the 10/40-window peoples who at that time will scarcely be able to recall their Muslim or Hindu or Buddhist roots?

May God use the life of Adoniram Judson to stir many of us to give our lives to this great cause!

Deep Faith in the Sovereignty of God

Adoniram Judson lived on the great truths of God's sovereign grace. He would have been known as a Calvinist, but not the kind that wears his Calvinism on his sleeve.[4] You can see the evidence for his Reformed convictions in Thomas J. Nettles's *By His Grace and for His Glory*.[5]

His father, who was a pastor of the Third Congregational Church of Plymouth, Massachusetts, had studied with Jonathan Edwards's

---

[2] David Barrett, ed., *World Christian Encyclopedia* (New York: Oxford University Press, 1982), 202.

[3] Patrick Johnstone and Jason Mandryk, eds., *Operation World* (Carlisle: Paternoster, 2001), 462.

[4] Erroll Hulse, *Adoniram Judson and the Missionary Call* (Leeds: Reformation Today Trust, 1996), 48. "When we come to the doctrines of grace we find that he believed them implicitly rather than by explicit exposition."

[5] Thomas J. Nettles, *By His Grace and for His Glory* (Grand Rapids, MI: Baker, 1986), 148–54.

student Joseph Bellamy. Five years after his son had left for Asia, the father became convinced of the Baptist way and risked his livelihood by resigning from his Congregational church. Adoniram, as we will see, received from his father both the Reformed theology and the courage to put his life on the line rather than compromise his beliefs.

The importance this has for our purpose here is to stress that this deep confidence in God's overarching providence through all calamity and misery sustained him to the end. He said, "If I had not felt certain that every additional trial was ordered by infinite love and mercy, I could not have survived my accumulated sufferings."[6] He loved what he called "the Doctrines of Grace." What he saw in them was the power for sacrifice and self-denial, not the ammunition for argument. "That faith which consists merely in a correct belief of the Doctrines of Grace and prompts no self denial . . . is no faith at all."[7]

This was the unshakable confidence of all three of his wives, Ann (also called Nancy), Sarah, and Emily. For example, Ann, who married Judson on February 5, 1812, and left with him on the boat for Asia on February 19 at age twenty-three, bore three children to Adoniram. All of them died. The first baby, nameless, was born dead just as they sailed from India to Burma. The second child, Roger Williams Judson, lived seventeen months and died. The third, Maria Elizabeth Butterworth Judson, lived to be two and outlived her mother by six months and then died.

When her second child died, Ann Judson wrote:

> Our hearts were bound up with this child; we felt he was our earthly all, our only source of innocent recreation in this heathen land. But God saw it was necessary to remind us of our error, and to strip us of our only little all. O, may it not be vain that he has done it. May we so improve it that he will stay his hand and say "It is enough."[8]

In other words, what sustained this man and his three wives was a rock-solid confidence that God is sovereign and God is good. And all things come from his hand for the good—sometimes the incredibly *painful* good—of his children.

---

[6] Adoniram Judson, quoted in Eugene Myers Harrison, *Giants of the Missionary Trail* (Chicago: Scripture Press Foundation, 1954), 73.
[7] Nettles, *By His Grace and for His Glory*, 154.
[8] Anderson, *To the Golden Shore*, 193.

The Roots of Confidence in God's Good Providence

There are roots of this missionary-sustaining confidence in God's goodness and providence. One, as we have seen, is the legacy that his father left him. That's what his father believed, and that's what he lived. A second source of this confidence was the Bible. Judson was a lover of the Word of God. The main legacy of his thirty-eight years in Burma was a complete translation of the Bible into Burmese and a dictionary that all the later missionaries could use.

Once when a Buddhist teacher said that he could not believe that Christ suffered the death of the cross because no king allows his son such indignity, Judson responded,

> Therefore you are not a disciple of Christ. A true disciple inquires not whether a fact is agreeable to his own reason, but whether it is in the book. His pride has yielded to the divine testimony. Teacher, your pride is still unbroken. Break down your pride, and yield to the word of God.[9]

The Bible was a friend closer and more lasting than Judson's wife. When the bottom fell out some years later and he struggled with the darkest spiritual depression, he disappeared into the tiger-infested jungle to live alone. But he did not leave his Bible behind. This unbreakable attachment to the Bible saved his life and defined the final outcome.

A Remarkable Conversion

A third source of his confidence in the goodness and detailed providence of God was the way God saved him. It is a remarkable story. Adoniram was a brilliant boy. His mother taught him to read in one week when he was three to surprise his father when he came home from a trip.[10] He read his father a chapter from the Bible to surprise him.

When he was sixteen, he entered Brown University as a sophomore and graduated at the top of his class three years later in 1807. What his godly parents didn't know was that Adoniram was being lured away from the faith by a fellow student named Jacob Eames, who was a deist. By the time Judson was finished, he had no Christian faith. He kept this concealed from his parents until his twentieth birthday, August 9, 1808, when he broke their hearts with his announcement that he had

---

[9] Ibid., 240.
[10] Ibid., 14.

no faith and that he intended to go to New York and learn to write for the theater—which he did six days later, riding on a horse his father gave him as part of his inheritance.

It didn't prove to be the life of his dreams. He attached himself to some strolling players and, as he said later, lived "a reckless, vagabond life, finding lodgings where he could, and bilking the landlord where he found opportunity."[11] His disgust with what he found there was the beginning of several remarkable providences.

He went to visit his Uncle Ephraim in Sheffield but found there instead "a pious young man" who stunned him by being firm in his Christian convictions without being "austere and dictatorial."[12] Strange that he should find this young man there instead of his uncle.

The next night he stayed in a small village inn where he had never been before. The innkeeper apologized that his sleep might be interrupted because there was a man critically ill in the next room. Through the night he heard comings and goings and low voices and groans and gasps. It bothered him to think that the man next to him may not be prepared to die. He wondered about himself and had terrible thoughts of his own dying. He felt foolish because good deists weren't supposed to have these struggles.

When he was leaving in the morning, he asked if the man next door was better. "He is dead," said the innkeeper. Judson was struck with the finality of it all. On his way out he asked, "Do you know who he was?" "Oh yes. Young man from the college in Providence. Name was Eames, Jacob Eames."[13]

Judson could hardly move. He stayed there for hours pondering the death of his unbelieving friend. If Eames were right, then this was a meaningless event. But Judson could not believe it. "That hell should open in that country inn and snatch Jacob Eames, his dearest friend and guide, from the next bed—this could not, simply could not, be pure coincidence."[14] His conversion was not immediate. But now it was sure that God was on his trail—like the apostle Paul on the Damascus Road—and there was no escape. Months of struggle were to follow.

---

[11] Ibid., 193.
[12] Ibid., 42.
[13] Ibid., 44. The source of this story is oral reports from family members recorded in Francis Wayland, *A Memoir of the Life and Labors of the Rev. Adoniram Judson, D.D.*, 2 vols. (Boston: Phillips, Sampson, and Co., 1854), 1:24–25.
[14] Anderson, *To the Golden Shore*, 45.

The Path to Marriage

He entered Andover Seminary in October 1808 and on December 2 made solemn dedication of himself to God. The fire was burning for missions at Andover and at Williams College. (The Haystack Prayer Meeting had taken place in August 1806 near Williams College, and two from there had come to Andover.)

On June 28, 1810, Judson and others presented themselves to the Congregationalists for missionary service in the East. He met Ann Hasseltine that same day and fell in love. After knowing Ann for one month, he declared his intention to become a suitor and wrote to her father the following letter:

> I have now to ask, whether you can consent to part with your daughter early next spring, to see her no more in this world; whether you can consent to her departure, and her subjection to the hardships and sufferings of missionary life; whether you can consent to her exposure to the dangers of the ocean, to the fatal influence of the southern climate of India; to every kind of want and distress; to degradation, insult, persecution, and perhaps a violent death. Can you consent to all this, for the sake of him who left his heavenly home, and died for her and for you; for the sake of perishing, immortal souls; for the sake of Zion, and the glory of God? Can you consent to all this, in hope of soon meeting your daughter in the world of glory, with the crown of righteousness, brightened with the acclamations of praise which shall redound to her Savior from heathens saved, through her means, from eternal woe and despair?[15]

Her father, amazingly, said she could make up her own mind. She wrote to her friend Lydia Kimball:

> I feel willing, and expect, if nothing in Providence prevents, to spend my days in this world in heathen lands. Yes, Lydia, I have about come to the determination to give up all my comforts and enjoyments here, sacrifice my affection to relatives and friends, and go where God, in his Providence, shall see fit to place me.[16]

Between this engagement and the marriage, Judson made a trip to London to seek support from the London Missionary Society. Instead of support of that sort, he discovered the kind of support he would need far more. The ship he was on, the British *Packet*, was taken by a French

---

[15] Ibid., 83.
[16] Ibid., 84.

ship, *L'Invincible Napoleon*, and Judson was made prisoner with the crew. He was taken to Bayonne, France, and put in prison.

In this helpless situation for a twenty-two-year-old American, Judson learned of a kind of provision he would need again and again in Burma. Amazingly, a man from Philadelphia snuck Judson out of the prison by bribing the guards. He made his way to London and made his futile effort to solicit the support of the London Missionary Society. He left on June 18, 1811, and arrived in New York August 7 from a journey that seemed pointless—except for this: he always "regarded his detention in France as a very important, and, indeed, necessary part of his preparation for the duties which afterwards devolved upon him."[17]

Adoniram and Ann were married six months later on February 5, 1812, and sailed for India fourteen days later with two other couples and two single men[18] divided among two ships, in case one went down.

The Path to India and the Baptist Way

The voyage to India took 114 days. On the journey, Judson had been studying the issue of baptism and was becoming convinced from Scripture that his views on infant baptism were not biblical. In India, he and Ann lived for a short time with William Carey. In this context, Judson settled his views and became a Baptist. Ann followed, as did one of the single missionary men, Luther Rice.

This was a heart-wrenching and life-threatening decision at several levels. Ann expressed the internal doctrinal and emotional struggle for both of them:

> I . . . must acknowledge that the face of Scripture does favor the Baptist senti-
> ments. I intend to persevere in examining the subject. And [I] hope that I shall
> be disposed to embrace the truth, whatever it may be. It is painfully mortifying
> to my natural feelings, to think seriously of renouncing a system which I have
> been taught from infancy to believe and respect, and embrace one which I have
> been taught to despise. O that the Spirit of God may enlighten and direct my
> mind—may prevent my retaining an old error, or embracing a new one![19]

Moreover, they had been sent out by a Congregational board. Their support would very likely not be continued. And perhaps worst of all

---

[17] Ibid., 93.
[18] Luther Rice, Gordon Hall, Samuel and Harriet Newell, Samuel and Roxana Nott.
[19] Anderson, *To the Golden Shore*, 144–45.

was that this change split the group of missionaries who went out together. They loved each other, and as Ann said, "We are perfectly united with our brethren in every other respect, and are much attached to them."[20] But how would they plant and structure a church when their views on baptism differed so much? Ann captured the situation and the cost with these words:

> Thus, we are confirmed Baptists, not because we wanted to be, but because truth compelled us to be. We have endeavored to count the cost, and be prepared for the many severe trials resulting from this change of sentiment. We anticipate the loss of reputation, and of the affection and esteem of many of our American friends. But the most trying circumstances attending this change, and that which has caused us most pain, is the separation which must take place between us and our dear missionary associates. . . . We feel that we are alone in the world, with no real friend but each other, no one on whom we can depend but God.[21]

As with all events under God's merciful providence, this painful circumstance had some remarkably positive effects. The Judsons and Rice knew that someone would need to go home to make official the departure from the Congregational oversight and seek support from the Baptists. Rice was single, and it made sense for him to return. He entered New York harbor in September 1813. From that time until he died in 1836, he became a stateside advocate for Baptist Missions. He never returned to join the Judsons. His labor gave cohesion to the Baptist movement in America and gave support to Baptist missions abroad.[22] His influence was extraordinary.

The story would be very different for Adoniram and Ann Judson. After a time in India, they chose to take the risks of venturing to a new field. They arrived in Rangoon, Burma, on July 13, 1813.

The Beginnings of Their Sufferings

There began a lifelong battle in 108-degree heat with cholera, malaria, dysentery, and unknown miseries that would take two of Judson's

---

[20] Ibid., 144.

[21] Ibid., 146.

[22] Largely owing to the untiring advocacy by Luther Rice for Baptist unity and missions, Baptists met for their first national gathering at Philadelphia in May 1814. It was called "The General Missionary Convention of the Baptist Denomination in United States of America, for Foreign Missions."

wives, seven of his thirteen children, and colleague after colleague in death.

The first news from home arrived two years later on September 5, 1815. They had died to the nearness of family. Adoniram would never see his mother or father or brother again. He would not return for thirty-three years. "Missionary time" in those days was very slow. It was a world of difference from today. If someone was sick enough, the typical remedy to save the life was a sea voyage. So a marriage or the entire work could be put on hold, so to speak, for three to six months as someone was sent out to sea.

Or it could be longer. Eight years into their mission, Ann was so ill that the only hope was a trip home. She sailed on August 21, 1821. She returned on December 5, 1823, two years and four months later. And when she arrived, Judson had not heard from her for ten months. If you are married and you love your wife, and you are both called to the Great Work, this is the way you die day after day for a greater good and a greater joy.

One of the joys was seeing some of God's goodness in the dark providences. For example, when Ann was recovering in the States, she wrote a book titled *An Account of the American Baptist Mission to the Burman Empire*. It had a huge influence in stirring up recruits and prayer and finances. This would have never happened without her sickness and two-year absence. But most of the time, God's wise purposes in their pain were not that clear.

The Price of Breakthrough

Through all the struggles with sickness and interruptions, Judson labored to learn the language, translate the Bible, and do evangelism on the streets. Six years after they arrived, they baptized their first convert, Maung Nau. The sowing was long and hard, the reaping even harder for years. But in 1831, nineteen years after their arrival, there was a new spirit in the land. Judson wrote:

> The spirit of inquiry . . . is spreading everywhere, through the whole length and breadth of the land." [We have distributed] nearly 10,000 tracts, giving to none but those who ask. I presume there have been 6000 applications at the house. Some come two or three months' journey, from the borders of Siam and China—"Sir, we hear that there is an eternal hell. We are afraid of it. Do

give us a writing that will tell us how to escape it." Others, from the frontiers of Kathay, 100 miles north of Ava—"Sir, we have seen a writing that tells about an eternal God. Are you the man that gives away such writings? If so, pray give us one, for we want to know the truth before we die." Others, from the interior of the country, where the name of Jesus Christ is a little known—"Are you Jesus Christ's man? Give us a writing that tells us about Jesus Christ."[23]

But there had been an enormous price to pay between the first convert in 1819 and this outpouring of God's power in 1831.

In 1823, Adoniram and Ann moved from Rangoon to Ava, the capital, about three hundred miles inland and further up the Irrawaddy River. It was risky to be that near the despotic emperor. In May of the next year, a British fleet arrived in Rangoon and bombarded the harbor. All Westerners were immediately viewed as spies, and Adoniram was dragged from his home. On June 8, 1824, he was put in prison. His feet were fettered, and at night a long horizontal bamboo pole was lowered and passed between the fettered legs and hoisted up until only the shoulder and heads of the prisoners rested on the ground.

Years later, when his wife was dealing with deep darkness in her own soul, he recounted to her that he kept his sanity during the prison months partly by reciting repeatedly the lines of William Cowper,

> Beware of desp'rate steps; the darkest day
> (Live till tomorrow) will have passed away.[24]

As horrible as the conditions were in prison, Judson was spared his reason. He could still think through the possibilities of how this would all work out for the advancement of the gospel. He said to a fellow prisoner named Gouger,

> Here I have been ten years preaching the gospel to timid listeners who wish to embrace the truth but dare not, and beseeching the Emperor to grant liberty of conscience to his people but without success, and now when all human means seem at an end, God opens the way by leading a Christian nation to subdue the country. It is possible my life will be spared; if so, with what ardor shall I pursue my work! If not—his will be done. The door will be opened for others who would do the work better.[25]

---

[23] Anderson, *To the Golden Shore*, 398–99.
[24] William Cowper, "The Needless Alarm, Moral" (1794).
[25] Anderson, *To the Golden Shore*, 333–34.

Ann was pregnant, but she walked the two miles daily to the palace to plead that Judson was not a spy and that they should have mercy. She got some relief for him so that he could come out into a courtyard. The prisoners got vermin in their hair amid the rotting food and had to be shaved bald. Almost a year later, they were suddenly moved to a more distant village prison, gaunt, with hollow eyes, dressed in rags, crippled from the torture. There the mosquitoes from the rice paddies almost drove them mad on their bloody feet.

The daughter, Maria, had been born by now, and Ann was almost as sick and thin as Adoniram, but she still pursued him, with her baby, to take care of him as she could. Her milk dried up, and the jailer had mercy on them and actually let Judson take the baby each evening into the village fettered and beg for women to nurse his baby.

On November 4, 1825, Judson was suddenly released. The government needed him as a translator in negotiations with Britain. The long ordeal was over—seventeen months in prison and on the brink of death, with his wife sacrificing herself and her baby to care for him as she could. Ann's health was broken. Eleven months later she died (October 24, 1826). And six months later their daughter died (April 24, 1827).

When the Darkness Does Not Lift

While he was suffering in prison, Adoniram had been sustained with hope and with a spirit deeply submissive to the providence of God. We heard it in the words to his fellow prisoner: "It is possible my life will be spared; if so, with what ardor shall I pursue my work! If not—his will be done. The door will be opened for others who would do the work better."[26] But now that his wife and daughter were gone, darkness began to settle over his soul. Then in July, three months after the death of his little girl, he got word that his father had died eight months earlier.

The psychological effect of these losses was devastating. Self-doubt overtook his mind, and he wondered if he had become a missionary for ambition and fame, not humility and self-denying love. He began to read Catholic mystics like Madame Guyon, Fenelon, and Thomas à Kempis who led him into solitary asceticism and various forms of self-mortification. He dropped his Old Testament translation work, the love

---

[26] Ibid., 334.

of his life, and retreated more and more from people and from "any-thing that might conceivably support pride or promote . . . pleasure."[27]

He refused to eat outside the mission. He destroyed all letters of commendation. By writing a letter to the *American Baptist Magazine*, he formally renounced the honorary Doctor of Divinity that Brown University had given him in 1823. He gave all his private wealth (about six thousand dollars) to the Baptist Board. He asked that his salary be reduced by one quarter and promised to give more to missions himself. In October 1828, he built a hut in the jungle some distance from the Moulmein mission house and moved in on October 24, 1828, the second anniversary of Ann's death, to live in total isolation.

He wrote in one letter home to Ann's relatives, "My tears flow at the same time over the forsaken grave of my dear love and over the loath-some sepulcher of my own heart."[28] He had a grave dug beside the hut and sat beside it contemplating the stages of the body's dissolution. He ordered all his letters in New England destroyed. He refused to return a legal document his sister needed unless his demand were carried out. He retreated for forty days alone further into the tiger-infested jungle and wrote in one letter that he felt utter spiritual desolation. "God is to me the Great Unknown. I believe in him, but I find him not."[29]

His brother Elnathan died May 8, 1829, at the age of thirty-five. Paradoxically, this proved the turning point of Judson's recovery, be-cause he had reason to believe that the brother that he had left in un-belief seventeen years earlier had died in faith. All through the year of 1830, Adoniram was climbing out of his darkness.

Recall that it was 1831—the next year—when he experienced the great outpouring of spiritual interest across the land. "The spirit of inquiry . . . is spreading everywhere, through the whole length and breadth of the land."[30] Is that a coincidence? Or is that a God-ordained pattern for spiritual breakthrough in a dark and unreached place?

A Finished Bible and a New Wife

Central to his missionary labors from the beginning, and especially at this juncture in his life, was the translation of the Bible. Judson knew

---

[27] Ibid., 387.
[28] Ibid., 388.
[29] Ibid., 391.
[30] Ibid., 398.

the original languages and worked from the Greek and Hebrew. Four years after he arrived in Burma (May 1817), he had completed the Gospel of Matthew, and then began work on a Burmese dictionary.

Now in these years without a wife and children, he confined himself to a small room built for the purpose of being able to devote almost all his energy to refining the New Testament translation and pressing on with the Old Testament. At the end of 1832, three thousand copies of the completed New Testament were printed. He finished the Old Testament on January 31, 1834, and wrote on that day:

> Thanks be to God, I can now say I have attained. I have knelt down before him, with the last leaf in my hand, and imploring his forgiveness for all the sins which have polluted my efforts in this department, and his aid in future efforts to remove the errors and imperfections which necessarily cleave to the work, I have commended it to his mercy and grace; I have dedicated it to his glory. May he make his own inspired word, now complete in the Burman tongue, the grand instrument of filling all Burma with songs of praise to our great God and Savior Jesus Christ. Amen.[31]

With the first draft of the Bible in Burmese complete, it seems as though God smiled on these labors with the favor of a new wife. Three years earlier, another missionary in Burma named George Boardman had died. His widow, Sarah, stayed in Burma and became a legend in her own right, pressing into the interior with her baby, George.[32] In February 1834, Judson received a letter from Sarah. On April 1, he left Moulmein for Tavoy resolved to court her. On April 10, they were married. Judson wrote in his journal about their two departed spouses and their new love:

> Once more, farewell to thee, Boardman, and thy long-cherished grave. May thy memory be ever fresh and fragrant, as the memory of the other beloved, whose beautiful, death-marred form reposes at the foot of the hopia tree. May we, the survivors, so live as to deserve and receive the smiles of the sainted ones who have gone before us. And at last may we all four be reunited before the throne of glory, and form a peculiarly happy family, our mutual loves all purified and consummated in the bright world of love.[33]

[31] Ibid., 411.
[32] Ibid., 402.
[33] Ibid., 414.

These were to be some of his happiest times in Burma, but not without pain, and not to last much more than a decade. "She was a blue eyed beauty and he at 47 had a full head of hair with no gray and was strong and healthy and was coming it seemed into a season of peace and joy with Sarah."[34] She would bear Adoniram eight children. Five of them would live beyond their childhood.

After marriage to Sarah, Adoniram gave himself to the revision of the Old Testament and, for a season, preached seven messages a week, one on Sunday morning and one on the other evenings of the week.[35] Sarah was a gifted partner and knew the language better than any but Judson himself. She translated *The Pilgrim's Progress* during these years before her untimely death.

Another Wife Given Up in Death

After bearing eight children in eleven years, Sarah became so ill that the family decided to travel to America in the hopes that the sea air would work healing. They set sail April 26, 1845, with their three oldest children and the intention of leaving them for education in the United States when they returned. They left the three youngest behind, one of whom died before Judson returned.

Judson had not been to America now for thirty-three years and was only returning for the sake of his wife. As they rounded the tip of Africa in September 1845, Sarah died. Adoniram recorded her dying on the ship in tender detail:

> Her mind became liable to wander; but a single word was sufficient to recall and steady her recollection. On the evening of the 31st of August, she appeared to be drawing near to the end of her pilgrimage. The children took leave of her, and retired to rest. I sat alone to the side of her bed during the hours of the night, endeavoring to administer relief to the distressed body, and consolation to the departing soul. At 2 o'clock in the morning, wishing to obtain one more token of recognition, I roused her attention, and said "Do you still love the Savior?" "O, yes," she replied, "I ever love the Lord Jesus Christ." I said again, "Do you still love me?" She replied in the affirmative by a peculiar expression of her own. "Then give me one more kiss," and we exchanged that token of love for the last time. Another hour passed,

---

[34] Ibid., 417.
[35] Ibid., 418.

life continued to recede, and she ceased to breathe. For a moment I traced her upward flight, and thought of the wonders which were opening to her view. I then closed her sightless eyes, dressed her, for the last time, in the drapery of death; and being quite exhausted with many sleepless nights, I threw myself down and slept.[36]

The ship dropped anchor at St. Helena Island long enough to dig a grave and bury a wife and mother and then sail on. This time Adoniram did not descend into the depths of depression as before. He had his children. But even more, his sufferings had disengaged him from hoping for too much in this world. He was learning how to "hate his life" in this world (John 12:25) without bitterness or depression.

He had one passion: to return and give his life for Burma. So he planned for his stay in the States to be just long enough to get his children settled and find a ship back. All that was left of the life he knew in New England was his sister. She had kept his room exactly as it had been thirty-three years earlier and would keep it that way to the day she died.

He landed Wednesday, October 15, 1845. His first wife's book, *An Account of the American Baptist Mission to the Burman Empire*, and the publishing of the *Memoir of Mrs. Ann Judson* by James Knowles in 1829, had been read by hundreds of thousands. Adoniram Judson was a celebrity. Countless parents had named their children after him. He had been the topic of thousands of sermons. His homecoming was a sensation.

God Planned Another Marriage, but Not a Long One

Judson's stay in the States did not go according to plan. To everyone's amazement, he fell in love a third time, this time with Emily Chubbuck, and married her on June 2, 1846. She was twenty-nine; he was fifty-seven. She was a famous writer and left her fame and writing career to go with Judson to Burma.[37] They arrived in November 1846. And God gave them four of the happiest years that either of them had ever known. On their first anniversary (June 2, 1847), she wrote,

---

[36] Ibid., 440.

[37] Emily's pen name was Fanny Forester. She had "skyrocketed to literary fame" with a children's book called *Charles Linn* and another book, *Trippings in Author Land*. When Judson met her he said, "How can you reconcile it with your conscience to employ such noble talents in writing so little useful and spiritual as those sketches I read?" He resolved that she should write Sarah's memoir and that she should be his next wife. Ibid., 454.

It has been far the happiest year of my life; and, what is in my eyes still more important, my husband says it has been among the happiest of his. . . . I never met with any man who could talk so well, day after day, on every subject, religious, literary, scientific, political, and—nice baby-talk.[38]

They had one child. Things looked bright, but then the old sicknesses attacked Adoniram one last time. The only hope was to send the desperately ill Judson on a voyage. On April 3, 1850, they carried Adoniram onto *The Aristide Marie* bound for the Isle of France with one friend, Thomas Ranney, to care for him. In his misery, he would be roused from time to time by terrible pain ending in vomiting. One of his last sentences was, "How few there are who . . . who die so hard!"[39]

At 4:15 on Friday afternoon, April 12, 1850, Adoniram Judson died at sea, away from all his family and the Burmese church. That evening the ship hove to.

The crew assembled quietly. The larboard port was opened. There were no prayers. . . . The captain gave the order. The coffin slid through the port into the night. The location was latitude 13 degrees North, longitude 93 degrees East, almost in the eastward shadow of the Andaman Islands, and only a few hundred miles west of the mountains of Burma. The Aristide Marie sailed on toward the Isle of France.[40]

Ten days later, Emily gave birth to their second child, who died at birth. She learned four months later that her husband was dead. She returned to New England that next January and died of tuberculosis three years later at the age of thirty-seven.

The Burmese Bible was done. The dictionary was done. Hundreds of converts were leading the church. And today there are about 3,700 congregations of Baptists in Myanmar who trace their origin to this man's labors of love.

A Plea to Be a Part of What Judson and Christ Died For

Life is fleeting. In a very short time, we will all give an account before Jesus Christ, not only as to how well we have fulfilled our vocations but how well we have obeyed the command to make disciples of all nations.

---

[38] Ibid., 391.
[39] Ibid., 504.
[40] Ibid., 505.

Many of the peoples of the world are without any indigenous Christian movement today. Christ is not enthroned there, his grace is unknown there, and people are perishing with no access to the gospel. Most of these hopeless peoples do not want followers of Jesus to come. At least they think they don't. They are hostile to Christian missions. Today this is the final frontier. And the Lord still says, "Behold, I am sending you out as sheep in the midst of wolves. . . . [S]ome of you they will put to death. You will be hated by all for my name's sake. But not a hair of your head will perish" (Matt. 10:16; Luke 21:16–18).

Are you sure that God wants you to keep doing what you are doing? For most of you, he probably does. Your calling is radical obedience for the glory of Christ right where you are. But for many of you, the stories in this book are among a hundred things God is using to loosen your roots and plant you in another place. Some of you he is calling to fill up what is lacking in the sufferings of Christ, to fall like a grain of wheat into some distant ground and die, to hate your life in this world and so to keep it forever and bear much fruit. Judson wrote to missionary candidates in 1832:

> Bear in mind, that a large proportion of those who come out on a mission
> to the East die within five years after leaving their native land. Walk softly,
> therefore; death is narrowly watching your steps.[41]

The question is not whether we will die, but whether we will die in a way that bears much fruit.

---

[41] Adoniram Judson, "Advice to Missionary Candidates" (Maulmain, June 25, 1832), accessed May 21, 2008, http://www.wholesomewords.org/missions/bjudson4.html.

Conclusion

This Momentary Affliction
for Eternal Glory

The position we are in at the beginning of the twenty-first century is one that cries out for tremendous missionary effort and great missionary sacrifice. Patrick Johnstone writes in *Operation World* that only in the 1990s did we get a reasonably complete listing of the world's peoples. For the first time, we can see clearly what is left to be done.

There are about 12,000 ethnolinguistic[1] peoples in the world. About 3,500 of these peoples have, on average, 1.2 percent Christian populations—about twenty million of the 1.7 billion people in these groups, using the broadest, nominal definition of Christian.[2] Most of these least-reached 3,500 peoples are in the 10/40 window[3] and are religiously unsympathetic to Christian missions. That means that we—the body of Christ, from the West and from the Global South[4]—must go to these peoples with the gospel. There is no indigenous church capable of evangelizing its own people in these groups. That's what it means to be *unreached*. Where a faithful indigenous church exists, the role of outsiders is humble partnership and helpfulness. But that is not the case for these

---

[1] The term *ethnolinguistic* is used to designate people groups categorized by ethnicity and language, in distinction from the term *geopolitical* that has reference to peoples categorized according to political and geographic boundaries.

[2] Patrick Johnstone and Jason Mandryk, eds., *Operation World* (Carlisle: Paternoster, 2001), 15–16.

[3] A term representing a huge swath of territory from the west coast of Africa to the eastern edge of south Asia and from 10 degrees north to 40 degrees north. You can see a map of the region and keep up with the ever-changing picture of unreached peoples at http://joshuaproject.net/resources/articles/10_40_window.

[4] *Global South* is a relatively new term that tries to capture the reality that a map of the "statistical center of gravity of global Christianity shows that center moving steadily southward, from a point in northern Italy in 1800, to central Spain in 1900, to Morocco by 1970, and to a point near Timbuktu [in Mali, West Africa] today [2006]. The Southward trajectory will continue unchecked through the coming century" (Philip Jenkins, *The New Faces of Christianity: Believing the Bible in the Global South* [Oxford: Oxford University Press, 2006], 9). In other words, without an astonishing spiritual awakening and reformation to reverse the trends of the past century, the centers of vitality and influence and mission sending will increasingly move from the traditional points of power in Europe and America to South America, Africa, and Asia.

unreached peoples. Reaching them, as Jesus commands, will be danger-ous and costly. Some of us, and some of our children, will be killed.

The Lure to Leave the Hardship

The temptation under these circumstances will be to give up. This has always been the case. Sitting in my comfortable study in Minneapolis, it is too easy for me to plead for perseverance in suffering for the sake of the nations. I pray that I am always willing to be endangered for Christ and his kingdom. I know that mine, for now, is a relatively secure min-istry. But others have given the plea for perseverance more authentically than I. Here is the way Adoniram Judson put it in a letter that he wrote to missionaries on June 25, 1832:

> Beware of the greater reaction which will take place after you have acquired the language, and become fatigued and worn out with preaching the gospel to a disobedient and gainsaying people. You will sometimes long for a quiet retreat, where you can find a respite from the tug of toiling at native work—the incessant, intolerable friction of the missionary grindstone. And Satan will sympathize with you in this matter; and he will present some chapel of ease, in which to officiate in your native tongue, some government situa-tion, some professorship or editorship, some literary or scientific pursuit, some supernumerary translation, or, at least, some system of schools; any-thing, in a word, that will help you, without much surrender of character, to slip out of real missionary work. Such a temptation will form the crisis of your disease. If your spiritual constitution can sustain it, you recover; if not, you die.[5]

God knows there are times to flee and times to stand. As John Bunyan said, "There are few rules in this case. The man himself is best able to judge concerning his present strength, and what weight this or that ar-gument has upon his heart to stand or fly."[6] Bunyan, who spent twelve years in prison when a simple pledge not to preach would have provided his freedom, has written compassionately and biblically about the ten-sion between flying for safety and standing to suffer. To the question *May we try to escape?* Bunyan answers,

---

[5] Adoniram Judson, "Advice to Missionary Candidates" (Maulmain, June 25, 1832), accessed May 17, 2008, http://www.wholesomewords.org/missions/bjudson4.html.
[6] John Bunyan, *Seasonable Counsels, or Advice to Sufferers*, in *Works of John Bunyan*, ed. George Offor, 3 vols. (orig. 1854; Edinburgh: Banner of Truth, 1991), 2:726.

Thou mayest do in this as it is in thy heart. If it is in thy heart to fly, fly: if it be in thy heart to stand, stand. Any thing but a denial of the truth. He that flies, has warrant to do so; he that stands, has warrant to do so. Yea, the same man may both fly and stand, as the call and working of God with his heart may be. Moses fled, Ex. 2:15; Moses stood. Heb. 11:27. David fled, 1 Sam. 19:12; David stood. 24:8. Jeremiah fled, Je. 37:11–12; Jeremiah stood. 38:17. Christ withdrew himself, Luke 9:10; Christ stood. John 18:1–8. Paul fled, 2 Cor. 11:33; Paul stood. Acts 20:22–23. . . .

There are therefore few rules in this case. The man himself is best able to judge concerning his present strength, and what weight this or that argument has upon his heart to stand or fly. . . . Do not fly out of a slavish fear, but rather because flying is an ordinance of God, opening a door for the escape of some, which door is opened by God's providence, and the escape countenanced by God's Word (Matt. 10:23). . . .

If, therefore, when thou hast fled, thou art taken, be not offended at God or man: not at God, for thou art his servant, thy life and thy all are his; not at man, for he is but God's rod, and is ordained, in this, to do thee good. Hast thou escaped? Laugh. Art thou taken? Laugh. I mean, be pleased which way soever things shall go, for that the scales are still in God's hand.[7]

My hope for this book is that our hearts and minds have been shaped more deeply by the work of the Spirit so that when the crisis comes, we will be guided more by the ways of God and less by the worldly assumptions of security and comfort.

How Likely Is the Crisis of Martyrdom?

Indeed, I pray that the backbone of our courage would be steeled by these stories of faithfulness so that when the necessity of martyrdom comes, we would be ready. How likely is that crisis? It depends on where you live and where you are willing to go.

Each year David Barrett, Todd Johnson, and Peter Crossing publish their annual "Status of Global Mission, Presence, and Activities, AD 1800–2025." One of the most sobering items in this seventy-nine-item report is called "Average Christian Martyrs per Year." The global number for 2008 was 175,000. That's 479 Christians every day who lost their lives as a result of being a Christian.

---

[7] Ibid.

These are not martyrs who die at their own hands like so many jihadists who kill others as they kill themselves. That is not the way of Jesus. Followers of Christ do not kill in order to spread the gospel about Christ who died so that his enemies could live. Christian martyrdom is not suicide. But it is willingly accepted if necessary.

Judson loved life and cherished three wives and all his children. He exercised faithfully to preserve health and life. He told missionary candidates, "Beware of that indolence which leads to a neglect of bodily exercise. The poor health and premature death of most Europeans in the East must be eminently ascribed to the most wanton neglect of bodily exercise."[8]

Paton faced down fierce opposition at the risk of his life again and again, but also chose to flee from hundreds of crazed enemies by hiding in a tree and finding a boat to get off the island of Tanna. He was not eager to die. He wanted to spend his long life evangelizing the New Hebrides. And he was granted his heart's desire. He was eighty-two when he died.

Tyndale did not want to die. He was only forty-two. He had not yet married. He was in a foreign land. His cause was just. He was a promising scholar and preacher. But when the decision was rendered that he would be burned, he accepted it as the will of God. He was imbued with the spirit of 1 Peter 4:19: "Let those who suffer according to God's will entrust their souls to a faithful Creator while doing good."

This was the pattern for thousands of frontline peacemakers from the earliest times to this very day. For example, on July 17, 180, in one of the Roman provinces of Africa, six Christians were put on trial for refusing to render full homage to the emperor, even though they kept the laws and paid their taxes. Their names were Speratus, Nartzalus, Cittinus, Donata, Secunda, and Vestia. They were being tried by proconsul Saturninus along with others. The dialogue of their last hours was recorded:

> The proconsul Saturninus said: "Have no part in this madness."
> Cittinus said: "We have none other to fear save the Lord our God who is in heaven."

---

[8] Judson, "Advice to Missionary Candidates."

Donata said: "Give honor to Caesar as unto Caesar, but fear to God."

Vestia said: "I am a Christian."

Secunda said: "I wish to be none other than what I am."

The proconsul Saturninus said to Speratus: "Do you persist in remaining a Christian?"

Speratus said: "I am a Christian." And all were of one mind with him.

The proconsul Saturninus said: "Do you desire any space for consideration?"

Speratus said: "When the right is so clear there is nothing to consider."

The proconsul Saturninus said: "What have you in your case?"

Speratus said: "The Books, and the letters of a just man, one Paul."

The proconsul Saturninus said: "Take a reprieve of thirty days and think it over."

Speratus again said: "I am a Christian." And all were of one mind with him.

The proconsul Saturninus read out the sentence from his notebook: "Whereas Speratus, Nartzalus, Cittinus, Donata, Vestia, Secunda, and the rest have confessed that they live in accordance with the religious rites of the Christians, and, when an opportunity was given them of returning to the usage of the Romans, persevered in their obstinacy, it is our pleasure that they should suffer by the sword."

Speratus said: "Thanks be to God."

Nartzalus said: "Today we are martyrs in heaven: thanks be to God!"

The proconsul Saturninus commanded that proclamation be made by the herald: "I have commanded that Speratus, Nartzalus, Cittinus, Veturius, Felix, Aquilinus, Laetantius, Januaria, Generosa, Vestia, Donata, Secunda be led forth to execution."

They all said: "Thanks be to God!"

And so all were crowned with martyrdom together, and reign with the Father and the Son and the Holy Spirit for ever and ever. Amen.[9]

How the Death of Martyrs Blossoms

How likely is the crisis of martyrdom today? Perhaps a better question is: How important is martyrdom today? How important is suffering for the sake of taking the gospel to the nations? George Otis Jr. shocked many at the Second Lausanne Congress on World Evangelization in Manila in 1989 when he asked, "Is our failure to thrive in Muslim

---

[9] "The Martyrs of Scilli in Africa Proconsularis, 17 July 180," in *A New Eusebius: Documents Illustrative of the History of the Church to A.D. 337*, ed. J. Stevenson (London: SPCK, 1968), 41–42.

countries owing to the absence of martyrs? Can a covert church grow in strength? Does a young church need martyr models?"

Fittingly, he concludes his book *The Last of the Giants* with a chapter entitled "Risk Safety."

> Should the Church in politically or socially trying circumstances remain covert to avoid potential eradication by forces hostile to Christianity? Or would more open confrontation with prevailing spiritual ignorance and deprivation—even if it produced Christian martyrs—be more likely to lead to evangelistic breakthroughs? Islamic fundamentalists claim that their spiritual revolution is fueled by the blood of martyrs. Is it conceivable that Christianity's failure to thrive in the Muslim world is due to the notable absence of Christian martyrs? And can the Muslim community take seriously the claims of a Church in hiding? . . . The question is not whether it is wise at times to keep worship and witness discreet, but rather how long this may continue before we are guilty of "hiding our light under a bushel." . . . The record shows that from Jerusalem and Damascus to Ephesus and Rome, the apostles were beaten, stoned, conspired against and imprisoned for their witness. Invitations were rare, and never the basis for their missions.[10]

Otis would have agreed with Gregory the Great (pope from 590 to 604) when he said, "The death of the martyrs blossoms in the lives of the faithful."[11]

None of this is without divine meaning and design. God saved us by the suffering and death of his Son. It is his pattern to send this message of salvation to the world by displaying a realistic picture of those sufferings in the suffering of his servants. The reason for this pattern is to make clear to us and to the world that the surpassing and successful effect of this mission belongs to God and not to us. Paul shows us this divine purpose through his own life:

> We were so utterly burdened beyond our strength that we despaired of life itself. Indeed, we felt that we had received the sentence of death. But *that was to make us rely not on ourselves but on God* who raises the dead. . . . But we have this treasure in jars of clay, to show that *the surpassing power belongs to*

---

[10] George Otis Jr., *The Last of the Giants: Lifting the Veil on Islam and the End Times* (Grand Rapids, MI: Chosen, 1991), 261, 263. This account of George Otis at Lausanne is based on my own notes from being there and hearing him. I recorded this also in *Desiring God* (Colorado Springs: Multnomah, 2011), 273.
[11] Quoted in Joseph Tson, "A Theology of Martyrdom" (Wheaton, IL: The Romanian Missionary Society, n.d.), 1.

God and not to us. . . . "*My power* is made perfect in weakness." (2 Cor.1:8–9; 4:7; 12:9).

In the end, the message, the method, and the final outcome of missions will all work together to make us humbly dependent on God, and to show God graciously powerful to save. If we must suffer along the way to put Christ's sacrificial love on display, it will be a small price for the inheritance to come. "I consider that the sufferings of this present time are not worth comparing with the glory that is to be revealed to us" (Rom. 8:18). "This light momentary affliction is preparing for us an eternal weight of glory beyond all comparison" (2 Cor. 4:17).

Walk Softly to the Nations

Therefore, we may receive Adoniram Judson's final counsel with peace. After observing that "a large proportion of those who come out on a mission to the East die within five years," he says, "Walk softly, therefore; death is narrowly watching your steps."[12]

Indeed, death is watching our steps. We are as fragile as a flower that fades. Let there be no triumphalistic swagger. No cocky self-assurance. Let us accept humbly that we are "a mist that appears for a little time and then vanishes" (James 4:14). And let us resolve to set our faces like flint on the path of obedience and never turn back. And with a full grasp of the possible cost before us, and with full courage because of Christ, let us walk softly to every unreached people that remains.

---

[12] Judson, "Advice to Missionary Candidates."

The Swans Are Not Silent

Book 6

Seeing Beauty and Saying Beautifully

*The Power of Poetic Effort in the Work of
George Herbert, George Whitefield,
and C. S. Lewis*

In memory of
Clyde S. Kilby
whose classroom poetic effort
made us savor what he saw

Seeing Beauty and Saying Beautifully

Book 6

Contents

Preface

When Eraclius, the successor to Augustine as bishop of Hippo in AD 400, said of his awe-inspiring predecessor, "The swan is silent," he compared his own voice to Augustine's as a chirping cricket. He was not referring mainly to the beauty of Augustine's eloquence but to the beauty and power and fullness of his ideas.

But when I say of George Herbert and George Whitefield and C. S. Lewis that these swans are not silent, I have in mind precisely the way their eloquence and their ideas relate to each other. The aim of this volume of The Swans Are Not Silent is to probe the interrelationship between seeing beauty and saying it beautifully.

George Herbert, Pastor-Poet

George Herbert died in 1633 just short of his fortieth birthday. Late in that short life, he became an Anglican country pastor. He wrote a book called *The Country Parson*. But he is known today because of his peerless combination of poetic craftsmanship and profound Christian faith. If any swan should be considered when pondering the relationship between seeing the beauty of Christ and saying it with unparalleled technical, artistic skill, it is George Herbert. He is "arguably the most skillful and important British devotional lyricist of [the seventeenth century] or any other time."[1]

George Whitefield, Preacher-Dramatist

George Whitefield was an English Christian evangelist who lived from 1714 to 1770. He crossed the Atlantic thirteen times and is buried, not in his homeland, but in Newburyport, Massachusetts. Along with John

[1] "George Herbert," *Poetry Foundation*, accessed February 21, 2014, http://www.poetryfoundation.org/bio/george-herbert.

Wesley in England, Howell Harris in Wales, and Jonathan Edwards in America—but more international than any of them—Whitefield was a primary catalyst of the First Great Awakening.

The preaching pace he set for thirty years was almost superhuman. Sober estimates are that he spoke about one thousand times every year for thirty years. That included at least eighteen thousand sermons and twelve thousand talks and exhortations.[2] But it is not the pace that concerns us in this book, but the power—specifically the connections between the power of his biblical perception, the power of his natural eloquence, and the power of his spiritual effectiveness.

Jonathan Edwards's wife Sarah said that Whitefield was a "born orator."[3] Benjamin Franklin, who rejected Whitefield's entire theology, said, "Every accent, every emphasis, every modulation of voice, was so perfectly well turned, and well-placed, that without being interested in the subject, one could not help being pleased with the discourse."[4] So people have asked, "Was, then, Whitefield's effectiveness only natural rather than spiritual and eternal?" J. C. Ryle certainly did not think so: "I believe that the direct good which he did to immortal souls was enormous. I will go further—I believe it is incalculable."[5]

George Whitefield was not a poet in the strict sense the way George Herbert was. But his preaching craft, with all its verbal and emotional and physical dimensions, was such a work of art that Benjamin Franklin said that listening was "a pleasure of much the same kind with that received from an excellent piece of music."[6] Therefore, Whitefield provides us with a second historical seedbed for our question about the relationship between seeing beauty and saying beautifully.

C. S. Lewis, Scholar-Novelist

C. S. Lewis is the third focus of our study. Peter Kreeft stands in awe of Lewis and says, "Clive Staples Lewis was not a man: he was a

---

[2] Michael A. G. Haykin, ed., *The Revived Puritan: The Spirituality of George Whitefield* (Dundas: Joshua Press, 2000), 32–33. Arnold Dallimore, *George Whitefield: The Life and Times of the Great Evangelist of the Eighteenth-Century Revival*, 2 vols. (Edinburgh: Banner of Truth, 1970), 2:522.
[3] Haykin, *Revived Puritan*, 35–37.
[4] Harry S. Stout, *The Divine Dramatist: George Whitefield and the Rise of Modern Evangelicalism* (Grand Rapids, MI: Eerdmans, 1991), 204.
[5] J. C. Ryle, *Select Sermons of George Whitefield with an Account of his Life* (Edinburgh: Banner of Truth, 1958), 28.
[6] Stout, *Divine Dramatist*, 204.

world."[7] Lewis lived from 1898 to 1963 and spent his working life as a professor of Medieval and Renaissance Literature at Oxford and Cambridge. But he is known most widely as the author of the children's books (which adults love) The Chronicles of Narnia, some of which have been made into movies.[8]

Lewis wanted to be a great poet. But he admits at age fifty-six that his poetry met "with little success."[9] Nevertheless, he says,

> The imaginative man in me is . . . continuously operative. . . . It was he . . . who led me to embody my religious belief in symbolical . . . forms, ranging from Screwtape to a kind of theologized science-fiction. And it was of course he who has brought me, in the last few years, to write the series of Narnian stories for children.[10]

This "imaginative man" who wanted to be a great poet remained a real poet in all his prose. Alister McGrath expressed it well when he said that much of Lewis's power was "his ability to write prose tinged with a poetic vision, its carefully crafted phrases lingering in the memory because they have captivated the imagination. The qualities we associate with good poetry . . . [abound] in Lewis's prose."[11]

Lewis had the eyes and the pen of a poet. Of all the people I have ever read, Lewis—like Jonathan Edwards, but for different reasons—sees beauty and wonder in what he looks at, and awakens my mind to do the same. He saw beauty, and what he saw, he said beautifully. The combination has given him lasting power. He is the most widely read twentieth-century apologist today. He is more popular and influential now than he ever was in his lifetime.

Three Anglicans and Their Poetic Effort

This is a book about the interrelationship between seeing beauty and saying it beautifully—and the impact that the effort has on our lives. It is rooted in the life and work of three Anglican Christians—

---

[7] Peter Kreeft, *C. S. Lewis: A Critical Essay* (Grand Rapids, MI: Eerdmans, 1969), 4.
[8] Most recently, *The Lion, the Witch, and the Wardrobe* (2005), *Prince Caspian* (2008), and *The Voyage of the Dawn Treader* (2010).
[9] Walter Hooper, ed., *The Collected Letters of C. S. Lewis: Narnia, Cambridge, and Joy, 1950–1963*, 3 vols. (San Francisco: HarperCollins, 2007), 3:517.
[10] Ibid.
[11] Alister McGrath, *C. S. Lewis—A Life: Eccentric Genius, Reluctant Prophet* (Carol Stream, IL: Tyndale, 2013), 108.

a pastor-poet, a preacher-dramatist, and a scholar-novelist. All of them, in their own ways, made sustained poetic effort in what they spoke and wrote. This book is about that effort and how it relates to seeing beauty and awakening others to see it—especially the beauty of Jesus Christ.

Acknowledgments

John Donne is usually acknowledged to be the greatest of the so-called metaphysical poets. He was twenty-one years older than George Herbert, and a close friend of Herbert's mother. Donne's influence on Herbert was significant. Some of his most famous lines are:

> No man is an island,
> Entire of itself,
> Every man is a piece of the continent,
> A part of the main. . . .
>
> And therefore never send to know for whom the bell tolls;
> It tolls for thee.[1]

The older I get and the more of my life on this earth is behind me rather than before me, the more I feel the truth of this. I am what I am as a thread in a fabric, a grape in a cluster, a spark in a fire, a bee in a hive, a nerve in a body, an ingredient in a recipe, a stone in a wall, or a drop in an ocean.

To be sure, I deeply value individuality, and loathe the horrors of constrained, homogenous, communistic sameness. God made individuals with stunning distinctiveness and as absolutely unique refractions of his glory. Nevertheless, the greatest glory is when these refractions compose a unified display of God's greatness, as a stained-glass window with thousands of fragments reveals one bright picture—not *in spite of* the differences among the fragments, but *because* of them. Or like a tapestry with millions of matchless threads—yellow, orange, blue, and crimson fragmentary alone—being woven into a perfect whole.

So it is no artificial humility for me to say that I am more thankful at

---

[1] John Donne, "Meditation 17" (1623) in *The Complete Poetry and Selected Prose of John Donne*, ed. Charles M. Coffin (New York: Random, 1952), 440–41.

age sixty-eight than I have ever been for the people who have made this book possible. They are more than I can remember or honor. Dozens of those who have made this book possible are dead. They have been dead for centuries and are as much a part of my life as many of the living. In my home, and in high school, and college, and seminary, and graduate school, and college teaching, and pastoring, there have been hundreds of people who have shaped the way I think and the way I respond to the world and to God.

And there are the obvious ones who are close and precious. My wife and children and even grandchildren shape my heart in these days. Noël and Talitha make a home for me as the three of us eat and sleep and talk and read and pray together.

David Mathis, the executive editor at desiringGod.org, and Marshall Segal, my executive assistant, protect, distill, provide, suggest, correct, refine, and encourage with devotion and excellence so that I can flourish in the ministry of the Word.

Since stepping down as pastor for preaching at Bethlehem Baptist Church in March of 2013, Desiring God has been my new base of operations. I'm called founder and teacher. They pay my salary. They share me with Bethlehem College and Seminary so that I can function as chancellor and teach part-time. All this means that I am surrounded and sustained by an amazing team of partners (at DG and BCS) committed to spreading a passion for the supremacy of God in all things for the joy of all peoples through Jesus Christ.

I thank God for this beautiful fabric of life into which I have been woven.

Crossway has again been willing to publish another volume, this one the sixth, in the series The Swans Are Not Silent. Because of this partnership, the fruit of all the other influences of my life are made available to the public. May God continue to weave, with this book, tens of thousands of threads into the great tapestry of his Christ-exalting purpose in the world.

I am not an island. When the bell tolls for a thousand losses in the lives of others, it tolls for me. And with this book, even more of us will be woven together. The tapestry grows, the beauties increase, and the sorrows multiply—until the last stitch is made and all is beauty.

Christ did not send me to baptize but to preach the gospel, and not with words of eloquent wisdom, lest the cross of Christ be emptied of its power. For the word of the cross is folly to those who are perishing, but to us who are being saved it is the power of God. . . . Where is the debater of this age? Has not God made foolish the wisdom of the world? . . .

For the foolishness of God is wiser than men, and the weakness of God is stronger than men. . . . And I, when I came to you, brothers, did not come proclaiming to you the testimony of God with lofty speech or wisdom. For I decided to know nothing among you except Jesus Christ and him crucified.

1 Corinthians 1:17–2:2

Introduction

"Not with Lofty Speech or Wisdom"

Does the Bible Warrant Poetic Effort?

This book is about the relationship between *poetic effort* on the one hand, and perceiving, relishing, and portraying truth and beauty on the other hand—especially the truth and beauty of God in Christ. By *poetic effort*, I don't mean the effort to write poetry. Those who make the greatest poetic effort, as I am using the term, may never write a poem. Only one of the three men in this book is known mainly for his poetry—George Herbert. But all three of them made poetic effort in their Christ-exalting communications. They made poetic effort to *see* and *savor* and *show* the glories of Christ. This effort was the God-dependent intention and exertion to find striking, penetrating, imaginative, and awakening ways of expressing the excellencies they saw. My thesis is that this effort to say beautifully is, perhaps surprisingly, a way of seeing and savoring beauty.

For example, when I hear my daughter singing worship songs in her bedroom, my heart is glad. But when I make the effort to put into suitable words what I love about her song—in a conversation, in a birthday card, in a poem—I hear more, see more, love more. This is how it is with all truth and beauty—the wonders of nature, the stunning turns of redemptive history, and the glories of Christ. In making the poetic effort to find fitting words for these wonders, we see and savor them more deeply and speak them with more power. George Herbert, George Whitefield, and C. S. Lewis discovered this long before I did. It has been a profound joy to follow their discovery and use of poetic effort—for Christ and his kingdom.

My Biggest Fear

My biggest fear in writing this book is that I might contradict the apostle Paul when he says, "Christ did not send me . . . to preach the gospel . . . *with words of eloquent wisdom,* lest the cross of Christ be emptied of its power" (1 Cor. 1:17),[1] or when he said, "I . . . did not come proclaiming to you the testimony of God *with lofty speech or wisdom*" (1 Cor. 2:1).[2] There is a way to speak the gospel—a way of eloquence or cleverness or human wisdom—that nullifies the cross of Christ.

James Denney said, "No man can give the impression that he himself is clever and that Christ is mighty to save."[3] This statement has been my constant companion for the last three decades. I long to show that Christ is mighty to save. I dread nullifying the cross. Therefore, the implicit exhortation throughout this book—to make poetic effort and to find striking ways to speak truth—runs the risk of contradicting Scripture. That is a fearful thing.

Indispensable Words

But the risk is unavoidable. Every person who seeks to commend Christ with words faces this issue. And we cannot do without words in commending Christ. We know him in the words of Scripture, and the Scriptures themselves teach us how indispensable words are in the Christian life. God has designed the world and human beings in such a way that his ultimate and highest aims for humanity come about through human words. For example,

- The *new birth* comes about through words (1 Pet. 1:23–25): "You have been born again . . . through the living and abiding word of God. . . . This word is the good news that was preached to you" (also, James 1:18).

---

[1] The NIV 1984 translates 1 Cor. 1:17, "Not with words of human wisdom"; the NASB, "Not in cleverness of speech"; and the KJV, "Not with wisdom of words."

[2] The NIV translates 1 Cor. 2:1, "I did not come with *eloquence or human wisdom*"; the NASB, "I did not come with *superiority of speech or of wisdom*"; and the KJV, "[I] came not with *excellency of speech or of wisdom.*"

[3] James Denney, quoted in John Stott, *Between Two Worlds: The Art of Preaching in the Twentieth Century* (Grand Rapids, MI: Eerdmans, 1982), 325.

- Saving *faith* comes about through words (Rom. 10:17): "Faith comes from hearing, and hearing through the word of Christ."
- The grace of *edification* comes through words (Eph. 4:29): "[Let only speech come from your mouth] as fits the occasion, that it may give grace to those who hear."
- Christian *love* and purity of heart and a good conscience come through words (1 Tim. 1:5): "The aim of our charge [our words] is love that issues from a pure heart and a good conscience and a sincere faith."
- The *joy* of Christ in the believer comes through words (John 15:11): "These things I have spoken to you, that my joy may be in you, and that your joy may be full."
- *Freedom* from the power of sin comes through words (John 8:32): "You will know the truth, and the truth will set you free."
- That is, *sanctification* comes through words (John 17:17): "Sanctify them in the truth; your word is truth."
- And final *salvation* comes though teaching with words (1 Tim. 4:16): "Keep a close watch . . . on the teaching. Persist in this, for by so doing you will save both yourself and your hearers."

God's Decisive Work

Of course, if that's all we said about the cause of these great accomplishments (new birth, faith, love, holiness, and salvation), then one might be tempted to think that our giftedness in using words effectively is decisive in bringing these things about. Poetic effort and "wordsmithing" would be paramount. But in fact, our words are not decisive in producing any of these glorious effects. God is.

- *God* made his people alive while they were dead in their sins (Eph. 2:5), so that they could even hear the words of the gospel.
- By the grace *of God*, our people come to have faith. "This is not [their] own doing; it is the gift of God" (Eph. 2:8).
- When our people achieve any measure of holiness, it is *God* "working in [them] that which is pleasing in his sight" (Heb. 13:21).
- If they experience any Christ-honoring love or joy or peace, it is the fruit of *God's* Spirit (Gal. 5:22).
- If they fight successfully against any sin, it is "by [*God's*] Spirit" that they put to death the deeds of the body (Rom. 8:13).
- And if they are saved in the end, it is decisively because *God* "saved [them] . . . not because of [their] works but because of his own

purpose and grace" (2 Tim. 1:9). *God* kept them from stumbling (Jude 24); *God* completed the work that he began (Phil. 1:6).

In other words, all the highest aims of language are decisively the work of God. They are decisively supernatural. And no amount of poetic effort or expertise in the use of words can bring about the great aims of life if God withholds his saving power. Which raises the question: Does, then, the way we use words—does poetic effort—make any difference in whether the great aims of life are achieved?

The Importance of How We Use Words

The New Testament answers yes, at least in regard to the clarity of the words and the attitude of their delivery. The *clarity* of the words matters: "Pray also for us . . . that I may make it *clear*, which is how I ought to speak" (Col. 4:3–4). "If with your tongue you utter speech that is not intelligible, how will anyone know what is said? For you will be speaking into the air" (1 Cor. 14:9, cf. v. 19). And the *attitude* of the delivery matters. Paul pleads for prayer, "that words may be given to me in opening my mouth *boldly* to proclaim the mystery of the gospel . . . as I ought to speak" (Eph. 6:18–20).

This leaves us asking: If God is the decisive cause of the aims of our ministry, and yet God wills that the *clarity* and *attitude* of our words make a difference in their effectiveness, are there other aspects of language (besides clarity and attitude) that might make a difference in their effectiveness? What about poetic effort? What about the effort to find words and ways of putting them together that is surprising and striking and provocative and awakening and creative and imaginative?

Unavoidable Choices of Words

We are not forcing this question on the text of Scripture. It is not we but God who has made words indispensable for the greatest events of the world—spiritual events with eternal effects. And we cannot just quote Scripture. We must talk about it. Explain it. Exult in it. Defend it. Commend it. Herald it. Pray it. And each time we must choose words. Which words will we choose?

We know that different words have different associations and connotations and effects. We must choose how to put these words together in sentences and paragraphs. We must choose how to say them: softly or loudly, quickly or slowly, pausing or not pausing, tenderly or toughly, emotionally or dispassionately, joyfully or sadly, with gestures or without gestures, walking or standing still, smiling or frowning, looking people in the eye or looking past them. We cannot escape this. We must make these choices. We either do it consciously or unconsciously.

Forward with the Risk

So I don't take this risk of writing this book because I want to, but because I have had to make these choices every day of my Christian life. Of course, I don't have to write a book about it. But is not writing a book less of a risk? Should I make these choices without reflection? Should I make them without Christian models to help me—like Herbert and Whitefield and Lewis? Should I do the hard work of thinking about these things but not share it with anyone? It seems to me that the risk of each of those options is greater than the risk of writing this book.

So we ask: Did the apostle Paul in 1 Corinthians 1 and 2 intend to discourage all poetic effort in commending the truth and beauty of God in Christ? Did he mean that we should make no prayerful, Bible-guided, God-dependent exertion to find striking, penetrating, imaginative, awakening ways of expressing the excellencies of Christ? I don't think so.[4] And I have six reasons. The most important is the context of 1 Corinthians itself and what kind of eloquence Paul actually meant to condemn.

1. What Kind of Eloquence Did Paul Actually Condemn?

Let's make our way back into Paul's mind through a recent book on eloquence by Denis Donoghue, Professor of English and American Letters at New York University. In his book *On Eloquence*, he argues that eloquence is a surprising, impacting style that is an end in itself.

> A speech or an essay may be eloquent, but if it is, the eloquence is incidental to its aim. Eloquence, as distinct from rhetoric, has no aim: it is a play of words or other expressive means. . . . The main attribute of eloquence is gratuitousness.[5]

---

[4] In the following paragraphs, I am drawing heavily on my chapter "Is There Christian Eloquence: Clear Words and the Wonder of the Cross," in *The Power of Words and the Wonder of God*, ed. John Piper and Justin Taylor (Wheaton, IL: Crossway, 2009), 67–80.
[5] Denis Donoghue, *On Eloquence* (New Haven, CT: Yale University Press, 2008), 3.

> Eloquence does not serve a purpose or an end in action. . . . In rhetoric, one is trying to persuade someone to do something: in eloquence, one is discovering with delight the expressive resources of the means at hand.[6]

I doubt that most people would agree with that definition of eloquence, as if eloquence cannot intentionally stand in the service of a great aim— say the eloquence of Martin Luther King Jr. in the cause of civil rights, or the eloquence of Winston Churchill in the cause of British national defense. But here is why Donoghue's view is important.

The Sophists in Corinth

It expresses the view that was probably behind the "eloquence" in Corinth that Paul wanted no part of. Donoghue agrees with E. M. Cioran that this notion of gratuitous eloquence began with the sophists two thousand years ago.

> The sophists were the first to occupy themselves with a meditation upon words, their value, propriety, and function in the conduct of reasoning: the capital step toward *the discovery of style, conceived as a goal in itself, as an intrinsic end*, was taken [by the sophists].[7]

One of the most compelling books on the background of Paul's words about eloquence in 1 Corinthians is Bruce Winter's *Philo and Paul among the Sophists*. Winter's argument is that it is precisely the sophists, and their view of eloquence, that form the backdrop of what Paul says about his own speech and how he ministered in Corinth.[8]

---

[6] Ibid., 148.

[7] Ibid., 136, emphasis added.

[8] "The wise, the well born and the powerful epitomized the class from which the sophists came and which the latter helped perpetuate through an elitist educational system which emphasized the art of rhetoric. Given the great sin of the sophistic movement was its boasting . . . Paul made the Jeremiah prohibition against boasting about wisdom, status and achievement a primary text in this critique of the Corinthian sophistic movement." Bruce Winter, *Philo and Paul among the Sophists: Alexandrian and Corinthian Responses to a Julio-Claudian Movement*, 2nd ed. (Grand Rapids, MI: Eerdmans, 2002), 253–54. Duane Litfin makes a similar case, arguing that Paul is defining his role as a "herald" over and against the classical "orator" or rhetoric of Corinth: "Both his physical appearance and his speaking itself were deficient, even contemptible, by the sophisticated standards of Greek rhetoric (2 Cor. 10:10). Paul was simply out of his league. These people were accustomed to the *euglottia* ("beautiful speech") of orators of the caliber of Favorinus, that paragon of Greek culture whose eloquence was both *sophos* ("wise") and *potimos* ("sweet, pleasant") [Philostratus, *Lives of the Sophists* (Cambridge, MA: Harvard University Press, 1998), 489, 491]. . . . Such a one as this could impress the Corinthians. But by this standard the apostle was an embarrassing figure. Whatever else one could say for him, he was woefully short by the stringent criteria of genuine Greek eloquence. He was simply a layman (*idiotes*, 2 Cor. 11:6) as a speaker. He appeared to lack the high-octane ability to discover convincing arguments and then sculpt them at will into irresistible phrases. He came far short of the polish and sophistication in word choice, in diction, in voice, in physical charm and self-possession that was indispensable to impress and move a Greco-Roman crowd." Duane Litfin, "Swallowing Our Pride: An Essay on the Foolishness of Preaching," in *Preach the Word: Essays*

So let's consider briefly Paul's words in 1 Corinthians to see if he gives us enough clues to show what sort of eloquence he is rejecting. Given my definition of poetic effort (which I would call a kind of eloquence), it is clear to me that in the very act of rejecting Greek eloquence, Paul is making poetic effort. For example, in 1 Corinthians 1:25, he says, "The foolishness of God is wiser than men, and the weakness of God is stronger than men." He cannot be unconscious that it is shocking to say that the gospel is "the foolishness of God" and "the weakness of God." This risks blasphemy. He could have spared us preachers the work of explaining this daring, over-the-top description of God's greatest work as foolish and weak. But no! He chose a shocking way to say it. He used irony. He made an effort to select words that would make an impact and force people to wake up and think. That is what I mean by poetic effort. And Paul does it while condemning a certain kind of "eloquence."

"Not with Words of Eloquent Wisdom"

What then is he condemning? We know from 2 Corinthians 10:10 that Paul's opponents mocked him for lacking eloquence. They said, "His letters are weighty and strong, but his bodily presence is weak, and *his speech of no account.*" We also know from at least six sources that the sophists were present and influential in Corinth.[9] Unlike Paul, they put a huge premium on style and form as evidence of education and power and wisdom. They had probably influenced some in the church to admire their kind of eloquence and look for it in Christian teachers. Bruce Winter says, "Paul deliberately adopts an anti-sophistic stance and thus defends his church-planting activities in Corinth against a backdrop of sophistic conventions, perceptions, and categories."[10]

That's what we find in 1 Corinthians 1:17: "Christ did not send me to baptize but to preach the gospel, and *not with words of eloquent wisdom*, lest the cross of Christ be emptied of its power." So the way Paul is going to oppose the eloquence of the sophists is to show that it empties the cross. Why is that? Why does this view of eloquence empty the cross of power?

---

on Expository Preaching: In Honor of R. Kent Hughes, ed. Leland Ryken and Todd A. Wilson (Wheaton, IL: Crossway, 2007), 120.

[9] Winter, *Philo and Paul*, 7–9, gives six sources for our knowledge of the sophist movement in Corinth. He concludes, "There can be no doubt . . . that sophists and their students were prominent in Corinth and played an important role in the life of the city." Ibid., 140.

[10] Ibid., 141.

Verse 18 gives part of the reason: "For the word of the cross is folly to those who are perishing, but to us who are being saved it is the power of God." The reason the cross can't fit in with the eloquence of the sophists is that it is folly to them—that is, it is so destructive of human pride that those who aim at human praise through "rhetorically elaborated eloquence"[11] and "an elitist educational system"[12] could only see the cross as foolishness. The cross is the place our sin is seen as most horrible and where God's free grace shines most brightly. Both of these mean we deserve nothing. Therefore, the cross undercuts pride and exalts Christ, not us, and that made it foolish to the sophists.

We see this confirmed in verse 20: "Where is the one who is wise? Where is the scribe? Where is the debater of this age?"—the debater, the man who is so nimble with his tongue that he can take either side and win. He is smooth and clever and verbally agile. Truth and content are not the issue; rhetorical maneuvering is. Paul says at the end of verse 20, "Has not God made foolish the wisdom of the world?" The wisdom in view is not any deep worldview over against Christianity; it's the sophistry of using language to win debates and show oneself clever and eloquent and powerful.

So the eloquence Paul is rejecting is not so much any particular language conventions but the exploitation of language to exalt self and belittle or ignore the crucified Lord. Notice the contrast again in chapter 2, verses 1–2: "And I, when I came to you, brothers, did not come proclaiming to you the testimony of God with lofty speech or wisdom. For I decided to know nothing among you except Jesus Christ and him crucified." The point is: Wherever I meet scribes and debaters who bolster their ego with language jousting and leave the cross in the shadows, I am going to bring it out of the shadows and showcase it totally. I will refuse to play their language games.

The Marks of Good Eloquence

So if there is good eloquence (what I mean by poetic effort) and bad eloquence (what Paul is condemning in 1 Corinthians), we are now seeing two criteria of what is good. The good eloquence humbles itself and

---

[11] Ibid., 144n16.
[12] Ibid., 253.

exalts Christ. This is most clearly seen in 1 Corinthians 1:26–31. Paul turns the tables on the sophists' love affair with boasting.[13]

> Consider your calling, brothers: not many of you were wise according to worldly standards, not many were powerful, not many were of noble birth. But God chose what is foolish in the world to shame the wise; God chose what is weak in the world to shame the strong; God chose what is low and despised in the world, even things that are not, to bring to nothing things that are, so that no human being might boast in the presence of God.

God's design, both in the cross and in election, is "that no human being might boast in the presence of God" (v. 29). That is the first criterion of good eloquence: *It does not come from pride or feed boasting. It does not come from an ego in search of exaltation through clever speech.*

Then he continues in verses 30–31:

> And because of him you are in Christ Jesus, who became to us wisdom from God, righteousness and sanctification and redemption, so that, as it is written, "Let the one who boasts, boast in the Lord."

The second design of God, not only in the cross and in election, but also in the sovereign grace of regeneration (*"Because of him* you are in Christ Jesus," v. 30) is that all boasting be boasting in the Lord Jesus—the one who was crucified and raised. "Let the one who boasts, boast in the Lord." So the second criterion of good eloquence is that it exalts Christ—*especially the crucified Christ.*

Self-Humbling, Christ-Exalting Poetic Effort

So here is the first reason why I don't think this book contradicts 1 Corinthians 1:17, where Paul says, "*Not with words of eloquent wisdom,*" or 1 Corinthians 2:1–2, where he says, "*[Not] with lofty speech or wisdom.*" The point of both these texts is not that all poetic effort (or call it Christ-exalting eloquence) is wrong. The point is that pride-sustaining, self-exalting use of words for a show of human wisdom is incompatible with finding your life and your glory in the cross of Christ. Rather, we should govern our use of words by these double criteria: self-humiliation and Christ-exaltation.

If we put these two criteria in front of all our poetic effort—all

---

13 "The great sin of the sophistic movement was its boasting." Ibid.

our attempts to make an impact through word selection and word arrangement and word delivery—we will be guarded from the kind of eloquence Paul rejected.

2. Christ-Exalting Christian Eloquence May Not Be the Reason the Cross Is Rejected

The second reason I don't think poetic effort is alien to Christ-exalting, self-humbling communication is this: accusations that eloquence is the problem are sometimes misdirected. This is not proof of the point. It is simply a removal of a misused counterargument.

Benjamin Franklin's Stumbling Block

In the spring of 1740, George Whitefield was in Philadelphia preaching outdoors to thousands of people. Benjamin Franklin attended most of these messages. Franklin, who did not believe what Whitefield was preaching, commented on these perfected sermons:

> His delivery . . . was so improved by frequent repetition, that every accent, every emphasis, every modulation of voice, was so perfectly well turned, and well placed, that *without being interested in the subject, one could not help being pleased with the discourse*: a pleasure of much the same kind with that received from an excellent piece of music.[14]

This is a fearful thing—to speak for Christ and be praised for our eloquence, not our Christ. But before we jump to the conclusion that Whitefield was neglecting Paul's counsel not to empty the cross by his eloquence, consider this: I believe there are people who have listened to my own preaching for years without grasping with their hearts what I was saying. They remained spiritually dead to what I was saying in spite of many changes in the manner of preaching—from the simplest to the most complex, from the tenderest to the toughest, from suspenseful story to careful argument. Yet they kept coming back, not because they loved what I said, but because they enjoyed the way I said it. They would tell me so. I have met with them one-on-one, pleaded with them, warned them, rebuked them, prayed over them. Yet, as far as I could tell, they remained blind to "the light of the gospel of the glory

---

[14] Harry Stout, *The Divine Dramatist* (Grand Rapids, MI: Eerdmans, 1991), 104, emphasis added.

of Christ" (2 Cor. 4:4). I detected no spiritual taste for the truth and beauty of Christ.

I do not believe this was because I had emptied the cross of its power through vain eloquence in all those messages. Rather, I believe it was owing to what Paul said in 2 Corinthians 2:15–16: "We are the aroma of Christ to God among those who are being saved and among those who are perishing, to one a fragrance from death to death, to the other a fragrance from life to life." In other words, the preacher's vanity and carnal eloquence are not the only stumbling blocks to faith.

Jesus, John the Baptist, and the Stumbling Block of Truth

Herod would one day behead John the Baptist, but he could not stop listening to him: "When he heard him, he was greatly perplexed, and yet he heard him gladly" (Mark 6:20). Similarly with Jesus himself: "The great throng heard him gladly" (Mark 12:37), but very few understood what he was saying and truly believed. Jesus and John the Baptist were not tickling the ears of kings and people with clever speech or vain eloquence. They were not nullifying the words of Paul. Yet their speech was "seasoned with salt" (Col. 4:6) and caused kings and commoners to keep coming back.

Jesus said, "I told you, and you do not believe. The works that I do in my Father's name bear witness about me, but you do not believe because you are not among my sheep. My sheep hear my voice, and I know them, and they follow me" (John 10:25–27). Perhaps Jesus would have spoken this over Benjamin Franklin when he refused to believe in the message of George Whitefield. Perhaps Whitefield's eloquence was not an obstacle to his faith but an excuse of his unbelief, while others found it to be the pathway to the cross.

3. God Inspired Men to Make Poetic Effort

The third reason I don't think the apostle Paul (or any other biblical writer) ruled out poetic effort in the service of Christ is that God himself inspired men to make poetic effort in the writing of Scripture. We have already seen that in the very argument against vain human eloquence, Paul chose words that were highly out of the ordinary to strike an unforgettable blow: "the foolishness of God" and "the weakness of

God" (1 Cor. 1:25). This is the kind of thing I mean by poetic effort. This is a kind of shock-eloquence, and he used it while condemning vain eloquence.

Paul's Poetic Effort

This wasn't the only place Paul chose words that were unusual or metaphorical or emotionally impactful when he could have used words less surprising or moving or stabbing. For example,

- he called loveless speaking in tongues "a noisy gong or a clanging cymbal" (1 Cor. 13:1);
- he described our incomplete knowledge on this earth compared with knowledge in heaven as the difference between a child's stammering and an adult's reasoning, and as seeing in a mirror dimly (1 Cor. 13:11–12);
- he dared to compare the Lord's coming again to the coming of a thief (1 Thess. 5:2);
- he sought to waken the Thessalonians to his affections by saying, "We were gentle among you, like a nursing mother taking care of her own children" (1 Thess. 2:7);
- in 2 Corinthians 11 and 12, he dared to play on the enemy's field of boasting, beat them at their own game, then called himself a fool for doing it: "I am speaking as a fool—I also dare to boast of that" (2 Cor. 11:21) and "I have been a fool!" (2 Cor. 12:11);
- he calls his own weak body a jar "of clay" (2 Cor. 4:7), and in another place, a "tent" (2 Cor. 5:2);
- he refers to himself and the apostles as "the filth of the world, and . . . the offscouring of all things" (1 Cor. 4:13 KJV);
- he says that his highest moral attainments without Christ are "rubbish" (Phil. 3:8);
- he refers to fickle listeners as having "itching ears" (2 Tim. 4:3); and
- he describes our sins as written in a record and nailed with Jesus to the cross (Col. 2:14).

This is what I mean by poetic effort. All these words are images laden with verbal power and evocative potential. He strove not to be boring. Not to be bland. He aimed to strike blows with feathers ("nursing mother") and stones ("fool," "rubbish," and "filth").

The Pervasive Poetic Effort of Scripture

Whole books have been written on the stunning richness and variety of language in the Bible. Addressing the question of how much of God's inspired Word is poetry, Leland Ryken asks and answers,

> Given the combined presence of parallelism and a heavy reliance on figurative language, how much of the Bible ranks as poetry? One-third of the Bible is not too high an estimate. Whole books of the Bible are poetic: Job, Psalms, Proverbs, Song of Solomon. A majority of Old Testament prophecy is poetic in form. Jesus is one of the most famous poets of the world. Beyond these predominantly poetic parts of the Bible, figurative language appears throughout the Bible, and whenever it does, it requires the same type of analysis given to poetry.[15]

In Hosea 12:10, God himself says, "I have also spoken by the prophets, and I have multiplied visions, and used similitudes" (KJV). In other words, God himself claims to have put it in the minds of biblical writers to think of analogies and comparisons and metaphors and similes and symbols and parables—to search out words that point to reality in indirect ways, rather than always describing things directly with the least imaginative words.

The poet John Donne says, "The Holy Ghost in penning the Scriptures delights himself, not only with a propriety, but with a delicacy, and harmony, and melody of language; with height of Metaphors, and other figures, which may work greater impressions upon the Readers."[16] John Calvin cites Isaiah as an example: "Let us pay attention to the style of Isaiah, which is not only pure and elegant, but also is ornamented with high art—from which we may learn that eloquence may be of great service to faith."[17]

Pascal and Paul on Pleasing the Hearer

The point is not that these verbal choices are decisive in bringing about the greatest goals of language. God alone decides that. The point is that, short of these highest goals, God seems to have ordained that typically

---

[15] Leland Ryken, "'I Have Used Similitudes': The Poetry of the Bible," *Bibliotheca Sacra* 147 (July 1990), 259–60.
[16] John Donne, *The Sermons of John Donne*, ed. George R. Potter and Evelyn M. Simpson (Berkeley, CA: University of California Press, 1953–1962), 6:55.
[17] B. B. Warfield, quoted in "Calvin and the Bible," in *Selected Shorter Writings of Benjamin B. Warfield*, ed. John E. Meeter, 2 vols. (Phillipsburg, NJ: P&R, 1970), 1:398.

some uses of language awaken, hold interest, and provoke to thought better than others so that the message might more clearly be seen and considered. Pascal writes,

> Eloquence is an art of saying things in such a way—(1) that those to whom we speak may listen to them without pain and with pleasure; (2) that they feel themselves interested, so that self-love leads them more willingly to reflection upon it.[18]

No doubt, there is eloquence that displeases the hearer, but Pascal's main point is that arresting and holding the listener (or reader) is a means to other ends. Surely the apostle Paul would have included his speech in the "everything" when he said, "I try to please everyone in everything I do, not seeking my own advantage, but that of many, that they may be saved" (1 Cor. 10:33). It is not the pleasing that saves. God saves. But Paul believed acting (and speaking) a certain way could advance that salvation better than other ways. And he believed this, even though God can use any kind of speech he pleases as a means of salvation.

At the merely natural level, we are all dull and are served well when language claps its hands and wakes us up to pay attention. George Eliot in the novel *Middlemarch* speaks to this through one of her characters,

> We do not expect people to be deeply moved by what is not unusual. . . . If we had a keen vision and feeling of all ordinary human life, it would be like hearing the grass grow and the squirrel's heartbeat, and we should die of that roar which lies on the other side of silence. As it is, the quickest of us walk about well wadded with stupidity.[19]

Proverbs and Isaiah for Example

This may be one reason why the Bible is filled with every manner of literary device to add natural impact: acrostics, alliteration, analogies, anthropomorphism, assonance, cadence, chiasmus, consonance, dialogue, hyperbole, irony, metaphor, meter, onomatopoeia, paradox, parallelism, repetition, rhyme, satire, simile—they're all there, and more. Take a small sampling of these images from Proverbs and Isaiah only. They could be increased hundreds of times.

---

[18] Blaise Pascal, *Pensées* (New York: Dutton, 1958), Kindle Edition.
[19] George Eliot, *Middlemarch*, chap. 20 (1874), quoted in Donoghue, *On Eloquence*, 77.

Bread gained by deceit is sweet to a man,
  but afterward his mouth will be full of gravel. (Prov. 20:17)

The lips of knowledge are a precious jewel. (Prov. 20:15)

A king's wrath is like the growling of a lion,
  but his favor is like dew on the grass. (Prov. 19:12)

Gracious words are like a honeycomb,
  sweetness to the soul and health to the body. (Prov. 16:24)

The name of the LORD is a strong tower;
  the righteous man runs into it and is safe. (Prov. 18:10)

Whoever trusts in his riches will fall,
  but the righteous will flourish like a green leaf. (Prov. 11:28)

A rich man's wealth is his strong city;
  the poverty of the poor is their ruin. (Prov. 10:15)

The tongue of the righteous is choice silver;
  the heart of the wicked is of little worth. (Prov.10:20)

Like vinegar to the teeth and smoke to the eyes,
  so is the sluggard to those who send him. (Prov. 10:26)

Can a man carry fire next to his chest
  and his clothes not be burned?
Or can one walk on hot coals
  and his feet not be scorched?
So is he who goes in to his neighbor's wife;
  none who touches her will go unpunished. (Prov. 6:27–29)

Save yourself like a gazelle from the hand of the hunter,
  like a bird from the hand of the fowler. (Prov. 6:5)

Poverty will come upon you like a robber,
  and want like an armed man. (Prov. 6:11)

The lips of a forbidden woman drip honey,
  and her speech is smoother than oil. (Prov. 5:3)

[Wisdom] is a tree of life to those who lay hold of her;
  those who hold her fast are called blessed. (Prov. 3:18)

Wisdom cries aloud in the street,
>   in the markets she raises her voice. (Prov. 1:20)

Wine is a mocker, strong drink a brawler,
>   and whoever is led astray by it is not wise. (Prov. 20:1)

The terror of a king is like the growling of a lion;
>   whoever provokes him to anger forfeits his life. (Prov. 20:2)

The spirit of man is the lamp of the LORD,
>   searching all his innermost parts. (Prov. 20:27)

The heart of Ahaz and the heart of his people shook as the trees of the forest shake before the wind. (Isa. 7:2)

Do not let your heart be faint because of these two smoldering stumps of firebrands, at the fierce anger of Rezin and Syria and the son of Remaliah. (Isa. 7:4)

In that day the LORD will whistle for the fly [Pharaoh] that is at the end of the streams of Egypt, and for the bee [Sennacherib] that is in the land of Assyria. (Isa. 7:18)

They rejoice before you
>   as with joy at the harvest,
>   as they are glad when they divide the spoil. (Isa. 9:3)

Shall the axe boast over him who hews with it,
>   or the saw magnify itself against him who wields it?
As if a rod should wield him who lifts it,
>   or as if a staff should lift him who is not wood! (Isa. 10:15)

The remnant of the trees of his forest will be so few
>   that a child can write them down. (Isa. 10:19)

Behold, the Lord GOD of hosts
>   will lop the boughs with terrifying power;
the great in height will be hewn down,
>   and the lofty will be brought low. (Isa. 10:33)

There shall come forth a shoot from the stump of Jesse,
>   and a branch from his roots shall bear fruit. (Isa. 11:1)

They shall not hurt or destroy
>   in all my holy mountain;

for the earth shall be full of the knowledge of the LORD
    as the waters cover the sea. (Isa. 11:9)

    They will be in anguish like a woman in labor.
    . . . Their faces will be aflame. (Isa. 13:8)

And like a hunted gazelle,
    or like sheep with none to gather them,
each will turn to his own people,
    and each will flee to his own land. (Isa. 13:14)

Like fleeing birds,
    like a scattered nest,
so are the daughters of Moab
    at the fords of the Arnon. (Isa. 16:2)

Behold, the LORD . . . will seize firm hold on you and whirl you around and around, and throw you like a ball into a wide land. (Isa. 22:17–18)

And I will fasten him like a peg in a secure place, and he will become a throne of honor to his father's house. And they will hang on him the whole honor of his father's house. (Isa. 22:23–24)

    Moab shall be trampled down in his place,
    as straw is trampled down in a dunghill.
And he will spread out his hands in the midst of it
    as a swimmer spreads his hands out to swim,
    but the LORD will lay low his pompous pride. (Isa. 25:10–11)

Like a pregnant woman
    who writhes and cries out in her pangs
    when she is near to giving birth,
so were we because of you, O LORD;
we were pregnant, we writhed,
    but we have given birth to wind. (Isa. 26:17–18)

As when a hungry man dreams, and behold, he is eating
    and awakes with his hunger not satisfied,
or as when a thirsty man dreams, and behold, he is drinking
    and awakes faint, with his thirst not quenched,
so shall the multitude of all the nations be
    that fight against Mount Zion. (Isa. 29:8)

This iniquity shall be to you
> like a breach in a high wall, bulging out, and about to collapse,
> whose breaking comes suddenly, in an instant. (Isa. 30:13)

A thousand shall flee at the threat of one;
> at the threat of five you shall flee,
till you are left
> like a flagstaff on the top of a mountain,
> like a signal on a hill. (Isa. 30:17)

The Invitation to Join Scripture in Its Poetic Effort

If the poetic effort of the wise man in Proverbs and the prophet Isaiah are not undermining to the spiritual purpose of Scripture to humble pride, point to Christ, waken hope, and lead to faith, then we will not be surprised that it seems God invites us to join him in this creativity of impactful and striking imagery in language. He beckons us with words like these:

To make an apt answer is a joy to a man,
> and a word in season, how good it is! (Prov. 15:23)

The wise of heart is called discerning,
> and sweetness of speech increases persuasiveness. (Prov. 16:21)

A word fitly spoken
> is like apples of gold in a setting of silver. (Prov. 25:11)

Like a lame man's legs, which hang useless,
> is a proverb in the mouth of fools. (Prov. 26:7)

Let your speech always be gracious, seasoned with salt. (Col. 4:6)

Whatever you do, in *word* or deed, do everything in the name of the Lord Jesus, giving thanks to God the Father through him. (Col. 3:17)

In other words, give thought to the aptness and seasonableness and fitness and timing and appropriateness of your words. And make all of them an honor to the name of the Lord Jesus.

4. Many Who Have Made Poetic Effort Have Been Humble, Others-Oriented People

I know that many have been vain and self-exalting in their use of eloquence. If that were not true, Paul would not have written 1 Corinthians 1–4, and I would not be writing this introduction the way I am. Not only have there been such people, but we ourselves are prone to be that way. Pride lurks in every human heart. Christ died for this sin so that we might die to it and live in humble righteousness (1 Pet. 2:24). But while we live in this fallen world, we must reckon it to be dead again and again. We must, so to speak, put it to death daily (Luke 9:23; 1 Cor. 15:31; Col. 3:5).

George Herbert: Less Than the Least of God's Mercies

Nevertheless, there have been truly humble persons who have aimed their poetic effort at the benefit of others and not at their self-exaltation. George Herbert, as we will see shortly, was a country pastor whose unpublished poems he offered on his deathbed to his trusted friend Nicholas Ferrar, with these words to the courier:

> Sir, I pray deliver this little book to my dear brother Ferrar, and tell him he shall find in it a picture of the many spiritual conflicts that have passed betwixt God and my soul, before I could subject mine to the will of Jesus my Master, in whose service I have now found perfect freedom; desire him to read it: and then, if he can think it may turn to the advantage of any dejected poor soul, let it be made public; if not, let him burn it; for I and it are less than the least of God's mercies.[20]

Here is the combination of humility ("Less than the least of God's mercies") and love for others ("If he can think it may turn to the advantage of any dejected poor soul"). Yet I doubt that there ever has been a more accomplished craftsman of poetic language than George Herbert.

Whitefield Humbled by the Doctrine of Election

George Whitefield, the eighteenth-century British evangelist, was the sensation of his day—on both sides of the Atlantic. Yet God led him to biblical views of sin and salvation that cut him down to size. He said,

> For my part I cannot see how true humbleness of mind can be attained without a knowledge of [the doctrine of election]; and though I will not say, that every one who denies election is a bad man, yet I will say, with that sweet singer, Mr. Trail, it is a very bad sign: such a one, whoever he be, I think

---

[20] Quotation from Izaak Walton, *The Life of Mr. George Herbert* (1670), in *George Herbert: The Complete English Poems*, ed. John Tobin (New York: Penguin, 1991), 310–11.

cannot truly know himself; for, if we deny election, we must, partly at least, glory in ourselves; but our redemption is so ordered, that no flesh should glory in the Divine presence; and hence it is, that the pride of man opposes this doctrine, because, according to this doctrine, and no other, "he that glories must glory only in the Lord."[21]

The testimony of others, especially the lowly, is that he was a man of love. They did not smell the stench of pride or manipulation or abuse in his eloquence. They felt loved. For example, Phillis Wheatley, a black servant girl at age seventeen, wrote a poetic tribute to Whitefield titled,

An Elegiac Poem on the Death of That Celebrated Divine, and Eminent Servant of Jesus Christ, the Late Reverend, and Pious George Whitefield

It contained these lines:

When his AMERICANS were burden'd sore,
When streets were crimson'd with their guiltless gore!
Unrival'd friendship in his breast now strove:
The fruit thereof was charity and love.[22]

She was referring to American blacks. So, at least in her case, the eloquence of the man became not the exaltation of self but the expression of love.

C. S. Lewis's "Magisterial Humility"

C. S. Lewis was perhaps the most popular apologist for Christianity in the twentieth century. He is certainly the most widely read apologist today from the twentieth century. But Lewis, too, had come to Christ as the center of his world and the Savior of mind and soul and verbal skill. Owen Barfield, who knew him well, describes him as having a "magisterial humility."[23] I take this to mean that he carried his magisterial knowledge and ability lightly.

---

[21] Michael A. G. Haykin, ed., *The Revived Puritan: The Spirituality of George Whitefield* (Dundas: Joshua Press, 2000), 97–98.

[22] Phillis Wheatley, "An Elegiac Poem on the Death of That Celebrated Divine, and Eminent Servant of Jesus Christ, the Late Reverend, and Pious George Whitefield" (1771), in *A Celebration of Women Writers*, ed. Mary Mark Ockerbloom, accessed January 13, 2014, http://www.digital.library.upenn.edu/women /wheatley/whitefield/whitefield.html.

[23] C. S. Lewis, *Poems*, ed. Walter Hooper (New York: Harcourt, Brace & World, 1964), vi.

Lewis gives an unwitting description of himself when he says that the early Protestants had a "buoyant humility." "From this buoyant humility, this farewell to the self with all its good resolutions, anxiety, scruples, and motive-scratchings, all the Protestant doctrines originally sprang. . . . Relief and buoyancy are the characteristic notes."[24] Walter Hooper, his secretary, says,

> Although Lewis owned a huge library, he possessed few of his own works. His phenomenal memory recorded almost everything he had read except his own writings—an appealing fault. Often, when I quoted lines from his own poems he would ask who the author was. He was a very great scholar, but no expert in the field of C. S. Lewis.[25]

One gets the impression that his "omnivorous attentiveness"[26] to the world and the people outside him had freed him in a wonderfully healthy way from the kind of self-preoccupation that angles for attention or praise. His poetic effort—whether in fiction or nonfiction—was strewn with imaginative ways of seeing and saying things, but it all seemed to serve others. One of the most striking things he ever said for an Oxford professor of literature was this:

> The Christian knows from the outset that the salvation of a single soul is more important than the production or preservation of all the epics and tragedies in the world: and as for superiority, he knows that the vulgar, since they include most of the poor, probably include most of his superiors.[27]

Poetic Effort That Does Not Empty the Cross

The human heart is deceitful above all things and desperately corrupt. We are capable of taking the most humbling theology and the most humbling experiences and turning them into props for pride. I am sure Herbert, Whitefield, and Lewis fell prey to that temptation. But I don't believe it was their deepest identity. Their egos had been humbled by the gospel of Jesus Christ, and their hearts had been turned outward toward the world. When they made poetic effort, they did it not to exalt

---

[24] C. S. Lewis, *Poetry and Prose in the Sixteenth Century: The Oxford History of English Literature* (Oxford: Clarendon, 1954), 33–34.
[25] Lewis, *Poems*, vii.
[26] Alan Jacobs, *The Narnian* (New York: Harper One, 2005), xxi.
[27] C. S. Lewis, "Christianity and Literature" in *Christian Reflections* (Grand Rapids, MI: Eerdmans, 1967), 10.

themselves and empty the cross but to see and savor and show the truth and beauty of God—that is, they did it out of love.

5. Saying Newly Is a Way of Seeing and Savoring Newly

A fifth reason I don't think Paul meant to condemn all poetic effort is that from my own experience, poetic effort is not only helpful for others in *speaking* the glories of Christ but also helpful for me in *seeing* them and *savoring* them. This is the real origin of this book. George Herbert was the main inspiration.

Poetic Effort as Fellowship with Christ

In his poem called "Quidditie," Herbert has these lines about what writing poetry is for him:

> It is no office, art, or news;
> Nor the Exchange, or busie Hall;
> But it is that which while I use
> I am with Thee. . . . [28]

His poems are "that which while I use I am with Thee." This put into words what I have found to be true for decades. The effort to put the truth of God, and all his ways and works, into fresh language—something that may have never been spoken before—is a way of coming near to God, because of seeing and feeling more suitably. "While I use [that is, while I make poetic effort], I am with Thee."

Herbert confirmed for me in his experience what has been an indispensable part of my preaching and writing. I don't mean just the writing of poems but also the writing of sermons and books and letters and most anything else that matters. Every sermon was an opportunity not just to *say* but to *see* and *savor*. Every effort to speak the wonders of the Word of God became a fresh seeing and a fresh savoring. The pressure to prepare a fresh word from God week by week was one of the greatest gifts of my life. The effort to say beautifully was a way of seeing beauty. The effort to put a glimpse of glory into striking or moving words made the glimpse grow. The effort to find worthy words for Christ opened to me more fully the worth of Christ.

---

[28] George Herbert, "The Quidditie," in *The English Poems of George Herbert*, ed. Helen Wilcox (Cambridge: Cambridge University Press, 2007), 254.

I think this is true for everyone. And that is one of the reasons I have written this book.

6. Three Great Examples: George Herbert, George Whitefield, and C. S. Lewis

Finally, I believe that self-humbling, Christ-exalting eloquence—or poetic effort, as I am calling it in this book—is valid and important for Christian living and speaking because the three subjects of this book bear it out in their lives. I commend them to you for your own inspiration and guidance. All three of them, of course, are vastly more gifted than I am and perhaps than you are. Don't let that put you off. I come nowhere close to the poetic gifting of George Herbert, the dramatic power of George Whitefield, or the imaginative power of C. S. Lewis. But, oh, what they have shown me of truth and beauty and how to see them and say them. The glory of Christ is brighter and clearer and sweeter for me because of their poetic effort—the effort to see and savor and speak the glories they have seen in fresh and powerful ways. I thank God for them.

Yes, there is humble, Christ-exalting eloquence. Yes, poetic effort is good. It is not the decisive factor in salvation. God is. But faith and all its fruits come by hearing, and hearing by the Word (Rom. 10:17; Gal. 3:5). That Word in the Bible is pervasively eloquent—words are put together in a way to give great impact. And God invites us to create our own fresh phrases for his glory, not ours. And in the mystery of his sovereign grace, he will glorify himself in us and in the hearts of others in spite of and because of the words we have chosen. In that way, he will keep us humble and get all the glory for himself.

My God, a verse is not a crown,
No point of honour, or gay suit,
No hawk, or banquet, or renown,
Nor a good sword, nor yet a lute:

It cannot vault, or dance, or play;
It never was in *France* or *Spain*;
Nor can it entertain the day
With a great stable or demain:

It is no office, art, or news;
Nor the Exchange, or busie Hall;
But it is that which while I use
I am with Thee: and *Most take all*.
George Herbert
"The Quiddite"

1

"While I Use I Am with Thee"

The Life and Poetry of George Herbert

If you go to the mainstream poetry website *Poetry Foundation* and click on George Herbert, what you read is this: "He is . . . enormously popular, deeply and broadly influential, and arguably the most skillful and important British devotional lyricist of this or any other time."[1] This is an extraordinary tribute to a man who never published a single poem in English during his lifetime and died as an obscure country pastor when he was thirty-nine. But there are reasons for his enduring influence. And some of those reasons are why I have written this book.

His Short Life

George Herbert was born April 3, 1593, in Montgomeryshire, Wales. He died a month before his fortieth birthday on March 1, 1633. He was the seventh of ten children born to Richard and Magdalene Herbert, but his father died when he was three, leaving ten children, the oldest of which was thirteen. This didn't put them in financial hardship, however, because Richard's estate, which he left to Magdalene, was sizable.

It was twelve years before Magdalene married again, this time to Sir John Danvers who was twenty years younger than she was and just two years older than her eldest son. But he was a good father to the family during the eighteen years of marriage until Magdalene's death in

---

[1] "George Herbert," *Poetry Foundation*, accessed December 9, 2013, http://www.poetryfoundation.org/bio/george-herbert.

1627. George Herbert kept in touch with his stepfather and eventually made him the executor of his will. Herbert never knew him as a father in the home because the year John and Magdalene married was the year Herbert began his studies at Trinity College Cambridge.

Herbert had been an outstanding student at a Westminster preparatory school, writing Latin essays when he was eleven years old that would later be published. And now at Cambridge, he distinguished himself in the study of classics. He graduated second in a class of 193 in 1612 with a bachelor of arts, and then in 1616, he took his master of arts and became a major Fellow of the university.

In 1619, he was elected public orator of Cambridge University. This was a prestigious post with huge public responsibility. Herbert wrote to his stepfather what it meant to be elected the orator.

> The finest place in the University, though not the gainfullest. . . . For the Orator writes all the University letters, makes all the orations, be it to King, Prince, or whatever comes to the University, to requite these pains, he takes place next to the Doctors, is at all their assemblies and meetings, and sits above the Proctors. . . . And such like Gaynesses. Which will please a young man well.[2]

This is going to be one of the most important insights into his life because the academic stimulation, the prominence even in the king's court,[3] and the pleasures of it all would prove the great battleground over his call to the pastoral ministry.

Eleven years after his election to the oratorship, on the day of his induction to the parish ministry at Bemerton, he would say,

> I can now behold the Court with an impartial eye, and see plainly that it is made up of fraud, titles and flattery, and many other such empty, imaginary and painted pleasures: pleasures that are so empty as not to satisfy when they are enjoyed.[4]

But for now, there seemed good reasons to give himself to public service for the sake of the university and its relation to the wider civic life

---

[2] George Herbert, quoted in Margaret Bottrall, *George Herbert* (London: John Murray, 1954), 13.

[3] "The Court was not merely a spring-board for men ambitious of public office; it was the focus of all talent, literary and artistic, and its patronage extended to preachers and divines as well as to the playwrights and poets." Ibid., 16.

[4] George Herbert, quoted in Pat Magee, *George Herbert: Rector of Bemerton* (Moxham Printers, 1977), 15.

of the country. On top of the oratorship, he added a one-year term in Parliament in 1623–1624.

But the conflict of his soul over a call to the pastoral ministry intensified that year. And a vow he had made to his mother during his first year at Cambridge took hold in his heart. He submitted himself totally to God and to the ministry of a parish priest. He was ordained as a deacon in the Church of England in 1626 and then became the ordained priest of the little country church at Bemerton in 1630. There were never more than a hundred people in his church. The last three years of his life, he was a parson to a remote country parish.

At the age of thirty-six and in failing health, Herbert married Jane Danvers the year before coming to Bemerton, March 5, 1629. As the name suggests, she was a kinswoman of his stepfather. We only know about Herbert's marriage because of Izaak Walton's *Life of Mr George Herbert*, published in 1670. He says it was a happy four years. He and Jane never had children, though they adopted three nieces who had lost their parents. After fewer than three years in the ministry, Herbert died of tuberculosis, which he had suffered from most of his adult life. He was thirty-nine years old. His body lies under the chancel of the church, and there is only a simple plaque on the wall with the initials *GH*.

His Dying Gift

That's the bare outline of Herbert's life. And if that were all there was, nobody today would have ever heard of George Herbert. Even the fact that he wrote a short book known as *The Country Parson* would probably not have secured his place in memory. The reason anyone knows of George Herbert today, and the reason he is included in this volume, is because of something climactic that happened a few weeks before he died.

His close friend Nicholas Ferrar sent a fellow pastor, Edmund Duncon, to see how Herbert was doing. On Duncon's second visit, Herbert knew that the end was near. So he reached for his most cherished earthly possession and said to Duncon,

> Sir, I pray deliver this little book to my dear brother Ferrar, and tell him he shall find in it a picture of the many spiritual conflicts that have passed betwixt God and my soul, before I could subject mine to the will of Jesus my Master, in whose service I have now found perfect freedom; desire him to

read it: and then, if he can think it may turn to the advantage of any dejected poor soul, let it be made public; if not, let him burn it; for I and it are less than the least of God's mercies.[5]

That little book was a collection of 167 poems. Herbert's friend Nicholas Ferrar published it later that year, 1633, under the title *The Temple*. It went through four editions in three years, was steadily reprinted for a hundred years, and is still in print today. It established Herbert as one of the greatest religious poets of all time, though not one of these poems was published during his lifetime.

Centuries of Accolades

Forty-eight years after Herbert's death, Richard Baxter said, "Herbert speaks to God like one that really believeth a God, and whose business in this world is most with God. Heart-work and heaven-work make up his books."[6] William Cowper cherished Herbert's poetry in his struggle with depression.[7] Samuel Taylor Coleridge, nineteenth-century poet and critic, wrote to a member of the Royal Academy, "I find more substantial comfort now in pious George Herbert's *Temple* [the collection of his poems] . . . than in all the poetry since the poetry of Milton."[8]

Herbert's poetry is found in virtually every anthology of English literature. He is one of the very few great poets who is loved both by specialists and nonspecialists. He is loved for his technical rigor and his spiritual depth. T. S. Eliot said, "The exquisite variations of form in the . . . poems of *The Temple* show a resourcefulness of invention which seems inexhaustible, and for which I know no parallel in English poetry."[9] Margaret Bottrall agrees that Herbert "was an exquisite craftsman."[10] He was part of an era that prized meticulous care with language and poetry. Peter Porter writes that the fact "that Herbert is perhaps the most honest poet

---

[5] Quotation from Izaak Walton, *The Life of Mr. George Herbert* (1670), quoted in John Tobin, ed., *George Herbert: The Complete English Poems* (New York: Penguin, 1991), 310–11.
[6] Richard Baxter, quoted in Helen Wilcox, ed., *The English Poems of George Herbert* (Cambridge: Cambridge University Press, 2007), xxi.
[7] Jane Falloon, *Heart in Pilgrimage: A Study of George Herbert* (Bloomington, IN: Author-House, 2007), ix.
[8] Samuel Taylor Coleridge, quoted in Bottrall, *George Herbert*, 145.
[9] T. S. Eliot, *George Herbert* (Plymouth: Northcote, 1962), 36. In the introduction to this same volume, Peter Porter writes, "We begin by admiring the abruptness, go on to wonder at the singularity of the argument, sometimes even its bizarreness, but end up being awed by the moral rightness of what is said. We see why invention matters, why cleverness is not the enemy of seriousness. What else could have kept Herbert's poetry so fresh? Matthew Arnold's 'melancholy long withdrawing roar' of the sea of faith is no match for the ageless freshness of Herbert's epiphanic sound."
[10] Bottrall, *George Herbert*, 1.

who ever wrote in English does not prevent his being also one of the most accomplished technicians of verse in the whole [Western] canon."[11]

Reformed, Poetic Ministry for an Opium Addict

We will come back to his craftsmanship shortly. But linger with me over the power of his poetry to minister deeply to the likes of an opium addict such as Samuel Coleridge. One of the reasons for this is the solid rock of God's sovereignty that Coleridge felt under Herbert's poems. This is a dimension of Herbert's poetry that, I would guess, few English literature classes address. But it is essential for understanding his poems. Gene Edward Veith wrote his doctoral dissertation on Herbert as a representative of *Reformation spirituality*. He comments, to the surprise of many,

> Serious studies of George Herbert invariably come upon his Calvinism. Rather than its being seen as a solution, though, it has been treated as something of a problem. How is it that a theology associated with determinism, austerity, the impoverishment of the liturgy, and "Puritanism," with all of its negative connotations, can produce such winsome religious verse?[12]

Not What We Often Think about the Earliest Protestants

In partial answer to this question, Veith points out,

> Calvinism, attacked now for its strictness, was originally attacked for its permissiveness. Far from being ascetic, Calvinism was in conscious reaction to monastic asceticism, which rejected marriage and sexuality and insisted upon fasts and mortification of the flesh. Far from being a "theology of fear," Calvinism offered to believers, who had been taught to continually be terrified of hell, the assurance that salvation is free and that it can never be lost.[13]

Unless we put ourselves back into that period of history, we will likely bring some wrong assumptions to the task of grasping Herbert's Calvinism. C. S. Lewis wrote what remains one of the most authoritative histories of sixteenth-century literature, overflowing into the early 1600s. In it he makes this same point as he tries to free modern readers from misconceptions about the earliest Calvinists. Lewis observes that Charles

---

[11] Peter Porter, introduction to T. S. Eliot, *George Herbert*, 2.
[12] Gene Edward Veith, *Reformation Spirituality: The Religion of George Herbert* (Cranbury, NJ: Associated University Presses, 1985), 23.
[13] Ibid., 28.

Dickens's nineteenth-century character, "Mrs. Clennam, trying to expiate her early sin by a long life of voluntary gloom, was doing exactly what the first Protestants [of the sixteenth century] would have forbidden her to do."[14] The early Protestant experience was radically different:

> It springs directly out of a highly specialized religious experience. . . . The experience is that of catastrophic conversion. The man who has passed through it feels like one who has waked from nightmare into ecstasy. Like an accepted lover, he feels that he has done nothing, and never could have done anything, to deserve such astonishing happiness. . . . His own puny and ridiculous efforts would be as helpless to retain the joy as they would have been to achieve it in the first place. . . . From this buoyant humility, this farewell to the self with all its good resolutions, anxiety, scruples, and motive-scratchings, all the Protestant doctrines originally sprang. . . . Relief and buoyancy are the characteristic notes.[15]

Rethinking "Puritan"

The implication of this, Lewis says, is that "every association which now clings to the word *Puritan* has to be eliminated when we are thinking of the early Protestants. Whatever they were, they were not sour, gloomy, or severe; nor did their enemies bring any such charge against them."[16] For the Roman Catholic—Thomas More, for example—the Puritans were "dronke of the new must of lewd lightnes of mind and vayne gladnesse of harte."[17] "Protestantism," Lewis concludes, "was not too grim, but too glad, to be true."[18]

The Reformation doctrine of God's absolute sovereignty over the world, Lewis says, was "unemphasized because it was unquestioned, that every event, every natural fact, and every institution, is rooted in the supernatural. Every change of winds at sea, every change of dynasty at home, all prosperity and all adversity, is unhesitatingly referred to God. The writers do not argue about it, they know."[19]

Lewis ventures a comparison to help us break out of our misconceptions of the early Calvinists. He admits the analogy is risky: "It may be

---

[14] C. S. Lewis, *Poetry and Prose in the Sixteenth Century: The Oxford History of English Literature* (Oxford: Clarendon, 1954), 33.
[15] Ibid., 33–34.
[16] Ibid., 34.
[17] Ibid., original spelling of More's *Dialogue*, 3.2.
[18] Ibid.
[19] Ibid., 38.

useful to compare the influence of Calvin on that age with the influence of Marx on our own; or even Marx and Lenin in one, for Calvin had both expounded the new system in theory and set it going in practice."[20] The point he's making is not about communism but about the youth and revolutionary impulse of the Calvinists:

> This will at least serve to eliminate the absurd idea that Elizabethan Calvinists were somehow grotesque, elderly people, standing outside the main forward current of life. In their own day they were, of course, the very latest thing. Unless we can imagine the freshness, the audacity, and (soon) the fashionableness of Calvinism, we shall get our whole picture wrong. . . . The fierce young don, the learned lady, the courtier with intellectual leanings, were likely to be Calvinists.[21]

So when Gene Veith writes an entire book on George Herbert's Calvinism, we must be careful not to import our own misconceptions. Herbert was not a Puritan in his own time. He was a high-church Episcopalian. "During Herbert's lifetime, however, Calvinism was the norm, both for Episcopalian factions and for Presbyterian ones."[22] "The Anglican Church of Herbert's day, in its mainstream, was both ceremonial in its liturgy and Calvinist in its theology."[23]

What Made the Difference from John Donne

But not all clergy in the Church of England embraced Herbert's Calvinistic Reformation spirituality. It is illuminating to note that John Donne, the close friend of Herbert's mother, did not share Herbert's Calvinism. Though his style influenced Herbert significantly, there is a marked difference in their devotional poetry. Here's the way Veith puts it:

> It has been observed that Herbert never worries about hell, in marked contrast to John Donne's obsessive fear of damnation. This is perhaps the clearest evidence of Herbert's Calvinism, the point where dogma touches religious experience. For a Calvinist, hell is not a possibility for a Christian. Herbert believed in the perseverance of the saints, a doctrine that is perhaps the litmus test of a truly Calvinist spirituality.[24]

---

[20] Ibid., 42.
[21] Ibid., 43.
[22] Ibid., 27.
[23] Ibid., 30.
[24] Veith, *Reformation Spirituality*, 34.

Therefore, as Veith shows, "The dynamics of Calvinism are also the dynamics of Herbert's poetry."[25] The heart of these "dynamics" is the sovereign intervention of God's grace into the rebellious human heart to subdue the mutiny against heaven and give a new allegiance to the true King of the world, Jesus Christ. Herbert experienced this, wrote about this, preached this, and prayed this.

> Thou hast exalted thy mercy above all things, and hast made our salvation, not our punishment, thy glory: so that then where sin abounded, not death but grace superabounded—accordingly, when we had sinned beyond any help in heaven or earth, then thou saidest, Lo, I come![26]

When there was no help from anywhere—when the case of the human heart is hopeless in its rebellion—God breaks in and saves. That is the heart of his Calvinism. Veith says Herbert's poem "The Collar" is "the supreme Calvinist poem, dramatizing the depraved human will that insists on serving itself rather than God, in a state of intrinsic rebellion and growing chaos until God intervenes intruding upon the human will in a way that cannot be resisted, calling the sinner, effecting a response, and restoring order."[27]

> I struck the board, and cry'd, No more.
> I will abroad.
> What? shall I ever sigh and pine?
> My lines and life are free; free as the rode,
> Loose as the winde, as large as store.
> Shall I be still in suit?
> Have I no harvest but a thorn
> To let me bloud, and not restore
> What I have lost with cordiall fruit?
> Sure there was wine
> Before my sighs did drie it: there was corn
> Before my tears did drown it.
> Is the yeare onely lost to me?
> Have I no bayes to crown it?
> No flowers, no garlands gay? all blasted?
> All wasted?

---

25 Ibid.
26 George Herbert, "The Author's Prayer before Sermon," in *A Priest to the Temple; Or, The Country Parson: His Character, and Rule of Life*, in Tobin, *George Herbert*, 261.
27 Veith, *Reformation Spirituality*, 34.

Not so, my heart: but there is fruit,
                        And thou hast hands.
          Recover all thy sigh-blown age
On double pleasures: leave thy cold dispute
Of what is fit, and not forsake thy cage,
                        Thy rope of sands,
Which pettie thoughts have made, and made to thee
          Good cable, to enforce and draw,
                        And be thy law,
While thou didst wink and wouldst not see.
                        Away; take heed:
                        I will abroad.
Call in thy deaths head there: tie up thy fears.
                        He that forbears
          To suit and serve his need,
                        Deserves his load.
But as I rav'd and grew more fierce and wilde
                        At every word,
Me thoughts I heard one calling, *Childe*:
          And I reply'd, *My Lord*.[28]

The Best News Coleridge Ever Heard

In other words, just as Herbert had prayed, "When we had sinned beyond any help in heaven or earth, then thou saidest, Lo, I come!" This sovereign intervention into the rebellious human heart—like the opium-addicted heart of Samuel Coleridge—was the best of news, and Coleridge saw more clearly than most people in his day that the criticisms of Calvinism often obscured the comfort of the doctrine itself. Here's the way he put it:

> If ever a book was calculated to drive men to despair, it is Bishop Jeremy Taylor's *On Repentance*. It first opened my eyes to Arminianism, and that Calvinism is *practically* a far more soothing and consoling system. . . . Calvinism (Archbishop Leighton's for example) compared with Taylor's Arminianism, is the lamb in wolf's skin to the wolf in the lamb's skin: the one is cruel in the phrases, the other in the doctrine.[29]

Remember, as we noted earlier, Coleridge had said, "I find more substantial comfort now in pious George Herbert's *Temple*, which I

---

[28] George Herbert, "The Collar," in *English Poems of George Herbert*, ed. Wilcox, 526.
[29] Veith, *Reformation Spirituality*, 117.

used to read to amuse myself with his quaintness, in short, only to laugh at, than in all the poetry since the poetry of Milton." This is because, as Veith argues, Herbert was the "clearest and most consistent poetic voice"[30] of the Calvinism that Coleridge found to be life giving. Veith comments on Coleridge's words,

> Herbert is a lamb clothed in the wolf-skin of Calvinism. . . . Calvinism [as Coleridge says] "is cruel in the phrases," with its dreadful language of depravity and reprobation; Arminianism has gentle phrases (free will, universal atonement), but is cruel "in the doctrine." Coleridge, perhaps faced with the incapacity of his own will, his inability, for instance, to simply choose to stop taking opium, saw the consolation in a theology that based salvation not on the contingency of human will and efforts, but on the omnipotent will and unceasing effort of God.[31]

God's Daily Sovereign Work to "Make" Us

Herbert knew the answer to Coleridge's need. It was the answer to his own struggles. And it was not free will. It was not even an initial act of sovereign, delivering grace. It was *daily*, lifelong, sovereign sustaining grace. In his poem "Giddinesse," Herbert laments the fragmented, fickle nature of man's heart—his heart.

> Oh what a thing is man! how farre from power,
>   From setled peace and rest!
> He is some twentie sev'rall men at least
>   Each sev'rall houre.

What is the remedy? Not just one act of new creation at the beginning of our life in Christ, but rather, God's *daily* sovereign work as Creator to *make* us, not just mend us.

> Lord, mend or rather make us: one creation
>   Will not suffice our turn:
> Except thou make us dayly, we shall spurn
>   Our own salvation.[32]

Herbert continually celebrates the grace of God not only in his initial salvation but in God's ongoing returns and rescues from spiritual and

---

[30] Ibid., 35.
[31] Ibid., 131–32.
[32] George Herbert, "Giddinesse," in *English Poems of George Herbert*, ed. Wilcox, 446.

emotional death. "How fresh, O Lord, how sweet and clean are thy returns! . . . After so many deaths I live."[33] Again, in a poem titled "Nature," he celebrates God's great "art" of subduing human rebellion and taking us captive repeatedly:

> Full of rebellion, I would die,
> Or fight, or travail, or denie
> That thou hast ought to do with me.
>   O tame my heart;
>   It is thy highest art
> To captivate strong holds to thee.[34]

Sweet Security through Many Conflicts of Soul

Herbert called his poems the record of his conflict with God.[35] But through them all, there is the resounding note of solid confidence in God's covenant with his people. This is why Coleridge found such help. And thousands of others have as well. Perhaps the clearest poem about our security in God's provision, even of our faith and our daily confession, is "The Holdfast."

> I threatened to observe the strict decree
>   Of my deare God with all my power & might.
>   But I was told by one, it could not be;
> Yet I might trust in God to be my light.
>
> Then will I trust, said I, in him alone.
>   Nay, ev'n to trust in him, was also his:
>   We must confesse, that nothing is our own.
> Then I confess that he my succor is:
>
> But to have naught is ours, not to confesse
>   That we have nought. I stood amaz'd at this,
>   Much troubled, till I heard a friend expresse,
> That all things were more ours by being his.
>
>   What Adam had, and forfeited for all,
>   Christ keepeth now, who cannot fail or fall.[36]

---

33 George Herbert, "The Flower," in ibid., 568.
34 George Herbert, "Nature," in ibid., 155.
35 Tobin, *George Herbert*, 310–11.
36 George Herbert, "The Holdfast," in *English Poems of George Herbert*, ed, Wilcox, 499.

This is what Coleridge felt as a precious gift from Herbert's poems: utter honesty about what Herbert called "the many spiritual conflicts that have passed betwixt God and my soul"[37] and the God-given confidence that all our faith, all our perseverance, all our safety, lies in Christ. "Nay, ev'n to trust in him, was also his." The sovereign, keeping power of God's love proves to be a profound comfort.

> We all acknowledge both thy power and love
> To be exact; transcendent, and divine;
> Who dost so strongly and so sweetly move,
> While all things have their will, yet none but thine.[38]

This is the sovereign permeation of all our supposed autonomy that every enslaved sinner desperately needs. "While all things have their will, yet none but thine." For an addict like Coleridge, this was the comforting sheep in wolf's clothing. This was the secret of hope for the hopelessly enchained—everyone.

The Beauty of His Craftsmanship

So from the springs of his Anglican[39], Reformed[40] spiritual heritage, Herbert has nurtured wounded and hungry souls for centuries. And he has done it as one of the most gifted craftsmen the world of poetry has ever known. Not only is he regarded by many as "the greatest devotional poet in English,"[41] his skill in the use of language has earned him high praises in the twentieth century from T. S. Eliot,[42] W. H. Auden,[43] Gerard Manley Hopkins, Elizabeth Bishop, and Seamus Heaney.[44]

---

[37] Tobin, *George Herbert*, 311.

[38] George Herbert, "Providence," in *English Poems of George Herbert*, ed. Wilcox, 417.

[39] Gerard Manley Hopkins found his love of Herbert "his strongest tie to the English Church." Bottrall, *George Herbert*, 95.

[40] "George Herbert, the loyal Anglican, was more 'Puritan' in literary temper, than Andrew Marvell, the civil servant of the Puritan government." Veith, *Reformation Spirituality*, 31.

[41] Wilcox, *English Poems of George Herbert*, xxi. See also Veith's estimate: "George Herbert, measured by any standard—his craftsmanship, his mastery of language, his poetic and religious subtlety, the profoundness of his spiritual experience—may well be the greatest of all religious poets." Veith, *Reformation Spirituality*, 20.

[42] "When we take Herbert's collected poems and read industriously through the volume we cannot help being astonished both at the considerable number of pieces which are as fine as those in any anthology, and at what we may consider the spiritual stamina of the work. Throughout there is brainwork, and a very high level of intensity; his poetry is definitely an *oeuvre*, to be studied entire, and our gradual appreciation of the poetry gives us a new impression of the man." T. S. Eliot, quoted in Jane Falloon, *Heart in Pilgrimage*, x–xi.

[43] Auden said that George Herbert was one of the few artists of genius that he would have liked to have known personally. Cited from Peter Porter, introduction to Eliot, *George Herbert*, 3.

[44] Wilcox, *English Poems of George Herbert*, xxi.

Herbert loved crafting language in new and powerful ways. It was for him a way of seeing and savoring and showing the wonders of Christ. The central theme of his poetry was the redeeming love of Christ,[45] and he labored with all his literary might to see it clearly, feel it deeply, and show it strikingly. We don't have a single sermon that he ever preached. None has survived the vagaries of history. One can only imagine that they would have been rich with the beauties of Christ. What we have is his poetry. And here the beauty of the *subject* is wedded to the beauty of his *craft*. What we are going to see is not only that the beauty of the subject inspired the beauty of the poetry, but more surprisingly, the effort to find beautiful poetic form helped Herbert see more of the beauty of his subject. The craft of poetry opened more of Christ for Herbert—and for us.

Of the 167 poems in *The Temple*, 116 are written with meters that are not repeated. This is simply incredible when you think about it. He created new kinds of structures for seventy percent of his poems. Peter Porter expresses the amazement poets feel when they encounter Herbert: "The practicing poet examining a Herbert poem is like someone bending over a Rolls-Royce engine. How is it all done? Why can't I make something so elaborate and yet so simple? Why is a machine which performs so well also so beautiful?"[46]

Beauty and Beauteous Words

Herbert could not conceive of such a thing as a formless poem. The modern concept of free verse would probably have been incomprehensible to him. The poet's duty was to perceive and communicate beauty—which for Herbert meant the beauty of God. In the process, he would construct out of the chaos of experience and the mass of language an object that would reflect the beauty of the subject.[47]

> True beautie dwells on high: ours is a flame
> > But borrow'd thence to light us thither.
> Beautie and beauteous words should go together.[48]

---

[45] "His most frequent and dearest theme is the redemptive love of Christ." Bottrall, *George Herbert*, 88.
[46] Porter, introduction to Eliot, *George Herbert*, 4.
[47] Joseph H. Summers, *George Herbert: His Religion and Art* (Cambridge, MA: Harvard University Press, 1954), 93.
[48] George Herbert, "Forerunners," in *English Poems of George Herbert*, ed. Wilcox, 612.

Beauty originates in God. It lights our little candle of beauty here as a way to lead us to God. Therefore, "beautie and beauteous words should go together." They should go together as a witness to the origin of beauty in God and as a way of leading us home to God.

All Consecrated to God's Glory

In other words, Herbert never aimed at art for art's sake—technique for technique's sake. When he was seventeen years old, he wrote two sonnets for his mother. He sent them to her with a vow. He seemed to know already that he would give much of his life to poetry. The letter accompanying the poems to his mother lamented "the vanity of those many love poems that are daily writ, and consecrated to Venus" and that "so few are writ that look towards God and heaven." Then came his vow: "That my poor abilities in poetry, shall be all and ever consecrated to God's glory."[49]

He kept that vow in a radical way. "Not a single lyric in *The Temple* is addressed to a human being or written in honor of one."[50] He writes all 167 poems of *The Temple* as a record of his life with God. Herbert was moved to write with consummate skill because his only subject was consummately glorious. "The subject of every single poem in *The Temple*," Helen Wilcox says, "is, in one way or another, God."[51]

> How should I praise thee, Lord! how should my rymes
> > Gladly engrave thy love in steel,
> > If what my soul doth feel sometimes,
> > > My soul might ever feel![52]

His aim was to feel the love of God and to engrave it in the steel of human language for others to see and feel. Poetry was entirely for God, because everything is entirely for God. He wrote "The Elixer" precisely to give an account of how doing all things for God's sake turns them into something supremely valuable—whether it be sweeping a room or writing poetry.

---

[49] Joan Bennett, *Five Metaphysical Poets* (Cambridge: Cambridge University Press, 1964), 51.
[50] Bottrall, *George Herbert*, 134.
[51] Wilcox, *English Poems of George Herbert*, xxi.
[52] George Herbert, "The Temper (I)," in *English Poems of George Herbert*, ed. Wilcox, 193.

"For Thy Sake"

"An *elixir* (conventional modern spelling) is a preparation used by alchemists in the attempt to change base metals into gold."[53] In this poem, it is the same as the "tincture" that makes the "mean" and lowly "grow bright and clean." It is the "famous stone" that turns all to gold. And what is this elixir? This tincture? This stone? It is the heart's intention: "For thy sake" (stanza four). So the truth he is celebrating in this poem is that intentionally referring all things to God gives them great worth (gold!), whatever they are. This is what he vowed to his mother he would do with all his poems.

> Teach me, my God and King,
>   In all things thee to see,
> And what I do in any thing,
>   To do it as for thee:
>
> Not rudely, as a beast,
>   To runne into an action;
> But still to make thee prepossest,
>   And give it his perfection.
>
> A man that looks on glasse,
>   On it may stay his eye;
> Or if he pleaseth, through it passe,
>   And then the heav'n espie.
>
> All may of thee partake:
>   Nothing can be so mean,
> Which with his tincture (for thy sake)
>   Will not grow bright and clean.
>
> A servant with this clause
>   Makes drudgerie divine:
> Who sweeps a room, as for thy laws,
>   Makes that and th' action fine.
>
> This is the famous stone
>   That turneth all to gold:
> For that which God doth touch and own
>   Cannot for lesse be told.[54]

---

[53] Wilcox, *English Poems of George Herbert*, 641.
[54] George Herbert, "The Elixer," in *English Poems of George Herbert*, ed. Wilcox, 640–41.

In every stanza the "elixir" that turns all of life and poetry to gold is expressed in different ways:

Stanza one: "What I do in any thing to, do it as for thee."

Stanza two: "To make [God] prepossest" (having preeminence and ownership).

Stanza three: Looking not just at, but through, all things to see heaven.

Stanza four: "For thy sake."

Stanza five: "With this clause [for thy sake]," we beautify drudgery.

Stanza six: God is the one who touches the ordinary and turns it into gold.

"Secretarie of Thy Praise"

Poetry is one of those simple tasks of God's servant that needs to be touched by the elixir, the tincture, the stone, and turned into God's praise. Herbert believed that since God ruled all things by his sacred providence, everything revealed God. Everything spoke of God. The role of the poet is to be God's echo. Or God's secretary. To me, Herbert's is one of the best descriptions of the Christian poet: "Secretarie of thy praise."

> O Sacred Providence, who from end to end
> Strongly and sweetly movest! shall I write,
> And not of thee, through whom my fingers bend
> To hold my quill? shall they not do thee right?
>
> Of all the creatures both in sea and land
> Only to Man thou hast made known thy wayes,
> And put the penne alone into his hand,
> And made him Secretarie of thy praise.[55]

God bends Herbert's fingers around his quill. "Shall they not do thee right?" Shall I not be faithful secretary of thy praise—faithfully rendering, beautifully rendering—the riches of your truth and beauty? This is a high calling. And this is why so many of his poems are laments about his dullness and his impending loss of powers. He mourns the diminishing ability to "do thee right"—to be God's faithful secretary, to "praise thee brim-full."

---

[55] Herbert, "Providence," 416.

> Why do I languish thus, drooping and dull,
>   As if I were all earth?
> O give me quicknesse, that I may with mirth
>   Praise thee brim-full![56]

Living and Writing to Show God's Power

Herbert would die of tuberculosis at the age of thirty-nine. He was weakened by this disease most of his adult life—enduring "so many deaths." Therefore, his powers to write poetry came and went. This was a great sorrow. He lived to preach and write about the greatness of God in Christ. When his strength was taken away, it was a heavy stroke. And when the strength occasionally returned, he picked up his pen with joy because he did "relish versing."

> And now in age I bud again,
> After so many deaths I live and write;
>   I once more smell the dew and rain,
> And relish versing: O my onely light,
>   It cannot be
>   That I am he
> On whom thy tempests fell all night.[57]

He loved to see and savor and speak the saving, restoring power of God. This is what he lived for:

> I live to shew his power, who once did bring
> My *joyes* to *weep*, and now my *griefs* to *sing*.[58]

The Discovery That Saying Leads to Seeing

But Herbert discovered, in his role as the secretary of God's praise, that the poetic effort to speak the riches of God's greatness gave him deeper sight into that greatness. Writing poetry was not merely the expression of his experience with God that he had *before* the writing. The writing was part of the experience of God. It was, in the making, a way of seeing more of God. Deeper communion with God happened *in* the writing. Probably the poem that says this most forcefully is called "The Quidditie"—that is, the essence of things. And his point is that poetic

---

[56] George Herbert, "Dulnesse," in *English Poems of George Herbert*, ed. Wilcox, 410.
[57] Herbert, "The Flower," 568.
[58] George Herbert, "Josephs Coat," in *English Poems of George Herbert*, ed. Wilcox, 546, emphasis added.

verses are nothing in themselves, but are everything if he is with God in them.

> My God, a verse is not a crown,
> No point of honour, or gay suit,
> No hawk, or banquet, or renown,
> Nor a good sword, nor yet a lute:
>
> It cannot vault, or dance, or play;
> It never was in *France* or *Spain*;
> Nor can it entertain the day
> With a great stable or demain:
>
> It is no office, art, or news;
> Nor the Exchange, or busie Hall;
> But it is that which while I use
> I am with Thee, and *Most take all*.[59]

His poems are "that which while I use I am with Thee." Or as Joseph Summers says, "The writing of a verse gave to Herbert 'The Quidditie' of the spiritual experience."[60] Or as Helen Wilcox says, "This phrase makes clear that it is not the finished 'verse' itself which brings the speaker close to God, but the act of 'using' poetry—a process which presumably includes writing, revising, and reading."[61]

"My Utmost Art . . . and Cream of All My Heart"

For Herbert, this experience of seeing and savoring God was directly connected with the care and rigor and subtlety and delicacy of his poetic effort—his craft, his art. Thus he says in his poem called "Praise (II)":

---

[59] George Herbert, "The Quidditie," in ibid., 253–54. There is little consensus about the meaning of the last phrase: "And Most take all." F. E. Hutchinson gives J. Middleton Murray's explanation: "The titles to esteem, which verse is not, are first detailed; then it is declared that verse nevertheless is the quiddity of them all, in the very real sense that Herbert in his poetry comes nearest to God and most partakes of the creative power that sustains all these excellences." F. E. Hutchinson, *The Works of George Herbert* (Clarendon, 1941), Kindle Edition. Helen Wilcox suggests: "[Most take all] recalls 'Winner takes all' from the card game Primero (a game referred to in *Jordan (I)*); . . . The echo suggests that by giving up worldly interests and trusting in God—as the players give up their cards (and their money) and trust to the luck of the game—the speaker gains everything. There are thus two winners in the writing of divine poetry: God, and the writer, who 'wins by being won by an omnipotent God' (Nardo 92)." Wilcox, *English Poems of George Herbert*, 255.

[60] Summers, *George Herbert: His Religion and Art*, 107.

[61] Wilcox, *English Poems of George Herbert*, 255.

Wherefore with my utmost art
   I will sing thee,
And the cream of all my heart
   I will bring thee.[62]

The bringing of his *heart* and the singing with utmost *art* are not an incidental rhyme. They are profoundly united in his experience of God. There is, you might say, an ontological rhyme. God himself has established a connection between the "cream of heart" and the "utmost art." To labor in faith to speak the beauty of God in beautiful ways awakens—at least it did for Herbert—the heart's cream of seeing and savoring.

"To the Advantage of Any Poor Dejected Soul"

Yet Herbert had in view more than the joys of his own soul as he wrote. He wrote (and dreamed of publishing after death) with a view of serving the church. Pressing in to his "utmost art" and giving form to "the cream of all [his] heart" was not only for this own soul's joy in God. True, he had never published them during his lifetime, though we know he had been writing seriously for twenty-three years. So they were clearly for his own soul—his way of seeing and savoring the glories of God. But when he came to die, he sent this life collection of poems to his friend Nicholas Ferrar and said, "[If you] can think it may turn to the advantage of any dejected poor soul, let it be made public."[63]

This is, in fact, what he hoped for, because in the introductory poem to the entire collection, he wrote:

Hearken unto a Verser, who may chance
Ryme thee to good, and make a bait of pleasure.
   A verse may finde him, who a sermon flies,
   And turn delight into a sacrifice.[64]

He believed that the delights he had found in God by writing the poems could become a sacrifice of worship for the reader as well. It may be, he thought, that I can "ryme thee to good."

[62] George Herbert, "Praise (II)," in *English Poems of George Herbert*, ed. Wilcox, 507.
[63] Walton, *The Life of Mr. George Herbert*, in Tobin, *George Herbert*, 311.
[64] George Herbert, "The Church-porch," in *English Poems of George Herbert*, ed. Wilcox, 50.

Poetic Effort Not in Vain

And this is, in fact, what has happened. People have met God in Herbert's poems, and their lives have been changed. Joseph Summers said of Herbert's poems, "We can only recognize . . . the immediate imperative of the greatest art: 'You must change your life.'"[65] Simone Weil, the French philosopher, was totally agnostic toward God and Christianity but encountered Herbert's poem "Love (III)" and became a kind of Christian mystic,[66] calling this poem "the most beautiful poem in the world."[67]

> Love bade me welcome: yet my soul drew back,
>   Guiltie of dust and sinne.
> But quick-ey'd Love, observing me grow slack
>   From my first entrance in,
> Drew nearer to me, sweetly questioning
>   If I lack'd any thing.
>
> A guest, I answer'd, worthy to be here:
>   Love said, you shall be he.
> I the unkinde, ungratefull? Ah my deare,
>   I cannot look on thee.
> Love took my hand, and smiling did reply,
>   Who made the eyes but I?
>
> Truth Lord, but I have marr'd them: let my shame
>   Go where it doth deserve.
> And know you not, sayes Love, who bore the blame?
>   My deare, then I will serve.
> You must sit down, sayes Love, and taste my meat:
>   So I did sit and eat.[68]

It is a beautiful poem. Beautiful in form and beautiful in substance. It is the poem Herbert apparently chose to close the entire collection of his life's work. In that position, at the end of *The Temple*, it takes on a climactic resolution and peacefulness.

He had told his friend Nicholas Ferrar shortly before his death that in this collection of poems, which were his life's work, he would find "a

---

[65] Summers, *George Herbert: His Religion and Art*, 190.
[66] Falloon, *Heart in Pilgrimage*, 200.
[67] Wilcox, *English Poems of George Herbert*, xxi.
[68] George Herbert, "Love (III)," in *English Poems of George Herbert*, ed. Wilcox, 661.

picture of the many spiritual conflicts that have passed betwixt God and my soul." But then he added, "Before I could subject mine to the will of Jesus my Master, in whose service I have now found perfect freedom." This final, peaceful subjection and freedom is the spirit of this concluding poem in *The Temple*, "Love (III)."

Chana Bloch argues that "Love (III)" "contains *The Temple* in brief" proceeding "by a series of careful balancings . . . until it comes to rest in the last line emphatically on the side of God's love."[69] Gene Veith says similarly, "The final poem . . . is the capstone of *The Temple*, recapitulating and resolving once and for all the paradoxes of sin and grace, guilt and love, that are Herbert's continual themes. . . . The feast portrayed in 'Love (III)' is the goal of all the preceding poems."[70] Indeed, Veith circles back to what we saw earlier and says, "Just as there are few religious poems so positive or joyful in their message and in their effects, so there are few poems that are so Calvinistic."[71]

Relief and Buoyancy: The Characteristic Notes

Again we must recall what C. S. Lewis reminded us of earlier about the early Calvinist of Herbert's day:

> Like an accepted lover, he feels that he has done nothing, and never could have done anything, to deserve such astonishing happiness. . . . His own puny and ridiculous efforts would be as helpless to retain the joy as they would have been to achieve it in the first place. . . . Relief and buoyancy are the characteristic notes.[72]
>
> [This kind of Protestantism] was not too grim, but too glad, to be true.[73]

In other words, one of the marks of this Calvinism was that God's sovereign self-exaltation was supremely expressed in preventing man from putting God in the place of a dependent master who needs servants to sustain him. Instead God expresses his sovereignty in putting humble and dependent man finally and permanently where God will serve him with the inexhaustible resources of the riches of his glory. Hence the last lines of Herbert's poem and Herbert's life work:

---

[69] Chana Bloch, quoted in Wilcox, *English Poems of George Herbert*, 660.
[70] Veith, *Reformation Spirituality*, 171–72.
[71] Ibid.
[72] Lewis, *Poetry and Prose*, 33–34.
[73] Ibid.

> And know you not, sayes Love, who bore the blame?
>> My deare, then I will serve.
> You must sit down, sayes Love, and taste my meat:
>> So I did sit and eat.[74]

Herbert protests that he will return God the favor of bearing his blame: "My deare, then I will serve." But this Lover will not have it. "Nor is he served by human hands, as though he needed anything, since he himself gives to all mankind life and breath and everything" (Acts 17:25). "The Son of Man came not to be served but to serve, and to give his life as a ransom for many" (Mark 10:45). No, eternity will not be spent with human beings paying back the debt of grace we owe. Grace that can be paid back is not grace. Rather, for all eternity, we will be the beneficiaries of God's kindness. This Lover saves us so that "in the coming ages he might show the immeasurable riches of his grace in kindness toward us in Christ Jesus" (Eph. 2:7).

> You must sit down, sayes Love, and taste my meat:
>> So I did sit and eat.[75]

This is the end of the matter. No more striving. No more struggle. No more "spiritual conflicts [passing] betwixt God and my soul." Instead, Love himself serves the poet's soul as he sits and receives.

Love's Yoke Is Easy

This is not the excess of a poet's imagination. This is the dream come true of a poet whose mind is saturated with the Bible. You might say that these last lines are a lucid echo of the promise of Jesus in Luke 12:37. Jesus portrays his second coming as the return of a master who, instead of demanding service, serves:

> Blessed are those servants whom the master finds awake when he comes. Truly, I say to you, he will dress himself for service and have them recline at table, and he will come and serve them.

Herbert has struggled all his life to know that Love's yoke is easy and its burden is light. He had come to find that this is true. And he ended his

---

[74] Herbert, "Love (III)," 661.
[75] Ibid.

poems and his life with the most astonishing expression of it in all the Bible: the King of kings will "dress himself for service and have them recline at table, and he will come and serve them."

> You must sit down, sayes Love, and taste my meat:
> So I did sit and eat.[76]

A Pearl That Cost Him the World

Herbert hoped that the record of his own encounters with God in his poetry would do good to others. And they have. God had brought him through so many afflictions and so many temptations that his poems bore the marks not only of his "utmost art"[77] but also of utmost reality. Sitting finally in peace at his Master's table did not come without the temptations of all that the world had to offer—the lure of academia, the pull of political power, the raw pleasures of the body that are open to such positions—he had known access to them all.

His poem called "The Pearle" includes in the title "Matth. 13." It's a reference to Matthew 13:45–46, "The kingdom of heaven is like a merchant in search of fine pearls, who, on finding one pearl of great value, went and sold all that he had and bought it." The poem unfolds Herbert's experience of the world and how he came to purchase the pearl.

> I know the wayes of *learning*; both the head
> And pipes that feed the presse, and make it runne;
>
> . . .
>
> I know the wayes of *honour*, what maintains
> The quick returns of courtesie and wit:
>
> . . .
>
> I know the wayes of *pleasure*, the sweet strains,
> The lullings and the relishes of it;
>
> . . .
>
> I know all these, and have them in my hand.
> Therefore not sealed, but with open eyes
> I fly to thee, and fully understand
> Both the main sale, and the commodities;
> And at what rate and price I have thy love; . . . [78]

---

[76] Ibid.
[77] Herbert, "Praise (II)," 507.
[78] George Herbert, "The Pearle. *Matth. 13*" in *English Poems of George Herbert*, ed. Wilcox, 322–23, emphasis added.

"Weariness May Toss Him to My Breast"

He had found, at last, satisfaction and rest in Christ, not because he didn't know any alternatives but because he knew them well and found that they were not enough. One of his most famous poems, "The Pulley," describes how God himself gave wonderful gifts in this world but plotted to protect man from idolatry by withholding rest.

> When God at first made man,
> Having a glasse of blessings standing by;
> Let us (said he) poure on him all we can:
> Let the worlds riches, which dispersed lie,
> 　　Contract into a span.
>
> 　So strength first made a way;
> Then beautie flow'd, then wisdome, honour, pleasure:
> When almost all was out, God made a stay,
> Perceiving that alone of all his treasure
> 　　Rest in the bottome lay.
>
> 　For if I should (said he)
> Bestow this jewell also on my creature,
> He would adore my gifts instead of me,
> And rest in Nature, not the God of Nature:
> 　　So both should losers be.
>
> 　Yet let him keep the rest,
> But keep them with repining restlesnesse:
> Let him be rich and wearie, that at least,
> If goodnesse leade him not, yet wearinesse
> 　　May tosse him to my breast.[79]

"Guilded Clay"

Beauty, wisdom, honor, pleasure—good gifts of God, but oh, so dangerous. Herbert tasted them both ways. And found, by the sovereign grace of God, that restlessness would finally toss him to his Master's breast and seat him at his Master's table. God granted the miracle of the human heart—to see before it is too late that this world, without God, is "guilded clay." Hence his poem "Frailtie" begins,

---

[79] George Herbert, "The Pulley," in ibid., 548–49.

> Lord, in my silence how do I despise
> What upon trust
> Is styled *honour, riches,* or *fair eyes*;
> But is *fair dust*!
> I surname them *guilded clay,*
> *Deare earth, fine grasse* or *hay*;
> In all, I think my foot doth ever tread
> Upon their head.

But even in this poem that begins so confidently, the conflict between God and his soul breaks out again:

> But when I view abroad both Regiments;
> The worlds, and thine:
> Thine clad with simplenesse, and sad events;
> The other fine,
> Full of glorie and gay weeds,
> Brave language, braver deeds:
> That which was dust before, doth quickly rise,
> And prick mine eyes.
>
> O brook not this, lest if what even now
> My foot did tread,
> Affront those joyes, wherewith thou didst endow
> And long since wed
> My poore soul, ev'n sick of love:
> It may a Babel prove
> Commodious to conquer heav'n and thee
> Planted in me.[80]

"That which was dust before [in stanza one!], doth quickly rise, and prick mine eyes." The world that was unattractive in one moment, rises up and lures his eyes again. So he pleads with God. "O brook not this." Don't let this happen. Forbid it. Just now my foot was treading on the "gay weeds" of this world's temptations. Oh, let them not rise up and prove to be a Tower of Babel in me, rising up to oppose heaven and God himself.

---

[80] George Herbert, "Frailtie," in ibid., 260, emphasis added.

The Triumph of Seeing and Saying Divine Beauty

So when Herbert finally came to rest from the battle and take his seat at the Master's table, it was not because there were no powerful conflicts. He had known them, fought them, and won them. And among his weapons of his triumph were both the *seeing* and the *saying* of divine beauty. The power of knowing God and the poetic effort of showing God had won the day.

Thus George Herbert's impact as a poet was owing to his deep Reformed spirituality—that is, his proven theology of grace, centered on the cross—and to the conflicts of his soul that brought him through the lures of the world to the love of Christ, and to his poetic effort to express all this with his "utmost art" and the "cream of all his heart."[81]

A Modest Proposal: Poetic Effort

In keeping with the focus of this book, I will close this chapter with an exhortation for everyone who is called to speak about great things. I think that includes everyone—at least everyone who has been called out of darkness by Jesus Christ. "But you are . . . a people for his own possession, *that you may proclaim the excellencies of him who called you* out of darkness into his marvelous light" (1 Pet. 2:9). Every Christian is called to speak of God's excellencies.

My exhortation is that it would be fruitful for your own soul, and for the people you speak to, if you also made a *poetic effort* to see and savor and show the glories of Christ. I don't mean the effort to write poetry. Very few are called to do that. I mean the effort to see and savor and show the glories of Christ by giving some prayerful effort to finding striking, penetrating, and awakening ways of saying the excellencies that we see.

Collecting Proverbs as Poetic Effort

There are two little-appreciated habits of George Herbert that point to the kind of poetic effort for nonpoets that I am commending. First, Herbert collected proverbs. These were first published in 1640 in the periodical *Witts Recreation*, under the title: "Outlandish Proverbs Selected by Mr. G. H." Most of them were translations of proverbs from French, Spanish, and Italian sources. That's why they were called "Out-

---

[81] Herbert, "Praise (II)," 507.

landish Proverbs," which simply meant, at that time, *outside our own land*, that is, *foreign*. There were at least 1,184 of these proverbs, which are available today in F. E. Hutchinson's *The Works of George Herbert*.

Collecting proverbs was not an unusual practice at the time. We know, for example, that Francis Bacon, Erasmus, and two of Herbert's brothers collected proverbs. Herbert's collection included sayings like:

2. He begins to die, that quits his desires.
12. A good bargain is a pick-purse.
13. The scalded dog fears cold water.
14. Pleasing ware is half sold.
35. He loses nothing, that loses not God.
199. I wept when I was borne, and every day shows why.
258. I had rather ride on an ass that carries me, than a horse that throws me.
456. Good finds good.
698. Though you see a Church-man ill, yet continue in the Church still.
769. One foot is better then two crutches.
1059. Heresy may be easier kept out, than shook off.
1074. Two sparrows on one Ear of Corn make an ill agreement.
1121. We must recoil a little, to the end we may leap the better.
1122. No love is foul, nor prison fair.
1159. A man is known to be mortal by two things, Sleep and Lust.
1174. Civil Wars of France made a million of Atheists, and thirty thousand Witches.
1182. Money wants no followers.

Language That Strikes Home

Jane Falloon gives one explanation of Herbert's practice of collecting such proverbs:

> He showed a delight in them, and used them in his poems, especially in the long poem "The Sacrifice," in which many of the verses contain a proverb. Herbert must have collected them as other people collect stamps or match-boxes: a light-hearted hobby with underlying gleams of seriousness, in the succinct wisdom so many of them hold.[82]

---

[82] Falloon, *Heart in Pilgrimage*, 53.

I agree. But I would add this: Herbert was committed to speaking of the glories of Christ with language that struck home. Part of his poetic effort was to understand why certain ways of saying things had attained proverbial status. Why do these words strike and stick? And his aim was to form the habit of speaking and writing with this pungency.

When you read Herbert's poems, you can see the effect of the pithy, epigrammatic influence of proverbial diction. Some of the proverbs are manifestly poetic: "No love is foul, nor prison fair." Others are shrewd: "Pleasing ware is half sold." Others are humorously illuminating: "The scalded dog fears cold water." Others are profound: "He loses nothing, that loses not God." And all of them bear the kind of short, sharp, compact, aphoristic mark that we find in so many of Herbert's poems. For example, his line: "While all things have their will, yet none but thine."[83] Or: "A verse may find him, who a sermon flies."[84] Or: "Beauty and beauteous words should go together."[85] Or: "What Adam had, and forfeited for all, Christ keepeth now, who cannot fail or fall."[86]

So my point is this: whether you aim to write poetry or not, there are things you can do that make your speech more savory, more compelling, more like the point of Proverbs 25:11, "A word fitly spoken is like apples of gold in a setting of silver." Or Proverbs 15:23: "To make an apt answer is a joy to a man, and a word in season, how good it is!"

The Poetic Effort of Loving Music

I mentioned that there were two habits Herbert had which were part of his poetic effort. One was collecting proverbs. The other was the pursuit and enjoyment of music. He was an accomplished lutenist and played the viol. About a fourth of his poems refer to music.[87] He said once, "Music points the way to heaven as it frees us, for the moment, from the limitations of our bodily being and gives us strength back to believe in final harmony."[88] His earliest biographer wrote:

> His chiefest recreation was Music, in which heavenly art he was a most excellent master, and did himself compose many Divine Hymns and Anthems,

---

[83] Herbert, "Providence," 417.
[84] Herbert, "The Church-porch," 50.
[85] Herbert, "Forerunners," 612.
[86] Herbert, "The Holdfast," 499.
[87] Summers, *George Herbert: His Religion and Art*, 157.
[88] Magee, *George Herbert: Rector of Bemerton*, 23.

which he set and sang to his lute or viol: and though he was a lover of re-
tiredness, yet his love of Music was such, that he went usually twice every
week, on certain appointed days, to the Cathedral Church in Salisbury; and
at his return would say "that his time spent in prayer, and Cathedral-music
elevated his soul, and was his Heaven upon earth."[89]

It seems to me that for Herbert, music functioned to shape both the
source and the style of his poetry. By source, I mean his soul. If the soul
has no harmony, the mind will have no poetry. Music shaped his soul
and put him in a frame of mind that could see and savor beauty. And
music shaped his style. He is lyrical. His poems don't just say; they sing.
There is a musical flow.

So music was part of Herbert's poetic effort. That is, it was a part
of his life that contributed to the compelling way he spoke and wrote.
Whether it is in collecting pungent proverbs or loving beautiful music,
there are ways to enrich and refine and sharpen the penetrating power
of your language. This is part of what I mean by poetic effort.

Saying as a Way of Seeing

For Herbert, these habits supported the main path of seeing and savoring the beauty of Christ—the path of writing poetry. This path was
not only a way of saying but a way of seeing. What I am proposing is
that Herbert's effort to write with unusual poetic power was a way of
meditating on the glories of Christ. I am suggesting that poetic effort is
a fruitful means of meditation.

In this, I'm proposing one answer (among many) to the question:
What does it mean to meditate on the excellencies—the glories—of
Christ? What ways has God given us for lingering over the glory-laden
Word of God until that glory is seen and savored in our minds and
hearts in a way that is worthy of its supreme value? What steps can we
take to help us fruitfully meditate on the glory of Christ until we see?

Of course, one essential biblical answer is to pray. Pray prayers like,
"Open my eyes, that I may behold wondrous things" (Ps. 119:18). Or
as Paul prays, "[Have] the eyes of our hearts enlightened" (Eph. 1:18).
We often fail to see glory because we don't earnestly ask to see it.

But then what? Suppose you have prayed earnestly for God to open

---

[89] Falloon, *Heart in Pilgrimage*, 48.

the eyes of your heart so that ordinary words in the Bible become radiant with glory, beauty, and excellence. Now what? After we have asked God to do his part, what is our part? Through what human means does God intend to do his part? The answer I am proposing in this book is this: *poetic effort.* And the conviction behind it is this: *The effort to say freshly is a way of seeing freshly. The effort to say strikingly is a way of seeing strikingly. The effort to say beautifully is a way of seeing beauty.* And you don't have to write poetry to make this "poetic" effort.

For George Herbert, poetry was a form of meditation on the glories of Christ mediated through the Scriptures. Conceiving and writing poems was a way of holding a glimpse of divine glory in his mind and turning it around and around until it yielded an opening into some aspect of its essence or its wonder that he had never seen before—or felt.

This is meditation: getting glimpses of glory in the Bible or in the world and turning those glimpses around and around in your mind, looking and looking. And for Herbert, this effort to *see* and *savor* the glory of Christ was the effort to *say* it as it had never been said before.

The Greatest Example of Turning the Diamond

One of the best examples of Herbert's meditation on a single glory by turning it around and around before his eyes is his poem on the glorious reality of prayer. My guess is that when you read my phrase "glorious reality of prayer," you feel a disconnect between my big language and your small experience of prayer. Yes. So do I. But just a moment's reflection and you realize, prayer is glorious. How could talking to the Creator of the universe personally not be glorious? How could something not be glorious that cost the Son of God his life, so that sinners may come boldly to a throne, not of judgment, but of grace? Herbert tasted this glory, and he wanted to see more. So he turned this diamond around and around. Read Herbert's meditation on prayer slowly.

> Prayer the Churches banquet, Angels age,
>> God's breath in man returning to his birth,
>> The soul in paraphrase, heart in pilgrimage,
> The Christian plummet sounding heav'n and earth;
>
> Engine against th' Almightie, sinners towre,
>> Reversed thunder, Christ-side-piercing spear,

The six-daies world transposing in an houre,
A kinde of tune, which all things heare and fear;

Softnesse, and peace, and joy, and love, and blisse,
Exalted Manna, gladnesse of the best,
Heaven in ordinarie, man well drest,
The milkie way, the bird of Paradise,

Church-bels beyond the starres heard, the souls bloud,
The land of spices; something understood.[90]

Twenty-five images of prayer. My favorite is "reversed thunder." Think of it! Where did these pictures, these images, these words, come from? They came from long, focused, prayerful, Bible-saturated brooding over a single glorious reality. They came from humble, prayerful *poetic effort*. Before this effort, prayer was a word. Perhaps a wonderful word. Perhaps a rich experience. But now, on this side of the poetic effort, prayer is seen to be more than we ever dreamed. Herbert *saw* as he labored to *say*.

Putting into Words as a Way of Seeing Worth

Herbert found, as most poets have, that the effort to put the glimpse of glory into striking or moving words makes the glimpse grow. The effort to say deeply what he saw made the seeing deeper. The effort to put the wonder in an unexpected rhyme, a pleasing rhythm, a startling cadence or meter, an uncommon metaphor, a surprising expression, an unusual juxtaposition, or in words that blend agreeably with assonance or consonance—all this effort (I'm calling it *poetic effort* quite apart from poem writing) caused his heart's eyes to see the wonder in new ways. *The poetic effort to say beautifully was a way of seeing beauty.* The effort to find worthy words for Christ opens to us more fully the worth of Christ—and the *experience* of the worth of Christ. As Herbert says of his own poetic effort: "It is that which, while I use, I am with thee."[91]

My point of application is that this can be true for all of us—all those who have tasted and seen that the Lord is good. All who have

---

[90] Herbert, "Prayer (I)," in *English Poems of George Herbert*, ed. Wilcox, 178.
[91] See note 59 on the poem "Quidditie." His poem, "Prayer (I)," is one of the clearest examples of the fruit of lingering over a glory—in this case, the glory of prayer—and seeing the wonders of it by the poetic effort to say it in ways it had never been said before.

been called out of darkness into the light of marvelous realities—"unsearchable riches of Christ" (Eph. 3:8). Preachers have this job supremely. But all of us, Peter says, are called out of darkness to "proclaim the excellencies" (1 Peter 2:9). When we were converted to Christ, we were thrown into an ocean of wonder. In this life, we are to get a start on the eternity we will spend going deeper and higher into the "unsearchable riches." And my point here for all of us is *the effort to put the excellencies into worthy words is a way of seeing the worth of the excellencies. The effort to say more about the glory than you have ever said is a way of seeing more than you have ever seen.*

Poetry is a pointer to this. What poetry emphasizes—poetry from George Herbert and poetry throughout the Bible—is that the effort to say it surprisingly and provocatively and beautifully uncovers truth and beauty that you may not find any other way. I say it carefully. I do not claim that poetic effort is a *necessary* way of seeing a facet of Christ's beauty. God may open our eyes by other means—by some act of obedience, by hard study, by watching the mountains, by the gift of your own cancer, or by the death of your spouse or your child. But the poetic effort *is* a way—a pervasively biblical way, a historically proven way—of seeing and savoring and showing the glory of God.

Therefore, I commend it to you. And I commend one of its greatest patrons, the poet-pastor, George Herbert.

Hail, happy Saint, on thine immortal throne!
To thee complaints of grievance are unknown;
We hear no more the music of thy tongue,
Thy wonted auditories cease to throng.
Thy lessons in unequal'd accents flow'd!
While emulation in each bosom glow'd;
Thou didst, in strains of eloquence refin'd,
Inflame the soul, and captivate the mind.
Unhappy we, the setting Sun deplore!
Which once was splendid, but it shines no more;
He leaves this earth for Heav'n's unmeasur'd height;
And worlds unknown, receive him from our sight.
There WHITEFIELD wings, with rapid course his way,
And sails to Zion, through vast seas of day.

Phillis Wheatley
"An Elegiac Poem on the Death of . . . George Whitefield"

2

"I Will Not Be a Velvet-Mouthed Preacher!"

The Life and Eloquence of George Whitefield

The facts about George Whitefield's preaching as an eighteenth-century itinerant evangelist are almost unbelievable. Can they really be true? Judging by multiple attestations of his contemporaries—and by the agreement of sympathetic and unsympathetic biographers—they seem to be so.

From his first outdoor sermon on February 17, 1739, at the age of twenty-four, to the coal miners of Kingswood near Bristol, England, until his death thirty years later on September 30, 1770, in Newburyport, Massachusetts (where he is buried), his life was one of almost daily preaching. Sober estimates are that he spoke about one thousand times every year for thirty years. That included at least eighteen thousand sermons and twelve thousand talks and exhortations.[1]

Speaking More Than Sleeping

The daily pace he kept for thirty years meant that many weeks he was speaking more than he was sleeping. Henry Venn, vicar of Huddersfield, who knew Whitefield well, expressed amazement for us all when he wrote,

---

[1] Michael A. G. Haykin, ed., *The Revived Puritan: The Spirituality of George Whitefield* (Dundas: Joshua Press, 2000), 32–33. Arnold Dallimore, *George Whitefield: The Life and Times of the Great Evangelist of the Eighteenth-Century Revival* (Edinburgh: Banner of Truth, 1970), 2:522.

> Who would think it possible that a person . . . should speak in the compass
> of a single week (and that for years) in general forty hours, and in very many,
> sixty, and that to thousands; and after this labor, instead of taking any rest,
> should be offering up prayers and intercessions, with hymns and spiritual
> songs, as his manner was, in every house to which he was invited.[2]

Make sure you hear that accurately. Many weeks he was actually speaking (not preparing to speak, which he had virtually no time to do) for *sixty* hours (60, not 16). On the slower weeks, that's almost six hours a day, seven days a week, and on the heavier weeks, over eight hours a day.

Preaching, Preaching, Preaching

In all of my reading about Whitefield, I have found no references to what we today would call *vacations* or *days off*. When he thought he needed recuperation, he spoke of an ocean voyage to America. He crossed the Atlantic thirteen times in his life—an odd number (not even) because he died and was buried in America, not in England. The trips across the Atlantic took eight to ten weeks each. That's about two years of his life on a boat! And even though he preached virtually every day on the ship,[3] the pace was different, and he was able to read and write and rest.[4]

But on land, the preaching pace was unremitting. Two years before he died at the age of fifty-five, he wrote in a letter, "I love the open bracing air." And the following year, he said, "It is good to go into the highways and hedges. Field-preaching, field-preaching forever!"[5] Day after day all his life, he went everywhere preaching, preaching, preaching.

Speaking to Thousands

And keep in mind that most of these messages were spoken to gatherings of thousands of people—usually in difficulties of wind and competing noise. For example, in the fall of 1740, for over a month he preached almost every day in New England to crowds of up to eight

---

[2] J. I. Packer, "The Spirit with the Word: The Reformational Revivalism of George Whitefield," in *Honouring the People of God, The Collected Shorter Writings of J. I. Packer*, 4 vols. (Carlisle: Paternoster, 1999), 4:40.
[3] Harry S. Stout, *The Divine Dramatist: George Whitfield and the Rise of Modern Evangelicalism* (Grand Rapids, MI: Eerdmans, 1991), 59.
[4] Dallimore, *George Whitefield: The Life and Times*, 2:284.
[5] Haykin, *Revived Puritan*, 30.

thousand people. That was when the population of Boston, the largest city in the region, was not much larger than that.[6]

He recounts that in Philadelphia that same year, on Wednesday, April 6, he preached on Society Hill twice in the morning to about six thousand and in the evening to nearly eight thousand. On Thursday, he spoke to "upwards of ten thousand," and it was reported at one of these events that his expression of the text, "He opened his mouth and taught them saying," was distinctly heard at Gloucester point, a distance of two miles by water down the Delaware River.[7] Do you see why I say such things are nearly unbelievable? And there were times when the crowds reached twenty thousand or more.[8] This meant that the physical exertion to project his voice to that many people for so long, in each sermon, for so many times every week, for thirty years, was Herculean.[9]

One Scarcely Interrupted Sermon

Add to this the fact that he was continually traveling, in a day when it was done by horse or carriage or ship. He covered the length and breadth of England repeatedly. He regularly traveled and spoke throughout Wales. He visited Ireland twice, where he was almost killed by a mob from which he carried a scar on his forehead for the rest of his life.[10] He traveled fourteen times to Scotland and came to America seven times, stopping once in Bermuda for eleven weeks—all for preaching, not resting. He preached in virtually every major town on the Eastern seaboard of America. Michael Haykin reminds us, "What is so remarkable about all of this is that Whitefield lived at a time when travel to a town but 20 miles away was a significant undertaking."[11]

J. C. Ryle summed up Whitefield's life like this:

> The facts of Whitefield's history . . . are almost entirely of one complexion. One year was just like another; and to attempt to follow him would be only going repeatedly over the same ground. From 1739 to the year of his death, 1770, a period of 31 years, his life was one uniform employment. He

---

[6] Mark Noll, *The Old Religion in a New World: The History of North American Christianity* (Grand Rapids, MI: Eerdmans, 2002), 52.
[7] Dallimore, *George Whitefield: The Life and Times*, 1:480.
[8] Haykin, *Revived Puritan*, 31–32.
[9] Once when I was speaking to about two hundred people outdoors on a windy day, the generator for the sound system died. I finished my message for maybe fifteen minutes trying to be heard, and found it to be a strain. That was two hundred, not two thousand.
[10] Stout, *Divine Dramatist*, 209.
[11] Haykin, *Revived Puritan*, 33.

was eminently a man of one thing, and always about his Master's business. From Sunday mornings to Saturday nights, from 1 January to 31 December, excepting when laid aside by illness, he was almost incessantly preaching Christ and going about the world entreating men to repent and come to Christ and be saved.[12]

Another nineteenth-century biographer said, "His whole life may be said to have been consumed in the delivery of one continuous, or scarcely interrupted sermon."[13]

A Phenomenon in Church History

He was a phenomenon not just of his age but in the entire two-thousand-year history of Christian preaching. There has been nothing like the combination of his preaching pace and geographic extent and auditory scope and attention-holding effect and converting power. Ryle is right: "No preacher has ever retained his hold on his hearers so entirely as he did for thirty-four years. His popularity never waned."[14]

His contemporary Augustus Toplady (1740–1778) remembered him as "the apostle of the English Empire."[15] He was "Anglo America's most popular eighteenth-century preacher and its first truly mass revivalist."[16] He was "the first colonial-American religious celebrity."[17] Eight years of his life were spent in America. He loved the American ethos. He was more American in his blood, it seems, than he was English.

America's First Celebrity

Harry Stout points out, "As tensions between England and America grew [Whitefield] saw he might have to choose. Wesley would remain loyal to England, and Whitefield could not. His institutional attachments and personal identification with the colonies were stronger than his loyalty to the crown."[18]

Estimates are that 80 percent of the entire population of the Ameri-

---

[12] J. C. Ryle, *Select Sermons of George Whitefield: With an Account of His Life* (Edinburgh: Banner of Truth, 1958), 21–22.
[13] Dallimore, *George Whitefield: The Life and Times*, 2:522.
[14] Ryle, *Select Sermons of George Whitefield*, 32.
[15] Augustus Toplady, quoted in Haykin, *Revived Puritan*, 23.
[16] Stout, *Divine Dramatist*, xiii.
[17] Ibid., 92.
[18] Ibid., 261.

can colonies (this is before TV or radio) heard Whitefield at least once. Stout shows that Whitefield's impact on America was such that

> he can justly be styled America's first cultural hero. Before Whitefield, there was no unifying inter-colonial person or event. Indeed, before Whitefield, it is doubtful any name other than royalty was known equally from Boston to Charleston. But by 1750 virtually every American loved and admired White-field and saw him as their champion.[19]

William Cowper, who died when Whitefield was twenty-nine, already called him "the wonder of the age."[20]

Preaching Was Everything

This was all the effect of the most single-minded, oratorically enthrall-ing, thunder-voiced devotion to daily evangelistic preaching that history has ever known. Preaching was everything. Perhaps most of his biogra-phers would agree that Whitefield, to quote Stout,

> demonstrated a callous disregard for his private self, both body and spirit. The preaching moment engulfed all, and it would continue to do so, for in fact there was nothing else he lived for. . . . The private man and the fam-ily man had long since ceased to exist. In the final scene, there was only Whitefield in his pulpit.[21]

Howell Harris was one of Whitefield's closest friends—at least in his early ministry. Harris introduced Whitefield to open-air preaching, taught him courage in the pulpit, and later found him a wife. Before Harris introduced Whitefield to the widow Elizabeth James, Whitefield had been rejected by Elizabeth Delamotte, whom he had proposed to in a letter from America in 1740. From this letter, we get a sense of how pragmatic Whitefield was about marriage. He emphasized not a romantic attraction to her but his need for help, for example with his "increasing family" of orphans. He wrote,

> You need not be afraid of sending me a refusal. For, I bless God, if I know anything of my own heart, I am free from that foolish passion which the world calls *Love*. . . . The passionate expressions which carnal courtiers

---

[19] Harry S. Stout, "Heavenly Comet," *Christian History* 38 (1993): 13–14.
[20] Haykin, *Revived Puritan*, 23.
[21] Stout, *Divine Dramatist*, 276–77.

use, I think, ought to be avoided by those that would marry in the Lord. . . .
I trust, I love you only for God, and desire to be joined to you only by his
command and for his sake.[22]

This Elizabeth rejected the proposal. The other Elizabeth had been
a widow for ten years; she was neither pretty nor much attracted to
Whitefield. But Harris persuaded them both that the union would be
good. They were married on November 14, 1741, in Abergavenny,
South Wales. In a letter to Gilbert Tennent, Whitefield mentioned his
marriage: "About 11 weeks ago I married, in the fear of God, one who
was a widow, of about 36 years of age, and has been a housekeeper for
many years; neither rich in fortune, nor beautiful as to her person, but,
I believe, a true child of God."[23]

After two years, they had a son named John. He died in infancy,
even though Whitefield had had a strong impression that he would be a
great preacher. Elizabeth endured four miscarriages, but the Whitefields
remained childless. They were often separated for months at a time,
and from February 1747 to June 1749, she remained in America while
he was away. There was never any fear or accusation of unfaithfulness,
as both of them were committed to the highest standards of sexual
faithfulness. But the marriage seemed more functional than amorous.

On August 9, 1768, Elizabeth died after twenty-seven years of marriage to Whitefield. Whatever grief he felt was consumed in the passion
for evangelism. He wrote only days after her death, "Let us work whilst
it is day."[24] Two weeks later he was preparing to leave for America
again.

Whitefield's marriage, like John Wesley's, was not the model of
wholeness. Surely this is in part because Whitefield himself was the
fruit of a very broken family. His father died when he was two, leaving
a widow, an inn, and seven children. Eight years later his mother married Capel Longden, who tried to get the inn for himself, and failing,
deserted the family.[25] Thus Whitefield grew up not only without a father
but with a very poor example in the one father figure he briefly knew.
This is not to excuse the emotional distance he felt from Elizabeth. But

[22] Ibid., 167.
[23] Ibid., 170.
[24] Ibid., 267.
[25] Ibid., 2.

it is valuable to know some of the roots of the imperfections of our fallible heroes.

Natural and Spiritual Power

What shall we make of the public phenomenon of George Whitefield? What was the key to his power? Asking this question leads us into issues similar to what we saw in the ministry of George Herbert. Herbert's poetic effort focused on the making of poems. Whitefield's poetic effort focused on the making of sermons. And I don't mean the writing of sermons but the astonishing moment of delivering sermons. When I say *poetic effort*, I mean the entire energy of mind and soul and body that created, in the electrifying moment of preaching, something more than just intelligible words transmitting information. Specific biblical passages and doctrines were chosen, and specific words, sequences, consonances, assonances, cadences, images, narratives, characters, tones, pathoses, gestures, movements, facial expressions—all combined for an astonishing impact on believer and unbeliever alike.

Just as Herbert's poetry is studied and admired by many who do not share his faith in Christ and do not use his poetry the way he hoped they would, so also Whitefield's oratory was admired and studied then, as it is now, by people who did not share his faith and who did not respond to his messages the way he prayed they would. Therefore, in the case of George Whitefield, as with George Herbert, we must face the issue of how the natural and supernatural intersect in his poetic effort.

At one level, Whitefield's power was the natural power of eloquence, and at another it was the spiritual power of God to convert sinners and transform communities. There is no reason to doubt that he was the instrument of God in the salvation of thousands. J. C. Ryle said,

> I believe that the direct good which he did to immortal souls was enormous. I will go further—I believe it is incalculable. Credible witnesses in England, Scotland, and America have placed on record their conviction that he was the means of converting thousands of people.[26]

The Bible makes clear that true conversion to Christ is not a merely natural event. It is not mere information, argument, emotion, and words connecting persuasively with someone's brain and altering the

---

[26] Ryle, *Select Sermons of George Whitefield*, 28.

way they think and feel about Jesus. True conversion is a miracle of new birth, or new creation, brought about by the Spirit of God through the message of the gospel. There is an intersection of natural and supernatural. Without the supernatural, the "natural man" would never be converted, Paul says, "The natural person does not accept the things of the Spirit of God, for they are folly to him, and he is not able to understand them because they are spiritually discerned" (1 Cor. 2:14). The only way the "natural person" can be brought to see and believe is for God to act supernaturally: "I planted, Apollos watered, but God gave the growth" (1 Cor. 3:6).

When a rich man turned away from Jesus, he said, "It is easier for a camel to go through the eye of a needle than for a rich person to enter the kingdom of God" (Mark 10:25). When his disciples asked, "Then who can be saved?" Jesus said, "With man it is impossible, but not with God. For all things are possible with God" (Mark 10:26–27). Yes, and *only* possible with God. How does the New Testament say that?

- When Peter confessed Christ as the Son of God, Jesus said, "Flesh and blood has not revealed this to you, but my Father who is in heaven" (Matt. 16:17).
- When Lydia believed on Christ, Luke explains the conversion like this: "The Lord opened her heart to pay attention to what was said by Paul" (Acts 16:14).
- When Paul explained how unbelievers cease to be blinded by the Devil to the glory of Christ in the gospel, he said, "God, who said, 'Let light shine out of darkness,' has shone in our hearts to give the light of the knowledge of the glory of God in the face of Jesus Christ" (2 Cor. 4:6).
- When Peter explains this miracle, he says that it happens through the preaching of the gospel: "You have been born again, not of perishable seed but of imperishable, through the living and abiding word of God; . . . And this word is the good news that was preached to you" (1 Pet. 1:23–25).
- Similarly James says that the miracle of being born of God comes by the Word: "Of his own will he brought us forth by the word of truth" (James 1:18).

So the Bible and the witnesses of his own day combine to testify that Whitefield's converts were not merely the product of natural talent or oratory. Many of them were truly born of God—supernaturally changed. This was true of the wider movement of the day called the Great Awakening. Real conversions by supernatural means were happening, but they were happening through real flesh-and-blood people preaching sermons with both poetic effort and supernatural anointing.

Whitefield was the main international instrument of God in this first Great Awakening. No one else in the eighteenth century was anointed like this in America and England and Wales and Scotland and Ireland. This preaching was not a flash in the pan. Deep and lasting things happened.

His Effect on Edwards and Wilberforce

In February of 1740, Jonathan Edwards sent an invitation to Whitefield in Georgia asking him to come preach in his church. On October 19, Whitefield recorded in his journal, "Preached this morning, and good Mr. Edwards wept during the whole time of exercise. The people were equally affected."[27] Edwards reported that the effect of Whitefield's ministry was more than momentary—"In about a month there was a great alteration in the town."[28]

The impact of Whitefield, the Wesleys, and the Great Awakening in England changed the face of the nation. William Wilberforce, who led the battle against the slave trade in England, was eleven years old when Whitefield died. Wilberforce's father had died when he was nine, and Wilberforce went to live for a time with his aunt and uncle, William and Hannah Wilberforce. This couple was good friends with George Whitefield.[29]

This was the evangelical air Wilberforce breathed even before he was converted. And after his conversion, Whitefield's vision of the gospel was the truth and the spiritual dynamic that animated Wilberforce's lifelong battle against the slave trade. This is only one small glimpse of the lasting impact of Whitefield and the awakening he served.

So I do not doubt that Whitefield's contemporary, Henry Venn, was right when he said, "[Whitefield] no sooner opened his mouth as a preacher, than God commanded an extraordinary blessing upon his

---

[27] Dallimore, *George Whitefield*, 1:538.
[28] Stout, *Divine Dramatist*, 126.
[29] John Pollock, *Wilberforce* (London: Constable and Company, 1977), 4–5.

word."[30] Thus, at one level, the explanation of Whitefield's phenomenal impact was God's exceptional anointing on his life.

His Natural Oratorical Gifts

But at another level, Whitefield held people in thrall who did not believe a single doctrinal word that he said. In other words, we must come to terms with the natural oratorical gifts that he had. How are we to think about these in relation to his effectiveness? Benjamin Franklin, who loved and admired Whitefield[31]—and totally rejected his theology—said,

> Every accent, every emphasis, every modulation of voice, was so perfectly well turned, and well-placed, that without being interested in the subject, one could not help being pleased with the discourse: a pleasure of much the same kind with that received from an excellent piece of music.[32]

Virtually everyone agrees with Sarah Edwards when she wrote to her brother about Whitefield's preaching:

> He is a born orator. You have already heard of his deep-toned, yet clear and melodious voice. O it is perfect music to listen to that alone! . . . You remember that David Hume thought it worth going 20 miles to hear him speak; and Garrick [an actor who envied Whitefield's gifts] said, 'He could move men to tears . . . in pronouncing the word Mesopotamia.' . . . It is truly wonderful to see what a spell this preacher often casts over an audience by proclaiming the simplest truths of the Bible.[33]

And then she raised one of the questions that has given rise to this book:

> A prejudiced person, I know, might say that this is all theatrical artifice and display; but not so will anyone think who has seen and known him. He is a very devout and godly man, and his only aim seems to be to reach and influence men the best way. He speaks from the heart all aglow with love, and pours out a torrent of eloquence which is almost irresistible.[34]

How does Whitefield's poetic effort—his God-given oratorical abilities—relate to the supernatural effect that we believe he had?

---

[30] Ryle, *Select Sermons of George Whitefield*, 29.
[31] Franklin's comment in a letter about Whitefield was, "He is a good man and I love him." Stout, *Divine Dramatist*, 233.
[32] Ibid., 204.
[33] Haykin, *Revived Puritan*, 35–37.
[34] Ibid.

Edwards's Misgivings about Whitefield's Oratory

The story of Jonathan and Sarah Edwards's sincere appreciation for Whitefield is well known. Less known is Edwards's cautions to his people concerning their enthusiasm for Whitefield in the months that followed. I mention this because Edwards's mixed feelings about Whitefield's ministry are part of the issue we are wrestling with—the intersection of the divine and the human in his oratory—his poetic effort.

Whitefield arrived in Northampton on October 17, 1740, stayed four days, and preached four times in Edwards's meeting house. Edwards's wife Sarah commented, "It is wonderful to see what a spell he casts over an audience. . . . I have seen upwards of a thousand people hang on his words with breathless silence, broken only by an occasional half-suppressed sob."[35] When Whitefield was gone, Edwards observed, "the minds of the people in general appeared more engaged in religion, shewing a greater forwardness to make religion the subject of their conversation . . . and to embrace all opportunities to hear the Word preached."[36] Five years had gone by since the fading of the first phase of the Great Awakening in Edwards's parish. Now things were stirring again. And Whitefield seemed to be the decisive instrument.

Nevertheless, Edwards was cautious of uncritical approval and took opportunity to confront Whitefield, gently it seems, concerning several matters such as Whitefield's being guided by "impulses" and Whitefield's too easy judgment of some ministers as unconverted. This dampened the relationship. Edwards says in a letter from 1744, "It is also true (though I don't know that ever I spake of it before) that I thought Mr. Whitefield liked me not so well, for my opposing these things: and though he treated me with great kindness, yet he never made so much of an intimate of me, as of some others."[37]

We can hear echoes of Edwards's concerns in a series of nine sermons he preached the month after Whitefield had left, a series on the parable of the sower from Matthew 13:3–8. He did not name Whitefield, so far as we know, but the cautions he gives shows that he was

---

[35] Quoted in Ava Chamberlain, "The Grand Sower of the Seed: Jonathan Edwards's Critique of George Whitefield," *The New England Quarterly* 70, no. 3 (September 1997): 368.

[36] Ibid., 369.

[37] Jonathan Edwards, quoted in *Letters and Personal Writings*, ed. George S. Claghorn, vol. 16 of *The Works of Jonathan Edwards* (New Haven, CT: Yale University Press, 1998), 157.

wrestling with the very poetic effort we are dealing with in its relation to God's supernatural work in the preacher and the hearer.

For example, he says in these messages that people may experience joy when "exceedingly taken with the eloquence of the preacher" and when "pleased with the aptness of expression, and with the fervency, and liveliness, and beautiful gestures of the preacher." But affections grounded in superficial characteristics such as these are not gracious.[38] Whitefield testified to Edwards's tears as he listened to Whitefield preach. But Edwards cautioned later that "men may shed a great many tears and yet be wholly ignorant of this inward, refreshing, life-giving savor" that is the true foundation for genuine religious affections. If not followed by a "lasting alteration in the frame of the heart," Edwards says, the tears may be simply "hypocritical."[39]

Still speaking without naming Whitefield, Edwards warns the people about "talking much of the man, and setting forth the excellency of his manner of delivery, his fervency, affections, and the like." And he remarks that some of his parishioners are "almost ready to follow the preacher to the ends of the earth."[40]

None of these warnings halted the emergence of another phase of the Great Awakening, nor did Edwards intend for them to. Rather, they had the effect he hoped for.

> There are indications that the Northampton revival did take place on Edwards's, and not on Whitefield's, terms. By his own assessment, Edwards was able to avoid the mistakes that, out of ignorance, he had failed to forestall during the earlier awakening. During "the years 1740 and 1741," he reported, "the work seemed to be much more pure, having less of a corrupt mixture, than in the former great outpouring of the Spirit in 1735 and 1736."[41]

Harry Stout, professor of history at Yale, is not optimistic about the purity of Whitefield's motives or the likelihood that his effects were decisively supernatural. He leans toward the judgment of the contemporary of Whitefield, Alexander Garden of South Carolina, who believed that Whitefield "would equally have produced the same Effects, whether he had acted his Part in the Pulpit or on the Stage. . . . It was

---

[38] Chamberlain, "Grand Sower of the Seed," 378.
[39] Ibid., 379.
[40] Ibid., 380.
[41] Ibid., 382.

not the Matter but the Manner, not the Doctrines he delivered, but the Agreeableness of the Delivery," that explained the unprecedented crowds that flocked to hear him preach.[42] Stout's biography, *The Divine Dramatist: George Whitefield and the Rise of Modern Evangelicalism*, is the most sustained piece of historical cynicism I have ever read.

The Consummate Actor?

But the challenge does need to be faced. And I think if we face it head on, what we find is something deeper than what Stout finds. Stout contends that Whitefield never left behind his love for acting and his skill as an actor that was prominent in his youth before his conversion. Thus he says the key to understanding him is "the amalgam of preaching and acting."[43] Whitefield was "the consummate actor."[44] "The fame he sought was . . . the actor's command performance on center stage."[45] "Whitefield was not content simply to talk about the New Birth; he had to sell it with all the dramatic artifice of a huckster."[46] "Tears became Whitefield's . . . psychological gesture."[47] "Whitefield became an actor-preacher, as opposed to a scholar-preacher."[48]

And, of course, this last statement is true, in one sense. He was an actor-preacher as opposed to a scholar-preacher. He was not a Jonathan Edwards. He preached totally without notes,[49] and his traveling pulpit was more of a tiny stage than it was a traditional pulpit.[50] Unlike most of the preachers in his day, he was full of physical action when he preached. Cornelius Winter, Whitefield's young assistant in later years, said,

> I hardly ever knew him go through a sermon without weeping . . . sometimes he exceedingly wept, stamped loudly and passionately, and was frequently so overcome, that, for a few seconds, you would suspect he never could recover; and when he did, nature required some little time to compose himself.[51]

---

[42] Ibid., 384.
[43] Stout, *Divine Dramatist*, xviii.
[44] Ibid., 42.
[45] Ibid., xxi.
[46] Ibid., 40.
[47] Ibid., 41.
[48] Ibid., xix.
[49] Dallimore, *George Whitefield: The Life and Times*, 2:225.
[50] See a picture in Dallimore, *George Whitefield*, between pages 2:303–4, and see a picture of an example of his preaching in Haykin, *Revived Puritan*, 96.
[51] Stout, *Divine Dramatist*, 41. Cornelius Winter also said, "My intimate knowledge of him admits of my acquitting him of the charge of affectation." Eric Carlsson, review of *The Divine Dramatist: George Whitefield and the Rise of Modern Evangelicalism*, by Harry S. Stout, *TrinJ* 14 no. 2 (Fall 1993): 241.

And another contemporary from Scotland, John Gillies, reported how Whitefield moved with "such vehemence upon his bodily frame" that his audience actually shared his exhaustion and "felt a momentary apprehension even for his life."[52]

Therefore, in one sense, I do not doubt that Whitefield was "acting" as he preached. That is, that he was taking the part of the characters in the drama of his sermons and pouring all his energy—his poetic effort—into making their parts real. As when he takes the part of Adam in the garden and, with a bold and near-blasphemous statement, says to God, "If thou hadst not given me this woman, I had not sinned against thee, so thou mayest thank thyself for my transgression."[53]

Why Was He Acting?

But the question is: *Why was Whitefield "acting"?* Why was he so full of action and drama? Was he, as Stout claims, "plying a religious trade"?[54] Pursuing "spiritual fame"?[55] Craving "respect and power"?[56] Driven by "egotism"?[57] Putting on "performances"[58] and "integrating religious discourse into the emerging language of consumption"?[59]

I think the most penetrating answer comes from something Whitefield himself said about acting in a sermon in London. In fact, I think it's a key to understanding the power of *his* preaching—and all preaching. James Lockington was present at this sermon and recorded this verbatim. Whitefield is speaking.

> "I'll tell you a story. The Archbishop of Canterbury in the year 1675 was acquainted with Mr. Butterton the [actor]. One day the Archbishop . . . said to Butterton . . . 'Pray inform me Mr. Butterton, what is the reason you actors on stage can affect your congregations with speaking of things imaginary, as if they were real, while we in church speak of things real, which our congregations only receive as if they were imaginary?' 'Why my Lord,' says Butterton, 'the reason is very plain. We actors on stage speak of things imaginary, as if they were real and you in the pulpit speak of things real as if they were imaginary.'"

---

[52] Stout, *Divine Dramatist*, 141.
[53] Ryle, *Select Sermons of George Whitefield*, 165. The sermon is "Walking with God."
[54] Stout, *Divine Dramatist*, xvii.
[55] Ibid., 21.
[56] Ibid., 36.
[57] Ibid., 55.
[58] Ibid., 71.
[59] Ibid., xviii.

"Therefore," added Whitefield, 'I will bawl [shout loudly], I will not be a velvet-mouthed preacher!'"[60]

This means that there are three ways to speak. First, you can speak of an unreal, imaginary world as if it were real—that is what actors do in a play. Second, you can speak about a real world as if it were unreal—that is what half-hearted pastors do when they preach about glorious things in a way that implies they are not as terrifying or as wonderful as they are. And third, you can speak about a real spiritual world as if it were wonderfully, terrifyingly, magnificently real, because it is.

Out-Acting the Actors

So if you ask Whitefield, "Why do you preach the way you do?" he would probably say, "I believe what I read in the Bible is real." So let me venture this claim: *George Whitefield is not a repressed actor, driven by egotistical love of attention. Rather, he is consciously committed to out-acting the actors because he has seen what is ultimately real.* His oratorical exertion—his poetic effort—is not in *place* of God's revelation and power but in the *service* of them. It is not an expression of ego but of love—for God and for the lost. It is not an effort to get a hearing at any cost but to pay a cost suitable to the beauty and worth of the truth.

He is acting with all his might, not because it takes greater gimmicks and charades to convince people of the unreal, but because he had seen something more real than actors on the London stage had ever known. In the very acting, the very speaking, he was seeing, experiencing, the reality of which he spoke. The poetic effort to speak and act in suitable ways wakened in him the reality he wanted to communicate. For him the truths of the gospel were so real—so wonderfully, terrifyingly, magnificently real—that he could not and would not preach them as though they were unreal or merely interesting. He would not treat the greatest facts in the universe as unworthy of his greatest efforts to speak with fitting skill and force.

Acting in the Service of Reality

This was not a repressed acting. This was a released acting. It was not acting in the service of imagination. It was imaginative acting in

---

[60] Ibid., 239–40.

the service of reality. This was not rendering the imaginary as real. It was rendering the realness of the real as awesomely, breathtakingly real. This was not affectation. This was a passionate re-presentation—replication—of reality. This was not the mighty microscope using all its powers to make the small look impressively big. This was the desperately inadequate telescope turning every power to give some small sense of the majesty of what too many preachers saw as tiresome and unreal.

I don't deny that God uses *natural* vessels to display his *supernatural* reality. And no one denies that George Whitefield was a stupendous natural vessel. He was driven, affable, eloquent, intelligent, empathetic, single-minded, steel-willed, venturesome, and had a voice like a trumpet that could be heard by thousands outdoors—and sometimes at a distance of two miles. All of these, I venture to say, would have been part of Whitefield's natural gifting even if he had never been born again.

Whitefield Born Again

But something happened to Whitefield that made all these natural gifts subordinate to another reality. It made them all come into the service of another reality—the glory of Christ in the salvation of sinners. It was the spring of 1735. He was twenty years old. He was part of the Holy Club at Oxford with John and Charles Wesley, and the pursuit of God was all discipline.

> I always chose the worst sort of food. . . . I fasted twice a week. My apparel was mean. . . . I wore woolen gloves, a patched gown, and dirty shoes. . . . I constantly walked out in the cold mornings till part of one of my hands was quite black. . . . I could scarce creep upstairs, I was obliged to inform my kind tutor . . . who immediately sent for a physician to me.[61]

He took a break from school, and there came into his hands a copy of Henry Scougal's *Life of God in the Soul of Man*. Here is what happened, in his own words:

> I must bear testimony to my old friend Mr. Charles Wesley, he put a book into my hands, called, *The Life of God and the soul of man*, whereby God showed me, that I must be born again, or be damned. I know the place: it may be superstitious, perhaps, but whenever I go to Oxford, I cannot help running

---

[61] Ibid., 25–26.

to that place where Jesus Christ first revealed himself to me, and gave me the new birth. [Scougal] says, a man may go to church, say his prayers, receive the sacrament, and yet, my brethren, not be a Christian. How did my heart rise, how did my heart shutter, like a poor man that is afraid to look into his account-books, lest he should find himself a bankrupt: yet shall I burn that book, shall I throw it down, shall I put it by, or shall I search into it? I did, and, holding the book in my hand, thus addressed the God of heaven and earth: Lord, if I am not a Christian, if I am not a real one, for Jesus Christ's sake, show me what Christianity is, that I may not be damned at last. I read a little further, and the cheat was discovered; oh, says the author, they that know anything of religion know it is a vital union with the son of God, Christ formed in the heart; oh what a way of divine life did break in upon my poor soul. . . . Oh! With what joy—Joy unspeakable—even joy that was full of, and big with glory, was my soul filled.[62]

The power and depth and the supernatural reality of that change in Whitefield is something Harry Stout—and others who reduce the man to his natural abilities—does not sufficiently reckon with. What happened there was that Whitefield was given the supernatural ability to see what was real. His mind was opened to new reality. Here is the way he described it.

Above all, my mind being now more opened and enlarged, I began to read the holy Scriptures upon my knees, laying aside all other books, and praying over, if possible, every line and word. This proved meat indeed and drink indeed to my soul. I daily received fresh life, light, and power from above. I got more true knowledge from reading the book of God in one month than I could ever have acquired from all the writings of men.[63]

This means that Whitefield's acting—his passionate, energetic, whole-souled preaching—was the fruit of his new birth because his new birth gave him eyes to see "life and light and power from above." He saw the glorious facts of the gospel as real. Wonderfully, terrifyingly, magnificently real. This is why he cries out, "I will not be a velvet-mouthed preacher!"

None of his natural abilities vanished. They were all taken captive to obey Christ (2 Cor. 10:5). "Let my name be forgotten, let me be trodden under the feet of all men, if Jesus may thereby be glorified."[64]

---

[62] Haykin, *Revived Puritan*, 25–26. From a sermon in 1769.
[63] Ryle, *Select Sermons of George Whitefield*, 15.
[64] Carlsson, review of *Divine Dramatist*, 244.

Fighting Pride, Confessing Foolishness

Of course he fought pride. Who doesn't fight pride—pride because we *are* somebody, or pride because we *want* to be somebody? But what the record shows is that he fought this fight valiantly, putting to death again and again the vanity of human praise. "It is difficult," he said, "to go through the fiery trial of popularity and applause untainted."[65]

"Commendations," he wrote to a friend, "or even the hinting at them, are poison to a mind addicted to pride. A nail never sinks deeper than when dipt in oil. . . . Pray for me, dear Sir, and heal the wounds you have made. To God alone give glory. To sinners nothing belongs, but shame and confusion."[66]

He confessed publicly the foolishness and mistakes of his earlier years.[67] He confessed to a friend in 1741, "Our most holy thoughts are tinctured with sin, and want the atonement of the Mediator."[68] He cast himself on the free grace that he preached so powerfully:

> I am nothing, have nothing, and can do nothing without God. What although I may, like a polished sepulcher appear a little beautiful without, yet within I am full of pride, self-love and all manner of corruption. However, by the grace of God I am what I am, and if it should please God to make me instrumental to do the least good, not unto me, but unto him, be all the glory.[69]

Making Real Things Real

So Whitefield had a new nature. He had been born again. And this new nature enabled him to see what was real. And Whitefield knew in his soul: *I will never speak of what is real as though it is imaginary. I will not be a velvet-mouthed preacher.* He would not abandon acting. He would out-act the actors in his preaching, because they became actors to make imaginary things look real, and he became the preacher-actor to make real things look like what they are. This was Herbert's passion with his crafted poetry and Whitefield's passion with his dramatic preaching. They both sought to use words—crafted words, heralded words—in such a way as to waken the reader and the listener to things that no mere words could communicate.

---

[65] Haykin, *Revived Puritan*, 68.
[66] Ibid., 83.
[67] Dallimore, *George Whitefield: The Life and Times*, 2:168, 241.
[68] Haykin, *Revived Puritan*, 50.
[69] Ibid., 103.

Whitefield didn't pause in his preaching to have a little drama off to the side—like some preachers do today, a little skit, a little clip from a movie—that would have missed the whole point. Preaching *was* the play. Preaching *was* the drama. The reality of the gospel had consumed *him*. That *was* the witness. The preaching itself had become the active word of God. God was speaking. Reality was not simply being shown. Reality was happening in the preaching.

Not Acting in the Theatrical Sense

What this means is that in the end, Whitefield's "acting" was not acting in the theatrical sense at all. If a woman has a role in a movie, say, the mother of a child caught in a burning house, and as the cameras are focused on her, she is screaming to the firemen and pointing to the window in the second floor, we all say she is acting. But if a house is on fire in your neighborhood, and you see a mother screaming to the firemen and pointing to the window in the second floor, nobody says she's acting. Why not? They look exactly the same.

It's because there really is a child up there in the fire. This woman really is the child's mother. There is real danger that the child could die. Everything is real. And that's the way it was for Whitefield. The new birth had opened his eyes to what was real and to the magnitude of what was real: God, creation, humanity, sin, Satan, divine justice and wrath, heaven, hell, incarnation, the perfections of Christ, his death, atonement, redemption, propitiation, resurrection, the Holy Spirit, saving grace, forgiveness, justification, reconciliation with God, peace, sanctification, love, the second coming of Christ, the new heaven and the new earth, and everlasting joy. These were real. Overwhelmingly real to him. And infinitely important. He had been born again. He had eyes to see.

When he warned of wrath, pleaded for people to escape, and lifted up Christ, he wasn't playacting. He was calling down the kind of emotions and actions that correspond with such realities. That's what preaching does. It seeks to exalt Christ, and describe sin, and offer salvation, and persuade sinners with words and actions and emotions that correspond to the weight of these realities. George Herbert stuns us again and again with new glimpses of Christ in his startling turns of phrase, his unexpected endings that do anything but end our vision.

Whitefield stunned his audiences with the glimpses of Christ in his dramatic reenactments of the greatest realities in the world.

If you see these realities with the eyes of your heart, and if you feel the weight of them, you will know that such poetry is not pretense and such preaching is not playacting. The house is burning. There are people trapped on the second floor. We love them. And there is a way of escape.

The Preciousness of "the Doctrines of Grace"

Let's be more specific. What did George Whitefield see as real? Unlike so much preaching today, the preaching of the eighteenth-century awakening—including the evangelistic preaching of Whitefield and Wesley—was doctrinally specific and not vague. When you read the sermons of Whitefield, you are struck with how amazingly doctrinal they are.

What Whitefield saw within months after his conversion, just as George Herbert saw so differently from John Donne, was the preciousness and power of the "doctrines of grace."[70] What was real for him was classical evangelical Calvinism. "From first to last," Stout says, "he was a Calvinist who believed that God chose him for salvation and not the reverse."[71] J. I. Packer observes that "Whitefield was entirely free of doctrinal novelties."[72]

Embracing the Calvinistic Scheme

His guide as he read the Bible in those formative days was not John Calvin but Matthew Henry.[73] "I embrace the Calvinistic scheme," he said, "not because Calvin, but Jesus Christ has taught it to me."[74] In fact, he wrote to John Wesley in 1740, "I never read anything that Calvin wrote."[75]

He believed these biblical truths—which he sometimes called "the doctrines of the Reformation"—did the most to "debase man and exalt

---

[70] He used the term freely for the fullness of the Reformation and Calvinistic teaching about salvation by sovereign grace. Writing on February 20, 1741, to Anne Dutton, he refers to his settlement in Georgia and says, "My family in Georgia was once sadly shaken, but now, blessed be God, it is settled, and, I hope, established in the doctrines of grace." Ibid., 127. On his second trip to America, he was critical of many pastors, saying, "Many ministers are so sadly degenerated from their pious ancestors, that the doctrines of grace, especially the personal, all-sufficient righteousness of Jesus is but too seldom, too slightly mentioned." Stout, *Divine Dramatist*, 97.
[71] Stout, *Divine Dramatist*, xxiii.
[72] Packer, "Spirit with the Word," 56.
[73] Haykin, *Revived Puritan*, 26.
[74] Packer, " Spirit with the Word," 47.
[75] Dallimore, *George Whitefield: The Life and Times*, 1:574.

the Lord Jesus. . . . All others leave free will in man, and make him, in part at least, a Savior to himself."[76] And not only did that diminish the work of the Savior, it made our position in Christ insecure.

The Link between Election and Perseverance

What Whitefield saw as real with his new eyes was the link between election and perseverance. God had chosen him unconditionally, and God would therefore keep him invincibly. This was his rock-solid confidence and a fire in his bones and the power of his obedience. He wrote in 1739 from Philadelphia,

> Oh the excellency of the doctrine of election, and of the saints' final perseverance, to those who are truly sealed by the Spirit of promise! I am persuaded, till a man comes to believe and feel these important truths, he cannot come out of himself; but when convinced of these, and assured of the application of them to his own heart, he then walks by faith indeed, not in himself but in the Son of God, who died and gave himself for him. Love, not fear, constrains him to obedience.[77]

And a year later he wrote to John Wesley, "The doctrine of election, and the final perseverance of those that are truly in Christ, I am ten thousand times more convinced of, if possible, then when I saw you last."[78] He loved the assurance he had in the mighty hands of God. "Surely I am safe, because put into his almighty arms. Though I may fall, yet I shall not utterly be cast away. The Spirit of the Lord Jesus will hold, and uphold me."[79]

Telling the Gospel with All His Might

And he didn't just quietly enjoy these realities for himself. George Whitefield and George Herbert had seen the beauties of God's grace and the horrors of sin, and neither could leave these things unexpressed. Neither would keep them to himself. Herbert hoped his work would bless many, but he left it to his friend Nicholas Ferrar to render that judgment. Just before he died he sent his life's work of unpublished poems through a common acquaintance with the words: "If [Nicholas]

---

[76] Haykin, *Revived Puritan*, 76.
[77] Ibid., 71–72.
[78] Ibid., 113.
[79] Ibid., 76.

can think it may turn to the advantage of any dejected poor soul, let it be made public; if not, let him burn it; for I and it are less than the least of God's mercies."[80]

Similarly, Whitefield would not keep his passion for the glories of Christ and the doctrines of grace to himself. They were woven into all his evangelistic messages.

He said to Wesley, "I must preach the Gospel of Christ, and this I cannot now do without speaking of election."[81] In his sermon based on 1 Corinthians 1:30 called "Christ the Believer's Wisdom, Righteousness, Sanctification, and Redemption," he exults in the doctrine (remember he is lifting up his voice to thousands):

> For my part I cannot see how true humbleness of mind can be attained without a knowledge of [the doctrine of election]; and though I will not say, that every one who denies election is a bad man, yet I will say, with that sweet singer, Mr. Trail, it is a very bad sign: such a one, whoever he be, I think cannot truly know himself; for, if we deny election, we must, partly at least, glory in ourselves; but our redemption is so ordered, that no flesh should glory in the Divine presence; and hence it is, that the pride of man opposes this doctrine, because, according to this doctrine, and no other, "he that glories must glory only in the Lord."
>
> But what shall I say? Election is a mystery that shines with such resplendent brightness, that, to make use of the words of one who has drunk deeply of electing love, it dazzles the weak eyes even of some of God's children; however, though they know it not, all the blessing they receive, all the privileges they do or will enjoy, through Jesus Christ, flow from the everlasting love of God the Father.[82]

Offering Jesus Freely to Every Soul

And Whitefield reminds Wesley—and us—in a letter of 1741, "Though I hold particular election, yet I offer Jesus freely to every individual soul."[83] Indeed, Whitefield does not hide his understanding of the Calvinistic doctrines of definite atonement or irresistible grace as he pleads with men to come to Christ. In a sermon on John 10:27–28 called "The

---

[80] Quotation from Izaak Walton's *The Life of Mr. George Herbert* (1670), in *George Herbert: The Complete English Poems*, ed. John Tobin (New York: Penguin, 1991), 310–11.
[81] Dallimore, *George Whitefield: The Life and Times*, 2:41.
[82] Haykin, *Revived Puritan*, 97–98.
[83] Ibid., 145.

Good Shepherd," he speaks clearly of the particular sense in which Christ died for his own.

> If you belong to Jesus Christ, he is speaking of you; for says he, "I know my sheep." "I know them"; what does that mean? Why, he knows their number, he knows their names, he knows every one for whom he died; and if there were to be one missing for whom Christ died, God the Father would send him down again from heaven to fetch him.[84]

And then he mounts his passionate plea on the basis of irresistible sovereign grace:

> O come, come, see what it is to have eternal life; do not refuse it; haste, sinner, haste away: may the great, the good Shepherd, draw your souls. Oh! If you never heard his voice before, God grant you may hear it now. . . . O come! Come! Come to the Lord Jesus Christ; to him I leave you. . . . Amen.[85]

The Prominence of Justification

Among the doctrines of the Reformation that filled his great evangelistic sermons, the most prominent was the doctrine of justification. His signature sermon, if there was one, seemed to be "The Lord Our Righteousness" based on Jeremiah 23:6. He never elevated justification to the exclusion of regeneration and sanctification. In fact, he was explicit in his effort to keep them in balance:

> We must not put asunder what God has joined together; we must keep the medium between the two extremes; not insist so much on the one hand upon Christ without, as to exclude Christ within, as evidence of our being his, and as a preparation for future happiness; nor on the other hand, so depend on inherent righteousness or holiness wrought in us, as to exclude the righteousness of Jesus Christ without us.[86]

The Glory of Jesus's Obedience Imputed

But oh, how jealous he is again and again to press home to the masses the particularities of this doctrine, especially the imputation of Christ's obedience. He lamented in one sermon,

---

[84] Ryle, *Select Sermons of George Whitefield*, 193.
[85] Ibid., 199. Also see page 112 for another illustration of how he pleads with people even while drawing their attention to the fact that they cannot change themselves.
[86] Ibid., 106.

I fear they understand justification in that low sense, which I understood it in a few years ago, as implying no more than remission of sins; but it not only signifies remission of sins past, but also a *federal right* to all good things to come. . . . As the obedience of Christ is imputed to believers so his perseverance in that obedience is to be imputed to them also.[87]

Never did greater or more absurdities flow from the denying any doctrine, than will flow from denying the doctrine of Christ's imputed righteousness.[88]

The world says, because we preach faith we deny good works; this is the usual objection against the doctrine of imputed righteousness. But it is a slander, an impudent slander.[89]

Relentlessly Devoted to Good Deeds

And, indeed, it was a slander in the life of George Whitefield. Whitefield was relentless in his devotion to good deeds and his care for the poor—constantly raising funds for orphans and other mercy ministries.[90] Benjamin Franklin, who enjoyed one of the warmest friendships Whitefield ever had, in spite of their huge religious differences, said, "[Whitefield's] integrity, disinterestedness and indefatigable zeal in prosecuting every good work, I have never seen equaled, I shall never see excelled."[91]

In other words, Whitefield's impassioned belief in the imputation of Christ's righteousness did not hinder the practical pursuit of justice and love—it empowered it. This connection between doctrine and practical duties of love was one of the secrets of Whitefield's power. The masses believed, and believed rightly, that he practiced what he preached. The new birth and justification by faith made a person good.

A Contradictory Figure

But it didn't make a person perfect. It didn't make Whitefield perfect. In fact, one of the effects of reading history, and biography in particular,

---

[87] Ibid., 107.
[88] Ibid., 129.
[89] Ibid., 189.
[90] "[Whitefield] was doctrinally pure in his insistence that salvation came only through God's grace, *but* he was nevertheless [sic] deeply involved in charitable work, and his year-long tour through America was to raise money for an orphanage in Georgia. He raised more money than any other cleric of his time for philanthropies, which included schools, libraries, and almshouses across Europe and America." Walter Isaacson, *Benjamin Franklin: An American Life* (New York: Simon & Schuster, 2003), 110.
[91] Carlsson, review of *Divine Dramatist*, 245.

is the persistent discovery of contradictions and paradoxes of sin and righteousness in the holiest people.

Whitefield is no exception, and he will be more rightly honored if we are honest about his blindness as well as his doctrinal faithfulness and goodness. The most glaring blindness of his life—and there were others—was his support for the American enslavement of blacks.

Slaveholder

Before it was legal to own slaves in Georgia, Whitefield advocated for the legalization with a view to making the orphanage he built more affordable.[92] In 1748, he wrote to the trustees of Bethesda, the name of his orphanage and settlement,

> Had a Negro been allowed, I should now have had a sufficiency to support a great many orphans, without expending about half the sum which hath been laid out. . . . Georgia never can or will be a flourishing province without negroes [sic] are allowed. . . . I am as willing as ever to do all I can for *Georgia* and the orphan house, if either a limited use of negroes is approved of, or some more indentured servants sent over. If not, I cannot promise to keep any large family, or cultivate the plantation in any considerable manner.[93]

In 1752, Georgia became a royal colony. Slavery was legalized, and Whitefield joined the ranks of the slave owners that he had denounced in his earlier years.[94]

Ardent Slave Evangelist

That, in itself, was not unusual. Most of the slaveholders were professing Christians. But in Whitefield's case things were more complex. He didn't fit the mold of a wealthy, Southern plantation owner. Almost all of them resisted evangelizing and educating the slaves. They knew intuitively that education would tend toward equality, which would undermine the whole system. And evangelism would imply that slaves could become children of God, which would mean

---

[92] "Whitefield spent much of his time in the South actively promoting the legalization of slavery in Georgia." Stout, *Divine Dramatist*, 198.
[93] Ibid., 199.
[94] "There was no longer a need for the South Carolina plantation. All resources were transferred to Bethesda, including a force of slaves for whom, Whitefield rejoiced, 'Nothing seems to be wanted but a good overseer, to instruct the negroes in selling and planting.'" Ibid., 218.

that they were brothers and sisters to the owners, which would also undermine the whole system. That's why the apparent New Testament tolerance of slavery is in fact a very powerful subversion of the institution.

Ironically, Whitefield did more to bring Christianity to the slave community in Georgia than anyone else.[95] Whitefield wrote letters to newspapers defending the evangelism of slaves and arguing that to deny them this was to deny that they had souls (which many did deny). Harry Stout observes, "In fact, the letters represented the first journalistic statement on the subject of slavery. As such, they marked a precedent of awesome implications, beyond anything Whitefield could have imagined."[96]

Whitefield said he was willing to face the "whip" of Southern planters if they disapproved of his preaching the new birth to the slaves.[97] He recounts one of his customary efforts among the slaves in North Carolina on his second trip to America:

> I went, as my usual custom . . . among the negroes belonging to the house. One man was sick in bed, and two of his children said their prayers after me very well. This more and more convinces me that negro children, if early brought up in the nurture and admonition of the Lord, would make as great proficiency as any among white people's children. I do not despair, if God spares my life, of seeing a school of young negroes singing the praises of Him Who made them, in a psalm of thanksgiving. Lord, Thou has put into my heart a good design to educate them; I doubt not but Thou wilt enable me to bring it to good effect.[98]

Gary B. Nash dates "the advent of black Christianity" in Philadelphia to Whitefield's first preaching tour. He estimates that perhaps one thousand slaves heard Whitefield's sermons in Philadelphia. What they heard was that they had souls just as surely as the white people. Whitefield's work for the slaves in Philadelphia was so effective that Philadelphia's most prominent dancing master, Robert Bolton, renounced his old vocation and turned his school over to blacks. "By summer's end, over 50 'black Scholars' had arrived at the school."[99]

---

[95] Ibid., 101.
[96] Ibid., 123.
[97] Ibid., 100.
[98] Ibid., 101.
[99] Ibid., 107–8.

Sowing the Seeds of Equality

From Georgia to North Carolina to Philadelphia, Whitefield sowed the seeds of equality through heartfelt evangelism and education—blind as he was, it seems, to the contradiction of this equality with buying and selling slaves.

Whitefield ended his most famous sermon, "The Lord Our Righteousness," with this appeal to the blacks in the crowd:

> Here, then, I conclude; but I must not forget the *poor negroes*: no, I must not. Jesus Christ has died for them, as well as for others. Nor do I mention you last, because I despise your souls, but because I would have what I shall say make the deeper impression upon your hearts. O that you would seek the Lord to be your righteousness! Who knows but he may be found of you? For in Jesus Christ there is neither male nor female, bond nor free; even you may be the children of God, if you believe in Jesus. . . . Christ Jesus is the same now as he was yesterday, and will wash you in his own blood. Go home then, turn the word of the text into a prayer, and entreat the Lord to be your righteousness. Even so. Come Lord Jesus, come quickly in all our souls. *Amen*. Lord Jesus, *amen*, and *amen*!

This kind of preaching infuriated many slave owners. One wonders if there was a rumbling in Whitefield's own soul because he really did perceive where such radical evangelism would lead. He went public with his censures of slave owners and published words like these: "God has a quarrel with you" for treating slaves "as though they were Brutes." If these slaves were to rise up in rebellion, "all good Men must acknowledge the judgment would be just."[100]

This was incendiary. But it was too early in the course of history. Apparently Whitefield did not perceive fully the implications of what he was saying. What was clear was that the slave population loved Whitefield. For all his imperfections and blindness to the contradiction between advocating slavery and undermining slavery, when he died, it was the blacks who expressed the greatest grief in America.[101] More than any other eighteenth-century figure, Whitefield established Christian faith in the slave community. Whatever else he failed in, for this service they were deeply thankful.

---

[100] Ibid., 101–2.
[101] Ibid., 284.

A seventeen-year-old black Boston servant girl named Phillis Wheatley (1753–1784) wrote one of his most famous elegies. Wheatley would become one of the best-known poets in pre-nineteenth-century America.

> Pampered in the household of prominent Boston commercialist John Wheatley, lionized in New England and England, with presses in both places publishing her poems, and paraded before the new republic's political leadership and the old empire's aristocracy, Phillis was the abolitionists' illustrative testimony that blacks could be both artistic and intellectual. Her name was a household word among literate colonists and her achievements a catalyst for the fledgling antislavery movement.[102]

It was the Whitefield elegy that brought Wheatley national renown. "Published as a broadside and a pamphlet in Boston, Newport, and Philadelphia, the poem was published with Ebenezer Pemberton's funeral sermon for Whitefield in London in 1771, bringing her international acclaim."[103] In it she paid her due in tribute to Whitefield's love for "Africans."

> He offer'd THAT he did himself receive,
> A greater gift not GOD himself can give:
> He urg'd the need of HIM to every one;
> It was no less than GOD's co-equal SON!
>
> . . . .
>
> Take HIM ye *Africans*, he longs for you;
> Impartial SAVIOUR, is his title due;
> If you will choose to walk in grace's road,
> You shall be sons, and kings, and priests to GOD.[104]

Indeed, it is a beautiful providence that Whitefield's spiritual power and poetic eloquence should find their first and (at that time) most influential expression in a poem of a black slave. It is worth reading in full:

---

[102] "Phillis Wheatley," *Poetry Foundation*, accessed August 2, 2013, http://www.poetryfoundation.org/bio /phillis-wheatley.
[103] Ibid.
[104] Phillis Wheatley, "An Elegiac Poem on the Death of That Celebrated Divine, and Eminent Servant of Jesus Christ, the Late Reverend, and Pious George Whitefield," (1771), *A Celebration of Women Writers*, ed. Mary Mark Ockerbloom, accessed January 13, 2014, www.digital.library.upenn.edu/women/wheatley /whitefield/whitefield.html.

**An Elegiac Poem, on the Death of That Celebrated
Divine, and Eminent Servant of Jesus Christ,
the Late Reverend, and Pious George Whitefield**

Hail, happy Saint, on thine immortal throne!
To thee complaints of grievance are unknown;
We hear no more the music of thy tongue,
Thy wonted auditories cease to throng.
Thy lessons in unequal'd accents flow'd!
While emulation in each bosom glow'd;
Thou didst, in strains of eloquence refin'd,
Inflame the soul, and captivate the mind.
Unhappy we, the setting Sun deplore!
Which once was splendid, but it shines no more;
He leaves this earth for Heav'n's unmeasur'd height;
And worlds unknown, receive him from our sight.
There WHITEFIELD wings, with rapid course his way,
And sails to Zion, through vast seas of day.

When his AMERICANS were burden'd sore,
When streets were crimson'd with their guiltless gore!
Unrival'd friendship in his breast now strove:
The fruit thereof was charity and love
Towards *America*—couldst thou do more
Than leave thy native home, the *British* shore,
To cross the great Atlantic's wat'ry road,
To see *America's* distress'd abode?
Thy prayers, great Saint, and thy incessant cries,
Have pierc'd the bosom of thy native skies!
Thou moon hast seen, and ye bright stars of light
Have witness been of his requests by night!
He pray'd that grace in every heart might dwell:
He long'd to see *America* excell;
He charg'd its youth to let the grace divine
Arise, and in their future actions shine;
He offer'd THAT he did himself receive,
A greater gift not GOD himself can give:
He urg'd the need of HIM to every one;
It was no less than GOD's co-equal SON!
Take HIM ye wretched for your only good;
Take HIM ye starving souls to be your food.

Ye thirsty, come to this life giving stream:
Ye Preachers, take him for your joyful theme:
Take HIM, "my dear AMERICANS," he said,
Be your complaints in his kind bosom laid:
Take HIM ye *Africans*, he longs for you;
Impartial SAVIOUR, is his title due;
If you will chuse to walk in grace's road,
You shall be sons, and kings, and priests to GOD.

Great COUNTESS![105] we *Americans* revere
Thy name, and thus condole thy grief sincere:
We mourn with thee, that TOMB obscurely plac'd,
In which thy Chaplain undisturb'd doth rest.
New-England sure, doth feel the ORPHAN's smart;
Reveals the true sensations of his heart:
Since this fair Sun, withdraws his golden rays,
No more to brighten these distressful days!
His lonely *Tabernacle*, sees no more
A WHITEFIELD landing on the *British* shore:
Then let us view him in yon azure skies:
Let every mind with this lov'd object rise.
No more can he exert his lab'ring breath,
Seiz'd by the cruel messenger of death.
What can his dear AMERICA return?
But drop a tear upon his happy urn,
Thou tomb, shalt safe retain thy sacred trust,
Till life divine re-animate his dust.[106]

A Sinner Fit to Preach Free Grace

So the greatest preacher of the eighteenth century, perhaps in the history of the Christian church, was a paradoxical figure. There was, as he himself so freely confessed, sin remaining in him. And that is what we have found in every human soul on this earth—except one. Which is why our lives are meant to point to him—that sinless one. Christ's perfect obedience, not ours, is the foundation of our acceptance with God. If then, our sin, as well as our righteousness, can point people away from ourselves to Christ, we will rejoice even as we repent.

---

[105] The Countess of Huntington, who gave hearty support to the evangelical awakening in England and for whom Whitefield functioned as a chaplain.
[106] Wheatley, "An Elegiac Poem."

"I know no other reason," Whitefield said, "why Jesus has put me into the ministry, than because I am the chief of sinners, and therefore fittest to preach free grace to a world lying in the wicked one."[107] Yes. But as we have seen, God would make not only his unworthiness redound to the grace of God, but also his passionate oratory, his natural dramatic giftedness, and his poetic effort. This too, imperfect as it was, no doubt contaminated as it was with flawed motives, God made the instrument of his supernatural work of salvation. No eloquence can save a soul. But the worth of salvation and the worth of souls impels preachers to speak and write with all their might in ways that say: there is more, there is so much more beauty—so much more glory—for you to see than I can say.

---

[107] Haykin, *Revived Puritan*, 157–58.

Mythologies . . . are products of imagination in the sense that their content is imaginative. The more imaginative ones are "near the mark" in the sense that they communicate more Reality to us.
C. S. Lewis
Personal letter

[The epic of Oedipus] may not be "like real life" in the superficial sense: but it sets before us an image of what reality may well be like at some more central region.

A great romance is like a flower whose smell reminds you of something you can't quite place. . . . I've never met Orcs or Ents or Elves—but the feel of it, the sense of a huge past, of lowering danger, of heroic tasks achieved by the most apparently unheroic people, of distance, vastness, strangeness, homeliness (all blended together) is so exactly what living feels like to me.
C. S. Lewis
"On Stories"

C. S. Lewis—Romantic, Rationalist, Likener, Evangelist

How Lewis's Paths to Christ Shaped His Life and Ministry

We begin with an accolade from Peter Kreeft, professor of philosophy at Boston College:

> Once upon a dreary era, when the world of . . . specialization had nearly made obsolete all universal geniuses, romantic poets, Platonic idealists, rhetorical craftsmen, and even orthodox Christians, there appeared a man (almost as if from another world, one of the worlds of his own fiction: was he a man or something more like elf or Angel?) who was all of these things as amateur, as well as probably the world's foremost authority in his professional province, Medieval and Renaissance English literature. Before his death in 1963 he found time to produce some first-quality works of literary history, literary criticism, theology, philosophy, autobiography, biblical studies, historical philology, fantasy, science fiction, letters, poems, sermons, formal and informal essays, a historical novel, a spiritual diary, religious allegory, short stories, and children's novels. Clive Staples Lewis was not a man: he was a world.[1]

Those are the kinds of accolades you read again and again. Which means there must have been something extraordinary about the man. Indeed, there was.

Speaking personally, ever since I began to take him and his Reformed counterpart, Jonathan Edwards, seriously in my early twenties,

---

[1] Peter Kreeft, *C. S. Lewis: A Critical Essay* (Grand Rapids, MI: Eerdmans, 1969), 4.

I have never been the same. I don't see myself as an imitator of Lewis and Edwards. The kind of Joy that Lewis and Edwards spoke of cannot be imitated. It's a gift. You don't make it happen. And both these men are intellectual giants in the land. I don't have their intellectual ability. In their ability to see and think and feel, they are almost without peer. Their capacities to see and feel the freshness and wonder of things was childlike, and their capacities to describe it and understand it and defend it was massively manly.

Ruth Pitter was a poet and close friend of Lewis, and described it so well. She said,

> His whole life was oriented and motivated by an almost uniquely-persisting child's sense of glory and of nightmare. The adult events were received into a medium still as pliable as wax, wide open to the glory, and equally vulnerable, with a man's strength to feel it all, and a great scholar's and writer's skills to express and to interpret.[2]

So I can't imitate Lewis, but I can listen. And I have been listening for decades, and what I have heard and seen echoes almost everywhere in my life and work. His influence is simply enormous.

Childhood, Schooling, and Becoming the Voice

The focus of this chapter is not mainly on Lewis's biographical details, but we do need an outline of his life to see what kind of life gave birth to his ideas. So here is a short summary of his life—the hard facts, you might say. Lewis loved hard facts. The kind you want under your house when the rains come down and the floods come up.

Lewis was born in 1898 in Belfast, Ireland. His mother died when he was nine years old, and his father never remarried. Between the death of his mother in August 1908 and the fall of 1914, Lewis attended four different boarding schools. Then for two and a half years, he studied with William Kirkpatrick, whom he called "the Great Knock." And there his emerging atheism was confirmed and his reasoning powers were refined in an extraordinary way. Lewis said, "If ever a man came near to being a purely logical entity that man was Kirk."[3] He described himself later as a seventeen-year-old rationalist.

---

[2] Ruth Pitter, quoted in Alan Jacobs, *The Narnian* (New York: HarperOne, 2005), xxii.
[3] C. S. Lewis, *Surprised by Joy* (New York: Harcourt, Brace, & World, 1955), 135.

But just as his rationalism was at its peak, he stumbled onto George MacDonald's fantasy novel *Phantastes*. "That night," he said, "my imagination was, in a certain sense, baptized."[4] Something had broken in—a "new quality," a "bright shadow," he called it.[5] The romantic impulse of his childhood was again awake. Only now it seemed real, and holy (though he would not have called it that yet).

At eighteen he took his place at Oxford University, but before he could begin his studies he entered the army, and in February 1918 was wounded in France and returned to England to recover. He resumed his studies at Oxford in January 1919, and over the next six years took three First Class Honors in classics, humanities, and English literature. He became a teaching Fellow in October 1925, at the age of twenty-six.

Six years later in 1931, he professed faith in Jesus Christ and was settled in the conviction that Christianity is true. Within ten years, he had become the "voice of faith" for the nation of England during the Second World War, and his broadcast talks in 1941–1942 "achieved classic status."[6]

Lewis in Full Flower

He was now in the full flower of his creative and apologetic productivity. In his prime, he was probably the world's leading authority on Medieval English literature, and according to one of his adversaries, "the best read man of his generation."[7] But he was vastly more. Books of many kinds were rolling out: *Pilgrim's Regress*, *The Allegory of Love*, *The Screwtape Letters*, and *Perelandra*. Then in 1950, he began the Chronicles of Narnia. All these titles were of different genres and showed the amazing versatility of Lewis as a writer and thinker and imaginative visionary.

He appeared on the cover of *Time* magazine in 1947. Then, after thirty years at Oxford, he took a professorship in Medieval and Renaissance English at the University of Cambridge in 1955. The next year, at the age of fifty-seven, he married Joy Davidman. And just short of their fourth anniversary, she died of cancer. Three and a half years later—two

---

4 Ibid., 181.
5 Ibid., 179.
6 Alister McGrath, *C. S. Lewis—A Life: Eccentric Genius, Reluctant Prophet* (Carol Stream, IL: Tyndale, 2013), 210.
7 Ibid., 166.

weeks short of his sixty-fifth birthday, on November 22, 1963—Lewis followed her in death.

Lewis as an author is more popular today than at any time during his life. The Chronicles of Narnia alone have gone on to sell over one hundred million copies in forty languages.[8] One of the reasons for this appeal, I will argue, is that Lewis is a "romantic rationalist" to an exceptionally high and healthy degree. His poetic effort and his rational effort combined in a kind of writing and speaking that was exceptionally illuminating on almost everything he touched.

Lewis's Defective Views

Before I unfold what that means, it's important to confess that, for all the accolades, Lewis is not exemplary in all his views. Some readers may see quickly the common denominator between George Herbert and George Whitefield on the one hand, and C. S. Lewis on the other— namely, the conviction and demonstration that poetic effort is a path to seeing more truth and more beauty. That is what we have seen in the experience of Herbert and Whitefield. Now Lewis says, it is often the case that highly imaginative stories "are 'near the mark' in the sense that *they communicate more Reality to us.*"[9] Ironically, then, the effort to describe reality in creative and wondrous language often takes us deeper into that reality. If you see this common denominator, the inclusion of Herbert and Whitefield and Lewis in one volume will make sense.

But some readers will realize that Lewis was not the kind of historic, Reformed evangelical Christian that Herbert and Whitefield were. Doctrinally his differences from them, and from me, are significant. We would do him a disservice not to take this into account.

Scripture, Reformation, Catholicism

For example, Lewis doesn't believe in the inerrancy of Scripture. He claims Jesus predicted his second coming within one generation and calls this prediction an "error."[10] He treats the Reformation as an un-

---

[8] Jonathan Luxmoore, "C. S. Lewis 'Couldn't Touch Anything without Illuminating It,'" *National Catholic Reporter*, accessed December 18, 2013, http://www.ncronline.org/news/art-media/cs-lewis-couldnt-touch -anything-without-illuminating-it.

[9] Walter Hooper, ed., *The Collected Letters of C. S. Lewis: Books, Broadcasts, and War, 1931–1949* (San Francisco: HarperCollins, 2007), 2:445, emphasis added.

[10] C. S. Lewis, "The World's Last Night" in *C. S. Lewis: Essay Collection and Other Short Pieces*, ed. Lesley Walmsley (London: HarperCollins, 2000), 45. See also Michael Christensen's study of Lewis's view

necessary intramural fracas and thinks it could have been avoided. He calls aspects of it farcical.[11] He steadfastly refused in public or in letters to explain why he was not a Roman Catholic but remained in the Church of England.

Salvation without Knowing Christ?

He makes room for at least some people to be saved through imperfect representations of Christ in other religions. After visiting Greece with his dying wife, he wrote, "At Daphne it was hard not to pray to Apollo the Healer. But somehow one didn't feel it would have been very wrong—would only have been addressing Christ *sub specie Apollinis*."[12] In this way of talking about possibly praying to Christ through Apollo, he is suggesting something similar to the counsel he gave a mother who feared her son loved Aslan more than Jesus:

> Laurence can't really love Aslan more than Jesus, even if he feels that's what he's doing. For the things he loves Aslan for doing or saying are simply the things Jesus really did and said. So that when Laurence thinks he is loving Aslan, he is really loving Jesus: and perhaps loving him more than he ever did before.[13]

The most familiar instance of suggesting people can be saved without knowing Jesus is the entrance of Emeth into heaven at the end of *The Last Battle*. Emeth is the Hebrew word for "faithful" or "true" and represents a sincere seeker in a religion that does not know Aslan, at least not by his real name.[14]

The most sweeping statement of this view that some are saved without knowing Christ is found in his answer to a Mrs. Johnson, who wrote to him and asked, "What happens to Jews who are still waiting for the Messiah?" Lewis answers:

---

of Scripture, *C. S. Lewis on Scripture* (Waco, TX: Word, 1979), 91. And the very helpful essay by Philip Ryken, "Inerrancy and the Patron Saint of Evangelicalism: C. S. Lewis on Holy Scripture," in *The Romantic Rationalist: God, Life, and Imagination in the Work of C. S. Lewis*, ed. John Piper and David Mathis (Wheaton, IL: Crossway, 2014), 39–64.

11 "The process whereby 'Faith and Works' became a stock gag in the commercial theater is characteristic of that whole tragic farce which we call the history of the Reformation." C. S. Lewis, *English Literature in the Sixteenth Century: Excluding Drama* (Oxford: Oxford University Press, 1953), 37.

12 Lewis to Chad Walsh, 23 May 1960, in *Letters of C. S. Lewis*, ed. W. H. Lewis and Walter Hooper, rev. ed. (New York: Harcourt Brace Jovanovich, 1993), 488.

13 C. S. Lewis to a mother, *Letters to Children*, ed. Lyle W. Dorsett and Marjorie Lamp Mead (New York: Macmillian, 1985), 57.

14 C. S. Lewis, *The Last Battle* (New York: Macmillan, 1957), 155–57.

I think that every prayer which is sincerely made even to a false god, or to a very imperfectly conceived true God, is accepted by the true God and that Christ saves many who do not think they know Him. For He is (dimly) present in the good side of the inferior teachers they follow. In the parable of the Sheep & Goats (Matt. 25:31 and following) those who are saved do not seem to know that they have served Christ. But of course our anxiety about unbelievers is most usefully employed when it leads us not to speculation but to earnest prayer for them and the attempt to be in our own lives such good advertisements for Christianity as will make it attractive.[15]

Free Will and Atonement

On another point, Lewis's case for free will as a way to explain why there is suffering in the world seems to run counter to biblical texts on the sovereignty of God.[16] But we must be careful here because he did not give us a systematic statement of his views, and they do not all point toward a traditional view of free will as ultimate self-determination.[17]

Finally, I should mention that Lewis speaks of the atonement with reverence, but he puts little significance on any of the explanations for how it actually saves sinners. To a Roman Catholic, he wrote in 1941,

Yes—I think I gave the impression of going further than I intended in saying that all theories of the atonement were "to be rejected if we don't find them helpful." What I meant was "need not be used"—a very different thing. Is there, on your view, any real difference here: that the Divinity of Our Lord has to be believed whether you find it helpful or a "scandal" (otherwise you

---

[15] Walter Hooper, ed., *The Collected Letters of C. S. Lewis: Narnia, Cambridge, and Joy, 1950–1963* (San Francisco: HarperCollins, 2007), 3:245–46. I have written a book which tries to show this is a seriously mistaken understanding of Scripture, *Jesus: The Only Way to God: Must You Hear the Gospel to Be Saved?* (Grand Rapids, MI: Baker, 2010).

[16] C. S. Lewis, *The Problem of Pain* (New York: Macmillan, 1962), 26–88.

[17] Lewis's view is not simple or completely transparent. He could say, "You will certainly carry out God's purpose, however you act, but it makes a difference to you whether you serve like Judas or like John." Lewis, *Problem of Pain*, 111. And one wonders if by "free will" Lewis sometimes only means "voluntary," rather than "having ultimate self-determination." For example, he writes, "After all, when we are most free, it is only with freedom God has given us; and when our will is most influenced by Grace, it is still *our will*. And if what our will does is not voluntary, and if 'voluntary' does not mean 'free', what are we talking about?" W. H. Lewis and Hooper, *Letters of C. S. Lewis* (1966), 246. And perhaps most significantly, after saying that a fallen soul "could still turn back to God," he adds this footnote: "Theologians will note that I am not here intending to make any contribution to the Pelagian-Augustinian controversy. I mean only that such a return to God was not, even now, an impossibility. Where the initiative lies in any instance of such return is a question on which I am saying nothing." Lewis, *Problem of Pain*, 83. See Douglas Wilson, "Undragoned: C. S. Lewis on the Gift of Salvation," in *Romantic Rationalist*, ed. Piper and Mathis, 65–80.

are not a Christian at all) but the Anselmic theory of Atonement is not in that position. Would you admit that a man was a Christian (and could be a member of your church) who said "I believe that Christ's death redeemed man from sin, but I can make nothing of the theories as to how!" You see, what I wanted to do in these talks was simply to give what is common to us all, and I've been trying to get a *nihil obstat* from friends in various communions. . . . It therefore doesn't much matter how you think of my own theory, because it is advanced only as my own.[18]

These are some of the examples of how Lewis is out of step with Whitefield and Herbert doctrinally. Lewis rarely shows his exegesis. He doesn't deal explicitly with many texts. He is not an expositor. His value is not in his biblical exegesis. It lies elsewhere. And in this chapter, we will see some of what that is.

The Irony of Strengthening My Doctrinal Positions

If you wonder whether Lewis has had a weakening effect on my commitment to the doctrines where we disagree, the answer is: just the opposite. There was something at the core of his work—his mind—that had the ironic effect on me of awakening lively affections and firm convictions that he himself would not have shared.

There was something about the way he read Scripture that made my own embrace of inerrancy tighter, not looser. There was something about the way he spoke of grace and God's power that made me value the particularities of the Reformation more, not less. There was something about the way he portrayed the wonders of the incarnation that made me more suspicious of his own inclusivism (salvation in other religions), not less. There was something about the way he spoke of doctrine as the necessary roadmap that leads to reality,[19] and the way he esteemed truth and reason and precision of thought, that made me cherish more, not less, the historic articulations of the biblical explanations of *how* the work of Christ saves sinners—the so-called theories of the atonement.

---

[18] W. H. Lewis and Hooper, *Letters of C. S. Lewis* (1966), 197–98. Surely Iain Murray is right to say, "'Substitution' is not one 'theory' of the atonement, it is the heart of the message. This is not the case with Lewis." (Personal correspondence to author, October 10, 2009, quoted with permission.) I think Lewis would have regarded the biblical presentations of justification and reconciliation and propitiation and redemption with greater importance and preciousness if he had attended more carefully the particular texts.
[19] "For Lewis the doctrines were always absolutely necessary as maps toward one's true destination—they should never be the *goal* of the Christian life." Jacobs, *The Narnian*, 293.

Life Calling: Display and Defend "Mere Christianity"

It may be that others have been drawn away by Lewis from these kinds of convictions and experiences. I doubt that more people, on the whole, have been weakened in true biblical commitments than have been strengthened by reading Lewis. Nevertheless, I am sure it happens. Some, for example, who have taken the road to Roman Catholicism away from evangelicalism, say Lewis has played a part in that pilgrimage. He devoted his whole Christian life to defending and adorning what he called "mere Christianity"—"the Christian religion as understood *ubique et ab omnibus* [everywhere by everyone]."

> To a layman, it seems obvious that what unites the Evangelical and the Anglo-Catholic against the "Liberal" or "Modernist" is something very clear and momentous, namely, the fact that both are thoroughgoing supernaturalists, who believe in the Creation, the Fall, the Incarnation, the Resurrection, the Second Coming, and the Four Last Things [death, judgment, heaven, hell]. This unites them not only with one another, but with the Christian religion as understood *ubique et ab omnibus* [everywhere by everyone].
>
> The point of view from which this agreement seems less important than their divisions, or than the gulf which separates both from any non-miraculous version of Christianity, is to me unintelligible. Perhaps the trouble is that as supernaturalists, whether "Low" or "High" Church, thus taken together, they lack a name. May I suggest "Deep Church"; or, if that fails in humility, Baxter's "mere Christians"?[20]

Or, as he says in *The Problem of Pain*, "I have believed myself to be re-stating ancient and orthodox doctrines. . . . I have tried to assume nothing that is not professed by all baptized and communicating Christians."[21] He believed that when one looks at Christianity across the centuries, it has an astounding unity which has great apologetic power.

> I myself was first led into reading the Christian Classics, almost accidentally, as a result of my English studies. Some, such as Hooker, Herbert, Traherne, Taylor and Bunyan, I read because they are themselves great English writers; others such as Boethius, St. Augustine, Thomas Aquinas and Dante because they were "influences." . . . They are, you will note, a mixed bag, representative of many Churches, climates and ages. And that brings me to

---

[20] C. S. Lewis, a letter to R. D. Daunton-Fear, February 8, 1952, in *God in the Dock: Essays on Theology and Ethics*, ed. Walter Hooper (Grand Rapids, MI: Eerdmans, 1970), 336.
[21] Lewis, *Problem of Pain*, 10.

yet another reason for reading them. The divisions of Christendom are un-
deniable and are by some of these writers most fiercely expressed. But if any
man is tempted to think—as one might be tempted who read only contemporaries—that "Christianity" is a word of so many meanings that it means
nothing at all, he can learn beyond all doubt, by stepping out of his own
century, that this is not so. Measured against the ages "mere Christianity"
turns out to be no insipid interdenominational transparency, but something positive, self consistent, and inexhaustible . . . —so unmistakably the
same; recognizable, not to be evaded, the odour which is death to us until
we allow it to become life. . . .

I know, for I saw it; and well our enemies know it. That unity any of us
can find by going out of his own age. . . . You have now got on to the great
level viaduct which crosses the ages and which looks so high from the val-
leys, so low from the mountains, so narrow compared to the swamps, and
so broad compared to the sheep tracks.[22]

What "Mere Christianity" Did Not Mean

This means that Lewis rarely tried to distance himself from Roman Catholicism or any other part of Christendom. He rarely spoke about any
debates within Christianity itself.[23] But it would be a mistake to take
Lewis's focus on "mere Christianity" as a belief that Christian denominations are unnecessary, or that they do not have a valuable place. This
is important to see for two reasons. First, some have used his emphasis
on "mere Christianity" to discount the theological distinctions among
denominations, which Lewis did not do. Second, seeing what he really
thought about denominations shows how supremely important doctrinal truth is for him.

In the introduction to *Mere Christianity*, he writes,

I hope no reader will suppose that "mere" Christianity is here put forward as
an alternative to the creeds of the existing communions—as if a man could
adopt it in preference to Congregationalism or Greek Orthodoxy or anything
else. It is more like a hall out of which doors open into several rooms. If I can
bring anyone into that hall I shall have done what I attempted. But it is in the

---

[22] C. S. Lewis, "On the Reading of Old Books," in *God in the Dock*, 203–4.
[23] "I think we must admit that the discussion of these disputed points has no tendency at all to bring outsiders into the Christian fold. . . . Our divisions should never be discussed except in the presence of those
who have already come to believe that there is one God and that Jesus Christ is his only son." C. S. Lewis,
quoted in Jacobs, *The Narnian*, 215.

rooms, not in the hall, that there are fires and chairs and meals. The hall is a place to wait in, a place from which to try the various doors, not a place to live in. For that purpose the worst of the rooms (whichever that may be) is, I think, preferable. It is true that some people may have to wait in the hall for a considerable time. . . .

You must keep on praying for light: and, of course, even in the hall you must begin trying to obey the rules which are common to the whole house. And above all you must be asking which door is the true one; not which pleases you best by its paint and paneling. In plain language, the question should never be: "Do I like that kind of service?" but "Are these doctrines true: Is holiness here? Does my conscience move me towards this?"

When you have reached your own room, be kind to those who have chosen different doors, and to those who are still in the hall. If they are wrong they need your prayers all the more; and if they are your enemies, then you are under orders to pray for them. That is one of the rules common to the whole house.[24]

Unlike so many ecumenical enthusiasts in his day and ours, Lewis elevated truth to the decisive point: "Above all you must be asking which door is the true one." As you consider which room to live in, ask, above all, "Are these doctrines true?" As your conscience witnesses to that truth, go through that door.

Radically Different from Liberalism

In spite of all Lewis's aberrations from the understanding of salvation that I hold so dear, there was a radical difference between him and most modern liberal theology and postmodern slipperiness. The way he deals with Joy and with absolute truth puts him in another world—a world where I am totally at home, a world where I find both my heart and my mind awakened and made more alive and perceptive and responsive and earnest and hopeful and amazed and passionate for the glory of God. It's this combination of experiencing the stab of God-shaped Joy and defending objective, absolute truth, because of the absolute reality of God, that sets Lewis apart as a rare and wonderful "dinosaur" in the modern world.[25] To my knowledge, there is simply no one else who puts these two things together the way Lewis does.

---

[24] C. S. Lewis, *Mere Christianity* (New York: Macmillan, 1960), xi–xii.
[25] In "*De Descriptione Temporum*," Lewis's inaugural lecture from the chair of Medieval and Renaissance Literature at Cambridge University in 1954, Lewis says,

My Thesis in This Chapter

My thesis in this chapter is that Lewis's romanticism and his rationalism were the paths on which he came to Christ, and they are the paths on which he lived his life and did his work. They shaped him into a teacher and writer with extraordinary gifts for logic and likening—and evangelism. What I mean by "likening," as we will see, is almost identical with what I have called *poetic effort* or *dramatic effort* in the previous chapters. Lewis discovered that joy and reason, longing and logic, pointed beyond this world, and thus to the deeper meaning of this world. And he found that this effect of longing and logic (romanticism and rationalism) called forth a kind of language—a poetic effort, an imaginative use of likening—that illumined the reality of what *is* by describing it in a way that it is *not*. Thus he spent his life pointing people, even in his rigorous prose, beyond the world to the meaning of the world, Jesus Christ.

1. Lewis the Romantic

So we will look first at his romanticism, and then at his rationality, and how they conspired together to lead him to Christ. Then we will see how this path led him to see language as a vehicle of this romanticism and rationalism, and how this led him to be one of the most effective Christian evangelists in the twentieth century. Along with George Herbert and George Whitefield, Lewis demonstrated that the effort to speak and write creatively, imaginatively—which I have called *poetic effort*—was a way of seeing and showing truth and beauty—ultimately the truth and beauty of God in Christ.

I myself belong far more to that Old Western order than to yours. I am going to claim that this, which in one way is a disqualification for my task, is yet in another a qualification. The disqualification is obvious. You don't want to be lectured on Neanderthal Man by a Neanderthaler, still less on dinosaurs by a dinosaur. And yet, is that the whole story? If a live dinosaur dragged its slow length into the laboratory, would we not all look back as we fled? What a chance to know at last how it really moved and looked and smelled and what noises it made! And if the Neanderthaler could talk, then, though his lecturing technique might leave much to be desired, should we not almost certainly learn from him some things about him which the best modern anthropologist could never have told us? He would tell us without knowing he was telling. . . . Ladies and gentlemen, . . . I read as a native text that you must read as foreigners. . . . It is my settled conviction that in order to read Old Western literature aright you must suspend most of the responses and unlearn most of the habits you have acquired in reading modern literature. And because this is the judgment of a native, I claim that, even if the defense of my conviction is weak, the fact of my conviction is a historical datum to which you should give full weight. That way, where I fail as a critic, I may yet be useful as a specimen. I would even dare to go further. Speaking not only for myself but for all other Old Western men whom you may meet, I would say, use your specimens while you can. There are not going to be many more dinosaurs. "Full Text of 'De Descriptione Temporum,'" *Internet Archive*, accessed October 10, 2013, http://www.archive.org /stream/DeDescriptioneTemporum/DeDescriptioneTemporumByC.S.Lewis_djvu.txt.

Removing an Old Confusion

In August 1932, Lewis sat down and wrote his first novel in fourteen days, less than a year after professing faith in Christ.[26] *The Pilgrim's Regress* is a two-hundred-page allegory of his own pilgrimage to faith in Christ. The subtitle goes like this: "An Allegorical Apology for Christianity, Reason, and Romanticism." So he is defending being a romantic, a rationalist, and a Christian.

But ten years later, when the third edition of the book appeared, he added a ten-page preface to apologize for obscurity and to explain what he means by being a romantic. He said, "The cause for obscurity was the (unintentionally) 'private' meaning I then gave to the word 'Romanticism.'"[27] The word, as he used it, he said, described "the experience which is central in this book."

> What I meant by "Romanticism" . . . and what I would still be taken to mean on the title page of this book—was . . . a particular recurrent experience which dominated my childhood and adolescence and which I hastily called "Romantic" because inanimate nature and marvelous literature were among the things that evoked it.[28]

Romanticism and Stabs of Joy

When we examine his description of the experience he refers to, it turns out to be identical with what ten years later in his autobiography he calls Joy.[29]

> The experience [of romanticism] is one of intense longing. It is distinguished from other longings by two things. In the first place, though the sense of want is acute and even painful, yet the mere wanting is felt to be somehow a delight. . . . This hunger is better than any other fullness; this poverty better than all other wealth.[30]

---

[26] He wrote to his friend Arthur Greeves, October 1, 1931, "I have just passed on from believing in God to definitely believing in Christ—in Christianity." Walter Hooper, ed., *The Collected Letters of C. S. Lewis: Family Letters, 1905–1931* (San Francisco: HarperSanFrancisco, 2004), 1:974.

[27] C. S. Lewis, *The Pilgrim's Regress* (Grand Rapids, MI: Eerdmans, 1958), 5.

[28] Ibid., 7.

[29] In *Surprised by Joy*, 17–18, Lewis said that this Joy is the experience "of an unsatisfied desire which is itself more desirable than any other satisfaction. I call it Joy, which is here a technical term and must be sharply distinguished both from Happiness and from Pleasure. Joy (in my sense) has indeed one characteristic, and one only, in common with them; the fact that any one who has experienced it will want it again. Apart from that, and considered only in its quality, it might almost equally well be called a particular kind of unhappiness or grief. But then it is the kind we want. I doubt whether anyone who has tasted it would ever, if both were in his power, exchange it for all the pleasures in the world. But then Joy is never in our power and pleasure often is."

[30] Lewis, *Pilgrim's Regress*, 7.

There is a peculiar mystery about the *object* of this Desire. Inexperienced people (and inattention leaves some inexperienced all their lives) suppose, when they feel it, that they know what they are desiring. [Some past event, some perilous ocean, some erotic suggestion, some beautiful meadow, some distant planet, some great achievement, some quest or great knowledge, etc.]

But every one of these impressions is wrong. The sole merit I claim for this book is that it is written by one who has proved them all to be wrong. There is no room for vanity in the claim I know them to be wrong not by intelligence but by experience. . . . For I have myself been deluded by every one of these false answers in turn, and have contemplated each of them earnestly enough to discover the cheat.[31]

If a man diligently followed this desire, pursuing the false objects until their falsity appeared and then resolutely abandoning them, he must come out at last into the clear knowledge that the human soul was made to enjoy some object that is never fully given—nay, cannot even be imagined as given—in our present mode of subjective and spatio-temporal existence.[32]

A Lived Ontological Proof

Lewis called this experience a kind of lived ontological proof of God— or at least of something beyond the created world. "The dialectic of Desire," he said, "faithfully followed, would . . . force you not to propound, but to live through, a sort of ontological proof."[33]

Later when he wrote *Mere Christianity*, he would state it most famously: "If I find in myself a desire which no experience in this world can satisfy, the most probable explanation is that I was made for another world."[34]

From Atheism to Christ

So the essence of his romanticism is Lewis's experience of the world that repeatedly awakened in him a sense that there is always more than this created world—something other, something beyond the natural world. At first, he thought the stabbing desire and longing was what he really wanted. But his conversion to theism and then to Christ would clear

---

[31] Ibid., 8.
[32] Ibid., 10.
[33] Ibid.
[34] Lewis, *Mere Christianity*, 106.

the air and show him what all the longing had been for. God overcame Lewis's atheism in the spring term of 1929. He was thirty years old.

> You must picture me alone in that room in Magdalen, night after night, feeling, whenever my mind lifted even for a second from my work, the steady, unrelenting approach of Him Whom I so earnestly desired not to meet. That which I greatly feared had come upon me. In the Trinity Term of 1929 I gave in, and admitted that God was God, and knelt and prayed: perhaps, that night, the most dejected and reluctant convert in all England. . . . Who can duly adore that love which will open the high gates to a prodigal who is brought in kicking, struggling, resentful, darting his eyes in every direction for a chance of escape?[35]

That was not the end of the struggle. It was two years later, on October 1, 1931, that he wrote to his friend Arthur, "I have just passed on from believing in God to definitely believing in Christ—in Christianity."[36] The great story really is true. God really sent his Son. He really died for our sins. We really can have forgiveness and eternal life in the presence of the One to whom all the Joy was pointing.

The Meaning of Joy: Made for God

Lewis looked back on all his experiences of Joy differently now. Now he knew why the desire was inconsolable and yet pleasant. It was a desire for God. It was evidence that he was made for God.

> The books or the music in which we thought the beauty was located will betray us if we trust to them; it was not *in* them, it only came *through* them, and what came through them was longing. These things—the beauty, the memory of our own past—are good images of what we really desire; but if they are mistaken for the thing itself, they turn into dumb idols, breaking the hearts of their worshipers. For they are not the thing itself; they are only the scent of a flower we have not found, the echo of the tune we have not heard, news from a country we have never yet visited.[37]

All his life, he said, "an unattainable ecstasy has hovered just beyond the grasp of [my] consciousness."[38] "The sweetest thing of all my life

---

[35] Lewis, *Surprised by Joy*, 228–29. See Alister McGrath, *C. S. Lewis—A Life*, 141–46, for a slight redating of Lewis's conversion to about a year later.
[36] Hooper, *Collected Letters of C. S. Lewis: Family Letters, 1905–1931*, 974.
[37] C. S. Lewis, *The Weight of Glory* (Grand Rapids, MI: Eerdmans, 1949), 4–5.
[38] Lewis, *Problem of Pain*, 148.

has been the longing . . . to find the place where all the beauty came from."[39] But when Lewis was born again to see the glory of God in Christ, he never said again that he didn't know where the beauty came from. Now he knew where all the Joy was pointing. On the last page of his autobiography, he explains the difference in his experience of Joy now and before.

> I believe . . . that the old stab, the old bittersweet, has come to me as often and as sharply since my conversion as at any time of my life whatever. But I now know that the experience, considered as a state of my own mind, had never had the kind of importance I once gave it. It was valuable only as a pointer to something other and outer. While that other was in doubt, the pointer naturally loomed large in my thoughts. When we are lost in the woods the sight of the signpost is a great matter. He who first sees it cries, "Look!" The whole party gathers round and stares. But when we have found the road and are passing signposts every few miles, we shall not stop and stare. They will encourage us and we shall be grateful to the authority that set them up. But we shall not stop and stare, or not much; not on this road, though their pillars are of silver and their lettering of gold. "We would be at Jerusalem."[40]

No Less Romantic Joy as a Christian

So Lewis stopped turning Joy into an idol when he found, by grace, that it was "a pointer to something other and outer," namely, to God. Clyde Kilby gave the highest estimation of this theme in Lewis:

> [For Lewis, Joy is] a desire which no natural happiness can ever satisfy, the lifelong pointer toward heaven . . . which gave us such delight and yet are the meager signs of the true rapture He has in heaven for redeemed souls. . . . The culmination of *Sehnsucht* [longing, Joy] in the rhapsodic joy of heaven is, for me at least the strongest single element in Lewis. In one way or other it hovers over nearly every one of his books and suggests to me that Lewis's apocalyptic vision is perhaps more real than that of anyone since St. John on Patmos.[41]

This "other and outer" had been wonderful even before he knew that what he was longing for was God. And now that he was a Christian, the piercing longing did not go away just because he knew who it was:

---

[39] Lewis, *Till We Have Faces: A Myth Retold* (New York: Harcourt, 1956), 75.
[40] Lewis, *Surprised by Joy*, 238.
[41] Clyde S. Kilby, *The Christian World of C. S. Lewis* (Grand Rapids, MI: Eerdmans, 1964), 187.

"That the old stab, the old bittersweet, has come to me as often and as sharply since my conversion as at any time of my life."

The Central Story of Every Life

Alan Jacobs says, "Nothing was closer to the core of his being than this experience."[42] And Lewis himself says, "In a sense the central story of my life is about nothing else."[43] When you read his repeated descriptions of this experience of romanticism or Joy in *Surprised by Joy* and *Pilgrim's Regress* and *The Problem of Pain* and *The Weight of Glory*, you realize Lewis doesn't see this as a quirk of his personality but as a trait of humanness. All of us are romantics in this sense. Devin Brown says Lewis's "use of the inclusive *you* in these passages . . . makes it clear that Lewis believes this is a longing we have all felt. . . . You might say this is the central story of everyone's life."[44]

For example, in *The Problem of Pain*, Lewis makes the case that even people who think they have never desired heaven don't see things clearly.

> There have been times when I think we do not desire heaven, but more often I find myself wondering whether, in our heart of hearts, we have ever desired anything else . . . tantalizing glimpses, promises never quite fulfilled, echoes that died away just as they caught your ear. But if . . . there ever came an echo that did not die away but swelled into the sound itself—you would know it. Beyond all possibility of doubt you would say, "here at last is the thing I was made for."[45]

So Lewis saw in his own experience of romanticism the universally human experience. We are all romantics. All of us experience from time to time—some more than others, and some more intensely than others—a longing this world cannot satisfy, a sense that there must be more.

2. Lewis the Rationalist

We turn now to Lewis's rationalism. And, as with the term *romanticism*, I mean something different from some of its common philosophical uses. All I mean is his profound devotion to being rational—to the

---

[42] Jacobs, *The Narnian*, 42.
[43] Lewis, *Surprised by Joy*, 17.
[44] Devin Brown, *A Life Observed: A Spiritual Biography of C. S. Lewis* (Grand Rapids, MI: Brazos, 2013), 5.
[45] Lewis, *Problem of Pain*, 145–46.

principle that there is true rationality and that it is rooted in absolute reason, God's reason.

A Lover of the Law of Noncontradiction

Remember that the subtitle of *The Pilgrim's Regress* is *An Allegorical Apology for Christianity, Reason, and Romanticism.* We've seen what he meant by romanticism. Now what did he mean by reason, and what was his defense of its use?

The simplest way to get at the heart of Lewis's rationality is to say he believed in the law of noncontradiction, and he believed that where this law was abandoned, not only was truth imperiled, but romanticism and Joy were imperiled as well. The law of noncontradiction is simply that contradictory statements cannot both be true at the same time and in the same way.

Lewis saw logic as a real expression of ultimate reality. The laws of logic are not human conventions created differently from culture to culture. They are rooted in the way God is. And these laws of logic make true knowledge of reality possible. "I conclude," he writes, "then that logic is a real insight into the way in which real things have to exist. In other words, the laws of thought are also the laws of things: of things in the remotest space and the remotest time."[46]

Logic as a Parallel Path to God

This commitment to the basic laws of logic, or rationality, led Lewis on the philosophical path to the same Christ that he had found on the path of romanticism or Joy. He put it like this: "This lived dialectic [of my romanticism], and the merely argued dialectic of my philosophical progress, seem to have converged on one goal,"[47] namely, the reality of theism and Christianity and Christ as the Savior of the world.

On the romantic path, Lewis was led again and again to look beyond nature for ultimate reality—finally to God in Christ—because his desires could not be explained as a product of this world. Now how did that same thing happen by the use of his reason?

He looked at the philosophical, scientific cosmology emerging in the modern world and found it self-contradictory.

---

[46] C. S. Lewis, "*De Futilitate,*" in *C. S. Lewis: Essay Collection*, ed. Walmsley, 674.
[47] Lewis, *Pilgrim's Regress*, 10.

If I swallow the scientific cosmology as a whole (that excludes a rational, personal God), then not only can I not fit in Christianity, but I cannot even fit in science. If minds are wholly dependent on brains, and brains on biochemistry, and biochemistry (in the long run) on the meaningless flux of the atoms, I cannot understand how the thought of those minds should have any more significance than the sound of the wind in the trees. And this is to me the final test.[48]

In other words, modern people construct a worldview that treats their thoughts as equivalent to wind in the trees. And then they call these thoughts true. Lewis said that's a contradiction. Atheistic man uses his mind to create a worldview that nullifies the use of his mind.

This is what Lewis meant by the title of his book *The Abolition of Man*. If there is no God as the foundation of logic (like the law of non-contradiction) and the foundation of value judgments (like justice and beauty), then man is abolished. His mind is no more than the rustling of leaves, and his value judgments are no more than ripples on a pond.

The rebellion of new ideologies against the Tao [the absoluteness of first principles—and ultimately against God] is a rebellion of the branches against the tree: if the rebels could succeed they would find that they had destroyed themselves.[49]

Lewis compares atheistic cosmology to dreaming and Christian theology to being awake. When you are awake, you can explain wakefulness and dreaming. But when you are dreaming, you don't have the capacity to explain wakefulness. Similarly:

Christian theology can fit in science, art, morality, and the sub-Christian religions. The scientific point of view cannot fit in any of these things, not even science itself. I believe in Christianity as I believe that the Sun has risen not only because I see it but because by it I see everything else.[50]

The Path to Closure with Christ

Here's how he describes the way these thoughts brought him on the path of reason to see Christianity as true:

On these grounds and others like them one is driven to think that whatever else may be true, the popular scientific cosmology at any rate is certainly

---

[48] C. S. Lewis, "Is Theology Poetry?" in *C. S. Lewis: Essay Collection*, ed. Walmsley, 21.
[49] C. S. Lewis, *The Abolition of Man* (New York: Macmillan, 1947), 56.
[50] Lewis, "Is Theology Poetry?" in *C. S. Lewis: Essay Collection*, ed. Walmsley, 21.

not. . . . Something like philosophical idealism or Theism must, at the very worst, be less untrue than that. And idealism turned out, when you took it seriously, to be disguised Theism. And once you accepted Theism you could not ignore the claims of Christ. And when you examine them it appeared to be that you could adopt no middle position. Either he was a lunatic or God. And he was not a lunatic.[51]

Truth and Joy, Logic and Longing—Two Paths, One Goal

So we have seen that both Lewis's romanticism and his rationalism brought him to Christ. His lifelong, recurrent experience of the inbreaking of a longing he could not explain by this world led beyond the world to God and finally to Christ. And his lifelong experience of reason and logic led him to see that truth and beauty and justice and science would have no validity at all if there were no transcendent God in whom they were all rooted.

Indeed, the most precious experience of his life—the longing for God and the finding—would all be empty nothingness if there were no absolute truth and no valid rationality for knowing it.

When Lewis saw the historical Christ and the eternal, objective, absolutely real God as the object of his inconsolable longing (his Joy), he knew that if truth goes, if objective reality goes, if the possibility of knowing goes, if reason goes, then Joy becomes the mirage he feared all his life it might be. Christianity was the end of his quest precisely because it is true. Christ is real. God is real. Truth is real. Here's the way he describes the connection between truth and Joy.

> There was no doubt that Joy was a desire . . . but a desire is turned not to itself but to its object. . . . The form of the desired is in the desire. It is the object which makes the desire harsh or sweet, coarse or choice, "high" or "low." It is the object that makes the desire itself desirable or hateful. I perceived (and this was a wonder of wonders) that just as I had been wrong in supposing that I really desired the Garden of the Hesperides, so also I have been equally wrong in supposing that I desired Joy itself. Joy itself, considered simply as an event in my own mind, turned out to be of no value at all. All the value lay in that of which Joy was the desiring. And that object, quite clearly, was no state of my own mind or body at all.[52]

---

[51] Ibid., 20.
[52] Lewis, *Surprised by Joy*, 220.

No Truth, No Joy

Here is the crucial link between truth and Joy. "Joy itself, considered simply as an event in my own mind, turned out to be of no value at all. All the value lay in that of which Joy was the desiring." So we see what is at stake. The entire modern world—and even more so the postmodern world—was moving away from this conviction. Liberal theology, and postmodern cynics who scorn propositions, have gone with the flow of unbelief—subjectivism and relativism. Lewis stood against it with all his might.[53]

Subjectivism and relativism means "the abolition of man." In the end, it means the destruction of civilization.[54] But long before that, it means the destruction of Joy, because, as Lewis had learned when he became a Christian, an attack on the objective reality of God is an attack on Joy. "Joy itself, considered simply as an event in my own mind, turned out to be of no value at all. All the value lay in that of which Joy was the desiring." All the value lay in God. Without God, the event in my mind called Joy is utterly trivial.

So for Lewis, the experience of Joy and truth, longing and logic, romanticism and rationalism, had conspired to lead him to Christ. And now these two paths would together preserve and deepen his experience of Christ, and would unleash a life of likening—of poetic effort—that would make him one of the most illuminating Christian writers of the twentieth century.

3. Lewis the Master Likener

Therefore, Lewis came to Christ as his Lord and God along the path of *romanticism*, or inconsolable longing on the one hand, and the path of *rationalism*, or logic, on the other hand. Both of these experiences demanded of him that he own the reality of something beyond this material world, something *other*, something *more* than this world. Both

---

[53] As we have seen, *The Abolition of Man* is Lewis's fury at the purveyors of modern subjectivism in textbooks for young people. He gives this example from one such textbook in his own words. The authors of the textbook refer to a story of Coleridge agreeing with a friend that the beauty of a certain waterfall is *sublime*. The authors comment, "When the man said *That is sublime*, he appeared to be making a remark about the waterfall. . . . Actually . . . he was not making a remark about the waterfall, but a remark about his own feelings. What he was saying was really *I have feelings associate in my mind with the word "Sublime,"* or shortly, *I have sublime feelings.* . . . This confusion is continually present in language as we use it. We appear to be saying something very important about something: and actually we are only saying something about our own feelings." Lewis, *Abolition of Man*, 14.
[54] Ibid., 39.

paths finally converged on Jesus Christ as the Creator, and Redeemer, and supreme fulfillment of all our longings, and the ground of all our reasoning.

Both romanticism and rationalism—longing and logic—led him out of this world to find the meaning and validity of this world. This world could not satisfy his deepest desires. And this world could not give validity to his plainest logic. Desires found full and lasting satisfaction and the truth claims of reason found legitimacy in God, not in this world.

Longing and Logic as the Key to Likening

This double experience of romanticism and rationalism, leading finally to God, gave Lewis a key to the power of language to reveal the deeper meaning of the world, namely, the key of *likening*. What I mean by the key of likening is this: *Likening some aspect of reality to what it is not can reveal more of what it is.*

God created what is not God. He made not-God the means of revealing and knowing God. And Lewis found the key to what the world really is by being led out of the world to something other than the world, namely, God. He found that this world was most honest and most true when it was pointing beyond itself.

He reasoned like this: if the key to the deepest meaning of this world lies outside this world, then the world will probably be illumined most deeply not simply by describing the world as what it is but by likening the world to what it is not.

Part of what makes Lewis so illuminating on almost everything he touches is his unremitting *rational clarity* and his pervasive use of *likening*. Metaphor, analogy, illustration, simile, poetry, story, myth—all of these are ways of *likening* aspects of reality to what it is *not*, for the sake of showing more deeply what it *is*.

The Paradox of Saying What Is Not to Show What Is

At one level, it seems paradoxical to liken something to what it is *not* in order to show more deeply what it *is*. But that's what life had taught Lewis. And he devoted his whole life to exemplifying and defending this truth. He wrote to T. S. Eliot in 1931 to explain an essay he had sent him and said, "The whole [of it], when completed . . . will re-affirm the romantic doctrine of *imagination as a truth-bearing faculty*, though not quite as the romantics understood it."[55]

Lewis had experienced this all his life—the power of verbal images to illumine reality. But when he became a Christian, this deep-seated way of seeing the world was harnessed for the sake of illumining truth in everything he wrote. In 1954, Lewis sent a list of his books to the Milton Society of America and explained what ties them together like this:

> The imaginative man in me is older, more continuously operative, and that sense more basic than either the religious writer or the critic. It was he who made me first attempt (with little success) to be a poet. . . . It was he who after my conversion led me to embody my religious belief in symbolical or mythopoeic forms, ranging from *Screwtape* to a kind of theologised science-fiction. And it was of course he who has brought me, in the last few years, to write the series of Narnian stories for children.[56]

Imagination for the Sake of Reality

He tells us in more than one place why he embraced imaginative literature as such a large part of his calling. All these forms of likening have the paradoxical effect of revealing aspects of the real that we often otherwise miss.

In 1940, he wrote in a letter, "Mythologies . . . are products of imagination in the sense that their content is *imaginative*. The more *imaginative* ones are 'near the mark' in the sense that *they communicate more Reality to us*."[57] In other words, by likening reality to what it is not, we learn more of what it is.

In his essay "On Stories," Lewis comments on the ancient myth of *Oedipus* and says, "It may not be 'like real life' in the superficial sense: but it sets before us an image of what reality may well be like at some more central region."[58]

Lewis calls Tolkien's Lord of the Rings trilogy a "great romance,"[59] and comments in a letter in 1958, "A great romance is like a flower whose smell reminds you of something you can't quite place. . . . I've

---

[55] Hooper, *Collected Letters of C. S. Lewis: Narnia, Cambridge, and Joy, 1950–1963*, 1523, emphasis added.

[56] Ibid., 516–17.

[57] Hooper, *Collected Letters of C. S. Lewis: Books, Broadcasts, and War, 1931–1949*, 445, emphasis added.

[58] C. S. Lewis, "On Stories," in *C. S. Lewis: Essay Collection*, ed. Walmsley, 501.

[59] Hooper, *Collected Letters of C. S. Lewis: Narnia, Cambridge, and Joy, 1950–1963*, 371.

never met Ents or Elves—but the feel of it, the sense of a huge past, of lowering danger, of heroic tasks achieved by the most apparently unheroic people, of distance, vastness, strangeness, homeliness (all blended together) is so exactly what living feels like to me."[60]

In the preface to *The Pilgrim's Regress*, he comments, "All good allegory exists not to hide but to reveal; to make the inner world more palpable by giving it an (imagined) concrete embodiment."[61] And in his poem "Impenitence," he defends imaginary talking animals by saying that they are

> Masks for Man, cartoons, parodies by Nature
> Formed to reveal us.[62]

In other words, heroic myth, penetrating allegory, great romance, and talking animals are "masks . . . formed to reveal." Again, the paradox of likening—depicting *some aspect of reality as what it is not in order to reveal more of what it is.*

A Likener Everywhere, Not Just in Poems and Stories

But lest I give the wrong impression that Lewis was a likener only in his poetry and fiction, I need to stress that he was a likener everywhere—in everything he wrote. Myths and allegories and romances and fairy tales are extended metaphors. But thinking and writing metaphorically, imaginatively, and analogically were present everywhere in Lewis's life and work.

Lewis was a poet and craftsman and image maker in everything he wrote. Alister McGrath observes that what captivated the reader of Lewis's sermons, essays, and apologetic works, not just his novels, was

> his ability to write prose tinged with a poetic vision, its carefully crafted phrases lingering in the memory because they have captivated the imagination. The qualities we associate with good poetry—such as an appreciation of the sound of words, rich and suggestive analogies and images, vivid description, and lyrical sense—are found in Lewis's prose.[63]

---

[60] Ibid., 971–72.
[61] Lewis, *Pilgrim's Regress*, 13.
[62] C. S. Lewis, "Impenitence," in *Poems*, ed. Walter Hooper (New York: Harcourt, Brace, and World, 1964), 2.
[63] McGrath, *C. S. Lewis—A Life*, 108.

I think this is exactly right, and it makes him not only refreshing and illuminating to read on almost any topic but also a great model for how to think and write about everything.

Walter Hooper puts it like this:

> A sampling of all Lewis's works will reveal the same man in his poetry as in his clear and sparkling prose. His wonderful imagination is the guiding thread. It is continuously at work. . . . And this is why, I think, his admirers find it so pleasant to be instructed by him in subjects they have hitherto cared so little for. Everything he touched had his kind of magic about it.[64]

It is indeed pleasant to be instructed by a master likener. Images and analogies and creative illustrations and metaphors and surprising turns of phrase are pleasant. "A word fitly spoken is like apples of gold in a setting of silver" (Prov. 25:11). Solomon even uses an image to celebrate the pleasure of images. But my point here has not been the *pleasure* of likening but its power of *illumination*, its power to reveal truth.

Lewis's romanticism and his rationalism—his inconsolable longing and his validity-demanding logic—pointed outside the world for the key to understanding the world. And he found that, if the key to the deepest meaning of this world lies outside this world—in its Maker and Redeemer, Jesus Christ—then the world itself will probably be illumined most deeply not simply by describing the world merely as what it is but by *likening* the world to what it's not.

Lewis's unrelenting commitment to *likening*—to the use of images and analogies and metaphor and surprising juxtapositions, even in his most logical demonstrations of truth—was not mainly owing to the greater pleasure it can give but to the deeper truth it can reveal. Lewis loved the truth. He loved objective reality. He believed that the truth of this world and the truth of God could be known. He believed that the use of reason was essential in knowing and defending truth. But he also believed that there are depths of truth and dimensions of reality that *likening* will reveal more deeply than reason.

"Only Supernaturalists *Can See Nature"*

Unless we see that this world is not ultimate reality but is only like it, we will not see and savor this world for the wonder that it is. Lewis is

---

[64] C. S. Lewis, *Poems*, ed. Walter Hooper (New York: Harcourt, Brace & World, 1964), vi.

at his metaphorical best as he explains this with his image-laden prose in this paragraph from *Miracles*.

> The Englishness of English is audible only to those who know some other language as well. In the same way and for the same reason, only Supernaturalists really see Nature. You must go a little way from her, and then turn round, and look back. Then at last the true landscape will become visible. You must have tasted, however briefly, the pure water from beyond the world before you can be distinctly conscious of the hot, salty tang of Nature's current. To treat her as God, or as Everything, is to lose the whole pith and pleasure of her [note: pith *and* pleasure]. Come out, look back, and then you will see . . . this astonishing cataract of bears, babies, and bananas: this immoderate deluge of atoms, orchids, oranges, cancers, canaries, fleas, gases, tornadoes, and toads. How could you ever have thought this was the ultimate reality? How could you ever have thought that it was merely a stage-set for the moral drama of men and women? She is herself. Offer her neither worship nor contempt. Meet her and know her. . . . The theologians tell us that she, like ourselves, is to be redeemed. The "vanity" to which she was subjected was her disease, not her essence. She will be cured in character: not tamed (Heaven forbid) nor sterilized. We shall still be able to recognize our old enemy, friend, playfellow and foster-mother, so perfected as to be not less, but more, herself. And that will be a merry meeting.[65]

"Only supernaturalists really see nature." The only people who can know the terrifying wonder of the world are those who know that the world is not the most wonderful and terrifying reality. The world is a likening. The path of romanticism taught Lewis that the world is a likening—the final satisfaction of our longing is not in this world. The path of rationality taught Lewis that the world is a likening. The final validation of our thinking is not in this world. And since this world is a likening—not the goal of our longing or the ground of our logic— therefore it is revealed for what it most profoundly is by likening.

4. Lewis the Evangelist

What was Lewis doing in all his works—in all his likening, in all this poetic effort, in all his likening-soaked reasoning? He was pointing. He was unveiling. He was depicting the glory of God in the face of Jesus.

---

[65] C. S. Lewis, *Miracles: A Preliminary Study* (New York: Macmillan, 1947), 67–68.

He was leading people to Christ. The two paths he knew best were the paths of romanticism and rationalism—longing and logic. So these are the paths on which he guided people to Christ.

The Real Business of Life

One of the things that makes him admirable to me, in spite of all our doctrinal differences, is his crystal-clear, unashamed belief that people are lost without Christ and that every Christian should try to win them, including world-class scholars of Medieval and Renaissance literature. And so unlike many tentative, hidden, vague, approval-craving intellectual Christians, Lewis says outright, "The salvation of a single soul is more important than the production or preservation of all the epics and tragedies in the world."[66] And again: "The glory of God, and, as our only means to glorifying Him, the salvation of human souls, is the real business of life."[67]

This is what he was doing in all his likening and all his reasoning. And when Norman Pittenger criticized him in 1958 for being simplistic in his portrayal of Christian faith, Lewis responded in a way that shows us what he was doing in all his work:

> When I began, Christianity came before the great mass of my unbelieving fellow-countrymen either in the highly emotional form offered by revivalists or in the unintelligible language of highly cultured clergymen. Most men were reached by neither. My task was therefore simply that of a translator—one turning Christian doctrine, or what he believed to be such, into the vernacular, into language that unscholarly people would attend to and could understand. . . . Dr. Pittenger would be a more helpful critic if he advised a cure as well as asserting many diseases. How does he himself do such work? What methods, and with what success, does he employ when he is trying to convert the great mass of storekeepers, lawyers, realtors, morticians, policemen and artisans who surround him in his own city?[68]

Lewis came to Christ on the converging paths of romanticism and rationalism. And as a Christian, he became a master thinker and master likener—a master of poetic effort in story and essay. This is who

[66] C. S. Lewis, "Christianity and Literature," in *Christian Reflections* (Grand Rapids, MI: Eerdmans, 1967), 10.
[67] C. S. Lewis, "Christianity and Culture," in *Christian Reflections*, 14.
[68] C. S. Lewis, "Rejoinder to Dr Pittenger," in *God in the Dock*, 183.

he was, and this is what he knew. And so this is how he did his evangelism. He bent every romantic effort and every rational effort to help people see what he had seen through his poetic effort—the glory of Jesus Christ, the goal of all his longings, and the solid ground of all his thoughts.

The heavens declare the glory of God,
and the sky above proclaims his handiwork.
Day to day pours out speech,
and night to night reveals knowledge.
There is no speech, nor are there words,
whose voice is not heard. . . .

The law of the LORD is . . .
more to be desired . . . than gold,
even much fine gold;
sweeter also than honey
and drippings of the honeycomb.
Psalm 19:1–3, 7, 10

Oh, taste and see that the LORD is good!
Psalm 34:8

Conclusion

Speak God's Wonders—
In His World and in His Word

Seasonable joyousness, honey sweetness, golden fitness, gracious saltiness—such are the descriptions of speech commended in the Bible.

> To make an apt answer is a joy to a man,
>   and a word in season, how good it is! (Prov. 15:23)

> The wise of heart is called discerning,
>   and sweetness of speech increases persuasiveness. (Prov. 16:21)

> A word fitly spoken
>   is like apples of gold in a setting of silver. (Prov. 25:11)

> Let your speech always be gracious, seasoned with salt. (Col. 4:6)

Of course, there are many other descriptions of good speech, such as
truth (Eph. 4:15), clarity (Col. 4:4), boldness (Eph. 6:20), sincerity
(2 Cor. 2:17), in the name of the Lord Jesus (Col. 3:17). But our focus
in this book has been on joyful, honey-like, strikingly fitting language
that is "seasoned with salt." I have called the mental, emotional, prayerful, God-dependent, self-humbling, Christ-exalting exertion it takes to
find and express these words *poetic effort.*

The aim has not been to suggest that all Christians write poems
(though I suspect we all will someday). Poetic effort is not the effort to
write poems. Poetic effort is the effort to see and savor and speak the
wonder—the divine glory—that is present everywhere in the world God
made, in the history God guides, and in the Word God inspired.

The Central Focus of This Book

The particular focus we have circled back to frequently is the insight that the effort to say beautifully is a way of also seeing beauty. By *beautifully*, I don't mean flowery or ostentatious or ornate or showy or elevated. I mean illuminating, well-timed, penetrating, creative, fresh, imaginative, striking, awakening, provocative—while not being trite, clichéd, clever, cute, silly, obtrusive, awkward, puerile, faddish, corny, or boring. The very fact that so many words exist to describe poorly chosen words shows how common they are. I am pleading for us to do better.

So the central point of this book—saying beautifully is a way of seeing beauty—doesn't mean, let's all create poems or let's all be artsy. It means that as you try to find words that seem worthy of the worth of what you have seen, the worth of what you have seen becomes clearer and deeper. That's the point.

The point is to waken us to go beyond the common awareness that using worthy words helps others feel the worth of what we have seen. Everybody knows that. It is a crucial and wise insight. And love surely leads us to it. But I am going beyond that. Or under that. Or before it. The point of this book has been that finding worthy words for worthy discoveries not only helps others feel their worth but also helps us feel the worth of our own discoveries. Groping for awakening words in the darkness of our own dullness can suddenly flip a switch and shed light all around what it is that we are trying to describe—and feel. Taking hold of a fresh word for old truth can become a fresh grasp of the truth itself. Telling of beauty in new words becomes a way of tasting more of the beauty itself.

George Herbert

George Herbert and C. S. Lewis virtually said this point explicitly. Why did Herbert labor to find extraordinary words and unprecedented ways of describing the glories of the love of Christ?

> [Poetry] is no office, art, or news,
> Nor the Exchange, or busie Hall;
> But it is that which while I use
> I am with thee. . . . [1]

---

[1] George Herbert, "The Quidditie," in *The English Poems of George Herbert*, ed. Helen Wilcox (Cambridge: Cambridge University Press, 2007), 254.

The very effort to find the words for Christ brought him closer to Christ. It opened the treasure chest of redeeming love. Yes, his poems illumine us. But first they illumined Herbert. He did not merely find the sweetness of Christ and then create words so we could taste. No. The creating of the words was part of finding the sweetness. He tasted Christ by means of the poetic effort to tell well.

George Whitefield

George Whitefield wrote little and preached almost ceaselessly—sometimes as much at sixty hours in a week. He did not reflect theoretically on his way of speaking. But from what he said, and what others experienced, we know that his verbal and theatrical poetic effort was a way of feeling and heralding the greatest realities in the world. This story is worth repeating:

> I'll tell you a story [Whitefield said]. One day the Archbishop . . . said to Butterton [a famous actor] . . . "Pray inform me Mr. Butterton, what is the reason you actors on stage can affect your congregations with speaking of things imaginary, as if they were real, while we in church speak of things real, which our congregations only receive as if they were imaginary?" "Why my Lord," says Butterton, "the reason is very plain. We actors on stage speak of things imaginary, as if they were real and you in the pulpit speak of things real as if they were imaginary." Therefore, I will bawl [shout loudly], I will not be a velvet-mouthed preacher![2]

We may readily admit that in one sense Whitefield was "acting" as he preached. That is, he was taking the part of the characters in the drama of his sermons and pouring all his energy—his poetic effort—into making their parts real. And this poetic effort was not only for his listeners but for himself. The key words in the story above are "as if." "We actors on stage speak of things imaginary, *as if* they were real and you in the pulpit speak of things real *as if* they were imaginary." Whitefield resolved to do neither. He would speak of things real *as if* they were real, because they *are* real. This "as if" is what I mean by poetic effort. It gropes not for words to make the unreal real but for words to see and savor and speak the real as real. The true as true. The glorious as

---

[2] Harry S. Stout, *The Divine Dramatist: George Whitefield and the Rise of Modern Evangelicalism* (Grand Rapids, MI: Eerdmans, 1991), 239–40.

glorious. The horrible as horrible. The tender as tender. The tough as tough. The joyful as joyful. And reaching for a voice that matches the truth—this is my point—wakens the speaker as well as the hearer.

C. S. Lewis

C. S. Lewis came to faith in Christ by learning that this world, for all its wonders and joys, is not what his heart was finally made for. All the joys of nature and literature were pointing to something—"something other and outer." God had revealed himself in terms of what he was not. The world and everything in it was a creative language pointing to the real thing. Which also meant that the realness of the world could only be known, in its true depth and beauty, by those who know that it is not everything.

> Only Supernaturalists really see Nature. You must go a little way from her, and then turn round, and look back. Then at last the true landscape will become visible. You must have tasted, however briefly, the pure water from beyond the world before you can be distinctly conscious of the hot, salty tang of Nature's current.[3]

So to truly know God, we must attend to what he has made—the world, the written Word, the flesh of the incarnate Son. And to know what he has made, we must attend to God. From this, Lewis drew out his understanding of myth and story and metaphor and poetry—and poetic effort. He saw that one can speak deeply and truly of God and this world only by reaching for the terms of the other—God in terms of the world, the world in terms of God. The world is not what it is without God, and God is not known for who he is except through the world. But this implied something else. Lewis also saw that one can *see* the world and God deeply and truly only by reaching for the terms of the other. We don't just *speak* the world and God truly by stretching for the words outside the world and outside God, but we also *see* the world and God that way. We would not see them for what they are if we did not try to think them and speak them in the terms of the other.

Thus Lewis provides us with a deeper foundation for the point of this book. Saying beautifully as way of seeing beauty—saying surprisingly and imaginatively, speaking in terms of "the other"—is rooted in

---

[3] C. S. Lewis, *Miracles: A Preliminary Study* (New York: Macmillan, 1947), 67.

the fact that God and nature are "other" from each other. Nature is not what it is apart from "the other" (God), and God is not known for what he is apart from "the other" (the world he made). This foundational truth trickles all the way down to our everyday speech. The words "just as" and "like" and "as if" are echoes of this foundational truth. We see more of what *is* when we describe it in terms of what it *is not*.

Benediction

May the Lord Jesus himself protect us from self-exalting, Christ-obscuring eloquence. But may he grant us a humble, Christ-exalting poetic habit of speaking his wonders—from the simplest in his world to the greatest in his Word—in words of seasonable joyousness, honey sweetness, golden fitness, and gracious saltiness. May he do it so that we ourselves might first taste, then tell.

The Swans Are Not Silent

Book 7

A Camaraderie of Confidence

*The Fruit of Unfailing Faith in the Lives of
Charles Spurgeon, George Müller, and Hudson Taylor*

To the Global Partners
who have gone out from Bethlehem Baptist Church
for the sake of the Name

A Camaraderie of Confidence

Book 7

Contents

Preface

This is book seven in the series of biographical studies called The Swans Are Not Silent. The series title comes from the story of Augustine's retirement as the bishop of Hippo in North Africa in AD 426. His successor, Eraclius, contrasted himself with Augustine by saying, "The cricket chirps, the swan is silent."[1] It was humble. But in a profound sense, it was untrue. Augustine became probably the most influential theologian in the history of the Christian church. The swan was not—and is not—silent.

So when I say "The Swans Are Not Silent," I mean: there are voices from church history that are still heard, and should be heard, in the ongoing history of the church. My hope is that this series will give voice to some of these swans. In this volume, the swans are Charles Spurgeon, the greatest preacher of the nineteenth century; George Müller, the great lover of orphans and supporter of missions; and Hudson Taylor, the founder of the China Inland Mission. Some of the things that bind them together are that they were all contemporaries, based in England, knew each other, encouraged each other, and took inspiration from each other's lives.

When one reads the history of evangelicalism in the nineteenth century,[2] and reads the lives of Spurgeon, Müller, and Taylor against that backdrop, one can't help but see that they were part of something much bigger than themselves. The waves of the Great Awakenings had broken over Britain and America, and remarkable advances were happening in the growth of the Christian movement. The Awakening of

---

[1] Peter Brown, *Augustine of Hippo* (Berkeley, CA: University of California Press, 1969), 408.
[2] The stories of the first and second halves of the century are told respectively by John Wolffe, *The Expansion of Evangelicalism: The Age of Wilberforce, More, Chalmers and Finney* (Downers Grove, IL: InterVarsity Press, 2007), and David W. Bebbington, *The Dominance of Evangelicalism: The Age of Spurgeon and Moody* (Downers Grove, IL: InterVarsity Press, 2005).

1859 was sending its ripple effects from Canada to Ireland, Scotland, Wales, and England. The time was right for these three evangelicals, and they were both very like and very unlike their era. But in their similarities and distinctives, they were bound together with each other and with the evangelical movement. They may seem like meteors in their own right. But they were part of a constellation.

Similarly, in our own day, I feel woven together with many people in all the undertakings of my life. For example, when it came to researching the relationships between Spurgeon, Müller, and Taylor, there was a community of friends and scholars I could turn to who love these heroes. Here at Desiring God, content strategist and staff writer Tony Reinke spearheaded the effort to gather insights about how these "swans" related to each other. With his help, I reached out to Michael Haykin, professor of church history and biblical spirituality at Southern Baptist Theological Seminary; Thomas Nettles, recently retired professor of historical theology at Southern; Christian George, assistant professor of historical theology and curator of the Spurgeon Library at Midwestern Baptist Theological Seminary; and Jim Elliff, president of Christian Communicators Worldwide. Mark Noll directed me to the work of Alvyn Austin on the history of the China Inland Mission.[3] These friends responded with generous pointers that have shaped this book.

Of course, it almost goes without saying that I am indebted to dozens of other researchers and writers who over the years have studied and written about Spurgeon, Müller, and Taylor. I did not have access to any original sources that are not available to everybody. Whatever is fresh about the stories I tell is not owing to fresh sources, but fresh reading and thinking and comparing. So I have a great debt to the biographies and articles in which others have presented the facts of these men's lives.

A new development in my own indebtedness to the community of scholars and students of history and Scripture is the extraordinary possibilities that now exist with Logos Bible Software (now part of Faithlife). Logos has made available the works of Spurgeon, Müller, and Taylor electronically so that one can search them for names and words and phrases almost instantaneously. Thus, it is possible in a

---

[3] Alvyn Austin, *China's Millions: The China Inland Mission and Late Qing Society, 1832–1905* (Grand Rapids, MI: Eerdmans, 2007).

matter of seconds to see every place where Spurgeon, for example, in his sixty-three volumes of sermons, refers to Müller or Taylor. You can easily imagine the possibilities of looking up terms and phrases. I am deeply thankful for how responsive Logos has been to requests I have made for the addition of certain works to its already massive library of electronic books.

Closer to home, as always, my life is freed and encouraged for the work of writing by Marshall Segal and David Mathis, both writers and editors for Desiring God. They provide the practical, critical, and visionary help to make me productive. They are part of the web of relationships without which my life would be a drab and lonely affair.

Saying thank you for the help I received on this book is complicated by the fact that the writing of it spans twenty years. The first draft of the Spurgeon section was written in 1995. The main constant relationships in my life over those years are Jesus and my wife, Noël. There are others, but without these—no books. God has been kind to me. When I ponder the relationships among Spurgeon, Müller, and Taylor, I feel a special gratitude for the matrix of relationships in my life. Only God knows what life would have been if anyone were missing.

I pray now that these three "swans" will sing their way into your life. What they have to teach us and show us about the camaraderie of confidence in God, in all his goodness, glory, and power, is enormous. Let them lead you into a life of greater faith and joy and radical commitment to Christ's mission in this world.

It was George Müller who said it, with that holy blessed life of faith at the back of every word; and I was like a child, sitting at a tutor's feet, to learn of him.

Charles Spurgeon

No mission now existing has so fully our confidence and good wishes as the work of Mr. Hudson Taylor in China. It is conducted on those principles of faith in God which most dearly commend themselves to our innermost soul. The man at the head is "a vessel fit for the Master's use." His methods of procedure command our veneration.

Charles Spurgeon

Introduction

A Camaraderie of Confidence in the Mighty Goodness of God

Indigenous, Transforming Exiles

In some ways Charles Spurgeon, "the greatest preacher" of the nine-teenth century,[1] and George Müller, who cared for thousands of or-phans, and Hudson Taylor, who founded the China Inland Mission, were men of their amazing age. In other ways, they were exiles on the earth—a camaraderie of confidence in something beyond this world. This is not an exceptional statement, since the same could be said of almost every Christian who believes the gospel and wants to serve the temporal and eternal needs of his fellow man.

The roots of this simple observation are in the Bible. On the one hand, we are told that Christians are "sojourners and exiles" (1 Pet. 2:11) whose "citizenship is in heaven" (Phil. 3:20). On the other hand, the apostle Paul said, "I have become all things to all people, that by all means I might save some" (1 Cor. 9:22). Not surprisingly, fruitful Christians are people of their age, and yet also people out of step with their age.

It is the divine genius of Christianity that incarnation and transforma-tion are built into the very nature of the coming of Christ. He was one of us. And he was infinitely different from us. He fit in. But he changed everything. Therefore, Christianity spreads in the same way—from age to age and from culture to culture. It adapts to culture and it alters culture. It puts on the culture's clothes and changes the culture's heart. Then that heart-change circles back around to the clothes—and everything.

---

[1] David W. Bebbington, *The Dominance of Evangelicalism: The Age of Spurgeon and Moody* (Downers Grove, IL: InterVarsity Press, 2005), 40, 267.

Andrew Walls, a former missions professor at the University of Edinburgh, calls these two truths the "indigenizing principle" and the "pilgrim principle." Both are rooted in the heart of the Christian faith—the doctrines of justification and sanctification. "On the one hand, it is the essence of the Gospel that God accepts us as we are, on the ground of Christ's work, alone, not on the ground of what we have become or are trying to become."[2] That means we bring our culturally conditioned ways of life into Christ.

But as Walls points out:

> [There is] another force in tension with this indigenizing principle, and this also is equally of the Gospel. Not only does God in Christ take people as they are: He takes them in order to transform them into what He wants them to be. . . . The Christian inherits the pilgrim principle, which whispers to him that he has no abiding city and warns him that to be faithful to Christ will put him out of step with his society; for that society never existed, in East or West, ancient time or modern, which could absorb the word of Christ painlessly into its system.[3]

Men of Their Age

Spurgeon, Müller, and Taylor were clearly nineteenth-century men. Müller's life spanned the century (1805–1898). Spurgeon was cut down early by gout and Bright's disease at the age of fifty-seven (1834–1892). Taylor died five years into the twentieth century (1832–1905). But what made them men of their age was not merely their dates. They were part of a great surge politically, industrially, and religiously. One could not live in the nineteenth century and fail to be affected by some of the biggest changes in the history of the world.

Citizens of a Great Empire

All three of these men were part of British culture, though Müller was born in Prussia and immigrated at the age of twenty-four. That meant that they were a part of an empire at the peak of its influence. There was only one monarch from 1837 to the end of the century, Queen Victoria—it was the Victorian Age. This stability was matched by a half-century of peace from 1850 onward. Globally, "Britain was at the height of its worldwide prestige."[4]

---

[2] Andrew Walls, *The Missionary Movement in Christian History: Studies in the Transmission of Faith* (Maryknoll, NY: Orbis Books, 2001), 7.
[3] Ibid., 8.
[4] Bebbington, *The Dominance of Evangelicalism*, 14.

The most prominent statesman of the mid-century, Lord Palmerston, expressed the significance of the British Empire to the effect that "just as anyone in the ancient world could announce that he was a Roman citizen and the might of Rome's Empire would protect him, so Britain's authority would shield all who could claim to be subjects of the crown wherever they might be."[5]

First Members of the Modern World

The Industrial Revolution and the age of invention were sweeping Britain into the modern world. In 1851, London hosted the Great Exhibition, with many new products on display. "But the overriding purpose was to celebrate the technical expertise of Britain, the first country to industrialize."[6] Between 1852 and 1892, the production of cotton in Britain tripled. The production of coal increased from 60 million tons in 1851 to 219 million tons fifty years later. It was the same in the United States. Coal production in that period jumped from 7 million to 268 million tons.

Railroads expanded dramatically. Steamships largely replaced sailing vessels. This was the age of Thomas Edison and Alexander Graham Bell, both born in 1847. Electric lights, radio, the telephone, and other inventions were transforming life across the world. Patterns of life common for millennia were giving way to a new world.

Medical discoveries abounded. "In Britain over seventy special hospitals were founded between 1800 and 1860.... Among the drugs isolated, concocted, or discovered between 1800 and 1840 were morphine, quinine, atropine, digitalin, codeine, and iodine."[7] Along with industry and invention and discovery, prosperity followed. "For the first time many families had money to spend over and above what had to go toward subsistence."[8]

Heirs of the Great Awakenings

The first and second Great Awakenings had given a lasting impetus to world Christianity. Along with the population in general, the churches

---

[5] Cited in ibid., 13.
[6] Ibid., 17.
[7] Bruce Haley, *The Healthy Body and Victorian Culture* (Cambridge, MA: Harvard University Press, 1987), n.p., cited at http://www.victorianweb.org/science/health/health12.html.
[8] Bebbington, *The Dominance of Evangelicalism*, 18.

were expanding significantly. For example, between 1800 and 1850, the number of Methodists in England expanded from 96,000 to 518,000. The same was true for churches in Wales and Scotland. In the United States, it was equally dramatic. "Methodists increased from rather over 1,250,000 to about 5,500,000 members over the second half of the 19th century. Baptists rose from about 750,000 to about 4,500,000."[9]

More specifically, the Awakening of 1859 had a direct effect especially on Taylor's effort to reach China by founding the China Inland Mission. Alvyn Austin describes it:

> In 1859, while Hudson Taylor was still in China [on his first term before founding the CIM], a revival broke out in Northern Ireland that led to a religious movement so pivotal in British religious history that it came to be called the Revival or "Awakening of '59." . . . Although Taylor missed the first phase of the revival, he arrived in Britain in time to reap its benefits. As J. Edwin Orr noted, "there is reason to believe that the whole [of the China Inland Mission's first] party [of 1866] was made up of converts and workers of the 1959 Awakening." . . . It is generally agreed that "something happened" in 1859–60, and that its ripples continued to reverberate for the rest of the century.[10]

It deserves mention in passing that this awakening was simultaneous with events that were hostile to the Christian faith. "In the secular realm, 1859 was equally momentous, with the publication of Darwin's *On the Origin of Species* and John Stuart Mill's essay *On Liberty*."[11] I mention this to show that we should be slow to assume that any particular cultural development (as in our own day, with the unraveling of the moral fabric of Western culture) should be seen as defining the trajectory of the future. God is always doing more than we know. Just when secular ways of seeing the world were intensifying, evangelical strength was also increasing.

At the end of the century, one estimate was that evangelicalism "represented the beliefs of 'not less, and probably many more, than sixty millions of avowed Christians in all parts of the world.'" David Bebbington endorses this estimate: "Including the converts of the

---

[9] Ibid., 253.
[10] Alvyn Austin, *China's Millions: The China Inland Mission and Late Qing Society, 1832–1905* (Grand Rapids, MI: Eerdmans, 2007), 82–83, 85.
[11] Ibid., 82

missionary movement, [this] estimate was probably not far wrong."[12] Evangelicalism was the dominant form of Christianity, and Britain was the dominant empire.

They Were Evangelicals

Bebbington has given one of the most compelling definitions of "evangelicalism" as a distinct movement rising out of the Great Awakening of the eighteenth century and continuing to this day. Spurgeon, Müller, and Taylor were supreme exemplars of this movement in their time.

Bebbington argues that evangelicalism is a movement within Christianity marked by "crucicentrism, conversionism, Biblicism, and activism."[13] Or, more simply, "Bible, cross, conversion and activism were the characteristic themes of the evangelical movement."[14] Evangelicals "were stirred by the teaching of the *Scriptures*; they were eager to proclaim the message of *Christ crucified*; and they were unflagging in their quest for *conversions*. Hence they were dedicated *activists* in the spread of the gospel."[15]

The mark of evangelicalism that linked Spurgeon, Müller, and Taylor most clearly to their age was their activism. For all the depth of their theology and spirituality, these three giants were consummate doers. Bebbington notes, "The final mark of the evangelicals was an eagerness to be up and doing."[16]

Activism Was in the Air

Activism for social betterment was in the air. It was the air that evangelicals breathed. For example, one of the legacies of John Wesley (1703–1791) was a rule of his societies that Christians ought to avoid "soft and needless self-indulgence." In 1883, a New York Methodist newspaper asked what these words meant, and the *Christian Advocate* gave the official reply. The words covered "over-feeding, over-sleeping, over-clothing, idleness, pampering the body, living an easy, idle life,

---

[12] Bebbington, *The Dominance of Evangelicalism*, 263.
[13] Ibid., 23.
[14] Ibid., 267.
[15] Ibid., 50 (emphasis added). To say it one more way, "evangelicalism typically chose to give prominence to conversion, the Bible, the cross and missionary activity. . . . These qualities renamed the defining features of evangelicalism down to the end of the century and beyond. . . . There were the typical emphases on the atoning work of Christ on the cross; the need for personal faith through conversion; the supreme value of the Bible; and the binding obligation of mission." Ibid., 22–23.
[16] Ibid., 36.

regarding work as an evil, and gratifying the appetites and passions."[17] We get the idea. The "idle life" is defective. Work is not evil. Self-indulgence is sin.

Social engagement for the betterment of the life of the oppressed was one pervasive expression of this activism. It may surprise some people today, but evangelicals were at the cutting edge of this social activism for the sake of the poor. Bebbington gives abundant illustrations of the truth that "a plethora of churches and church-sponsored organizations throughout the English-speaking world tackled aspects of social destitution."[18]

The suspicion that many of us have inherited concerning the dilution of evangelism amid social concern was not true in general of nineteenth-century evangelicalism. "The typical disparagement by fundamentalists of concern for physical welfare was only just beginning as the 20th century opened. Down to 1900, what would later be called holistic mission was part of the agreed program of evangelicalism."[19] Thus, there were a "host of evangelicals of all denominations who attempted to redress the social conditions of Victorian Britain."[20]

One of the most prominent burdens felt by society and church was the plight of orphans. This plight was a common theme in the novels of nineteenth-century writer Charles Dickens (1812–1870). One feels the plight in the description of Oliver Twist: "He was badged and ticketed, and fell into his place at once—a parish child—the orphan of a workhouse—the humble, half-starved drudge—to be cuffed and buffeted through the world—despised by all, and pitied by none."[21]

Caring for Orphans by Faith

Ministers across Great Britain founded institutions to relieve the plight of the orphan. And that social work carried over into pressure for reform of working conditions and public treatment of the poor.[22] Müller was the most famous of the founders of orphanages, not because he was the only one doing it, but because of how he did it—namely, without asking for money or going into debt. Spurgeon, in London, seventy

---

[17] Cited in ibid., 37.
[18] Ibid., 100–1.
[19] Ibid., 263.
[20] Ibid., 39.
[21] Charles Dickens, *Oliver Twist* (1838; repr., Ware, Hertfordshire, UK: Wordsworth, 1992), 5.
[22] Bebbington, *The Dominance of Evangelicalism*, 38.

miles from Bristol, where Müller's orphanages were, founded his own orphanages at Stockwell in 1867.

Taylor did not found a ministry directly for orphans, but the link with Müller's ministry is significant. Taylor's commitment to go to China as a missionary included his eagerness to be a blessing to the whole person, physical and spiritual. Hence, in 1851, on his nineteenth birthday, Taylor went to live with Dr. Robert Hardey in Hull as an apprentice in medicine.[23] While he was there, he became part of a Plymouth Brethren[24] fellowship where Müller was very highly esteemed.

Here is how Taylor's son, Frederick, recounts the importance of this connection with the Brethren and Müller, who himself was part of the Brethren:

[Hudson] was hungry for the Word of God, and their preaching was for the most part a thoughtful exposition of its truths. He needed a fresh vision of eternal things, and the presence of Christ was often so real on these occasions that it was like heaven on earth to be among them. He was facing a difficult future, and they set before him an example of faith in temporal as well as spiritual things that surpassed his utmost thought. For this meeting was in close touch with George Müller of Bristol, whose work was even then assuming remarkable proportions. He had already hundreds of orphan children under his care, and was looking to the Lord for means to support a thousand. But this did not exhaust his sympathies. With a deep conviction that these are the days in which the Gospel must be preached "for a witness unto all nations," he sustained in whole or part many missionaries, and was engaged in circulating the Scriptures far and wide in Roman Catholic as well as heathen lands. All this extensive work, carried on by a penniless man through faith in God alone, with no appeals for help or guarantee of stated income, was a wonderful testimony to the power of "effectual, fervent prayer." As such it made a profound impression upon Hudson Taylor, and

---

[23] Frederick Howard Taylor and Geraldine Taylor, *Hudson Taylor in Early Years: The Growth of a Soul* (Littleton, CO; Mississauga, ON; Kent, TN: OMF Books, 1995), 105.
[24] There is some ambiguity about the lifelong connection between the Plymouth Brethren and Taylor. The most extensive, scholarly study of the China Inland Mission and Taylor makes these observations: "Historians of the Brethren Movement claim Hudson Taylor as one of their own. As secretary Richard Hill whispered to Geraldine Guinness Taylor [Hudson Taylor's daughter-in-law], herself a second-generation Brethren: 'You know of course that the great majority of the earliest supporters were either or practically P.B.s [Plymouth Brethren].' Yet in her thirty books the word 'Brethren' never passed Mrs. Taylor's pen, hidden behind a cloud of euphemisms like 'chapel' and 'meeting.' A. J. Broomhall went to great lengths to deny the 'false label' that Taylor was connected with the Plymouth Brethren, that is, John Nelson Darby's Exclusives who practiced second-degree separation, which Taylor 'repudiated,' as well as the equally 'false label' that Taylor was a 'Baptist.' Broomhall did acknowledge that 'the non-sectarian, trans-denominational practices and principles of China Inland Mission . . . owed much' to the non-Plymouth or Open Brethren, like Berger, Grattan Guinness, and the Howard family." Austin, *China's Millions*, 94.

encouraged him more than anything else could have in the pathway he was about to enter.[25]

So even though Taylor did not found an orphanage the way Müller and Spurgeon did, he was inspired by such work and in his own way became no less an activist, mobilizing thousands of missionaries for China—which to this day is transforming the way the Chinese think about children.

The Pervasiveness of Practicality

Of course, Spurgeon's orphanage was the tip of the iceberg of his activism. By the time he was fifty years old, he had founded, or was overseeing, sixty-six organizations. Lord Shaftesbury commented that this was a "a noble career of good . . . for the benefit of mankind."[26]

It would be a huge mistake to describe Spurgeon's activism as if he were not a man of profound personal faith and deep reliance on the Lord, with powerful capacities for enjoying the beauties of Christ and his world. We must get out of our heads entirely, when thinking of Spurgeon, Müller, and Taylor, that their activism was like the pragmatic activism of some today, who replace piety and prayer and meditation and worship with endless work. As will become clear in the chapters to follow, all of these men were mystics in their own way. That is, each had a profound, heartfelt, personal relationship with the living Christ.

Nevertheless, one cannot miss the pragmatic cast that colors even the most spiritual acts of Spurgeon. This is strikingly evident in his own words about prayer:

> When I pray, I like to go to God just as I go to a bank clerk when I have [a] cheque to be cashed. I walk in, put the cheque down on the counter, and the clerk gives me my money, I take it up, and go about my business. I do not know that I ever stopped in a bank five minutes to talk with the clerks; when I have received my change I go away and attend to other matters. That is how I like to pray; but there is a way of praying that seems like lounging near the mercy seat as though one had no particular reason for being found there.[27]

---

[25] Taylor and Taylor, *Hudson Taylor in Early Years*, 111–13.

[26] Cited in Arnold Dallimore, *Spurgeon* (Chicago: Moody Press, 1984), 173.

[27] Cited in Erroll Hulse and David Kingdon, eds., *A Marvelous Ministry: How the All-Round Ministry of Charles Haddon Spurgeon Speaks to Us Today* (Ligonier, PA: Soli Deo Gloria , 1993), 46–47.

Again, it would be a caricature to take from these words the notion that Spurgeon did not believe in the sweetness of enjoying the presence of Christ in meditation and prayer. But one can hardly imagine someone talking like this three hundred years earlier. We are all profoundly shaped by the way the Holy Spirit meets us in our own age.

Modern Mavericks

Part of the spirit of activism that was woven into the fabric of evangelicalism and into the expansive nineteenth-century ethos was a measure of pragmatic individualism. Spurgeon, Müller, and Taylor exploited this freedom to the full. I am not referring to a crass pragmatism that compromises biblical principles for the sake of measurable results. Almost the opposite. I am referring to a willingness to adjust inherited ways and traditions to put personal biblical convictions to practical use. If that makes one a maverick, so be it. Hence the individualism.

Bebbington points out how prevalent this spirit of pragmatic, can-do individualism was in the age of Spurgeon, Müller, and Taylor, in both Britain and America:

> The strength and number of para-church organizations—at the time called benevolent associations in America—is a sign of the same spirit of adapting church life to contemporary requirements. The range of miscellaneous but vigorous groups was immense—including in England the Army Scripture Readers' Society, the Christian Vernacular Society for India, the Working Men's Lord's Day Rest Association and the Society for the Relief of Persecuted Jews. Evangelicalism characteristically spawned organizations beyond the control of strictly ecclesiastical bodies.[28]

Both Müller and Taylor were disillusioned with the existing organizations of the day. In another age, they might have simply adjusted and made the best of things through slow reform. But in the nineteenth century, one could actually dream of taking charge, creating a new institution, and running and funding it practically as one saw fit.

Müller's Large and Liberal Entrepreneurialism

In Müller's case, the orphan work was only one branch of a larger organization that he founded in 1834 (the year Spurgeon was born) called

---

[28] Bebbington, *The Dominance of Evangelicalism*, 145.

the Scripture Knowledge Institution for Home and Abroad. Through this Institution, he lavished his generosity (and remarkable fund-raising skill) on other causes of the gospel. For example, Müller became the largest donor to Taylor's China Inland Mission:

> In its early years he kept the mission afloat. From the fragmentary financial records, Moira McKay has ascertained that Müller contributed one-third of the CIM's income between 1866 and 1871, a total of £780 to the general fund and £560 to individual missionaries; this does not include money he gave Hudson Taylor personally for his own use, nor the money he remitted directly to China.[29]

Müller was committed not only to his own ministries. His large and entrepreneurial heart had a wider kingdom focus. But it should be mentioned that, for all the wideness of his generosity, he never lost his doctrinal bearings. There came a point, for example, when he withheld his contributions to Taylor's CIM until the resignation of a key leader who had come to embrace the view of annihilationism in place of the biblical view of hell as eternal, conscious torment.[30]

A. T. Pierson, Müller's authorized biographer, said Müller's Scripture Knowledge Institution "owed its existence to the fact that its founder devised large and liberal things for the Lord's cause."[31] Indeed, that banner could be waved over the lives of all three of these men: they "devised large and liberal things for the Lord's cause."

But the impetus for new ministries was not merely entrepreneurial. When asked why he did not use existing institutions, Müller answered that they were out of step with what he saw in the Scriptures. "We found, in comparing the then existing religious Societies with the word of God, that they departed so far from it, that we could not be united with them, and yet maintain a good conscience."[32] Specifically, he said, (1) they tended to be postmillennial, (2) too many unregenerate persons were involved in running them, (3) they asked unconverted people for money, (4) the rich and unregenerate

---

[29] Austin, *China's Millions*, 96.
[30] Ibid., 190.
[31] Arthur T. Pierson, *George Müller of Bristol: His Life of Prayer and Faith* (Grand Rapids, MI: Kregel, 1999), 248. Originally published as "Authorized Memoir" (Old Tappan, NJ: Revell, 1899).
[32] George Müller, *A Narrative of Some of the Lord's Dealings with George Muller, Written by Himself, Jehovah Magnified. Addresses by George Muller Complete and Unabridged*, vol. 1 (Muskegon, MI: Dust and Ashes Publications, 2003), 80.

even served on their boards, (5) they tended to look for persons of rank to lead them, and (6) they were willing to fund their ministries by going into debt.[33]

So Müller started his own agency and led it in the way he understood the Scriptures to teach. From this individual commitment and vision flowed enormous energy and fruit. Besides caring for more than ten thousand orphans in his lifetime, the Scripture Knowledge Institution spread day schools across continental Europe, eventually serving more than one hundred twenty-three thousand students.[34] And the Institution was among the first to get behind Taylor's China Inland Mission when it was founded in 1865.

Taylor Follows Müller's Model

Taylor's decision to start his own foreign mission sending agency was similarly driven by his disillusionment with the way other societies were run. He had gone to China in 1853 with the Chinese Evangelisation Society. But within four years, he resigned because he disagreed with the policy of the society to borrow money to pay its bills. "The Society itself was in debt. The quarterly bills which I and others were instructed to draw were often met with borrowed money, and a correspondence commenced which terminated in the following year by my resigning from conscientious motives."[35] Eight years later, he founded the China Inland Mission on principles like those of Müller's Institution. We tell that story in chapter 3.

The Modern Mavericks Were Very Unmodern—No Debt!

This issue of debt, together with the readiness to trust God to meet practical needs, is an example of how their very individualism and pragmatic adaptability could put Spurgeon, Müller, and Taylor not only in step with the spirit of the age, but radically out of step with it. All three of them rejected debt as a way of running any Christian ministry. And in its place, Müller and Taylor put a "faith principle"[36] that meant they would look to God and never directly ask another person for money.

---

[33] Ibid., 80–81.
[34] George Müller, *Autobiography of George Müller, or A Million and a Half in Answer to Prayer*, comp. G. Fred Bergin (Denton, TX: Westminster Literature Resources, 2003), ix.
[35] *The Works of J. Hudson Taylor* (Douglas Editions, 2009). Kindle edition, locations 1508–1510.
[36] Bebbington, *The Dominance of Evangelicalism*, 185–90, describes how this "faith principle" rose up in the nineteenth century and shaped most of the evangelical movement. "By 1900 Anglican evangelicals were

Müller's conscience was bound by Romans 13:8: "Owe no man any thing" (KJV). He said: "There is no promise that He will pay our debts,—the word says rather: 'Owe no man any thing.'"[37] He believed deeply that this way of life was the duty of every Christian and called on believers to repent if any were in debt. "The Lord helping us, we would rather suffer privation, than contract debts. . . . May I entreat the believing reader, prayerfully to consider this matter; for I am well aware that many trials come upon the children of God, on account of not acting according to Rom. xiii. 8."[38]

Müller went so far as to refuse to pay the milkman weekly, but would only pay him daily.[39] He did pay his workers a salary, but only with the understanding that "if the Lord should not be pleased to send in the means at the time when their salary is due, I am not considered their debtor."[40]

Taylor was born the year that Müller founded his Scripture Knowledge Institution. In due time, the reputation of Müller's faith made a huge impact on Taylor. The obituary that Thomas Champness wrote for Taylor in 1905 shows the extent of Müller's influence:

> HUDSON TAYLOR is no more! A Prince of Israel has been gathered home. He died in China, the land he loved more than life. Now that he has gone we shall hear more of him. In his way he was as great a man as George Müller. Like him, he had more faith in God than man. The China Inland Mission, of which he was the founder, was run on similar lines to the Orphanage at Bristol. What the writer of these lines owes to Hudson Taylor will never be known.[41]

Under Taylor's leadership, the China Inland Mission was never in debt and never directly asked for money.

The influence of Müller on Taylor was direct from the first time that they met:

> Although Müller had given financial contributions to Taylor since 1857, they do not seem to have met until 1863, when Taylor took Wang Lae-djün

---

predominantly Keswick in their spirituality, millennial in their view of the future and at least respectful toward the faith principle." Ibid., 259.
[37] Müller, *A Narrative*, vol. 1, 316.
[38] Ibid., 62.
[39] Ibid., 169.
[40] Ibid., 256.
[41] *In Memoriam: J. Hudson Taylor* (London: Morgan & Scott, 1906), 102.

to Bristol to sit at Müller's feet. . . . The grand old man—he was nearing sixty, almost gaunt-looking, with a white beard and unruly hair—bequeathed two gifts to the young man. The first were his mottoes, which became the watchwords of the CIM: "Ebenezer" ("Hitherto hath the Lord helped us") and "Jehovah-Jireh" ("the Lord will provide"). Taylor transcribed them into Chinese, and printed them on the cover of every issue of *China's Millions: Yi-ben-yi-shi-er* and *Ye-he-hua-yi-la.* Müller's second gift was his system for divine bookkeeping: each donor was given a numbered receipt, which Müller published in consecutive order, anonymously, on regular occasions.[42]

Like Müller and Taylor, Spurgeon said he hated debt the way Martin Luther hated the pope. All the buildings he built were entered debt-free.[43] But it does not appear that he embraced the principle of not asking for funds the way Müller and Taylor did. The explanation seems plain enough. He was a pastor charged with preaching the Scriptures to his flock and applying it, not merely to parachurch organizations, but specifically to his people's relationships. One of those relationships was with the local church to which they belonged—the Metropolitan Tabernacle. If any text a pastor touches involves the teaching that the members of a church should sustain the church financially, then not only *may* the pastor exhort the people to give, he would be untrue to the text if he didn't.

Spurgeon loved Müller as a close comrade in ministry and as one of his heroes. He conversed with him often[44] and called him his "dear friend." Müller preached occasionally in Spurgeon's Metropolitan Tabernacle.[45] Spurgeon's praise for Müller was unparalleled for any man in his day. "I never heard a man who spoke more to my soul than dear Mr. George Müller."[46] "I think, sometimes, that I would not mind changing places with George Müller for time and for eternity, but I do not know anybody else of whom I would say as much as that."[47]

---

[42] Austin, *China's Millions*, 95–96.

[43] Eric W. Hayden, *Highlights in the Life of C. H. Spurgeon* (Pasadena, TX: Pilgrim Publications, 1990), 95.

[44] Müller shared Spurgeon's affection and recalled several conversations when Spurgeon was on vacation in Mentone, France. "At Mentone I enjoyed especially the intercourse I had with Mr. Spurgeon, with whom I spent repeatedly a considerable time." George Müller, *Autobiography of George Muller: A Million and a Half in Answer to Prayer* (London: J. Nisbet, 1914), 532.

[45] "On our way to Sunderland, I preached in the large Metropolitan Tabernacle for Mr. Spurgeon." Ibid., 526.

[46] C. H. Spurgeon, *The Metropolitan Tabernacle Pulpit Sermons*, vol. 29 (London: Passmore & Alabaster, 1883), 389.

[47] C. H. Spurgeon, *The Metropolitan Tabernacle Pulpit Sermons*, vol. 49 (London: Passmore & Alabaster, 1903), 238.

Perhaps only slightly less was Spurgeon's admiration for Taylor. In the nature of the case, the relationship could not be as close, since Müller was only a few hours away in Bristol, while Taylor was often in China. Nevertheless, Spurgeon sang the praises of Taylor and the China Inland Mission:

> No mission now existing has so fully our confidence and good wishes as the work of Mr. Hudson Taylor in China. It is conducted on those principles of faith in God which most dearly commend themselves to our innermost soul. The man at the head is "a vessel fit for the Master's use." His methods of procedure command our veneration—by which we mean more than our judgment or our admiration; and the success attending the whole is such as cheers our heart and reveals the divine seal upon the entire enterprise.[48]

In other words, Spurgeon's unwillingness to trumpet the exact same funding strategy as Müller and Taylor did not diminish his affection and admiration and support for them. In fact, he admired their faith and their strategy.

The Unifying Root of Renegade Finances

Why did Taylor and Müller adopt the pattern of not asking people directly for funds?[49]

Müller gave the clearest answer. And this answer shows how he and Spurgeon and Taylor were utterly out of step with their age. Müller gave three reasons for establishing the orphan houses, and he gave them in the order of their importance in his mind:

> The three chief reasons for establishing an Orphan-House are: 1) That God may be glorified, should He be pleased to furnish me with the means, in its being seen that it is not a vain thing to trust in Him; and that thus the faith of His children may be strengthened. 2) The spiritual welfare of fatherless and motherless children. 3) Their temporal welfare.[50]

This is really astonishing, and a sure sign Müller was an exile and sojourner on the earth, with a true citizenship and treasure in heaven.

---

[48] C. H. Spurgeon, *The Sword and the Trowel: 1869* (London: Passmore & Alabaster, 1869), 7.
[49] In the following chapters, it will become clear that while *direct* appeals for funds were not given, nevertheless both Müller and Taylor were vigilant about making use of the latest means of communicating to the world how God was meeting their needs, and thus *indirectly* communicated their needs and pulled at people's hearts.
[50] Müller, *A Narrative*, vol. 1, 103.

The glory of God was preeminent for him, not the temporal welfare of the children. Caring for the children was the fruit of aiming to glorify God by showing him trustworthy. This is the highest and best gift he has for the children and for the world. Without this gift, all is in vain.

This is why Müller ran the orphanages the way he did—and in this goal, he was one with Spurgeon and Taylor. He wanted to give a living proof of the power and the trustworthiness of God, and the value of living by faith and prayer—without debt. When explaining why he never purchased anything for the orphan houses on credit, he said:

> The chief and primary object of the work was not the temporal welfare of the children, nor even their spiritual welfare (blessed and glorious as it is, and much as, through grace, we seek after it and pray for it); but the first and primary object of the work was: *To show before the whole world and the whole church of Christ, that even in these last evil days the living God is ready to prove Himself as the living God, by being ever willing to help, succour, comfort, and answer the prayers of those who trust in Him:* so that we need not go away from Him to our fellow-men, or to the ways of the world, seeing that He is both able and willing to supply us with all we can need in His service.[51]

Though there may have been minor differences in strategy and application, this passion for displaying God's faithfulness to the world bound these three friends together in their respective focuses of church (Spurgeon), orphan care (Müller), and world missions (Taylor).

Indigenous Pilgrims

Like every human being who lives in space and time—that is, in a particular culture and age—Charles Spurgeon, George Müller, and Hudson Taylor were shaped significantly by the explosive new world they inhabited. Their activism and individualism and pragmatism and resistance to elite privilege and identification with the common man (none of them had a theological degree) made them men of their age. Nevertheless, they were radically different from the unbelieving masses of their day.

What will become clear in the coming chapters is that, for all their differences, there was a profound camaraderie of confidence in God among them. They were indeed evangelical in their emphases on Scripture, the atoning work of Christ on the cross, the necessity of the new

---

[51] Ibid., 317. See also 105.

birth and conversion, and the resulting energy of activism and mission. But in each man's life, the suffering each would endure brought out an extraordinary confidence in the mighty goodness of God. Beneath all their talk of faith and the simplicity of trusting God to fulfill his promises for us in everyday life lay a massive vision of God's right and power to govern every detail of life, the evil and the good—with nothing able to stop him.

Taylor, who, among the three, was the least given to theological systematizing and labeling,[52] gave one of the strongest statements of this common conviction. When his wife Maria died after twelve years of marriage, Taylor was thirty-eight years old. He wrote to his mother, "From my inmost soul I delight in the knowledge that God does or permits all things, and causes all things to work together for good to those who love Him."[53] Fourteen years later, at the age of fifty-two, he wrote, "So make up your mind that God is an infinite Sovereign, and has the right to do as He pleases with His own, and He may not explain to you a thousand things which may puzzle your reason in His dealings with you."[54]

Spurgeon and Müller said the same in similar contexts—Müller at the death of his wife, Spurgeon in the face of debilitating suffering. This was the uniting foundation of their camaraderie in confidence in the goodness, glory, and power of God. This would be the key to Spurgeon's powerful preaching through relentless adversity, Müller's unshakable satisfaction in God, and Taylor's enjoyment of his lasting union with Jesus Christ.

---

[52] Spurgeon and Müller were self-confessed Calvinists. But in all the works by and about Taylor that I have seen, there is no clear statement on the matter. One pointer might be this excerpt from his commentary on the Song of Solomon: "In the little sister, as yet immature, may we not see the elect of GOD, given to CHRIST in GOD's purpose, but not yet brought into saving relation to Him?" Cited in J. Stuart Holden, "Foreword," in *Union and Communion; or, Thoughts on the Song of Solomon*, 3rd ed. (London: Morgan & Scott, 1914), 78.

[53] Cited in Dr. and Mrs. Howard Taylor, *Hudson Taylor's Spiritual Secret*, Kindle edition (May 25, 2013), 163.

[54] Cited in Jim Cromarty, *It Is Not Death to Die* (Fearn, Ross-shire, Scotland: Christian Focus, 2008), 8.

Causeless depression cannot be reasoned with, nor can David's harp charm it away by sweet discoursings. As well fight with the mist as with this shapeless, undefinable, yet all-beclouding hopelessness . . .

The iron bolt which so mysteriously fastens the door of hope and holds our spirits in gloomy prison, needs a heavenly hand to push it back.

Charles Spurgeon

1

Charles Spurgeon

Preaching through Adversity

For Pastors and the Rest of Us

Everyone faces adversity and must find ways to persevere through the oppressing moments of life. Everyone must get up and walk through the routines of making breakfast and washing clothes and going to work and paying bills and discipling children. We must, in general, keep life going when our hearts are breaking.

But it's different with pastors—not *totally* different, but different. The heart is the instrument of our vocation. Charles Spurgeon said, "Ours is more than mental work—it is heart work, the labour of our inmost soul."[1] When a pastor's heart is breaking, therefore, he must labor with a broken instrument. Preaching is the pastor's main work, and preaching is heart work, not just mental work. The question becomes, then, not just how you keep living when the marriage is blank or when the finances don't reach or when the pews are bare and friends forsake you, but *How do you keep preaching?*

When the heart is overwhelmed, it's one thing to survive adversity; it is something entirely different to continue preaching Sunday after Sunday, month after month.

Spurgeon said to the students of his Pastors' College: "One crushing stroke has sometimes laid the minister very low. The brother most relied upon becomes a traitor. . . . Ten years of toil do not take so much

[1] Charles Spurgeon, *Lectures to My Students* (Grand Rapids, MI: Zondervan, 1972), 156.

life out of us as we lose in a few hours by Ahithophel the traitor, or Demas the apostate."[2] The question for pastors is not, "How do you live through unremitting criticism and distrust and accusation and abandonment?"—but, *"How do you preach through it? How do you do heart work when the heart is under siege and ready to fall?"*

These are the uppermost questions for many pastors. Preaching great and glorious truth in an atmosphere that is not great and glorious is immensely difficult. To be reminded week in and week out that many people regard his preaching of the glory of God's grace as hypocrisy pushes a preacher not just into the hills of introspection, but sometimes to the precipice of self-extinction. I don't mean suicide—but something more complex. I mean the deranging inability to know any longer who you are.

What begins as a searching introspection for the sake of holiness and humility gradually leaves your soul, for various reasons, in a hall of mirrors. You look into one and you're short and fat; you look into another and you're tall and lanky; you look into another and you're upside down. Then the horrible feeling begins to break over you that you don't know who you are anymore. The center is not holding. If the center doesn't hold—if there is no fixed "I" able to relate to the fixed "thou" (namely, God), who is supposed to preach next Sunday?

When the apostle Paul said in 1 Corinthians 15:10, "By the grace of God I am what I am," he was saying something utterly essential for the survival of preachers in adversity. If the identity of the "I"—the "I" created by Christ and united to Christ, but still a human "I"—doesn't hold, there will be no more authentic preaching because there is no longer an authentic preacher. When the "I" is gone, there is only a collection of echoes.

Oh, how fortunate we are that we are not the first to face these things! I thank God for the healing history of the power of God in the lives of his saints and, in particular, for the life and ministry of Charles Spurgeon, who, for thirty-eight years at the New Park Street Chapel and the Metropolitan Tabernacle in London, modeled how to preach through adversity. And for those who have eyes to see, the lessons are not just for pastors, but for all of us.

---

[2] Ibid., 161.

Puritan Beginnings

Susannah Thompson, who became Spurgeon's wife for thirty-six years, was born in 1832, two years before her husband-to-be, and outlived him by eleven years. His life was enveloped in hers in more ways than one, as she served him, and the wider cause of Christ, even after she became an invalid twelve years into their marriage. She bore him two sons, twins, on September 20, 1856, Thomas and Charles Jr. Thomas would become the pastor of the Metropolitan Tabernacle after his father died, and Charles Jr. would take over the leadership of the Stockwell Orphanage that his father had founded.

George Müller was the great evangelical advocate for orphans in the nineteenth century, but Spurgeon, too, was passionate about this ministry. He started the Stockwell Orphanage in 1866, twelve years into his pastoral ministry in London. He loved to say, "The God who answers by orphanages, let him be Lord!"[3] Mrs. Hillyard, who belonged to Müller's Plymouth Brethren denomination, offered Spurgeon £20,000 if he would start an orphanage like the one he had described in *The Sword and the Trowel*, a magazine he founded in 1865. He had written that a school for the poor was needed where "all that we believe and hold dear shall be taught to the children of our poorer adherents."[4]

Spurgeon, who was born June 19, 1834, was himself a kind of orphan. His parents had not died, but they were not able to care for him at the beginning, and in his first year sent him to live with his grandparents. He recalls his exposure there to the riches of the Puritan books of his grandfather. He would be a lover of the Puritans for the rest of his life. He said he read *The Pilgrim's Progress* more than one hundred times.[5] His grandmother would give him a penny for each Isaac Watts hymn that he memorized. And his mother, after he moved back home in 1841, would read to him Puritan classics such as "Alleine's Alarm."[6]

Even before he was converted at fifteen through the preaching of a Methodist lay preacher, he knew his spiritual condition and the Puritan prescription for the remedy for his sins. He had read John Bunyan's

---

[3] Cited in Tom Nettles, *Living by Revealed Truth: The Life and Pastoral Theology of Charles Haddon Spurgeon* (Fearn, Ross-shire, Scotland: Christian Focus, 2013), 375.
[4] Cited in ibid.
[5] Eric W. Hayden, "Did You Know?" in *Christian History*, Issue 29, Volume X, No. 1, 2.
[6] Joseph Alleine, *An Alarm to the Unconverted* (1671; repr., Lafayette, IN: Sovereign Grace, 2007).

Grace Abounding, Richard Baxter's *Call to the Unconverted*, and John Angell James's *The Anxious Inquirer*. But God did not open his eyes to the sweetness of the gospel until January 6, 1850, in the Primitive Methodist Church in Colchester, where he had taken refuge from a snowstorm.

Whatever his estrangement was before—from his parents and his Creator—he was now adopted into the family of God. He never looked back. With no formal theological training, he was called at the age of seventeen to be the pastor of a Congregational church in Waterbeach. Just short of two years later, at the age of nineteen, he candidated at the New Park Street Chapel, London. He started his ministry there the next year (1854). The church changed its name to the Metropolitan Tabernacle when a new building was constructed. Spurgeon would be the pastor of this congregation for thirty-eight years until his death in 1892.

The Waves of Blessing on His Preaching

Preaching was the most renowned and effective part of Spurgeon's life. He preached more than six hundred times before he was twenty.[7] After the new building opened, he was typically heard by six thousand people on the Lord's Day. He once preached to the largest indoor crowd of his life, 23,654—without electronic amplification. His sermons would eventually sell about twenty-five thousand copies a week and be translated into twenty languages.

When he came to New Park Street Chapel, there were 232 members. Thirty-eight years later, there were 5,311, with a total addition of 14,460 (an average of 380 new members a year). All of this happened even though he had no formal theological education. He was self-taught and read voraciously—about six books a week, with a phenomenal memory. At his death, his library consisted of about twelve thousand volumes. To secure the legacy of preaching for other churches and times, he founded a Pastors' College, which trained nearly nine hundred men in his lifetime.[8]

But the ever-present Lord Jesus did not spare his friend and servant the "many tribulations" Paul promised to all who would enter

---

[7] Hayden, "Did You Know?," 2.
[8] Ibid.

the kingdom of heaven (Acts 14:22). His life was hard, and by the standard of his friend Müller, short. He stood before his people for the last time on June 7, 1891, and died the following January 31 from a painful combination of rheumatism, gout, and Bright's disease. He was fifty-seven.

Neither Spurgeon's death nor his life was easy. They were not pain-free. As I have walked with Spurgeon over the years, these lessons have helped me most—the lessons of living with loss and criticism and sickness and sorrow. This is what I focus on in this chapter. But first, we should see that there are other reasons why we—especially preachers—can learn so much from Spurgeon. I offer seven reasons.

1. Spurgeon Was a Preacher

We have seen already that Spurgeon's preaching, beyond question, was what gave his life such a powerful impact. The sheer quantity of his preaching is staggering. Today, his collected sermons fill sixty-three volumes, currently standing as the largest set of books by a single author in the history of Christianity.[9]

Even if his son Charles was biased, his assessment is close enough to the truth: "There was no one who could preach like my father. In inexhaustible variety, witty wisdom, vigorous proclamation, loving entreaty, and lucid teaching, with a multitude of other qualities, he must, at least in my opinion, ever be regarded as the prince of preachers."[10] Spurgeon was a preacher.

2. He Was a Truth-Driven Preacher

We should not be interested in how preachers deal with adversity if they are not first and foremost guardians and givers of unchanging biblical truth. If they find their way through adversity by other means than faithfulness to truth, they are no help to us.

Spurgeon defined the work of the preacher like this: "To know truth as it should be known, to love it as it should be loved, and then to proclaim it in the right spirit, and in its proper proportions."[11] He said to his students, "To be effective preachers you must be sound

---

[9] Ibid., 2.
[10] Cited in C. H. Spurgeon, *Autobiography*, vol. 2 (Edinburgh: Banner of Truth, 1973), 278.
[11] Charles Haddon Spurgeon, *An All-Round Ministry* (Edinburgh: Banner of Truth, 1960), 8.

theologians."[12] He warned that "those who do away with Christian doctrine are, whether they are aware of it or not, the worst enemies of Christian living . . . [because] the coals of orthodoxy are necessary to the fire of piety."[13]

Two years before he died, he said:

> Some excellent brethren seem to think more of the life than of the truth; for when I warn them that the enemy has poisoned the children's bread, they answer "Dear brother, we are sorry to hear it; and, to counteract the evil, we will open the window, and give the children fresh air." Yes, open the window, and give them fresh air, by all means. . . . But, at the same time, this ought you to have done, and not to have left the other undone. Arrest the poisoners, and open the windows, too. While men go on preaching false doctrine, you may talk as much as you will about deepening their spiritual life, but you will fail in it.[14]

Doctrinal truth was at the foundation of all Spurgeon's labors.

3. He Was a Bible-Believing Preacher

The truth that drove his preaching ministry was biblical truth, which he believed to be God's truth. He held up his Bible and said:

> These words are God's. . . . Thou book of vast authority, thou art a proclamation from the Emperor of Heaven; far be it from me to exercise my reason in contradicting thee. . . . This is the book untainted by any error; but it is pure unalloyed, perfect truth. Why? Because God wrote it.[15]

There is a difference in the hearts of preachers and people where this allegiance holds sway. I once had lunch with a man who bemoaned the atmosphere of his fledgling Sunday school class. He said the class typically centered around the group's discussion. One person would raise a topic and another would find a relevant Bible verse, but after the reading of the verse, the attitude became, "Now we have heard what Jesus thinks; what do you think?" Where that atmosphere begins to take over the pulpit and the church, defection from truth and weakness in holiness are not far behind.

---

[12] Ibid.
[13] Cited in Erroll Hulse and David Kingdon, eds., *A Marvelous Ministry: How the All-Round Ministry of Charles Haddon Spurgeon Speaks to Us Today* (Ligonier, PA: Soli Deo Gloria, 1993), 128.
[14] Spurgeon, *An All-Round Ministry*, 374.
[15] Cited in Hulse and Kingdon, *A Marvelous Ministry*, 47.

4. He Was a Soul-Winning Preacher

There was not a week that went by in Spurgeon's mature ministry that souls were not saved through his written sermons.[16] He and his elders were always on the "watch for souls" in the great congregation. "One brother," he said, "has earned for himself the title of my hunting dog, for he is always ready to pick up the wounded birds."[17]

Spurgeon was not exaggerating when he said:

> I remember, when I have preached at different times in the country, and sometimes here, that my whole soul has agonized over men, every nerve of my body has been strained and I could have wept my very being out of my eyes and carried my whole frame away in a flood of tears, if I could but win souls.[18]

He was consumed with the glory of God and the salvation of men.

5. He Was a Calvinistic Preacher

Spurgeon was my kind of Calvinist. Let me give you a flavor of why his Calvinism drew five thousand people a week to his church rather than driving them away. He said:

> To me, Calvinism means the placing of the eternal God at the head of all things. I look at everything through its relation to God's glory. I see God first, and man far down in the list. . . . Brethren, if we live in sympathy with God, we delight to hear Him say, "I am God, and there is none else."[19]

> Puritanism, Protestantism, Calvinism [are simply] poor names which the world has given to our great and glorious faith—the doctrine of Paul the apostle, the gospel of our Lord and Savior Jesus Christ.[20]

But he did make distinctions between the full system of Calvinism, which he did embrace, and some central, evangelical doctrines shared by others that bound him together with them. For example, his favorite was the doctrine of the substitution of Christ for sinners. He said, "Far be it from me to imagine that Zion contains none but Calvinistic Christians within her walls, or that there are none saved who do not hold our views."[21]

---

[16] Arnold Dallimore, *Spurgeon* (Chicago: Moody Press, 1984), 198.
[17] Spurgeon, *Autobiography*, vol. 2, 76.
[18] Cited in Hulse and Kingdon, *A Marvelous Ministry*, 49–50.
[19] Spurgeon, *An All-Round Ministry*, 337.
[20] Ibid., 160.
[21] Cited in Hulse and Kingdon, *A Marvelous Ministry*, 65.

He said, "I am not an outrageous Protestant generally, and I rejoice to confess that I feel sure there are some of God's people even in the Romish Church."[22] He chose a paedobaptist to be the first head of his Pastors' College, and did not make that issue a barrier to preaching in his pulpit. His communion was open to all Christians, but he said he "would rather give up his pastorate than admit any man to the church who was not obedient to his Lord's command [of baptism]."[23]

His first words in the Metropolitan Tabernacle, the place he built to preach in for thirty years, were:

> I would propose that the subject of the ministry in this house, as long as this platform shall stand and as long as this house shall be frequented by worshippers, shall be the person of Jesus Christ. I am never ashamed to avow myself a Calvinist; I do not hesitate to take the name of Baptist; but if I am asked what is my creed, I reply, "It is Jesus Christ."[24]

But Spurgeon believed that Calvinism honored Christ most fully because it was most true. And he preached it explicitly and tried to work it into the minds of his people because, he said, "Calvinism has in it a conservative force which helps to hold men to vital truth."[25]

Therefore, he was open and unashamed: "People come to me for one thing. . . . I preach to them a Calvinist creed and a Puritan morality. That is what they want and that is what they get. If they want anything else they must go elsewhere."[26]

6. He Was a Hard-Working Preacher

I do not look to soft and leisurely men to instruct me how to endure adversity. If the main answer is, "Take it easy," I look for another teacher. Take a glimpse of Spurgeon's capacity for work:

> No one living knows the toil and care I have to bear. . . . I have to look after the Orphanage, have charge of a church with four thousand members, sometimes there are marriages and burials to be undertaken, there is the weekly sermon to be revised, *The Sword and the Trowel* to be edited, and besides all that, a weekly average of five hundred letters to be answered. This,

---

[22] Spurgeon, *Autobiography*, vol. 2, 21.
[23] Cited in Hulse and Kingdon, *A Marvelous Ministry*, 43.
[24] Cited in Bob L. Ross, *A Pictorial Biography of C. H. Spurgeon* (Pasadena, TX: Pilgrim Publications, 1974), 66.
[25] Cited in Hulse and Kingdon, *A Marvelous Ministry*, 121.
[26] Cited in ibid., 38.

however, is only half my duty, for there are innumerable churches established by friends, with the affairs of which I am closely connected, to say
nothing of the cases of difficulty which are constantly being referred to me.[27]

At his fiftieth birthday, a list was read of sixty-six organizations that
he had founded and conducted. The Earl of Shaftesbury, a distinguished
English peer, was there and said, "This list of associations, instituted by
his genius, and superintended by his care, were more than enough to
occupy the minds and hearts of fifty ordinary men."[28]

He typically read six substantial books a week and could remember
what he read and where to find it.[29] He produced more than 140 books
of his own—such as *The Treasury of David*, which was twenty years in
the making, and *Morning and Evening* and *Commenting on Commentaries* and *John Ploughman's Talk* and *Our Own Hymnbook*.[30]

He often worked eighteen hours in a day. The missionary David Livingstone asked him once, "How do you manage to do two men's work
in a single day?" Spurgeon replied, "You have forgotten there are two
of us."[31] I think he meant the presence of Christ's energizing power that
we read about in Colossians 1:29, where Paul says, "I toil, struggling
with all his energy that he powerfully works within me."

Spurgeon's attitude toward sacrificial labor would not be acceptable
today, when the primacy of "wellness" seems to hold sway. He said:

> If by excessive labour, we die before reaching the average age of man, worn
> out in the Master's service, then glory be to God, we shall have so much less
> of earth and so much more of Heaven![32]

> It is our duty and our privilege to exhaust our lives for Jesus. We are not to be
> living specimens of men in fine preservation, but living sacrifices, whose
> lot is to be consumed.[33]

Behind this radical viewpoint were some deep biblical convictions
that came through the apostle Paul's teaching. One of these convictions Spurgeon expressed like this: "We can only produce life in others

---

[27] Spurgeon, *Autobiography*, vol. 2, 192.
[28] Cited in Dallimore, *Spurgeon*, 173.
[29] Hayden, "Did You Know?," 2.
[30] Dallimore, *Spurgeon*, 195.
[31] Hayden, "Did You Know?," 3.
[32] Spurgeon, *An All-Round Ministry*, 126–27.
[33] Spurgeon, *Lectures to My Students*, 157.

by the wear and tear of our own being. This is a natural and spiritual law—that fruit can only come to the seed by its spending and being spent even to self-exhaustion."[34]

The apostle Paul said, "If we are afflicted, it is for your comfort and salvation" (2 Cor. 1:6) and "Death is at work in us, but life in you" (4:12). And he said that his own sufferings were the completion of Christ's sufferings for the sake of the church (Col. 1:24).

Another biblical conviction behind Spurgeon's radical view of pastoral zeal is expressed like this:

> Satisfaction with results will be the [death] knell of progress. No man is good who thinks that he cannot be better. He has no holiness who thinks that he is holy enough.[35]

In other words, he was driven with a passion never to be satisfied with the measure of his holiness or the extent of his service (see Phil. 3:12). The year he turned forty, he delivered a message to his pastors' conference with the one-word title "Forward!"[36] In it, he said:

> In every minister's life there should be traces of stern labour. Brethren, do something; do something; *do something*. While Committees waste their time over resolutions, do something. While Societies and Unions are making constitutions, let us win souls. Too often we discuss, and discuss, and discuss, while Satan only laughs in his sleeve. . . . Get to work and quit yourselves like men.[37]

I think the word *indefatigable* was created for people like Spurgeon.

7. He Was a Maligned and Suffering Preacher

He knew the whole range of adversity that most preachers suffer—and a lot more.

Spurgeon knew the everyday, homegrown variety of frustration and disappointment from lukewarm members.

> [Pastors] understand what one cold-hearted man can do if he gets at you on Sunday morning with the information that Mrs. Smith and all her family are offended, and therefore, their pew is vacant. You did not want to

---

[34] Spurgeon, *An All-Round Ministry*, 177.
[35] Ibid., 352.
[36] Ibid., 32–58.
[37] Ibid., 55.

know of that Lady's protest just before entering the pulpit, and it does not help you.[38]

Or perhaps, even worse, it can happen after the service:

What terrible blankets some professors are! Their remarks after a sermon are enough to stagger you. . . . You have been pleading as for life or death and they have been calculating how many seconds the sermon occupied, and grudging you the odd five minutes beyond the usual hour.[39]

It's even worse, he says, if the calculating observer is one of your deacons: "Thou shalt not yoke the ox and the ass together was a merciful precept: but when a laborious, ox-like minister comes to be yoked to a deacon who is not another ox, it becomes hard work to plough."[40]

He also knew the extraordinary calamities that befall us once in a lifetime.

On October 19, 1856, he preached for the first time in the Music Hall of the Royal Surrey Gardens because his own church would not hold the people. The seating capacity of ten thousand was far exceeded as the crowds pressed in. Someone shouted, "Fire!" and there was great panic in parts of the building. Seven people were killed in the stampede and scores were injured.

Spurgeon was twenty-two years old and was overcome by this calamity. He said later, "Perhaps never soul went so near the burning furnace of insanity, and yet came away unharmed."[41] But not all agreed he was unharmed. The specter brooded over him for years, and one close friend and biographer said, "I cannot but think, from what I saw, that his comparatively early death might be in some measure due to the furnace of mental suffering he endured on and after that fearful night."[42]

Spurgeon also knew the adversity of family pain.

He had married Susannah on January 8 of the same year of the calamity at Surrey Gardens. His only two children, twin sons, were born the day after the calamity, on October 20. Susannah was never able to have more children. In 1865 (nine years later), when she was

---

[38] Ibid., 358.
[39] Spurgeon, *Lectures to My Students*, 310.
[40] Ibid., 311.
[41] Cited in *Great Preaching on the Deity of Christ*, comp. Curtis Hutson (Murfreesboro, TN: Sword of the Lord, 2000), 206.
[42] Cited in Darrel W. Amundsen, "The Anguish and Agonies of Charles Spurgeon," in *Christian History*, Issue 29, Vol. X, No. 1, 23.

thirty-three years old, she became a virtual invalid and seldom heard her husband preach for the next twenty-seven years until his death. Some kind of rare cervical operations were attempted in 1869 by James Simpson, the father of modern gynecology, but to no avail.[43] So to Spurgeon's other burdens were added the care of a sickly wife and the inability to have more children, though his own mother had given birth to seventeen.

Spurgeon knew unbelievable physical suffering.

He suffered from gout, rheumatism, and Bright's disease (inflammation of the kidneys). His first attack of gout came in 1869, at the age of thirty-five. It became progressively worse, so that "approximately one third of the last twenty-two years of his ministry was spent out of the Tabernacle pulpit, either suffering, or convalescing, or taking precautions against the return of illness."[44] In a letter to a friend, he wrote, "Lucian says, 'I thought a cobra had bitten me, and filled my veins with poison; but it was worse—it was gout.' That was written from experience, I know."[45]

So for more than half of his ministry, Spurgeon dealt with ever-increasing recurrent pain in his joints that cut him down from the pulpit and from his labors again and again. The diseases eventually took his life at age fifty-seven, when he was convalescing in Mentone, France.

In addition to the physical suffering, Spurgeon had to endure a lifetime of public ridicule and slander, sometimes of the most vicious kind.

In April 1855, the *Essex Standard* carried an article with these words:

> His style is that of the vulgar colloquial, varied by rant. . . . All the most solemn mysteries of our holy religion are by him rudely, roughly, and impiously handled. Common sense is outraged and decency disgusted. His rantings are interspersed with coarse anecdotes.[46]

The *Sheffield and Rotherham Independent* said:

> He is a nine days' wonder—a comet that has suddenly shot across the religious atmosphere. He has gone up like a rocket and ere long will come down like a stick.[47]

---

[43] Hulse and Kingdon, *A Marvelous Ministry*, 38–39.
[44] Iain H. Murray, ed., *Letters of Charles Haddon Spurgeon* (Edinburgh: Banner of Truth, 1992), 166n1.
[45] Cited in ibid., 165.
[46] Cited in Hulse and Kingdon, *A Marvelous Ministry*, 35.
[47] Cited in ibid.

His wife kept a bulging scrapbook of such criticisms from the years 1855–1856. Some of it was easy to brush off. Most of it wasn't. In 1857, he wrote, "Down on my knees have I often fallen, with the hot sweat rising from my brow under some fresh slander poured upon me; in an agony of grief my heart has been well-nigh broken."[48]

His fellow ministers from the right and left criticized him. From the left, Joseph Parker wrote:

> Mr. Spurgeon was absolutely destitute of intellectual benevolence. If men saw as he did they were orthodox; if they saw things in some other way they were heterodox, pestilent and unfit to lead the minds of students or inquirers. Mr. Spurgeon's was a superlative egotism; not the shilly-shallying, timid, half-disguised egotism that cuts off its own head, but the full-grown, over-powering, sublime egotism that takes the chief seat as if by right. The only colors which Mr. Spurgeon recognized were black and white.[49]

And from the right, James Wells, the hyper-Calvinist, wrote, "I have—most solemnly have—my doubts as to the Divine reality of his conversion."[50]

All the embattlements of his life came to a climax in the Downgrade Controversy, as Spurgeon fought unsuccessfully for the doctrinal integrity of the Baptist Union. In October 1887, he withdrew from the Union. And the following January, he was officially and publicly censured by a vote of the Union for his manner of protest.[51]

Eight years earlier, he had said: "Men cannot say anything worse of me than they have said. I have been belied from head to foot, and misrepresented to the last degree. My good looks are gone, and none can damage me much now."[52]

He gives an example of the kinds of distortions and misrepresentations that were typical in the Downgrade Controversy:

> The doctrine of eternal punishment has been scarcely raised by me in this controversy; but the "modern thought" advocates continue to hold it up on all occasions, all the while turning the wrong side of it outwards.[53]

---

48 Cited in Amundsen, "The Anguish and Agonies of Charles Spurgeon," 23.
49 Cited in Hulse and Kingdon, *A Marvelous Ministry*, 69.
50 Cited in ibid., 35.
51 Ibid., 126.
52 Cited in ibid., 159.
53 Cited in ibid., 288.

But even though he usually sounded rough and ready, the pain was overwhelming and deadly. In May 1891, eight months before he died, he said to a friend: "Good-bye; you will never see me again. This fight is killing me."[54]

Spurgeon had recurrent battles with depression.

This final adversity was the result of the others. It is not easy to imagine the omnicompetent, eloquent, brilliant, full-of-energy Spurgeon weeping like a baby for no reason that he could think of. In 1858, at age twenty-four, it happened for the first time. He said, "My spirits were sunken so low that I could weep by the hour like a child, and yet I knew not what I wept for."[55] He added:

> Causeless depression cannot be reasoned with, nor can David's harp charm it away by sweet discoursings. As well fight with the mist as with this shapeless, undefinable, yet all-beclouding hopelessness. . . . The iron bolt which so mysteriously fastens the door of hope and holds our spirits in gloomy prison, needs a heavenly hand to push it back.[56]

He saw his depression as his "worst feature." "Despondency," he said, "is not a virtue; I believe it is a vice. I am heartily ashamed of myself for falling into it, but I am sure there is no remedy for it like a holy faith in God."[57]

In spite of all these sufferings and persecutions, Spurgeon endured to the end, and was able to preach mightily until his last sermon at the Tabernacle on June 7, 1891. The question I have asked in reading this man's life and work is, *how did he preserve and preach through this adversity?*

Preaching through Adversity

There were innumerable strategies of grace in the life of Charles Spurgeon. The ones I have chosen to mention are limited, and I chose them mainly because they have impacted me personally, but the scope of this man's strategies and the wisdom of his warfare were immense.

1. *Spurgeon saw his depression as the design of God for the good of his ministry and the glory of Christ.*

---

[54] Cited in Amundsen, "The Anguish and Agonies of Charles Spurgeon," 25.
[55] Cited in ibid., 24.
[56] Spurgeon, *Lectures to My Students*, 163.
[57] Cited in Amundsen, "The Anguish and Agonies of Charles Spurgeon," 24.

I begin with the issue of despondency and depression because if this one can be conquered, all the other forms of adversity that feed into it will be nullified. What comes through again and again in Spurgeon's writings is his unwavering belief in the sovereignty of God in all his afflictions. More than anything else, it seems, this kept him from caving in to the adversities of his life. He writes:

> It would be a very sharp and trying experience to me to think that I have an affliction which God never sent me, that the bitter cup was never filled by his hand, that my trials were never measured out to me by him, nor sent to me by his arrangement of their weight and quantity.[58]

This is exactly the opposite strategy of modern thought, even much evangelical thought, which recoils from the implications of God's infinity. If God is God, he not only knows what is coming, but he knows it *because* he designed it (Isa. 46:10; Jer. 1:12). For Spurgeon, this view of God was not an argument for debate; it was a means of survival. Our afflictions are the health regimen of an infinitely wise Physician. Spurgeon told his students:

> I dare say the greatest earthly blessing that God can give to any of us is health, with the exception of sickness. . . . If some men that I know of could only be favoured with a month of rheumatism, it would, by God's grace mellow them marvelously.[59]

He meant this mainly for himself. Though he dreaded suffering and would avoid it, he said:

> I am afraid that all the grace that I have got of my comfortable and easy times and happy hours, might almost lie on a penny. But the good that I have received from my sorrows, and pains, and griefs, is altogether incalculable. . . . Affliction is the best bit of furniture in my house. It is the best book in a minister's library.[60]

He saw three specific purposes of God in his struggle with depression. The first is that it functioned like the apostle Paul's thorn to keep him humble, lest he be lifted up in himself. Spurgeon said the Lord's work is summed up in these words:

---

58 Cited in ibid., 25.
59 Spurgeon, *An All-Round Ministry*, 384.
60 Cited in Amundsen, "The Anguish and Agonies of Charles Spurgeon," 25.

"Not by might nor by power but by my Spirit, saith the Lord." Instruments shall be used, but their intrinsic weakness shall be clearly manifested; there shall be no division of the glory, no diminishing of the honor due to the Great Worker. . . . Those who are honoured of their Lord in public have usually to endure a secret chastening, or to carry a peculiar cross, lest by any means they exalt themselves, and fall into the snare of the devil.[61]

The second purpose of God in his despondency was the unexpected power it gave to his ministry:

One Sabbath morning, I preached from the text, "My God, My God, why has Thou forsaken Me?" and though I did not say so, yet I preached my own experience. I heard my own chains clank while I tried to preach to my fellow-prisoners in the dark; but I could not tell why I was brought into such an awful horror of darkness, for which I condemned myself. On the following Monday evening, a man came to see me who bore all the marks of despair upon his countenance. His hair seemed to stand up right, and his eyes were ready to start from their sockets. He said to me, after a little parleying, "I never before, in my life, heard any man speak who seemed to know my heart. Mine is a terrible case; but on Sunday morning you painted me to the life, and preached as if you had been inside my soul." By God's grace I saved that man from suicide, and led him into gospel light and liberty; but I know I could not have done it if I had not myself been confined in the dungeon in which he lay. I tell you the story, brethren, because you sometimes may not understand your own experience, and the perfect people may condemn you for having it; but what know they of God's servants? You and I have to suffer much for the sake of the people of our charge. . . . You may be in Egyptian darkness, and you may wonder why such a horror chills your marrow; but you may be altogether in the pursuit of your calling, and be led of the Spirit to a position of sympathy with desponding minds.[62]

The third design of his depression was what he called a prophetic signal for the future:

This depression comes over me whenever the Lord is preparing a larger blessing for my ministry; the cloud is black before it breaks, and overshadows before it yields its deluge of mercy. Depression has now become to me as a prophet in rough clothing, a John the Baptist, heralding the nearer coming of my Lord's richer benison.[63]

---

[61] Cited in ibid., 163–64.
[62] Spurgeon, *An All-Round Ministry*, 221–22.
[63] Spurgeon, *Lectures to My Students*, 160.

I would say with Spurgeon that in the darkest hours, it is the sovereign goodness of God that has given me the strength to go on—the granite promise that he rules over my circumstances and means it for good, no matter what anyone else means.

2. *Spurgeon supplemented his theological survival strategy with God's natural means of survival—his use of rest and nature.*

For all his talk about spending and being spent, he counsels us to rest and take a day off and open ourselves to the healing powers God has put in the world of nature.

"Our Sabbath is our day of toil," he said, "and if we do not rest upon some other day we shall break down."[64] Eric Hayden reminds us that Spurgeon "kept, when possible, Wednesday as his day of rest."[65] More than that, Spurgeon said to his students:

> It is wisdom to take occasional furlough. In the long run, we shall do more by sometimes doing less. On, on, on forever, without recreation may suit spirits emancipated from this "heavy clay," but while we are in this tabernacle, we must every now and then cry halt, and serve the Lord by holy inaction and consecrated leisure. Let no tender conscience doubt the lawfulness of going out of harness for a while.[66]

In my pastoral ministry experience, I can testify that time off is crucial for breathing a different spiritual air. When we take time away from the press of duty, Spurgeon recommends that we breathe country air and let the beauty of nature do its appointed work. He confesses that "sedentary habits have tendency to create despondency . . . especially in the months of fog." He then counsels, "A mouthful of sea air, or a stiff walk in the wind's face would not give grace to the soul, but it would yield oxygen to the body, which is next best."[67]

At this point, let me add a personal word to you who are younger. In my years of pastoral ministry, I noticed significant changes in my body and soul. They were partly owing to changing circumstances, but much was owing to a changing constitution. First, I had to reduce my calorie intake to keep from gaining unhelpful weight. During the course of my ministry and aging, my metabolism stopped functioning the way it once

---

[64] Ibid., 160.
[65] Eric W. Hayden, *Highlights in the Life of C. H. Spurgeon* (Pasadena, TX: Pilgrim Publications, 1990), 103.
[66] Spurgeon, *Lectures to My Students*, 161.
[67] Ibid., 158.

did. Second, I grew to become emotionally less resilient when I didn't get adequate sleep. There were early days when I would work without regard to sleep, and afterward I would feel energized and motivated. However, as I entered my forties, adequate sleep was no longer a matter of staying healthy, but a matter of staying in the ministry. It is irrational that my future should look bleaker when I get four or five hours of sleep for several nights in a row, but that point is irrelevant. The fact is that my future *felt* bleaker, and I must live within the limits of that fact. I commend sufficient sleep to you, for the sake of your proper assessment of God and his promises.

Spurgeon was right when he said:

> The condition of your body must be attended to.... A little more ... common sense would be a great gain to some who are ultra spiritual, and attribute all their moods of feeling to some supernatural cause when the real reason lies far nearer to hand. Has it not often happened that dyspepsia has been mistaken for backsliding, and bad digestion has been set down as a hard heart?[68]

3. Spurgeon consistently nourished his soul by communion with Christ through prayer and meditation.

It was a great mercy to me at an embattled point in my ministry that I discovered John Owen's book *Communion with God*. It nourished me again and again as my soul asked, "Can God spread a table in the wilderness?"

Spurgeon warned his students:

> Never neglect your spiritual meals, or you will lack stamina and your spirits will sink. Live on the substantial doctrines of grace, and you will outlive and out-work those who delight in the pastry and syllabubs of "modern thought."[69]

I think one of the reasons Spurgeon was so rich in language and full in doctrinal substance and strong in the spirit, in spite of his despondency and his physical oppression and his embattlements, is that he was always immersed in a great book—six books a week. Most of us cannot match that number, but we can always be walking with some great

---

[68] Ibid., 312.
[69] Ibid., 310.

"see-er" of God. Over the years, I've learned that the key in all good reading of theology is to strive in the reading for utterly real fellowship with Christ. Spurgeon said:

> Above all, feed the flame with intimate fellowship with Christ. No man was ever cold in heart who lived with Jesus on such terms as John and Mary did of old. . . . I never met with a half-hearted preacher who was much in communion with the Lord Jesus.[70]

In many ways, Spurgeon was a child in his communion with God. He did not speak in complex terms about anything too strange or mystical. In fact, as we noted in the introduction, his prayer life seems to have been more businesslike than contemplative:

> When I pray, I like to go to God just as I go to a bank clerk when I have [a] cheque to be cashed. I walk in, put the cheque down on the counter, and the clerk gives me my money, I take it up, and go about my business. I do not know that I ever stopped in a bank five minutes to talk with the clerks; when I have received my change I go away and attend to other matters. That is how I like to pray; but there is a way of praying that seems like lounging near the mercy seat as though one had no particular reason for being found there.[71]

This may not be entirely exemplary. It may dishonor the Lord to treat him like a bank clerk rather than like a mountain spring. But we would make a mistake if we thought that Spurgeon's businesslike praying was anything other than childlike communion with his Father.

The most touching description I have read of his communion with God comes from 1871, when he was in terrible pain with gout:

> When I was racked some months ago with pain, to an extreme degree, so that I could no longer bear it without crying out, I asked all to go from the room, and leave me alone; and then I had nothing I could say to God but this, "Thou are my Father, and I am thy child; and thou, as a Father art tender and full of mercy. I could not bear to see my child suffer as thou makest me suffer, and if I saw him tormented as I am now, I would do what I could to help him, and put my arms under him to sustain him. Wilt thou hide thy face from me, my Father? Wilt thou still lay on a heavy hand, and not give me a smile from thy countenance?" . . . So I pleaded, and I ventured to say, when I was quiet, and

---

[70] Ibid., 315.
[71] Cited in Hulse and Kingdon, *A Marvelous Ministry*, 46–47.

they came back who watched me: "I shall never have such pain again from this moment, for God has heard my prayer." I bless God that ease came and the racking pain never returned.[72]

If we are going to preach through adversity, we have to live in communion with God on such intimate terms—speaking to him our needs and our pain, and feeding on the grace of his promises and the revelations of his glory.

4. Spurgeon rekindled his zeal and passion to preach by fixing his eyes on eternity rather than on the immediate price of faithfulness.

The apostle Paul saw that the outer nature was wasting away. What kept him going was the abiding assurance that his momentary affliction was working for him an eternal weight of glory. And so he looked to the things that are eternal (2 Cor. 4:16–18). So did Spurgeon:

> O brethren, we shall soon have to die! We look each other in the face to-day in health, but there will come a day when others will look down upon our pallid countenances as we lie in our coffins. . . . It will matter little to us who shall gaze upon us then, but it will matter eternally how we have discharged our work during our lifetime.[73]

When our hearts grow faint and our zeal wavers for the task of preaching, Spurgeon calls us to:

> Meditate with deep solemnity upon the fate of the lost sinner. . . . Shun all views of future punishment which would make it appear less terrible, and so take off the edge of your anxiety to save immortals from the quenchless flame. . . . Think much also of the bliss of the sinner saved, and like holy Baxter derive rich arguments from "the saints' everlasting rest." . . . There will be no fear of your being lethargic if you are continually familiar with eternal realities.[74]

Short of eternity, he took the long view when it came to his own persecution. In the Downgrade Controversy, Spurgeon said:

> Posterity must be considered. I do not look so much at what is to happen to-day, for these things relate to eternity. For my part, I am quite willing to be eaten of dogs for the next fifty years; but the more distant

---

[72] Cited in Amundsen, "The Anguish and Agonies of Charles Spurgeon," 24.
[73] Spurgeon, *An All-Round Ministry*, 76.
[74] Spurgeon, *Lectures to My Students*, 315.

future shall vindicate me. I have dealt honestly before the living God. My brother, do the same.[75]

To keep on preaching in storms of adversity, you must look well beyond the crisis and feelings of the hour. You must look to what history will make of your faithfulness, and most of all, what God will make of it at the last day.

5. *Spurgeon had settled who he was and would not be paralyzed by external criticism or internal second-guessing.*

One of the great perils of living under continual criticism is that it is a constant call for you to be other than what you are. This is especially problematic because a humble saint always wants to be a better person than he is.

Tim Stafford, a freelance writer and senior writer for *Christianity Today*, warns us against taking Spurgeon's counsel in the wrong way—a way that short-circuits the process of sanctification. He tells his story by way of illustration:

> I was shy, and often shy people retreat into themselves, unknowingly giving the impression of unfriendly aloofness. In college, I began to realize that other people's image of me did not match my image of myself. Those who did not know me well saw me as stern, aloof, and judgmental. Nobody told me so directly. Once I began to catch on, however, I was hit by the message from all sides.
>
> This pained me deeply, because it was not true. I knew what was inside me. I was as aloof as a puppy dog. I was soft-hearted, if anything. I cared about people. I craved friendship.
>
> I began to try to rewrite my life. I began consciously to say nice things to people, to let them know that I appreciated and liked them. I tried to act warmly. I began to hold my tongue when I had something to say that might be construed as critical or snobbish.
>
> And I hated it. It felt horribly unnatural. I despised having to watch my words, having to mull over every interaction to see whether I had handled it well and gotten my message across. Why couldn't I just be myself? I was, I suppose, a true child of the sixties: I believed that acting sincerely was enough. Now I felt that I was acting insincerely, putting on an act.
>
> My changes did bring noticeably better results, though. People told me I was different. They told me I seemed warmer, happier. People opened up

to me. People sought me out. I liked those differences. And I found that I got used to the act I was putting on. Over months and years it grew comfortable. Eventually, it became liberating. It became me.[76]

That is a good and wise caution against using "Be yourself" as an excuse to never change more fully into the likeness of Christ. The New Testament everywhere presumes that change is possible through Christ and is to be pursued—"from one degree of glory to another" (2 Cor. 3:18).

But Spurgeon knew this as well as we do. When he spoke of change, he was talking about something different. He was pointing out that in the clash of tongues, when your adversaries are saying that you cast out demons by the prince of demons, you'd better know if that is true or not. If you doubt yourself because of such criticism, you will not survive in the ministry. There is a great danger here of losing your bearings in a sea of self-doubt and not knowing who you are—not being able to say with Paul, "By the grace of God I am what I am" (1 Cor. 15:10). Spurgeon felt this danger keenly.

In comparing one ministerial identity with another, he reminded other pastors that at Jesus's Last Supper, there was a chalice for drinking the wine and there was a basin for washing feet. Then he said:

> I protest that I have no choice whether to be the chalice or the basin. Fain would I be whichever the Lord wills so long as he will but use me. . . . So you, my brother, you may be the cup, and I will be the basin; but let the cup be a cup, and the basin a basin, and each one of us just what he is fitted to be. Be yourself, dear brother, for, if you are not yourself, you cannot be anybody else; and so, you see, you must be nobody. . . . Do not be a mere copyist, a borrower, a spoiler of other men's notes. Say what God has said to you, and say it in your own way; and when it is so said, plead personally for the Lord's blessing upon it.[77]

I would also add, plead to the Lord personally that his purifying blood be upon it, too, because none of our best labors is untainted. The danger, though, is to let the truth paralyze you with fear of man and doubt of self.

Eleven years later, in 1886, Spurgeon struck the same anvil again:

---

[76] Tim Stafford, "Can We Talk?" in *Christianity Today*, Oct. 2, 1995.
[77] Spurgeon, *An All-Round Ministry*, 73–74.

Friend, be true to your own destiny! One man would make a splendid preacher of downright hard-hitting Saxon; why must he ruin himself by cultivating an ornate style? . . . Apollos has the gift of eloquence; why must he copy blunt Cephas? Every man in his own order.[78]

Spurgeon illustrates with his own struggle to be responsive to criticism during the Downgrade Controversy. For a season, he tried to adapt his language to the critics. But there came a time when he had to be what he was.

I have found it utterly impossible to please, let me say or do what I will. One becomes somewhat indifferent when dealing with those whom every word offends. I notice that, when I have measured my words, and weight my sentences most carefully, I have then offended most; while some of my stronger utterances have passed unnoticed. Therefore, I am comparatively careless as to how my expressions may be received, and only anxious that they may be in themselves just and true.[79]

If you are to survive and go on preaching in an atmosphere of controversy, there comes a point where you have done your best to weigh the claims of your critics and take them to heart, and must now say, "By the grace of God I am what I am." We must bring an end to the deranging second-guessing that threatens to destroy the very soul.

6. *Spurgeon found the strength to go on preaching in the midst of adversity and setbacks from the assured sovereign triumph of Christ.* This, we saw in the introduction, is what bound him together with George Müller and Hudson Taylor in the great camaraderie of confidence in the goodness, glory, and power of God. Near the end of his life, around 1890, in his last address at his pastors' conference, Spurgeon compared adversity and the ebb of truth to the ebbing tide:

You never met an old salt, down by the sea, who was in trouble because the tide had been ebbing out for hours. No! He waits confidently for the turn of the tide, and it comes in due time. Yonder rock has been uncovered during the last half-hour, and if the sea continues to ebb out for weeks, there will be no water in the English Channel, and the French will walk over from Cherbourg. Nobody talks in that childish way, for such an ebb will never come. Nor will we speak as though the gospel would be routed, and eternal

---

[78] Ibid., 232–33.
[79] Ibid., 282–83.

truth driven out of the land. We serve an almighty Master. . . . If our Lord does but stamp his foot, he can win for himself all the nations of the earth against heathenism, and Mohammedanism, and Agnosticism, and Modern-thought, and every other foul error. Who is he that can harm us if we follow Jesus? How can his cause be defeated? At his will, converts will flock to his truth as numerous as the sands of the sea. . . . Wherefore be of good courage, and go on your way singing [and preaching!]:

> The winds of hell have blown
> The world its hate hath shown,
> Yet it is not o'erthrown.
> Hallelujah for the Cross!
> It shall never suffer loss!
> The Lord of hosts is with us,
> the God of Jacob is our refuge.[80]

---

[80] Ibid., 395–96.

If it is really good for me, my darling wife will be raised up again; sick as she is. God will restore her again. But if she is not restored again, then it would not be a good thing for me. And so my heart was at rest. I was satisfied with God. And all this springs, as I have often said before, from taking God at His word, believing what He says.

George Müller

2

George Müller

A Strategy for Showing God—Simple Faith,
Sacred Scripture, Satisfaction in God

An Immigrant with Large Vision

George Müller was a native German (a Prussian). He was born in Krop-penstaedt on September 27, 1805, and lived almost the entire nineteenth century. He died March 10, 1898, at the age of ninety-two. He saw the great Awakening of 1859, which, he said, "led to the conversion of hundreds of thousands."[1] He did follow-up work for D. L. Moody,[2] preached for Charles Spurgeon,[3] and inspired the missionary faith of Hudson Taylor.[4]

He spent most of his life in Bristol, England, and pastored the same church there for over sixty-six years—a kind of independent, premillennial,[5] Calvinistic[6] Baptist[7] church that celebrated the Lord's supper weekly[8] and admitted non-baptized people into membership.[9] If this sounds unconventional, that would be accurate. He was a maverick not only in his church life, but in almost all the areas of his life. But his

---

[1] George Müller, *A Narrative of Some of the Lord's Dealings with George Müller, Written by Himself, Jehovah Magnified. Addresses by George Müller Complete and Unabridged*, 2 vols. (Muskegon, MI: Dust and Ashes, 2003), 1:646.
[2] Ibid., 2:675.
[3] Arthur T. Pierson, *George Müller of Bristol: His Life of Prayer and Faith* (Grand Rapids, MI: Kregel, 1999), 248. Originally published as "Authorized Memoir" (Old Tappan, NJ: Revell, 1899).
[4] Ibid., 354.
[5] Müller, *A Narrative*, 1:41.
[6] Ibid., 1:39–40.
[7] Ibid., 1:53.
[8] Ibid., 1:191.
[9] Ibid., 1:140.

eccentricities were almost all large-hearted and directed outward for the good of others. A. T. Pierson, who wrote the biography that Müller's son-in-law endorsed as authoritative,[10] captured the focus of this big-hearted eccentricity when he said that Müller "devised large and liberal things for the Lord's cause."[11]

A New and Different Institution

In 1834 (when he was twenty-eight), Müller founded the Scripture Knowledge Institution for Home and Abroad[12] because he was disillusioned with the postmillennialism, the liberalism, and the worldly strategies (such as going into debt[13]) of existing mission organizations.[14] This Institution eventually developed five branches that oversaw: (1) schools for children and adults to teach Bible knowledge, (2) Bible distribution, (3) book and tract distribution, (4) missionary support, and (5) "to board, clothe and Scripturally educate *destitute* children who have lost BOTH parents by death."[15]

The accomplishments of all five branches were significant. In Müller's own words, here is a summary of accomplishments up to May 1868:

> Above Sixteen Thousand Five Hundred children or grown up persons were taught in the various Schools, entirely supported by the Institution; more than Forty-Four Thousand and Five Hundred Copies of the Bible, and above Forty Thousand and Six Hundred New Testaments, and above Twenty Thousand other smaller portions of the Holy Scriptures, in various languages, were circulated from the formation of the Institution up to May 26, 1868; and about Thirty-one Millions of Tracts and Books, likewise in several languages, were circulated. There were, likewise, from the commencement, Missionaries assisted by the funds of the Institution, and of late years more than One Hundred and Twenty in number. On this Object alone Seventy six Thousand One Hundred and Thirty-seven Pounds were expended from the beginning, up to May 26, 1868. Also 2,412 Orphans were under our care,

---

[10] Pierson, *George Müller*, 13.

[11] Ibid., 264.

[12] Müller, *A Narrative*, 1:80.

[13] "Are you in debt? Then make confession of sin respecting it. Sincerely confess to the Lord that you have sinned against Rom. xiii. 8. And if you are resolved no more to contract debt, whatever may be the result, and you are waiting on the Lord, and truly trust in Him, your present debts will soon be paid. Are you out of debt? then whatever your future want may be, be resolved, in the strength of Jesus, rather to suffer the greatest privation, whilst waiting upon God for help, than to use unscriptural means, such as borrowing, taking goods on credit, etc., to deliver yourselves. This way needs but to be tried, in order that its excellency may be enjoyed." Ibid., 1:251.

[14] Ibid., 1:80–81.

[15] Ibid., 2:365–75. The italics and capital letters are Müller's.

and five large houses, at an expense of above One Hundred and Ten Thousand Pounds were erected, for the accommodation of 2,050 Orphans. With regard to the spiritual results, eternity alone can unfold them; yet even in so far as we have already seen fruit, we have abundant *cause for* praise and thanksgiving.[16]

A Lover of Orphans

But of all these accomplishments of the Institution, the one Müller was known for around the world—in his own lifetime, and still today—was the orphan ministry. He built five large orphan houses and cared for 10,024 orphans in his lifetime. When he started in 1834, there were accommodations for thirty-six hundred orphans in all of England, and twice that many children under eight were in prison.[17] One of the great effects of Müller's ministry was to inspire others so that "fifty years after Mr. Müller began his work, at least one hundred thousand orphans were cared for in England alone."[18]

He prayed in millions of dollars (in today's currency) for the orphans, and never asked anyone directly for money. He never took a salary in the last sixty-eight years of his ministry, but trusted God to put in people's hearts to send him what he needed. He never took out a loan or went into debt.[19] And neither he nor the orphans were ever hungry.

A Dream of Missions Come True

He did all this while he was preaching three times a week from 1830 to 1898, at least ten thousand times.[20] And when he turned seventy, he fulfilled a lifelong dream of missionary work for the next seventeen years, until he was eighty-seven. He traveled to forty-two countries,[21] preaching an average of once a day[22] and addressing some three million

---

[16] Ibid., 2:314. The italics are Müller's.
[17] Pierson, *George Müller*, 274.
[18] Ibid.
[19] "In looking back upon the Thirty One years, during which this Institution had been in operation, I had, as will be seen, by the Grace of God, kept to the original principles, on which, for His honour, it was established on March 5, 1834. For 1, during the whole of this time I had avoided going in debt; and never had a period been brought to a close, but I had some money in hand. Great as my trials of faith might have been, I never contracted debt; for I judged, that, if God's time was come for any enlargement, He would also give the means, and that, until He supplied them, I had quietly to wait His time, and not to act before His time was fully come." Müller, *A Narrative*, 2:291. On his view of debt, see also 1:25, 62, 83, 169, 172, 213, 251, 259, 316–17, 403.
[20] Pierson, *George Müller*, 305.
[21] George Müller, *Autobiography of George Müller, or A Million and a Half in Answer to Prayer*, comp. G. Fred Bergin (Denton, TX: Westminster Literature Resources, 2003), ix.
[22] Pierson, *George Müller*, 305.

people.[23] He preached nine times in my hometown of Minneapolis in 1880 (nine years after the founding of Bethlehem Baptist Church, where I served as pastor).

From the end of his travels in 1892 (when he was eighty-seven) until his death in March 1898, he preached in his church and worked for the Scripture Knowledge Institution. At age ninety-two, not long before he died, he wrote, "I have been able, every day and all the day, to work, and that with ease, as seventy years since."[24] He led a prayer meeting at his church on the evening of Wednesday, March 9, 1898. The next day, a cup of tea was taken to him at seven in the morning, but no answer came to the knock on the door. He was found dead on the floor beside his bed.[25]

The funeral was held the following Monday in Bristol, where he had served for sixty-six years. "Tens of thousands of people reverently stood along the route of the simple procession; men left their workshops and offices, women left their elegant homes or humble kitchens, all seeking to pay a last token of respect."[26] A thousand children gathered for a service at the Orphan House No. 3. They had now "for a second time lost a 'father.'"[27]

Precious Wives

Müller had been married twice: to Mary Groves when he was twenty-five and to Susannah Sangar when he was sixty-six. Mary bore him four children. Two were stillborn. One son, Elijah, died when he was a year old. Müller's daughter Lydia married James Wright, who succeeded him as the head of the Institution. But she died in 1890 at fifty-seven years of age. Five years later, Müller lost his second wife, just three years before he died. And so he outlived his family and was left alone with his Savior, his church, and two thousand children. He had been married to Mary for thirty-nine years and to Susannah for twenty-three years. He preached Mary's funeral sermon when he was sixty-four[28] and preached Susannah's funeral sermon when he was ninety.[29] It's what he said in the face of this loss and pain that gives us the key to his life.

---

[23] Ibid., 257.
[24] Cited in ibid., 283.
[25] Ibid., 285.
[26] Ibid., 285–86.
[27] Ibid., 286.
[28] Ibid., 2:389–401.
[29] Pierson, *George Müller*, 279.

Mary's Death and the Key to His Life

We have the full text of his message at Mary's funeral and we have his own recollections of this loss. To feel the force of what he said, we have to know that they loved each other deeply and enjoyed each other in the work they shared:

> Were we happy? Verily we were. With every year our happiness increased more and more. I never saw my beloved wife at any time, when I met her unexpectedly anywhere in Bristol, without being delighted so to do. I never met her even in the Orphan Houses, without my heart being delighted so to do. Day by day, as we met in our dressing room, at the Orphan Houses, to wash our hands before dinner and tea, I was delighted to meet her, and she was equally pleased to see me. Thousands of times I told her—"My darling, I never saw you at any time, since you became my wife, without my being delighted to see you."[30]

Then came the diagnosis: "When I heard what Mr. Pritchard's judgment was, viz., that the malady was rheumatic fever, I naturally expected the worst. . . . My heart was nigh to be broken on account of the depth of my affection."[31] The one who had seen God answer ten thousand prayers for the support of the orphan did not get what he asked this time. Or did he?

Twenty minutes after four on the Lord's Day, February 6, 1870, Mary died. "I fell on my knees and thanked God for her release, and for having taken her to Himself, and asked the Lord to help and support us."[32] He recalled later how he strengthened himself during these hours. And here we see the key to his life:

> The last portion of Scripture which I read to my precious wife was this: "The Lord God is a sun and shield, the Lord will give grace and glory, no good thing will he withhold from them that walk uprightly." Now, if we have believed in the Lord Jesus Christ, we have received grace, we are partakers of grace, and to all such he will give glory also. I said to myself, with regard to the latter part, "no good thing will he withhold from them that walk uprightly"—I am in myself a poor worthless sinner, but I have been saved by the blood of Christ; and I do not live in sin, I walk uprightly before God. Therefore, if it is really good for me, my darling wife will be raised up again;

[30] Müller, *A Narrative*, 2:392–93.
[31] Ibid., 2:398.
[32] Ibid., 2:400.

sick as she is. God will restore her again. But if she is not restored again, then it would not be a good thing for me. And so my heart was at rest. I was satisfied with God. And all this springs, as I have often said before, from taking God at his word, believing what he says.[33]

Here is the cluster of unshakable convictions and experiences that are the key to Müller's remarkable life. "I am in myself a poor worthless sinner." "I have been saved by the blood of Christ." "I do not live in sin." "God is sovereign over life and death. If it is good for her and for me, she will be restored again. If it is not, she won't." "My heart is at rest." "I am satisfied with God."

All this comes from taking God at his word. There you see the innermost being of George Müller and the key to his life—the Word of God, revealing his sin, revealing his Savior, revealing God's sovereignty, revealing God's goodness, revealing God's promise, awakening his faith, satisfying his soul. "I was satisfied with God."

The Gift of Faith vs. the Grace of Faith

So, were his prayers for Mary answered? To understand how Müller himself would answer this question, we have to see the way he distinguished between the extraordinary *gift* of faith and the more ordinary *grace* of faith. He constantly insisted, when people put him on a pedestal, that he did *not* have the gift of faith just because he would pray for his own needs and the needs of the orphans, and the money would arrive in remarkable ways:

> Think not, dear reader, that I have *the gift of faith*, that is, that gift of which we read in 1 Corinthians 12:9, and which is mentioned along with "the gifts of healing," "the working of miracles," "prophecy," and that on that account I am able to trust in the Lord. *It is true* that the faith, which I am enabled to exercise, is altogether God's own gift; it is true that He alone supports it, and that He alone can increase it; it is true that, moment by moment, I depend upon Him for it, and that, if I were only one moment left to myself, my faith would utterly fail; but *it is not true* that my faith is that gift of faith which is spoken of in 1 Corinthians 12:9.[34]

---

[33] Ibid., 2:745. In the actual funeral sermon, Müller took as a text Psalm 119:68, "Thou art good, and doest good" (KJV). He opened it like this: "'The Lord is good, and doeth good,' all will be according to His own blessed character. Nothing but that, which is good, like Himself, can proceed from Him. If he pleases to take my dearest wife, it will be good, like Himself. What I have to do, as His child, is to be satisfied with what my Father does, that I may glorify Him. After this my soul not only aimed, but this, my soul, by God's grace, attained to. I was satisfied with God." Ibid., 2:398–99.
[34] Ibid., 1:302. The italics are Müller's.

The reason he is so adamant about this is that his whole life—especially in the way he supported the orphans by faith and prayer without asking anyone but God for money—was consciously planned to encourage Christians that God could really be trusted to meet their needs. We will never understand Müller's passion for the orphan ministry if we don't see that the good of the orphans was second to this.

> The three chief reasons for establishing an Orphan-House are: 1) That God may be glorified, should He be pleased to furnish me with the means, in its being seen that it is not a vain thing to trust in Him; and that thus the faith of His children may be strengthened. 2) The spiritual welfare of fatherless and motherless children. 3) Their temporal welfare.[35]

Make no mistake about it: the order of those three goals is intentional. He makes that explicit over and over in his *Narrative*: *the orphan houses exist to display that God can be trusted and to encourage believers to take him at his word*. This was a deep sense of calling with Müller. He said that God had given him the mercy of "being able to take God by His word and to rely upon it."[36] He was grieved that "so many believers . . . were harassed and distressed in mind, or brought guilt on their consciences, on account of not trusting in the Lord."[37] This grace that he had to trust God's promises, and this grief that so many believers didn't trust his promises, shaped Müller's entire life. This was his supreme passion: *to display with open proofs that God could be trusted with the practical affairs of life*. This was the higher aim of building the orphan houses and supporting them by asking God, not people, for money:

> It seemed to me best done, by the establishing of an Orphan-House. It needed to be something which could be seen, even by the natural eye. Now, if I, a poor man, simply by prayer and faith, obtained, without asking any individual, the means for establishing and carrying on an Orphan-House: there would be something which, with the Lord's blessing, might be instrumental in strengthening the faith of the children of God besides being a testimony to the consciences of the unconverted, of the reality of the things of God. This, then, was *the primary reason*, for establishing the Orphan-House. . . . The *first and primary object* of the work was, (and still is) that God might be magnified by the fact, that the orphans under my care are provided, with all

---

[35] Ibid., 1:103.
[36] Ibid., 1:105.
[37] Müller, *Autobiography*, 148.

they need, only by prayer and faith, without any one being asked by me or my fellow-laborers, whereby it may be seen, that God is FAITHFUL STILL and HEARS PRAYER STILL.[38]

That was the chief passion and unifying aim of Müller's ministry: *to live a life and lead a ministry in a way that proves God is real, God is trustworthy, and God answers prayer.* He built orphanages the way he did to help Christians trust God. He says it over and over again.[39]

Now we see why he was so adamant that his faith was *not* the gift of faith mentioned in 1 Corinthians 12:9, which only some people have, but was the grace of faith that all Christians should have.[40] Now we are ready to see this crucial distinction he made between the gift of faith and the grace of faith. His entire aim in life hung on this. If Christians simply say, "Müller is in a class by himself; he has the gift of faith," then we are all off the hook and he is no longer a prod and proof and inspiration for how we ought to live. Here is what he says:

> The difference between the *gift* and the *grace* of faith seems to me this. According to the *gift* of faith I am able to do a thing, or believe that a thing will come to pass, the not doing of which, or the not believing of which would not be sin; according to the *grace* of faith I am able to do a thing, or believe that a thing will come to pass, respecting which I have the word of God as the ground to rest upon, and, therefore, the not doing it, or the not believing it would be sin. For instance, the gift of faith would be needed, to believe that a sick person should be restored again though there is no human probability: for there is no promise to that effect; the grace of faith is needed to believe that the Lord will give me the necessaries of life, if I first seek the kingdom of God and His righteousness: for there is a promise to that effect. Matthew 6:33.[41]

Müller did not think he had any biblical ground for being certain that God would spare his wife Mary. He admits that a few times in his life he was given "something like the gift (not grace) of faith so that unconditionally I could ask and look for an answer,"[42] but he did not

---

[38] Müller, *A Narrative*, 1:105. Italics added. The capital letters are his.
[39] Ibid., 1:131, 250, 285, 317, 443, 486, 548, 558, etc.
[40] "All believers are called upon, in the simple confidence of faith, to cast all their burdens upon Him, to trust in Him for every thing, and not only to make every thing a subject of prayer, but to expect answers to their petitions which they have asked according to His will, and in the name of the Lord Jesus." Ibid., 1:302.
[41] Ibid., 1:65.
[42] Ibid.

have that rare gift in Mary's case. And so he prayed for her healing conditionally—namely, if it would be good for them and for God's glory. But most deeply he prayed that they would be satisfied in God, whatever God did. And God did answer that prayer by helping Müller believe Psalm 84:11: "No good thing will God withhold." God withheld no good thing from him, and he was satisfied with God's sovereign will. All this, he says, "springs . . . from taking God at his word, believing what he says."[43]

How Did Müller Get to This Position?

Let's go back and let Müller tell the story—essential parts of which are omitted from all the biographies I have looked at.

His father was an unbeliever, and George grew up a liar and a thief, by his own testimony.[44] His mother died when he was fourteen, and he records no impact that this loss had on him except that while she was dying he was roving the streets with his friends, "half intoxicated."[45] He went on living a bawdy life, then found himself in prison for stealing when he was sixteen years old. His father paid to get him out, beat him, and took him to live in another town (Schoenbeck). Müller used his academic skills to make money by tutoring in Latin, French, and mathematics. Finally his father sent him to the University of Halle to study divinity and prepare for the ministry because that would be a good living. Neither he nor George had any spiritual aspirations. Of the nine hundred divinity students in Halle, Müller later estimated that maybe nine feared the Lord.[46]

Then, on a Saturday afternoon in the middle of November 1825, when Müller was twenty years old, he was invited to a Bible study and, by the grace of God, felt the desire to go. "It was to me as if I had found something after which I had been seeking all my life long. I immediately wished to go."[47] "They read the Bible, sang, prayed, and read a printed sermon."[48] To his amazement, Müller said, "the whole made a deep impression on me. I was happy; though, if I had been asked, why I was happy I could not have clearly explained it. . . . I have not the least

[43] Ibid., 2:745.
[44] Ibid., 1:10.
[45] Ibid.
[46] Ibid., 1:16.
[47] Ibid., 1:17.
[48] Ibid., 1:16.

doubt, that on that evening, [God] began a work of grace in me. . . . That evening was the turning point in my life."[49]

That's true. But there was another turning point four years later that the biographies do not open for the reader, but which, for Müller, was absolutely decisive in shaping the way he viewed God and the way he did ministry.

A Decisive Turning Point: Confidence in the Sovereign Goodness of God

He came to England in the hope of being a missionary with the London Missionary Society. Soon he found his theology and ministry convictions turning away from the LMS, until there was a break. In the meantime, a momentous encounter happened.

Müller became sick (thank God for providential sickness!), and in the summer of 1829, he went for recovery to a town called Teignmouth. There, in a little chapel called Ebenezer, he made at least two crucial discoveries: the preciousness of reading and meditating on the Word of God[50] and the truth of the doctrines of grace.[51] For ten days Müller lived with a nameless man who changed his life forever: "Through the instrumentality of this brother, the Lord bestowed a great blessing upon me, for which I shall have cause to thank Him throughout eternity."[52]

> Before this period I had been much opposed to the doctrines of election, particular redemption, and final persevering grace; so much so that, a few days after my arrival at Teignmouth, I called election a devilish doctrine. . . . I knew nothing about the choice of God's people, and did not believe that the child of God, when once made so, was safe for ever. . . . But now I was brought to examine these precious truths by the word of God.[53]

Müller was led to embrace the doctrines of grace—the robust, mission-minded, soul-winning, orphan-loving Calvinism that marked William Carey, who died in 1834, and that would mark Charles Spurgeon, who

---

[49] Ibid., 1:17.
[50] "For when it pleased the Lord in August, 1829, to bring me really to the Scriptures, my life and walk became *very* different." Ibid., 1:28–29.
[51] "Between July, 1829, and January, 1830, I had seen the leading truths connected with the second coming of our Lord Jesus; I had apprehended the all-sufficiency of the Holy Scriptures as our rule, and the Holy Spirit as our teacher; I had seen clearly the precious doctrines of the grace of God, about which I had been uninstructed for nearly four years after my conversion." Ibid., 2:720.
[52] Ibid., 1:39.
[53] Ibid., 1:46.

was born in 1834. The doctrines changed his life. They had a profound effect on the holiness of his behavior:

> Being made willing to have no glory of my own in the conversion of sinners, but to consider myself merely as an instrument; and being made willing to receive what the Scriptures said; I went to the Word, reading the New Testament from the beginning, with a particular reference to these truths. To my great astonishment I found that the passages which speak decidedly for election and persevering grace, were about four times as many as those which speak apparently against these truths; and even those few, shortly after, when I had examined and understood them, served to confirm me in the above doctrines.
>
> As to the effect which my belief in these doctrines had on me, I am constrained to state, for God's glory, that though I am still exceedingly weak, and by no means so dead to the lusts of the flesh, and the lust of the eyes, and the pride of life, as I might and as I ought to be, yet, by the grace of God, I have walked more closely with Him since that period. My life has not been so variable, and I may say that I have lived much more for God than before.[54]

About forty years later, in 1870, Müller spoke to some young believers about the importance of what had happened to him at Teignmouth. He said that his preaching had been fruitless for four years from 1825 to 1829 in Germany, but then he came to England and was taught the doctrines of grace:

> In the course of time I came to this country, and it pleased God then to show to me the doctrines of grace in a way in which I had not seen them before. At first I hated them, "If this were true *I* could do nothing at all in the conversion of sinners, as all would depend upon God and the working of His Spirit." But when it pleased God to reveal these truths to me, and my heart was brought to such a state that I could say, "I am not only content simply to be a hammer, an axe, or a saw, in God's hands; but I shall count it an honor to be taken up and used by Him in any way; and if sinners are converted through my instrumentality, from my inmost soul I will give Him all the glory"; the Lord gave me to see fruit; the Lord gave me to see fruit in abundance; sinners were converted by scores; and ever since God has used me in one way or other in His service.[55]

---

[54] Ibid. "Thus, I say, the electing love of God in Christ (when I have been able to *realize it*) has often been the means of producing holiness, instead of leading me into sin." Ibid., 1:40.
[55] Ibid., 1:752.

Asking God (and Using Means) to Move Men's Hearts

This discovery of the all-encompassing sovereignty of God became the foundation of Müller's confidence in God to answer his prayers for money. He gave up his regular salary.[56] He refused to ask people directly for money:

> [The gifts have been given to me] without one single individual having been asked by me for any thing. The reason why I have refrained altogether from soliciting any one for help is, that the hand of God evidently might be seen in the matter, that thus my fellow-believers might be encouraged more and more to trust in Him, and that also those who know not the Lord, may have a fresh proof that, indeed, it is not a vain thing to pray to God.[57]

He prayed and published his reports about the goodness of God and the answers to his prayer. These yearly reports were circulated around the world, and they clearly had a huge effect in motivating people to give to the orphan work.

Müller walked a narrow line: on the one hand, he wanted to give God all the credit for answering prayer for meeting all his needs, and so he did not ask people directly for help. But on the other hand, he wanted this work of God to be known so that Christians would be encouraged to trust God for answered prayer. But in the very publication of the work of God, he was making known how much he depended on the generosity of God's people, and thus motivating them by human means to give.

Müller knew that God used means. In fact, he loved to say, "Work with all your might; but trust not in the least in your work."[58] He was open and unashamed in saying that the reports of God's provision motivated people to give:

> I do not mean to say that God does not use the Reports as instruments in procuring us means. They are written in order that I may thus give an ac-

---

[56] "Upon our first coming to Bristol we declined accepting anything in the shape of regular salary. . . . We did not act thus because we thought it wrong that those who were ministered unto in spiritual things should minister unto us in temporal things; but . . . because we would not have the liberality of the brethren to be a matter of constraint, but willingly." Ibid., 1:275.

[57] Ibid., 1:132.

[58] Ibid., 1:611. "This is one of the great secrets in connexion with successful service for the Lord; to work as if everything depended upon our diligence, and yet not to rest in the least upon our *exertions*, but upon the blessing of the Lord." Ibid., 2:290. "Speak also for the Lord, as if everything depended on your exertions; yet trust not in the least in your exertions, but in the Lord, who *alone* can cause your efforts to be made effectual." Ibid., 2:279.

count of my stewardship, but particularly, in order that, by these printed ac-
counts of the work, the chief end of this Institution may be answered, which
is to raise another public testimony to an unbelieving world, that in these
last days the Living God is still the Living God, listening to the prayers of His
children, and helping those who put their trust in Him; and in order that
believers generally may be benefited and especially be encouraged to trust
in God for everything they may need, and be stirred up to deal in greater
simplicity with God respecting everything connected with their own particular position and circumstances; in short, that the children of God may be
brought to the practical use of the Holy Scriptures, as the word of the Living
God.—But while these are the primary reasons for publishing these Reports,
we doubt not that the Lord has again and again used them as instruments in
leading persons to help us with their means.[59]

But he also insisted that his hope was in God alone, not his exertions
and not the published reports. These means could not account for the
remarkable answers that he received.

Sovereign Goodness

Müller's faith that his prayers for money would be answered was rooted
in the sovereignty of God. When faced with a crisis in having the means
to pay a bill, he would say, "*How* the means are to come, I know not;
but I know that God is almighty, that the hearts of all are in His hands,
and that, if He pleaseth to influence persons, they will send help."[60]
That was the root of his confidence: *God is almighty, the hearts of all
men are in his hands,*[61] *and when God chooses to influence their hearts,
they will give.*

He had come to know and love this absolute sovereignty of God
in the context of the doctrines of *grace*, and therefore he cherished it
mainly as sovereign *goodness*.[62] This gave him a way to maintain a personal peace beyond human understanding in the midst of tremendous

---

[59] Ibid., 1:662.
[60] Ibid., 1:594.
[61] "There is scarcely a country, from whence I have not received donations; yet all come unsolicited, often
anonymously, and in by far the greater number of cases from entire strangers, who are led by God, in answer
to our prayers, to help on this work which was commenced, and is carried on, only in dependence on the
Living God, in whose hands are the hearts of all men." Ibid., 2:387. "Our Heavenly Father has the hearts
of all men at His disposal, and we give ourselves to prayer to Him, and He, in answer to *our* prayers, lays
the necessities of this work on the hearts of his stewards." Ibid., 2:498. "We should not trust in the Reports,
and expect that they would bring in something, but trust in the Living God, who has the hearts of all in
His hands, and to whom all the gold and silver belongs." Ibid., 2:80.
[62] "Remember also, that God delights to bestow blessing, but, generally, as the result of earnest, believing
prayer." Ibid., 2:279.

stress and occasional tragedy. "The Lord never lays more on us," he said, "in the way of chastisement, than our state of heart makes needful; so that whilst He smites with the one hand, He supports with the other."[63] In the face of painful circumstances, he said, "I bow, I am satisfied with the will of my Heavenly Father, I seek by perfect submission to His holy will to glorify Him, I kiss continually the hand that has thus afflicted me."[64]

And when he was about to lose a piece of property that he wanted for the next orphan house, he said, "If the Lord were to take this piece of land from me, *it would be only for the purpose of giving me a still better one; for our Heavenly Father never takes any earthly thing from His children except He means to give them something better instead.*"[65] This is what I mean by confidence in God's sovereign goodness. This confidence was the root of Müller's faith and ministry.

The Aroma of Müller's Calvinism: Satisfaction and Glad Self-Denial

But there was an aroma about Müller's Calvinism that was different from many stereotypes. For him, the sovereign goodness of God served, first and foremost, the satisfaction of the soul. And then the satisfied soul was freed to sacrifice and live a life of simplicity and risk and self-denial and love. But everything flowed from the soul that was first satisfied in the gracious, sovereign God. Müller is clearer on this than anyone I have ever read. He is unashamed to sound almost childishly simple:

> According to my judgment the most important point to be attended to is this: above all things see to it that your souls are happy in the Lord. Other things may press upon you, the Lord's work may even have urgent claims upon your attention, but I deliberately repeat, it is of supreme and paramount importance that you should seek above all things to have your souls truly happy in God Himself! Day by day seek to make this the most important business of your life. This has been my firm and settled condition for the last five and thirty years. For the first four years after my conversion I knew not its vast importance, but now after much experience I specially commend this point to the notice of my younger brethren and sisters in Christ:

---

[63] Ibid., 1:61.
[64] Ibid., 2:401.
[65] Ibid., 1:505. The italics are Müller's.

the secret of all true effectual service is joy in God, having experimental acquaintance and fellowship with God Himself.[66]

Why is this the "most important" thing? Why is daily happiness in God "of supreme and paramount importance"? One answer he gives is that it glorifies God. After telling about one of his wife's illnesses when he almost lost her, he says, "I have . . . stated this case so fully, to show the deep importance to be satisfied with the will of God, not only for the sake of glorifying Him, but as the best way, in the end, of having given to us the desire of our hearts."[67] Being satisfied in God is "of supreme and paramount importance" because it glorifies God. It shows that God is gloriously satisfying.

But there is another answer, namely, that happiness in God is the only source of durable and God-honoring self-denial and sacrifice and love. In reference to lifestyle changes and simplicity, he says:

We should begin the thing in a right way, *i.e.* aim after the right state of heart; begin *inwardly* instead of *outwardly*. If otherwise, it will not last. We shall look back, or even get into a worse state than we were before. But oh! how different if joy in God leads us to any little act of self denial. How gladly do we do it then![68]

"Glad self-denial" is the aroma of Müller's Calvinism. How can there be such a thing? He answers: "Self-denial is not so much an *impoverishment* as a *postponement*: we make a sacrifice of a present good for the sake of a future and greater good."[69] Therefore, happiness in God is of "supreme importance" because it is the key to love that sacrifices and takes risks. "Whatever be done . . . in the way of giving up, or self-denial, or deadness to the world, should result from the joy we have in God."[70]

A well-to-do woman visited him once to discuss a possible gift to the Institution. He did not ask her for the money. But when she was gone, he asked God for it. And the way he did reveals his understanding of how the human heart works:

---

[66] Ibid., 2:730–31. "I saw more clearly than ever, that the first great and primary business to which I ought to attend every day was, to have my soul happy in the Lord. The first thing to be concerned about was not, how much I might serve the Lord, how I might glorify the Lord; but how I might get my soul into a happy state, and how *my* inner man might be nourished." Ibid., 1:271.
[67] Ibid., 2:406.
[68] Ibid., 1:355.
[69] Cited in Pierson, *George Müller*, 374.
[70] Müller, *A Narrative*, 1:355.

After she was gone, I asked the Lord, that He would be pleased to make this dear sister so happy in Himself and enable her so to realize her true riches and inheritance in the Lord Jesus, and the reality of her heavenly calling, that she might be constrained by the love of Christ, cheerfully to lay down this 500 [pounds] at His feet.[71]

How Do We Get and Keep Our Happiness in God?

If happiness in God is "of supreme and paramount importance" because it is the spring of sacrificial love that honors God, then the crucial question becomes, how do we get it and keep it?

> But in what way shall we attain to this settled happiness of soul? How shall we learn to enjoy God? How obtain such an all-sufficient soul-satisfying portion in him as shall *enable us to let go the things of this world* as vain and worthless in comparison? I answer, This happiness is to be obtained through the study of the Holy Scriptures. God has therein revealed Himself unto us in the face of Jesus Christ.[72]

Happiness in God comes from seeing God revealed to us in the face of Jesus Christ through the Scriptures. "In them . . . we become acquainted with the character of God. Our eyes are divinely opened to see what a lovely Being God is! And this good, gracious, loving, heavenly Father is ours, our portion for time and for eternity."[73] Knowing God is the key to being happy in God:

> The more we know of God, the happier we are. . . . When we became a little acquainted with God . . . our true happiness . . . commenced; and the more we become acquainted with him, the more truly happy we become. What will make us so exceedingly happy in heaven? It will be the fuller knowledge of God.[74]

Therefore, the most crucial means of fighting for joy in God is to immerse oneself in the Scriptures, where we see God in Christ most clearly. When he was seventy-one years old, Müller spoke to younger believers:

> Now in brotherly love and affection I would give a few hints to my younger fellow-believers as to the way in which to keep up spiritual enjoyment. It is absolutely

---

[71] Ibid., 1:326.
[72] Ibid., 2:731.
[73] Ibid., 2:732.
[74] Ibid., 2:740.

needful in order that happiness in the Lord may continue, that the Scriptures be regularly read. These are God's appointed means for the nourishment of the inner man.... Consider it, and ponder over it.... Especially we should read regularly through the Scriptures, consecutively, and not pick out here and there a chapter. If we do, we remain spiritual dwarfs. I tell you so affectionately. For the first four years after my conversion I made no progress, because I neglected the Bible. But when I regularly read on through the whole with reference to my own heart and soul, I directly made progress. Then my peace and joy continued more and more. Now I have been doing this for 47 years. I have read through the whole Bible about 100 times and I always find it fresh when I begin again. Thus my peace and joy have increased more and more.[75]

Müller was seventy-one, and he would live and read on for another twenty-one years. But he never changed his strategy for satisfaction in God. When he was seventy-six, he wrote the same thing he did when he was sixty, "I saw more clearly than ever, that the first great and primary business to which I ought to attend every day was, to have my soul happy in the Lord."[76] And the means stayed the same:

I saw that the most important thing I had to do was to give myself to the read-ing of the word of God, and to meditation on it.... What is the food of the inner man? Not *prayer*, but *the word of God*; and ... not the simple reading of the word of God, so that it only passes through our minds, just as water runs through a pipe, but considering what we read, pondering over it, and applying it to our hearts.[77]

This brings us back to the satisfaction of Müller's soul at the death of his wife, Mary. Remember, he said: "My heart was at rest. I was sat-isfied with God. And all this springs, as I have often said before, from taking God at his word, believing what he says."[78]

The aim of George Müller's life was to glorify God by helping people take God at his word.[79] To that end, he saturated his soul with the Word of God. At one point, he said that he read the Bible five or ten times more than he read any other books.[80] His aim was to see God in

---

[75] Ibid., 2:834.
[76] Ibid., 1:271.
[77] Ibid., 1:272–73.
[78] Ibid., 2:745.
[79] "I have not served a hard Master, and that is what I delight to show. For, to speak well of His name, that thus my beloved fellow-pilgrims, who may read this, may be encouraged to trust in Him, is the chief purpose of my writing." Ibid., 1:63.
[80] Ibid., 1:101.

Jesus Christ crucified and risen from the dead in order that he might maintain the happiness of his soul in God. By this deep satisfaction in God, Müller was set free from the fears and lusts of the world. And in this freedom of love, he chose a strategy of ministry and style of life that put the reality and trustworthiness and beauty of God on display. To use his own words, his life became a "visible proof to the unchangeable faithfulness of the Lord."[81]

Müller was sustained in this extraordinary life by his deep convictions that God is sovereign over the human heart and can turn it where he wills in answer to prayer; that God is sovereign over life and death; and that God is good in his sovereignty and withholds no good thing from those who walk uprightly. He strengthened himself continually in his wife's final illness with the words of a hymn:

> Best of blessings He'll provide us,
> Nought but good shall e'er betide us,
> Safe to glory He will guide us,
> Oh how He loves![82]

An Exhortation and Plea

I will let Müller have the closing word of exhortation and pleading for us to join him in the path of radical, joyful faith:

> My dear Christian reader, will you not try this way? Will you not know for yourself . . . the preciousness and the happiness of this way of casting all your cares and burdens and necessities upon God? This way is as open to you as to me. . . . Every one is invited and commanded to trust in the Lord, to trust in Him with all his heart, and to cast his burden upon Him, and to call upon Him in the day of trouble. Will you not do this, my dear brethren in Christ? I long that you may do so. I desire that you may taste the sweetness of that state of heart, in which, while surrounded by difficulties and necessities, you can yet be at peace, because you know that the living God, your Father in heaven, cares for you.[83]

---

[81] Ibid., 1:105.
[82] Ibid., 2:399.
[83] Ibid., 1:521.

It is *only* in the trial of GOD's grace that its *beauty and power* can be seen. Then all our trials of temper, circumstances, provocation, sickness, disappointment, bereavement, will but give a higher burnish to the mirror, and enable us to reflect more fully and more perfectly the glory and blessedness of our MASTER.
Hudson Taylor

3

Hudson Taylor

An Enduring and Expansive Enjoyment of Union with Jesus Christ

Our focus in this chapter will be on how Hudson Taylor experienced union with Christ. The warning flags go up immediately, because it is well known that Taylor was significantly influenced by the Keswick Movement and its views of sanctification, which, in the worst exponents, are seriously flawed. My conclusion is that Taylor was *not* one of those worst exponents, and that he was protected from Keswick's worst flaws by his allegiance to the Bible, his experience of lifelong suffering and sorrow, and his belief in the sovereignty of God.[1]

There Is More of God Yet to Be Enjoyed

All of this means that there are glorious things to see in the life of Hudson Taylor and wonderful lessons to be learned about abiding in Christ and about faith and prayer and obedience and suffering. Whatever else Keswick's teaching may have gotten wrong, it was not wrong to say to all Christians that there is more joy, more peace, more love, more power, and more fruit to be enjoyed in Christ than we are presently enjoying.

[1] It is important to note that Keswick teaching has changed considerably in recent decades. As Andy Naselli writes: "Beginning in the 1920s, the Keswick Convention's view of sanctification began to shift from the view promoted by the leaders of the early convention. William Scroggie (1877–1958) led that transformation to a view of sanctification closer to the Reformed view. The official Keswick Convention that now hosts the annual Keswick conferences holds a Reformed view of sanctification and invites speakers who are confessionally reformed." Andrew D. Naselli, "Why 'Let Go and Let God' Is a Bad Idea," *Tabletalk*, October 2011, 74.

- 1 Thessalonians 4:1—"As you received from us how you ought to walk and to please God, just as you are doing, . . . do so *more and more.*"
- 1 Thessalonians 4:9–10—"Concerning brotherly love . . . we urge you, brothers, to do this *more and more.*"
- Philippians 1:9—"It is my prayer that your love may abound *more and more.*"
- Ephesians 5:18–19—"Be *filled* with the Spirit, addressing one another in psalms and hymns and spiritual songs, singing and making melody to the Lord with your heart."
- 1 Peter 1:2—"May grace and peace *be multiplied* to you."
- And most amazing of all: Ephesians 3:16–19—"According to the riches of his glory, . . . may [the Father] grant you to be strengthened with power through his Spirit in your inner being, so that Christ may dwell in your hearts through faith—that you, being rooted and grounded in love, may have strength to comprehend with all the saints what is the breadth and length and height and depth, and to know the love of Christ that surpasses knowledge, that you may be *filled with all the fullness of God.*"

Any view of the Christian life that does not promote the desire for, and the pursuit of, this inexpressible fullness—this more—is as defective as the view that says its usual way of coming is through a single crisis experience of full consecration.

A Prayer for the Reader

The link between Taylor's pursuit of this fullness and the legacy of the China Inland Mission is enormously instructive. It is relevant for everyone who wants to experience the peace that passes all understanding (Phil. 4:7). It is relevant for any one of you who wants to see your life bear fruit wonderfully out of proportion with your limitations.

That is what I hope God does with this story of Hudson Taylor: lead you into a deeper experience of union with Christ and inspire you to venture more for his glory than you ever have.

When Taylor wrote one of his most famous sayings, "Depend upon it, GOD's work done in GOD's way will never lack GOD's supplies,"[2] he meant every kind of need that we have—money and health and faith and peace and strength. And that is my prayer for this chapter: that

---

[2] Cited in Frederick Howard Taylor and Geraldine Taylor, *Hudson Taylor and the China Inland Mission: The Growth of a Work of God* (Littleton, CO; Mississauga, ON; Kent, TN: OMF Books, 1995), 42.

you will see and experience new possibilities for your life—more faith, more joy, more peace, more love, and all the money you need to do his will—which may be none.

And all of that is because of your union with Christ, as is put so well in one of Taylor's favorite texts: "My God will supply every need of yours according to his riches in glory *in Christ Jesus*" (Phil. 4:19). And then, because of all that, I pray you will launch into some venture, some dream of ministry, beyond all your real or perceived inadequacies, for the glory of Christ.

He Was Not a Short-Lived Meteorite

Unlike Robert and Hannah Smith, who were among those who gave early influence to Keswick thinking, Taylor did not make shipwreck of his faith. From his conversion to his death at age seventy-three in 1905, he was unwavering in his allegiance to Jesus Christ and Christ's purpose to evangelize all the provinces of China. Whatever his views of the Christian life, they served him well, and the legacy of his steadfast faith and obedience and fruitfulness is astonishing. He did not have a flashy experience and then fade away. He had an experience indeed, and then he proved Christ over and over, as the old song says: "Jesus, Jesus, how I trust Him, How I've proved Him o'er and o'er."[3] So his life is worth looking at.

A Dramatic Conversion

Hudson Taylor was born May 21, 1832, at Barnsley, England, into a devout Methodist home. At the age of seventeen, he was dramatically converted through the prayers of his mother. His friend Charles Spurgeon tells the story dramatically. Spurgeon was two years younger than Taylor, and, as we have seen, a great admirer of Taylor's faith and zeal for the gospel. They knew each other from at least 1864, when Taylor took his wife, Maria, and Wang Lae-djün to the Metropolitan Tabernacle. Spurgeon invited him to address a weekday meeting and to give a lecture on China. "A mutual admiration which never faded grew from that beginning."[4] Here's how Spurgeon weaves the story of his friend's conversion into one of his sermons:

---

[3] From the hymn "'Tis So Sweet to Trust in Jesus" by Louisa M. R. Stead, 1882.
[4] Alvyn Austin, *China's Millions: The China Inland Mission and Late Qing Society, 1832–1905* (Grand Rapids, MI: Eerdmans, 2007), 87.

Oh, that some here may have faith to claim at this moment the salvation of their friends! May desire be wrought into expectancy, and hope become certainty! Like Jacob at Jabbok, may we lay hold of God, saying, "I will not let thee go, except thou bless me." To such faith the Lord will give a quick response. He that will not be denied shall not be denied.

My friend, Hudson Taylor, who has done such a wonderful work for China, is an instance of this. Brought up in a godly home, he, as a young man, tried to imitate the lives of his parents, and failing in his own strength to make himself better, he swung to the other extreme, and began to entertain skeptical notions. One day, when his mother was from home, a great yearning after her boy possessed her, and she went up to her room to plead with God that "even now" he would save him. If I remember aright, she said that she would not leave the room until she had the assurance that her boy would be brought to Christ.

At length her faith triumphed, and she rose quite certain that all was well, and that "even now" her son was saved. What was he doing at that time? Having half an hour to spare, he wandered into his father's library, and aimlessly took down one book after another to find some short and interesting passage to divert his mind. He could not find what he wanted in any of the books; so, seeing a narrative tract, he took it up with the intention of reading the story, and putting it down when the sermon part of it began. As he read, he came to the words "the finished work of Christ", and almost at the very moment in which his mother, who was miles away, claimed his soul of God, light came into his heart. He saw that it was by the finished work of Christ that he was to be saved; and kneeling in his father's library, he sought and found the life of God.

Some days afterwards, when his mother returned, he said to her, "I have some news to tell you." "Oh, I know what it is!" she answered, smiling, "You have given yourself to God." "Who told you?" he asked, in astonishment. "God told me," she said, and together they praised him, who, at the same moment, gave the faith to the mother, and the life to the son, and who has since made him such a blessing to the world. It was the mother's faith, claiming the blessing "even now", that did it. I tell you this remarkable incident that many others may be stirred up to the same immediate and importunate desire for the salvation of their children and relatives. There are some things we must always pray for with submission as to whether it is the will of God to bestow them upon us: but for the salvation of men and women we may ask without a fear. God delights to save and to bless; and when the faith is given to us to expect an immediate answer to such a prayer, thrice happy are we. Seek such faith even now, I beseech you, "even now."[5]

---

[5] C. H. Spurgeon, *The Metropolitan Tabernacle Pulpit Sermons*, vol. 38 (London: Passmore & Alabaster, 1892), 151–52.

The newly converted Taylor was at first part of the Wesleyan Methodist Connection, the church of his family. But his independent, Bible-oriented spirit showed itself very soon. In his application to the Chinese Evangelisation Society a year later, he wrote:

> At first I joined the Wesleyan Methodists, as my parents and friends were members of that body. But not being able to reconcile the late proceedings with the doctrines and precepts of Holy Scripture, I withdrew, and am at present united to the branch Society.[6]

Alvyn Austin comments:

> Having left the church of his fathers, Hudson Taylor . . . never "joined" another church, though he felt free to share communion with all. He was (re)baptized by the Plymouth Brethren and in a burst of enthusiasm, baptized his sister Amelia in a local stream. Later he was ordained by the Baptists, though this too was not publicized lest the CIM be identified with one church which would reduce its interdenominational appeal.[7]

No Debt, New Marriage

Within four years, Taylor was in China. During these four years, he entered rudimentary medical studies as an apprentice to Robert Hardey. Then, at the age of twenty-one, on September 19, 1853, he sailed for China with the Chinese Evangelisation Society. He had no formal training in theology or missions. Five and a half months later, he landed in Shanghai on March 1, 1854.

He learned the language quickly and, in his first two years in China, engaged in ten extended evangelistic journeys to the interior. But after four years, Taylor resigned from the Chinese Evangelisation Society because he had a deep conviction—shared with Spurgeon and George Müller—that borrowing money to sustain Christ's work was wrong:

> To borrow money implied, to my mind, a contradiction of Scripture—a confession that GOD had withheld some good thing, and a determination to get for ourselves what He had not given. . . . To satisfy my conscience I

---

[6] Cited in Austin, *China's Millions*, 47.
[7] Ibid. Even into the 1890s, the CIM was combatting rumors that it required members of the mission to be rebaptized as Baptists. Taylor replied, "'The statements you have heard of proselytism are entirely false. . . . Though a Baptist myself,' . . . the CIM had set aside certain districts for Baptists, Presbyterians, Anglicans, Methodists, and Plymouth Brethren." Cited in ibid., 342.

was therefore compelled to resign connection with the Society which had hitherto supplied my salary.[8]

That was the beginning of a lifetime of never being in financial debt and never explicitly asking anyone for money[9]—following the lead of his hero, Müller.

On January 20, 1858, when he had been in China almost five years, Taylor married another missionary, Maria Dyer. They were married for twelve years. When Maria died at age thirty-three, she had given birth to eight children. Three died at birth and two in childhood, and the ones who lived to adulthood all became missionaries with the mission their father founded, the China Inland Mission.

The Birth of the China Inland Mission

In July 1860, two years into their marriage, Hudson and Maria sailed for England. He was seriously ill with hepatitis, but what seemed like a setback would soon give rise to the most decisive event of his life.[10] His burden for China grew for the next four years. He could not shake the idea that a new mission agency was needed. But he did not know if he could lead it. However, in the same period it took the Americans to fight the Civil War, God birthed in Taylor a dream that would change the history of the largest nation on earth. The moment came one Lord's Day on the beach near Brighton, England, which he describes like this:

> On Sunday, June 25th, 1865, unable to bear the sight of a congregation of a thousand or more Christian people rejoicing in their own security, while millions were perishing for lack of knowledge, I wandered out on the sands alone, in great spiritual agony; and there the LORD conquered my unbelief, and I surrendered myself to GOD for this service. I told Him that all the responsibility as to issues and consequences must rest with Him; that as His servant, it was mine to obey and to follow Him—His, to direct, to care for, and to guide me and those who might labour with me. Need I say that peace at once flowed into my burdened heart? There and then I asked Him for twenty-four fellow-workers, two for each of eleven inland provinces which

---

[8] Cited in J. H. Taylor, *A Retrospect*, 3rd ed. (Toronto: China Inland Mission, n.d.), 99.
[9] "Inland China opened to the Gospel largely as an outcome of this life, . . . a mission which has never made an appeal for financial help, yet has never been in debt, that never asks man or woman to join its ranks." Dr. and Mrs. Howard Taylor, *Hudson Taylor's Spiritual Secret*, Kindle edition (May 25, 2013), 2.
[10] "Little did I then realize that this long absence from the work was a necessary step towards the formation of an agency that GOD would bless as He has blessed the China Inland Mission." Cited in M. G. Guinness, *The Story of the China Inland Mission*, 3rd ed. (London: Morgan & Scott, 1894), 1:193.

were without a missionary, and two for Mongolia; and writing the petition on the margin of the Bible I had with me, I returned home with a heart enjoying rest such as it had been a stranger to for months.[11]

That was the birthplace of the China Inland Mission. Taylor was thirty-three years old. The missionaries were to have no guaranteed salaries, they were not to appeal for funds, and they were to adopt Chinese dress and press the gospel to the interior. On May 26, 1866, Hudson, Maria, and their children left England with the largest group of missionaries that had ever sailed to China—sixteen besides themselves. Taylor was to be the leader and settle all disputes.[12] Not everyone appreciated his leadership and the demands he made on himself and everyone else. One missionary accused him of tyranny and had to be dismissed.[13]

The Decisive Moment

Three years later, after Taylor had experienced prolonged frustration with his own temptations and failures in holiness, the epoch-making experience happened—the one that stamps him as a part of the Keswick Movement.

Notice what he was experiencing leading up to the great change. He wrote to his mother:

[The need for your prayer] has never been greater than at present. Envied by some, despised by many, hated by others, often blamed for things I never heard of or had nothing to do with, an innovator on what have become established rules of missionary practice, an opponent of mighty systems of heathen error and superstition, working without precedent in many respects and with few experienced helpers, often sick in body as well as perplexed in mind and embarrassed by circumstances—had not the Lord been specially gracious to me, had not my mind been sustained by the conviction that the work is His and that He is with me, . . . I must have fainted or broken down. But the battle is the Lord's, and He will conquer.

---

[11] Cited in J. H. Taylor, *A Retrospect.*

[12] "We came out as God's children at God's command [was Mr Taylor's simple statement] to do God's work, depending on Him for supplies; to wear native dress and to go inland. I was to be the leader in China. . . . There was no question as to who was to determine points at issue." Cited in Dr. and Mrs. Howard Taylor, *Hudson Taylor's Spiritual Secret,* 110.

[13] "Lewis Nicol, who accused Taylor of tyranny, had to be dismissed. Some CIM missionaries, in the wake of this and other controversies, left to join other missions, but in 1876, with 52 missionaries, CIM constituted one-fifth of the missionary force in China." *Hudson Taylor, Faith Missionary to China,* ChristianHistory.net, August 8, 2008, http://www.christianitytoday.com/ch/131christians/missionaries/htaylor.html?start=1.

We may fail—do fail continually—but He never fails. . . . I have continu-ally to mourn that I follow at such a distance and learn so slowly to imi-tate my precious Master. I can not tell you how I am buffeted sometimes by temptation. I never knew how bad a heart I have. Yet I do know that I love God and love His work, and desire to serve Him only and in all things. And I value above all else that precious Saviour in whom alone I can be accepted. Often I am tempted to think that one so full of sin can not be a child of God at all. . . . May God help me to love Him more and serve Him better.[14]

The stage was set for the crisis that happened on September 4, 1869, in Zhenjiang. He exulted to one of his associates: "Oh, Mr. Judd, God has made me a new man! God has made me a new man!"[15] What happened that day was not ephemeral. He looked back almost thirty years later, giving thanks for the abiding experience of it:

We shall never forget the blessing we received through the words, in John iv. 14, "Whosoever drinketh of the water that I shall give him SHALL NEVER THIRST," nearly thirty years ago. As we realized that Christ literally meant what He said—that "shall" meant shall, and "never" meant never, and "thirst" meant thirst—our heart overflowed with joy as we accepted the gift. Oh, the thirst with which we had sat down, but oh, the joy with which we sprang from our seat, praising the Lord that the thirsting days were all past, and past for ever![16]

We should beware of being cynical here. Taylor was not naïve. He was speaking of a thirty-year-long experience in which he battled with some very low times. "The thirsting days were all past" does not mean he never had desires for Jesus again. It doesn't mean he never longed for more of Christ. We will turn to what it does mean shortly. But for now, we should simply be aware that, as his most thorough biographer wrote, his whole life "came to be revolutionized"[17] by this experience.

The Most Difficult Year of His Life

And just in time, too. The next year, 1870, was the most difficult of his life. His son Samuel died in January. Then in July, Maria gave birth to a

---

[14] Cited in Dr. and Mrs. Howard Taylor, *Hudson Taylor's Spiritual Secret*, 140–41.

[15] Cited in Frederick Howard Taylor and Geraldine Taylor, *Hudson Taylor and the China Inland Mission*, 173.

[16] Cited in James Hudson Taylor, *Separation and Service or Thoughts on Numbers VI, VII.*, Kindle edition, Locations 519–524.

[17] A. J. Broomhall, *The Shaping of Modern China: Hudson Taylor's Life and Legacy, Vol. 2 (1868–1990)* (Pasadena, CA: William Carey Library, Piquant Editions, 2005), 109 (originally published as vols. 5–7 of *Hudson Taylor and China's Open Century*).

son, Noel, who died two weeks later. And to crown Hudson's sorrows, on July 23, Maria died of cholera. She was thirty-three years old, and left the thirty-eight-year-old Hudson with four living children.

It was as though God had given Taylor his extraordinary experience of the all-satisfying Christ not as a kind of icing on the cake of conversion, but rather as a way of surviving and thriving in the worst of sorrows, which came to him almost immediately.

A New Marriage, a Life at Sea, a Loss of Life

A year later, Taylor sailed for England. While he was there, on November 28, 1871, he married the woman with whom he would spend nearly the rest of his life, Jennie Faulding. They were married for thirty-three years before she died in 1904, the year before he did. They had a son and a daughter besides the four children from Maria. During one period, from 1881 to 1890, Jennie was in England while Hudson traveled to China twice, separating them for a total of about six years.

In his lifetime, Taylor made ten voyages to China, which means, as I calculate it, that he spent between four and five years on the water in transit—a good reminder, I suppose, that he was a pilgrim here. Over time, his ministry became increasingly global as the ambassador for China and for the China Inland Mission. He was the general director from 1865 to 1902, when he handed over the role to Dixon Hoste.

Taylor lived to see the horrible Boxer Rebellion, which raged against all Christians and foreigners in China in 1900. The China Inland Mission lost more members than any other agency: fifty-eight adults and twenty-one children were killed. But the next year, when the allied nations were demanding compensation from the Chinese government, Taylor refused to accept payment for loss of property or life. His aim was to win the Chinese, not demand justice.

Death and Legacy

In February 1905, Taylor sailed for China for the last time. After a tour of some of the mission stations, he died on June 3 at Changsha, Hunan, at the age of seventy-three. He was buried at Chinkiang by the side of his first wife and the children who had died in China. This was not owing to a superior relationship to Maria, but to the distances involved. Jennie had died in Switzerland the year before. The cemetery in China was destroyed as part of the Cultural Revolution, and today industrial buildings stand over the site.

At the time of Taylor's death, the China Inland Mission was an international body with 825 missionaries living in all eighteen provinces of China; more than three hundred mission stations; more than five hundred local Chinese helpers; and twenty-five thousand Christian converts.[18] Among the better-known luminaries who served China with CIM are the Cambridge Seven,[19] William Borden,[20] James Fraser,[21] and John and Betty Stam.[22]

Today, about sixteen hundred missionaries work for what is now known as OMF International.[23] Its international headquarters is in Singapore, and the mission is led by Patrick Fung, who is Chinese. The mission statement is: "We share the good news of Jesus Christ in all its fullness with East Asia's peoples to the glory of God." And the vision statement is: "Through God's grace, we aim to see an indigenous, biblical church movement in each people group of East Asia, evangelizing their own people and reaching out in mission to other peoples."

The year 2015 marked the 150th anniversary of the mission that Taylor founded. In 1900, there were one hundred thousand Christians in China, and today there are probably around 150 million.[24] This growth is God's work: one plants, another waters, but God gives the growth (1 Cor. 3:6). Nevertheless, it is the fruit of faithful labor. And Taylor labored longer and harder than most. That labor was sustained by union with Christ. So we turn to look at what this union meant for Taylor.

The Sentence That Removed the Scales

On September 4, 1869, when he was thirty-seven years old, Taylor found a letter waiting for him at Zhenjiang from John McCarthy. God

---

[18] Ralph R. Covell, "James Hudson Taylor: 1832–1905," *Biographical Dictionary of Chinese Christianity*, http://www.bdcconline.net/en/stories/t/taylor-james-hudson.php

[19] John Pollock, *The Cambridge Seven: The True Story of Ordinary Men Used in No Ordinary Way* (Fearn, Ross-Shire, Scotland: Christian Focus, 2006).

[20] Howard Taylor, *Borden of Yale* (Minneapolis: Bethany House, 1988).

[21] Geraldine Taylor, *Behind the Ranges: The Life-Changing Story of J. O. Fraser* (Littleton, CO: OMF Publications, 1998).

[22] Geraldine Taylor, *The Triumph of John and Betty Stam* (Chicago: Moody Publishers, 1935).

[23] In 1964, the China Inland Mission was renamed Overseas Missionary Fellowship, which was then shortened to OMF International.

[24] For how this can be computed from official statistics in China, see http://www.billionbibles.org/china/how-many-christians-in-china.html.

used the letter to revolutionize Taylor's life. "When my agony of soul was at its height, a sentence in a letter from dear McCarthy was used to remove the scales from my eyes, and the Spirit of God revealed to me the truth of our oneness with Jesus as I had never known it before."[25]

Notice two things about that sentence. One is that the change in Taylor didn't come through new information. Taylor knew his Bible, and he knew what Keswick teachers were saying. Just that year, the magazine *Revival* had carried a series of articles by Robert Pearsall Smith on "the victorious life"[26]—one of the catchphrases of the Keswick teaching. These articles had been the inspiration for McCarthy's own experience that he was now sharing with Taylor. It was not a new teaching. It was one familiar sentence. We have all had experiences of this sort: the same truth we have read a hundred times explodes with new power in our lives. That happened for Taylor.

The other thing to notice is that the truth that exploded was his "oneness with Jesus." And Taylor says it carefully: "the Spirit of God revealed to me the truth of our oneness with Jesus *as I had never known it before.*" He knew it before, but this time the Holy Spirit gave him a new sight of the wonder of it. This is exactly the way he understood it.

The prayer of Ephesians 1:18 was answered as never before: "having the eyes of your hearts enlightened, that you may know . . ." Taylor said: "As I read, I saw it all! . . . I looked to Jesus and saw (and when I saw, oh, how joy flowed!) that He had said, 'I will never leave thee.'"[27]

> I saw not only that Jesus will never leave me, but that I am a member of His body, of His flesh and of His bones. The vine is not the root merely, but all—root, stem, branches, twigs, leaves, flowers, fruit. And Jesus is not that alone—He is soil and sunshine, air and showers, and ten thousand times more than we have ever dreamed, wished for or needed. Oh, the joy of seeing this truth![28]

This was not new information. This was the miracle of the eyes of the heart being opened to taste and see at a deeper level than had been tasted and seen before. "Oh, taste and see that the LORD is good!" (Ps. 34:8). And the center of what he saw and tasted was union with

---

25 Cited in Dr. and Mrs. Howard Taylor, *Hudson Taylor's Spiritual Secret*, 149.
26 Broomhall, *The Shaping of Modern China*, 109.
27 Cited in Dr. and Mrs. Howard Taylor, *Hudson Taylor's Spiritual Secret*, 149.
28 Cited in ibid., 149–50.

Christ: "The sweetest part, if one may speak of one part being sweeter than another, is the rest which full *identification* with Christ brings."[29] The experience came to be known as the "exchanged life" because of Galatians 2:20: "I have been crucified with Christ. It is no longer I who live, but Christ who lives in me. And the life I now live in the flesh I live by faith in the Son of God, who loved me and gave himself for me."

Along with a new sight of Christ's fullness and his union with Christ, there was also a new yieldedness: "Surrender to Christ he had long known, but this was more; this was a new yieldedness, a glad, unreserved handing over of self and everything to Him."[30] This new yieldedness was so powerful and so sweet—so supernatural—that it rose up like an indictment against all vain striving. When you have been swept up into the arms of Jesus, all previous efforts to jump in seem vain.

At the heart of the discovery was this: the fruit of the vine comes from abiding, not striving:

> To let my loving Saviour work in me His will, my sanctification, is what I would live for by His grace. Abiding, not striving nor struggling; looking off unto Him; trusting Him for present power; resting in the love of an almighty Saviour.[31]

> From the consciousness of union springs the power to abide. Let us, then—not seek, not wait, not pursue—but now accept by faith the Saviour's word—"Ye *are* the branches."[32]

Taylor experienced such a powerful revelation of the inexpressible reality of union with Christ, as an absolute and glorious fact of security and sweetness and power, that it carried in it its own effectiveness. It gave vivid meaning to the difference between the works of the flesh and the fruit of the Spirit: "Work is the outcome of effort; fruit, of life. A bad man may do good work, but a bad tree cannot bear good fruit."[33] "How to get faith strengthened? Not by striving after faith, but by resting on the Faithful One."[34]

---

[29] Cited in ibid. Italics added.
[30] Ibid., 154.
[31] Cited in ibid., 144.
[32] Cited in J. H. Taylor, *Hudson Taylor's Choice Sayings: A Compilation from His Writings and Addresses* (London: China Inland Mission, n.d.), 7.
[33] Cited in James Hudson Taylor, *A Ribband of Blue And Other Bible Studies*, Kindle edition (May 12, 2012), Locations 246–49.
[34] Cited in Dr. and Mrs. Howard Taylor, *Hudson Taylor's Spiritual Secret*, 149.

Unlike many who claimed a higher-life experience, Taylor really was lifted to a plane of joy and peace and strength that lasted all his life. He wrote, "Never again did the unsatisfied days come back; never again was the needy soul separated from the fullness of Christ."[35] Just before turning sixty, Taylor was in Melbourne, Australia. An Episcopalian minister had heard of Keswick, and after spending time with Taylor, he wrote: "Here was the real thing, an embodiment of 'Keswick teaching' such as I had never hoped to see. It impressed me profoundly. Here was a man almost sixty years of age, bearing tremendous burdens, yet absolutely calm and untroubled."[36]

Decades of Resting in Jesus

Why did this crisis experience bear such lasting fruit for Hudson Taylor? There are at least three reasons.

1. *Taylor was saturated with the Bible, and his interpretation of his experience was chastened by the Bible.*

This means that in his experience, the walk of faith was not as passive as he made it sound. William Berger, Taylor's friend and the leader of the China Inland Mission in England, made plain to Taylor that he did not approve of "overstressing of the passive, receptive aspect of 'holiness.'"[37] He emphasized the need for active resistance to evil and of effort to obey God the way J. C. Ryle was to balance the Keswick Movement's emphases a few years later.[38]

Over the years, Taylor embraced this counsel, but never lost the wonder of being *really* united to the vine. He acknowledged: "Union is not identical with abiding: union is uninterrupted, but abiding may be interrupted. If abiding be interrupted, sin follows."[39] He not only recognized that abiding in Christ can be interrupted, leading to sin, but also that our best obedience needs cleansing: "We are sinful creatures, and our holiest service can only be accepted through Jesus Christ our Lord."[40]

His life was one resounding affirmation that God uses means to

---

[35] Cited in ibid., 153.

[36] Cited in ibid., 215.

[37] Broomhall, *The Shaping of Modern China*, 111.

[38] See J. I. Packer's treatment of Ryle's view of sanctification and Ryle's own book, *Holiness*, in *Faithfulness and Holiness: The Witness of J. C. Ryle* (Wheaton, IL: Crossway, 2010).

[39] Cited in J. H. Taylor, *Hudson Taylor's Choice Sayings*, 1.

[40] Cited in J. H. Taylor, "Consecration and Blessing," in T. J. Shanks, ed., *College Students at Northfield; or, A College of Colleges, No. 2* (New York; Chicago: Revell, 1888), 78.

preserve and deepen and intensify our experience of union with Christ. These means are a kind of *effort*. To be sure, there are different kinds of effort. There is slavish effort and there is trusting effort—effort that leans on the flesh and effort that leans on God. "I worked harder than any of them, though it was not I, but the grace of God that is with me" (1 Cor. 15:10). "Whoever serves, [let him serve] as one who serves by the strength that God supplies" (1 Pet. 4:11). "The life I now live . . . I live by faith" (Gal. 2:20).

But in this *effort of faith* there are things to be done. In Taylor's own words: "Communion with Christ requires our coming to Him. Meditating upon His person and His work requires the diligent use of the means of grace, and specially the prayerful reading of His Word. Many fail to abide because they habitually fast instead of feed."[41] Taylor's new pattern was to go to bed earlier and then rise at five a.m. "to give time to Bible study and prayer (often two hours) before the work of the day began."[42]

Taylor never saw these disciplines in contradiction to his glorious experience of union with Christ. Jesus is the vine and his Father is the vinedresser. Both the power of the vine from within and the providence of the vinedresser from without serve the fullness of the experience of joy-filled, peace-filled, love-filled union with Christ.

2. The second reason Taylor's life-changing experience lasted was that he saw suffering as God's way of deepening and sweetening his experience of union with Christ.

The vinedresser does many things for the branches. But the one task Jesus focused on in John 15 was pruning or cutting. The aim of this is to preserve and intensify and make fruitful the branch's union with the vine. Taylor said:

---

[41] Cited in J. H. Taylor, *Hudson Taylor's Choice Sayings*, 2.

[42] Dr. and Mrs. Howard Taylor, *Hudson Taylor's Spiritual Secret*, 145. One of the most moving scenes from his closing months is given by his son in describing how Taylor found time for prayer and the Word every day, no matter how busy: "To him, the secret of overcoming lay in daily, hourly fellowship with God; and this, he found, could only be maintained by secret prayer and feeding upon the Word through which He reveals Himself to the waiting soul. It was not easy for Mr Taylor, in his changeful life, to make time for prayer and Bible study, but he knew that it was vital. Well do the writers remember travelling with him month after month in northern China, by cart and wheelbarrow, with the poorest of inns at night. Often with only one large room for coolies and travellers alike, they would screen off a corner for their father and another for themselves, with curtains of some sort; and then, after sleep at last had brought a measure of quiet, they would hear a match struck and see the flicker of candlelight which told that Mr. Taylor, however weary, was poring over the little Bible in two volumes always at hand. From two to four A.M. was the time he usually gave to prayer; the time when he could be most sure of being undisturbed to wait upon God. That flicker of candlelight has meant more to them than all they have read or heard on secret prayer; it meant reality, not preaching but practice. The hardest part of a missionary career, Mr. Taylor found, is to maintain regular, prayerful Bible study. 'Satan will always find you something to do,' he would say, 'when you ought to be occupied about that, if it is only arranging a window blind.'" Cited in ibid., 223.

It is *only* in the trial of GOD'S grace that its *beauty and power* can be seen. Then all our trials of temper, circumstances, provocation, sickness, disappointment, bereavement, will but give a higher burnish to the mirror, and enable us to reflect more fully and more perfectly the glory and blessedness of our MASTER.[43]

It is in the path of obedience and self-denying service that God reveals Himself most intimately to His children. When it costs most we find the greatest joy. We find the darkest hours the brightest, and the greatest loss the highest gain. While the sorrow is short lived, and will soon pass away, the joy is far more exceeding, and it is eternal. Would that I could give you an idea of the way in which God has revealed Himself to me in China, and to others whom I have known. In the presence of bereavement, in the deepest sorrows of life, He has so drawn near to me that I have said to myself, Is it possible that the precious one who is in His presence can have more of the presence of God than I have?[44]

In other words, the experience of the fullness of union with Christ, with all its joy and peace and power and love, comes not only from the preciousness of the vine but also from the pruning of the vinedresser. God uses the means of pain as well as prayer and Bible reading. "All these difficulties," Taylor said, "are only platforms for the manifestation of His grace, power and love."[45]

3. Finally, his experience of sweet union with Christ lasted because he embraced the absolute goodness and sovereignty of God over his suffering and his union with Christ.

This is how Taylor could retain such composure in Christ in the most oppressive and dangerous and sorrowful and painful circumstances. He believed that the key to joy and peace and fruitfulness lay in being sure not only of the vine's all-satisfying sap, but also of the vinedresser's all-controlling sovereignty.

When he was fifty-two and confined to bed and feeling forgotten, he wrote, "So make up your mind that God is an infinite Sovereign, and has the right to do as He pleases with His own, and He may not explain to you a thousand things which may puzzle your reason in His

---

[43] Cited in J. H. Taylor, *Days of Blessing in Inland China: Being an Account of Meetings Held in the Province of Shan-Si, &c.,* 2nd ed. (London: Morgan & Scott, 1887), 61.
[44] Cited in *China's Millions,* No. 110, Vol. IX, August 1884, 102.
[45] Cited in Dr. and Mrs. Howard Taylor, *Hudson Taylor's Spiritual Secret,* 202. "The highest service demands the greatest sacrifice, but it secures the fullest blessing and the greatest fruitfulness." *The Works of J. Hudson Taylor* (Douglas Editions, 2009), Kindle edition, Location 2955.

dealings with you."[46] Taylor lost his wife Maria when she was thirty-three and he was thirty-eight. As noted in the introduction, he wrote to his mother, "From my inmost soul I delight in the knowledge that God does or permits all things, and causes all things to work together for good to those who love Him."[47]

Though Satan is real and causes much evil in the world, Taylor was strengthened by the assurance that God never loses control: "Oftentimes shall we be helped and blessed if we bear this in mind—that Satan is servant, and not master, and that he, and wicked men incited by him, are only permitted to do that which GOD by His determinate counsel and foreknowledge has before determined shall be done."[48] In other words, the vinedresser may use anything and anyone he pleases to prune the branch that he loves (John 15:1–2).

Conclusion

So I conclude that, while the Keswick teaching may in many cases have overemphasized the passivity of the pursuit of holiness and may have overemphasized a distinct crisis experience of consecration as the means of entering the "higher life," nevertheless Hudson Taylor's life bears witness to the possibility of living with more peace and more joy and more fruit in hardship than most of us enjoy.

Paul said he had learned this secret:

> I have learned in whatever situation I am to be content. I know how to be brought low, and I know how to abound. In any and every circumstance, I have learned the secret of facing plenty and hunger, abundance and need. I can do all things through him who strengthens me. (Phil. 4:11–13)

The learning is both *information* and *realization*. The *information* is the truth of Scripture that the vine is infinitely sufficient and satisfying for our souls' hunger, and that the vinedresser is all-controlling in care for the branches. And the *realization* is the miracle of actually resting in this truth, actually experiencing Christ and the Father becoming for us experientially all that they are.

Whether God gives you a crisis moment of this realization that lasts a lifetime, as he did Hudson Taylor, or leads you deeper gradually over

---

[46] Cited in Jim Cromarty, *It Is Not Death to Die* (Fearn, Ross-shire, Scotland: Christian Focus, 2008), 8.
[47] Cited in Dr. and Mrs. Howard Taylor, *Hudson Taylor's Spiritual Secret*, 163.
[48] Cited in James Hudson Taylor, *A Ribband of Blue And Other Bible Studies*, Locations 375–76.

time, don't settle for anything less than what Paul experienced in Philippians 4 and what he prayed for in Ephesians 3:19—that we might be "filled with all the fullness of God." Don't stop wanting this fullness and pursuing it.

If Hudson Taylor were here, he would say: "It is yours in Christ. Possess it. Enjoy it. Who knows? God may birth a ministry through you that lasts 150 years."

If his glory will come of it, shall I not even crave the honour of being the agent of his glory, even though it be by lying passive and enduring in anguish.
Charles Spurgeon

The Lord will give me the necessaries of life, if I first seek the kingdom of God and His righteousness: for there is a promise to that effect. Matthew 6:33.
George Müller

Let us see that we keep God before our eyes; that we walk in His ways, and seek to please and glorify Him in everything, great and small. Depend upon it, God's work done in God's way will never lack God's supplies.
Hudson Taylor

Conclusion

Perhaps the most striking and uniting thread in the interwoven lives of Charles Spurgeon, George Müller, and Hudson Taylor was their great confidence that God could and would fulfill all his promises of care to each of his children. And it follows, they believed, that all of us who, through Christ, know God as our heavenly Father should trust him implicitly to fulfill those promises very specifically and practically for us in our daily lives. And, they believed, our aim in that practical faith should be that God would be glorified through his Son as an all-powerful, all-wise, all-loving, promise-keeping God for those who trust him. Theirs was a camaraderie of confidence in the goodness, glory, and power of God.

This confidence was based on explicit promises in the Bible that, they believed, it would be sin not to believe:

- "Seek first the kingdom of God and his righteousness, and all these things will be added to you" (Matt. 6:33).
- "The Lord God is a sun and shield; the Lord bestows favor and honor. No good thing does he withhold from those who walk uprightly" (Ps. 84:11).
- "And we know that for those who love God all things work together for good, for those who are called according to his purpose" (Rom. 8:28).
- "Oh, fear the Lord, you his saints, for those who fear him have no lack!" (Ps. 34:9).

Each of these promises is conditional: seek the kingdom; walk uprightly; love God; fear the Lord. Taylor clarified for us that this does not mean that we must be perfect in order to enjoy these promises:

"No good thing will He withhold from them that walk uprightly." Not, "from them that walk perfectly, or sinlessly"—no one does that; not, "from them that are blameless"—though we all should be that; but if we are honestly and uprightly seeking to serve Him, no good thing will He withhold. What a rich promise this is![49]

Indeed, it is rich. It is staggeringly rich. It means we will always have what we *need* if we trust him and walk uprightly. These three friends did not believe God had promised that we will always have what we *want*. Nor did they believe that God had promised to spare them suffering and death. "There is no promise to that effect. . . . [Rather] the Lord will give me the necessaries of life, if I first seek the kingdom of God and His righteousness: for there is a promise to that effect. Matt. vi."[50]

Thus, when Paul says, "My God will supply every need of yours according to his riches in glory in Christ Jesus" (Phil. 4:19), they understood "need" the way Paul does a few verses earlier:

> Not that I am speaking of being in *need*, for I have learned in whatever situation I am to be content. I know how to be brought low, and I know how to abound. In any and every circumstance, I have learned the secret of facing plenty and hunger, abundance and *need*. I can do all things through him who strengthens me. (vv. 11–13)

Paul says he always has what he *needs*—which includes times of being "brought low" and times of being in "hunger" and "need." In other words, Paul has no need when he is in need! He has no need when he is in hunger.

What does that mean? It means that Paul puts Jesus Christ and his glory above all earthly needs, and says, "If Christ is with me, and if Christ is my supreme treasure, and if Christ is deciding what is good for me, then I am content with what he decides, and have no needs."

> Whatever gain I had, I counted as loss for the sake of Christ. Indeed, I count everything as loss because of the surpassing worth of knowing Christ Jesus my Lord. For his sake I have suffered the loss of all things and count them as rubbish, in order that I may gain Christ. (vv. 7–8)

The glory of God was always the preeminent issue in the life of faith for Spurgeon, Müller, and Taylor. If God should will that the time for their death had come, they would say with Paul, "It is my eager expectation

---

[49] J. Hudson Taylor, *A Ribband of Blue and Other Bible Studies* (Toronto: China Inland Mission, n.d.), 107–8.
[50] George Müller, *A Narrative of Some of the Lord's Dealing with George Muller, Written by Himself, Jehovah Magnified. Addresses by George Muller Complete and Unabridged*, vol. 1 (Muskegon, MI: Dust and Ashes Publications, 2003), 65.

and hope that . . . Christ will be honored in my body, whether by life or by death" (Phil. 1:20). They would not think the promises of God's care had failed. What would it mean in this situation that God "withholds no good thing"? It would mean that he did not withhold the grace to die in a way that would magnify Christ. This was the greatest "need" they felt.

Thus Spurgeon spoke of his own suffering. If it served the glory of God according to God's will, then suffering was his desire—not his physical pleasure, to be sure, but his deepest desire. His deepest "need," which would not be withheld from him, was that God be glorified in his life and death:

> Moreover, we should not only bear all things because the Lord ordains them, but because he orders all things for a wise, kind, beneficent purpose. He doth not afflict willingly. He takes no delight in the sufferings of his children. Whenever adversity must come it is always with a purpose; and, if a purpose of God is to be subserved by my suffering, would I wish to escape from it? If his glory will come of it, shall I not even crave the honour of being the agent of his glory, even though it be by lying passive and enduring in anguish.[51]

Therefore, the camaraderie of confidence in God that these friends shared did not include the confidence that they would never get sick or that they would be able to pray their loved ones out of the hospital. Both Müller and Taylor laid two wives in their graves because of illness. They both lost children. And Spurgeon died early because of a body wracked with disease.

Their confidence was not that God would prevent sickness and death, but that God would give them all they needed to do his will and give him glory in life and death. Taylor famously said, "Depend upon it, God's work done in God's way will never lack God's supplies."[52] This is a paraphrase of 2 Corinthians 9:8: "God is able to make all grace abound to you, so that having all sufficiency in all things at all times, you may abound in every good work." What does "every good work" mean? It does not refer to the "good works" required of someone else on the other side of the world. Rather, it refers to the works God is calling you to do today. Thus, Taylor expanded his motto: "The Lord does not require anything outside of that which He has given to His people, to accomplish His present purposes, whatever they may be."[53]

---

[51] C. H. Spurgeon, *The Metropolitan Tabernacle Pulpit Sermons*, vol. 22 (London: Passmore & Alabaster, 1876), 38.

[52] J. H. Taylor, *Hudson Taylor's Choice Sayings: A Compilation from His Writings and Addresses* (London: China Inland Mission, n.d.), 65.

[53] Ibid., 60.

Nor should we leave the life stories of this book thinking that Müller and Taylor chose their particular strategy of trusting God, without asking people for help, because it was the only obedient way. They did not believe it was sin to ask someone for help. Müller made it clear that his way was not for everyone. He chose it because it seemed to him that this was God's way for him to put God's glory most clearly on display:

> I do not mean to say that it would be acting against the precepts of the Lord to seek for help in His work by personal and individual application to believers, (though it would be in direct opposition to His will to apply to unbelievers, 2 Cor. vi. 14–18); but I act in the way in which I do for the benefit of the Church at large, cheerfully bearing the trials, and sometimes the deep trials connected with this life of faith (which however brings along with it also its precious joys), if by any means a part at least of my fellow believers might be led to see the reality of dealing with God only, and that there is such a thing as the child of God having power with God by prayer and faith.[54]

This was the great aim—that people might "be led *to see.*" To see the glory of God. To see his power, his wisdom, his care, his readiness to answer prayer, and his absolute commitment to meet every need we have, as we trust in him. Spurgeon and Müller would all rejoice to say "Amen" to these words of Hudson Taylor:

> In the greatest difficulties, in the heaviest trials, in the deepest poverty and necessities, He has never failed me; but, because I was enabled by His grace to trust in Him, He has always appeared for my help. I delight in speaking well of His Name.[55]

These three swans are not silent. Their lives and their words to this day are "speaking well of His name." And I delight to put the modest megaphone of this book to their lips. They would be glad, I think (in their very practical bent!), if we end on Taylor's own note of exhortation, full of hope:

> Let us see that we keep God before our eyes; that we walk in His ways, and seek to please and glorify Him in everything, great and small. Depend upon it, God's work done in God's way will never lack God's supplies.[56]

---

[54] Müller, *A Narrative*, 1:322 (emphasis added).
[55] Cited in Frederick Howard Taylor and Geraldine Taylor, *Hudson Taylor and the China Inland Mission: The Growth of a Work of God* (Littleton, CO; Mississauga, ON; Kent, TN: OMF Book, 1995), 183.
[56] J. H. Taylor, *Hudson Taylor's Choice Sayings*, 65.

Publication Information

• • •

• • •